NEW YORK

CONVENTION MANUAL

PREPARED IN PURSUANCE OF

CHAPTERS 194 AND 458, OF THE LAWS OF 1867,

UNDER THE DIRECTION OF

FRANCIS C. BARLOW, Secretary of State,
THOMAS HILLHOUSE, Comptroller, and
JOHN H. MARTINDALE, Attorney-General.

By FRANKLIN B. HOUGH.

PART II.
STATISTICS.

I0836617

ALBANY, N. Y.:
WEED, PARSONS & COMPANY, PRINTERS.
1867.

CONTENTS.

DELEGATES TO CONSTITUTIONAL CONVENTION OF 1867.

President,............................... WILLIAM A. WHEELER.
Secretary,............................... LUTHER CALDWELL.

DELEGATES AT LARGE.

Waldo Hutchins,............................... New York.
William M. Evarts, ... New York.
George Opdyke,............................... New York.
Augustine J. H. Duganne, ... New York.
George William Curtis,..................... New York.
Horace Greeley,............................... Westchester county.
Joshua M. Van Cott, ... Brooklyn, Kings county.
Ira Harris, ... Albany, Albany county.
Erastus Cooke, ... Kingston, Ulster county.
Martin I. Townsend,......................... Troy, Rensselaer county.
William A. Wheeler,......................... Malone, Franklin county.
Charles Andrews, ... Syracuse, Onondaga county.
Tracy Beadle, ... Elmira, Chemung county.
Charles J. Folger, ... Geneva, Ontario county.
Erastus S. Prosser, ... Buffalo, Erie county.
Augustus Frank, ... Warsaw, Wyoming county.
Augustus Schell, ... New York.
George Law, ... New York.
Henry C. Murphy, ... Brooklyn, Kings county.
Homer A. Nelson,............................. Poughkeepsie, Dutchess county.
David L. Seymour,........................... Troy, Rensselaer county.
Jacob Hardenburgh,......................... Kingston, Ulster county.
Smith M. Weed, ... Plattsburgh, Clinton county.
Alonzo C. Paige, ... Schenectady, Schenectady Co.
Francis Kernan, ... Utica, Oneida county.
George F. Comstock, ... Syracuse, Oneida county.
John Magee, ... Watkins, Schuyler county.
Henry D. Barto,............................... Trumansburgh, Tompkins Co.
Sanford E. Church,.......................... Albion, Orleans county.
Henry O. Chesebro, ... Canandaigua, Ontario county.
Joseph G. Masten, ... Buffalo, Erie county.
Marshall B. Champlain, ... Cuba, Allegany county.

FIRST SENATORIAL DISTRICT—*Queens, Richmond and Suffolk Counties.*

Selah B. Strong, ... Setauket, Suffolk county,
Solomon Townsend,.......................... Oyster Bay, Queens county.
William Wickham, ... Cutchogue, Suffolk county.
Erastus Brooks, ... New York.

SECOND SENATORIAL DISTRICT—*The 1st, 2d, 3d, 4th, 5th, 7th, 11th. 13th, 15th, 19th and 20th Wards of the City of Brooklyn, in the County of Kings.*

John P. Rolfe,.................................... Brooklyn, Kings county.
Daniel P. Barnard, ... Brooklyn, Kings county.
Charles Lowrey, ... Brooklyn, Kings county.
Walter L. Livingston,....................... Brooklyn, Kings county.

THIRD SENATORIAL DISTRICT—*The 6th, 8th, 9th, 10th, 12th, 14th, 16th, 17th and 18th Wards of the City of Brooklyn, and the Towns of Kings County.*

Teunis G. Bergen,............................. Brooklyn, Kings county.
William D. Veeder, ... Brooklyn, Kings county.
John G. Schumaker, ... Brooklyn, Kings county.
Stephen I. Colahan,.......................... Brooklyn, Kings county.

FOURTH SENATORIAL DISTRICT—*The 1st, 2d, 3d, 4th, 5th, 6th 7th, 13th and 14th Wards of New York City.*

Charles P. Daly,............................ New York.
Samuel B. Garvin, ... New York.
Abraham R. Lawrence, Jr.,........... New York.
John E. Burrill,.............................. New York.

FIFTH SENATORIAL DISTRICT—*The 8th, 9th, 15th and 16th Wards of New York City.*

Nathaniel Jarvis Jr., ... New York.
Elbridge T. Gerry, ... New York.
Henry Rogers,................................ New York.
Norman Stratton, ... New York.

SIXTH SENATORIAL DISTRICT.—*The 10th, 11th and 17th Wards of New York City.*

Frederick W. Loew,........................ New York.
Gideon J. Tucker, ... New York.
Abraham D. Russell,....................... New York.
Magnus Gross,................................ New York.

SEVENTH SENATORIAL DISTRICT—*The 18th, 20th and 21st Wards of New York City.*

Samuel J. Tilden. .... New York.
Anthony L. Robertson, ... New York.
Edwards Pierrepont,....................... New York.
James Brooks, ... New York.

EIGHTH SENATORIAL DISTRICT—*The 12th, 19th and 22d Wards of New York City.*

Richard L. Larremore,.................... New York.
Claudius L. Monell,........................ New York.
John E. Develin,............................ New York.
William Hitchman,......................... New York.

NINTH SENATORIAL DISTRICT—*The Counties of Westchester, Rockland and Putnam.*

Abraham B. Conger,....................... Haverstraw, Rockland county.
Abraham B. Tappen,....................... Fordham, Westchester county.
Robert Cochran,............................. White Plains, Westchester Co.
William H. Morris,........................ Cold Spring, Putnam county.

TENTH SENATORIAL DISTRICT—*The Counties of Orange and Sullivan.*

Stephen W. Fullerton, ... Newburgh, Orange county.
William H. Houston,...................... Florida, Orange county.
Clinton V. R. Ludington, ... Monticello, Sullivan county.
Gideon Wales,................................. Pike Pond, Sullivan county.

ELEVENTH SENATORIAL DISTRICT—*The Counties of Dutchess and Columbia.*

B. Platt Carpenter,........................ Poughkeepsie, Dutchess county.
John Stanton Gould,....................... Hudson, Columbia county.
Wilson B. Sheldon,......................... Green Haven, Dutchess county.
Francis Silvester,........................... Kinderhook, Columbia county.

TWELFTH SENATORIAL DISTRICT—*The Counties of Rensselaer and Washington.*

John M. Francis,............................ Troy, Rensselaer county.
Jonathan P. Armstrong,................. Hoosick, Rensselaer county.
Cornelius L. Allen,......................... Salem, Washington county.
Adolphus F. Hitchcock, ... Kingsbury, Washington county.

THIRTEENTH SENATORIAL DISTRICT—*The County of Albany.*

Erastus Corning,............................ Albany, Albany county.
William Cassidy,............................ Albany, Albany county.
Amasa J. Parker, ... Albany, Albany county.
James Roy,...................................... West Troy, Albany county.

FOURTEENTH SENATORIAL DISTRICT—*The Counties of Greene and Ulster.*

Marius Schoonmaker, ... Kingston, Ulster county.
Solomon G. Young, ... Highland, Ulster county.
Manly B. Mattice, ... Oak Hill, Greene county.
Ezekiel P. More, ... Prattsville, Greene county.

FIFTEENTH SENATORIAL DISTRICT—*The Counties of Saratoga, Montgomery, Fulton, Hamilton and Schnectady.*

Alembert Pond, ... Saratoga Springs, Saratoga Co.
Hezekiah Baker, ... St. Johnsville, Montgomery Co.
Judson S. Landon, ... Schenectady, Schenectady Co.
Horace E. Smith, ... Johnstown, Fulton county.

SIXTEENTH SENATORIAL DISTRICT—*The Counties of Warren, Essex and Clinton.*

George M. Beckwith, ... Plattsburgh, Clinton county.
Matthew Hale, ... Elizabethtown, Essex county.
Nathan G. Axtell, ... Peru, Clinton county.
Andrew J. Cheritree, ... Luzerne, Warren county.

SEVENTEENTH SENATORIAL DISTRICT—*The Counties of St. Lawrence and Franklin.*

William C. Brown, ... Ogdensburgh, St. Lawrence Co.
Edwin A. Merritt, ... Potsdam, St. Lawrence county.
Leslie W. Russell, ... Canton, St. Lawrence county.
Joel J. Seaver, ... Malone, Franklin county.

EIGHTEENTH SENATORIAL DISTRICT—*The Counties of Jefferson and Lewis.*

Edward A. Brown, ... Lowville, Lewis county.
Marcus Bickford, ... Carthage, Jefferson county.
James A. Bell, ... Dexter, Jefferson county.
Milton H. Merwin, ... Watertown, Jefferson county.

NINETEENTH SENATORIAL DISTRICT—*The County of Oneida.*

Richard U. Sherman, ... Utica, Oneida county.
Theodore W. Dwight, ... New York.
Benjamin N. Huntington, ... Rome, Oneida county.
George Williams, ... Delta, Oneida county.

TWENTIETH SENATORIAL DISTRICT—*The Counties of Herkimer and Otsego.*

Elijah E. Ferry, ... Schenevus, Otsego county.
John Eddy, ... Milford, Otsego county.
Ezra Graves, ... Herkimer, Herkimer county.
Oliver B. Beals, ... Cedarville, Herkimer county.

TWENTY-FIRST SENATORIAL DISTRICT—*The Counties of Oswego and Madison.*

Elias Root, ... Oswego, Oswego county.
Lester M. Case, ... Cazenovia, Madison county.
M. Lindley Lee, ... Fulton, Oswego county.
Loring Fowler, ... Canastota, Madison county.

TWENTY-SECOND SENATORIAL DISTRICT—*The Counties of Onondaga and Cortland.*

Thomas G. Alvord, ... Syracuse, Onondaga county.
Frank Hiscock,* .... Syracuse, Onondaga county.
Patrick Corbett, ... Syracuse, Onondaga county.
Horatio Ballard, ... Cortland Village, Cortland county.

TWENTY-THIRD SENATORIAL DISTRICT—*The Counties of Chenango, Delaware and Schoharie.*

Elizur H. Prindle, ... Norwich, Chenango county.
John Grant, ... Margaretville, Delaware county.
Samuel F. Miller, ... Franklin, Delaware county.
Hobart Krum, ... Schoharie C. H., Scho'e county.

* In place of L. Harris Hiscock, deceased.

TWENTY-FOURTH SENATORIAL DISTRICT — *The Counties of Broome, Tioga and Tompkins.*

Stephen D. Hand, ... Binghamton, Broome county.
Charles E. Parker, ... Owego, Tioga county.
Oliver H. P. Kinney, ... Waverly, Tioga county.
Milo Goodrich, ... Dryden, Tompkins county.

TWENTY-FIFTH SENATORIAL DISTRICT—*The Counties of Cayuga and Wayne.*

George Rathbun, ... Auburn, Cayuga county.
Charles C. Dwight, ... Auburn, Cayuga county.
Leander S. Ketcham, ... Clyde, Wayne county.
Ornon Archer, ... Palmyra, Wayne county.

TWENTY-SIXTH SENATORIAL DISTRICT—*The Counties of Ontario, Yates and Seneca.*

Elbridge G. Lapham, ... Canandaigua, Ontario county.
Angus McDonald, ... Geneva, Ontario county.
Sterling G. Hadley, ... Waterloo, Seneca county.
Melatiah H. Lawrence, ... Penn Yan, Yates county.

TWENTY-SEVENTH SENATORIAL DISTRICT—*The Counties of Chemung, Schuyler and Steuben.*

Elijah P. Brooks, ... Elmira, Chemung county.
David Rumsey, ... Bath, Steuben county.
Abraham Lawrence, ... Lawrence, Schuyler county.
George T. Spencer, ... Corning, Steuben county.

TWENTY-EIGHTH SENATORIAL DISTRICT—*The County of Monroe.*

Jerome Fuller, ... Brockport, Monroe county.
Lorenzo D. Ely, ... Rochester, Monroe county.
William A. Reynolds, ... Rochester, Monroe county.
Freeman Clarke, ... Rochester, Monroe county.

TWENTY-NINTH SENATORIAL DISTRICT — *The Counties of Niagara, Orleans and Genesee.*

Seth Wakeman, ... Batavia, Genesee county.
Levi F. Bowen, ... Lockport, Niagara county.
Thomas T. Flagler, ... Lockport, Niagara county.
Ben Field, ... Albion, Orleans county.

THIRTIETH SENATORIAL DISTRICT—*The Counties of Wyoming, Livingston and Allegany.*

Edward J. Farnum, ... Wellsville, Allegany county.
Isaac L. Endress, ... Dansville, Livingston county.
John M. Hammond .... Filmore, Allegany county.
William H. Merrill, ... Warsaw, Wyoming county.

THIRTY-FIRST SENATORIAL DISTRICT—*The County of Erie.*

Israel T. Hatch .... Buffalo, Erie county.
Isaac A. Verplanck, ... Buffalo, Erie county.
Allen Potter .... Buffalo, Erie county.
George W. Clinton, ... Buffalo, Erie county.

THIRTY-SECOND SENATORIAL DISTRICT—*The Counties of Chautauqua and Cattaraugus.*

George Barker, ... Fredonia, Chautauqua county.
Augustus F. Allen, ... Jamestown, Chàutauqua county.
Norman M. Allen, ... Dayton, Cattaraugus county.
George Van Campen, ... Allegany, Cattaraugus county.

STANDING COMMITTEES OF THE CONVENTION.

---

1. *On the preamble and the bill of rights.*

Mr. Evarts, New York.
Mr. Spencer, Steuben.
Mr. A. R. Lawrence, New York.
Mr. Bowen, Niagara.
Mr. Paige, Schenectady.
Mr. Frank, Wyoming.
Mr. Hardenburgh, Ulster.

2. *On the Legislature, — its organization, and the number, apportionment, election, tenure of office, and compensation of its members.*

Mr. Merritt, St. Lawrence.
Mr. Cooke, Ulster.
Mr. Sherman, Oneida.
Mr. Monell, New York.
Mr. Barker, Chautauqua.
Mr. Jarvis, New York.
Mr. Merwin, Jefferson.

3. *On the powers and duties of the Legislature, except as to matters otherwise referred.*

Mr. Rathbun, Cayuga.
Mr. Rumsey, Steuben.
Mr. Robertson, New York.
Mr. E. A. Brown, Lewis.
Mr. Fields, Orleans.
Mr. M. H. Lawrence, Yates.
Mr. Burrill, New York.

4. *On the right of suffrage, and the qualifications to hold office.*

Mr. Greeley, Westchester.
Mr. Endress, Livingston.
Mr. Cassidy, Albany.
Mr. Merrill, Wyoming.
Mr. Williams, Oneida.
Mr. L. W. Russell, St. Lawrence.
Mr. Schumaker, Kings.

5. *On the Governor and Lieutenant-Governor, their election, tenure of office, compensation, powers and duties, except as otherwise referred.*

Mr. C. L. Allen, Washington.
Mr. E. P. Brooks, Chemung.
Mr. A. J. Parker, Albany.
Mr. Flagler, Niagara.
Mr. Wakeman, Genesee.
Mr. Miller, Delaware.
Mr. Garvin, New York.

6. *On the Secretary of State, Comptroller, Treasurer, Attorney-General, and State Engineer and Surveyor, their election or appointment, tenure of office, compensation, powers and duties.*

Mr. Tucker, New York.
Mr. Baker, Montgomery.
Mr. Duganne, New York.
Mr. Fuller, Monroe.
Mr. Ely, Monroe.
Mr. Ketcham, Wayne.
Mr. A. R. Lawrence, New York.

7. *On town and county officers, other than judicial, their election or appointment, tenure of office, compensation, powers and duties.*

Mr. Smith, Fulton.
Mr. Bickford, Jefferson.
Mr. Rolfe, Kings.
Mr. A. Lawrence, Schuyler.
Mr. Kinney, Tioga.
Mr. Sheldon, Dutchess.
Mr. Roy, Albany.

8. *On the judiciary.*

Mr. Folger, Ontario.
Mr. Evarts, New York.
Mr. Comstock, Onondaga.
Mr. Van Cott, Kings.
Mr. Daly, New York.
Mr. Barker, Chautauqua.
Mr. Kernan, Oneida.
Mr. Hutchins, New York.
Mr. Masten, Erie.
Mr. T. W. Dwight, Oneida.
Mr. A. J. Parker, Albany.
Mr. Andrews, Onondaga.
Mr. Hale, Essex.
Mr. Goodrich, Tompkins.
Mr. Pierrepont, New York.

9. *On the finances of the State, the public debt, revenues, expenditures, and taxation, and restrictions on the powers of the Legislature in respect thereto.*

Mr. Church, Orleans,
Mr. Frank, Wyoming.
Mr. Corning, Albany.
Mr. Opdyke, New York.
Mr. Tilden, New York.
Mr. Clarke, Monroe.
Mr. Van Cott, Kings.
Mr. Schell New York.
Mr. W. C. Brown, St. Lawrence.
Mr. Nelson, Dutchess.
Mr. A. F. Allen, Chautauqua.
Mr. Hatch, Erie.
Mr. Carpenter, Dutchess.
Mr. Barto, Tompkins.
Mr. Hardenburgh, Ulster.

10. *On canals.*

Mr. Lapham, Ontario.
Mr. Alvord, Onondaga.
Mr. Clinton, Erie.
Mr. Prosser, Erie.
Mr. Seymour, Rensselaer.
Mr. Beckwith, Washington.
Mr. Schoonmaker, Ulster.
Mr. Hutchins, New York.
Mr. Champlain, Allegany.
Mr. Root, Oswego.
Mr. Bell, Jefferson.
Mr. Magee, Schuyler.
Mr. Prindle, Chenango.
Mr. Bergen, Kings.
Mr. Tappen, Westchester.

11. *On cities, their organization, government and powers.*

Mr. Harris, Albany.
Mr. Opdyke, New York.
Mr. Murphy, Kings.
Mr. Francis, Rensselaer.
Mr. Paige, Schenectady.
Mr. Alvord, Onondaga.
Mr. Verplanck, Erie.
Mr. Bowen, Niagara.
Mr. Law, New York.
Mr. Fullerton, Orange.
Mr. E. Brooks, Richmond.
Mr. Graves, Herkimer.
Mr. Weed, Clinton.
Mr. Hand, Broome.
Mr. Chesebro, Ontario.

12. *On counties, towns and villages, their organization, government and powers.*

Mr. Hadley, Seneca.
Mr. N. M. Allen, Cattaraugus.
Mr. Lowrey, Kings.
Mr. Ferry, Otsego.
Mr. Fowler, Madison.
Mr. Corbett, Onondaga.
Mr. Wickham, Suffolk.

13. *On currency, banking and insurance.*

Mr. Beadle, Chemung.
Mr. Huntington, Oneida.
Mr. Veeder, Kings.
Mr. Eddy, Otsego.
Mr. Armstrong, Rensselaer.
Mr. Ludington, Sullivan.
Mr. Hitchman, New York.

14. *On corporations other than municipal, banking and insurance.*

Mr. Ballard, Cortland.
Mr. Stratton, New York.
Mr. S. Townsend, Queens.
Mr. Krum, Schoharie.
Mr. L. W. Russell, St. Lawrence.
Mr. Hitchcock, Washington.
Mr. Barnard, Kings.

15. *On State prisons, and the prevention and punishment of crime.*

Mr. Gould, Columbia.
Mr. C. C. Dwight, Cayuga.
Mr. A. D. Russell, New York.
Mr. Cochran, Westchester.
Mr. Lee, Oswego.
Mr. Axtell, Clinton.
Mr. Conger, Rockland.

16. *On the pardoning power.*

Mr. M. I. Townsend, Rensselaer.
Mr. Pond, Saratoga.
Mr. Develin, New York.
Mr. Landon, Schenectady.
Mr. Prindle, Chenango.
Mr. Lee, Oswego.
Mr. Gerry, New York.

17. *On the militia and military officers.*

Mr. Morris, Putnam.
Mr. Seaver, Franklin.
Mr. Barto, Tompkins.
Mr. C. C. Dwight, Cayuga.
Mr. Cheritree, Warren.
Mr. Stratton, New York.
Mr. Hammond, Allegany.

18. *On education and funds relating thereto.*

Mr. Curtis, New York.
Mr. Archer, Wayne.
Mr. Conger, Rockland.
Mr. Gould, Columbia.
Mr. Beals, Herkimer.
Mr. Clinton, Erie.
Mr. Larremore, New York.

19. *On charities and charitable institutions.*

Mr. E. Brooks, Richmond.
Mr. T. W. Dwight, Oneida.
Mr. Strong, Suffolk.
Mr. Spencer, Steuben.
Mr. Ludington, Sullivan.
Mr. Silvester, Columbia.
Mr. Livingston, Kings.

20. *On industrial interests, except those already referred.*

Mr. Duganne, New York.
Mr. Gross, New York.
Mr. Farnum, Allegany.
Mr. Armstrong, Rensselaer.
Mr. Wales, Sullivan.
Mr. Case, Madison.
Mr. More, Greene.

21. *On the salt springs of the State.*

Mr. Bell, Jefferson.
Mr. Comstock, Onondaga.
Mr. C. E. Parker, Tioga.
Mr. McDonald, Ontario.
Mr. Rolfe, Kings.
Mr. Houston, Orange.
Mr. Young, Ulster.

22. *On the relations of the State to the Indians residing therein.*

Mr. Van Campen, Cattaraugus.
Mr. Silvester, Columbia.
Mr. Bergen, Kings.
Mr. Axtell, Clinton.
Mr. S. Townsend, Queens.
Mr. McDonald, Ontario.
Mr. Colahan, Kings.

23. *On future amendments and revisions of the Constitution.*

Mr. E. A. Brown, Lewis.
Mr. Greeley, Westchester.
Mr. Robertson, New York.
Mr. Flagler, Niagara.
Mr. Murphy, Kings.
Mr. Grant, Delaware.
Mr. J. Brooks, New York.

24. *Privileges and elections.*

Mr. Landon, Schenectady.
Mr. Endress, Livingston.
Mr. Loew, New York.
Mr. Lowrey, Kings.
Mr. Mattice, Greene.

25. *Printing.*

Mr. Seaver, Franklin.
Mr. Francis, Rensselaer.
Mr. Potter, Erie.
Mr. Merrill, Wyoming.
Mr. Jarvis, New York.

26. *Contingent expenses.*

Mr. Ferry, Otsego.
Mr. Williams, Oneida.
Mr. Cochran, Westchester.
Mr. Reynolds, Monroe.
Mr. Rogers, New York.

27. *Engrossment and enrollment.*

Mr. Sherman, Oneida.
Mr. Archer, Wayne.
Mr. Cassidy, Albany.
Mr. Cheritree, Warren.
Mr. Mattice, Greene.

Select committee on the adulteration or sale of intoxicating liquors

Mr. Graves,
Mr. Livingston,
Mr. Ely,
Mr. Cochran,
Mr. Landon,
Mr. Hand,
Mr. Ray,
Mr. Verplanck.

STANDING RULES OF THE CONVENTION.

CHAPTER I.

Of the Powers and Duties of the President.

Rule 1. The President shall take the Chair each day at the hour appointed for the meeting of the session.

Rule 2. He shall possess the powers and perform the duties herein prescribed, viz.:

1. He shall preserve order and decorum.
2. He shall decide all questions of order, subject to appeal to the Convention. On every appeal he shall have the right, in his place, to assign his reasons for his decision.
3. He shall appoint all committees except where the Convention shall otherwise order.
4. He may substitute any member to perform the duties of the Chair for a period not exceeding two consecutive legislative days.
5. When the Convention shall be ready to go into Committee of the Whole, he shall name a Chairman to preside therein.
6. He shall designate the reporters for the public press, not exceeding fifteen in number, and shall assign to them their respective seats.

CHAPTER II.

Of the Daily Order of Business.

Rule 3. The first business of each day's session shall be the reading of the Journal of the preceding day, and the correction of any errors that may be found to exist therein. After which, except on days and at times set apart for the consideration of special orders, the order of business, which shall not be departed from except by unanimous consent, shall be as follows, viz.:

1. *The presentation of memorials.* Under which head shall be included petitions, remonstrances and communications from individuals and from public bodies.
2. Communications from the Governor.
3. Communications from State officers. Under which head shall be embraced also, communications from public officers and from corporations, in response to calls for information.
4. Notices.
5. Reports of Standing Committees.

C

6. Reports of select committees.
7. Resolutions.
8. Unfinished business of the general orders.
9. Special orders.
10. General orders.

CHAPTER III.

Of the Rights and Duties of Members.

Rule 4. The President, or any member, when he shall be recognized in his plaee, may present, under the proper order of business, any paper of a respectful character, addressed to the Convention, and the same, unless the Convention shall otherwise order, shall be referred to the appropriate committee.

Rule 5. Every member presenting a paper shall indorse the same; if a petition, memorial, remonstrance or communication in answer to a call for information, with a concise statement of its subject, adding his name; if a notice or resolution, with his name; if the report of a committee, with a statement of its subject, the name of the committee and of the member making the report; if a proposition of any other kind for the consideration of the Convention, with a statement of its subject, the proposer's name, and the reference, if any, desired.

Rule 6. Every member who shall be within the bar of the Convention when a question shall be stated from the chair, shall vote thereon unless he be excused or be personally interested in the question. No member shall be obliged to vote on any question unless within the bar when the question shall be put, but in the case of a division by yeas and nays, may vote if present before the last name shall be called. The bar of the Convention shall be deemed to include only the floor of the Assembly Chamber, and the open spaces adjacent thereto, within the doors.

Rule 7. Any member requesting to be excused from voting may make, when his name is called, or immediately after the roll shall have been called, and before the result shall be announced, a brief statement of the reasons for making such request, not exceeding five minutes in time, and the question shall then be taken without debate; and such request shall not be withdrawn without the consent of the Convention.

CHAPTER IV.

Of Order and Decorum.

Rule 8. No member rising to debate, to give a notice, make a motion or present a paper of any kind, shall proceed until he shall have addressed the President, and been recognized by him as entitled to the floor.

Rule 9. Where a member shall have the floor for any purpose, no member shall entertain any private discourse or pass between him and the chair.

Rule 10. While the President shall be putting a question, or a division by counting shall be had, no member shall leave his place, or speak, unless to make a privileged motion or state a question of privilege demanding immediate attention.

Rule 11. When a motion to adjourn, or for a recess, shall be affirmatively determined, no member or officer shall leave his place till the adjournment or recess shall be declared by the President.

CHAPTER V.

Of Order in Debate.

Rule 12. No member shall speak more than once to the same question, without leave of the Convention, until every member desiring to speak on the question pending shall have spoken.

Rule 13. No remarks reflecting personally upon the character or action of any member shall be in order in debate.

Rule 14. If any member, in speaking, shall transgress the rules of the Convention, the President shall, or any member may call to order, in which case the member so called to order, shall not proceed, unless to explain or speak in order.

CHAPTER VI.

Of Committees and their Duties.

Rule 15. Standing Committees shall be appointed by the President to consider and report severally upon the following subjects, and such others as may be referred to them, viz.:

To consist of seven members each.

1. On the preamble and bill of rights.
2. On the Legislature, its organization and the number, apportionment, election, tenure of office, and compensation of its members.
3. On the powers and duties of the Legislature, except as to matters otherwise referred.
4. On the right of suffrage and the qualifications to hold office.
5. On the Governor and Lieutenant-Governor, their election, tenure of office, compensation, powers and duties, except as otherwise referred.
6. On the Secretary of State, Comptroller, Treasurer, Attorney-General, and State Engineer and Surveyor, their election or appointment, tenure of office, compensation, powers and duties.
7. On town and county officers, other than judicial, their election or appointment, tenure of office, compensation, powers and duties.

To consist of fifteen members each.

8. On the judiciary.
9. On the finances of the State, the public debt, revenues, expenditures,

and taxation, and restrictions on the powers of the Legislature in respect thereto.

10. On canals.

11. On cities, their organization, government and powers.

To consist of seven members each.

12. On counties, towns and villages, their organization, government and powers.

13. On currency, banking and insurance.

14. On corporations other than municipal, banking and insurance.

15. On State prisons, and the prevention and punishment of crime.

16. On the pardoning power.

17. On the militia and military officers.

18. On education and funds relating thereto.

19. On charities and charitable institutions.

20. On industrial interests, except those already referred.

21. On the salt springs of the State.

22. On the relations of the State to the Indians residing therein.

23. On future amendments and revisions of the Constitution.

To consist of five members each.

24. Privileges and elections.

25. Printing.

26. Contingent expenses.

27. Engrossment and enrollment.

Rule 16. All reports of committees, embracing propositions for constitutional alterations, shall be referred, as of course, to the Committee of the Whole, for consideration therein, before final action by the Convention.

CHAPTER VII.

Of General and Special Orders.

Rule 17. The matters referred to the Committee of the Whole, shall constitute the General Orders, and shall be recorded by their titles or subjects, in a calendar to be kept for that purpose by the Secretary, in the order in which they shall be referred respectively.

Rule 18. Any particular report or other matter on the General Orders, may be made a Special Order for any particular day, or from day to day, with the assent of two-thirds of the members voting, and no Special Order shall be postponed or rescinded except by a similar vote.

CHAPTER VIII.

Of the Committee of the Whole.

Rule 19. The same rules shall be observed in Committee of the Whole as in the Convention, as far as applicable, except that the yeas and nays shall not be taken on a division.

Rule 20. A motion to rise and report progress shall be in order at any stage, and shall be decided without debate.

Rule 21. Subjects shall be taken up in Committee of the Whole in the order in which they shall stand on the General Orders, unless the Committee, by a two-thirds vote, shall, in any case, otherwise direct. The paper under consideration shall be first read at length, unless the Committee shall otherwise order, and shall then be read and considered by sections. All amendmeuts made in Committee of the Whole shall be reported to the Convention for action.

Rule 22. If at any time, in the Committeo of the Whole, it shall appear that no quorum be present, the Committee shall immediately rise, and the Chairman shall report the fact to the Convention.

CHAPTER IX.

Of Motions and their Precedence.

Rule 23. When a question shall be under consideration, no motion shall be received except as herein specified, and motions shall have precedence in the order stated, viz.:

1. For an adjournment.
2. For a recess.
3. A call of the Convention.
4. To lay on the table.
5. To postpone indefinitely.
6. To postpone to a day certain.
7. To commit to a Committee of the Whole.
8. To commit to a standing committee.
9. To commit to a select committee.
10. To amend.

Rule 24. The motion to adjourn for the day, for a recess, and to lay on the table, shall be decided without amendment or debate. The respective motions to postpone or commit shall preclude debate on the main question.

Rule 25. Every motion or resolution shall, after presentation, be first stated by the President, or on his order read by the Secretary before debate, and again, if desired by any member, immediately before putting the question. And every resolution and amendment shall be reduced to writing if the President or any member desire it.

Rule 26. After a proposition shall have been stated by the President, it shall be deemed to be in possession of the Convention, but may be withdrawn at any time before it shall be decided or amended.

Rule 27. The motions to adjourn or to take a recess shall be always in order when made by a member entitled to the floor.

Rule 28. A motion for reconsideration shall be in order at any time, and may be moved by any member of the Convention; but the question shall not be taken on the motion to reconsider on the same day on which the decision proposed to be reconsidered shall take place, unless by unanimous consent; and a motion to reconsider, being once put and lost, shall not be renewed, nor shall any subject be a second time reconsidered without the consent of the Convention. If the motion to reconsider shall not be made on the same day or the day after that on which the decision proposed to be reconsidered was made, three days' notice of the intention to make the motion shall be given.

CHAPTER X.

Of Resolutions.

Rule 29. The following classes of resolutions shall lie over one day for consideration, after which they may be called up as of course, under their appropriate order of business :

1. Resolutions containing calls for information from any of the Executive Departments, from State, county or municipal officers, or from any incorporate bodies.
2. Resolutions giving rise to debate, except such as shall relate to the disposition of business immediately before the Convention, to the business of the day on which they may be offered, or to adjournment or recesses.

Rule 30. All resolutions for the printing of an extra number of documents, shall be referred, as of course, to the Standing Committee on Printing, for their report thereon, before final action by the Convention.

Rule 31. All resolutions authorizing or contemplating expenditures for the purposes of the Convention, shall be referred to the Standing Committee on Contingent Expenses, for their report thereon before final action by the Convention.

CHAPTER XI.

Miscellaneous Provisions.

Rule 32. The privileges of admission to the floor of the Convention shall be confined to the following descriptions of persons, viz. :

1. The Governor and Lieutenant-Governor.
2. The Heads of the State Executive Departments and their Deputies.
3. Ex-Governors of the State.
4. Members of the United States Congress.
5. Officers of the Convention.
6. Reporters of the press, duly assigned as such by the President of the Convention.
7. Officers or ex-officers of the United States army or navy who have received the thanks of Congress by name on a special vote.
8. Judges and ex-Judges of the Court of Appeals, and the members of the two former Constitutional Conventions in this State.

Rule 33. In cases of the absence of a quorum at any session of the Convention, the members present may take such measures as they may deem necessary to secure the presence of a quorum, and may inflict such censure as they may deem just, on those who on being called on for that purpose shall render no sufficient excuse for their absence.

Rule 34. If any question contain several distinct propositions, it shall be divided by the President, at the request of any member; provided each subdivision, if left to itself, shall form a substantive proposition; but the motion to strike out and insert shall be indivisible.

Rule 35. The yeas and nays shall be taken and recorded in the journal on any question when demanded by fifteen members, except in cases where such a division shall have been already ordered on a pending question.

Rule 36. The journal of each day's proceedings shall be printed so that it shall be laid on the desks of members within one day after its approval.

Rule 37. Files of all documents ordered to be printed, shall be prepared and kept by the sergeant-at-arms, and one copy shall be placed upon the desk of each member of the Convention; one copy shall be supplied also to the secretary, one to each of his assistants, one to the stenographer, one to the librarian and one to each reporter for the press.

Rule 38. When a blank is to be filled and different sums or time shall be proposed, the question shall be first taken on the highest sum and the longest time.

Rule 39. No standing rule of the Convention shall be suspended, amended or rescinded, or additional rule or rules added, unless one day's notice of the motion therefor shall have been given; nor shall any such suspension, addition, amendment or repeal be then made, except by the vote of two-thirds of the members present, or that of a majority of all the members elected to the Convention. But such notice shall not be required on the last day's session. The notice and motion for a suspension, shall each state specifically the number of the rule and the object of the proposed suspension, and every suspension on such notice and motion, shall be held to apply only to the particular object or objects specified therein.

Rule 40. All questions relating to the priority of business, that is, the priority of one subject-matter over another, under the same order of business, the postponement of any special order, or the suspension of any rule, shall be decided without debate.

Rule 41. There shall be printed, as of course, and without any special order, eight hundred copies of all reports of committees on the subject of Constitutional revision, and of all reports and communications made in pursuance of the order or request of the Convention; and eight hundred copies of the journal; which numbers shall be denominated the usual number.

Rule 42. The Governor and each head of the State Executive departments shall be furnished by the printer with a copy of the official documents of the Convention out of the usual number printed.

Rule 43. The sergeant-at-arms shall receive from the printer all matter printed for the use of the Convention, and shall keep a record of the time of the reception of each document and the number of copies received, and shall cause a copy of each to be placed on the desks of the members, officers and reporters entitled to receive them, immediately after their reception by him.

Rule 44. There shall be bound, out of the usual number printed, three hundred copies of the journal and three hundred copies of the reports and documents of the Convention, to be distributed as follows, viz.: To each member of the Convention, one copy; State Library, five copies; the library of the Senate, sixteen copies; the library of the Assembly, fifty copies; the counties and public offices, sixty-nine copies.

Rule 45. The assistant sergeant-at-arms shall perform the duties of postmaster of the Convention, without any compensation for such services or claims for the same, other than that provided for by chapter 194 of the laws of 1867, and as such shall receive, distribute and dispatch such mail matter as may be deposited in his office, addressed to or by members of the Convention; and the sergeant-at-arms shall assign to the service of the acting postmaster such number of the messengers as he may need to aid him in the performance of his duty.

EXECUTIVE DEPARTMENT.

Under the present Constitution the Executive power is vested in a Governor, whose term of office is two years. No person is eligible to the office who is not a citizen of the United States, of the age of thirty years, and for five years next preceding his election, a resident within this State. He is constituted the Commander-in-Chief of the military and naval forces of the State; is empowered to convene the Legislature (or the Senate only) on extraordinary occasions; and to grant reprieves, commutations and pardons after conviction, for all offenses except treason and cases of impeachment, upon such conditions as he may determine. Upon conviction for treason, he may suspend sentence until the case shall be reported to the Legislature at its next meeting. He may also veto any bill passed by the Legislature, in which case a vote of two-thirds of the members present is necessary to its passage by the Legislature. He may remove from office Sheriffs, Clerks of Counties, including the Register and Clerk of the City and County of New York, Coroners and District Attorneys, giving to the officer removed a copy of the charges against him, and an opportunity of being heard in his defense. He may recommend the removal from office of any judicial officer, excepting Justices of the Peace, Judges and Justices of inferior courts not of record, Justices of the Supreme Court, and Judges of the Court of Appeals.

The following duties are imposed upon the Governor by the Constitution:

To communicate by message to the Legislature, at every session, the condition of the State, and to recommend such matters to them as he shall judge expedient. To transact all necessary business with the officers of government, both civil and military.

To expedite all measures resolved upon by the Legislature.

To enforce the laws.

To communicate annually to the Legislature the number of reprieves, commutations or pardons granted, with the names of the convicts and the circumstances attending the cases.

To nominate and, with the consent of the Senate, to appoint all Major-Generals and the Commissary-General.

To commission the commissioned officers of the militia.

Under the laws of the State, the Governor has power to nominate, and by and with the advice and consent of the Senate, to appoint the following named officers: The Auditor of the Canal Department; the Superintendent of the Insurance Department; the Superintendent of the Banking Department; three Canal Appraisers; three State Assessors; three Commissioners of Public Accounts; four Trustees for the State Asylum for Idiots; nine Managers of the State Lunatic Asylum; six Trustees for the Willard Asylum for the Insane; ten Managers for the Hudson River State Hospital for the Insane; nine Trustees for the State Institution for the Blind; fifteen Managers for the Western House of Refuge; eight State Commissioners of Public Charities; the Superintendent of the Onondaga Salt Springs; an Inspector of Gas Meters; the Agent of the Onondaga Indians; the Attorney of the Seneca Nation of Indians; three Commissioners of the New Capitol; eleven Harbor Masters for the port of New York, and one for the port of Albany; nine Port Wardens for the port of New York, and two special Wardens to reside at Quarantine; a Captain of the port of New York; the Hell Gate Pilots; one Health Officer of the port of New York; three Quarantine Commissioners of Emigration; two Trustees of the Nautical School; five Metropolitan Fire Commissioners; four Sanitary Commissioners in and for the Metropolitan Sanitary District; three Commissioners of Taxes and Assessments in and for the city and county of New York; three Capital Police Commissioners and two Advisory Commissioners; three Commissioners of Niagara Frontier Police District; Commissioners named in Chapter 289, Laws of 1840; Commissioners for loaning certain moneys of the United States; seven Trustees of the Seaman's Fund and Retreat; Notaries Public.

In addition to the foregoing, the Governor appoints Commissioners to take acknowledgments to be used in this State, residing in other States, and Great Britain; Railway Policemen; fifteen Wreck Masters in the county of Suffolk; twelve in the county of Queens, three in the county of Kings, two in the county of Richmond and two in the county of Westchester.

He is also authorized to appoint a Private Secretary, an Adjutant-General, an Inspector-General, an Engineer-in-Chief, a Judge-Advocate-General, a Surgeon-General, a Quartermaster-General, a Paymaster-General, a Chief of the Bureau of Military Statistics, six Aides-de-Camp, and a Military Secretary.

The Governor is, *ex-officio*, a Regent of the University, a Trustee of the Capitol, of the State Asylum for Idiots, of the Cornell University, and of Union College.

Number of Notaries Public allowed by law in each county.

County.	*Quota.*	*County.*	*Quota.*
Albany,	75	Clinton,	28
Allegany,	26	Columbia,	32
Broome,	26	Cortland,	18
Cattaraugus,	28	Delaware,	31
Cayuga,	43	Dutchess,	51
Chautauqua,	42	Erie, (Buffalo city not limited, 166),	33
Chemung,	22	Essex,	16
Chenango,	27		

County.	Quota.	County.	Quota.
Franklin,	18	Putnam,	11
Fulton,	14	Queens,	33
Genesee,	22	Rensselaer,	64
Greene,	21	Richmond,	16
Hamilton,	...	Rockland,	14
Herkimer,	29	St. Lawrence,	51
Jefferson,	48	Saratoga,	35
Kings, (now in office 421; number not limited.)		Schenectady,	14
		Schoharie,	21
Lewis,	19	Schuyler,	25
Livingston,	28	Seneca,	19
Madison,	32	Steuben,	43
Monroe,	69	Suffolk,	25
Montgomery,	26	Sullivan,	20
New York,	1000	Tioga,	22
Niagara,	34	Tompkins,	23
Oneida,	73	Ulster,	55
Onondaga,	67	Warren,	15
Ontario,	31	Washington,	36
Orange,	50	Wayne,	37
Orleans,	21	Westchester,	66
Oswego,	54	Wyoming,	19
Otsego,	36	Yates,	14

Chapter 508, Laws of 1863, allows one to every two thousand of population in each county, except in the county of Kings, the city of Buffalo, and the city and county of New York.

Chapter 29, Laws of 1864, allows one to each Bank, except in cities of Brooklyn, New York and Buffalo.

Chapter 420, Laws of 1867, allows one hundred additional for city of New York, and two for each Assembly District in the State.

Commissioners of Deeds for this State, appointed in other States, and now in office.

Alabama,	6	New Hampshire,	5
Arkansas,	1	New Jersey,	32
California,	13	North Carolina,	4
Colorado,	3	Ohio,	22
Connecticut,	31	Oregon,	1
Delaware,	4	Pennsylvania,	31
Florida,	4	Rhode Island,	8
Georgia,	10	South Carolina,	5
Illinois,	17	Tennessee,	9
Indiana,	3	Texas,	6
Iowa,	9	Vermont,	7
Kansas,	3	Virginia,	8
Kentucky,	8	West Virginia,	1
Louisiana,	10	Wisconsin,	22
Maine,	8	District of Columbia,	10
Maryland,	7	Idaho,	1
Massachusetts,	34	Montana,	7
Michigan,	28	Nebraska,	1
Minnesota,	4	Kingdom of Great Britain,	2
Mississippi,	5	Canada West,	3
Missouri,	13	Empire of France	...
Nevada,	10		

Numbers allowed by law, ten to each county.

Number allowed by law in Great Britain and France, three.

TABLE *showing the total number of Pardons, conditional or unconditional, Commutations of sentence and Restoration to citizenship in this State, by years since* 1846, *and the total from* 1777 *inclusive.**

YEARS.	FROM WHAT PUNISHMENT PARDONED.									COMMUTATION.		PARDONED CONDITIONALLY.					RESTORED		FROM WHAT CLASS CRIMES PARDONED.					GENERAL SUMMARY.		
	Fine.	Fines and imprisonment.	Fines, but not imprisonment.	Imprisonment, but not fines.	Penitentiary, jail, and local prisons.	State prisons, limited terms.	State prison for life.	Punishment not stated.	Fine partially remitted.	From death to State prison for life.	Other commutations.	To leave the State.	To leave the United States.	To leaving city.	To leaving county.	To abstain from use of intoxicating liquors.	To military privileges.	To rights of a citizen.	Against person.	Against property.	Forgery and against the currency.	Other offenses.	Respited in capital offenses.	Conditional pardons.	Unconditional pardons.	Total.
1847,	16	8	1	......	......	94	8	......	......	2	......	1	3	...	...	......	......	101	32	66	15	16	...	4	125	129
1848,	1	1	1	1	28	102	2	......	......	1	2	3	......	...	...	......	......	73	33	77	18	11	1	4	135	139
1849,	...	3	......	1	4	24	2	......	......	1	......	1	......	...	...	......	......	7	9	22	3	1	5	6	29	35
1850,	...	2	......	1	6	51	......	......	1	1	......	2	1	...	...	......	......	12	12	34	12	4	...	5	57	62
1851,	...	9	......	......	38	107	......	1	......	5	......	3	......	...	...	......	......	48	46	77	17	20	11	3	157	160
1852,	1	16	......	2	55	103	4	1	......	4	......	......	3	...	...	......	1	84	70	64	25	27	8	7	179	186
1853,	1	4	1	......	90	104	2	2	......	3	......	10	......	...	...	......	......	37	61	90	15	41	13	35	172	207
1854,	...	5	1	......	58	140	1	......	......	1	43	2	......	...	...	......	......	40	63	138	16	32	3	31	218	249
1855,	...	10	......	3	55	92	1	1	......	5	86	3	......	1	3	32	......	1	51	73	13	25	9	39	214	253
1856,	1	6	1	......	55	109	1	......	......	5	99	4	1	...	...	5	......	2	53	90	13	17	...	10	267	277
1857,	...	18	2	2	82	110	1	......	6	2	1	7	......	...	1	2	......	13	42	95	16	40	...	30	163	193
1858,	...	13	3	......	106	127	......	......	6	5	2	10	3	1	...	......	......	29	62	121	17	33	2	22	211	233
1859,	...	7	......	......	16	58	3	......	......	2	6	......	......	...	...	......	......	22	25	44	7	8	4	13	79	92
1860,	...	3	......	......	15	58	2	......	......	......	14	1	......	...	...	......	......	52	15	38	10	15	1	3	89	92
1861,	...	......	......	......	10	55	1	......	......	......	15	......	......	...	1	1	......	30	11	45	5	5	...	2	64	66
1862,	...	4	......	......	17	66	4	......	......	......	19	....	1	...	...	......	......	32	17	43	13	14	...	1	86	87
1863,	2	2	......	18	6	14	......	......	......	4	1	1	......	...	...	......	......	61	35	25	6	5	1	2	69	71
1864,	...	2	......	......	29	84	......	1	......	1	85	......	1	...	...	1	......	61	48	40	13	11	1	2	114	116
1865,	...	......	......	......	35	90	3	2	1	2	17	......	1	1	...	1	......	25	58	57	7	9	3	5	126	131
1866,	...	11	......	96	61	94	5	1	......	3	21	2	1	...	...	......	......	83	50	78	7	32	1	13	155	168
Total since 1846,	22	124	10	124	766	1,682	40	9	14	48	411	50	15	3	5	42	1	813	793	1,316	248	366	63	237	2,701	2,915
Total since '77, inc.,	163	311	26	168	1,772	6,414	580	268	30	81	466	1,074	222	3	5	42	2	1,218	1,784	5,801	1,444	580	81	1,782	8,793	10,577

Pardon conditioned to enlistment in navy, 52; to giving bonds for good behavior, 157.

* The appendix to the Report on Criminal Statistics in 1855 [Senate Doc., 79], contains by single years the statistics of pardons since the organization of a State government in 1777. The earlier pardons were recorded in the same volumes with commissions, but, since 1799, they have been separately recorded.

Number of Pardons Granted by each Executive, from the organization of a State Government in 1777.

George Clinton, 18 years (1777 to 1795),	166
John Jay, 6 years, (1795 to 1801),	160
George Clinton, 3 years (1801 to 1804),	142
Morgan Lewis, 3 years (1804 to 1807),	213
Daniel D. Tompkins, 9 years and 8 months (1807 to 1817),	1,693
John Tayler, 4 months (1817),	223
De Witt Clinton, 5 years and 6 months (1817 to 1822),	1,619
Joseph C. Yates, 2 years (1823 and 1824),	291
De Witt Clinton, 3 years and 2 months (1825 to Feb. 1828),	670
Nathaniel Pitcher, 10 months (Feb to Dec. 1828),	228
Martin Van Buren, 3 months (Jan. to March, 1829),	37
Enos T. Throop, 2 years and 9 months (March 1829 to Dec. 1832),	415
William L. Marcy, 6 years (1833 to 1838),	834
William H. Seward, 4 years (1838 to 1842),	377
William C. Bouck, 2 years (1843 and 1844),	279
Silas Wright, 2 years (1845 and 1846),	282
John Young, 2 years (1847 and 1848),	268
Hamilton Fish, 2 years (1849 and 1850),	97
Washington Hunt, 2 years (1851 and 1852),	346
Horatio Seymour, 2 years (1853 and 1854),	456
Myron H. Clark, 2 years (1855 and 1856),	530
John A. King, 2 years (1857 and 1858),	426
Edwin D. Morgan, 4 years (1859 to 1862),	337
Horatio Seymour, 2 years (1863 and 1864),	187
Reuben E. Fenton, 2 years (1865 and 1866),	299

This list does not include those respited for a limited time, nor simple restorations to citizenship of persons previously pardoned.

The indexes to the laws show that, under the first State Constitution, in which the power of pardoning for murder was reserved by the Legislature, three respites and five pardons were granted, in the latter cases including restoration of person and estate to the same condition as before sentences two general acts of indemnity and oblivion were passed, applying to offenders under obnoxious acts, and those engaged in the Vermont controversy. Those attainted and banished October 22, 1779, were subsequently allowed to return to the State, but not to recover their property. The first conditional pardon was granted by Governor George Clinton, the first commutation of death to imprisonment for life by Governor Jay, the first restoration to citizenship by Lieutenant-Governor Pitcher, and the first respite in capital offenses (except by the Legislature), by Governor Marcy.

SECRETARY OF STATE.

The office of Secretary of State has existed from the earliest period of the Government, and his records extend back through the English and Dutch colonial periods. He is the keeper of the State Archives and the Great seal, and, in his office are preserved the original laws and joint resolutions of the Legislature, land papers, Indian treaties, civil commissions, pardons, oaths of office, certificates of incorporation under most of the general laws, depositions of resident aliens intending to become citizens, and such other books, maps, records, parchments, papers and documents as have heretofore been or may, from time to time, be required by general or special laws. He issues certified copies of papers requiring the great seal, and certifies to the seal and signature of county and other officials, grants peddlers licenses, makes an annual report upon pauperism and crime, from reports of county officers, and once in ten years directs the taking of a State census.

The Secretary of State is, *ex officio*, a Regent of the University, a Commissioner of the Land Office and of the Canal Fund, a Member of the Canal Board, and of the Board of State Canvassers, a Trustee of the Capitol and of the State Hall, a Trustee of the Idiot Asylum and of Union College, and, in conjunction with the Comptroller, makes all contracts for printing and binding ordered by the Legislature, and not otherwise provided for. He has also specific duties in relation to the publication and distribution of the laws and documents ordered by the Legislature of this State, and the distribution of the Laws of Congress. At the opening of each session of the Legislature he attends and administers to the Assembly the Constitutional oath. He is elected biennially, and receives a salary of $2,500.

CRIMINAL STATISTICS.

Excepting the reports made by Inspectors of State Prisons, we have no statistics of crime in the several counties of this State, earlier than the revision of the statutes in 1828. It was therein made the duty of the several county clerks, to transmit, soon after the adjournment of every court, a statement of all the convictions had, to the Secretary of State. These reports were ordered to contain a description of the offense committed, abridged from the indictment, and sufficiently full to maintain the averments necessary to be made in any indictment against the same person for a second offense. The intention of these returns was to afford the legal evidence necessary to determine the penalty awarded for repeated offenses, but beyond this no use appears to have been originally contemplated.

On the 13th of April, 1837, a law was passed requiring the Secretary of State to report to the next and succeeding legislatures, a statement of all convictions had during the preceding year, with the dates of conviction, sentence, court at which tried, and crime. Under this authority, and the modifications of subsequent amendments, a report has been made annually since that period. For several years, these years contained no statistics indicating the habits, domestic relations, education, nativity, age, profession or previous convictions of the persons reported. These have since been included,* but unfortunately the returns have in some years been so defective as to greatly impair their value.

The limited space of this manual will not admit of summaries of habits, domestic relations, education, nativity, age, profession, and other details embraced in the present system.

---

*Laws of 1839, chapter 252, page 234.

General Summary of Crime during twenty years.

YEARS.	CONVICTIONS IN COURTS OF RECORD AS REPORTED BY COUNTY CLERKS.						RESULTS OF INDICTMENTS AND OF CONVICTIONS UPON CONFESSION AS REPORTED BY COUNTY CLERKS.						Whole number convicted in courts of special sessions.
	Whole number of convictions in courts of record.	Offenses against the person.	Offenses against property with violence.	Offenses against property without violence.	Offenses against the currency.	Other offenses.	Whole number of indictments tried.	Number on which convictions were had.	Number in which defendants were acquitted.	Number on which the jury did not agree.	Number of persons convicted on confession.	Number of indictments on which persons were discharged without trial.	
1846, ..	1,517	384	138	471	60	538	1,097	719	353	25	853	783	3,184
1847, ..	1,294	335	132	396	54	407	959	610	330	19	699	1,161	3,179
1848, ..	1,527	437	120	612	38	425	1,284	766	485	33	715	540	3,387
1849, ..	1,531	397	150	545	24	404	1,291	801	386	31	673	804	3,874
1850, ..	1,552	397	199	521	33	410	1,310	719	414	17	664	650	4,124
1851, ..	1,482	409	148	475	37	406	1,106	709	365	24	782	532	3,592
1852, ..	1,602	411	228	480	25	482	1,185	782	363	29	690	441	3,733
1853, ..	1,844	482	185	573	41	627	1,536	1,059	450	27	1,056	470	5,256
1854, ..	2,117	420	189	580	75	853	1,489	1,012	439	38	1,154	506	5,456
1855, ..	1,830	395	268	574	37	556	1,372	920	432	24	922	387	5,347
1856, ..	1,507	425	248	573	49	212	1,205	840	323	38	651	1,010	8,090
1857, ..	1,554	375	340	607	63	168	1,084	761	300	22	839	672	7,460
1858, ..	1,712	434	329	577	90	206	1,369	869	358	20	849	390	10,339
1859, ..	2,091	425	341	439	89	505	1,360	903	410	20	1,292	505	7,796
1860, ..	2,212	599	381	566	121	545	1,150	714	392	31	963	595	8,561
1861, ..	2,275	562	340	619	150	605	1,242	826	400	25	1,405	669	13,430
1862, ..	1,616	377	215	449	75	500	897	572	237	20	966	711	12,933
1863, ..	1,644	433	241	540	68	362	865	580	218	22	1,080	494	10,923
1864, ..	1,430	416	169	436	60	349	822	520	276	20	961	655	12,459
1865, ..	2,036	417	289	907	52	271	1,097	690	391	16	1,472	1,007	11,222

General classification of crimes.

YEARS.	Offenses against the person.	Offenses against property with violence.	Offenses against property without violence.	Offenses against the currency.	Other offenses not included in the foregoing.	Totals.
1847, ...	335	132	396	24	40	1,294
1848, ...	437	120	512	33	425	1,527
1849, ...	397	150	545	43	404	1,531
1850, ...	397	199	521	36	410	1,552
1851, ...	409	148	475	49	401	1,482
1852, ...	411	228	480	50	434	1,602
1853, ...	482	185	573	52	553	1,844
1854, ...	420	189	580	75	853	2,117
1855, ...	395	268	574	37	556	1,830
1856, ...	425	248	573	49	212	1,507
1857, ...	375	340	607	63	168	1,554
1858, ...	434	329	577	90	206	1,712
1859, ...	425	341	439	89	505	2,091
1860, ...	599	381	566	121	545	1,601
1861, ...	562	340	619	150	604	1,671
1862, ...	377	215	449	75	500	1,616
1863, ...	427	241	532	68	376	1,644
1864, ...	416	169	436	60	349	1,430
1865, ...	417	289	907	52	371	2,036
1866, ...	553	467	1,119	53	473	2,665

Crimes for which Convictions were had in Courts of Record in the State of New York, from 1854 to 1866, both years inclusive.

CRIME.	1854	1855	1856	1857	1858	1859	1860	1861	1862	1863	1864	1865	1866
Offenses against the person.													
Administering poison,							3						1
Abandoning infant,	1									1	2	3	
Abduction,						2	2			2			
Assault,	3	19	22	38	36	19	5		14	12	17	11	11
Assault and battery,	256	260	273	211	259	279	377	325	226	240	208	243	317
Assault, intent to ravish,							5						3
Assault and trespass,			3										
Assault on public officer,							10	7	8	11	9		9
Assault, &c., with intent to maim,							1					10	1
Assault, &c., with intent to kill,	24	17	24	22	24	26	56	80	34	21	12	16	16
Assault, &c., intent to commit rape,	16	14	9	22	13	14	12	21	8	13	5	14	14
Assault with deadly weapon,	22	19	22		1		48			19	12	24	15
Assault, &c., to com. manslaughter,										1			
Assault, &c., with intent to rob,	5	6	9	8	17	23	18	10	6	9	6	19	13
Assault and rescue,			4										
Assault, intent to do bodily harm,							2			13	13		22
Assisting to commit a rape,			1										
Attempt to murder,						2							
Attempt to poison,						2						2	
Attempt to procure abortion,			1			1							1
Incest and rape,						1							
Kidnapping,										1	1		
Larceny from the person,								38	22		24		45
Maiming,			8				1						
Manslaughter,	33	20	20	30	37	29	32	43	35	31	40	36	35
Murder,	9	8		6	11	7	7	15	11	12	12	18	15
Procuring abortion,										1			
Rape,	17	8	15	13	7	13	17	20	11	12	6	11	12
Riot and affray,											30		8
Riot and assault,					1					13			
Riot, assault and battery,	33	23	12	24	20	9	3			15	20	10	12
Seduction,	1	1	2	1		3		3	1	1	3		3
	420	395	425	375	434	425	599	562	377	427	416	417	553
Offenses against property, with violence.													
Attempt to commit larceny,							29	26	39	55	61		2
Attempt to commit burglary,	4	5	19	33	38	52	19	23	10	16	3	39	83
Attempt at felony,								4			5		
Attempt to rob,		2											2
Burglary,	137	226	178	220	205	184	247	230	124	108	48	154	264
Burglary and larceny,	36	19	30	59	65	83	57	23	23	33	29	51	64
Felony,							4	10	1	1	1		5
Forcible entry,										1	2		
Robbery,	12	16	12	38	21	22	25	24	15	27	20	45	47
	189	268	248	340	329	341	381	340	215	241	169	289	467
Offenses against property, without violence.													
Arson,	11	12	8	14	12	10	18	16	19	11	13	17	17
Attempt to commit arson,	1			10	2	10				3			5
Attempt to commit grand larceny,	13	18	22	34	60							176	164
Attempt to commit petit larceny,						93							11
Embezzlement,	7	3	2	4	2						2	5	7
Grand larceny,	273	249	264	264	263	295	292	284	213	270	247	477	574
Larceny, 2d offense,			10	42						1			1
Obtaining prop. by false pretenses,	24	19	11	20	12	7	20	29	24	15	7	13	26
Petit larceny,	197	225	206	204	205		150	218	162	190	137	181	256
Petit larc'y after convit'n of felony,	3				1	5	10			7		1	3
Petit larceny, 2d offense,	28	20	33				63	48	20	27	17	26	26
Receiving stolen property,	23	28	17	15	20	19	13	24	11	8	11	11	27
Selling pretended title to land,											2		
	580	574	573	607	577	439	566	619	449	532	436	907	1119
Offenses against the currency.													
Accessory to forgery,										1			
Counterfeiting,	6	4										1	1

CRIME.	1854	1855	1856	1857	1858	1859	1860	1861	1862	1863	1864	1865	1866
Forgery,	59	33	47	58	90	89	100	147	70	58	51	46	50
Having counterfeit money in possession,	6	....	....	....	....	....	....	....	....	3	....	....	....
Passing counterfeit money,	4	....	2	4	....	....	21	3	5	6	9	5	2
	75	37	49	63	90	89	121	150	75	68	60	52	53
Other offences not included in the foregoing.													
Accessory to felony,	....	....	....	....	....	....	....	....	3	3	....	16	1
Advertising lottery tickets for sale,	3	....	....	....	....	....	1	....	....	....	....	....	....
Aiding an escape,	2	1	....	....	2	1	2	....	2	2	4	....	1
Aiding an escape and riot,	....	....	....	....	....	....	....	....	....	1	....	....	....
Attempt to break jail,	....	....	....	....	....	....	....	....	....	2	....	....	1
Bigamy,	12	5	11	17	10	11	8	9	9	22	11	14	19
Blasphemy,	....	....	3	....	....	....	....	....	....	....	2	....	6
Breaking jail,	9	3	6	....	4	5	2	....	1	3	4	2	1
Breach of the peace,	....	....	....	....	....	....	....	5	1	2	1	....	....
Bribery at election,	....	....	....	....	....	4	....	....	....	....	....	....	....
Buggery,	....	....	....	....	....	1	4	....	....	....	....	....	....
Carrying liquor in jail,	....	....	....	....	....	1	....	....	....	....	....	....	....
Carrying slung shot,	5	3	3	1	....	....	3	....	1	1	....	5	4
Compounding misdemeanor,	....	4	2	....	....	....	....	....	....	....	....	....	....
Contempt of court,	....	....	1	....	....	....	2	....	....	....	....	....	....
Cruelty to animals,	....	....	....	....	....	....	....	3	1	....	2	1	....
Disorderly persons,	....	2	1	23	3	1	....	....	....	....	....	....	4
Embezzlement,	....	....	....	....	....	....	4	4	2	7	7	....	....
Exposing the person,	5	8	2	....	1	....	....	5	4	1	....	....	....
Gaming,	10	3	3	1	....	2	....	3	....	....	....	....	1
Illegal voting,	6	20	2	3	12	6	5	5	3	4	4	4	....
Illegal registering name as voter,	....	....	....	1	....	....	....	....	....	....	....	....	....
Incest,	....	2	2	1	2	2	3	....	....	2	3	....	2
Intoxication,	....	....	....	....	21	5	22	22	8	9	6	3	9
Indecent exposure,	....	....	....	....	....	2	10	....	....	....	1	....	5
Keep'g disorderly or bawdy house,	56	33	29	31	26	29	26	36	....	14	5	42	16
Keeping disorderly house and selling liquor without license,	....	....	....	....	....	....	....	....	....	1	26	....	....
Keeping gaming house,	26	17	14	13	12	12	8	4	8	5	10	4	12
Keeping lottery office,	1	....	....	....	....	....	....	....	....	....	....	....	....
Letting bawdy house,	....	....	....	....	....	....	....	....	....	1	....	1	....
Libel,	14	3	1	....	....	....	3	....	1	....	....	1	1
Malicious mischief,	....	3	5	16	2	19	12	18	3	5	10	12	4
Marrying married person,	....	....	....	....	....	....	....	....	....	1	....	1	....
Mayhem,	....	....	....	....	2	5	....	....	....	....	2	....	1
Misdemeanor,	23	2	32	19	....	....	31	9	41	15	4	171	17
Nuisance,	15	8	12	3	2	3	7	2	8	10	4	10	4
Official malpractice,	1	3	....	....	....	....	....	....	....	....	....	....	1
Obstructing railroad track,	....	....	....	....	....	3	2	....	....	....	....	1	....
Perjury,	1	3	6	2	2	6	9	....	4	4	2	1	4
Prize fighting,	....	....	....	....	....	....	5	....	....	....	....	....	....
Resisting public officer,	10	2	5	....	....	....	3	....	....	4	....	....	9
Riot,	91	54	38	....	....	22	16	23	29	30	....	12	33
Selling goods at auction contrary to law,	....	....	2	....	....	....	....	....	....	....	....	....	....
Selling liquor to Indians,	....	....	....	....	2	....	2	....	....	....	....	....	....
Selling liquor without license,	508	358	26	12	94	361	338	439	323	216	223	68	301
Selling liquor to minors,	....	....	....	....	....	....	1	....	....	....	....	....	....
Selling liquor without license and to Indians,	....	....	....	....	....	....	....	....	....	1	....	....	....
Selling lottery tickets,	9	9	1	....	1	3	3	5	11	2	3	....	1
Selling unwholesome provisions,	....	....	....	....	....	1	....	....	....	....	1	....	....
Selling liquor on Sunday,	....	....	....	....	....	....	2	....	....	....	....	....	7
Subornation of perjury,	1	....	....	....	....	....	....	....	....	....	....	....	3
Trespass,	19	4	....	....	8	....	....	11	1	6	....	1	....
Unlawful assembly,	....	....	....	....	....	....	....	....	....	....	1	....	....
Usury,	....	1	....	....	1	....	....	1	....	....	....	....	....
Writing threatening letter,	....	....	....	....	....	....	....	....	....	....	....	1	....
Not given,	26	5	8	25	....	....	....	....	....	....	....	....	1
	853	556	212	168	206	505	545	604	500	376	349	371	473
Total,	2117	1830	1507	1554	1712	2091	1601	1671	1616	1644	1430	2036	2665

Whole number of Indictments tried, by

COUNTIES.	1847.	1848.	1849.	1850.	1851.	1852.	1853.	1854.	1855.
Albany, ...	38	60	57	27	46	34	50	47	40
Allegany, ...	7	15	3	18	18	21	20	24	40
Broome, ...	10	6	3	13	5	4	7	3	4
Cattaraugus, ...	6	4	5	14	20	14	14	8	8
Cayuga, ...	12	12	11	7	6	6	6	8	12
Chautauqua,......	11	11	17	8	13	10	30	9	12
Chemung, ...	6	17	15	19	13	19	21	12	9
Chenango,........	7	5	18	12	15	3	10	6	7
Clinton, ...	9	13	5	13	23	16	21	15	14
Columbia, ...	15	20	7	7	14	12	10	7	6
Cortland, ...	2	2	7	7	20	5	3	3	5
Delaware, ...	11	4	10	1	6	1	19	3	7
Dutchess, ...	14	27	11	44	26	15	13	29	18
Erie, ...	94	144	114	144	63	74	136	187	164
Essex,...........	....	7	13	10	2	7	1	3	4
Franklin,.........	3	3	7	8	2	6	4	10	7
Fulton, ...	5	10	10	10	11	13	4	6	6
Genesee, ...	6	5	7	10	17	13	14	11	14
Greene,...........	15	3	9	13	7	5	4	5	8
Hamilton, ...	....	....	....	....	....	*	*	*	....
Herkimer,........	6	16	14	20	5	3	5	7	8
Jefferson,.........	18	24	21	29	12	13	23	32	10
Kings,............	54	82	145	82	61	117	84	139	135
Lewis,............	4	4	3	3	3	3	5	7	2
Livingston,.......	14	16	18	15	19	21	19	20	18
Madison, ...	12	5	9	5	10	10	13	13	14
Monroe, ...	23	75	60	62	32	68	73	59	48
Montgomery, ...	10	10	2	5	9	8	11	4	6
New York, ...	25	303	292	308	292	338	487	410	369
Niagara,..........	6	9	5	8	14	6	8	4	18
Oneida, ...	27	32	17	42	....	5	14	25	13
Onondaga, ...	23	48	39	21	16	12	21	26	17
Ontario, ...	16	25	23	32	34	20	17	24	6
Orange, ...	24	23	22	20	20	20	14	9	7
Orleans, ...	12	7	19	21	15	10	2	16	14
Oswego,..........	22	32	31	33	22	17	20	24	20
Otsego,....... ...	12	16	8	12	20	1	10	8	5
Putnam,..........	7	1	14	1	4	5	9	1	2
Queens, ...	8	7	20	16	11	18	16	13	13
Rensselaer, ...	22	7	26	11	17	18	12	15	16
Richmond, ...	4	1	1	3	....	2	7	5	11
Rockland, ...	2	2	11	7	...	8	16	13	7
St. Lawrence, ...	16	18	34	26	19	32	47	31	25
Saratoga, ...	8	1	10	3	2	1	10	5	16
Schenectady, ...	12	5	12	.12	12	20	21	29	17
Schoharie, ...	3	5	....	5	2	3	7	*	6
Schuyler, ...	....	....	....	....	....	....	....	....	....
Seneca, ...	3	14	10	10	10	8	6	4	....
Steuben,..........	5	8	11	7	14	25	16	11	20
Suffolk,..........	1	6	8	1	9	8	11	19	24
Sullivan, ...	10	12	4	4	3	3	4	3	12
Tioga, ...	3	3	15	16	21	17	30	42	18
Tompkins, ...	4	6	10	20	7	*	35	4	9
Ulster, ...	5	13	4	12	12	20	12	5	15
Warren, ...	1	....	9	6	11	10	6	2	15
Washington, ...	8	16	12	13	8	7	5	7	10
Wayne,...........	11	6	5	6	...	2	12	7	5
Westchester, ...	14	12	8	21	21	1	17	32	24
Wyoming,........	7	5	9	4	6	20	11	7	6
Yates, ...	5	3	2	3	6	7	13	10	6
Total, ...	959	1,284	1,291	1,310	1,106	1,185	1,536	1,487	1,372

* No report.

counties, as reported by County Clerks.

1856.	1857.	1858.	1859.	1860.	1861.	1862.	1863.	1864.	1865.	1866
50	44	44	38	15	13	10	3	22	36	37
11	4	2	24	12	9	9	13	4	2	14
8	17	6	*	6	6	4	5	10	12	5
2	12	6	18	41	17	21	14	15	11	8
13	15	26	13	26	14	5	10	6	6	4
12	13	8	10	16	12	9	12	11	21	20
14	25	27	18	9	20	13	28	15	21	12
2	13	6	16	4	....	2	....	3	5	2
15	22	32	42	26	26	19	10	6	6	10
7	3	6	7	4	4	9	1	1	5	8
1	2	*	6	3	9	7	7	3	....	5
4	2	12	4	9	5	3	5	2	2	7
21	14	11	3	3	17	16	2	13	...	21
178	110	164	145	116	95	148	198	135	177	114
9	8	12	11	9	7	1	4	9	2	1
5	4	7	5	5	3	1	6	1	....	....
....	*	2	*	....	....	6	1	*	1	*
2	9	5	16	12	14	6	12	11	12	9
9	1	12	5	1	2	3	4	2	16	1
....	1	*	*	....	....	....	....	*	....	1
5	2	4	12	....	38	21	10	22	6	5
6	14	20	24	11	11	6	24	11	11	14
141	22	23	47	90	56	32	56	69	68	173
3	8	4	6	....	....	1	1	4	1	6
21	8	20	8	17	18	3	5	15	17	18
8	9	11	15	13	13	4	3	6	10	3
51	33	53	57	56	56	37	22	8	16	38
5	7	8	8	6	2	8	9	1	3	8
298	339	367	409	433	370	203	149	178	362	302
27	26	26	17	11	17	14	20	8	20	32
15	1	*	20	16	11	10	12	8	4	13
32	18	25	26	23	22	28	22	27	30	16
5	7	10	12	13	14	14	12	16	6	14
9	18	31	2	24	24	2	5	15	12	29
3	4	9	12	4	2	6	5	5	12	18
26	26	30	16	13	8	3	11	8	4	8
5	5	12	21	12	7	3	7	5	4	6
....	4	*	*	....	7	1	1	1	2	5
19	14	17	24	22	16	9	6	11	....	20
13	10	17	15	30	31	17	25	21	18	30
....	*	*	3	6	12	11	....	5	21	8
4	2	7	8	5	9	4	10	3	7	4
15	16	19	36	23	30	35	26	13	11	14
5	7	3	15	8	8	11	6	5	15	14
7	17	14	29	19	11	5	11	6	11	16
5	4	1	8	4	4	1	6	4	4	3
....	....	*	...	10	6	3	6	3	6	5
2	4	13	24	1	2	6	8	1	1	6
9	21	8	14	25	18	3	1	9	17	23
7	15	11	13	12	13	24	7	7	8	5
1	5	2	2	10	9	5	5	3	1	*
11	12	9	22	17	12	4	4	4	5	...
13	6	22	*	6	11	10	10	1	8	5
16	23	32	28	21	32	7	10	6	23	17
5	9	3	7	....	13	1	...	....	1	2
3	14	8	*	8	3	2	....	7	10	1
6	4	3	9	13	10	7	7	1	5	3
14	12	17	*	28	24	18	....	24	....	*
15	10	15	10	19	6	15	4	6	3	7
12	9	*	*	10	13	10	4	6	9	1
1,205	1,089	1,369	1,360	1,150	1,242	897	865	822	1,097	1,171

* No report.

Number of Indictments on which Convictions

COUNTIES.	1847.	1848.	1849.	1850.	1851.	1852.	1853.	1854.	1855.
Albany,	20	38	38	19	39	23	37	36	29
Allegany,	4	8	2	11	4	10	13	13	13
Broome,	9	5	....	6	4	2	4	1	4
Cattaraugus,	....	2	....	7	7	7	9	2	6
Cayuga,	6	6	6	7	5	2	5	7	9
Chautauqua,	6	4	13	4	8	6	22	6	10
Chemung,	2	8	9	12	3	15	13	6	7
Chenango,	3	3	8	7	4	2	9	2	4
Clinton,	5	9	3	7	17	12	18	13	11
Columbia,	12	13	5	4	12	9	6	4	5
Cortland,	1	1	4	1	13	1	...	2	3
Delaware,	8	1	6	1	2	1	13	3	4
Dutchess,	9	22	8	25	20	14	11	23	15
Erie,	53	77	72	92	42	48	98	136	131
Essex,	....	4	10	7	2	3	1	3	2
Franklin,	3	3	2	3	....	5	2	5	2
Fulton,	2	4	7	8	8	6	2	6	4
Genesee,	4	4	3	9	10	8	8	6	10
Greene,	11	1	4	11	4	2	3	3	2
Hamilton,	....	....	....	....	....	*	*	*	....
Herkimer,	3	9	7	9	4	3	2	6	2
Jefferson,	11	13	13	13	8	9	10	18	9
Kings,	41	51	70	62	48	75	64	106	86
Lewis,	1	1	1	2	1	1	3	4	2
Livingston,	9	3	5	8	11	9	12	11	10
Madison,	4	2	6	5	5	4	8	11	11
Monroe,	11	47	28	35	22	46	49	36	24
Montgomery,	4	4	1	2	6	7	7	2	5
New York,	172	196	197	205	195	233	324	244	227
Niagara,	5	5	....	6	8	5	7	4	9
Oneida,	12	21	13	24	....	2	8	13	7
Onondaga,	16	30	23	13	5	10	15	20	12
Ontario,	10	13	14	22	24	15	10	20	5
Orange,	16	13	14	15	14	14	8	7	6
Orleans,	10	4	17	19	12	7	2	8	6
Oswego,	14	21	21	19	13	10	15	20	17
Otsego,	5	7	3	8	2	1	6	3	3
Putnam,	5	....	8	1	3	4	9	1	2
Queens,	6	4	18	13	10	14	13	10	11
Rensselaer,	17	6	24	8	11	16	8	12	9
Richmond,	4	....	1	1	....	....	4	5	9
Rockland,	1	1	11	6	....	5	16	12	6
St. Lawrence,	11	27	16	2	10	16	29	30	18
Saratoga,	7	4	5	8	....	....	5	3	13
Schenectady,	9	2	6	5	3	10	15	22	5
Schoharie,	1	4	....	5	1	3	4	*	5
Schuyler,	....	....	....	....	....	....	....	....	....
Seneca,	1	8	9	9	7	7	3	2	....
Steuben,	....	5	4	5	7	15	12	5	13
Suffolk,	...	3	3	1	5	8	10	10	16
Sullivan,	8	8	3	2	3	2	2	2	8
Tioga,	2	3	13	12	16	11	30	36	15
Tompkins,	2	4	7	10	5	*	22	4	7
Ulster,	4	7	2	9	12	12	6	2	10
Warren,	1	....	1	4	9	9	5	2	13
Washington,	6	9	22	10	8	3	5	4	7
Wayne,	9	3	4	6	....	1	7	6	2
Westchester,	7	9	6	17	13	1	14	21	24
Wyoming,	5	4	2	4	3	13	9	6	3
Yates,	2	2	3	3	1	5	7	6	6
Total,	610	766	801	819	709	782	1,059	1,012	920

* No report.

were had, as reported by County Clerks.

1856.	1857.	1858.	1859.	1860.	1861.	1862.	1863.	1864.	1865.	1866.
45	30	34	33	11	11	7	2	12	21	21
4	2	2	19	6	7	3	11	3	2	11
4	16	6	*	4	....	...	3	7	10	5
1	9	6	9	31	13	11	8	8	3	2
8	11	12	6	12	10	5	2	6	1	3
9	11	7	6	12	12	8	9	9	12	14
4	19	5	15	8	10	13	28	13	14	7
1	11	4	9	2	...	....	....	2	3	2
14	13	23	22	22	22	15	5	4	3	6
5	....	5	5	2	1	2	1	1	4	7
1	1	*	4	2	5	5	4	2	....	2
1	1	9	2	4	4	2	3	2	1	5
10	14	5	2	2	11	11	2	8	....	17
113	72	102	78	61	61	67	103	90	135	70
6	6	7	8	5	4	1	4	6	1	...
3	2	7	3	4	1	1	6	1	....	....
. ..	*	2	*	....	....	6	....	*	1	*
2	5	3	10	6	8	4	6	4	6	7
4	1	10	5	4	2	....	3	1	2	1
....	1	*	*	....	....	....	....	*	....	.. .
5	2	2	7	....	37	18	4	10	5	7
5	11	12	23	9	8	3	13	5	9	9
109	17	21	36	76	46	22	42	47	47	105
1	5	3	5	....	....	....	1	2	1	1
9	6	14	3	8	16	3	4	8	16	9
5	5	6	6	4	10	7	3	5	9	2
33	19	32	38	40	41	33	15	4	12	25
5	4	8	7	3	1	4	7	1	2	6
220	241	241	246	216	215	115	103	104	194	159
19	14	12	5	9	14	8	14	6	16	27
9	1	*	7	12	6	8	8	4	2	9
23	17	21	24	14	15	16	13	17	19	15
5	5	7	8	....	10	10	8	11	4	8
7	11	23	2	17	13	1	5	7	6	17
2	4	8	8	3	2	6	5	5	11	14
22	24	21	12	5	2	2	8	6	1	5
2	2	3	17	3	2	1	6	3	3	4
...	4	*	*	....	6	....	1	1	2	4
14	14	16	26	21	16	14	5	6	....	15
5	8	12	10	16	19	9	13	10	12	25
....	*	*	2	5	7	9	....	4	8	6
4	2	6	8	4	5	3	7	2	4	3
10	8	2	26	9	18	23	16	10	6	9
5	3	9	9	3	5	7	5	4	4	10
5	10	1	22	17	9	5	11	6	9	13
4	2	9	8	2	2	....	5	4	4	3
....	....	*	....	8	4	1	5	2	4	3
2	2	14	21	....	1	5	10	1	1	5
7	12	7	12	30	12	3	1	4	12	17
5	14	7	8	....	10	19	4	6	5	3
1	1	2	1	7	8	5	5	2	1	*
6	10	9	19	13	11	2	4	2	4	....
11	4	20	*	6	8	10	8	1	4	....
13	12	25	19	12	21	6	7	5	18	14
4	6	3	5	....	12	....	....	....	....	1
2	13	10	*	6	3	....	....	4	5	....
4	3	2	8	9	3	7	6	1	5	1
10	9	13	*	21	14	12	....	17	....	*
8	5	14	9	15	4	11	4	2	2	5
8	6	*	*	7	8	4	4	2	4	1
844	761	869	903	714	826	572	580	520	690	731

* No report.

Number of Indictments on which Defendants

COUNTIES.	1847.	1848.	1849.	1850.	1851.	1852.	1853.	1854.	1855.
Albany, ...	17	22	18	8	7	11	13	11	11
Allegany, ...	3	6	1	3	9	7	6	6	22
Broome, ...	1	1	3	....	1	2	3	1	....
Cattaraugus, ...	6	1	4	7	12	4	5	3	2
Cayuga, ...	6	6	5	....	1	4	1	1	3
Chautauqua, ...	5	7	4	4	5	4	8	3	2
Chemung, ...	4	9	5	5	10	4	6	6	2
Chenango, ...	3	2	10	5	11	1	1	3	....
Clinton, ...	2	4	2	5	6	4	3	2	3
Columbia, ...	3	6	2	2	1	2	3	3	1
Cortland, ...	1	1	3	1	7	4	2	1	2
Delaware, ...	2	3	1	....	4	....	6	....	2
Dutchess, ...	5	5	3	19	6	1	2	6	3
Erie, ...	36	63	35	48	19	24	35	46	32
Essex, ...	....	3	3	3	....	4	....	..	2
Franklin, ...	....	...	5	5	2	1	2	4	4
Fulton, ...	3	6	3	2	3	7	2	1	2
Genesee, ...	1	1	1	1	7	5	6	5	4
Greene, ...	4	2	4	2	2	2	....	2	5
Hamilton, ...	....	...	...	...	....	*	*	*	....
Herkimer, ...	2	5	7	11	1	....	3	....	6
Jefferson, ...	7	11	7	13	4	3	13	11	1
Kings, ...	13	31	20	17	10	31	19	33	48
Lewis, ...	3	3	2	1	2	2	2	3	....
Livingston, ...	4	12	9	4	7	12	7	2	4
Madison, ...	7	3	3	....	5	2	3	....	3
Monroe, ...	10	23	18	26	9	22	22	22	22
Montgomery, ...	5	6	1	3	1	1	3	2	1
New York, ...	78	107	95	103	97	105	163	166	142
Niagara, ...	1	3	...	2	6	1	1	....	9
Oneida, ...	14	10	5	17	....	3	4	11	6
Onondaga, ...	5	16	16	8	10	2	6	6	4
Ontario, ...	5	9	8	8	10	5	7	4	1
Orange, ...	8	9	8	5	6	6	5	2	1
Orleans, ...	2	2	3	2	2	3	....	7	7
Oswego, ...	8	9	7	13	6	4	4	4	3
Otsego, ...	7	9	3	1	20	....	4	5	2
Putnam, ...	2	1	2	....	2	1	....	....	....
Queens, ...	2	3	1	3	....	4	3	3	2
Rensselaer, ...	5	....	2	3	6	1	4	3	7
Richmond, ...	....	1	....	2	....	2	3	....	2
Rockland, ...	1	1	...	1	....	....	...	1	1
St. Lawrence, ...	2	19	16	1	8	16	15	1	7
Saratoga, ...	1	5	3	4	2	1	4	2	3
Schenectady, ...	3	3	6	....	5	9	6	7	11
Schoharie, ...	2	1	....	4	1	....	3	*	1
Schuyler, ...	....	....	....	....	...	....	....	....	....
Seneca, ...	2	6	1	16	3	1	3	2	....
Steuben, ...	5	2	7	2	7	10	4	3	7
Suffolk, ...	1	2	4	....	4	...	1	9	6
Sullivan, ...	2	4	....	2	....	1	1	1	4
Tioga, ...	1	....	2	4	5	6	....	6	3
Tompkins ...,....	1	2	3	8	1	*	13	....	2
Ulster, ...	1	5	1	3	....	7	5	2	5
Warren, ...	....	...	3	....	2	1	1	....	2
Washington, ...	2	6	1	3	....	4	....	2	3
Wayne, ...	3	3	1	....	....	1	4	1	3
Westchester, ...	7	3	2	4	4	....	3	10	...
Wyomihg, ...	2	1	6	....	2	4	2	....	1
Yates, ...	3	1	1	....	4	1	5	1	....
Total, ...	330	485	386	414	365	363	450	439	432

* No report.

were acquitted as reported by County Clerks.

1856.	1857.	1858.	1859.	1860.	1861.	1862.	1863.	1864.	1865.	1866.
5	13	9	5	1	2	3	1	10	15	15
6	2	2	5	1	2	3	2	1	....	2
2	1	....	*	1	6	1	1	3	1	....
1	3	....	9	9	5	9	3	6	8	6
5	4	13	3	8	4	....	7	....	5	1
3	2	1	1	4	1	1	3	2	9	6
7	4	2	2	....	4	2	....	2	6	3
1	2	2	7	2	....	....	....	1	2	....
1	8	9	10	1	3	3	5	2	3	3
2	3	1	2	1	2	7	....	....	1	1
....	....	*	2	1	4	2	3	1	....	1
3	1	3	2	5	1	....	1	....	1	2
11	....	4	1	1	6	5	....	5	....	4
63	36	50	44	31	33	27	51	36	42	43
3	3	3	3	4	3	....	....	3	1	1
....	2	....	2	....	2	....	....	....	....	....
....	*	....	*	....	....	....	1	*	....	*
....	4	2	6	3	7	2	4	7	6	5
5	....	2	....	....	....	....	1	1	14	....
....	....	*	*	....	....	....	....	*	....	1
....	....	2	5	....	1	3	6	12	1	1
....	3	6	1	3	3	3	11	6	2	5
30	5	2	11	11	10	10	17	22	21	66
2	2	1	1	....	....	....	....	2	....	5
7	2	8	3	5	2	....	1	5	1	6
1	2	3	7	2	1	....	....	1	1	1
18	14	22	19	15	15	4	7	3	4	13
....	2	....	1	1	1	4	2	....	1	2
77	98	126	163	189	155	81	45	74	168	143
7	12	13	12	1	1	6	5	2	4	7
6	....	*	10	3	5	2	3	3	1	3
9	1	4	4	6	8	8	5	9	11	1
....	2	3	2	2	3	2	3	5	1	5
2	6	8	....	7	9	1	....	6	5	11
1	....	1	1	1	....	....	....	....	1	4
2	1	8	2	5	6	....	2	1	2	2
3	3	8	3	7	4	....	1	2	1	2
....	....	*	*	....	1	1	....	....	....	1
2	....	1	5	3	4	....	1	5	....	4
5	2	4	4	12	11	7	11	8	6	5
....	*	*	1	1	3	1	....	1	12	2
....	....	1	....	1	4	1	2	....	2	1
4	6	5	9	8	14	9	3	3	4	5
....	2	1	6	1	2	2	1	1	1	3
2	6	2	6	2	2	....	....	....	2	4
1	2	....	....	....	3	1	....	....	....	....
....	....	*	....	2	2	1	1	1	....	2
....	2	3	3	....	1	1	1	....	....	1
2	7	4	7	2	5	....	....	4	5	6
2	1	4	4	....	3	4	2	1	3	2
....	4	....	1	3	....	....	....	1	....	*
5	2	....	3	1	1	2	....	2	1	....
2	2	2	*	....	3	....	1	....	4	5
3	11	7	8	9	11	1	3	1	4	3
1	3	....	2	....	1	....	1	....	1	1
1	1	....	*	1	....	....	....	1	3	1
2	1	1	1	3	7	....	....	....	....	2
2	2	4	*	6	9	8	....	7	....	*
4	4	1	1	4	2	3	....	2	....	2
2	1	*	*	2	2	6	....	2	4	....
323	300	358	410	392	400	237	218	276	391	421

* No report.

Number of Indictments on which Jury did

COUNTIES.	1847.	1848.	1849.	1850.	1851.	1852.	1853.	1854.	1855.
Albany,	1	....	....	....	....	....	....	....	....
Allegany,	....	1	....	2	4	4	1	5	5
Broome,	....	....	....	1	....	....	....	1	....
Cattaraugus,	....	1	....	....	....	3	....	3	....
Cayuga,	....	....	....	....	....	....	....	....	....
Chautauqua,	....	....	....	....	....	....	....	....	....
Chemung,	....	....	....	....	....	....	1	....	....
Chenango,	1	....	....	....	....	....	....	1	3
Clinton,	....	....	....	....	....	....	....	....	....
Columbia,	....	1	....	1	1	....	1	....	....
Cortland,	....	....	....	....	....	....	1	....	....
Delaware,	....	....	....	....	....	....	....	....	....
Dutchess,	....	....	....	....	....	....	....	....	....
Erie,	5	4	6	....	....	1	3	5	1
Essex,	....	....	....	....	....	....	....	....	....
Franklin,	....	....	....	....	....	....	....	....	1
Fulton,	....	....	....	....	....	....	....	....	....
Genesee,	1	....	....	....	....	....	....	....	....
Greene,	....	....	....	2	1	....	1	....	1
Hamilton,	....	....	....	....	....	*	*	....	...
Herkimer,	1	2	....	....	....	....	....	1	....
Jefferson,	....	....	1	3	....	1	....	3	....
Kings,	....	....	2	1	5	8	1	....	1
Lewis,	....	....	....	....	....	....	....	....	....
Livingston,	1	1	2	2	1	....	....	7	2
Madison,	1	....	....	....	....	1	2	2	....
Monroe,	2	5	2	....	1	....	2	1	2
Montgomery,	1	....	....	....	2	....	1	....	....
New York,	....	....	....	....	....	....	....	....	3
Niagara,	....	1	....	....	....	....	....	....	....
Oneida,	1	1	1	....	....	....	2	1	...
Onondaga,	2	2	1	....	1	....	....	....	1
Ontario,	1	3	....	....	....	....	....	....	....
Orange,	....	1	....	....	....	....	....	....	....
Orleans,	....	1	1	....	1	....	1	1	1
Oswego,	....	2	1	1	1	1	....	...	....
Otsego,	....	....	....	2	....	....	1	....	....
Putnam,	....	....	4	....	....	....	....	....	....
Queens,	....	....	1	....	1	....	....	....	....
Rensselaer,	....	1	....	....	....	1	....	....	....
Richmond,	....	....	....	....	....	....	....	....	....
Rockland,	....	....	....	....	....	3	....	....	....
St. Lawrence,	....	2	5	1	1	....	3	....	....
Saratoga,	....	....	....	....	....	....	1	....	....
Schenectady,	....	....	....	....	....	1	....	*	1
Schoharie,	....	....	....	....	....	....	....	....	....
Schuyler,	....	....	....	....	....	....	....	....	....
Seneca,	....	....	....	1	....	....	....	....	....
Steuben,	....	1	....	....	....	....	....	3	....
Suffolk,	....	1	1	....	....	....	....	....	2
Sullivan,	....	....	....	....	....	....	1	....	....
Tioga,	....	....	....	....	....	....	....	....	....
Tompkins,	1	....	....	....	1	*	....	....	....
Ulster,	....	1	....	....	....	1	1	1	....
Warren,	....	....	2	....	....	....	....	....	....
Washington,	....	1	....	....	....	....	....	1	....
Wayne,	....	....	....	....	....	....	1	....	....
Westchester,	....	....	....	....	....	....	....	1	....
Wyoming,	....	....	1	....	2	3	....	....	....
Yates,	....	....	....	....	1	1	1	1	....
Total,	19	33	31	17	24	29	27	38	24

* No report.

not agree, as reported by County Clerks.

1856.	1857.	1858.	1859.	1860.	1861.	1862.	1863.	1864.	1865.	1866.
....	1	2	....	2	....	....	....	....	....	....
1	....	....	....	....	....	2	....	....	....	1
2	....	....	*	1	....	....	1	....	1	....
....	....	....	....	1	....	1	3	2	....	....
....	....	1	2	3	....	....	1	....	....	....
....	....	....	....	....	....	....	....	....	....	....
3	2	1	1	1	2	....	....	....	....	2
....	....	....	....	....	*	....	*	....	1	....
....	1	....	....	1	1	1	....	....	....	1
....	....	....	....	1	1	....	....	....	....	....
....	1	*	....	....	....	....	....	....	....	2
....	....	....	....	....	....	1	....	....	....	....
....	....	....	....	....	....	....	....	....	....	....
2	2	3	....	....	1	....	1	....	....	1
....	....	....	....	....	....	....	....	....	....	....
2	....	....	....	....	....	....	....	....	....	....
....	*	....	*	....	*	....	....	*	....	*
....	....	....	....	....	....	....	1	....	....	....
....	....	....	....	....	....	....	....	....	....	....
....	....	*	*	....	*	....	*	*	....	....
....	....	....	....	....	....	....	....	....	....	....
1	....	2	....	1	....	....	....	....	....	....
2	....	....	....	1	....	....	....	....	....	2
....	1	....	....	....	*	1	....	....	....	....
5	....	1	2	2	....	....	....	2	....	3
2	2	2	2	1	2	....	....	....	....	....
....	....	....	....	....	....	....	1	1	....	....
....	1	....	....	....	....	....	....	....	....	....
1	....	....	....	....	....	....	....	....	....	....
1	....	....	....	....	2	1	....	....	....	1
....	....	*	1	1	2	....	1	2	1	....
....	....	....	....	....	1	4	4	1	....	....
....	....	....	2	7	1	2	1	....	1	1
....	1	....	....	....	2	....	....	2	1	1
....	....	....	2	....	....	....	....	....	....	....
2	1	1	2	1	....	1	1	....	1	1
....	....	1	1	1	1	....	1	....	....	....
....	....	*	*	....	....	....	....	....	....	....
3	....	....	....	....	....	....	....	....	....	1
3	....	1	1	....	2	....	2	3	....	....
....	*	*	....	....	2	....	*	....	1	1
....	....	....	....	....	....	....	....	....	1	....
1	1	....	1	2	....	2	2	....	1	....
....	2	3	....	....	1	2	....	....	....	1
....	1	....	1	....	....	....	....	....	....	....
....	....	1	....	....	....	....	1	....	....	....
....	....	*	....	....	....	....	....	....	2	....
....	....	....	....	....	....	....	....	....	....	....
....	1	....	....	....	1	....	....	1	....	....
....	....	....	1	....	....	....	1	....	....	....
....	....	....	....	....	....	....	....	....	....	*
....	....	....	....	1	....	....	....	....	....	....
....	....	....	*	....	....	....	....	....	....	....
....	....	....	1	....	....	....	....	....	1	....
....	....	....	....	....	....	....	*	....	....	....
....	....	1	*	1	....	....	*	2	2	....
....	....	....	....	....	....	....	....	....	....	....
2	1	....	*	1	....	1	*	....	....	*
3	1	....	....	....	....	1	....	2	1	....
2	2	*	*	1	3	....	....	2	1	....
38	22	20	20	31	25	20	22	20	16	19

* No report.

Number of Persons Convicted on Confession,

COUNTIES.	1847.	1848.	1849.	1850.	1851.	1852.	1853.	1854.	1855.
Albany, ...	63	34	35	26	38	20	....	39	37
Allegany, ...	2	5	7	...	13	8	6	21	22
Broome, ...	7	3	1	7	3	4	5	2	....
Cattaraugus, ...	2	1	2	1	5	16	1	6	4
Cayuga, ...	15	8	21	18	50	9	27	15	11
Chautauqua, ...	3	19	13	8	27	6	3	17	16
Chemung, ...	3	4	12	2	3	28	8	6	12
Chenango, ...	....	...	...	3	7	2	....	10	2
Clinton, ...	3	10	4	8	8	....	1	12	2
Columbia, ...	5	4	....	6	4	11	25	10	16
Cortland, ...	2	1	....	1	8	....	....	2	1
Delaware, ...	1	....	2	....	2	....	....	5	4
Dutchess, ...	15	6	6	3	10	2	11	7	15
Erie, ...	28	65	86	70	25	64	62	127	55
Essex, ...	1	....	....	....	3	...	....	....	3
Franklin, ...	1	4	4	7	2	9	23	15	16
Fulton, ...	1	3	3	....	2	7	9	2	....
Genesee, ...	3	5	6	18	10	5	7	11	2
Greene, ...	4	2	1	4	5	3	5	2	....
Hamilton, ...	....	....	....	....	....	*	*	....	....
Herkimer, ...	2	11	10	1	4	3	1	6	3
Jefferson, ...	13	5	4	....	25	9	1	6	4
Kings, ...	50	61	58	23	61	34	41	87	107
Lewis, ...	....	4	....	1	4	4	3	1	6
Livingston, ...	18	22	18	12	16	4	6	46	13
Madison, ...	9	3	4	3	14	5	4	....	1
Monroe, ...	62	44	41	44	20	30	37	37	45
Montgomery, ...	3	8	1	1	8	8	30	15	3
New York, ...	129	127	143	239	186	175	501	274	218
Niagara, ...	12	4	10	...	....	....	4	5	16
Oneida, ...	37	24	8	12	....	16	15	21	29
Onondaga, ...	15	20	11	1	12	19	2	12	23
Ontario, ...	4	19	21	6	1	....	8	19	16
Orange, ...	11	6	6	7	7	8	12	30	20
Orleans, ...	3	1	4	2	3	4	....	21	10
Oswego, ...	5	9	12	8	18	8	4	8	15
Otsego, ...	7	2	2	7	9	1	2	2	6
Putnam, ...	....	....	2	....	....	....	....	2	....
Queens, ...	5	2	....	3	6	5	4	14	14
Rensselaer, ...	9	17	20	16	20	11	9	6	12
Richmond, ...	2	...	...	....	....	1	1	8	8
Rockland, ...	2	30	29	6	21	23	4	4	2
St. Lawrence, ...	23	10	10	13	28	27	15	....	....
Saratoga, ...	2	2	10	....	10	4	14	43	18
Schenectady, ...	6	2	9	2	6	7	3	16	19
Schoharie, ...	3	8	2	3	2	1	....	*	2
Schuyler, ...	....	....	....	....	...	....	....	....	....
Seneca, ...	10	11	1	8	1	20	1	4	5
Steuben, ...	3	2	1	4	15	6	11	....	....
Suffolk, ...	2	1	1	....	2	1	....	4	1
Sullivan, ...	8	7	13	3	2	3	5	6	2
Tioga, ...	....	5	1	....	....	....	14	1	....
Tompkins, ...	2	2	....	1	....	*	8	6	2
Ulster, ...	5	3	2	....	....	....	7	....	5
Warren, ...	....	....	....	4	....	....	....	2	16
Washington, ...	18	15	5	27	25	33	33	52	37
Wayne, ...	35	15	1	11	5	7	12	29	21
Westchester, ...	7	4	5	7	15	1	36	43	....
Wyoming, ...	16	35	4	4	9	18	10	11	4
Yates, ...	2	....	1	....	2	....	5	4	1
Total, ...	699	715	673	664	782	690	1,056	1,154	922

* No report.

as reported by County Clerks.

1856.	1857.	1858.	1859.	1860.	1861.	1862.	1863.	1864.	1865.	1866.
39	75	15	62	67	80	37	46	37	77	108
3	1	8	7	21	15	21	6	6	1	9
6	1	2	*	10	....	....	9	19	16	15
....	....	....	....	....	4	2	6	1	6	6
4	17	36	38	7	6	20	12	21	12	19
11	17	17	10	9	10	6	14	26	13	27
....	4	4	13	12	14	6	1	7	35	30
3	....	6	22	3	*	13	*	5	7	13
....	5	7	....	....	....	5	21	15	27	18
6	15	9	9	12	5	7	4	2	7	14
....	....	*	3	2	3	3	4	3	3	26
3	....	....	....	1	3	7	3	4	16	8
13	3	9	....	3	17	11	1	....	....	21
25	33	39	46	53	75	64	62	77	97	131
1	5	1	15	13	15	6	7	8	....	9
3	....	5	32	19	11	2	10	18	17	3
1	*	1	*	....	*	....	1	*	1	*
3	5	2	10	20	28	29	25	36	14	14
1	6	6	3	4	1	....	2	6	1	2
....	....	*	*	....	*	*	*	*	....	1
....	1	6	1	....	....	....	18	14	48	50
....	....	....	....	4	....	1	3	7	2	13
2	8	1	41	238	266	197	140	80	58	198
3	1	2	6	....	*	1	....	....	1	1
6	5	3	9	....	6	1	7	3	15	42
5	15	10	17	14	9	5	8	15	13	28
36	28	30	61	28	31	21	4	4	25	63
3	8	7	12	12	2	4	8	3	2	11
300	383	493	611	582	477	218	350	271	657	681
....	6	....	4	....	9	16	76	30	30	24
23	1	*	8	25	20	17	19	20	15	29
28	20	32	40	26	19	23	27	26	47	62
....	....	4	36	6	12	9	14	4	8	14
5	7	14	....	24	44	40	21	18	15	55
4	....	8	6	2	2	5	....	1	....	....
20	12	12	19	22	3	9	18	4	11	34
5	4	11	6	10	7	8	10	9	8	4
....	....	*	*	....	1	....	....	7	4	....
2	1	10	16	10	14	11	6	10	4	6
16	19	29	18	16	18	12	22	24	31	34
....	*	*	....	....	3	1	*	....	....	8
5	....	....	....	....	8	1	....	2	....	2
3	8	....	39	26	6	4	3	29	23	22
7	9	9	17	2	11	19	8	10	20	31
2	9	8	4	....	3	....	3	....	....	4
....	1	....	....	1	1	2	....	2	....	6
....	....	*	8	....	6	....	1	4	4	5
1	4	....	3	9	5	2	3	12	1	12
6	19	6	16	21	26	11	2	9	14	36
2	4	6	4	....	1	....	10	5	6	11
....	1	1	....	....	2	....	....	....	1	*
1	....	....	10	1	10	28	31	18	5	15
....	....	....	*	....	9	2	1	1	12	9
....	4	12	8	3	1	10	6	8	7	1
....	....	....	....	....	8	2	*	1	....	4
8	22	27	*	46	29	14	*	1	11	6
14	17	2	11	44	22	15	3	1	2	3
19	31	37	*	22	4	13	*	5	....	*
....	4	....	....	....	12	2	8	6	5	10
3	....	*	*	....	11	3	15	6	17	9
651	839	849	1,292	963	1,405	966	1,080	961	1,472	2,015

* No report.

Number of Indictments on which Persons were

COUNTIES.	1847.	1848.	1849.	1850.	1851.	1852.	1853.	1854.	1855.
Albany, ...	111	42	75	92	7	8	1	2	13
Allegany, ...	5	5	1	14	10	9	11	13	16
Broome, ...	3	6	5	2	8	3	1	5	....
Cattaraugus, ...	4	2	....	7	5	4	4	10	9
Cayuga, ...	38	7	5	11	4	5	3	17	5
Chautauqua, ...	10	9	1	5	7	11	6	15	10
Chemung, ...	4	8	3	12	9	15	9	6	5
Chenango, ...	6	4	4	3	10	1	3	10	....
Clinton, ...	14	9	1	8	10	6	3	3	14
Columbia, ...	5	8	41	3	5	4	9	....	1
Cortland, ...	1	3	6	....	....	1	....	2	....
Delaware, ...	8	5	304	1	4	1	6	1	1
Dutchess, ...	17	10	34	26	7	14	2	7	2
Erie, ...	19	25	17	16	10	12	15	19	17
Essex, ...	....	2	....	1	1	2	....	1	3
Franklin, ...	8	3	15	2	13	2	8	3	4
Fulton, ...	3	13	...	....	....	3	7	4	3
Genesee, ...	3	3	4	5	9	2	7	3	1
Greene, ...	....	31	4	6	3	1	1	3	2
Hamilton, ...	....	...	...	....	....	*	*	....	....
Herkimer, ...	3	9	3	14	3	2	....	....	5
Jefferson, ...	7	2	3	12	19	2	....	9	....
Kings, ...	18	20	22	10	12	8	4	15	5
Lewis, ...	1	2	1	4	4	1	....	5	4
Livingston, ...	15	53	34	8	24	18	13	51	16
Madison, ...	17	12	5	2	19	4	5	10	3
Monroe, ...	24	20	15	12	3	8	24	20	33
Montgomery, ...	1	1	1	...	4	2	12	7	6
New York, ...	85	97	78	121	159	122	93	105	99
Niagara, ...	5	1	....	10	1	1	1	....	9
Oneida, ...	17	12	11	28	....	14	22	18	4
Onondaga, ...	45	13	5	13	45	50	15	43	....
Ontario, ...	49	5	5	3	14	....	4	5	....
Orange, ...	22	7	3	4	1	3	4	6	1
Orleans, ...	2	....	3	10	3	3	....	2	4
Oswego, ...	20	19	11	18	25	20	15	4	12
Otsego, ...	18	6	1	11	9	3	30	12	7
Putnam, ...	3	....	3	1	....	....	4	....	....
Queens, ...	3	6	....	10	2	6	1	10	5
Rensselaer, ...	444	1	27	59	6	3	3	....	....
Richmond, ...	7	....	...	3	....	1	4	2	4
Rockland, ...	2	4	....	4	....	7	1	....	3
St. Lawrence, ...	1	2	1	3	3	4	4	1	3
Saratoga, ...	1	1	3	2	1	....	5	1	7
Schenectady, ...	3	2	7	6	6	8	1	....	....
Schoharie, ...	13	2	....	1	1	....	4	*	1
Schuyler, ...	....	....	...	....	....	....	....	....	....
Seneca, ...	....	6	6	5	6	7	2	3	....
Steuben, ...	1	12	8	21	4	19	5	2	11
Suffolk, ...	1	1	....	3	1	2	5	3	3
Sullivan, ...	3	5	4	....	2	2	5	3	6
Tioga, ...	....	2	4	....	10	1	14	5	3
Tompkins ...,....	5	1	3	5	2	*	35	....	....
Ulster, ...	24	2	....	11	....	....	3	....	2
Warren, ...	....	....	4	...	4	2	2	....	....
Washington, ...	8	3	2	3	4	1	....	2	4
Wayne, ...	15	13	7	4	1	4	10	14	6
Westchester, ...	8	2	....	7	....	....	14	9	....
Wyoming, ...	4	2	3	8	8	8	7	8	9
Yates, ...	7	....	1	....	4	1	3	7	6
Total, ...	1,161	540	804	650	532	441	470	506	387

* No report.

discharged without trial, as reported by County Clerks.

1856.	1857.	1858.	1859.	1860.	1861.	1862.	1863.	1864.	1865.	1866.
14	8	9	3	18	3	7	1	11	97	31
7	4	5	11	7	9	3	....	1	...	1
....	....	....	*	....	....	3	3	1	....	...
....	10	2	6	7	1	3	5	1	5	10
46	4	14	39	12	6	9	12	3	7	1
38	7	5	8	12	8	10	14	9	13	12
42	27	....	16	20	21	25	9	8	26	7
18	2	2	2	3	*	17	*	8	41	3
5	13	8	10	3	2	3	5	8	19	6
8	9	2	6	....	2	13	1	12	4	12
....	....	*	3	3	6	2	5	4	....	11
3	3	12	....	8	3	8	1	2	6	6
59	....	....	17	....	33	2	1	5	....	5
116	65	25	25	19	15	34	31	50	38	252
5	1	1	....	1	4	2	6	....	9	3
9	6	11	11	7	7	....	3	4	4	2
....	*	....	*	....	*	....	....	*	....	*
5	3	4	1	6	9	8	8	15	5	8
1	....	2	3	1	7	....	2	9	4	4
....	....	*	*	....	*	*	*	*	....	....
....	....	1	2	....	6	9	2	6	1	7
....	3	2	5	....	....	1	8	3	6	4
16	....	1	2	28	20	19	5	1	11	64
8	1	1	5	....	*	10	....	2	3	5
123	27	9	9	4	13	3	....	3	1	14
12	13	8	9	7	12	6	2	4	5	6
18	9	12	21	27	11	6	....	4	15	18
4	5	1	10	14	2	6	6	5	....	14
109	223	86	93	134	224	128	173	203	309	241
7	10	7	4	4	2	9	10	1	10	13
41	2	*	10	33	41	18	27	52	55	39
40	19	63	76	29	54	64	39	83	131	61
....	8	....	1	....	1	....	4	2	....	3
4	....	14	...	2	....	...	4	18	4	19
1	3	6	1	18	....	....	5	....	1	3
9	79	11	1	14	18	25	32	10	21	36
5	3	2	10	9	8	3	10	10	5	10
....	....	*	*	....	....	1	....	....	1	1
7	17	3	14	7	7	64	7	10	6	12
1	....	8	4	54	18	17	11	15	51	10
....	*	*	2	4	3	4	*	....	10	16
5	....	2	5	....	3	....	2	2	....	1
1	1	7	5	3	2	10	5	3	2	....
1	3	5	....	5	....	3	1	1	5	3
....	....	...	6	....	....	2	....	1	....	2
7	8	1	2	7	....	1	....	4	3	7
....	....	*	7	10	5	....	9	2	3	2
....	2	....	....	1	1	6	3	....	....	4
14	24	8	2	12	7	2	1	5	17	16
6	1	....	1	8	....	3	....	4	2	2
....	5	....	....	6	2	3	....	1	....	*
3	6	1	4	1	7	8	15	6	9	4
42	3	2	*	....	....	....	....	....	3	....
19	19	10	6	5	9	15	7	7	18	5
....	3	1	2	....	4	....	*	....	13	6
95	7	5	*	....	11	....	*	1	2	....
9	3	....	2	5	13	7	3	4	3	8
12	2	4	*	12	18	1	*	14	....	*
19	6	2	3	4	1	7	3	6	....	1
1	5	*	*	1	10	2	3	5	3	....
1,010	672	390	505	595	669	711	494	655	1,007	1,031

* No report.

Whole number of Convictions in Courts of Record

COUNTIES.	1847.	1848.	1849.	1850.	1851.	1852.	1853.	1854.	1855.
Albany, ...	73	69	63	45	82	41	42	77	66
Allegany, ...	6	14	8	12	16	18	19	33	46
Broome, ...	19	8	1	13	5	5	9	3	4
Cattaraugus, ...	2	3	2	10	14	23	11	9	9
Cayuga, ...	24	17	28	26	55	9	40	22	21
Chautauqua,......	6	23	25	16	35	20	12	23	26
Chemung, ...	5	15	31	19	8	47	24	11	17
Chenango,........	3	3	10	10	16	6	12	12	5
Clinton, ...	8	23	5	28	16	10	18	31	15
Columbia, ...	24	19	5	10	28	19	21	14	19
Cortland, ...	3	2	3	8	3	3	5	2	6
Delaware, ...	10	1	8	4	7	9	12	8	8
Dutchess, ...	25	27	14	35	38	34	41	30	29
Erie, ...	91	142	115	177	72	193	159	176	196
Essex,............	1	4	10	7	4	2	1	3	4
Franklin,.........	6	7	11	13	2	15	26	22	20
Fulton, ...	3	7	10	8	9	13	10	7	5
Genesee, ...	11	12	21	31	33	22	19	21	15
Greene,..........	13	3	7	13	9	10	8	5	2
Hamilton, ...	....	....	....	....	....	....	....	....	....
Herkimer, ...	5	30	16	19	8	11	4	13	4
Jefferson,....	23	19	19	20	38	21	11	25	13
Kings,............	87	101	137	75	85	117	100	189	209
Lewis,............	1	6	1	3	2	5	6	5	8
Livingston,.......	28	25	29	18	11	21	19	53	25
Madison, ...	13	5	10	8	10	20	13	12	20
Monroe, ...	72	106	101	82	46	86	87	97	69
Montgomery, ...	7	12	2	2	14	15	36	18	9
New York, ...	257	295	294	338	315	329	539	484	351
Niagara,.........	16	9	10	19	14	16	12	9	23
Oneida, ...	52	47	21	40	....	17	22	49	37
Onondaga, ...	32	59	35	18	17	29	19	35	32
Ontario, ...	15	37	35	34	27	15	30	34	22
Orange, ...	26	18	23	23	22	26	28	42	34
Orleans, ...	14	5	21	32	19	11	2	19	15
Oswego,..........	21	33	46	29	33	22	21	31	40
Otsego,....... ...	12	9	5	12	11	2	8	5	8
Putnam,..........	5	....	10	1	3	3	5	3	2
Queens, ...	13	9	16	13	16	21	20	26	24
Rensselaer, ...	32	27	44	35	32	28	17	24	25
Richmond, ...	6	....	....	2	....	4	6	16	18
Rockland, ...	3	31	36	7	21	29	22	18	11
St. Lawrence, ...	34	38	32	4	38	48	40	31	17
Saratoga, ...	10	6	16	11	17	12	31	53	31
Schenectady, ...	15	5	15	6	10	12	19	38	28
Schoharie, ...	4	12	2	14	3	1	4	....	....
Schuyler, ...	....	....	....	....	...	...	....	....	....
Seneca, ...	12	24	10	22	10	25	8	8	5
Steuben,..........	3	6	21	10	24	30	29	5	16
Suffolk,..........	2	4	4	4	5	9	....	18	45
Sullivan, ...	16	21	13	5	5	4	2	7	9
Tioga, ...	2	1	11	13	16	12	42	43	17
Tompkins, ...	4	6	6	11	7	6	10	13	5
Ulster, ...	9	9	6	8	24	14	14	2	21
Warren, ...	1	....	1	6	14	9	6	8	29
Washington, ...	28	33	23	68	61	41	40	57	45
Wayne,...........	46	17	7	17	5	4	16	37	23
Westchester, ...	15	13	16	23	29	2	31	45	24
Wyoming,........	16	38	7	12	16	22	35	23	7
Yates, ...	4	2	4	3	2	4	14	14	8
Total, ...	1,294	1,527	1,531	1,552	1,482	1,602	1,844	2,117	1,842

in each year since 1846, as reported by County Clerks.

1856.	1857.	1858.	1859.	1860.	1861.	1862.	1863.	1864.	1865.	1866.
93	107	54	82	83	90	44	47	49	98	....
5	4	....	...	34	22	24	17	9	7	..
10	10	....	11	15	6	3	10	28	28	....
2	8	13	10	32	18	13	18	11	10	...
10	20	31	32	21	16	24	14	27	13	....
18	32	21	14	23	21	13	25	35	25	....
4	22	29	56	18	24	20	33	20	47	....
4	11	10	32	9	6	14	....	7	10	....
14	17	55	34	22	23	18	18	10	31	...
11	19	15	14	15	6	13	10	3	11	....
1	3	2	7	7	10	5	8	4	3	....
5	4	3	2	5	7	11	8	5	16	....
21	19	10	2	20	32	23	3	8	*	....
146	116	126	119	128	136	132	181	189	228	....
6	14	13	15	12	19	5	20	14	7	....
6	3	12	42	28	12	1	14	19	17	....
1	1	12	6	....	13	6	2	....	2	....
6	13	14	15	22	36	38	33	37	21	....
5	9	11	6	15	3	4	6	7	3	....
....	1	1	....	....	....	....	...	....	*	....
5	2	1	...	11	37	21	22	24	53	..
5	9	14	21	13	8	4	18	11	14	....
112	48	28	1	336	312	230	188	130	108	....
8	5	4	11	....	....	1	2	2	6	....
30	22	9	20	40	23	7	39	12	31	....
16	24	16	24	30	19	11	12	20	22	....
84	53	73	118	69	73	57	14	8	37	...
8	12	13	19	18	3	8	18	3	6	....
418	477	614	705	474	651	350	334	303	678	....
20	22	15	8	13	10	32	101	39	47	....
33	2	...	22	40	26	22	27	26	17	....
54	45	34	64	30	38	44	51	44	72	....
5	3	10	29	25	24	20	18	13	12	...
15	27	32	57	32	57	41	21	13	21	....
6	4	15	18	3	4	9	5	6	13	....
36	47	43	31	32	10	11	29	11	12	....
6	5	14	22	13	10	4	14	13	10	....
1	....	....	....	....	7	....	....	8	6	...
17	10	24	26	22	26	17	8	15	4	....
26	30	33	27	33	37	22	34	32	43	....
....	....	...	2	....	14	16	....	4	8	....
9	2	8	5	4	13	7	12	5	4	....
13	18	15	28	17	24	27	23	42	29	....
14	12	12	38	3	16	28	13	14	24	....
9	19	18	33	27	12	5	15	6	9	....
5	3	2	12	16	3	5	5	6	4	....
....	....	....	4	15	10	2	5	6	7	...
3	7	12	20	10	6	6	10	12	2	....
13	34	13	23	41	42	19	6	12	29	....
10	18	14	14	18	11	20	14	11	14	....
2	3	1	3	11	10	3	7	3	2	....
13	10	25	24	16	22	30	35	21	9	....
8	5	4	....	17	18	7	15	2	16	....
15	18	29	33	21	37	17	13	13	23	....
4	6	3	6	29	22	8	7	1	13	....
45	43	39	55	37	32	19	4	12	16	....
18	18	8	17	64	26	23	11	2	10	....
39	43	69	42	48	47	24	....	23	*	....
8	11	9	10	20	16	13	12	12	7	....
13	8	6	....	12	16	15	15	8	21	....
1,514	1,554	1,712	2,091	2,162	2,275	1,616	1,644	1,430	2,036	....

* No report.

Statistics of Pauperism.

Under the Revised Statutes of 1829, local officers having charge of expenditures for the poor, were required to make reports of the results of their labors to the Secretary of State, to be laid annually before the Legislature. In 1842, these inquiries were extended to embrace the name, sex, age, and native country of each pauper relieved or supported. The existing regulations are inadequate to obtain the requisite information, and the returns have always been more or less imperfect, some counties not reporting, and others sending only partial returns. It will be noticed that the war has not materially increased the expenses of public charity to the poor. The sudden changes in the numbers relieved by counties and towns, in some cases are to be attributed to a change in the mode of meeting these charges, rather than in the number of objects of charity. The years referred to in the following tables end on the first day of December.

YEARS.	WHOLE NUMBER OF TOWN AND COUNTY PAUPERS RELIEVED OR SUPPORTED.						
	Counties that reported.	Whole number of paupers relieved or supported during the year.	Number of county paupers relieved or supported.	Number of town paupers relieved or supported.	Number of persons temporarily relieved.	Expenses connected with the county poorhouse.	Expenses of administering temporary relief.
1847, ...	......	106,569	97,218	9,341	72,847	$421,218 38	$256,791 78
1848, ...	55	52,021	44,034	7,987	38,420	204,668 24	184,317 78
1849, ...	59	99,433	57,707	10,613	63,764	492,100 02	314,516 59
1850, ...	57	114,891	103,279	9,211	83,143	437,713 59	296,904 52
1851, ...	55	125,473	115,347	10,099	85,301	492,768 82	345,098 09
1852, ...	58	151,399	138,720	12,679	63,590	586,112 19	405,774 09
1853, ...	53	130,027	112,058	10,453	94,209	641,955 57	367,792 08
1854, ...	58	137,347	122,377	13,593	95,986	750,427 84	331,793 12
1855, ...	59	204,161	84,934	18,412	159,092	899,694 80	480,264 71
1856, ...	60	179,040	71,153	15,145	138,146	1,353,439 20	413,393 65
1857, ...	58	173,249	63,371	12,023	118,019	896,708 41	457,675 49
1858, ...	58	261,155	103,499	23,205	207,207	884,119 78	607,271 50
1859, ...	60	228,517	192,830	25,021	279,787	774,106 89	560,859 62
1860, ...	59	223,485	46,680	3,002	174,403	839,556 29	524,943 15
1861, ...	57	314,797	49,861	2,211	262,725	911,670 15	470,890 48
1862, ...	56	237,354	230,195	20,348	217,366	833,126 55	485,355 33
1863, ...	58	261,252	228,507	29,830	218,071	927,264 67	535,838 37
1864, ...	59	265,816	235,608	30,208	222,617	1,177,598 58	667,212 63
1865, ...	57	278,558	247,641	30,917	227,049	1,569,675 20	770,390 10
1866, ...	57	265,158	242,542	22,616	220,294	1,560,919 54	765,640 99

Statistics of Pauperism — (Continued).

YEARS.	Whole expense of support of county and town paupers for the year.	EXPENSES CONNECTED WITH COUNTY POORHOUSES.				
		Amount paid to superintendents for their services.	Amount paid to keepers and Poorhouse officers.	Amount paid to Constables and other officers.	Amount paid for supplies for the county Poorhouses.	Amount paid for the transportation of paupers.
1847,	$687,010 16	$18,516 71	$46,483 03	$1,685 37	$311,043 92	$10,675 84
1848,	388,986 02	15,886 96	24,029 13	970 58	124,863 34	8,559 43
1849,	816,858 90	41,494 31	28,199 61	1,097 98	396,317 93	10,361 89
1850,	734,881 11	39,229 95	27,692 14	1,518 56	314,487 98	8,287 02
1851,	857,866 91	39,366 97	28,243 45	3,837 20	365,330 47	9,061 53
1852,	991,886 28	40,583 17	28,659 11	5,535 45	412,958 02	11,157 56
1853,	1,009,747 65	22,553 16	50,288 29	1,791 74	434,031 16	10,377 16
1854,	1,121,904 00	28,713 45	53,654 53	1,367 63	505,323 49	11,223 12
1855,	1,379,959 51	30,901 97	62,594 39	1,212 43	683,610 33	11,739 27
1856,	1,769,332 85	31,438 94	70,778 95	1,028 09	704,097 00	8,621 13
1857,	1,354,383 90	31,127 54	80,910 73	1,489 35	664,201 80	10,232 94
1858,	1,491,391 28	27,619 87	91,764 40	3,241 53	649,864 91	12,073 14
1859,	1,334,966 51	47,489 46	74,087 40	2,665 81	575,217 67	10,784 67
1860,	1,365,499 54	30,439 21	106,287 80	3,024 17	631,522 68	11,195 65
1861,	1,382,560 63	34,389 37	96,349 92	1,716 23	672,378 56	10,717 60
1862,	1,318,481 88	36,520 97	93,734 32	864 00	602,013 88	10,927 44
1863,	1,463,102 04	34,981 33	99,918 69	1,068 50	675,528 07	9,704 98
1864,	1,853,906 36	35,895 99	104,539 37	1,659 81	888,109 44	10,171 34
1865,	2,339,865 30	39,111 13	135,453 42	1,422 48	1,183,497 63	10,895 33
1866,	2,327,060 53	46,670 48	162,291 14	2,719 88	1,160,290 11	10,673 41

YEARS.	EXPENSES CONNECTED WITH COUNTY POORHOUSES.			EXPENSES OF ADMINISTERING TEMPORARY RELIEF.			
	Amount paid to Physicians for attendance and medicines.	Amount paid for miscellaneous expenditures connected with the poorhouse.	Total.	Amount paid to overseers of the poor for their services.	Amount paid justices of the peace for their services.	Amount paid for relieving indigent persons temporarily not included in the two foregoing columns.	Total.
1847,	$8,985 52	$23 827 99	....	$18,107 96	$11,798 50	$226,885 22	....
1848,	8,057 79	22,301 10	$204,628 24	17,503 41	1,359 26	165,455 11	$184,317 78
1849,	10,914 94	30,713 36	492,100 02	34,871 98	2,982 30	275,493 39	314,516 59
1850,	13,570 26	32,927 88	437,713 59	28,950 16	1,764 68	264,990 65	296,904 49
1851,	14,980 95	31,948 25	492,768 82	44,896 95	1,730 24	298,470 90	345,098 09
1852,	13,275 20	73,943 68	586,112 19	38,149 19	1,884 01	365,740 93	405,774 09
1853.	14,297 95	108,616 11	641,955 57	35,386 48	1,806 13	330,599 48	367,792 08
1854,	27,852 50	122,293 12	750,427 84	38,324 09	1,359 74	331,793 12	371,476 95
1855,	35,637 12	73,999 29	899,694 80	40,211 36	2,847 11	437,206 24	480 264 71
1856,	32,057 45	75,807 17	923,828 73	40,050 53	1,411 75	375,750 51	425,740 25
1857,	37,692 26	74,433 13	900,087 75	41,292 80	877 32	411,862 01	454,032 13
1858,	34,264 43	65,301 50	884,129 78	57,309 11	2,550 42	547,411 97	607,274 50
1859,	30,735 34	33,364 79	774,106 89	53,559 25	8,506 25	498,794 12	560,859 62
1860,	29,247 59	27,839 19	839,556 29	53,907 04	3,669 72	467,366 39	524,943 15
1861,	36,829 59	59,288 88	911,670 15	43,354 83	22,477 70	405,057 95	470,890 48
1862,	38,793 49	47,125 60	833,126 55	47,160 74	3,087 93	425,046 68	485,355 33
1863,	42,744 28	64,828 22	927,264 67	48,056 71	2,474 42	472,827 91	535,838 37
1864,	55,344 28	76,119 82	1,177,598 58	57,347 39	1,858 43	567,570 00	667,216 63
1865,	68,542 79	118,580 12	1,569,475 20	50,901 03	2,504 19	698,824 62	770,390 10
1866,	73,325 42	104,949 10	1,560 919 59	47,744 74	2,932 17	661,973 78	765,640 99

Statistics of Pauperism — (Continued).

YEARS.	Value of labor of paupers.	Amount saved by labor of paupers.	Sum expended above the earnings for the support of each pauper.	Average weekly expense of each person.
1847,	$29,695 98	$31,972 87	$32 81	$0 63
1848,	29,700 02	33,447 11	34 75	66½
1849,	28,353 42	31,931 05	32 87	99¼
1850,	34,565 85	38,728 80	33 67	66
1851,	31,634 94	34,276 05	35 58	68½
1852,	38,203 49	43,107 23	38 85	70½
1853,	65,236 76	33,615 00	37 86	72½
1854,	27,839 37	29,599 44	45 20	86½
1855,	27,090 00	27,132 00	90 06	91¾
1856,	26,753 25	29,579 00	34 63	72
1857,	26,999 79	28,591 39	49 08	96¼
1858,	29,484 66	27,954 66	46 54	90½
1859,	30,836 00	30,513 05	60 90	91
1860,	35,182 00	22,938 50	42 52	82¾
1861,	32,015 00	29,191 00	42 12	85⅞
1862,	32,420 00	31,627 13	44 46	89⅞
1863,	33,814 19	43,388 58	46 65	89¾
1864,	30,575 00	35,270 92	58 61	1 12½
1865,	31,370 00	35,385 68	71 61	....
1866,	29,800 00	34,055 80	78 00	....

Description of Persons relieved and supported during the year.

YEARS.	CHANGES DURING THE YEAR IN THE COUNTY POORHOUSE.						NUMBER OF PERSONS IN POORHOUSES AT DATE OF REPORT.		
	Received.	Born.	Died.	Bound out.	Discharged.	Absconded.	Males.	Females.	Total.
1847,	23,648	489	2,824	452	14,728	1,420	4,560	4,073	8,633
1848,	12,895	219	1,384	306	8,036	1,015	3,078	2,315	5,393
1849,	26,658	375	3,200	601	19,913	1,224	4,775	5,395	10,170
1850,	25,227	636	2,156	848	18,049	1,013	4,542	5,444	9,986
1851,	29,338	564	2,621	972	20,843	1,555	6,221	5,339	11,560
1852,	34,046	775	2,967	873	26,504	982	6,173	5,430	11,603
1853,	28,129	715	2,351	953	12,442	10,135	5,768	5,345	11,163
1854,	33,167	841	3,266	934	23,654	2,185	6,433	5,672	12,105
1855,	37,887	896	2,616	589	25,028	1,183	5,722	6,275	11,997
1856,	31,840	754	2,125	662	20,075	1,221	5,313	5,829	11,142
1857,	31,663	752	2,262	506	23,335	763	6,227	6,965	13,192
1858,	38,582	849	2,584	646	30,400	1,107	6,919	7,203	13,422
1859,	36,550	812	2,428	654	27,475	884	6,389	7,042	13,431
1860,	26,560	774	2,713	678	28,411	942	5,587	6,552	12,139
1861,	38,394	786	3,012	670	29,386	952	5,238	6,880	12,118
1862.	29,996	713	2,493	788	21,774	1,024	6,132	6,117	12,249
1863,	28,613	774	2,906	726	21,883	1,170	6,219	5,940	12,318
1864,	32,998	819	3,257	603	22,310	1,203	6,597	6,088	12,685
1865,	41,008	1,020	3,865	445	31,092	1,016	6,782	6,573	13,480
1866,	33,983	1,010	4,336	521	30,517	1,899	7,213	7,108	14,321

Description of Persons relieved, &c. — (*Continued*).

YEARS.	CLASSES OF THE PRECEDING.				OF THE PERSONS RELIEVED AND SUPPORTED DURING THE YEAR, THERE WERE:			
	Foreigners.	Lunatics.	Idiots.	Mutes.	Foreigners.	Lunatics.	Idiots.	Mutes.
1847,	1,750	856	302	55	9,799	1,128	383	71
1848,	1,747	698	319	81	9,857	729	307	70
1849,	2,945	1,036	297	53	21,024	827	354	61
1850,	8,212	1,121	297	33	25,752	831	353	42
1851,	6,221	1,103	230	38	38,567	1,807	410	40
1852,	5,692	1,522	461	55	37,694	1,731	307	59
1853,	5,493	1,522	415	55	58,022	2,875	378	72
1854,	6,391	1,352	375	73	62,616	2,123	724	154
1855,	5,773	1,577	383	62	94,127	2,125	445	56
1856,	5,677	1,647	387	39	83,830	2,229	559	43
1857,	7,027	1,816	434	39	81,626	2,320	531	47
1858,	6,503	1,838	438	36	58,700	2,408	595	52
1859,	6,378	1,970	448	37	45,405	2,669	386	98
1860,	6,672	2,042	524	80	52,681	2,601	672	94
1861,	6,357	2,476	464	84	171,825	1,898	475	60
1862,	5,974	2,492	462	98	54,650	3,304	602	126
1863,	6,900	2,613	513	113	32,240	3,323	573	123
1864,	5,992	2,771	540	99	120,595	3,291	617	115
1865,	6,523	2,274	569	78	144,521	3,409	567	69
1866,	6,276	2,883	598	156	34,446	3,324	642	151

Statistics of Pauperism — (*Continued.*)

YEARS.	CHILDREN IN POOR-HOUSES.				NATIVE COUNTRY.					
					TOTAL.		UNITED STATES.		IRELAND.	
	Males under sixteen.	Females under sixteen.	Total number.	Number during the year.	Males.	Females.	Males.	Females.	Males.	Females.
1847,	1,804	1,175	2,979	2,057	24,942	19,227	10,622	8,258	9,827	7,807
1848,	900	551	1,451	1,738	20,491	15,943	9,004	7,150	7,157	5,473
1849,	1,755	1,120	2,875	2,639	27,349	24,134	10,424	9,638	12,276	10,447
1850,	1,960	1,275	3,235	2,635	80,042	24,357	35,033	10,083	32,195	10,273
1851,	1,977	1,152	3,128	2,849	28,501	25,104	10,667	10,366	12,400	10,059
1852,	1,992	1,155	3,147	3,193	71,384	59,746	20,028	17,872	38,634	31,725
1853,	1,871	1,142	3,013	3,219	53,198	46,513	21,265	19,064	21,884	19,109
1854,	2,083	1,347	3,430	3,299	62,680	74,853	21,655	28,826	20,853	26,873
1855,	1,806	1,461	3,267	3,066	89,078	111,862	32,643	47,681	33,708	43,084
1856,	1,946	1,105	3,051	2,933	69,132	93,010	35,776	38,148	32,809	44,659
1857,	2,974	2,424	5,403	3,037	73,146	90,624	26,902	37,368	33,450	42,024
1858,	2,776	3,045	5,821	3,219	177,966	143,107	45,174	59,570	42,212	50,504
1859,	3,510	2,752	6,262	2,972	101,147	117,282	40,654	53,847	40,000	44,763
1860,	1,868	1,254	3,122	4,010	95,283	112,303	35,664	43,805	44,072	54,585
1861,	4,154	3,808	7,962	394	127,482	175,964	44,721	66,675	61,603	26,741
1862,	12,832	12,129	24,961	3,012	102,787	144,196	39,183	57,615	49,320	68,874
1863,	11,999	11,617	23,616	4,112	97,135	144,939	39,924	61,593	43,311	65,600
1864,	8,562	9,682	18,244	2,680	96,237	149,569	36,326	60,906	44,837	68,924
1865,	11,940	10,211	22,151	2,872	100,084	155,448	37,557	63,217	45,118	69,758
1866,	13,364	12,887	26,251	2,642	101,156	147,316	36,819	58,148	45,726	67,244

Statistics of Pauperism—(Continued).

YEARS.	NATIVE COUNTRY.									
	England.		Scotland.		Germany.		France.		Canada.	
	Males.	Females.	Males.	Females	Males.	Females.	Males.	Females.	Males.	Females.
1847,	1,102	724	252	192	1,567	1,104	210	141	519	439
1848,	897	552	243	180	1,772	1,561	359	208	363	240
1849,	1,157	1,007	300	216	1,758	1,515	332	292	805	698
1850,	2,636	1,065	797	339	3,728	1,468	526	306	736	680
1851,	1,355	1,096	368	289	2,247	2,001	518	427	658	650
1852,	2,809	2,197	866	718	6,634	5,094	791	646	1,240	1,230
1853,	2,483	1,901	624	504	5,139	4,282	449	325	885	910
1854,	1,879	1,654	646	559	5,229	4,932	531	419	748	631
1855,	2,746	2,889	910	985	12,570	10,736	810	635	891	800
1856,	2,442	2,471	629	685	5,420	5,432	529	477	708	698
1857,	2,608	2,387	846	703	6,282	5,631	518	327	875	910
1858,	4,183	3,371	1,268	1,068	12,601	16,173	1,094	973	1,995	2,013
1859,	4,315	3,701	1,282	1,067	19,366	9,454	614	546	1,293	1,157
1860,	3,345	2,367	1,275	998	7,325	7,620	698	448	1,825	1,605
1861,	4,260	3,442	1,119	1,066	8,682	11,585	740	498	465	1,195
1862,	2,683	2,711	764	910	7,169	10,057	510	483	959	1,124
1863,	2,068	2,733	925	1,237	7,796	11,218	662	656	913	979
1864,	2,831	3,039	777	1,018	8,587	12,480	608	581	1,339	1,475
1865,	2,733	3,131	1,009	1,197	9,698	13,929	630	629	1,670	1,806
1866,	2,926	2,934	740	923	11,402	14,429	563	506	1,268	1,387

Causes of Pauperism.

YEARS.	Total.		Intemperance Direct.		Children, Intemper'e Parents.		Wives with intemperate husbands.	Debauchery.	
	Males.	Females.	Males.	Females.	Males.	Females.		Males.	Females.
1847,	24,942	19,227	3,617	1,270	1,320	972	347	49	406
1848,	20,491	15,943	4,387	1,125	834	735	571	44	394
1849,	28,248	22,373	7,373	2,944	2,102	1,871	1,413	191	516
1850,	28,495	25,086	5,063	3,239	2,455	2,100	1,091	251	532
1851,	29,144	27,921	4,679	1,844	2,507	2,237	1.922	240	516
1852,	69,984	57,009	9,204	3,352	3,037	2,757	1,972	368	761
1853,	54,956	47,134	7,006	3,193	2,005	1,918	1,495	347	640
1854,	62,681	74,853	6,032	2,587	2,493	1,832	2,156	329	513
1855,	89,078	111,862	8,815	4,549	7,190	3,812	3,938	784	974
1856,	70,869	95,702	7,263	3,734	3,718	3,733	3,202	249	395
1857,	71,453	90,715	7,482	3,330	4,426	3,799	2,885	339	626
1858,	117,736	143,337	16,669	9,164	5,627	5,133	3,140	543	622
1859,	100,661	116,115	13,000	9,330	4,404	4,582	2,728	980	635
1860,	95,300	11,457	11,817	5,718	3,740	3,569	2,694	1,303	851
1861,	126,454	175,899	16,287	10,246	3,613	3,681	2,161	961	760
1862,	103,017	143,240	13,099	9,326	3,030	3,442	2,462	737	927
1863,	98,520	143,856	12,904	7,725	2,960	3,177	2,185	551	794
1864,	98,162	145,343	12,935	8,120	3,124	3,136	1,849	347	560
1865,*	102,440	254,772	13,879	11,602	3,429	3,442	1,669	502	1,222
1866,	152,621	144,275	15,586	9,723	4,176	3,819	1,469	482	701

* From fifty-three counties.

Causes of Pauperism—(Continued).

YEARS.	Debauchery of Parents.		Idleness.		Vagrancy.		Idiocy.		Lunacy.	
	Males.	Females.	Males.	Females.	Males.	Females.	Males.	Females.	Males.	Females.
1847,	102	87	72	38	96	45	251	223	431	459
1848,	92	89	355	151	323	141	396	385	578	532
1849,	208	135	912	566	557	397	238	203	447	455
1850,	205	160	1, 147	1, 095	398	270	116	210	411	410
1851,	341	301	1, 556	1, 595	459	425	238	227	451	513
1852,	509	395	2, 357	1, 662	1, 301	728	308	291	972	1, 066
1853,	559	279	895	514	1, 221	1, 181	252	283	839	1, 017
1854,	249	255	2, 036	1, 612	656	473	401	358	990	1, 217
1855,	445	534	4, 756	3, 939	1, 053	559	274	250	1, 038	1, 195
1856,	2, 921	3, 412	1, 094	772	1, 167	729	481	580	881	1, 098
1857,	188	201	4, 187	3, 576	966	641	309	329	1, 064	1, 236
1858,	392	375	5, 582	4, 080	1, 417	904	431	441	1, 206	1, 533
1859,	321	322	5, 146	3, 337	1, 498	744	374	407	1, 446	1, 731
1860,	568	483	4, 967	3, 619	1, 045	577	478	457	1, 314	1, 669
1861,	361	250	5, 317	4, 131	2, 288	1, 147	426	375	1, 424	1, 814
1862,	472	532	4, 129	3, 832	1, 604	862	406	365	1, 554	2, 004
1863,	367	454	1, 064	746	1, 760	1, 266	380	366	1, 441	2, 096
1864,	392	373	1, 230	783	1, 013	768	335	275	1, 291	1, 894
1865,	400	751	993	763	1, 023	985	335	336	1, 386	1, 829
1866,	348	283	1, 026	621	1, 627	921	394	307	1, 435	2, 215

YEARS.	Blindness.		Lameness.		Sickness.		Decrepitude.	
	Males.	Females.	Males.	Females.	Males.	Females.	Males.	Females.
1847,	243	63	468	79	3, 757	2, 896	160	59
1848,	243	124	647	185	4, 465	3, 225	235	210
1849,	207	81	985	261	3, 331	2, 515	291	150
1850,	707	82	870	327	4, 425	3, 651	366	255
1851.	184	95	1, 056	500	3, 465	2, 839	342	262
1852,	210	101	1, 310	578	8, 228	7, 307	416	220
1853,	226	108	918	367	6, 101	4, 417	330	541
1854,	294	157	1, 120	498	7, 834	706	638	406
1855,	227	113	1, 371	497	8, 601	7, 097	587	397
1856,	250	104	1, 246	585	7, 918	7, 169	382	228
1857,	272	150	1, 056	450	8, 296	7, 246	420	352
1858,	353	165	1, 329	662	12, 667	10, 167	668	447
1859,	443	197	2, 154	545	11, 371	8, 937	794	413
1860,	509	190	1, 214	614	11, 468	8, 978	813	441
1861,	444	198	1, 240	510	10, 212	8, 208	829	473
1862,	374	154	1, 198	490	7, 502	9, 557	497	327
1863,	388	318	1, 103	516	7, 183	7, 927	471	393
1864,	309	238	1, 048	580	9, 362	8, 443	802	621
1865,	310	191	988	519	12, 094	13, 889	765	695
1866,	310	169	1, 483	584	11, 477	11, 752	487	383

Causes of Pauperism—(Continued).

YEARS.	Old Age.		Deaf and Dumb.		Indigent and Destitute.		Children having Destitute Parents.	
	Males.	Females.	Males,	Females.	Males.	Females.	Males.	Females.
1847,	371	265	29	18	1, 706	1, 832	834	577
1848,	442	352	34	28	4, 254	4, 697	547	322
1849,	821	570	33	19	4, 983	4, 301	4, 005	3, 748
1850,	644	500	37	23	4, 593	4, 614	4, 598	4, 569
1851,	745	649	39	43	7, 425	8, 745	2, 963	2, 795
1852,	1, 244	1, 425	28	17	8, 130	7, 478	4, 666	3, 806
1853,	854	814	27	29	28, 011	25, 353	3, 681	2, 921
1854,	1, 311	1, 077	73	47	20, 172	36, 476	3, 756	3, 105
1855,	1, 316	1, 011	47	26	40, 761	67, 191	4, 924	4, 227
1856,	1, 366	1, 244	49	24	33, 998	59, 791	4, 924	4, 787
1857,	1, 373	1, 481	39	29	33, 281	56, 686	4, 444	3, 876
1858,	1, 948	2, 077	40	32	50, 844	84, 881	6, 355	5, 930
1859,	1, 419	1, 185	38	26	59, 189	83, 599	6, 166	5, 683
1860,	1, 163	1, 189	53	43	45, 999	72, 133	5, 621	5, 135
1861,	1, 365	1, 131	67	48	73, 791	131, 277	5, 033	4, 941
1862,	1, 456	1, 337	154	146	56, 371	96, 725	5, 717	5, 184
1863,	1, 453	1, 501	55	48	59, 011	106, 268	4, 232	3, 852
1864,	1, 297	1, 300	55	38	59, 614	109, 465	4, 271	3, 655
1865,	1, 256	1, 085	49	46	56, 631	107, 228	4, 761	4, 438
1866,	1, 125	1, 110	79	63	56, 460	103, 947	4, 098	3, 499

YEARS.	Children having sick parents.		Wives with sick husbands.	Orphans.		Bastards.		Illegitimate children.		Not Reported.	
	Males.	Females.		Males.	Females.	Males.	Females.	Males.	Females.	Males.	Females.
1847,	1, 508	973	292	82	52	26	48	26	28	9, 650	7, 896
1848,	358	396	101	108	51	33	67	13	17	1, 548	1, 278
1849,	1, 290	1, 260	708	170	156	170	209	37	46	......	......
1850,	918	826	558	257	297	216	186	54	43	1, 304	......
1851,	1, 664	1, 886	779	213	173	210	217	37	29	29	39
1852,	1, 536	1, 603	598	472	343	292	239	102	141	25, 294	20, 169
1853,	1, 026	1, 117	406	315	223	211	186	57	69	40	34
1854,	1, 315	1, 225	765	468	333	243	244	64	82	12, 207	12, 129
1855,	1, 748	1, 897	844	578	461	300	283	77	69	8, 228	7, 728
1856,	1, 784	1, 826	1, 170	391	331	292	293	19	50	263	207
1857,	1, 584	1, 354	688	486	333	286	253	50	33	954	1, 093
1858,	2, 224	1, 958	1, 045	610	519	266	307	73	77	8, 391	9, 465
1859,	1, 847	1, 954	855	711	630	216	232	91	74	442	427
1860,	1, 455	1, 535	761	475	550	377	337	93	69	581	644
1861,	597	1, 392	654	804	741	257	254	357	288	450	387
1862,	1, 401	1, 475	1, 087	686	640	322	338	362	248	269	88
1863,	1, 120	1, 277	721	772	645	317	294	39	44	139	65
1864,	854	906	635	755	540	316	324	48	47	......	......
1865,	1, 092	976	723	771	699	214	232	142	150	39	37
1866,	783	887	617	808	699	228	200	259	251	......	......

Statistics of Pauperism — (Continued).

COUNTIES.	CITY OR TOWN WHERE POORHOUSES ARE LOCATED.	When established.	Acres of land attached.	Present value of property, from the State census of 1865.
Albany,	Albany City,	1823	115	$75,000
Allegany,	Angelica,	1831	283	8,000
Broome,	Binghamton,	1831	130	10,000
Cattaraugus,	Machias,	1835	200	8,000
Cayuga,	Sennett,	1825	96	30,000
Chautauqua,	Chautauqua,	1832	231⅛	18,000
Chemung,	Horseheads,	1841	175	10,700
Chenango,	Preston,	1828	170	13,700
Clinton,	Beekmantown,	1827	90	5,000
Columbia,	Ghent,	1839	216	40,000
Cortland,	Cortlandville,	1838	118	7,000
Delaware,	Delhi,	1827	200	12,600
Dutchess,	Washington,	1864	113	30,000
Erie,	Buffalo,	....	152	115,000
Essex,	Essex,	1834	100	10,000
Franklin,	Malone,	1836	162	5,180
Fulton,	Johnstown,	1855	100	6,000
Genesee,	Bethany,	1826	150	16,376
Greene,	Cairo,	1842	130	9,000
Hamilton,	None.			
Herkimer,	Herkimer,	1840	65	10,700
Jefferson,	Pamelia,	1834	107	10,000
Kings,	Flatbush,	1830	70	525,000
Lewis,	Lowville,	1828	59	4,000
Livingston,	Geneseo,	1828	118	20,000
Madison,	Eaton,	1828	172	15,000
Monroe,	Brighton,	1826	110	33,000
Montgomery,	Glen,	1831	160	6,000
New York,	New York city.			
Niagara,	Lockport,	1828	170	14,000
Oneida,	Rome,	1828	118	38,000
Onondaga,	Onondaga,	1827	36¼	30,000
Ontario,	Hopewell,	1826	212	25,200
Orange,	Goshen,	1830	265	19,200
Orleans,	Barre,	1830	121	14,278
Oswego	Mexico,	1826	60	10,000
Otsego,	Middlefield,	1827	153	18,000
Putnam,	Kent,	1830	106	10,000
Queens,	Hempstead,	1853	107	6,000
Rensselaer,	Troy city,	1820	144	28,800
Richmond,	Northfield,	1829	123	20,000
Rockland,	Ramapo,	1838	47	10,000
St. Lawrence,	Canton,	1826	130	6,000
Saratoga,	Milton,	1828	112	6,000
Schenectady,	Schenectady city,	1820	113	18,000
Schoharie,	Middleburgh,	....	112	10,000
Schuyler,	None.			
Seneca,	Fayette,	1830	126½	30,000
Steuben,	Bath,	1833	200	25,000
Suffolk,	(Town),	....	150	....
Sullivan,	Thompson,	1830	100	7,000
Tioga,	Owego,	1837	60	6,000
Tompkins,	Ulysses,	1826	100	8,000
Ulster,	New Paltz,	1827	140	13,000
Warren,	Warrensburgh,	1826	200	5,000
Washington,	Argyle,	1827	174	12,000
Wayne,	Lyons,	1830	193	10,000
Westchester,	Mount Pleasant,	1825	165	50,000
Wyoming,	Orangeville,	1844	111	9,000
Yates,	Jerusalem,	1831	185	10,000
Total,			7,826	$1,521,734

Resident Aliens.

The custom of naturalizing aliens, by an act of the General Assembly of New York, was introduced in 1718, and was continued by the State Legislature until the right was surrendered to the Federal Government in 1789. The number thus enabled to hold lands was as follows in each year:

1718,..............	7	1734,.............	10	1759,...........	127	1772,...........	19
1719,..............	3	1735,.............	16	1761,...........	170	1773,...........	93
1721,..............	5	1737,.............	24	1762,...........	78	1775,...........	37
1723,..............	30	1739,.............	18	1763,...........	23	1782,...........	2
1724,..............	7	1744,.............	2	1764,...........	16	1783,...........	4
1726,..............	18	1745,.............	2	1765,...........	12	1784,...........	115
1727,..............	8	1746,.............	19	1766,...........	15	1785,...........	57
1728,..............	4	1750,.............	1	1768,...........	39	1786,...........	93
1730,..............	16	1750,.............	36	1769,...........	31	1787,...........	50
1731,..............	7	1751,.............	5	1770,...........	43	1788,...........	67
1732,..............	8	1755,.............	74	1771,...........	51	1789,...........	181

The privilege was subsequently restricted to the right to hold lands, and the annual statute laws for many years after contain many names of persons who have thus been allowed a qualified right of citizenship. To relieve Legislation from this special business, an act was passed on the 21st of April, 1825, entitled "Act to enable resident aliens to hold real estate, and for other purposes." This authorized aliens who intended to become citizens to make affidavit of their intentions, and file the same in the office of the Secretary of State. In doing this they acquired the right to hold real estate, and became liable for all taxes, duties and assessments, and for the performance of military duty, in the same manner as citizens, but were not capable of holding an office, or of serving as jurors, excepting in cases of a jury *de medietate linguæ* being summoned. The results of this law have been as follows:

Resident aliens who have filed depositions.

YEARS.	Males.	Females.	Total.	YEARS.	Males.	Females.	Total.	YEARS.	Males.	Females.	Total.	YEARS.	Males.	Females.	Total.
1825, ..	61	3	64	1836, ..	356	17	373	1847, ..	121	58	179	1858, ..	234	349	583
1826, ..	73	2	75	1837, ..	194	21	215	1848, ..	338	268	606	1859, ..	239	373	612
1827, ..	101	1	102	1838, ..	145	19	164	1849, ..	341	280	621	1860, ..	267	336	603
1828, ..	62	1	63	1839, ..	148	20	168	1850, ..	524	302	826	1861, ..	198	325	523
1829, ..	43	1	44	1840, ..	159	19	178	1851, ..	738	393	1, 131	1862, ..	142	293	435
1830, ..	133	15	148	1841, .	115	14	129	1852, ..	959	471	1, 430	1863, ..	130	355	485
1831, ..	218	4	222	1842, ..	136	23	159	1853, ..	830	494	1, 324	1864, ..	207	642	849
1832, ..	213	7	220	1843, ..	142	30	172	1854, ..	693	630	1, 323	1865, ..	327	582	909
1833, ..	201	13	214	1844, ..	154	59	213	1855, ..	415	471	886	1866, ..	493	671	1, 164
1834, ..	279	14	293	1845, ..	181	77	258	1856, ..	324	421	745				
1835, ..	339	22	361	1846, ..	163	36	199	1857, ..	364	411	775		11, 500	8, 543	20, 043

CORPORATIONS FORMED UNDER GENERAL LAWS.

Under the provisions of Article VIII of the Constitution of 1846, the Legislature has provided for the formation of numerous classes of corporations. As a condition precedent, the Articles of Association are required to be filed in certain public offices, from which certified copies may be procured for the various legal or other purposes for which there may be need. The offices in which these papers are required to be filed are, the Secretary's office, Insurance Department, State Engineer and Surveyor, Regents of the University, County Clerks' and Town Clerks', according to the terms of their several acts. The following tables indicate the number of companies filing their articles of association in the office of the Secretary of State in each year, until the close of 1866, with some of the leading facts conneeted with each. In giving the titles of acts, we mention only the first, without reference to their subsequent amendments, unless the latter may have changed these titles. The brief time allowed in the preparation of this volume has prevented any attempt to analyze the annual reports, which some of these companies are required to make, or to notice proceedings for the increase or reduction of capital, change of location, reorganization, legal records relating to sale and transfer, or other statements.

Unquestionably very many of these corporations never had any real existence beyond the formalities of organization, being formed for speculative or other purposes, without any practical operation in the business for which they were nominally created. There are no means within reach for ascertaining the amount of capital now actually invested, in this State and elsewhere, under most of these general laws, and especially that relating to manufacturing, mining, mechanical and chemical companies.

Plank Roads and Turnpike Roads.

"An act to provide for the incorporation of companies to construct plank roads and to construct turnpike roads." (Chap. 210, Laws of 1847.) Passed May 7, 1847.

It is believed that most of these roads were constructed, and that with very few exceptions, they have been surrendered to the public many years since.

Plank Roads.

YEARS.	Companies formed.	Miles in length.	Capital.	YEARS.	Companies formed.	Miles in length.	Capital
1847, ...	20	246¾	$510,000	1854, ...	5	30½	$65,000
1848, ...	53	603⅛	1,104,950	1855, ...	3	17	30,000
1849, ...	79	888½	1,594,500	1858, ...	1	4	5,000
1850, ...	90	980½	1,833,600	1859, ...	2	6½	5,250
1851, ...	55	487	897,000	1863, ...	1	5	8,000
1852, ...	20	118⅔	262,000	1866, ...	1	6½	9,000
1853, ...	22	169½	396,000				
					352	3,563½	$6,720,300

Turnpikes.

YEARS.	Companies formed.	Miles in length.	Capital.	YEARS.	Companies formed.	Miles in length.	Capital.
1848, ...	4	21½	$22,500	1859, ...	1	3	$5,000
1850, ...	2	23	13,500	1860, ...	1	5	5,000
1851, ...	2	23	12,000	1861, ...	1	3	4,000
1852, ...	1	9½	7,000	1863, ...	2	9	8,500
1855, ...	3	26	29,000	1866, ...	1	6	6,600
1857, ...	1	10	10,000				
					19	139	$123,100

Gas Companies.

"An act to authorize the formation of gas companies." [Chap. 37, Laws of 1848.] Passed February 16, 1848.

YEARS.	Companies formed.	Capital.	YEARS.	Companies formed.	Capital.
1848, ...	6	$750,000	1859, ...	17	$1,986,000
1849, ...	2	150,000	1860, ...	14	526,000
1850, ...	4	220,000	1861, ...	9	282,000
1851, ...	2	87,000	1862, ...	5	94,000
1852, ...	13	2,430,000	1863, ...	8	17,990,000
1853, ...	10	795,000	1864, ...	13	7,703,500
1854, ...	7	1,650,000	1865, ...	1	10,000
1855, ...	7	327,000	1866, ...	3	1,035,000
1856, ...	11	1,307,000			
1857, ...	2	33,000	Total,...	139	$38,472,500
1858, ...	5	1,097 000			

Manufacturing, Mining, Mechanical and Chemical Companies.

"An act to authorize the formation of corporations for manufacturing, mining, mechanical or chemical purposes." [Chap. 40, Laws of 1848.] Passed February 17, 1848.

The title of this act was amended April 28, 1866 (chap. 838), to read as follows: "An act to authorize the formation of corporations for manufacturing, mining, mechanical, chemical, agricultural, horticultural, medical or curative, mercantile or commercial purposes."

YEARS.	Number of articles filed.	Capital.	YEARS.	Number of articles filed.	Capital.
1848, ...	27	$1,846 000	1859, ...	131	$40,068,700
1849, ...	24	947,600	1860, ...	119	27,887,900
1850, ...	22	1,939,500	1861, ...	86	17,406,500
1851, ...	26	1,851,000	1862, ...	70	16,316,000
1852, ...	56	6,062,750	1863, ...	220	131,150,400
1853, ...	115	33,449,000	1864, ...	728	672,845,450
1854, ...	259	89,441,500	1865, ...	1,590	966,421,300
1855, ...	156	45,504,963	1866, ...	797	489,030,150
1856, ...	123	25,152,200			
1857, ...	108	38,785,600	Total,...	4,781	$2,647,941,513
1858, ...	124	41,835,000			

The par value of shares of stock was fixed at $1 in 93 companies; $2 in 77; $3 in 30; $4 in 13; $5 in 716; $10 in 866; $20 in 111; $25 in 296; $50 in 498; $100 in 806; $500 in 98; $1,000 in 84; $5,000 in 5; $10,000 in 2, and variable sums in the remainder.

The number of trustees or directors, was 3 in 1,010 companies; 4 in 201; 5 in 1,578; 6 in 158; 7 in 1,023; 8 in 84; 9 in 444; 10 in 30; 11 in 63; 12 in 13, and 13 in 70. In the remainder it was not specified.

The place of business was located as follows: In Albany county, 43 companies; Allegany, 4; Broome, 15; Cattaraugus, 12; Cayuga, 19; Chautauqua, 14; Chemung, 12; Chenango, 6; Clinton, 4; Columbia, 27; Cortland, 5; Delaware, 2; Dutchess, 45; Erie, 88; Essex, 17; Franklin, 3; Fulton, 4; Genesee, 6; Greene, 5; Hamilton, 1; Herkimer, 13; Jefferson, 22; Kings, 167; Lewis, 6; Livingston, 5; Madison, 8; Monroe, 65; Montgomery, 8; New York, 3,358; Niagara, 30; Oneida, 52; Onondaga, 82; Ontario, 23; Orange, 56; Orleans, 5; Oswego, 28; Otsego, 6; Putnam, 13; Queens, 23; Rensselaer, 37; Richmond, 40; Rockland, 10; St. Lawrence, 26; Saratoga, 21; Schenectady, 7; Schoharie, 2; Schuyler, 1; Seneca, 7; Steuben, 12; Suffolk, 10; Sullivan, 9; Tioga, 6; Tompkins, 3; Ulster, 38; Warren, 3; Washington, 26; Wayne, 13; Westchester, 77; Wyoming, 2; Yates, 14; uncertain, 115.

An attempt at classification of the objects for which these companies were formed was made, founded upon that used in the National Patent Office. From the uncertain indications of the titles of the acts in some cases, the result did not prove fully satisfactory, but will not vary much from the following. In a few cases the same company was placed in two classes:

Class	I.	Agricultural tools and implements,	78
"	II.	Metallurgy and manufacture of metals, and instruments therefor,	452
"	III.	Manufactures of fibrous and textile substances, including machines for preparing the fibres of cotton, silk, fur, paper, &c.,	229
"	IV.	Chemical processes, manufactures and compounds, including medicine, pharmacy, dyeing, coloring and painting, baking, distilling, brewing, soap and candle making, &c.,	1,603
"	V.	Calorifics—comprising lamps, stoves, grates, and apparatus for cooking, heating, &c.,	50
"	VI.	Steam engines, boilers, locomotives, &c., and parts thereof,	60
"	VII.	Navigation, and maritime implements—comprising shipbuilding and rigging,	95
"	VIII.	Mathematical, philosophical and optical instruments, including clocks and watches,	24
"	IX.	Civil engineering and architecture — comprising mining, quarrying, building, &c.,	1,367
"	X.	Land conveyance, including wagons, carriages, cars and other vehicles, and their parts,	62
"	XI.	Hydraulics and pneumatics, including pumps, fire engines, &c.,	29
"	XII.	Lever, screw and other mechanical powers, including instruments for weighing, lifting, &c.,	21
"	XIII.	Grinding Mills, mill gearing, &c.,	34
"	XIV.	Lumber, including machines and tools for preparing and manufacturing wood, and the trades connected therewith,	76
"	XV.	Stone, clay, cement, pottery and glass, including the making, dressing and preparing of brick and stone, and the trades connected therewith,	235
"	XVI.	Leather, including tanning and dressing, the manufacture of boots, shoes, saddlery, trunks, harnesses, &c.,	32

CLASS XVII.—	Household furniture, machines and implements for domestic purposes, including upholstering, decorating and furnishing dwellings, ...	42
" XVIII.—	Arts, polite, fine and ornamental, including music, painting, sculpture, engraving, books, stationery, printing, binding, jewelry, &c., and the trades connected therewith, ...	122
" XIX.—	Fire arms and implements of war, and parts thereof, including the manufacture of shot and powder,.....	52
" XX.—	Surgical, medical and dental instruments and apparatus, ...	4
" XXI.—	Wearing apparel, articles for the toilet, &c., including instruments for manufacturing, and the trades connected therewith, &c., ...	55
" XXII.—	Miscellaneous manufactures,....................................	101

The number of petroleum and other oil companies formed in 1860–6, was 1,036. The number each year, and the amount of nominal capital, was as follows:

1860, 3 companies,.........	$1,200,000	1864, 276 companies,......$219,759,125
1861, 11 "	1,623,600	1865, 680 " 334,497,400
1863, 2 "	750,000	1866, 64 " 35,404,500

Total, 1,036 companies,..$593,234,625

Of cheese factories: the State census of 1865 contains returns from 435 establishments, more or less complete. The number of these formed under the general manufacturing law of 1848, was 31. Of these, 6 were in 1863; 5 in 1864; 8 in 1865; and 12 in 1866. The capital of these companies amounted to $432,075.

Railroad Companies.

"An act to authorize the formation of railroad companies." [Chap. 140, Laws of 1848.] Passed March 27, 1848.

"An act to authorize the formation of railroad corporations, and to regulate the same." [Chap. 140, Laws of 1850.] Passed April 2, 1850.

YEARS.	Companies formed.*	Length in miles.	Capital.	YEARS.	Companies formed,	Length in miles.	Capital.
1849, ...	4	180	$3,650,000	1859, ...	11	164¾	$5,235,000
1850, ...	5	248	3,100,000	1860, ...	15	208¾	8,445,000
1851, ...	17	621	9,235,000	1861, ...	8	122	5,650,000
1852, ...	22	1,129½	22,330,000	1862, ...	8	94	3,813,000
1853, ...	26	1,147½	29,775,000	1863, ...	30	460½	13,823,000
1854, ...	4	330	8,800,000	1864, ...	22	479½	26,880,000
1855, ...	3	56	1,310,000	1865, ...	24	427¼	22,272,000
1856, ...	3	39½	900,000	1866, ...	37	1,093½	69,670,000
1857, ...	3	151½	1,690,000				
1858, ...	2	14½	325,000	Total,...	244	6,967¾	$236,903,000

* In preparing this table, we have taken no account of companies reorganized upon the sale or transfer of roads already constructed, nor of increase or reduction of capital. The table includes the several street railroads built and projected. In a few instances the length of roads was not mentioned in the articles, and the omission was supplied from the best means of estimate within reach.

Telegraph Companies.

"An act to provide for the incorporation and regulation of telegraph companies." [Chap. 265, Laws of 1848.] Passed April 12, 1848.

YEARS.	Companies formed.	Capital.	YEARS.	Companies formed.	Capital.
1848, ...	2	$198, 600	1858, ...	2	$140, 000
1849, ...	1	42, 300	1860, ...	2	20, 000
1850, ...	3	425, 000	1861, ...	3	301, 000
1851, ...	4	422, 000	1862, ...	1	26, 000
1852, ...	10	1, 287, 450	1863, ...	5	400, 000
1853, ...	3	271, 250	1864, ...	15	13, 994, 700
1854, ...	4	227, 500	1865, ...	9	18, 182, 850
1855, ...	5	483, 000	1866, ...	......	51, 251, 200
1856, ...	2	265, 000			
1857, ...	2	400, 000	Total,...	73	$88, 337, 850

Benevolent, Charitable, Scientific and Missionary Societies.

"An act for the incorporation of Benevolent, Charitable, Scientific and Missionary Societies." [Chap. 319, Laws of 1848.] Passed April 12, 1848.

YEARS.	Total number of societies.	Asylums and Hospitals.	Bible and Tract Societies.	Charitable Associations and relief of the poor.	Educational purposes.	Farm Associations.	Historical Societies.	For Literary and moral improvement.	Medical Societies, Dispensaries, &c.	Missionary Societies.	Monument Associations.	Musical Societies.	Mutual aid in sickness, and burial of members. Aid to widows and orphans of members.	Publication Societies.	Reform Societies.	Scientific and Literary Societies, Lectures, Libraries, Lyceum.	Soldiers' Aid Societies.
1848, ...	23	....	1	1	1	....	....	.....	1	2	....	....	16	....	1	......	....
1849, ...	34	3	....	6	....	....	....	......	2	2	...	1	13	....	1	6	....
1850, ...	25	2	1	2	1	1	....	2	3	1	....	....	9	1	1	1	....
1851, ...	48	6	....	2	...	1	....	2	5	1	1	....	24	1	2	3	....
1852, ...	36	6	....	1	....	....	....	3	5	1	...	....	14	....	....	6	...
1853, ...	37	1	....	4	3	....	1	4	1	3	....	1	17	....	....	2	....
1854, ...	32	4	...	3	1	....	....	1	2	3	....	....	16	....	2	......	....
1855, ...	30	8	....	5	1	....	....	3	2	1	....	....	9	...	...	1	....
1856, ...	31	2	2	......	1	....	1	.....	2	4	...	1	13	1	...	2	....
1857, ...	26	1	....	4	2	....	...	1	......	2	....	1	10	1	....	4	....
1858, ...	32	1	....	6	....	....	....	......	3	4	....	....	15	1	1	1	....
1859, ...	26	2	....	......	1	....	....	4	2	....	....	...	15	....	....	2	....
1860, ...	30	2	....	5	4	....	2	2	......	2	....	....	12	....	1	......	..
1861, ...	36	....	....	6	2	....	...	......	2	6	....	....	14	....	....	4	2
1862, ...	33	2	...	1	2	...	....	1	3	5	....	....	17	1	....	1	....
1863, ...	32	2	....	1	3	....	2	3	1	....	...	1	17	....	....	1	1
1864, ...	57	5	....	3	2	....	....	3	......	4	1	....	30	3	1	2	3
1865, ...	63	6	...	6	1	...	....	6	1	3	1	...	35	....	1	3	....
1866, ...	92	3	1	6	1	....	....	5	1	8	....	....	67	....	....	......	...
	723	56	5	62	26	2	6	40	36	52	3	5	363	9	13	39	6

Of the societies formed for mutual benefit, aid to the sick, burials, aid to widows and orphans of members, &c., the language of the titles indicates the following nationalities: African, 1; French, 7; German, 37; Hungarian, 1; Italian, 3; Irish, 50; Jews, 112; Netherlands, 2; Polish, 1; Scotch, 4; Spanish, 1; Swedish, 1; Swiss, 3; Welsh, 1.

Ocean Navigation Companies.

"An act for the incorporation of companies formed to navigate the ocean by steamships." [Chap. 228, Laws of 1852.] Passed April 12, 1852.

YEARS.	Companies formed.	Capital,	YEARS.	Companies formed.	Capital.
1852, ...	2	$520, 000	1861, ...	1	$87, 500
1853, ...	7	5, 605, 000	1862, ...	2	312, 000
1854, ...	2	460, 000	1863, ...	2	4, 135, 000
1855, ...	2	1, 200, 000	1864, ...	4	5, 000, 000
1856, ...	1	150, 000	1865, ...	9	16, 220, 000
1857, ...	...	....	1866, ...	10	8, 000, 000
1858, ...	2	550, 000			
1859, ...	5	6, 200, 000	Total,...	51	$48, 699, 500
1860, ...	2	270, 000			

Building Companies.

"An act to authorize the formation of companies for the erection of buildings." [Chap. 117, Laws of 1853.] Passed April 5, 1853.

YEARS.	Companies formed.	Capital.	YEARS.	Companies formed.	Capital.
1853, ...	4	$210, 000	1861, ...	1	$50, 000
1854, ...	10	820, 000	1863, ...	2	450, 000
1856, ...	1	150, 000	1864, ...	1	250, 000
1857, ...	1	10, 000	1865, ...	2	1, 000, 000
1858, ...	2	35, 000	1866, ...	5	540, 000
1859, ...	1	10, 000			
1860, ...	1	200, 000	Total,...	31	$3, 725, 000

Of these three were in Albany county, two in Chemung, one in Kings, nine in New York, one in Onondaga, two in Oswego, one in Queens, four in Rensselaer, one in Schoharie, and three in Westchester.

Ferry Companies.

"An Act to authorize the formation of corporations for ferry purposes." [Chap. 135, Laws of 1853.] Passed April 9, 1853.

YEARS.	Companies formed.	Capital.	YEARS.	Companies formed.	Capital.
1853, ...	7	$1, 630, 500	1863, ...	2	$700, 000
1854, ...	2	812, 000	1864, ...	3	350, 000
1855, ...	2	903, 000	1865, ...	2	75, 000
1856, ...	1	100	1866, ...	1	100, 000
1859, ...	3	350, 000			
1860, ...	3	230, 000	Total,....	26	$5, 150, 600

Free Churches.

"An Act for the incorporation of societies to establish free churches." [Chap. 218, Laws of 1854.] Passed April 13, 1854.

Under this act nineteen churches have been formed, of which four were in 1855, one in 1856, one in 1858, four in 1859, one in 1860, three in 1861, one in 1862, one in 1863, one in 1864, and two in 1866. Their locations were: Columbia, one; Dutchess, one; Erie, one; Lewis, two; Monroe, two; New York, four; Niagara, one; Queens, four; Schoharie, one; Schuyler, one; and Seneca, one.

River and Lake Navigation Companies.

"An Act for the incorporation of companies formed to navigate the lakes and rivers." [Chap. 232, Laws of 1854.] Passed April 15, 1854.

YEARS.	Companies formed.	Capital.	YEARS.	Companies formed.	Capital.
1854, ...	3	$170,000	1862, ...	5	$420,000
1855, ...	4	2,120,000	1863, ...	7	631,000
1856, ...	8	1,327,000	1864, ...	4	475,000
1857, ...	3	420,000	1865, ...	4	510,000
1858, ...	1	80,000	1866, ...	7	2,280,000
1859, ...	6	6,000			
1860, ...	...	....	Total,....	53	$8,483,000
1861, ...	1	44,000			

Companies for Improving Breed of Horses.

"An Act for the incorporation of associations for improving the breed of horses." [Chap. 269, Laws of 1854.] Passed April 15, 1854.

Three companies have been formed under this act, previous to 1857, viz.: In Queens, two, and in Orange, one. One was formed in 1854, and two in 1855. Capital of two, $350,000, and of one not given.

Agricultural and Horticultural Societies.

"An act to facilitate the forming of Agricultural and Horticultural Societies." [Chap. 339, Laws of 1853.] Passed June 8, 1853. [Chap. 425, Laws of 1855.] Passed April 13, 1855.

Under general laws, passed in 1841, societies were formed in most of the counties, and some of these, it is believed, are still in existence under that law. The following table gives the dates of organization of county agricultural societies under the law of 1853–'55:

COUNTIES.	Date of filing articles of association.	COUNTIES.	Date of filing articles of association.
Albany, ...	Aug. 23, 1853; June 7, 1862.	Chemung, ...	Feb. 20, 1860.
Allegany, ...	Nov. 1, 1859.	Columbia, ...	March 8, 1856.
Broome, ...	June 29, 1858.	Erie, ...	Nov. 17, 1856.
Cattaraugus, ..	Feb. 1, 1856.	Franklin, ...	Aug. 30, 1856.
Cayuga, ...	June 24, 1856.	Fulton, ...	Aug. 1, 1865.

COUNTIES.	Date of filing articles of association.	COUNTIES.	Date of filing articles of association.
Genesee, ...	Sept. 24, 1856.	Queens, ...	Dec. 3, 1857.
Greene, ...	Oct. 22, 1856.	Rensselaer, ...	March 28, 1861.
Jefferson, ...	Dec. 9, 1854; March 29, 1865.	St. Lawrence, .	June, 1856.
Lewis, ...	Feb. 1, 1860.	Schoharie, ...	March 31, 1865.
Livingston, ...	July 5, 1855.	Schuyler, ...	March 29, 1855.
Madison, ...	Feb. 15, 1856.	Seneca, ...	January 28, 1856.
Monroe, ...	March 28, 1856.	Tioga, ...	Aug. 13, 1855.
Montgomery, .	Dec. 16, 1864	Tompkins, ...	Feb., 1858.
Niagara, ...	Dec. 14, 1858.	Ulster, ...	March 27, 1858.
Onondaga, ...	Feb. 15, 1856.	Warren, ...	March 5, 1857.
Ontario, ...	May 22, 1854.	Washington, .	March 22, 1865.
Orange, ...	Feb. 27, 1866.	Wayne, ...	May 12, 1855.
Orleans, ...	Oct. 20, 1856.	Wyoming, ...	Feb, 26, 1856.
Oswego, ...	Dec. 29, 1855.	Yates, ...	January 22, 1855.
Otsego, ...	Feb. 1, 1856.		

In addition to the foregoing, 93 Town and Union Agricultural, Horticultural and other societies had been formed under this act previous to the beginning of 1867. Of these 2 were in 1855; 9 in 1856; 12 in 1857; 8 in 1858; 15 in 1859; 10 in 1860; 8 in 1861; 10 in 1862; 4 in 1863; 5 in 1864; and 5 in 1865. They were distributed as follows among the counties: In Albany, 2; Allegany, 1; Cattaraugus, 7; Cayuga, 2; Chautauqua, 1; Chenango, 7; Cortland, 1; Delaware, 1; Erie, 1; Essex, 2; Herkimer, 2; Jefferson, 2; Livingston, 1; Madison, 5; Monroe, 1; Niagara, 6; Oneida, 6; Onondaga, 8; Ontario, 3; Orange, 3; Oswego, 4; Otsego, 4; St. Lawrence, 4; Schoharie, 2; Seneca, 4; Steuben, 1; Suffolk, 1; Tioga, 1; Tompkins, 3; Ulster, 1; Washington, 1; Wayne, 1; Westchester, 3; Wyoming, 1; and Yates, 1.

Roman Catholic Churches.

"An act supplementary to an act entitled 'An act to provide for the incorporation of religious societies,"' passed April 5, 1813. [Chap. 45, Laws of 1863.] Passed March 25, 1863.

Applies to Roman Catholic churches, and requires articles to be filed in Secretary's office.

The number of churches incorporated under this law were 75, of which 2 were in 1863; 4 in 1864; 52 in 1865, and 17 in 1866. They were located in the following counties: Albany, 3; Chautauqua, 1; Chemung, 2; Erie, 5; Kings, 25; Livingston, 1; Monroe, 5; New York, 4; Niagara, 1; Queens, 14; Steuben, 2; Suffolk, 6; Tompkins, 1: Ulster, 1, and Wyoming, 4.

Agricultural Companies.

"An act to authorize the formation of corporations for agricultural purposes." [Chap. 234, Laws of 1865.] Passed March 29, 1865.

In 1860, the company's capital was $1,000,000.

Clubs for Social and Recreative Purposes.

"An act for the incorporation of societies or clubs for certain social and recreative purposes." [Chap. 368, Laws of 1865.] Passed April 11, 1865.

In 1865, 3, viz.: Kings Co., 1; New York, 2.

In 1866, 22, viz.: Chemung, 1; Kings, 2, New York, 12; Oneida, 2; Onondaga, 1; Rensselaer, 1; Steuben, 1; Suffolk, 1.

Among the objects for which these clubs were formed were the following: Arts, Athletic games, Boating, Breeding and Training of horses, Fishing, Literature, Mutual improvement, Musical entertainment, Social amusement and Yachting.

Masonic Lodges and Chapters.

"An act to enable lodges and chapters of free and accepted masons to take, hold and convey real and personal estate." [Chap. 317, Laws of 1866.] Passed April 2, 1866.

In 1866, 8 lodges, and in 1867 (up to May 15th), 32 lodges and 4 chapters had filed their articles under this act. Of these there were in Allegany, 1; Cayuga, 2; Chemung, 1; Chenango, 1; Delaware, 1; Dutchess, 1; Erie, 1; Franklin, 2; Greene, 1; Herkimer, 1; Jefferson, 2; Livingston, 3; Monroe, 1; Montgomery, 1; New York, 3; Oneida, 2; Oswego, 2; Otsego, 5; Rensselaer, 4; Rockland, 2; St. Lawrence, 1; Schuyler, 1; Seneca, 1; Ulster, 1; Washington, 1; and Yates, 2.

Mineral Claims.

Reservations of gold and silver mines were made in most of the original land patents. In 1789, a law was passed securing rights for a limited term to discoverers, and this law has been incorporated into the Revised Statutes. Part I, Chap. IX, Title XI. Under this provision of the statutes, 53 claims were filed from 1846 to 1867, viz.: For gold, Franklin, 2; Putnam, 1; for gold and silver, Clinton, 2, Essex, 1, Franklin, 1, Hamilton, 8, Herkimer, 2, Lewis, 1, Orange, 1, Putnam, 2, St. Lawrence, 1, and Ulster, 3; for silver, Essex, 3, Franklin, 1, Hamilton, 7, Herkimer, 1, Jefferson, 1, Lewis, 2, Montgomery, 1, Orange, 1, Oswego, 1, Putnam, 2, Rockland, 1, St. Lawrence, 3, and Warren, 1; for silver and lead, Putnam, 1; for silver and copper, Rockland, 1; and for coal, Cattaraugus, 1. Of these 5 were filed in 1853; 2 in 1854; 3 in 1858; 6 in 1860; 4 in 1861; 1 in 1863; 3 in 1864; 18 in 1865; and 11 in 1866.

We believe that since the passage of this law in 1789, neither the State nor any individual has realized any profits whatever under its provisions.

Amount of fees of Secretary of State.

YEARS.	Amount.	YEARS.	Amount.
1847,	$1,604 59	1858,	$1,661 51
1848,	1,950 98	1859,	1,551 41
1849,	1,550 30	1860,	2,416 92
1850,	2,110 71	1861,	1,698 17
1851,	2,371 24	1862,	1,896 63
1852,	3,111 69	1863,	2,361 95
1853,	4,194 25	1864,	3,643 95
1854,	3,792 33	1865,	5,297 33
1855,	2,286 24	1866,	5,457 46
1856,	2,076 34		
1857,	2,739 52		$53,773 52

COMPTROLLER'S DEPARTMENT.

Office of Comptroller.

The office of Comptroller was created soon after the close of the war of the Revolution, and during the administration of Governor JAY. By the act, chapter 21, Laws of 1797, it was provided that an officer should be appointed to be called Comptroller, at an annual compensation for salary and clerks of $3,000, the act being limited in its operation to the period of three years. By subsequent acts, the office was continued down to the year 1812, when, by the act chapter 18 of that year, it was made permanent. By section 6 of article 4 of the Constitution of 1821, which provided that the Comptroller should be appointed by the Legislature, to hold his office for three years, unless sooner removed by concurrent resolution of the Senate and Assembly, the office was placed on a permanent basis, and there were no changes in the tenure until the adoption of the Constitution of 1846, which made the office elective, and reduced the term of service to two years.

The duties of the Comptroller are numerous and important. By the act of 1797, he was empowered to draw warrants on the treasury, to examine and liquidate claims against the State, to cause suits to be brought against persons indebted to the State, to loan surplus moneys belonging to the State, to attend during the session of the Legislature, and to borrow money when necessary to pay appropriations made by that body. These powers were enlarged by subsequent acts, and especially by the Revised Statutes, where they are enumerated in detail and with great particularity.

In addition to his general powers and duties, the Comptroller has at different periods been invested with special powers of equal importance and responsibility. At one time time he exercised nearly all the powers now devolving on the Auditor and the Superintendents of the Bank and Insurance Departments. In 1817, when certain funds were set apart to be devoted to the construction of the public works of the State then in progress, he was made ex-officio a member of the Board of Commissioners created for their management. He has also been ex-officio a member of the Canal Board from its institution, and of the Board of Commissioners of the Land Office since its reorganization in 1813. These functions were originally conferred by law; but having been incorporated in the present Constitution, they have thus been withdrawn from the control of the Legislature, and become permanently attached to the office.

The Comptroller is also, by virtue of his office, a Trustee of the public buildings and of Union College, and a member of the Board of State Canvassers.

By the fifth article of the Constitution the Comptroller is to receive an annual salary of $2,500 which can neither be increased nor diminished during his official term. His present salary is $2,500.

Explanations of the accompanying Statements.

Statement "A" shows the amount of the State debt on the 30th September, 1845, and the 30th September, 1866; the items of which it was made up at each period; the dates when it becomes payable; the rate of interest; the amount of the debt, after deducting the unapplied balances of the Sinking Funds, on the 30th September, 1866, applicable to its redemption, and the amount of principal and interest paid in each fiscal year on the State stock issued to railroad companies which became a charge on the treasury.

Statement "B" shows the operations of the General Fund debt Sinking Fund from 1846 to 1866 inclusive.

Statement "C" shows the annual receipts and payments on account of the General Fund, from all sources, from 1846 to 1866 inclusive.

Statement "D" shows the capital of the Common School Fund; its annual increase; the annual receipts and payments on account of the revenue of the fund from 1846 to 1866, and the changes in the character of the investments during that period.

Statement "E" shows the capital of the U. S. Deposit Fund; the receipts on account of revenue from 1837 to 1866; the losses by counties during the same period, and the annual payments from the revenue to Colleges, Universities, Academies, Common Schools, &c., from 1838 to 1866 inclusive.

Statement "F" shows the capital of the Literature Fund on the 30th September, 1866, and its increase from 1845.

Statement "G" shows the capital of the College Land Scrip Fund on the 30th September, 1866.

Statement "H" shows the receipts and payments on account of the several State prisons, from 1842 to 1866, inclusive; amount annually paid for transportation of convicts, salaries of Inspectors, traveling expenses, &c.

Statement "I" shows the aggregate valuations of real and personal property in the several counties of this State, from 1846 to 1866, inclusive; the annual rate per cent of increase and decrease. Also, the State tax levied for the same period, and the annual rate per cent increase and decrease.

Statement "J" shows the valuation of real and personal property, the State and local taxes, and the rate per cent for each year from 1845 to 1866, inclusive.

Statement "K" contains a classified list of the moneyed or stock corporations of this State, with their respective capitals and the value of their real estate; amount of their stock taxable, deducting real estate, and the total valuation as given in the annual returns of the several boards of supervisors.

Statement "L" contains the local indebtedness by counties, and the objects and purposes for which it was incurred, so far as can be ascertained from the returns made to this department.

Statement "M" shows the amounts due for principal and interest on loans from the Common School Fund to corporations, &c., and bonds for lands under contract, to 30th September, 1866.

(A.)

State Debt, 1845.

The aggregate debt of the State on the 30th September, 1845, as given in the Comptroller's report for that year was as follows, viz.:

General Fund debt,	$5,885,549 24
Canal debt,	19,690,020 77
Contingent debt,	1,713,000 00
Aggregate amount of debt direct and contingent,	$27,288,570 01

The General Fund debt, as above stated, consisted of the following items, viz.:

Stock issued to J. J. Astor, 5 per cent,	$561,500 00
Stock issued for loans from the bank fund, 5 per cent,	348,107 00
Stock issued to the Ithaca and Owego R. R. Co., 4½ and 5½ per cent,	315,700 00
Stock issued to the Canajoharie and Catskill R. R. Co., 5 per cent,	200,000 00
Stock issued to the New York and Erie R. R. Co., 4½, 5½ and 6 per cent,	3,000,000 00
Indian annuities, 6 per cent,	122,694 87
Temporary loans to the treasury, 5, 6 and 7 per cent,	597,395 59
Balance due specific funds,	740,151 78
	$5,885,549 24

The canal debt, as above stated, included the following items, viz.:

Erie and Champlain canal, old debt,	$111,365 54	
Erie and Champlain canal, new debt,	341,474 52	
		$452,840 06
Erie Canal enlargement,		9,933,000 00
Oswego canal,		421,304 00
Cayuga and Seneca canal,		237,000 00
Chemung canal,		648,600 58
Crooked Lake canal,		120,000 00
Chenango canal,		2,420,000 00
Black River canal,		1,544,000 00
Genesee Valley canal,		3,794,000 00
Oneida Lake canal,		50,000 00
Oneida River improvement,		69,276 13
		$19,690,020 77

The contingent debt, as above stated, was for stock issued to the following companies, viz.:

Delaware and Hudson Canal Company,	$793,000 00
Auburn and Syracuse R. R. Co.,	200,000 00
Auburn and Rochester R. R. Co.,	200,000 00
Hudson and Berkshire R. R. Co.,	150,000 00
Tonawanda R. R. Co.,	100,000 00
Long Island R. R. Co.,	100,000 00
Schenectady and Troy R. R. Co.,	100,000 00
Tioga Coal, Iron Mining and Manufacturing Company,	70,000 00
	$1,713,000 00

Of this amount $150,000 became a charge upon the State treasury, by the failure of the Hudson and Berkshire Railroad Co.

State Debt, 1866.

The aggregate debt of the State, on the 30th September, 1866, was as follows, viz.:

General Fund debt,	$5,642,622 22
Contingent,	218,000 00
Canal,	18,248,460 00
Bounty,	27,644,000 00
Aggregate amount of debt, direct and contingent,	$51,753,082 22

The General Fund debt, on the 30th September, 1866, included the following items, viz.:

Astor stock, chap. 302, Laws of 1827, and chap. 86, Laws of 1832,	$561,500 00
Deficiency loans under chapter 216, Laws of 1848,	4,880,848 82
Comptroller's bonds,	71,578 53
Indian annuities,	122,694 87
Not paying interest,	6,000 00
	$5,642,622 22

The principal of this debt is payable as follows, viz.:

On demand,	$35,578 53
1868,	942,961 05
1870,	700,000 00
1875,	900,000 00
1878,	800,000 00
At pleasure,	2,258,082 64
	$5,636,622 22
Not paying interest,	6,000 00
	$5,642,622 22

The contingent debt, on the 30th September, 1866, included the following items, viz.:

Stock issued to the Schenectady and Troy R. R. Co., per chapter 299, Laws of 1840, redeemable July 1st, 1867,	$100,000 00
To the Long Island R. R. Co., per chapter 193, Laws of 1840, redeemable August 1st, 1861; redemption deferred to August, 1876, chapter 36, Laws of 1858,	68,000 00
To the Tioga Coal, Iron Mining and Manufacturing Co., per chapter 296, Laws of 1840, redeemable at the pleasure of the Legislature,	50,000 00
	$218,000 00

The canal debt paying interest on the 30th September, 1866, includes the following items, viz.:

Under article 7, section 1, of the Constitution,	$4,899,600 00
Under article 7, section 3, of the Constitution,	11,567,000 00
Under article 7, section 12, of the Constitution,	1.700,000 00
	$18,166,600 00

The principal of this debt is payable as follows, viz.:

1868,	$899,600 00
1871,	67,000 00
1872,	3,050,000 00
1873,	6,000,000 00
1874,	6,750,000 00
1875,	500,000 00
1877,	900,000 00
Debt paying interest,	$18,166,600 00
Debt not paying interest,	81,860 00
Total debt,	$18,248,460 00

The Bounty Debt, on the 30th September, 1866, included the following items, viz.:

Comptroller's Bonds not converted, issued under chapter 56, Laws of 1865,	$3,358,500 00
Coupon bonds, issued under chapter 325, Laws of 1865,	2,559,000 00
Registered Stock, issued under chapter 209, Laws of 1866,	21,726,500 00
	$27,644,000 00

The principal of this debt is payable April 17, 1877.

State Debt and Rate of Interest, 30th September, 1866.

	5 per cent.	5½ per cent.	6 per cent.	7 per cent.	Total.
General Fund, ..	$2,277,898 99	....	$2,658,723 23	$700,000 00	$5,636,622 22
Contingent,.....	68,000 00	$50,000 00	100,000 00	....	218,000 00
Canal, ...	5,466,600 00	....	12,700,000 00	....	18,166,600 00
Bounty,.........	....	....	....	27,644,000 00	27,644,000 00
	$7,812,498 99	$50,000 00	$15,458,723 23	$28,344,000 00	$51,665,222 22
Paying no interest,	....	....	....	....	87,860 00
					$51,753,082 22

State Debt after deducting balances in the Sinking Funds, on the 30th September, 1866.

	Debt on the 30th Sept., 1866.	Balances of Sinking Funds, 30th September, 1866.	Balance of Debt after applying Sinking Funds.
General Fund,....................	$5,642,622 22	$217,127 05	$5,425,495 17
Contingent,....................	218,000 00	8,304 32	209,695 68
Canal,............................	18,248,460 00	2,563,623 23	15,684,836 77
Bounty,..........................	27,644,000 00	....	*27,644,000 00
	$51,753,082 22	$2,789,054 60	$48,964,027 62

*The amount of the Bounty Debt as here given has been since reduced by the payment and cancellation of $600,000 of the stock and bonds by which it is represented.

TABLE *showing the amount of principal and interest paid in each year, on the State stock issued to railroad companies, which became a charge upon the State Treasury.*

YEARS.	Principal.	Interest.	Total.
1842,	....	$155,702 99	$155,702 99
1843,	....	191,986 50	191,986 50
1844,	....	191,986 50	191,986 50
1845,	....	191,986 50	191,986 50
1846,	....	191,986 50	191,986 50
1847,	....	191,986 50	191,986 50
1848,	....	191,986 48	191,986 48
1849,	....	191,986 48	191,986 48
1850,	....	191,986 50	191,986 50
1851,	....	191,986 50	191,986 50
1852,	....	191,986 50	191,986 50
1853,*	....	204,621 88	204,621 88
1854,	....	200,236 52	200,236 52
1855,	....	200,236 52	200,236 52
1856,	....	200,236 52	200,236 52
1857,	....	200,236 52	200,236 52
1858,	....	198,986 52	198,986 52
1859,	$421,000 00	188,062 77	609,062 77
1860,	269,000 00	175,861 52	444,861 52
1861,	1,459,000 00	117,486 52	1,576,486 52
1862,	1,011,000 00	60,236 52	1,071,236 52
1863,	26,000 00	22,736 52	48,736 52
1864,	240,700 00	13,026 63	253,726 63
1865,	228,000 00	9,405 00	237,405 00
1866,	5,000 00	....	5,000 00
	†$3,659,700 00	$3,866,937 91	$7,526,637 91

* The Hudson and Berkshire Railroad Company failed to pay the interest.
† $6,000 of the New York and Erie Railroad Co. stock has not been presented for redemption.
NOTE.—The above stock was issued to the following companies, viz.:

Canajoharie and Catskill Railroad Co.,	....	$200,000 00	at 5 per cent.
Ithaca and Owego	do	287,700 00	at 4½ do
do do	do	28,000 00	at 5½ do
Hudson and Berkshire	do	150,000 00	at 5½ do
New York and Erie	do	1,600,000 00	at 5½ do
do do	do	1,100,000 00	at 6 do
do do	do	300,000 00	at 4½ do
		$3,665,700 00	

(B.)

Operations of the General Fund Debt Sinking Fund, from 1846 *to* 1866 *inclusive.*

RECEIPTS.

YEARS.	General Fund for Deficiencies.	Surplus Canal Revenues.	Interest on Investments and Advances.	Deficiency Loans.	Premium on Loans.	Miscellaneous.	Total.
1846,*	....	$116,666 66	$5,250 00	....	....	....	$121,916 66
1847,	....	350,000 00	....	....	....	....	350,000 00
1848,	....	350,000 00	7,000 00	....	....	....	357,000 00
1849,	....	350,000 00	7,000 00	....	....	....	357,000 00
1850,	....	350,000 00	8,026 66	....	....	....	358,026 66
1851,	....	350,000 00	4,005 20	....	....	....	354,005 20
1852,	....	350,000 00	4,005 20	....	....	....	354,005 20
1853,	....	350,000 00	3,975 20	$432,961 05	$34,038 95	....	820,975 20
1854,	....	350,000 00	4,089 20	10,000 00	1,000 00	....	365,089 20
1855,	....	350,000 00	3,009 20	348,107 00	....	....	701,116 20
1856,	....	350,000 00	3,009 20	....	....	$26 30	353,035 50
1857,	....	262,500 00	1,582 60	....	....	....	264,082 60
1858,	....	....	....	100,000 00	2,911 50	04	102,911 54
1859,	$840,179 21	....	....	350,000 00	3,702 50	....	1,193,881 71
1860,	352,455 99	....	....	250,000 00	....	....	602,455 99
1861,	330,964 47	....	....	1,950,000 00	31,162 20	....	2,312,126 67
1862,	....	350,000 00	....	800,000 00	83,870 20	....	1,233,870 20
1863,	....	350,000 00	....	....	....	....	350,000 00
1864,	....	350,000 00	....	....	....	....	350,000 00
1865,	....	950,000 00	....	....	....	....	950,000 00
1866,	....	537,500 00	†273,344 27	....	....	....	810,844 27
	$1,523,599 67	$6,416,666 66	$324,296 73	$4,241,068 05	$156,685 35	$26 34	$12,662,342 80

Two years contributions from the canal revenues, due as per above statement, were paid Oct. 3, 1866.

PAYMENTS.

YEARS.	Interest on Debt.	Principal of Debt.	Interest on Advances.	Indian Annuities.	Total.
1846,	$110,579 36	....	....	....	$110,579 36
1847,	335,940 40	$13,000 00	....	$7,061 67	356,002 07
1848,	324,455 15	27,147 50	$6,679 88	5,061 67	363,344 20
1849,	327,580 34	....	7,060 53	8,861 66	343,502 53
1850,	344,380 23	....	6,726 18	7,161 67	358,268 08
1851	331,413 02	....	5,807 68	7,961 67	345,182 37
1852,	359,535 04	....	3,392 53	7,361 67	370,289 24
1853,	354,155 86	467,000 00	4,080 21	7,361 67	832,597 74
1854,	348,885 96	10,000 00	3,573 58	7,361 67	369,821 21
1855.	347,244 33	348,107 00	3,686 49	7,361 67	706,399 49
1856,	347,181 83	....	5,420 53	7,361 67	359,964 03
1857,	339,871 60	....	7,485 02	7,387 96	354,744 58
1858,	354,679 55	....	15,102 31	7,361 67	377,143 53
1859,	347,820 57	421,000 00	....	7,361 67	776,182 24
1860,	345,119 32	269,000 00	....	7,361 67	621,480 99
1861,	354,764 98	1,709,000 00	....	7,361 67	2,071,126 65
1862,	362,048 17	1,011,000 00	....	6,861 67	1,379,909 84
1863,	‡382,327 91	26,000 00	....	7,753 91	416,081 82
1864,	350,235 68	240,700 00	....	7,444 43	598,380 11
1865,	346,037 80	228,000 00	....	7,340 53	581,378 33
1866,	337,145 05	408,332 15	....	7,360 14	752,837 34
	$7,051,402 15	$5,178,286 65	$69,014 94	$146,512 01	$12,445,215 75

Total receipts as per foregoing statement, ... $12,662,342 80
Total payments as per foregoing statement, ... 12,445,215 75

Balance in the treasury 30th September, 1866, ... $217,127 05

* Received in 1847. † Includes $245,461.01 interest on deferred payments from canal revenues.
‡ Includes $22,833.59 premium on coin.

The payments on account of the principal of the debt include the following items, viz.:

Comptroller's bonds,	$1,170,479 65
State stock,	348,107 00
Stock issued to the New York and Erie Railroad Company,	2,994,000 00
" " Ithaca and Owego Railroad Company,	315,700 00
" " Canajoharie and Catskill Railroad Company,	200,000 00
" " Hudson and Berkshire Railroad Company,	150,000,00
	$5,178,286 65

(C.)

Statement showing the Receipts on account of the General Fund, from 1846 to 1866, inclusive.

YEARS.	(1) Auction Duties.	(2) Salt duties.	(3) State tax.	(4) Sales of General Fund lands.
1846,	$139,312 22	$75,507 34	$346,811 47	$1,140 50
1847,	87,932 17	32,398 64	310,037 00	*34,473 96
1848,	103,901 35	43,847 67	238,706 39	16,322 86
1849,	93,025 46	51,598 98	278,843 10	18,579 00
1850,	85,909 69	44,364 03	272,422 45	†43,362 33
1851,	102,567 02	45,458 58	320,847 94	10,222 86
1852,	115,198 43	47,928 17	480,933 88	20,625 42
1853,	94,443 14	52,159 85	260,864 50	38,729 40
1854,	109,143 69	54,987 88	1,256,969 72	3,237 49
1855,	145,022 73	57,777 90	922,810 88	40,022 99
1856,	107,709 01	60,975 82	1,547,698 41	33,139 09
1857,	132,220 22	53,476 91	1,222,923 82	9,800 00
1858,	100,527 95	58,138 18	3,071,331 05	2,534 74
1859,	119,998 68	69,026 54	2,761,441 40	4,469 05
1860,	125,929 83	65,875 51	2,315,173 33	43,508 11
1861,	75,318 83	66,299 57	3,331,655 75	801 24
1862,	77,358 57	87,418 98	4,544,985 29	1,603 28
1863,	108,604 67	76,090 75	4,700,952 77	2,904 34
1864,	154,425 86	88,125 31	5,812,564 97	3,040 30
1865,	195,608 65	62,765 64	6,082,771 30	2,087 42
1866,	269,720 23	70,411 66	5,674,875 25	2,351 66
	$2,543,878 40	$1,264,133 91	$45,755,620 67	$332,956 04

YEARS.	(5) Pedlers' licenses.	(6) Arrears of county taxes.	(7) Interest on county taxes.	(8) Sales of lands for county taxes.
1846,	$2,445 00	$57,643 53	$7,484 96	$35 71
1847,	3,080 00	55,808 56	11,734 84	....
1848,	2,290 00	44,285 65	12,095 10	....
1849,	1,445 00	53,359 20	16,797 17	203,341 55
1850,	1,700 00	25,048 46	4,273 19	586 55
1851,	1,875 00	24,719 35	4,437 81	706 49
1852,	1,985 00	33,353 60	7,329 36	....
1853,	1,595 00	57,781 31	13,673 64	38,102 20
1854,	1,875 00	30,431 71	6,945 67	168,265 67
1855,	1,495 00	35,758 08	2,125 52	38,060 97
1856,	1,210 00	33,920 95	2,876 55	9,666 89
1857,	1,060 00	31,285 74	2,828 71	1,713 34
1858,	545 00	39,741 32	4,857 19	9 29
1859,	430 00	55,282 48	10,578 37	495 84
1860,	855 00	43,907 94	10,360 36	122,886 57
1861,	665 00	27,857 18	5,228 81	106,956 50
1862,	3,400 00	32,936 65	5,788 92	16,604 10
1863,	605 00	42,778 70	10,118 88	31 69
1864,	535 00	61,784 82	15,055 03	504 43
1865,	1,105 00	55,766 78	8,996 69	....
1866,	1,210 00	113,848 50	25,271 32	4 16
	$31,405 00	$957,300 51	$188,858 09	$707,971 95

* Includes $33,284.87 for lands on Staten Island, sold to the United States for military purposes.
† Includes $30,000 for State Arsenal grounds, in the city of New York.

Receipts on account of the General Fund—(Continued).

YEARS.	(9) Redemption of lands sold for taxes.	(10) Interest on treasury deposits and advances.	(11) Tax on Foreign Insurance Companies.	(12) Fees of Secretary of State's office.
1846,	$3,054 55	$8,376 02	$3,310 75	$1,515 35
1847,	1,317 51	6,821 20	8,588 36	1,604 59
1848,	611 10	10,972 65	4,810 14	1,950 98
1849,	21,107 74	21,488 65	5,052 16	1,550 30
1850,	34,230 47	19,950 52	802 79	2,110 71
1851,	102,430 99	18,581 35	479 47	2,371 24
1852,	3,551 90	9,435 31	129 93	3,111 69
1853,	6,588 13	7,765 59	621 48	4,194 25
1854,	24,584 26	8,880 81	113 48	3,792 33
1855,	30,592 12	9,901 37	62 53	2,286 24
1856,	96,811 51	13,940 51	152 45	2,076 34
1857,	13,362 85	37,543 37	....	2,739 52
1858,	1,944 91	29,488 22	3,750 13	1,661 51
1859,	246 73	15,398 96	3,023 84	1,551 41
1860,	19,000 19	22,899 33	3,413 90	2,416 92
1861,	14,011 07	21,179 42	2,900 06	1,698 17
1862,	155,279 69	18,235 05	2,296 60	1,896 63
1863,	4,348 38	25,883 21	1,641 19	2,361 95
1864,	3,573 32	17,500 78	1,895 87	3,643 95
1865,	469 35	20,844 63	1,142 73	5,297 33
1866,	204 31	26,528 92	852 94	5,457 46
	$537,321 08	$371,615 87	$45,040 80	$55,288 87

YEARS.	(13) Fees of Comptroller's office.	(14) Fees of Surveyor General's office.	(15) Fees of Clerk of Court of Appeals office.	(16) Registers' and Clerks' fees.
1846,	$794 49	$30 08	....	$34,896 47
1847,	290 93	66 75	....	30,857 76
1848,	193 84	35 62	$832 32	9,456 54
1849,	199 85	16 87	1,534 60	775 37
1850,	166 42	....	556 15	33 69
1851,	611 48	4 50	1,114 87	....
1852,	308 35	....	1,021 15	....
1853,	184 52	18 75	506 60	....
1854,	2,462 54	....	461 86	....
1855,	2,299 00	....	227 24	....
1856,	2,595 09	....	261 26	....
1857,	2,612 11	....	506 73	....
1858,	2,647 73	....	195 69	....
1859,	2,703 58	... .	532 09	....
1860,	*415 25	....	200 00	....
1861,	39 14	....	400 00	....
1862,	588 29	....	407 29	....
1863,	288 69	....	....	... .
1864,	169 50	....	599 91	....
1865,	142 40	....	1,317 90	... .
1866,	124 40	....	748 60	....
	$19,837 60	$172 57	$11,424 26	$76,019 83

* Insurance Department created as a separate Bureau.

Receipts on account of the General Fund—(Continued).

YEARS.	(17) Surplus canal revenues.	(18) Sales of Natural History of New York.	(19) Temporary loans to the treasury.	(20) Bank department for expenses.
1846,	*$400,000 00	$28,077 47	$13,994 42	$9,035 29
1847,	200,000 00	3,808 46	10,000 00	12,040 13
1848,	200,000 00	4,137 00	21,000 00	14,983 70
1849,	200,000 00	1,730 83	15,000 00	3,759 12
1850,	200,000 00	855 00	....	28,806 96
1851,	200,000 00	898 00	....	21,517 57
1852,	200,000 00	899 00	....	18,772 98
1853,	200,000 00	1,603 00	....	18,770 87
1854,	§200,000 00	3,772 74	....	22,824 93
1855,	....	3,099 38	237,000 00	20,600 39
1856,	....	1,926 69	250,000 00	21,631 77
1857,	....	62 00	....	26,983 74
1858,	....	29 00	50,000 00	24,607 95
1859,	....	48 00	150,000 00	31,367 40
1860,	....	44 00	200,000 00	26,440 62
1861,	....	21 00	1,150,000 00	29,197 82
1862,	....	1,428 74	1,500,000 00	27,626 70
1863,	200,000 00	1,350 50	2,000,000 00	33,020 33
1864,	200,000 00	315 44	1,000,000 00	31,166 73
1865,	151,113 40	114 00	4,984,000 00	33,386 85
1866,	....	25 00	525,000 00	26,390 08
	$2,551,113 40	$54,245 25	$12,505,994 42	$482,931 93

YEARS.	(21) Military fines and commutations.	(22) Expenses of military to aid sheriff, &c.	(23) Gas light companies.	(24) Insurance Department, fees and assessments.
1846,	....	$1,138 50	....	....
1847,	$9,603 02	1,250 00	....	....
1848,	50 71	1,054 00	....	....
1849,	68 61	1,000 00	....	....
1850,	....	1,434 97	....	....
1851,	....	500 00	....	....
1852,	....	300 00	....	....
1853,	....	....	....	....
1854,	....	1,024 80	....	....
1855,	....	....	....	....
1856,	....	....	....	....
1857,	....	....	....	....
1858,	....	....	....	....
1859,	....	....	....	....
1860,	35 00	....	....	$7,000 00
1861,	....	....	....	7,000 00
1862,	....	....	....	10,700 00
1863,	69,901 37	....	$954 24	14,694 22
1864,	1,209 00	....	5,595 79	15,671 00
1865,	2,846 00	....	1,763 67	17,162 03
1866,	....	....	2,928 51	25,364 81
	$83,713 71	$7,702 27	$11,242 21	$97,592 06

* Two years contribution.

§ Of this amount, $194,062.71 was refunded to the Canal Fund as an over-payment. Chap. 449, Laws of 1859.

Receipts on account of the General Fund — (Continued).

YEARS.	(25) Railroad Companies, for expenses.	(26) Sales of Colonial History.	(27) Auburn Prison.	(28) Clinton Prison.
1846,	....	....	....	....
1847,	....	....	....	....
1848,	....	....	....	....
1849,	....	....	....	....
1850,	....	....	....	....
1851,	....	....	....	....
1852,	....	....	....	....
1853,	....	....	....	....
1854,	....	....	$26,807 50	$2,339 91
1855,	....	....	71,156 08	857 70
1856,	$936 63	$735 00	74,518 48	6,151 04
1857,	13,210 16	1,477 00	64,121 42	26,050 54
1858,	12,030 76	23 00	33,300 00	3,762 04
1859,	3,280 68	635 82	75,917 62	17,313 94
1860,	1,554 76	171 75	98,286 53	23,273 02
1861,	4,983 32	....	48,067 85	16,090 46
1862,	5,420 78	....	110,684 44	36,611 73
1863,	3,266 33	....	105,762 54	38,582 14
1864,	11,986 51	....	119,350 65	43,074 50
1865,	3,914 10	....	80,712 51	46,562 89
1866,	16,652 29	....	95,841 00	86,386 96
	$77,236 32	$3,042 57	$1,004,526 62	$347,056 87

YEARS.	(29) Sing Sing prison	(30) Costs of suits.	(31) One mile of tolls on Cayuga Lake inlet.	(32) Sale of timber purch'd in pursuance of chap. 294, Laws of 1861.
1846,	....	$124 82	....	....
1847,	....	....	....	....
1848,	....	....	....	....
1849,	....	98 17	$60 75	....
1850,	....	247 00	102 98	....
1851,	....	3 00	95 20	....
1852,	....	....	115 07	....
1853,	....	1,267 00	135 89	....
1854,	$24,388 24	....	155 58	....
1855,	82,079 46	220 50	163 93	....
1856,	86,935 60	....	164 06	....
1857,	81,867 92	....	193 91	....
1858,	39,818 92	....	95 09	....
1859,	89,208 71	516 54	86 97	....
1860,	99,993 77	....	86 72	....
1861,	28,780 80	....	73 99	....
1862,	43,747 80	....	120 97	$1,055 14
1863,	122,780 62	....	193 20	39,268 51
1864,	116,526 91	....	175 92	10,000 00
1865,	102,012 94	....	135 02	27,297 25
1866,	121,929 00	....	143 22	....
	$1,040,070 69	$2,477 03	$2,298 47	$77,620 90

Receipts on account of the General Fund—(Continued.)

YEARS.	(33) U. S. on account of advances in raising troops, return of dut's, sale of arms and am'tion.	(34) Int. on Comptroller's bonds of N. Y. city.**	(35) Micellaneous.	Total.
1846,	....	....	$7,995 21	$1,142,724 15
1847,	....	....	*940,507 79	1,762,221 67
1848,	....	....	5,364 16	736,401 78
1849,	....	....	2,019 21	992,451 69
1850,	....	....	720 98	767,685 34
1851,	....	....	11,389 19	870,831 91
1852,	....	....	†192,328 91	1,137,328 15
1853,	....	....	1,606 87	800,611 99
1854,	....	....	2,061 61	1,955,527 42
1855,	....	....	13,207 21	1,716,827 22
1856,	....	....	7,376 27	2,363,409 42
1857,	....	....	‡277,490 5[illegible]	2,003,530 51
1858,	....	....	5,129 61	3,486,169 28
1859,	....	....	338 41	3,413,893 06
1860,	....	....	5,044 32	3,238,772 73
1861,	....	....	6,981 74	5,346,207 72
1862,	$1,210,598 50	$21,008 25	§20,016 40	7,937,818 79
1863,	191,288 46	18,000 00	5,550 38	7,821,223 06
1864,	....	18,000 00	‖50,527 01	7,787,018 51
1865,	....	18,000 00	5,040 13	11,912,376 61
1866,	262,763 17	18,000 00	¶116,606 17	7,489,639 62
	$1,664,650 13	$93,008 25	$1,677,302 08	$74,682,670 63

Payments on account of the General Fund, from 1846 to 1866, inclusive.

YEARS.	(1) Salaries, Clerk hire, and office expenses of officers of gov'm'nt.	(2) Expenses attending the administration of justice.	(3) Legislature.	(4) Printing.
1846,	$38,264 68	$108,410 67	$96,509 80	$69,739 27
1847,	39,602 53	97,875 32	94,021 98	38,457 59
1848,	45,956 02	146,333 23	144,171 11	64,935 21
1849,	47,511 18	119,976 10	82,290 34	75,448 37
1850,	50,476 25	107,768 09	87,962 09	92,528 53
1851,	55,950 62	105,505 82	130,787 71	121,448 49
1852,	67,465 87	107,787 60	105,385 78	138,224 88
1853,	60,037 37	107,055 07	138,844 15	135,363 95
1854,	62,027 36	109,899 55	95,288 64	128,460 58
1855,	65,216 58	110,939 77	110,994 73	156,617 50
1856,	69,023 66	109,933 24	80,344 02	109,549 04
1857,	82,799 36	113,105 93	153,982 32	109,935 93
1858,	84,070 67	126,595 78	139,741 62	124,264 43
1859,	86,024 95	122,679 80	125,905 10	158,929 88
1860,	89,208 98	132,678 85	124,299 15	181,796 76
1861,	79,160 05	130,043 60	116,956 62	132,496 25
1862,	86,252 12	131,421 38	117,071 01	102,498 85
1863,	87,455 00	140,115 88	145,422 79	102,252 80
1864,	102,159 45	146,423 74	165,000 06	155,715 20
1865,	110,522 12	143,323 76	198,156 24	214,161 50
1866,	125,010 22	147,752 16	183,040 52	193,221 59
	$1,534,195 04	$2,565,645 34	$2,636,175 78	$2,606,046 60

* Of this amount $939,318.80 was transferred from General Fund State Debt, for balances due the specific funds, 30 September, 1846.
† Includes $185,641.48 common school tax, erroneously paid to the General Fund and refunded.
‡ Includes $275,000.00 for sale of the State arsenal in the city of New York.
§ Includes $15,000.00 judgment against Mutual Safety Insurance Company.
‖ Includes $42,759.61 for advances to purchase coin to pay interest on a portion of the Canal Debt.
¶ Includes $65,250.00 paid by the city of Albany, chap. 648, Laws of 1865, also $30,000 interest on $107,251.80 Richmond county bonds issued per chap. 93, Laws of 1860, and $10,000 for account of Col. Edward Jardine, per chap. 536, Laws of 1866.
** These bonds amounting to $300,000 were received on sale of West Washington Market, and other property in the city of New York.

Payments on account of the General Fund—(Continued).

YEARS.	(5) Expenses of State Prisons and Building.	(6) Deaf and Dumb.	(7) Blind, N. Y.	(8) Blind, Chapter 587, Laws of '65.
1846,	$99,077 15	$25,192 99	$17,575 48	....
1847,	68,532 32	25,910 03	17,438 66	....
1848,	138,400 39	31,000 00	18,252 89	....
1849,	84,394 71	40,778 34	33,476 89	....
1850,	82,376 97	25,784 10	11,918 85	....
1851,	70,390 05	25,800 00	12,361 19	....
1852,	81,364 94	26,287 50	31,430 83	....
1853,	101,637 20	29,223 08	11,151 40	....
1854,	183,651 24	30,915 63	22,004 62	....
1855,	490,162 18	57,215 81	18,155 16	....
1856,	270,136 28	37,126 25	28,760 63	....
1857,	291,361 14	43,837 50	22,096 63	....
1858,	311,170 97	66,740 84	20,785 69	....
1859,	389,740 80	34,552 07	21,431 36	....
1860,	426,631 97	56,799 60	20,766 16	....
1861,	387,143 65	50,080 98	21,486 51	....
1862,	311,744 81	51,113 23	20,501 30	....
1863,	385,541 97	52,472 65	26,996 64	....
1864,	409,996 20	57,718 98	25,686 96	....
1865,	578,909 38	73,331 40	59,312 65	....
1866,	692,294 96	82,758 00	52,472 81	$31,637 59
	$5,854,659 28	$924,638 98	$514,063 31	$31,637 59

YEARS.	(9) Society for the Reformation of Juvenile Delinquents, N. Y.	(10) House of Refuge, Western N. Y.	(11) Lunatic Asylum.	(12) Idiot Asylum.
1846,	....	$3,234 66	$38,947 86	....
1847,	....	15,000 00	39,942 44	....
1848,	$5,333 33	26,615 34	5,577 48	....
1849,	6,000 00	19,300 00	12,306 86	....
1850,	8,000 00	18,000 00	9,429 92	....
1851,	8,000 00	18,000 00	8,322 79	....
1852,	33,000 00	21,000 00	10,476 61	$9,987 96
1853,	29,000 00	22,000 00	23,373 73	12,546 73
1854,	85,000 00	31,611 00	44,458 06	19,022 40
1855,	31,000 00	30,000 00	45,259 52	56,305 30
1856,	18,000 00	20,000 00	11,060 85	19,042 17
1857,	34,400 00	29,789 31	69,311 14	29,500 00
1858,	32,400 00	25,000 00	81,630 04	24,000 00
1859,	23,600 00	25,000 00	12,057 87	15,000 00
1860,	49,000 00	30,000 00	17,975 49	23,500 00
1861,	74,786 00	56,000 00	16,244 08	23,000 00
1862,	49,000 00	25,000 00	9,524 78	23,000 00
1863,	24,000 00	33,000 00	8,216 84	18,000 00
1864,	24,000 00	25,000 00	18,614 82	18,000 00
1865,	52,000 00	52,000 00	19,008 26	27,000 00
1866,	53,172 36	45,000 00	21,368 94	27,000 00
	$639,691 69	$570,550 31	$523,108 38	$344,904 56

Payments on account of the General Fund—(Continued).

YEARS.	(13) Willard Asylum for the Insane.	(14) Hospitals and other Charitable Institutions.	(15) Orphan Asylums.	(16) Dispensaries and Infirmaries.
1846,	....	$22,500 00	$1,000 00	....
1847,	....	22,500 00	1,000 00	....
1848,	....	23,000 00	500 00	$4,500 00
1849,	....	28,500 00	6,500 00	....
1850,	....	26,500 00	1,500 00	5,500 00
1851,	....	23,000 00	9,000 00	2,000 00
1852,	....	52,500 00	26,500 00	4,750 00
1853,	....	24,300 00	35,300 00	6,000 00
1854,	....	48,800 00	500 00	....
1855,	....	49,178 00	36,619 89	18,700 00
1856,	....	47,500 00	37,594 41	8,700 00
1857,	....	74,249 91	28,769 62	10,500 00
1858,	....	63,700 00	44,117 43	10,200 00
1859,	....	58,500 00	30,966 29	8,300 00
1860,	....	29,050 00	31,012 44	5,975 00
1861,	....	11,585 00	....	....
1862,	....	31,500 00	34,179 17	....
1863,	....	43,500 00	51,947 72	....
1864,	....	60,999 97	63,557 86	10,000 00
1865,	$639 89	101,750 00	47,228 99	8,150 00
1866,	64,622 42	117,750 00	44,624 73	25,500 00
	$65,262 31	$960,862 88	$532,418 55	$128,775 00

YEARS.	(17) Support of foreign poor in New York and other counties.	(18) Militia and national guard.	(19) Bureau of Military Statistics.	(20) Relief of Sick and Wounded Soldiers.
1846,	$10,000 00	$32,917,31	....	....
1847,	10,000 00	40,735,96	....	....
1848,	10,000 00	58,296,17	....	....
1849,	6,000 00	43,656,65	....	....
1850,	20,000 00	21,195,59	....	....
1851,	....	23,091,11	....	....
1852,	....	39,252,99	....	....
1853,	....	21,161,72	....	....
1854,	....	18,579,36	....	....
1855,	....	23,031,10	....	....
1856,	....	21,856,84	....	....
1857,	....	31,135,47	....	....
1858,	....	160,447,56	....	....
1859,	....	173,245,79	....	....
1860,	....	62,062,69	....	....
1861,	....	31,214,20	....	....
1862,	....	343,509,99	....	$7,337 98
1863,	....	548,833,31	$4,703 94	43,468 31
1864,	....	583,647,75	15,699 28	131,478 37
1865,	....	696,694,46	19,148 69	142,311 93
1866,	....	556,799,86	20,673 25	127,575 64
	$56,000 00	$3,531,365 88	$60,225 16	$452,172 23

Payments on account of the General Fund—(Continued).

YEARS.	(21) Military expenditures incident to the wars, including bount's to volunteers.	(22) State Library.	(23) State Library Building.	(24) State Hall
1846,	....	$6,886 93	....	$1,698 73
1847,	....	11,785 24	....	3,127 73
1848,	....	9,234 91	....	5,281 44
1849,	....	7,901 37	....	5,093 15
1850,	....	6,937 52	....	4,715 36
1851,	....	5,949 98	....	2,354 53
1852,	$24,960 00	7,049 98	$40,000 00	4,707 49
1853,	15,082 00	7,150 00	39,900 00	2,382 23
1854,	7,380 00	5,116 66	12,000 00	5,333 73
1855,	990 00	12,461 01	3,000 00	7,041 56
1856,	288 00	8,934 48	....	4,545 28
1857,	....	18,939 29	....	6,514 51
1858,	....	14,975 28	....	5,999 36
1859,	....	12,302 38	....	13,836 94
1860,	3,297 00	10,413 71	....	12,955 87
1861,	2,446,166 42	10,856 24	....	6,146 84
1862,	530,964 20	9,585 81	....	4,612 84
1863,	4,744,855 21	12,630 71	....	6,389 27
1864,	4,130,735 26	13,471 53	....	6,553 40
1865,	5,008,167 97	12,135 60	....	6,828 96
1866,	636,400 35	12,432 33	....	10,702 93
	$17,549,286 41	$217,150 96	$94,900 00	$126,822 15

YEARS.	(25) Old State Hall.	(26) Capitol.	(27) Geological Hall.	(28) Geological Hall Building.
1846,	$144 72	$7,471 50	$809 47	....
1847,	103 86	6,025 54	975 05	....
1848,	3,030 94	10,714 64	1,372 32	....
1849,	2,293 84	5,402 88	1,836 25	....
1850,	440 59	5,441 24	2,019 23	....
1851,	474 69	7,443 55	2,502 54	....
1852,	1,329 37	8,868 39	2,599 98	....
1853,	960 96	9,504 56	2,600 00	....
1854,	1,410 12	9,384 29	1,600 00	....
1855,	1,147 40	§34,763 79	1,783 34	$11,911 65
1856,	....	4,670 83	2,762 44	28,318 25
1857,	....	16,264 89	4,789 79	13,370 85
1858,	....	12,211 86	5,781 28	8,396 12
1859,	....	15,929 86	6,333 52	....
1860,	....	27,204 66	6,682 69	....
1861,	....	13,818 41	4,850 80	....
1862,	....	12,456 54	5,135 16	....
1863,	....	*67,324 94	5,106 80	....
1864,	....	‡29,584 91	5,810 76	....
1865,	....	‖29,209 08	7,412 38	....
1866,	....	†85,969 24	7,667 91	....
	$11,336 49	$419,665 60	$80,431 71	$61,996 87

§ Includes $25,000 for extension of building and fitting up Committee Rooms.
* Includes $51,593.66 for real estate, &c.
‡ Includes $9,453.55 for real estate, &c.
‖ Includes $10,860 08 for real estate, &c.
† Includes $65,250.00 for real estate, &c.

Payments on account of the General Fund — (Continued).

YEARS.	(29) Natural History.	(30) Advances for County Taxes, Redemptions, &c. refunded.	(31) Onondaga Salt Springs.	(32) Onondaga Salt Springs, purchase of lands.
1846,	$29, 908 93	$62, 665 45	$18, 917 78	....
1847,	27, 980 96	34, 136 14	30, 547 95	....
1848,	20, 391 95	31, 664 99	25, 520 21	....
1849,	13, 724 26	52, 194 18	29, 754 05	....
1850,	16, 918 82	56, 333 35	29, 027 00	$18, 372 20
1851,	1, 451 00	127, 171 60	30, 000 00	....
1852,	24, 901 00	21, 985 53	34, 911 53	....
1853,	13, 463 63	18, 620 03	24, 826 70	2, 279 50
1854,	8, 747 20	40, 441 62	25, 250 00	....
1855,	8, 741 12	45, 640 37	51, 000 00	26, 878 67
1856,	1, 573 75	94, 139 21	43, 000 00	....
1857,	4, 617 00	38, 853 93	66, 000 00	45, 622 48
1858,	4, 338 20	26, 199 17	61, 300 00	28, 563 21
1859,	7, 869 77	20, 133 31	56, 000 00	....
1860,	6, 043 42	33, 222 30	51, 416 00	....
1861,	8, 853 04	42, 070 88	63, 500 00	....
1862,	9, 492 62	183, 524 33	43, 074 44	....
1863,	5, 428 31	45, 894 96	32, 000 00	....
1864,	5, 276 62	36, 149 56	50, 000 00	....
1865,	9, 006 22	72, 557 08	48, 000 00	....
1866,	8, 092 16	84, 113 56	49, 184 00	....
	$236, 819 98	$1, 167, 711 55	$863, 229 66	$121, 716 06

YEARS.	(33) Bounties on coal, lead, gypsum, empty casks, and silks.	(34) Constitutional Convention.	(35) Interest on temporary loans.	(36) Indian affairs.
1846,	$20, 459 09	$35, 332 50	*$300, 769 62	‡$8, 645 53
1847,	121 45	31, 828 07	....	784 28
1848,	33 04	527 83	....	473 22
1849,	....	2 00	....	646 90
1850,	....	....	1, 436 26	1, 209 77
1851,	....	....	2, 160 00	900 60
1852,	....	....	2, 226 00	747 49
1853,	....	....	1, 080 00	743 91
1854,	....	....	3, 240 00	815 81
1855,	....	....	4, 461 37	856 33
1856,	....	....	15, 978 80	975 28
1857,	....	....	18, 063 29	886 08
1858,	....	....	2, 967 22	1, 012 99
1859,	....	....	2, 160 00	2, 217 13
1860,	....	....	2, 160 00	1, 032 70
1861,	....	....	2, 160 00	1, 049 36
1862,	....	....	133, 548 02	†10, 707 64
1863,	....	....	67, 814 24	938 59
1864,	....	....	2, 160 00	1, 175 00
1865,	....	....	641, 767 57	683 64
1866,	....	....	1, 535, 100 12	894 52
	$20, 613 58	$67, 690 40	$2, 739, 252 51	$37, 396 77

* Interest on General Fund Debt prior to the creation of the General Fund Debt Sinking Fund.
‡ Includes $7, 961.67 annuities.
† Includes $10,000 for a meeting house.

Payments on account of the General Fund—(Continued).

YEARS.	(37) Costs of suits and counsel fees	(38) Expenses public lands.	(39) Regents of the University.	(40) Rivers, roads and bridges.
1846,	$1,664 38	$312 11	$1,382 32	$1,621 77
1847,	1,184 23	457 95	105 44	4,684 50
1848,	1,642 26	814 98	24 16	5,588 73
1849,	8,547 21	1,753 51	1,414 87	....
1850,	2,073 58	1,352 02	4,181 74	4,875 00
1851,	6,994 42	279 94	3,500 00	12,570 90
1852,	8,020 30	1,194 73	2,600 00	24,258 78
1853,	5,252 91	1,241 25	2,600 00	19,405 62
1854,	5,482 71	711 86	3,300 00	38,863 64
1855,	3,576 67	1,140 00	2,500 00	27,048 85
1856,	4,487 34	456 77	2,200 00	15,482 03
1857,	12,285 57	847 31	3,166 00	20,933 48
1858,	15,355 54	850 96	4,107 51	29,548 92
1859,	7,323 47	1,390 52	4,200 00	4,535 27
1860,	3,056 95	809 79	4,983 33	6,132 21
1861,	5,162 54	14,687 72	2,200 00	399 41
1862,	4,367 59	4,413 56	2,700 00	....
1863,	2,985 77	1,276 81	2,500 00	1,500 00
1864,	4,778 76	1,602 80	3,000 00	7,620 22
1865,	10,094 48	3,174 23	4,570 00	8,000 00
1866,	7,291 49	4,047 26	4,205 86	5,500 00
	$121,628 17	$42,816 08	$59,441 23	$238,569 33

YEARS.	(41) Temporary Loans.	(42) State tax and other appropriations for canal purposes.	(43) Promotion of Agriculture.	(44) Purchase of Indian lands.
1846,	$115 50	$56,503 47	$6,968 50	$2,478 53
1847,	....	119,410 30	7,120 75	885 51
1848,	....	....	7,417 00	4,000 00
1849,	....	1,496 93	6,563 00	36 00
1850.	30,000 00	....	6,107 00	649 16
1851,	....	9,610 01	7,358 00	294 25
1852,	....	18,102 67	7,027 50	....
1853,	....	12,629 28	7,762 00	....
1854,	....	668,119 40	8,649 00	....
1855,	50,000 00	35,196 24	8,886 00	....
1856,	150,000 00	344,629 28	6,043 00	....
1857,	287,000 00	295,783 17	8,526 00	....
1858,	50,000 00	1,265,929 28	7,745 00	....
1859,	150,000 00	1,028,579 12	8,758 00	....
1860,	....	1,179,707 69	8,186 00	....
1861,	200,000 00	884,681 56	10,472 00	....
1862,	1,540,000 00	2,804,436 31	5,767 00	....
1863,	1,505,000 00	1,457,317 73	12,867 78	....
1864,	5,000 00	586,003 22	10,917 00	....
1865,	2,000,000 00	978,919 34	15,204 25	....
1866,	1,000,000 00	2,207,615 86	9,968 75	....
	$6,967,115 50	$13,954,670 86	$178,313 53	$8,343 45

Payments on account of the General Fund—(Continued).

YEARS.	(45) Expenses of military &c., called into service to aid sheriffs, &c.	(46) Bank Department.	(47) Transfers to the specific funds for interest on money in the Treasury.	(48) State Census.
1846,	$70,134 83	$10,787 89	...	...
1847,	198 04	8,743 03	...	...
1848,	...	16,215 43	...	...
1849,	2,879 97	17,399 96	$14,935 10	...
1850,	...	19,348 43	18,204 58	...
1851,	...	19,802 73	18,864 83	...
1852,	...	19,065 91	21,737 43	...
1853,	...	20,292 34	26,663 35	...
1854,	...	22,955 80	31,312 49	...
1855,	...	20,928 75	32,732 34	...
1856,	...	24,377 78	37,282 88	$7,650 30
1857,	...	26,623 22	39,707 39	3,762 80
1858,	...	28,497 46	38,722 79	...
1859,	...	28,116 20	34,026 65	...
1860,	...	28,965 83	36,945 69	...
1861,	...	29,422 44	31,035 52	...
1862,	...	29,405 16	31,478 07	...
1863,	...	31,749 62	26,186 00	...
1864,	...	32,378 20	39,592 61	...
1865,	...	27,652 07	51,987 33	6,196 31
1866,	...	25,216 63	79,808 92	35,194 03
	$73,212 84	$487,944 88	$611,223 97	$52,803 44

YEARS.	(49) Quarantine.	(50) Transportation of Journals and Documents of Legislature, packages for public offices, &c.	(51) Improvement of the Hudson River.	(52) Insurance Department.
1846,	...	$442 56	...	...
1847,	...	835 02	...	...
1848,	...	1,785 94	...	...
1849,	...	1,999 72	$7,000 00	...
1850,	...	2,922 62	1,000 00	...
1851,	...	4,229 59	2,000 00	...
1852,	...	5,365 78	9,746 70	...
1853,	...	3,269 64	125 95	...
1854,	...	1,516 02	...	...
1855,	...	3,783 73	...	...
1856,	...	3,255 92	...	...
1857,	$50,018 50	3,204 85	5,000 00	...
1858,	11,491 02	3,842 62	19,950 22	...
1859,	96,358 97	5,022 32	...	...
1860,	28,244 96	3,849 39	...	$5,900 65
1861,	572 00	3,323 14	...	8,860 46
1862,	6,641 34	5,200 96	...	9,582 68
1863,	...	4,353 88	20,299 64	11,874 95
1864,	50,437 49	5,565 28	149,029 42	15,411 56
1865,	50,240 10	10,471 35	91,206 25	29,137 55
1866,	95,561 71	8,822 12	232,836 44	21,569 27
	$389,566 09	$83,062 45	$538,194 62	$102,337 12

Payments on account of the General Fund—(Continued).

YEARS.	(53) Railroad Companies.	(54) Gas-Light Companies.	(55) Albany and Susquehanna Railroad.	(56) Cayuga Marshes.
1846,				
1847,				
1848,				
1849,				
1850,				
1851,				
1852,				$420 00
1853,				
1854,				11,375 89
1855,	$973 22			31,114 35
1856,	13,668 27			32,739 08
1857,	11,881 89			64,212 53
1858,	4,977 48			31,553 99
1859,	2,791 25			9,942 09
1860,	6,523 23	$1,500 00		12,413 25
1861,	7,613 71	1,500 00		8,216 89
1862,	4,117 07	4,125 00		
1863,	8,119 40	2,500 09		
1864,	10,686 62	2,500 00		
1865,	12,830 67	2,500 00	$500,000 00	225 00
1866,	14,171 64	2,500 00		
	$98,354 45	$17,125 00	$500,000 00	$202,213 07

YEARS.	(57) Normal School Building.	(58) Transferred to the School and Literature Funds, for losses on bonds, sales of lands, and loans.	(59) Academies, Institutes, Universities and Colleges.	(60) Colonial History.
1846,				
1847,				
1848,				
1849,	$28,500 00			
1850,	2,300 00			
1851,				
1852,		$48,155 56	$8,000 00	
1853,				
1854,				
1855,				
1856,		10,906 83	7,800 00	
1857,			5,000 00	
1858,			38,000 00	
1859,			44,800 00	
1860,				
1861,				$6,480 80
1862,			5,000 00	5,963 00
1863,		4,880 50	10,000 00	1,937 34
1864,		1,140 00		
1865,				
1866,				
	$30,800 00	$65,082 89	$118,600 00	*$14,381 14

* Balance of expenditures carried to printing account.

Payments on account of the General Fund—(Continued).

YEARS.	(61) Court of Impeachment.	(62) United States Direct Tax.	(63) Deficiencies in General Fund Debt Sinking Fund.	(64) Kansas for relief.
1846,	....	....	....	....
1847,	....	....	....	....
1848,	....	....	....	....
1849,	....	....	....	....
1850,	....	....	....	....
1851,	....	....	....	....
1852,	....	....	....	....
1853,	$4,958 20	....	....	....
1854,	11,932 04	....	....	....
1855,	108 18	....	....	....
1856,	9 50	....	....	....
1857,	520 86	....	....	....
1858,	....	....	....	....
1859,	....	....	$840,179 21	....
1860,	....	....	352,455 99	....
1861,	....	....	330,964 47	$38,762 12
1862,	....	$400,000 00	....	....
1863,	....	....	....	....
1864,	....	....	....	....
1865,	....	....	....	....
1866,	....	....	....	....
	$17,528 78	$400,000 00	$1,523,599 67	$38,762 12

YEARS.	(65) New York Harbor Commissioners.	(66) Pilot Commissioners of New York.	(67) Miscellaneous.	Total.
1846,	....	....	$21,710 92	$1,231,202 90
1847,	....	....	20,062 56	822,120 43
1848,	....	....	16,154 98	884,780 14
1849,	....	....	24,713 90	842,228 49
1850,	....	....	21,765 70	826,571 56
1851,	....	....	30,234 28	909,805 22
1852,	....	....	‡237,941 17	1,341,338 25
1853,	....	....	31,981 21	1,031,769 67
1854,	....	....	12,694 26	1,817,850 98
1855,	....	....	§58,438 47	1,786,498 95
1856,	$28,792 89	....	¶31,770 18	1,815,365 76
1857,	56,848 07	....	31,380 80	2,285,398 81
1858,	489 86	....	††55,447 68	3,093,120 05
1859,	....	$17,000 00	31,861 79	3,737,601 68
1860,	....	3,993 33	21,496 86	3,140,350 59
1861,	....	5,270 00	‖56,220 88	5,375,514 59
1862,	....	4,987 66	15,182 76	7,170,124 38
1863,	....	4,438 51	21,567 16	9,835,665 97
1864,	....	4,074 75	†33,540 94	7,457,894 55
1865,	....	4,500 00	§§41,671 12	12,227,997 82
1866,	....	4,351 03	*132,606 33	8,934,099 51
	$86,130 82	$48,615 28	$1,148,443 95	$76,567,300 30

‡ Includes $185,641.48 erroneously paid into the treasury by the city of New York, and refunded; also $18,758 to Syracuse Salt Company, for damages, &c.

§ Includes $16,256 paid Syracuse Salt Company, for damages, &c., and $18,455 paid W. G. Barnhardt and others, for damages for being dispossessed of certain lands.

¶ Includes $13,184 paid Syracuse Salt Company for removal of salt vats.

†† Includes $13,981.24 paid Little & Co. for damages on contract, and $4,000 for digest of claims.

‖ Includes $5,100 for completion of map of harbor of New York, and $7,500 paid Lake Ontario and Hudson River Railroad Company, and $5,000 for expenses of Peace Commissioners.

† Includes $157,138.06 Free School tax, erroneously credited to General Fund, and $53,034.20 premium on coin to pay interest on portion of State debt.

§§ Includes $15,437.03 expenses in connection with soldiers voting.

* Includes $80,000 borrowed by Superintendent of Public Instruction, pursuant to section 4, title 3, chapter 555, Laws of 1864; $10,000 to Col. Jardine, chapter 536, Laws of 1866, and $13,516 for Baxter's Island, chapter 533, Laws of 1866.

RECAPITULATION.

Receipts.

1.	Auction duties,	$2,543,878 40
2.	Salt duties,	1,264,133 91
3.	State tax,	45,755,620 67
4.	Sales of General Fund lands,	332,956 04
5.	Pedlers' licenses,	31,405 00
6.	Arrears of county taxes,	957,300 51
7.	Interest on county taxes,	188,858 09
8.	Sales of lands for county taxes,	707,971 95
9.	Redemption of lands sold for taxes,	537,321 08
10.	Interest on treasury deposits and advances,	371,615 87
11.	Tax on foreign insurance companies,	45,040 80
12.	Fees of Secretary of State's office,	55,288 87
13.	Fees of Comptroller's office,	19,837 60
14.	Fees of Surveyor-General's office,	172 57
15.	Fees of Clerk of Court of Appeals office,	11,424 26
16.	Fees of registers and clerks,	76,019 83
17.	Surplus canal revenues,	2,551,113 40
18.	Sales of Natural History of New York,	54,245 25
19.	Temporary loans to the treasury,	12,505,994 42
20.	Bank Department, for expenses,	482,931 93
21.	Military fines and commutations,	83,713 71
22.	Expenses of military to aid sheriffs, &c.,	7,702 27
23.	Gas-light companies,	11,242 21
24.	Insurance Department, fees and assessments,	97,592 06
25.	Railroad companies, for expenses,	77,236 32
26.	Sales of Colonial History,	3,042 57
27.	Auburn prison,	1,004,526 62
28.	Clinton prison,	347,056 87
29.	Sing Sing prison,	1,040,070 69
30.	Costs of suits,	2,477 03
31.	Tolls of Cayuga Lake inlet,	2,298 47
32.	Sales of timber purchased in pursuance of chapter 294, Laws of 1861,	77,620 90
33.	United States, on account of advances in raising troops, return of duties, sale of arms and ammunition,	1,664,650 13
34.	Interest on Comptroller's bonds, New York city,	93,008 25
35.	Miscellaneous,	1,677,302 08
		$74,682,670 63

Payments.

1.	Salaries, clerk hire, and office expenses of officers of government,	$1,534,195 04
2.	Expenses attending the administration of justice,	2,565,645 34
3.	Legislature,	2,636,175 78
4.	Printing,	2,606,046 60
5.	Expenses of State prisons and building,	5,854,659 28
6.	Deaf and dumb,	924,638 98
7.	Blind, New York,	514,063 31
8.	Blind, chapter 587, Laws of 1865,	31,637 59
9.	Society for the reformation of juvenile delinquents, New York,	639,691 69
10.	House of Refuge, Western New York,	570,550 31
11.	Lunatic asylum,	523,108 38
12.	Idiot asylum,	344,904 56
13.	Willard asylum for the insane,	65,262 31
14.	Hospitals and other charitable institutions,	960,862 88
15.	Orphan asylums,	532,418 55
16.	Dispensaries and infirmaries,	128,775 00
17.	Support of foreign poor in New York and other counties,	56,000 00
18.	Militia and National Guard,	3,531,365 88
19.	Bureau of Military Statistics,	60,225 16
20.	Relief of sick and wounded soldiers,	452,172 23
21.	Military expenditures incident to the war, including bounties to volunteers,	17,549,286 41
22.	State Library,	217,150 96
23.	State Library, for building,	94,900 00
24.	State Hall	126,822 15
25.	Old State Hall,	11,336 49
26.	Capitol,	419,665 60
27.	Geological Hall,	80,431 71
28.	Geological Hall building,	61,996 87
29.	Natural History,	236,819 98
30.	Advances for county taxes, redemptions, &c., refunded,	1,167,711 55
31.	Onondaga Salt Springs,	863,229 66
32.	Onondaga Salt Springs, purchase of lands,	121,716 06
33.	Bounties on coal, lead, gypsum, empty casks and silk,	20,613 58
	Carried forward,	$45,504,079 89

Brought forward,	$45,504,079 89
34. Constitutional Convention,	67,690 40
35. Interest on temporary loans,	2,739,252 51
36. Indian affairs,	37,396 77
37. Costs of suits and counsel fees,	121,628 17
38. Expenses of public lands,	42,816 08
39. Regents of the University,	59,441 23
40. Rivers, roads and bridges,	238,569 33
41. Temporary loans,	6,967,115 50
42. State tax and other appropriations for canal purposes	13,954,670 86
43. Promotion of agriculture,	178,313 53
44. Purchase of Indian lands,	8,343 45
45. Expenses of military, &c., called into service to aid sheriffs, &c.,	73,212 84
46. Bank Department,	487,944 88
47. Transfers to specific funds for interest on money in the treasury,	611,223 97
48. State census,	52,803 44
49. Quarantine,	389,566 09
50. Transportation of journals and documents of Legislature, packages for public offices, &c.,	83,062 45
51. Improvement of the Hudson river,	538,194 62
52. Insurance Department,	102,337 12
53. Railroad companies,	98,354 45
54. Gas-light companies,	17,125 00
55. Albany and Susquehanna Railroad Company,	500,000 00
56. Cayuga marshes,	202,213 07
57. Normal School building,	30,800 00
58. Transferred to the School and Literature Funds, for losses on bonds, sales of lands and loans,	65,082 89
59. Academies, institutes, universities and colleges,	118,600 00
60. Colonial History,	14,381 14
61. Court of Impeachment,	17,528 78
62. United States direct tax,	400,000 00
63. Deficiencies in the General Fund debt sinking fund,	1,523,599 67
64. Kansas, for relief,	38,762 12
65. New York harbor commissioners,	86,130 82
66. Pilot commissioners, New York,	48,615 28
67. Miscellaneous,	1,148,443 95
	$76,567,300 30

Total amount of payments from 1846 to 1866, inclusive,		$76,567,300 30
Balance due specific fund 30th September, 1845,		740,151 78
Warrants unpaid 30th September, 1845,		594 36
		$77,308,046 44
Total amount of receipts from 1846 to 1866, inclusive,	$74,682,670 63	
Warrants cancelled	961 99	
Warrants unpaid 30th September, 1866,	776 14	
		74,684,408 76
Deficiency 30th September, 1866,		$2,623,637 68

There was due on the 30th September, 1866, on account of taxes levied in 1865 from the city and county of New York, $2,435,903.09. Deducting this sum would make the actual deficiency on that day $187,734.59.

(D.)

Common School Fund.

The amount of the productive capital of this fund is,		$2,799,630 04
There remained invested on the 30th of September, 1866, as follows, viz.:		
State stock, 5 per cent,	$230,015 91	
do 6 do	905,041 33	
do 7 do	30,000 00	
	$1,165,057 24	
Comptroller's bonds, 6 per cent,	36,000 00	
Bank stock, Manhattan Company, New York,	50,000 00	
Bonds for lands, 6 and 7 per cent,	290,303 17	
Bonds for loans, 6 and 7 do	197,388 54	
Loan of 1840, 7 per cent,	49,326 00	
	$1,788,074 95	
And a balance in the treasury which has been used to defray expenses of government, and is drawing interest at the rate of six per cent per annum, in pursuance of chap. 382, Laws of 1849,	1,011,555 09	
		$2,799,630 04

There has been received into the treasury from the 30th September, 1866, to the 1st of April, 1867, on account of principal of bonds for lands, bonds for loans, and sales of lands $24,875.14, which added to $1,011,555.09, balance in the treasury at the close of the last fiscal year makes the sum of $1,036,430.23 of the capital in the treasury.

There also belongs to the capital of this fund 23,840 acres of land, valued at about $30,000.

Common School Fund—(Continued).

The following table exhibits the Capital of the School Fund, according to the annual reports of the Comptroller, from 1846 to 1866 inclusive; also the annual interest or revenue derived from the Fund; the amount annually paid from the State Treasury, and the increase of the capital each year for twenty-one years.

YEARS.	Capital.	Annual revenue or interest.	Sum annually paid from the State Treasury.	Increase of capital from year to year.
1846, ...	$2,133,943 01	$123,458 12	$106,073 81	....
1847, ...	2,170,514 47	131,554 21	110,820 32	$36,571 46
1848, ...	2,211,475 14	117,220 25	119,902 00	40,960 67
1849, ...	2,243,563 36	119,903 76	79,407 14	32,088 22
1850, ...	2,290,673 23	135,792 10	161,030 06	47,109 87
1851, ...	2,325,449 72	132,009 15	76,001 81	34,776 49
1852, ...	2,354,530 09	140,295 42	179,242 09	29,080 37
1853, ...	2,383,257 23	146,303 76	95,010 60	28,727 14
1854, ...	2,425,211 97	144,116 97	169,961 40	41,954 74
1855, ...	2,457,520 86	143,127 73	145,513 26	32,308 89
1856, ...	2,491,916 14	159,849 17	145,638 98	34,395 28
1857, ...	2,526,392 24	169,160 59	185,178 45	34,476 10
1858, ...	2,551,260 52	159,544 28	204,864 00	24,868 28
1859, ...	2,586,251 16	164,249 77	160,206 71	34,990 64
1860, ...	2,607,036 68	152,992 82	160,071 05	20,785 52
1861, ...	2,625,476 94	153,010 51	182,508 57	18,440 26
1862, ...	2,658,116 42	158,656 18	183,977 54	32,639 48
1863, ...	2,694,552 33	157,649 42	167,906 42	36,435 91
1864, ...	2,734,213 15	154,882 30	160,485 76	39,660 82
1865, ...	2,765,760 77	186,462 20	161,560 79	31,547 62
1866, ...	2,799,630 04	170,580 65	163,142 58	33,869 27
		$3,120,819 36	$3,118,503 34	$665,687 03

NOTE.—The receipts and payments, as given in the above table, are exclusive of $165,000 annually transferred from the income of the United States Deposit Fund, and included in the annual reports of the Comptroller in the receipts and payments on account of the School Fund.

Balance of revenue in the treasury on the 30th September, 1845, ...	$86,828 96
Received into the treasury from October 1, 1845, to 30th September, 1866, ...	3,120,819 36
	$3,207,648 32
Paid from the treasury during the same period, ...	3,118,503 34
Balance of revenue in the treasury on the 30th of September, 1866, ...	$89,144 98

Changes in the investments of the Capital of the Common School Fund, from 1846 *to* 1866 *inclusive.*

YEARS.	Bonds for lands.	Bonds for loans.	Loan of 1792.	Loan of 1808.	Loan of 1840.
1846, ...	$887,024 23	$293,941 43	$105,232 60	$208,469 84	$8,200 00
1847, ...	826,149 19	257,865 33	103,054 15	202,693 03	8,200 00
1848, ...	744,854 97	236,901 74	97,363 14	198,772 03	8,200 00
1849, ...	703,438 29	246,131 75	89,893 50	191,588 32	13,200 00
1850, ...	710,975 40	198,269 02	17,982 86	21,757 81	41,326 00
1851, ...	652,435 30	209,034 72	379 50	3,543 46	49,326 00
1852, ...	584,010 87	217,485 36	....	946 45	49,326 00
1853, ...	567,829 02	236,754 17	....	679 45	49,326 00
1854, ...	540,932 91	248,963 97	....	299 31	49,326 00
1855, ...	551,458 12	248,967 29	....	299 31	49,326 00
1856, ...	535,926 19	234,233 05	....	299 31	49,326 00
1857, ...	529,697 66	310,227 29	....	....	49,326 00
1858, ...	515,198 78	349,193 11	....	....	49,326 00
1859, ...	488,146 07	381,213 09	....	....	49,326 00
1860, ...	459,210 53	370,253 41	....	....	49,326 00
1861, ...	422,575 87	408,469 71	....	....	49,326 00
1862, ...	412,163 73	375,747 61	....	....	49,326 00
1863, ...	370,388 96	339,461 05	....	....	49,326 00
1864, ...	335,189 17	285,028 15	....	....	49,326 00
1865, ...	317,168 48	254,902 83	....	....	49,326 00
1866, ...	290,303 17	197,388 54	....	....	49,326 00

Changes in the investments of the Capital of the Common School Fund — (Continued).

YEARS.	Bank Stock, Manhattan Co.	State Stock.	Comptroller's Bonds.	Money in the Treasury.	Total.
1846, ...	$50,000 00	$115,500 96	$51,645 49	$413,928 46	$2,133,943 01
1847, ...	50,000 00	115,500 96	51,645 49	555,406 32	2,170,514 47
1848, ...	50,000 00	280,500 96	451,645 49	143,236 81	2,211,475 14
1849, ...	50,000 00	228,200 96	656,445 49	64,6[illegible]5 05	2,243,563 36
1850, ...	50,000 00	213,200 96	884,981 65	152,179 53	2,290,673 23
1851, ...	50,000 00	213,200 96	1,034,981 65	112,548 13	2,325,449 72
1852, ...	50,000 00	193,200 96	1,052,981 65	206,578 80	2,354,530 09
1853, ...	50,000 00	193,200 96	1,054,986 16	230,481 47	2,383,257 23
1854, ...	50,000 00	193,200 96	1,043,341 33	299,147 49	2,425,211 97
1855, ...	50,000 00	231,460 96	1,043,341 33	282,667 85	2,457,520 86
1856, ...	50,000 00	231,460 96	1,043,341 33	347,320 30	2,491,916 14
1857, ...	50,000 00	231,460 96	1,043,341 33	312,339 00	2,526,392 24
1858, ...	50,000 00	936,502 29	356,300 00	294,740 34	2,551,260 52
1859, ...	50,000 00	936,502 29	356,300 00	324,763 71	2,586,251 16
1860, ...	50,000 00	936,502 29	356,300 00	385,444 45	2,607,036 68
1861, ...	50,000 00	1,135,057 24	356,300 00	203,748 12	2,625,476 94
1862, ...	50,000 00	1,135,057 24	356,300 00	279,521 84	2,658,116 42
1863, ...	50,000 00	1,135,057 24	356,300 00	394,019 08	2,694,552 33
1864, ...	50,000 00	1,135,057 24	356,300 00	523,312 59	2,734,213 15
1865, ...	50,000 00	1,135,057 24	356,300 00	603,006 22	2,765,760 77
1866, ...	50,000 00	1,165,057 24	36,000 00	1,011,555 09	2,799,630 04

The receipts on account of the revenue of the Common School Fund, during the fiscal year ending 30th September, 1866, were as follows, viz.:

Interest on bonds for lands, ...	$16,100 58	
Interest on bonds for loans, ...	15,326 52	
Interest on State stock, ...	65,803 27	
Interest on Comptroller's bonds, ...	21,378 00	
Interest on loan of 1840, ...	2,627 21	
Rent of lands, ...	98 50	
Interest on money in the treasury, during the year, ...	42,751 57	
Dividends on stock of the Manhattan Company, ...	6,495 00	
		$170,580 65

The payments during the same period were as follows, viz.:

Common school dividends, ...	$264,000 00	
School commissioners, for salaries, ...	55,620 29	
Indian schools, ...	4,175 54	
For support of Normal School, ...	4,000 00	
For maintenance of the School for colored children at Flatbush, ...	200 00	
Teachers' Institutes, ...	146 75	
	$328,142 58	
Less amount paid from the revenue of the U. S. Deposit Fund, ...	165,000 00	
		$163,142 58

(E.)

United States Deposit Fund.

CAPITAL.

The capital of this Fund is the amount received from the United States, ...		$4,014,520 71
Of this sum there remained loaned on mortgage and county bonds in the several counties of this State, on the 30th September, 1866, ...	$3,589,888 79	
Invested in State stock, 6 per cent, ...	274,739 44	
Invested in State stock, 5 per cent, ...	142,500 00	
Money in the treasury, ...	7,392 48	
		$4,014,520 71

Receipts on account of the Revenue of the United States Deposit Fund, from 1837 to 1866, inclusive, viz.:

YEARS.	Int'st on loans and other investments.	Sales of lands and bonds for lands.	Total.	Transf'd to capital for losses on sales, failures of title, and defalcations.	Net revenue.
1837,	$45,307 34	....	$45,307 34	....	$45,307 34
1838,	37,879 47	....	37,879 47	....	37,879 47
1839,	199,795 75	....	199,795 75	....	199,795 75
1840,	269,607 46	....	269,607 46	....	269,607 46
1841,	268,797 97	....	268,797 97	$63,020 72	205,777 25
1842,	256,032 03	....	256,032 03	15,361 29	240,670 74
1843,	256,526 35	$150 00	256,676 35	34,018 51	222,657 84
1844,	261,438 48	64,816 50	326,254 98	106,412 55	219,842 43
1845,	254,677 82	22,389 28	277,067 10	20,031 08	257,036 02
1846,	253,759 07	54,518 95	308,278 02	15,287 13	292,990 89
1847,	258,846 28	12,479 78	271,326 06	5,638 00	265,688 06
1848,	246,065 39	13,231 31	259,296 70	5,269 00	254,027 70
1849,	254,165 54	8,862 55	263,028 09	8,009 00	255,019 09
1850,	251,841 88	11,317 14	263,159 02	9,332 70	253,826 32
1851,	252,619 05	10,979 03	263,598 08	1,982 00	261,616 08
1852,	249,222 13	1,599 00	250,821 13	900 00	249,921 13
1853,	259,668 70	2,766 56	262,435 26	850 00	261,585 26
1854,	255,558 31	2,030 00	257,588 31	154 00	257,434 31
1855,	244,844 09	100 00	244,944 09	2,279 64	242,664 45
1856,	256,463 73	....	256,463 73	4,510 96	251,952 77
1857,	251,274 19	600 00	251,874 19	8,275 82	243,598 37
1858,	248,637 97	100 00	248,737 97	1,569 95	247,168 02
1859,	249,117 87	4,355 00	253,472 87	4,899 67	248,573 20
1860,	250,395 55	750 00	251,145 55	16,994 00	234,171 55
1861,	247,061 27	1,620 00	248,681 27	2,001 00	246,680 27
1862,	258,242 48	170 00	248,412 48	1,611 25	256,801 23
1863,	256,994 98	1,475 00	258,469 98	13,871 04	244,598 94
1864,	255,994 18	4,424 49	260,418 67	3,465 76	256,952 91
1865,	247,967 70	7,075 00	255,042 70	....	255,042 70
1866,	246,395 41	1,355 00	247,750 41	....	247,750 41
	$7,145,198 44	$227,164 59	$7,372,363 03	$345,725 07	$7,026,637 96

List of the Counties in which Losses have occurred, with the amount in each case.

County	Amount	County	Amount
Albany,	$14,760 00	Oneida,	$2,450 00
Broome,	100 00	Onondaga,	1,409 00
Cattaraugus,	125 00	Orange,	2,000 00
Cayuga,	188 64	Orleans,	350 25
Chautauqua,	102 70	Oswego,	3,189 75
Chemung,	256 00	Otsego,	500 00
Chenango,	200 00	Queens,	7,573 70
Clinton,	775 00	Rensselaer,	9,702 43
Columbia,	50 00	Richmond,	1,700 00
Delaware,	1,365 75	Saratoga,	2,792 33
Dutchess,	4,595 71	Schoharie,	1,709 00
Erie,	6,912 91	St. Lawrence,	2,134 64
Essex,	1,619 78	Steuben,	275 50
Franklin,	45 00	Suffolk,	2,840 00
Genesee,	1,662 00	Tompkins,	691 00
Herkimer,	122 00	Ulster,	1,749 63
Jefferson,	983 00	Warren,	204 00
Kings,	13,825 24	Wayne,	147 70
Lewis,	130 00	Westchester,	4,239 00
Monroe,	38,460 25	Wyoming,	1,319 00
Montgomery,	300 00		
New York,	29,660 00		$167,626 55
Niagara,	4,410 64		

Payments from the Revenue of the United States Deposit Fund, on account of appropriations to Colleges, Universities, Academies, Common Schools, Teachers' Institutes, Orphan Asylums, &c., from 1838 to 1866 inclusive:

1838,	$15,000 00	
1839,	208,000 00	
1840,	208,000 00	
1841,	218,700 00	
1842,	214,896 75	
1843,	242,016 81	
1844,	233,431 33	
1845,	240,611 79	
1846,	246,086 61	
1847,	238,526 75	
1848,	225,711 61	
1849,	236,620 74	
1850,	235,472 09	
1851,	222,316 23	
1852,	220,114 45	
1853,	219,925 00	
1854,	224,120 00	
1855,	230,913 00	
1856,	230,820 00	
1857,	242,161 21	
1858,	237,738 44	
1859,	226,889 95	
1860,	227,077 12	
1861,	205,000 00	
1862,	205,000 00	
1863,	222,997 75	
1864,	231,496 88	
1865,	230,562 57	
1866,	248,398 78	
		$6,388,605 86
Transferred from the revenue of this fund to the capital of the Common School Fund, in pursuance of chapter 237, Laws of 1838,	$154,021 62	
Transferred to the capital of the Common School Fund, in pursuance of article 9 of the Constitution,	500,000 00	
Transferred to the General Fund, being proportion of surplus of the income on the 30th September, 1839,	14,334 92	
Losses to the fund charged to 30th September 1866,	118,560 48	
		786,917 02
		$7,175,522 88
Amount of revenue from 1837 to 1866,	$7,145,198 44	
Received from the treasury, pursuant to chapter 265, Laws of 1850,	2,391 02	
Received from the treasury, pursuant to chapter 347, Laws of 1852,	2,397 54	
Received from unexpended balances and erroneous payments refunded,	97 32	
Revenue overdrawn 30th September, 1866,	25,438 56	
		$7,175,522 88

Appropriations of the Income of the United States Deposit Fund, for the fiscal year ending September 30, 1867, *under Chapter* 476, *Laws of* 1866.

Common Schools, including salaries of School Commissioners,	$165,000 00
Academies,	28,000 00
Capital of the Common School Fund,	25,000 00
Common School Teachers for their instruction,	18,000 00
State Normal School,	16,000 00
Normal and Training School at Oswego,	10,000 00
Teachers' Institutes,	12,000 00
	$274,000 00

NOTE.—It will appear from the foregoing table that the net revenue of this fund from 1837 to 1866 was $7,026,637.96. To this should be added $5,204 for appraised value of premises remaining unsold. Deducting $35,350.21 for ascertained losses not yet transferred to the capital, and $83,186.81 received in 1837 and 1838, leaves $6,913,304.94 as the net revenue for twenty-eight years, being an average of $246,903.75 per annum, or 6.15-100 per cent.

The amount transferred from the revenue to the capital for losses on sales of premises, failures of title and defalcations by Commissioners, was $345,725.07. To approximate to the actual loss the sum of $35,350.21, being the ascertained losses not transferred, should be added, and $227,164.59, the amount realized from sales of lands, and $5,204, the value of premises remaining unsold deducted. This would make the loss $148,706.69, which is less by the sum of $18,919.86 than the losses as given by counties. The difference is accounted for by sales of premises in several of the counties by the Commissioners of the Land Office for sums exceeding the amount of principal due which are not deducted in the latter statement, as it is intended to show the whole amount of losses that have occurred in each county, and also by the sums paid as interest on resales of lands bid in for the State.

(F.)

Literature Fund.

The Capital of this Fund amounted on the 30th September, 1845, to, ...		$268,990 57
Capital of the Fund, 30th September, 1866.		
State Stock, 6 per cent, ...	$10,000 00	
do 5 do	20,347 00	
Comptroller's Bonds, 5 per cent, ...	25,330 94	
Albany Insurance Company Stock, ...	3,000 00	
Money in the Treasury, ...	211,774 18	
		270,452 12
Increase since 30th September, 1845, ...		$1,461 55

There also belongs to the capital of this fund 640 acres of land, in Hamilton county, valued at about seventy cents per acre.

(G.)

College Land Scrip Fund.

The capital of this Fund on the 30th of September, 1866, consisted of the following items, viz.:

State stock, 7 per cent, redeemable April 7, 1877, ...	$64,000 00
Bond of Ezra Cornell, 7 per cent, redeemable Nov. 24, 1875, ...	50,000 00
do do do do August 4, 1871, ...	30,000 00
Money in the treasury, ...	440 00
	$144,440 00

NOTE.—By the act of Congress, approved July 2, 1862, it was provided that there should be distributed to the several States, out of the public lands, a quantity equal to 30,000 acres for each Senator and Representative in Congress, the income to be derived from its location and sale to be devoted to the maintenance and support of at least one Institution for the benefit of Agriculture and the Mechanic Arts.

The portion to which each State was entitled, was represented by land scrip, of which the State of New York received for her share 6,187 pieces, each of 160 or 989,920 acres.

By the act, chapter 511, Laws of 1863, the income and revenue to be derived from the proceeds of the sale of the lands thus granted, were directed to be paid over from time to time, to the trustees of the People's College, and appropriated for the benefit of that Institution, on the condition set forth in the act. The trustees of the People's College having failed to comply with the terms of the grant, it was transferred by the act, chapter 585, Laws of 1865, to the Cornell University.

By the act, chapter 481, Laws of 1866, the Comptroller was authorized to dispose of the scrip then unsold, consisting of 5,087 certificates, to the trustees of the Cornell University, or if this should not be practicable, the Commissioners of the Land Office were empowered to dispose of it to any person or persons who would agree and give security for the performance of such agreement, that the net avails from sales of the lands, should, as they were realized, "be paid over and devoted to the purposes of such Institution or Institutions as have been or shall be created under the act, chapter 485, Laws of 1865." The trustees of the Cornell University having made no application for the purchase of the scrip, the Commissioners of the Land Office subsequently sold to Hon. Ezra Cornell, all that was then undisposed of, at the price limited in the act, 30 cents per acre, the purchaser agreeing to account for and pay over the profits as received into the treasury of the State, of which a portion, equal to 30 cents per acre, is to be added to the College Land Scrip Fund, and the balance is to form a distinct fund, to be called the Cornell Endowment Fund, to be kept and managed by the State, the principal to remain inviolate, and the income to be devoted to the support of the Cornell University. The security for the performance of the agreement on the part of Mr. Cornell, to be mortgages or assignments of the certificates of location, on the lands as located. There has been delivered to Mr. Cornell under the contract, to May 20, 1867, scrip representing 200,000 acres. This is irrespective of scrip representing 176,000 acres sold to Mr. Cornell and others, under the act, chapter 460, Laws of 1863.

(H.)

Expenditures and Earnings of Auburn Prison and the Asylum for the Insane Convicts at Auburn, in each fiscal year, from 1842 *to* 1866, *inclusive, viz.:*

YEARS.	Expenditures for support, repairs, &c.	Asylum for Insane Convicts, support, &c.	Total expenditures.	Earnings.	Excess of earnings over expenditures.	Excess of expenditures over earnings.
1842,	$67,870 79	....	$67,870 79	$64,441 12	....	$3,429 67
1843,	56,505 04	....	56,505 04	55,541 36	....	963 68
1844,	67,885 21	....	67,885 21	67,342 10	....	543 11
1845,	53,601 46	....	53,601 46	56,160 83	$2,559 37	....
1846,	52,483 60	....	52,483 60	62,912 20	10,428 60	....
1847,	52,625 36	....	52,625 36	53,054 89	429 53	....
1848,	67,298 97	....	67,298 97	53,458 55	....	13,840 42
1849,	56,775 67	....	56,775 67	63,226 27	6,450 60	....
1850,	71,264 07	....	71,264 07	68,737 31	....	2,526 76
1851,	88,546 00	....	88,546 00	70,355 02	....	18,190 98
1852,	86,358 40	....	86,358 40	52,769 70	....	33,588 70
1853,	80,716 37	....	80,716 37	69,425 56	....	11,290 81
1854,	72,460 58	....	72,460 58	77,297 35	4,836 77	....
1855,	67,786 60	....	67,786 60	71,156 08	3,369 48	....
1856,	70,115 52	....	70,115 52	74,518 48	4,402 96	....
1857,	74,580 35	....	74,580 35	64,121 42	....	10,458 93
1858,	77,213 98	....	77,213 98	33,300 00	....	43,913 98
1859,	78,234 16	$25,316 79	103,550 95	75,917 62	....	27,633 33
1860,	81,517 60	17,493 10	99,010 70	98,286 53	....	724 17
1861,	87,296 94	14,222 53	101,519 47	48,067 85	....	53,451 62
1862,	84,350 32	12,767 41	97,117 73	110,684 44	13,566 71	....
1863,	*100,467 11	11,567 64	112,034 75	105,762 54	....	6,272 21
1864,	104,625 45	15,073 38	119,698 83	119,350 65	....	348 18
1865,	109,427 85	†23,103 35	132,531 20	80,712 51	....	51,818 69
1866,	140,199 77	16,929 87	157,129 64	95,841 00	....	61,288 64
	$1,950,207 17	$136,474 07	$2,086,681 24	$1,792,441 38	$46,044 02	$340,283 88

Excess of expenditures over earnings, ... $294,239.86

* Includes expenses for September, 1862.
† Includes $5,000 for steam pipe and heating apparatus.

Expenditures and Earnings of the Clinton Prison in each fiscal year, from 1848 *to* 1866, *inclusive, viz.:*

YEARS.	Expenditures.	Earnings.	Excess of expenditures over receipts.	Excess of receipts over expenditures.
1848,	$39,900 98	$734 16	$39,166 82	....
1849,	*50,123 47	9,210 97	40,912 50	....
1850,	37,793 97	12,601 95	25,192 02	....
1851,	25,958 13	12,364 10	13,594 03	....
1852,	40,144 65	10,029 79	30,114 86	....
1853,	49,583 14	21,104 47	28,478 67	....
1854,	59,532 73	23,186 29	36,346 44	....
1855,	49,254 30	1,267 57	47,986 73	....
1856,	55,549 25	6,567 45	48,981 80	....
1857,	47,947 29	26,050 54	21,896 75	....
1858,	56,025 65	3,762 04	52,263 61	....
1859,	71,126 40	17,313 94	53,812 46	....
1860,	63,352 61	23,273 02	40,079 59	....
1861,	66,069 15	16,090 46	49,978 69	....
1862,	56,488 91	36,611 73	19,877 18	....
1863,	†76,145 96	‡38,582 14	37,563 82	....
1864,	75,160 56	43,074 50	32,086 06	....
1865,	§180,793 38	46,562 89	134,230 49	....
1866,	¶243,788 11	‖268,395 61	....	$24,607 50
	$1,344,738 64	$616,783 62	$752,562 52	$24,607 50

Excess of expenditures over earning, ... $727,955.02

* Includes $11,139.84 for old indebtedness.
† Includes expenses for September, 1862.
‡ Exclusive of receipts in September, 1863.
§ Includes $76,473 85 on manufacturing account.
¶ Includes $130,720.35 on manufacturing account, and $8,000.00 for completion of road from prison to Forest Station.
‖ Includes $182,003.65 stock on hand on manufacturing account, 30th September, 1866.

Expenditures and Earnings of the Sing Sing Prison (formerly known as Mount Pleasant), in each fiscal year, from 1842 to 1866 inclusive, viz.:

YEARS.	Expenditures.	Earnings.	Excess of expenditures over receipts.
1842,	$72,769 20	$53,935 10	$18,834 10
1843,	66,675 10	36,970 37	29,704 73
1844,	63,762 98	45,098 82	18,664 16
1845,	85,825 19	64,658 31	21,166 88
1846,	77,467 80	58,965 19	18,502 61
1847,	73,303 59	65,961 04	7,342 55
1848,	*120,082 98	51,352 77	68,730 21
1849,	82,725 04	53,668 51	29,056 53
1850,	95,978 64	53,479 39	42,499 25
1851,	79,477 52	71,437 07	8,040 45
1852,	85,481 09	79,728 62	5,752 47
1853,	121,018 73	81,609 84	39,408 89
1854,	†156,042 75	84,777 49	71,265 26
1855,	117,736 55	82,872 52	34,864 03
1856,	101,257 48	87,936 92	13,320 56
1857,	109,986 55	81,867 92	28,118 63
1858,	119,387 74	39,818 92	79,568 82
1859,	129,194 95	89,208 71	39,986 24
1860,	138,335 36	99,993 77	38,341 59
1861,	136,686 52	28,780 80	107,905 72
1862,	‡130,319 86	43,747 80	86,572 06
1863,	‖172,047 10	§122,780 62	49,266 48
1864,	183,851 31	116,526 91	67,324 40
1865,	239,294 37	102,012 94	137,281 43
1866,	253,315 50	121,929 00	131,386 50
	$3,012,023 90	$1,819,119 35	$1,192,904 55

* Includes $38,424.96 debt incurred previous to January, 1848.
† Includes $19,659.96 judgment obtained against the agent.
‡ Includes $9,000 for Croton water for 5 years, at $1.800.
‖ Includes expenses for August and September, 1862.
§ Includes receipts of September, 1862.
¶ Includes $21,000 for judgment against agent, and counsel fees defending suit

Amount paid for salaries and traveling expenses of the Inspectors and Agents of State Prisons, and for transportation of convicts and apprehension of escaped convicts in each fiscal year, from 1842 to 1866, inclusive, viz.:

YEARS.	Salaries of Inspectors.	Traveling expenses of Inspectors.	Traveling expenses of Agents.	Transportation of convicts.	Apprehension of escaped convicts.
1842,	$976 88	....	$196 83	$8,968 98	....
1843,	960 30	....	222 14	12,107 89	$95 88
1844,	1,516 66	....	112 00	13,193 94	38 50
1845,	863 15	....	100 38	13,545 07	46 86
1846,	1,480 60	....	80 25	12,742 28	50 00
1847,	1,692 70	....	225 88	10,037 67	80 88
1848,	2,822 20	....	292 33	8,493 44	457 04
1849,	4,800 00	....	395 56	12,017 34	275 62
1850,	4,800 00	....	178 04	10,796 05	92 37
1851,	4,800 00	....	675 40	13,478 90	73 58
1852,	4,800 00	....	360 90	13,300 10	50 00
1853,	4,800 00	....	452 99	15,368 80	....
1854,	4,800 00	....	548 72	16,006 65	....
1855,	4,800 00	$450 00	266 14	15,253 48	....
1856,	4,800 00	150 00	....	16,158 83	....
1857,	4,800 00	1,200 00	....	17,060 80	....
1858,	4,800 00	2,175 00	....	20,399 53	....
1859,	4,800 00	2,700 00	....	24,826 15	....
1860,	4,800 00	2,305 46	....	20,017 00	....
1861,	4,800 00	1,655 75	....	22,550 27	....
1862,	4,800 00	1,540 36	....	13,906 20	....
1863,	4,800 00	1,874 67	....	18,586 30	....
1864,	4,800 00	1,753 28	....	16,560 00	....
1865,	4,800 00	1,415 03	....	20,075 40	....
1866,	4,800 00	2,515 31	....	30,746 40	....
	$96,712 49	$19,734 86	$4,107 56	$396,197 47	$1,260 73

RECAPITULATION.

	Expenditures.	Earnings.	Excess of expenditures over earnings.
Auburn prison including asylum for insane convicts,	$2,086,681 24	$1,792,441 38	$294,239 86
Clinton prison,	1,344,738 64	616,783 62	727,955 02
Sing Sing prison,	3,012,023 90	1,819,119 35	1,192,904 55
	$6,443,443 78	$4,228,344 35	$2,215,099 43
Salaries of Inspectors,	....	....	96,712 49
Traveling expenses of inspectors,	....	....	19,734 86
Traveling expenses of agents,	....	....	4,107 56
Transportation of convicts,	....	....	396,197 47
Apprehension of escaped convicts,	....	....	1,260 73
			$2,733,112 54

(I.)

Statement showing the aggregate valuations of real and personal property in the several counties of this State, from 1846 to 1866 inclusive, and the annual rate per cent of increase and decrease; also the State tax levied for the same period, and the annual rate per cent of increase and decrease.

COUNTIES.	1846.	1847.	1848.	1849.	1850.
Albany,	$16,353,717	$16,510,667	$16,299,936	$17,393,366	$17,393,366
Allegany,	3,360,864	3,360,864	3,659,303	3,797,863	4,362,183
Broome,	2,048,139	2,076,346	2,066,676	2,118,612	2,114,594
Cattaraugus,	3,108,761	3,377,633	3,642,483	3,824,598	4,105,462
Cayuga,	9,852,227	10,410,625	10,533,516	10,797,141	11,162,522
Chautauqua,	4,310,511	4,809,859	5,053,667	5,324,257	5,324,257
Chemung,	2,664,381	2,730,999	2,907,196	3,058,073	3,887,234
Chenango,	4,149,005	4,204,767	4,297,813	4,295,632	4,939,212
Clinton,	1,673,581	1,721,677	1,743,131	1,779,567	2,289,868
Columbia,	9,210,324	9,288,856	9,272,541	9,272,541	8,938,632
Cortland,	2,183,978	2,194,868	2,222,646	2,262,196	2,298,380
Delaware,	3,663,890	3,674,952	3,684,873	3,737,810	3,769,528
Dutchess,	19,518,471	19,385,998	19,195,029	19,390,632	19,871,033
Erie,	12,570,440	13,595,411	15,099,723	15,727,545	17,319,987
Essex,	1,483,136	1,593,337	1,593,337	1,610,668	1,646,831
Franklin,	1,475,278	1,529,305	1,766,819	1,773,985	1,773,985
Fulton,	1,327,983	1,327,983	1,443,351	1,246,556	1,239,189
Genesee,	5,814,614	6,126,737	6,136,640	6,420,656	6,461,305
Greene,	2,910,500	3,021,572	3,025,749	2,746,933	2,937,346
Hamilton,	314,122	302,798	302,798	332,231	333,207
Herkimer,	6,261,041	6,377,584	6,237,655	6,496,298	7,708,664
Jefferson,	6,625,874	6,673,202	7,213,636	7,200,881	7,951,660
Kings,	33,335,602	36,049,605	38,292,425	39,915,592	44,980,866
Lewis,	1,658,000	1,664,000	1,618,000	1,622,000	2,361,000
Livingston,	9,159,628	9,815,775	10,191,600	10,723,489	11,226,654
Madison,	6,497,764	6,492,648	6,702,488	6,690,654	6,967,032
Monroe,	14,396,364	14,493,892	14,769,740	15,187,190	15,566,910
Montgomery,	3,568,185	3,570,994	3,545,398	3,614,146	3,599,813
New York,	244,952,004	247,152,303	254,192,527	254,192,527	286,061,816
Niagara,	4,938,413	4,918,027	5,149,223	5,278,988	5,591,385
Oneida,	12,042,531	12,178,214	12,446,643	12,862,660	13,147,231
Onondaga,	15,480,848	15,537,933	16,806,658	16,747,303	17,992,066
Ontario,	12,629,547	13,357,026	13,565,564	13,836,470	14,437,897
Orange,	11,607,619	11,657,205	11,751,424	12,159,987	12,159,987
Orleans,	4,864,192	4,880,786	4,968,187	5,043,114	5,203,069
Oswego,	5,312,692	5,971,371	6,245,242	7,118,859	8,038,778
Otsego,	5,429,800	5,384,470	5,539,399	5,555,155	5,435,953
Putnam,	2,831,363	2,829,881	2,989,064	3,293,825	3,289,188
Queens,	11,945,525	11,530,300	11,683,275	11,600,330	12,484,750
Rensselaer,	13,276,223	13,589,364	14,046,576	14,106,476	14,106,476
Richmond,	1,373,279	1,703,198	1,816,053	1,903,688	6,759,459
Rockland,	2,356,528	2,472,824	2,506,181	2,503,695	6,628,101
Saratoga,	6,795,089	6,795,089	7,207,809	7,401,586	7,440,101
Schenectady,	2,849,218	2,929,359	2,997,273	3,112,417	3,112,408
Schoharie,	1,947,306	1,904,967	1,795,587	1,818,328	1,826,141
Schuyler,	....	....	....	....	....
Seneca,	5,822,083	5,931,988	5,967,714	6,197,920	6,633,281
St. Lawrence,	3,506,321	3,520,034	3,604,911	3,587,629	5,077,177
Steuben,	6,172,414	6,172,414	6,811,614	6,811,614	8,050,689
Suffolk,	6,106,018	6,092,965	6,137,597	6,095,798	6,227,934
Sullivan,	1,468,283	1,443,978	1,443,978	1,557,458	1,548,668
Tioga,	1,819,160	1,887,175	1,903,080	1,938,146	1,985,496
Tompkins,	4,034,660	4,058,204	4,125,450	4,070,808	5,631,634
Ulster,	5,311,396	5,213,745	5,249,251	5,436,713	5,805,727
Warren,	978,476	997,761	1,083,206	1,023,307	1,081,003
Washington,	6,173,997	6,226,547	6,269,233	6,559,840	6,495,194
Wayne,	7,003,593	7,089,172	7,138,147	7,220,736	7,430,575
Westchester,	10,036,317	14,580,393	15,304,283	20,018,964	20,018,964
Wyoming,	4,157,131	4,261,106	4,384,099	4,099,712	4,497,931
Yates,	4,106,549	4,049,430	4,172,178	4,325,572	4,772,784
	$616,824,955	$632,699,993	$651,619,595	$665,850,737	$727,494,583
Agg. val'n per'l prop.,	$119,880,236	$121,162,201	$125,663,318	$129,926,625	$153,183,486

Statement of Real and Personal Property, &c. — (*Continued*).

COUNTIES.	1851.	1852.	1853.	1854.
Albany,	$33,068,549	$31,619,050	$33,005,780	$33,978,219
Allegany,	8,864,208	8,795,777	9,330,424	9,437,354
Broome,	7,024,393	6,592,471	7,063,810	8,003,917
Cattaraugus,	7,468,841	8,305,784	8,813,494	8,688,645
Cayuga,	20,805,734	20,806,767	20,909,331	20,711,045
Chautauqua,	12,267,859	13,116,859	15,345,181	15,459,190
Chemung,	8,897,260	8,482,641	9,436,643	8,628,253
Chenango,	12,605,953	11,878,320	11,898,564	11,622,278
Clinton,	7,138,386	7,203,099	7,243,766	7,188,186
Columbia,	9,925,528	10,148,230	13,899,854	14,019,262
Cortland,	5,601,111	5,602,087	5,778,521	5,704,016
Delaware,	8,854,463	8,641,006	8,675,189	8,675,189
Dutchess,	21,135,353	21,131,353	27,350,622	27,836,706
Erie,	34,081,545	34,927,057	34,927,057	45,620,589
Essex,	1,646,831	4,942,935	4,588,769	4,712,243
Franklin,	3,758,199	3,803,346	4,094,860	4,320,090
Fulton,	1,239,189	3,635,214	4,647,172	4,802,504
Genesee,	12,807,370	12,546,874	13,323,025	14,101,380
Greene,	9,221,532	8,242,557	8,212,757	7,828,562
Hamilton,	477,524	372,246	512,094	471,785
Herkimer,	13,895,737	13,254,172	12,892,787	12,640,602
Jefferson,	17,220,810	17,945,560	18,923,156	18,923,156
Kings,	60,806,394	74,175,594	74,175,594	94,044,093
Lewis,	5,825,000	5,680,000	5,615,000	5,688,000
Livingston,	16,947,895	16,762,823	17,838,243	18,396,766
Madison,	13,277,740	12,155,131	12,299,874	12,411,308
Monroe,	31,612,686	32,298,397	34,588,990	35,855,748
Montgomery,	9,458,081	4,885,649	9,111,999	8,903,308
New York,	286,061,816	351,768,396	413,631,432	462,237,550
Niagara,	16,217,062	16,505,804	17,416,146	17,671,945
Oneida,	19,379,166	17,457,344	17,566,198	17,566,198
Onondaga,	25,792,852	25,783,459	27,682,358	28,482,112
Ontario,	20,796,367	20,486,294	21,123,808	21,396,883
Orange,	23,446,322	23,791,013	24,799,432	25,578,980
Orleans,	11,103,809	10,935,056	11,208,363	11,500,459
Oswego,	13,699,990	13,620,612	13,895,129	14,681,784
Otsego.	12,599,011	12,599,011	11,988,940	12,106,828
Putnam,	5,940,691	5,273,447	5,154,232	4,966,257
Queens,	14,711,925	16,006,510	17,957,115	19,263,495
Rensselaer,	14,177,593	30,509,829	28,682,164	28,557,243
Richmond.	7,559,022	7,559,022	7,331,510	11,302,729
Rockland,	4,563,976	4,859,518	5,168,194	5,458,848
Saratoga,	14,103,943	13,227,881	13,227,881	13,068,840
Schenectady,	7,149,113	6,317,936	6,480,976	6,480,976
Schoharie,	7,921,210	7,892,093	7,621,258	7,351,848
*Schuyler,	....	....	....	5,263,866
Seneca,	11,716,434	11,270,527	11,029,328	10,713,832
St. Lawrence,	13,487,642	13,807,979	14,561,665	15,721,231
Steuben,	17,035,375	16,851,742	17,634,652	17,634,652
Suffolk,	11,272,875	10,521,988	10,462,433	10,645,459
Sullivan,	5,100,560	4,708,905	4,191,286	4,712,190
Tioga,	6,995,614	6,861,476	7,060,179	6,007,004
Tompkins,	13,137,328	13,088,965	13,359,858	13,359,858
Ulster,	16,620,306	16,803,081	16,217,690	16,574,644
Warren,	2,292,638	2,342,719	2,510,612	2,625,035
Washington,	15,802,002	15,734,877	15,848,549	15,770,042
Wayne,	13,813,057	13,942,963	14,802,083	14,802,083
Westchester,	32,175,517	32,406,363	35,505,852	36,328,734
Wyoming,	8,124,609	8,664,729	9,260,612	9,234,342
Yates,	9,099,634	8,784,699	8,784,699	8,416,284
	$1,077,831,630	$1,168,335,237	$1,266,666,190	$1,364,154,625
Agg. valuations of pers'l prop.	$196,538,263	$221,802,950	$249,720,727	$272,638,110

* Erected in 1854, from parts of the counties of Steuben, Chemung and Tompkins.

Statement of Real and Personal Property, &c.—(Continued).

COUNTIES.	1855.	1856.	1857.	1858.
Albany,	$35,148,412	$35,811,465	$38,149,640	$39,241,648
Allegany,	9,548,790	9,755,736	9,379,454	9,005,907
Broome,	8,230,168	8,051,355	7,891,395	7,558,308
Cattaraugus,	8,967,759	9,046,423	8,759,067	7,496,380
Cayuga,	20,682,775	21,033,480	20,795,102	19,554,754
Chautauqua,	15,428,913	15,050,161	15,026,361	14,819,090
Chemung,	8,671,893	8,415,632	7,676,407	7,219,012
Chenango,	11,519,102	11,507,229	11,594,762	11,298,141
Clinton,	7,194,359	6,901,138	6,848,472	6,310,674
Columbia,	14,025,969	14,544,199	14,706,684	14,700,000
Cortland,	5,882,844	5,801,317	6,180,525	5,821,167
Delaware,	8,817,003	8,846,456	8,974,818	8,672,675
Dutchess,	28,422,309	28,837,097	29,181,461	28,870,074
Erie,	49,212,605	51,538,658	53,046,535	50,170,619
Essex,	4,712,243	4,732,701	4,761,599	4,548,079
Franklin,	4,332,715	4,373,926	4,407,041	4,371,510
Fulton,	4,721,961	4,643,080	4,581,294	4,358,122
Genesee,	15,928,083	14,891,572	14,894,220	13,118,493
Greene,	7,876,557	7,572,107	7,494,977	7,377,756
Hamilton,	582,810	525,401	549,490	474,755
Herkimer,	12,823,766	12,601,391	11,865,222	10,316,833
Jefferson,	17,785,049	17,249,563	16,949,202	16,192,864
Kings,	99,992,827	101,509,032	104,724,735	104,296,566
Lewis,	5,688,000	5,528,000	5,129,000	5,130,000
Livingston,	18,396,766	18,561,800	16,764,011	14,734,707
Madison,	12,576,058	12,209,151	12,189,484	11,686,942
Monroe,	35,647,293	36,117,103	34,931,514	28,781,527
Montgomery,	9,058,220	9,308,120	8,694,812	8,782,486
New York,	487,060,838	511,740,491	520,545,282	531,222,642
Niagara,	17,916,420	18,667,075	14,887,113	13,774,764
Oneida,	17,566,198	17,846,240	17,318,630	16,864,140
Onondaga,	30,974,914	30,756,662	30,760,000	28,145,028
Ontario,	21,457,309	21,554,406	21,121,495	17,744,984
Orange,	25,332,489	25,777,830	26,369,366	25,605,331
Orleans,	11,582,818	11,574,608	11,206,613	10,592,223
Oswego,	14,750,721	15,346,681	15,343,000	10,929,869
Otsego,	12,294,598	12,193,957	12,115,295	12,063,554
Putnam,	4,922,336	5,175,968	5,349,967	5,155,760
Queens,	19,379,220	20,297,850	20,120,325	19,930,770
Rensselaer,	28,537,243	28,505,002	27,583,761	26,674,215
Richmond,	11,302,729	8,879,321	8,880,000	7,437,318
Rockland,	5,379,997	5,457,943	5,511,847	5,533,985
Saratoga,	12,050,707	11,860,942	11,946,587	11,932,166
Schenectady,	6,052,012	6,146,161	5,888,128	5,715,286
Schoharie,	6,941,524	6,786,008	6,763,827	6,532,814
Schuyler,	5,209,807	5,112,912	4,955,264	4,807,662
Seneca,	11,085,191	11,267,087	11,169,329	10,662,940
St. Lawrence,	16,481,722	16,702,829	16,846,948	17,037,831
Steuben,	16,270,534	16,422,598	16,267,309	14,978,432
Suffolk,	10,763,535	10,948,630	11,008,765	10,972,106
Sullivan,	4,712,190	4,451,706	4,387,690	4,276,586
Tioga,	5,715,978	5,790,931	5,919,835	5,634,893
Tompkins,	13,359,858	11,210,994	8,831,263	7,481,838
Ulster,	16,179,948	15,868,563	15,839,139	15,509,818
Warren,	2,664,544	2,751,172	2,561,283	2,575,761
Washington,	15,831,827	15,874,740	16,087,398	15,976,169
Wayne,	14,802,083	15,200,247	14,737,399	14,480,481
Westchester,	36,328,734	37,582,633	38,996,294	39,563,401
Wyoming,	9,629,757	9,468,494	9,434,309	8,525,234
Yates,	8,416,284	8,149,720	8,358,968	7,660,589
	$1,402,849,304	$1,430,334,696	$1,433,309,713	$1,404,907,679
Agg. valuat'n personal prop.,	$294,012,564	$316,506,930	$319,897,155	$307,049,165

Statement of Real and Personal Property, &c.— (Continued).

COUNTIES.	1859.	1860.	1861.	1862.
Albany,	$38, 544, 737	$39, 044, 737	$39, 444, 737	$39, 354, 490
Allegany,	8, 035, 120	8, 035, 120	8, 035, 120	9, 269, 046
Broome,	8, 491, 423	8, 391, 423	8, 391, 423	9, 012, 963
Cattaraugus,	6, 620, 148	6, 620, 148	6, 620, 148	8, 574, 454
Cayuga,	19, 214, 844	19, 214, 844	19, 214, 814	21, 942, 079
Chautauqua,	14, 270, 102	14, 270, 102	14, 270, 102	14, 208, 799
Chemung,	6, 272, 762	6, 472, 762	6, 472, 762	7, 078, 341
Chenango,	10, 962, 405	10, 500, 000	10. 500, 000	10, 412, 793
Clinton,	5, 727, 775	5, 727, 775	5, 727, 775	5, 929, 031
Columbia,	18, 365, 430	18, 365, 430	18, 365, 430	21, 714, 722
Cortland,	6, 465, 933	6, 165, 923	6, 165, 923	6, 541, 188
Delaware,	8, 210, 352	8, 210, 352	8, 210, 352	7, 826, 163
Dutchess,	30, 979, 280	29, 979, 280	29, 979, 280	33, 857, 806
Erie,	46, 757, 841	47, 251, 841	47, 251, 841	46, 538, 000
Essex,	3, 824, 027	3, 824, 027	3, 824, 027	3, 348, 442
Franklin,	4, 149, 270	4, 149, 270	4, 149, 270	4, 195, 271
Fulton,	4, 054, 412	4, 054, 412	4, 054, 412	4, 152, 490
Genesee,	11, 650, 136	11, 650, 136	11, 650, 136	13, 075, 604
Greene,	8, 650, 084	7, 950, 084	7, 950, 084	8, 240, 450
Hamilton,	470, 333	470, 333	470, 333	630, 266
Herkimer,	10, 144, 567	10, 144, 567	10, 144, 567	11, 144, 484
Jefferson,	15, 935, 769	15, 935, 769	15, 035, 769	16, 566, 882
Kings,	104, 295, 591	106, 295, 591	108, 295, 591	93, 231, 884
Lewis,	4, 995, 200	4, 495, 200	4, 495, 200	5, 279, 275
Livingston,	14, 306, 555	14, 306, 555	14, 306, 555	18, 357, 339
Madison,	11, 072, 782	11, 072, 782	11, 072, 782	13, 281, 535
Monroe,	26, 232, 076	26, 732, 076	26, 732, 076	29, 607, 232
Montgomery,	7, 354, 077	7, 354, 077	7, 354, 077	9, 442, 013
New York,	532, 903, 476	550, 078, 778	571, 078, 798	549, 624, 306
Niagara,	12, 823, 822	12, 823, 822	12, 823, 822	15, 414, 219
Oneida,	25, 639, 379	25, 639, 379	25, 639, 379	24, 709, 962
Onondaga,	28, 350, 128	28, 350, 128	28, 350, 128	26, 301, 687
Ontario,	16, 445, 575	16, 445, 575	16, 445, 575	19, 768, 497
Orange,	24, 828, 254	24, 525, 254	24, 525, 254	25, 855, 071
Orleans,	9, 682, 789	9, 682, 749	9, 682, 749	10, 764, 583
Oswego,	14, 254, 368	14, 254, 368	14, 254, 368	12, 226, 322
Otsego,	12, 172, 302	12, 072, 302	12, 072, 302	12, 407, 330
Putnam,	7, 114, 055	6, 114, 055	6, 114, 035	5, 272, 968
Queens,	22, 343, 083	21, 343, 083	21, 343, 083	21, 178, 286
Rensselaer,	26, 078, 926	26, 278, 926	26, 278, 926	31, 153, 496
Richmond,	9, 728, 402	9, 728, 402	8, 728, 402	5, 727, 740
Rockland,	5, 440, 264	5, 440, 260	5, 440, 260	6, 028, 034
Saratoga,	12, 048, 356	12, 048, 356	12, 048, 356	12, 345, 230
Schenectady,	5, 602, 786	5, 602, 786	5, 602, 786	7, 126, 992
Schoharie,	7, 350, 681	6, 850, 681	6, 850, 681	7, 055, 559
Schuyler,	4, 280, 723	4, 280, 723	4, 280, 723	5, 507, 289
Seneca,	7, 809, 547	8, 159, 547	8, 159, 547	10, 875, 074
St. Lawrence,	15, 633, 359	15, 633, 359	15, 633, 359	15, 052, 841
Steuben,	13, 991, 732	13, 991, 732	13, 991, 732	12, 932, 122
Suffolk,	13, 050, 506	12, 050, 506	12, 050, 506	8, 548, 972
Sullivan,	4, 132, 995	4, 132, 995	4, 132, 995	4, 757, 745
Tioga,	9, 948, 318	5, 848, 318	5, 818, 318	7, 285, 346
Tompkins,	7, 874, 265	7, 874, 265	7, 874, 205	8, 715, 849
Ulster,	15, 567, 658	15, 567, 658	15, 567, 658	14, 834, 426
Warren,	2, 519, 380	2, 519, 380	2, 519, 380	2, 143, 459
Washington,	15, 331, 107	15, 331, 105	15, 331, 105	16, 431, 774
Wayne,	13, 857, 159	13, 887, 157	13, 887, 157	16, 536, 115
Westchester,	41, 012, 725	41, 012, 725	42, 012, 725	41, 185, 997
Wyoming,	7, 750, 822	7, 750, 822	7, 750, 822	10, 229, 568
Yates,	7, 293, 708	7, 293, 708	7, 293, 708	8, 494, 038
	$1, 404, 913, 679	$1, 419, 297, 520	$1, 441, 767, 430	$1, 449, 303, 948
Agg. valuat'ns of pers. prop.,	$307, 349, 155	....	....	....

NOTE.—The valuations from and including 1859, are given as fixed by the Board of Equalization.

Statement of Real and Personal Property, &c. — (Continued).

COUNTIES.	1863.	1864.	1865.	1866.
Albany,	$39,940,693	$41,765,376	$43,706,396	$42,403,645
Allegany,	9,148,321	8,705,183	8,041,047	8,160,188
Broome,	9,021,100	8,883,985	8,082,711	8,080,711
Cattaraugus,	8,548,366	8,832,564	7,855,045	7,806,045
Cayuga,	22,292,079	21,784,806	20,743,701	20,952,475
Chautauqua,	14,316,820	14,277,983	14,579,488	14,955,165
Chemung,	7,210,263	7,238,709	7,847,230	8,364,433
Chenango,	9,812,798	9,932,793	10,841,168	10,606,261
Clinton,	5,662,707	5,701,292	5,747,262	5,829,081
Columbia,	21,915,177	21,791,700	21,653,861	22,141,406
Cortland,	6,237,819	5,959,001	5,894,931	6,080,301
Delaware,	8,194,252	7,945,581	9,115,854	9,042,727
Dutchess,	33,971,584	34,439,528	32,387,534	32,352,153
Erie,	47,086,595	47,845,813	47,614,230	48,484,601
Essex,	3,355,377	3,467,970	3,948,238	4,300,018
Franklin,	4,227,845	4,340,429	4,433,136	4,795,784
Fulton,	4,154,490	4,181,032	4,123,242	3,957,924
Genesee,	15,934,530	11,785,706	14,088,179	14,274,653
Greene,	7,759,662	9,104,319	7,585,564	7,114,492
Hamilton,	605,016	503,200	509,286	483,976
Herkimer,	10,444,468	11,004,319	11,062,070	10,994,175
Jefferson,	16,458,826	16,270,677	16,178,456	15,993,372
Kings,	98,147,604	107,726,080	122,912,018	125,986,563
Lewis,	5,391,577	5,426,005	4,538,719	4,497,668
Livingston,	17,041,838	16,371,702	15,509,608	15,277,692
Madison,	13,380,498	12,945,535	12,444,430	12,031,059
Monroe,	30,174,825	30,967,924	30,024,998	29,144,314
Montgomery,	9,659,631	9,907,730	8,847,755	8,382,809
New York,	547,416,031	576,000,161	622,595,040	606,784,355
Niagara,	15,285,475	15,762,110	14,652,746	14,575,766
Oneida,	24,709,962	24,955,584	25,674,054	24,857,046
Onondaga,	26,676,600	27,912,019	28,424,497	27,888,085
Ontario,	19,181,263	18,892,384	18,106,122	18,210,024
Orange,	26,350,113	26,371,775	27,833,694	28,305,248
Orleans,	10,893,252	11,246,218	10,426,527	10,302,771
Oswego,	13,032,095	12,825,035	14,606,454	14,003,553
Otsego,	12,322,037	12,603,669	12,292,748	11,964,260
Putnam,	5,457,976	5,657,535	5,578,282	5,437,889
Queens,	21,345,348	21,976,780	21,406,735	22,127,400
Rensselaer,	30,153,490	32,104,673	29,481,008	26,110,481
Richmond,	5,694,715	6,058,265	6,540,500	6,731,396
Rockland,	5,966,243	6,012,956	5,934,996	5,819,329
Saratoga,	12,345,237	12,880,206	12,362,200	11,988,204
Schenectady,	7,305,794	7,780,563	5,908,080	5,756,482
Schoharie,	7,146,713	7,159,405	6,342,051	6,197,570
Schuyler,	5,507,289	6,424,723	4,951,143	4,893,395
Seneca,	10,523,440	10,459,568	10,302,676	10,237,730
St. Lawrence,	15,771,727	14,929,933	15,310,757	15,625,157
Steuben,	12,919,912	12,427,372	13,478,267	13,606,982
Suffolk,	8,452,188	8,536,575	9,077,986	9,608,451
Sullivan,	4,760,548	4,630,375	4,020,380	3,894,971
Tioga,	6,942,397	6,901,576	5,881,905	5,737,497
Tompkins,	8,715,849	8,918,886	8,011,892	7,874,645
Ulster,	14,883,049	14,989,490	14,436,139	14,652,561
Warren,	2,143,459	2,196,157	2,351,312	2,314,713
Washington,	16,503,401	16,526,559	16,307,065	15,922,305
Wayne,	16,036,115	17,101,036	15,688,167	15,213,967
Westchester,	41,685,997	43,767,924	45,797,919	44,971,213
Wyoming,	9,729,568	9,712,567	8,714,304	8,994,565
Yates,	8,503,276	8,270,856	8,066,982	8,127,929
	$1,454,454,817	$1,500,999,877	$1,550,879,685	$1,531,229,636
Agg. valuations of pers'l prop.	....	$339,249,877	$392,552,314	$334,826,220

Recapitulation of Aggregate Valuations, &c.

YEARS.	Valuations.	Annual rate per cent of increase.	Annual rate per cent of decrease.	State tax in mills.	Annual rate per cent of increase.	Annual rate per cent of decrease.
1846, ...	$616, 824, 955	....	....	6-10 mill.	....	....
1847, ...	632, 699, 993	2.5737	....	1-2 "	....	16.6666
1848, ...	651, 619, 595	2.9903	....	1-2 "	....	....
1849, ...	665, 850, 737	2.1839	....	1-2 "	....	....
1850, ...	727, 494, 583	9.2579	....	1-2 "	....	....
1851, ...	1, 077, 831, 630	48.1566	....	1-2 "	....	....
1852, ...	1, 168, 335, 237	8.3968	....	1-4 "	....	50.
1853, ...	1, 266, 666, 190	8.4163	....	1 "	300.	....
1854, ...	1, 364, 154, 625	7.6964	....	3-4 "	....	25.
1855, ...	1, 402, 849, 304	2.8365	....	1 1-4 "	66.6666	....
1856, ...	1, 430, 334, 696	1.9592	....	1 3-4 "	40.	....
1857, ...	1, 433, 309, 713	.2080	....	3 "	71.4285	....
1858, ...	1, 404, 907, 679	....	1.9816	2 1-2 "	....	16.6666
1859, ...	1, 404, 913, 679	.0004	....	2 1-2 "	....	....
1860, ...	1.419, 297, 520	1.0238	....	3 5-6 "	53.3333	....
1861, ...	1, 441, 767, 430	1.5832	....	3 7-8 "	1.0869	....
1862, ...	1, 449, 303, 948	.5227	....	4 3-4 "	22.5806	....
1863, ...	1, 454, 454, 817	.3554	....	5 "	5.2631	....
1864, ...	1, 500, 999, 877	3.2002	....	5 1-4 "	5.	....
1865, ...	1, 550, 879, 685	3.3229	....	4 53-80 "	....	11.1905
1866, ...	1, 531, 229, 636	....	1.2670	5 9-16 "	19.3029	....

(J.)

Statement showing the valuations of real and personal property, the State and local taxes, and the rate per cent for each year, from 1845 to 1866, both inclusive.

YEAR.	Aggregate valuations.	State taxes.	Town, county and school taxes.	Total taxes.	Rate of tax on $1; valuation in cents.
1845,.........	$605, 646, 095	$361, 309 62	$3, 809, 218 33	$4, 170, 527 95	0.688
1846,.........	616, 824, 955	370, 557 44	4, 276, 904 44	4, 647, 461 88	0.753
1847,.........	632, 699, 993	302, 579 27	4, 541, 046 33	4, 843, 625 60	0.765
1848,.........	651, 619, 595	325, 638 72	4, 969, 819 51	5, 295, 458 23	0.812
1849,.........	665, 850, 737	334, 555 96	5, 214, 425 32	5, 548, 981 28	0.833
1850,.........	727, 494, 583	364, 003 75	5, 948, 783 58	6, 312, 787 33	0.867
1851,.........	1, 077, 831, 630	578, 546 88	6, 180, 891 38	6, 759, 438 26	0.627
1852,.........	1, 168, 335, 237	292, 641 69	6, 715, 046 39	7, 007, 688 08	0.600
1853,.........	1, 266, 666, 190	1, 285, 124 88	8, 060, 097 03	9, 345, 221 91	0.737
1854,.........	1, 364, 154, 625	1, 020, 926 49	8, 615, 164 36	9, 636, 090 85	0.706
1855,.........	1, 402, 849, 304	1, 751, 717 78	9, 924, 454 52	11, 676, 172 30	0.832
1856,.........	1, 430, 334, 696	1, 430, 000 02	11, 312, 845 04	12, 742, 845 06	0.890
1857,.........	1, 433, 309, 713	3, 221, 775 42	11, 941, 362 94	15, 163, 138 36	1.057
1858,.........	1, 404, 907, 679	2, 457, 533 80	12, 968, 004 78	15, 425, 538 58	1.098
1859,.........	1, 404, 913, 679	2, 458, 599 10	13, 894, 687 46	16, 353, 286 56	1.164
1860,.........	1, 419, 297, 520	4, 376, 167 35	14, 579, 857 15	18, 956, 024 50	1.335
1861,.........	1, 441, 767, 430	4, 505, 523 19	15, 896, 753 29	20, 402, 276 48	1.415
1862,.........	1, 449, 303, 948	5, 797, 215 79	13, 659, 072 61	19, 456, 288 40	1.342
1863,.........	1, 454, 454, 817	6, 181, 432 97	16, 865, 367 69	23, 046, 800 66	1.584
1864,.........	1, 500, 999, 877	6, 754, 499 45	33, 119, 446 11	39, 873, 945 56	2 656
1865,.........	1, 550, 879, 685	6, 067, 816 77	39, 893, 623 85	45, 961, 440 62	2.963
1866,.........	1, 531, 229, 636	7, 369, 042 63	33, 199, 202 06	40, 568, 244 69	2.649

NOTE.—The valuations from and including 1859, are given as fixed by the Board of Equalization.

(K.)

Statement of the moneyed or stock corporations of this State, with the amount of the capital stock paid in, as appears from their annual reports to the various State departments; assessed value of their real estate; assessed value of their stock taxable, deducting real estate, and the total assessed valuation, as given in the annual returns of the several Boards of Supervisors.

STATE BANKS.

NAME OF BANK.	Capital stock paid in.	Assessed Valuation.		
		Amount of real estate.	Amount of stock taxable, deducting real estate.	Total valuation.
Addison Bank,	....	$1,000 00	....	$1,000 00
Bank of Attica,	$250,000 00	....	$3,895 00	3,895 00
Bank of Canton,	50,000 00	....	....	....
Bank of Chenango,	150,000 00	....	....	....
Bank of Cooperstown,	....	....	....	....
Bank of Dansville,	126,350 00	3,800 00	3,800 00	7,600 00
Bank of Lowville,	100,000 00	....	....	....
Bank of Newark,	40,000 00	....	....	....
Bank of Newport,	....	2,000 00	....	2,000 00
Bank of Ontario	50,000 00	....	....	....
Bank of Orangetown,	100,000 00	....	40,000 00	40,000 00
Bank of Otego,	100,000 00	....	25,000 00	25,000 00
Bank of Port Byron,	....	....	....	....
Bank of Silver Creek,	95,800 00	2,800 00	....	2,800 00
Bank of Trumansburg,	50,000 00	....	....	....
Bank of Watertown,	35,000 00	....	....	9,857 00
Black River Bank,	15,000 00	....	....	15,000 00
Brooklyn Bank,	300,000 00	6,000 00	294,000 00	300,000 00
Buffalo City Bank,	138,850 00	....	....	....
Central Bank, Brooklyn,	200,000 00	....	192,000 00	192,000 00
Central City Bank,	125,000 00	....	....	....
City Bank, Oswego (1865),	276,400 00	....	....	7,000 00
Columbia Bank,	100,000 00	....	65,000 00	65,000 00
Commercial Bank, Rochester,	....	....	....	....
Commercial Bank, Whitehall,	108,200 00	....	3,000 00	3,000 00
Farmers' Bank of Lansingburgh,	....	3,510 00	....	3,510 00
Frankfort Bank,	105,000 00	1,000 00	....	1,000 00
Fredonia Bank,	25,000 00	....	....	....
Frontier Bank,	6,110 00	2,000 00	....	2,000 00
Hope Bank of Albany,	50,000 00	....	44,000 00	44,000 00
Ilion Bank,	....	....	33,334 00	33,334 00
International Bank,	....	16,825 00	....	16,825 00
J. N. Westfall & Co.'s Bank,	25,000 00	....	....	....
Long Island Bank,	400,000 00	8,000 00	392,000 00	400,000 00
Manufacturers' & Traders' Bank,	500,000 00	200 00	....	200 00
Marine Bank, Buffalo,	200,000 00	....	....	....
Mechanics' Bank, Brooklyn,	500,000 00	37,200 00	460,000 00	497,200 00
Montgomery County Bank,	100,000 00	1,000 00	62,318 50	63,318 50
New York and Erie Bank,	300,000 00	....	15,680 00	15,680 00
Oliver Lee & Co.'s Bank,	....	8,000 00	....	8,000 00
Oneida County Bank,	125,000 00	3,000 00	....	3,000 00
Otsego County Bank,	....	....	....	....
Palisade Bank,	....	....	....	....
Patterson Bank,	....	1,400 00	....	1,400 00
People's Exchange Bank,	....	1,350 00	....	1,350 00
Phœnix Bank,	....	3,700 00	....	3,700 00
P. R. Westfall's Bank,	25,000 00	....	....	....
Rochester Bank,	100,000 00	....	....	....
Schenectady Bank (1865),	100,000 00	3,000 00	5,700 00	8,700 00
Setauket Bank,	....	....	....	....
Steuben County Bank,	150,000 00	4,500 00	128,420 00	132,920 00
Susquehanna Valley Bank,	100,000 00	4,000 00	....	4,000 00
Syracuse City Bank,	166,700 00	....	....	....
Trustees of the Bank of Owego,	....	2,000 00	....	2,000 00
Amount carried forward,	$5,388,410 00	$116,285 00	$1,768,147 50	$1,916,289 50

State Banks — (Continued).

NAME OF BANK.	Capital stock paid in.	Assessed Valuation. Amount of real estate.	Amount of stock taxable, deducting real estate.	Total valuation.
Amount brought forward,	$5,388,410 00	$116,285 00	$1,768,147 50	$1,916,289 50
Union Bank, Medina,	25,000 00	....	....	....
Weedsport Bank,	100,000 00	....	....	....
White's Bank,	200,000 00	....	....	....
	$5,713,410 00	$116,285 00	$1,768,147 50	$1,916,289 50
City of New York.				
Bank of America,	$3,000,000 00	$210,000 00	....	$210,000 00
Bull's Head Bank,	200,000 00	21,000 00	$121,525 00	142,525 00
Corn Exchange Bank,	1,000,000 00	105,000 00	105,947 00	210,947 00
Greenwich Bank,	200,000 00	12,000 00	....	12,000 00
Manhattan Company,	2,050,000 00	176,650 00	....	176,650 00
Manufacturers' & Merchants' Bank,	500,000 00	....	....	....
Nassau Bank,	1,000,000 00	120,000 00	....	120,000 00
New York Dry Dock Co.,	200,000 00	161,050 00	155,273 00	316,323 00
North River Bank,	400,000 00	69,600 00	312,235 00	381,835 00
Oriental Bank,	300,000 00	25,000 00	....	25,000 00
People's Bank,	412,500 00	50,000 00	....	50,000 00
Wooster Sherman's Bank,	30,000 00	....	....	....
	$9,292,500 00	$950,300 00	$694,980 00	$1,645,280 00
Individual Banks.				
Alonzo Wood & Co.'s Bank,	....	....	....	....
Bank of Cayuga Lake,	$5,000 00	....	....	....
Bank of Commerce of Putnam Co.,	16,200 00	....	$5,000 00	$5,000 00
Bank of Lima,	20,000 00	....	....	....
Bank of Seneca Falls,	....	....	....	....
Bank of Westfield,	10,000 00	....	....	....
Bellinger Bank,	....	....	....	....
Briggs' Bank,	....	....	....	....
Burnet Bank,	52,750 00	....	....	....
Farmers' Bank of Attica,	40,000 00	....	40,000 00	40,000 00
George Washington Bank,	....	....	....	....
Henry D. Barto & Co.'s Bank,	20,000 00	....	....	....
H. G. Hotchkiss & Co.'s Bank,	6,320 00	....	....	....
H. G. Messenger's Bank,	50,000 00	....	25,000 00	25,000 00
H. J. Miner & Co.'s Bank,	....	....	....	....
J. A. Clark & Co.'s Bank,	....	....	....	....
J. N. Hungerford's Bank,	6,000 00	....	....	....
Joshua Pratt & Co.'s Bank,	6,085 00	....	....	....
J. T. Raplee's Bank,	15,000 00	$2,500 00	6,500 00	9,000 00
Lake Shore Bank,	....	....	....	....
Lyons Bank,	43,212 00	....	....	....
O. Paddock & Co.'s Bank,	12,000 00	....	....	....
Q. W. Wellington & Co.'s Bank,	10,000 00	....	10,000 00	10,000 00
Randall Bank,	50,000 00	....	25,000 00	25,000 00
R. L. Ingersoll & Co.'s Bank,	5,000 00	....	....	....
Smith's Bank of Perry,	50,000 00	....	....	....
Suffolk County Bank,	20,000 00	....	....	....
T. O. Grannis & Co.'s Bank,	....	....	....	....
	$437,567 00	$2,500 00	$111,500 00	$114,000 00

NATIONAL BANKS.

NATIONAL BANK OF	Capital stock paid in.	Assessed Valuation.		
		Amount of real estate.	Amount of stock taxable, deducting real estate.	Total valuation.
Adams, First,	$75,000 00		$28,127 00	$28,127 00
Adams, Hungerford,	125,000 00			47,040 00
Albany, First,	300,000 00		300,000 00	300,000 00
Albany, Nat. Albany Exch.,	300,000 00	$25,000 00	267,666 00	292,666 00
Albany, Merchants',	200,000 00	35,000 00	161,664 00	196,664 00
Albany, Union,	500,000 00	25,000 00	484,550 00	509,550 00
Albany, New York State,	350,000 00	27,500 00	322,500 00	350,000 00
Albany, Nat. Mech. & Far.,	350,000 00	28,652 00	296,754 00	325,406 00
Albany, Albany City,	500,000 00	25,000 00	474,040 00	499,040 00
Albany, Nat. Commercial,	500,000 00	56,165 00	725,930 00	782,095 00
Albion, First,	100,000 00			
Albion, Orleans County,	100,000 00	2,500 00		2,500 00
Amenia, First,	100,000 00	4,000 00	96,000 00	100,000 00
Andes, First,	60,000 00	900 00	60,000 00	60,900 00
Angelica, First,	100,000 00			
Auburn, First,	100,000 00			
Auburn, Auburn City,	200,000 00			
Auburn, Cayuga County,	250,000 00			
Auburn,	200,000 00	3,200 00		3,200 00
Auburn, National Exchange,	200,000 00			
Aurora, First,	100,000 00			
Amsterdam, First,	125,000 00		50,000 00	50,000 00
Amsterdam, Farmers',	200,000 00		80,000 00	80,000 00
Baldwinsville, First,	140,000 00	500 00	139,500 00	140,000 00
Batavia, First,	75,000 00			
Batavia, Nat. B'k of Genesee,	114,400 00			
Bath, First,	100,000 00	6,000 00	94,000 00	100,000 00
Binghamton, First,	200,000 00			
Binghamton, City,	200,000 00	8,000 00		8,000 00
Binghamton, Nat. Broome Co.,	100,000 00	7,000 00		7,000 00
Brockport, First,	50,000 00	2,000 00		2,000 00
Brooklyn, Nassau,	300,000 00		303,700 00	303,700 00
Brooklyn, First,	500,000 00	10,000 00	490,000 00	500,000 00
Brooklyn, Far. & Citizens',	300,000 00	15,000 00	285,000 00	300,000 00
Brooklyn, National City,	300,000 00	10,000 00	282,002 00	292,002 00
Brooklyn, Atlantic,	500,000 00	20,000 00	480,000 00	500,000 00
Buffalo, First,	100,000 00			
Buffalo, Far. & Mechanics',	200,000 00			
Buffalo, Third,	250,000 00			
Ballston Spa, Ballston Spa,	100,000 00	2,000 00		2,000 00
Ballston Spa, First,	100,000 00			
Canandaigua, First,	75,000 00			
Candor, First,	50,000 00	500 00	48,000 00	48,500 00
Castleton,	100,000 00		98,500 00	98,500 00
Champlain, First,	150,000 00			
Chittenango, First,	150,000 00			
Clyde, First,	50,000 00		12,620 00	12,620 00
Cobleskill, First,	100,000 00		30,500 00	30,500 00
Cooperstown, First,	200,000 00	4,000 00		4,000 00
Cooperstown, Second,	300,000 00	6,000 00		6,000 00
Cooperstown, Worthington,	50,000 00			
Cortland, First,	125,000 00			
Canajoharie, Canajoharie,	125,000 00	2,000 00	50,000 00	52,000 00
Canajoharie, Nat. Spraker,	100,000 00	2,500 00	40,000 00	42.500 00
Cherry Valley, Nat. Central,	200,000 00	2,000 00		2,000 00
Carmel, Putnam County,	100,000 00			
Cuba, Cuba,	100,000 00			2,560 00
Catskill, Tanners'	150,000 00	4,500 00		4,500 00
Catskill, Catskill,	149,991 00	7,500 00		7,500 00
Cazenovia,	150,000 00			
Cohoes,	100,000 00		100,000 00	100,000 00
Chester, Chester,	125,500 00	4,500 00	121,000 00	125,500 00
Coxsackie,	112,000 00			
Canastota, Canastota,	110,000 00			
Dansville, First,	50,000 00			
Delhi, First,	100,000 00	2,000 00	88,000 00	90,000 00
Delhi, Delaware,	150,000 00	3,000 00	147,000 00	150,000 00
Deposit, Deposit,	125,000 00			
Amount carried forward,	$11,961,891 00	$351,917 00	$6,157,053 00	$6,558,570 00

National Banks — (Continued).

NATIONAL BANK OF	Capital stock paid in.	Assessed Valuation.		
		Amount of real estate.	Amount of stock taxable, deducting real estate.	Total valuation.
Amount brought forward,	$11,961,891 00	$351,917 00	$6,157,053 00	$6,558,570 00
Dover, Dover Plains,	100,000 00	3,600 00	90,060 00	93,660 00
Ellenville, First,	200,000 00	....	....	....
Elmira, First,	100,000 00	....	....	....
Elmira, Second,	200,000 00	....	2,000 00	2,000 00
Elmira, Chemung Canal,	100,000 00	....	....	....
Elmira, Nat. B'k of Chemung,	100,000 00	2,400 00	....	2,400 00
Fishkill Landing, First,	100,000 00	....	80,000 00	80,000 00
Fishkill,	200,000 00	4,000 00	160,000 00	164,000 00
Franklin, First,	100,000 00	....	50,000 00	50,000 00
Fort Plain, Nat. Fort Plain,	200,000 00	2,000 00	80,000 00	82,000 00
Fredonia, Fredonia,	50,000 00	....	....	....
Friendship, First,	75,000 00	....	....	....
Fulton, First,	115,000 00	....	....	....
Fulton, Citizens',	166,100 00	....	....	....
Fayetteville,	140,000 00	....	....	45,800 00
Fonda, Nat. Mohawk River,	100,000 00	3,000 00	40,000 00	43,000 00
Fort Edward.	200,000 00	....	....	1,700 00
Fort Edward, Farmers',	170,000 00	....	....	....
Geneseo, Genesee Valley,	150,000 00	6,000 00	....	6,000 00
Geneva, First,	50,000 00	2,940 00	....	2,940 00
Geneva, Geneva,	200,000 00	9,800 00	....	9,800 00
Greenport, First,	75,000 00	....	....	200 00
Glens Falls, First,	136,400 00	4,500 00	....	4,500 00
Glens Falls, Glens Falls,	112,000 00	5,000 00	....	5,000 00
Greenwich, Washington Co.,	200,000 00	....	....	....
Groton, First,	100,000 00	....	....	....
Goshen, Orange County,	110,000 00	2,500 00	115,400 00	117,900 00
Goshen, Goshen,	110,000 00	....	110,000 00	110,000 00
Gloversville, Fulton County,	150,000 00	1,500 00	146,204 00	147,704 00
Havana, First,	50,000 00	....	50,000 00	50,000 00
Havana, Second,	55,000 00	....	55,000 00	55,000 00
Hobart, First,	100,000 00	....	....	....
Hornellsville, First,	50,000 00	26,250 00	....	26,250 00
Hudson, First,	200,000 00	....	200,000 00	200,000 00
Hudson, Farmers',	300,000 00	7,000 00	300,000 00	307,000 00
Hudson, Hudson River,	250,000 00	5,000 00	250,000 00	255,000 00
Hamilton, Hamilton,	110,000 00	....	....	....
Ithaca, First,	200,000 00	....	200,000 00	200,000 00
Ithaca, Merch'ts' & Farmers',	50,000 00	....	50,000 00	50,000 00
Ithaca, Tompkins County,	250,000 00	12,798 00	240,202 00	253,000 00
Jamestown, First,	153,300 00	3,000 00	....	3,000 00
Jamestown, Second,	100,000 00	....	....	....
Jamestown, Chautauqua Co.,	100,000 00	3,000 00	....	3,000 00
Kinderhook, Nat. Union,	200,000 00	5,000 00	190,000 00	195,000 00
Kinderhook,	250,000 00	3,000 00	240,000 00	243,000 00
Kingston, First,	200,000 00	....	....	....
Kingston, State of N. Y.,	125,000 00	4,000 00	....	4,000 00
Kingston, Ulster County,	150,000 00	5,000 00	....	5,000 00
Kingston, Kingston,	150,000 00	7,000 00	....	7,000 00
Leonardsville, First,	50,000 00	....	....	....
Lockport, First,	200,000 00	....	....	....
Lockport, Niagara County,	150,000 00	....	....	....
Lockport Nat. Exchange,	150,000 00	4,500 00	....	4,500 00
Leroy, First,	150,000 00	3,000 00	....	3,000 00
Lowville, First,	50,000 00	....	....	....
Lyons, Lyons,	100,000 00	....	....	....
Little Falls, Herkimer Co.,	200,000 00	....	....	....
Lansingburgh,	150,000 00	5,000 00	148,688 00	153,688 00
Lansingburgh, Exchange,	100,000 00	4,000 00	97,890 00	101,890 00
Malone, Farmers',	150,000 00	....	....	....
Malone,	200,000 00	....	....	....
Medina, First,	50,000 00	....	....	....
Middletown, First,	100,000 00	....	100,000 00	100,000 00
Middletown, Middletown,	200,000 00	5,000 00	200,500 00	205,500 00
Middletown, Wallkill,	175,000 00	2,000 00	174,500 00	176,500 00
Moravia, First,	80,000 00	....	....	....
Amount carried forward,	$21,069,691 00	$503,605 00	$9,027,497 00	$10,128,502 00

National Banks — (Continued).

NATIONAL BANK OF	Capital stock paid in.	Assessed Valuation.		
		Amount of real estate.	Amount of stock taxable, deducting real estate.	Total valuation.
Amount brought forward,	$21,069,691 00	$503,605 00	$9,027,497 00	$10,128,502 00
Morrisville, First,	100,000 00	....	....	....
Mohawk, Mohawk Valley,	150,000 00	1,200 00	....	1,200 00
Mt. Morris, Genesee River,	100,.000 00	1,700 00	....	1,700 00
Monticello, Nat. Union,	150,000 00	1,880 00	....	1,880 00
Newark, First,	50,000 00	....	....	....
New Berlin, First,	60,000 00	....	....	....
Newburgh, Newburgh,	800,000 00	10,000 00	790,000 00	800,000 00
Newburgh, Highland,	450,000 00	9,000 00	441,000 00	450,000 00
Newburgh. Quassaick,	300,000 00	7,500 00	292,500 00	300,000 00
New Paltz, Huguenot,	125,000 00	....	....	....
Nyack, Rockland County,	100,000 00	....	148,350 00	148,350 00
N. White Cr'k, Camb'ge Val.,	172,500 00	700 00	....	700 00
Norwich,	125,000 00	....	....	....
Newport,	50,000 00	....	....	....
Oneida, First,	125,000 00	....	....	....
Oneida, Oneida Valley,	105,000 00	....	....	....
Oswego, First,	200,000 00	....	....	....
Oswego, Second,	120,000 00	....	....	....
Oswégo, National Marine,	200,000 00	....	....	....
Oswego, Lake Ontario,	325,000 00	....	....	8,950 00
Owego, Tioga,	100,000 00	2,000 00	98,000 00	100,000 00
Owego, First,	100,000 00	....	100,000 00	100,000 00
Owego, National Union,	100,000 00	2,000 00	98,000 00	100,000 00
Oxford, First,	150,000 00	....	....	....
Palmyra, First,	200,000 00	....	....	....
Plattsburgh, First,	100,000 00	....	....	....
Plattsburgh, Second,	100,000 00	....	....	....
Port Chester, First,	100,000 00	....	....	....
Potsdam,	50,000 00	....	....	....
Poughkeepsie, First,	160,000 00	....	160,000 00	160,000 00
Poughkeepsie, Fallkill,	400,000 00	5,000 00	400,000 00	405,000 00
Poughkeepsie, City,	200,000 00	5,000 00	200,000 00	205,000 00
Poughkeepsie, Poughkeepsie,	250,000 00	4,000 00	250,000 00	254,000 00
Poughkeepsie, Far's & Mf'rs',	400,000 00	5,000 00	400,000 00	405,000 00
Poughkeepsie, Merchants,	150,000 00	5,000 00	150,000 00	155,000 00
Pawling,	175,000 00	3,800 00	159,250 00	163,050 00
Pine Plains, Stissing	90,000 00	....	90,000 00	90,000 00
Port Jervis,	130,000 00	....	130,000 00	130,000 00
Peekskill. Westchester Co.,	200,000 00	11,800 00	....	11,800 00
Pulaski, Pulaski,	50,000 00	....	....	13,960 00
Rochester, First,	200,000 00	....	....	....
Rochester, Farm's & Mech's,	100,000 00	....	....	....
Rochester, Trader's,	250,000 00	....	....	....
Rochester, Flour City,	300,000 00	....	....	....
Rochester, Clarke,	200,000 00	8,000 00	....	8,000 00
Rondout, First,	300,000 00	....	....	....
Rondout, Rondout,	200,000 00	....	....	....
Red Hook, First,	150,000 00	....	141,000 00	141,000 00
Rhinebeck, First,	175,000 00	....	148,750 00	148,750 00
Rome, Central,	97,560 00	4,500 00	....	4,500 00
Rome, Fort Stanwix,	150,000 00	5,500 00	....	5,500 00
Rome, First,	100,000 00	3,500 00	....	3,500 00
Seneca Falls, First,	60,000 00	....	....	....
Seneca Falls, National Ex.,	100,000 00	....	....	....
Sandy Hill, First,	75,000 00	1,200 00	....	1,200 00
Skaneateles, First,	150,000 00	....	....	150,000 00
Sing Sing, First,	100,000 00	....	....	....
South Worcester, First,	175,000 00	....	....	....
St. Johnsville,	75,000 00	....	30,000 00	30,000 00
South East, Croton River,	200,000 00	....	....	....
Syracuse, First,	250,000 00	....	....	....
Syracuse, Second,	100,000 00	....	....	....
Syracuse, Third,	300,000 00	....	....	....
Syracuse, Fourth,	105,500 00	....	....	....
Syracuse, Salt Springs,	200,000 00	....	....	196,000 00
Syracuse, Syracuse,	200,000 00	....	....	10,000 00
Amount carried forward,	$32,395,251 00	$601,885 00	$13,254,347 00	$14,832,542 00

National Banks — (Continued).

NATIONAL BANK OF	Capital stock paid in.	Assessed Valuation.		
		Amount of real estate.	Amount of stock taxable, deducting real estate.	Total valuation.
Amount brought forward,	$32,395,251 00	$601,885 00	$13,254,347 00	$14,832,542 00
Syracuse, Merchants,	180,000 00	....	....	....
Syracuse, Mechanics,	140,000 00	....	....	11,000 00
Saratoga Springs, First,	100,000 00	....	....	....
Saratoga Springs, Commerc'l,	100,000 00	....	....	....
Saugerties, First,	150,000 00	2,850 00	....	2,850 00
Saugerties, Saugerties,	125,000 00	3,800 00	....	3,800 00
Salem,	150,000 00	....	....	....
Sherburne, Sherburne,	100,000 00	....	....	....
Schenectady, Mohawk,	100,000 00	4,000 00	15,825 00	19,825 00
Somers, Farmers' & Drovers',	111,150 00	....	....	....
Schuylerville,	100,000 00	....	1,200 00	1,200 00
Schoharie, Schoharie County,	100,000 00	....	70,000 00	70,000 00
Tarrytown, First,	100,000 00	....	....	....
Troy, First,	300,000 00	9,000 00	248,934 00	257,934 00
Troy, National Exchange,	100,000 00	12,000 00	65,200 00	77,200 00
Troy, Troy City,	500,000 00	30,000 00	450,260 00	480,260 00
Troy, Manufacturers',	150,000 00	9,000 00	107,441 00	116,441 00
Troy, Merch. & Mechanics',	300,000 00	9,000 00	290,583 00	299,583 00
Troy United,	300,000 00	12,000 00	288,000 00	300,000 00
Troy National State,	250,000 00	10,000 00	235,612 00	245,612 00
Troy Mutual,	234,500 00	28,450 00	206,190 00	234,640 00
Troy Union,	300,000 00	12,000 00	273,410 00	285,410 00
Troy Central,	300,000 00	10,000 00	272,636 00	282,636 00
Union Springs, First,	100,000 00	....	....	....
Utica, Second,	300,000 00	....	....	....
Utica, Utica City,	200,000 00	7,500 00	....	7,500 00
Utica, Oneida,	400,000 00	....	....	....
Utica, First,	600,000 00	8,500 00	....	8,500 00
Unadilla National, Unadilla,	....	....	....	....
Vernon,	100,000 00	2,000 00	....	2,000 00
Warwick, First,	100,000 00	....	50,000 00	50,000 00
Waterloo, First,	50,000 00	5,000 00	....	5,000 00
Watkins, First,	50,000 00	....	36,000 00	36,000 00
Watkins, Second,	75,000 00	....	45,700 00	45,700 00
Waverly, First,	50,000 00	2,500 00	54,268 00	56,768 00
Waverly, Waverly,	106,100 00	2,000 00	103,693 00	105,693 00
Westfield, First	100,000 00	....	....	....
Whitehall, First,	100,000 00	....	....	....
Whitehall, Old,	100,000 00	5,000 00	....	5,000 00
West Winfield, First,	100,000 00	....	42,500 00	42,500 00
Warsaw, Wyoming Co.,	100,000 00	....	....	....
Watertown, First,	125,000 00	....	75,000 00	75,000 00
Watertown, Second,	100,000 00	....	....	....
Watertown, Jefferson Co.,	148,800 00	....	....	88,280 00
Watertown National Union,	147,440 00	....	....	84,464 00
Watert'n Nat. B'k & Loan Co.	75,000 00	....	....	45,000 00
Waterford, Saratoga,	150,000 00	3,000 00	....	3,000 00
West Troy,	250,000 00	....	250,000 00	250,000 00
Waterville,	150,000 00	700 00	....	700 00
Whitestown,	120,000 00	....	....	....
Yonkers, First,	150,000 00	....	150,000 00	150,000 00
	$40,733,241 00	$790,185 00	$16,586,799 00	$18,582,038 00
City of New York.				
First,	$500,000 00	....	....	....
Second,	300,000 00	....	....	....
Third,	1,000,000 00	....	....	....
Fourth,	5,000,000 00	....	....	....
Fifth,	150,000 00	....	....	....
Sixth,	200,000 00	....	....	....
Eighth,	250,000 00	....	....	....
Ninth,	1,000,000 00	....	....	....
Tenth,	1,000,000 00	....	....	....
American Exchange,	5,000,000 00	$265,000 00	....	$265,000 00
American,	500,000 00	....	....	....
Amount carried forward,	$14,900,000 00	$265,000 00	$............	$265,000 00

National Banks — (Continued).

NATIONAL BANK OF	Capital stock paid in.	ASSESSED VALUATION.		
		Amount of real estate.	Amount of stock taxable, deducting real estate.	Total valuation
Amount brought forward,	$14,900,000 00	$265,000 00	$	$265,000 00
Atlantic,	300,000 00	....	....	....
Bank of N. Y. Nat. B'k'g Ass.	3,000,000 00	350,000 00	....	350,000 00
Bowery,	250,000 00	....	....	....
Butchers' and Drovers',	800,000 00	61,000 00	....	61,000 00
Central,	3,000,000 00	....	....	....
Chatham,	450,000 00	....	139,200 00	139,200 00
Chemical,	300,000 00	70,000 00	....	70,000 00
Continental,	2,000,000 00	200,000 00	1,211,954 00	1,411,954 00
Croton,	200,000 00	....	....	....
East River,	350,000 00	34,000 00	36,866 00	70,866 00
Fulton,	600,000 00	45,000 00	....	45,000 00
Gallatin,	1,500,000 00	57,000 00	....	57,000 00
Grocers',	300,000 00	28,000 00	193,218 00	221,218 00
Hanover,	1,000,000 00	....	4,813 00	4,813 00
Importers' and Traders',	1,500,000 00	122,400 00	....	122,400 00
Irving,	500,000 00	28,000 00	....	28,000 00
Leather Manufacturers',	600,000 00	60,000 00	340,776 00	400,776 00
Manufacturers',	252,000 00	....	....	....
Marine,	400,000 00	30,000 00	....	30,000 00
Market,	1,000,000 00	65,000 00	153,778 00	218,778 00
Mechanics',	2,000,000 00	262,100 00	166,956 00	429,056 00
Mechanics' and Traders',	600,000 00	40,000 00	328,155 00	368,155 00
Mercantile,	1,000,000 00	60,000 00	....	60,000 00
Merchants' Exchange,	1,235,000 00	50,000 00	312,000 00	362,000 00
Merchants',	3,000,000 00	170,000 00	....	170,000 00
Metropolitan,	4,000,000 00	270,000 00	857,608 00	1,127,608 00
National Bank of Commerce,	10,000,000 00	350,000 00	....	350,000 00
Nat. Bank of the Com'wealth,	750,000 00	185,000 00	....	185,000 00
Nat. Bank of North America,	1,000,000 00	85,000 00	215,000 00	300,000 00
National Bank of Republic,	2,000,000 00	175,000 00	1,097,300 00	1,272,300 00
Nat. Bank of State of N. Y.,	2,000,000 00	135,000 00	1,036,290 00	1,171,290 00
National Broadway,	1,000,000 00	140,000 00	....	140,000 00
National Citizens,	400,000 00	35,000 00	....	35,000 00
National City,	1,000,000 00	80,000 00	....	80,000 00
National Currency,	100,000 00	....	....	....
Nat. Mech. Banking Assoc'n,	500,000 00	....	....	....
National Park,	2,000,000 00	105,000 00	....	105,000 00
New York County,	200,000 00	....	31,300 00	31,300 00
New York National Exch'ge,	300,000 00	....	....	....
Ocean,	1,000,000 00	86,216 00	550,995 00	637,211 00
Pacific,	422,700 00	85,000 00	....	85,000 00
Phœnix,	1,800,000 00	160,000 00	....	160,000 00
Seventh Ward,	500,000 00	....	....	....
Shoe and Leather,	1,500,000 00	120,000 00	100,000 00	220,000 00
St. Nicholas,	1,000,000 00	90,000 00	....	90,000 00
Tradesmen's,	1,000,000 00	150,000 00	....	150,000 00
Union,	1,500,000 00	160,000 00	....	160,000 00
	$75,009,700 00	$4,408,716 00	$6,776,209 00	$11,184,925 00

NOTE.—Under the act, chapter 761, Laws of 1866, it is provided that bank shares shall be assessed to the holders. It has been the practice, however, with some institutions to assume and pay the tax. In these cases the returns show an apparent assessment against the corporation, when in reality it represents the amount for which the holders were assessed collectively.

SAVINGS BANKS.

NAME OF BANK.	Excess of assets.	Assessed Valuation.		
		Amount of real estate.	Amount of stock taxable, deducting real estate.	Total valuation.
City of Albany.				
Albany Savings Bank, ...	$102,408 00	...	...	...
Albany City Savings Inst,,...	...	...	...	...
Albany Exch. Savings Bank,.	668 00	...	...	...
Mech. & Far. Savings Bank,.	16,887 00	...	...	...
	$119,963 00	...	...	...
City of Auburn.				
Auburn Savings Institution,.	$46,529 00	...	...	...
Mut. Savings B'k of Auburn,.	3,653 00	...	...	...
	$50,182 00	...	...	...
City of Brooklyn.				
Brooklyn Savings Bank,.....	$409,643 00	$55,000 00	$282,486 00	$337,486 00
Dime Savings B'k, Brooklyn,	127,018 00	30,000 00	78,000 00	108,000 00
Dime Savings B'k, W'msb'h,	8,758 00	...	2,403 00	2,403 00
East Brooklyn Savings Bank,	8,599 00	...	8,435 00	8,435 00
Emig't Savings B'k, Br'klyn,	644 00	...	...	...
German Savings B'k, Br'klyn,	869 00	...	...	...
Kings Co. Savings Inst.,.....	35,173 00	9,000 00	...	9,000 00
L. I. Savings B'k of Br'klyn,.	1,372 00	...	...	...
South Br'klyn Savings Inst.,.	149,515 00	18,000 00	107,493 00	125,493 00
Williamsburgh Savings Bank	504,809 00	18,200 00	323,168 00	341,368 00
	$1,246,400 00	$130,200 00	$801,985 00	$932,185 00
City of Buffalo.				
Buffalo Savings Bank,.......	$185,446 00	...	$165,975 00	$165,975 00
Emig't Savings B'k of Buffalo,	309 00	...	2,180 00	2,180 00
Erie Co. Savings Bank,......	218,249 00	$4,900 00	170,920 00	175,820 00
West'n Sav. Bank of Buffalo,	30,972 00	...	27,870 00	27,870 00
	$434,976 00	$4,900 00	$366,945 00	$371,845 00
City of New York.				
Atlantic Savings Bank.......	$82,361 00	$22,000 00	...	$22,000 00
B'k for Sav. in city of N. Y.,.	1,242,665 00	75,000 00	...	75,000 00
Bowery Savings Bank,.......	1,659,095 00	105,000 00	...	105,000 00
Broadway Savings Inst.,.....	136,680 00	...	...	...
Citizens' Savings Bank, ...	166,359 00	...	...	...
Dry Dock Savings Inst.,.....	329,608 00	25,000 00	...	25,000 00
East River Savings Inst.,....	232,971 00	38,000 00	...	38,000 00
Emigrant Industrial Sav. B'k,	324,380 00	55,000 00	...	55,000 00
Franklin Savings Bank, ...	6,428 00	...	...	...
German Sav. Bank of N. Y.,.	140,355 00	...	...	...
Greenwich Savings Bank, ...	411,071 00	40,000 00	...	40,000 00
Harlem Savings Bank,.......	906 00	...	...	...
Inst. for Sav. of Merch's' Cl'ks,	223,457 00	55,000 00	...	55,000 00
Irving Savings Institution, ..	112,045 00	18,000 00	...	18,000 00
Manhattan Savings Inst.,....	208,090 00	68,100 00	...	68,100 00
Market Savings Bank,.... ..	11,774 00	...	...	...
Mechanics' and Traders' Savings Institution,..........	142,061 00	14,000 00	...	14,000 00
Metropolitan Savings Bank, (formerly Mariners' Savings Institution),..............	145,497 00	13,000 00	...	13,000 00
New York Savings Bank, (formerly Rose Hill Sav. Bank,)	37,202 00	...	...	...
North River Savings Bank,..	...	...	...	...
Seaman's Bank for Savings,.	913,344 00	115,000 00	...	115,000 00
Sixpenny Savings Bank of the Empire City,..........	8,064 00	...	...	...
Third Av. Sav. Bank, (formerly Bloomingdale Sav. Bank,)	150,069 00	25,000 00	...	25,000 00
Union Dime Sav. Institution,	160,110 00	...	...	...
Up Town Savings Bank,.....	...	...	...	...
	$6,844,592 00	$668,100 00	...	$668,100 00

Savings Banks— (Continued).

NAME OF BANK.	Excess of assets.	Assessed Valuation.		
		Amount of real estate.	Amount of stock taxable, deducting real estate.	Total valuation.
City of Rochester.				
Monroe County Sav. Bank,..	$127,605 00	$15,000 00	$83,000 00	$98,000 00
Rochester Savings Bank,....	202,514 00	38,000 00	126,000 00	164,000 00
	$330,119 00	$53,000 00	$209,000 00	$262,000 00
City of Syracuse.				
Onondaga County Sav. Bank,	$126,852 00	....	....	....
Syracuse Savings Institution,	67,972 00	....	....	$12,000 00
	$194,824 00	....	....	$12,000 00
City of Troy.				
Central Sav. Bank of Troy,..	....	....	....	....
Manufact's Sav. B'nk of Troy,	....	....	....	....
Mutual Sav. Bank of Troy, ..	....	....	....	....
State Savings Bank of Troy,.	$243 00	....	....	....
Troy Savings Bank, ...	54,772 00	$30,000 00	....	$30,000 00
	$55,015 00	$30,000 00	....	$30,000 00
City of Utica.				
Central City Sav. Institution,	$1,588 00	....	....	....
National Sav. B'k of Utica,..	1,126 00	....	....	....
Savings Bank of Utica,......	143,868 00	$3,000 00	....	$3,000 00
	$146,582 00	$3,000 00	....	$3,000 00
Other Localities.				
Chau'qua Co. Sav. B'k, Fred'a,	$5 00	....	....	....
Chena'o Co. Sav. B'k, Norw'h,	684 00	....	....	....
Cohoes Sav. Inst., Cohoes, ..	....	....	....	....
Cor'g Sav. B'k, Cor'g (clos'g),	172 00	....	....	....
Cortland Sav. B'k, Cortland,	....	....	....	....
Elm'a Sav. B'k, Elm'a(clos'g),	1,750 00	....	....	....
Fishkill Sav. Inst., Fishkill .	28,460 00	....	....	....
Hudson City Savings Institution, Hudson,.	29,286 00	....	$5,000 00	$5,000 00
Jefferson County Savings Bank, Watertown,...	7,099 00	....	....	....
Mechanics' Savings Bank of Fishkill, on the Hudson,...	....	....	....	....
Newburgh Sav. B'k, New'gh,	82,019 00	....	....	....
New Rochelle Savings Bank, New Rochelle,............	157 00	....	....	....
Niagara Co. Sav. B'k, Lock't,	248 00	....	....	....
Oneida Sav. Bank, Oneida, ..	553 00	....	....	....
Oswego City Sav. B'k, Osw'o,	14,229 00	....	....	....
Peekskill Sav. B'k, Peekskill,	22,899 00	....	19,250 00	19,250 00
Port Chester Saving Bank, Port Chester, ...	593 00	....	....	....
Poughk'psie Sav. B'k, Pough.	108,016 00	$4,000 00	....	4,000 00
Queens Co. Sav. B'k, Flush'g,	12,659 00	....	7,650 00	7,650 00
Rhineb'k Sav. B'k, Rhineb'k,	1,318 00	....	....	....
Rome Savings Bank, Rome, .	24,715 00	....	....	....
Sag Harbor Sav. B'k, Sag Har.	4,277 00	....	....	....
Schenect'y Sav. B'k, Schen'y,	10,689 00	....	....	....
Skaneat'les Sav. B'k, Skane's,	1,031 00	....	....	....
Sing Sing Sav. B'k, Sing S'ng,	14,466 00	....	....	....
Southold Sav. B'k, Southold,	13,684 00	....	....	....
Ulster Co. Sav. Inst. Kings'n,	21,867 00	....	....	....
West. Co. Sav. B'k, Tarryt'n,	19,963 00	....	....	....
Yonkers Sav. B'k, Yonkers,.	21,949 00	....	....	2,000 00
	$442,788 00	$4,000 00	$31,900 00	$37,900 00
Grand Total, ...	$9,865,441 00	$893,200 00	$1,409,830 00	$2,317,030 00

INSURANCE COMPANIES.

NEW YORK JOINT STOCK FIRE INSURANCE COMPANIES.	Capital.	Gross Assets.	Assessed Valuation. Amount of real estate.	Amount of stock taxable, deducting real estate.	Total Valuation.
Aetna Fire, New York,	$300,000 00	....	....	$139,000 00	$139,000 00
Adriatic Fire, New York,	200,000 00	....	....	130,000 00	130,000 00
Agricultural, Watertown,	100,000 00	....	$1,000 00	99,000 00	100,000 00
Albany, Albany,	150,000 00	....	....	106,500 00	106,500 00
Albany City, Albany,	200,000 00	....	....	61,675 00	61,675 00
American Fire, New York,	200,000 00	....	....	....	....
American Ex. Fire, N. Y.,	200,000 00	....	....	79,500 00	79,500 00
Arctic Fire, New York,	250,000 00	....	3,000 00	246,750 00	249,750 00
Astor Fire, New York	250,000 00	....	....	120,500 00	120,500 00
Atlantic Fire, Brooklyn,	300,000 00	....	....	38,000 00	38,000 00
Baltic Fire, New York,	200,000 00	....	2,500 00	200,000 00	202,500 00
Beekman Fire, New York,	200,000 00	....	....	165,000 00	165,000 00
Bergholtz Fire, Niag. Co.,	....	....	....	1,000 00	1,000 00
Brevoort Fire, New York,	....	....	....	10,000 00	10,000 00
Broadway, New York,	200,000 00	....	....	145,646 00	145,646 00
Brooklyn Fire, Brooklyn,	153,000 00	....	12,300 00	119,333 00	131,633 00
Capital City, Albany,	200,000 00	....	....	....	....
Central Park Fire, N. Y.,	....	....	....	125,000 00	125,000 00
Citizens, Brooklyn,	300,000 00	....	6,800 00	288,109 00	294,909 00
City Fire, New York,	210,000 00	....	2,000 00	144,665 00	146,665 00
Clinton Fire, New York,	250,000 00	....	....	164,000 00	164,000 00
Columbia Fire, New York,	250,000 00	....	....	200,800 00	200,800 00
Commerce, Albany,	400,000 00	....	31,400 00	147,600 00	179,000 00
Commerce Fire, N. Y.,	200,000 00	....	....	67,000 00	67,000 00
Commercial Fire, N. Y.,	200,000 00	....	....	86,400 00	86,400 00
Commonwealth Fire, N. Y.	250,000 00	....	....	195,000 00	195,000 00
Continental, New York,	500,000 00	....	92,000 00	155,098 00	247,098 00
Corn Exchange, N. Y.,	400,000 00	....	....	250,000 00	250,000 00
Croton Fire, New York,	....	....	....	22,205 00	22,205 00
Eagle Fire, New York,	300,000 00	....	63,449 00	240,011 00	303,460 00
Empire City Fire, N. Y.,	200,000 00	....	....	88,000 00	88,000 00
Excelsior Fire, New York,	200,000 00	....	45,604 00	103,845 00	149,449 00
Exchange Fire, New York,	150,000 00	....	7,000 00	100,000 00	107,000 00
Farm's' Joint St'ck, Merid.	100,000 00	....	....	....	....
Fireman's, New York,	204,000 00	....	....	101,000 00	101,000 00
Fireman's Fund, N. Y.,	150,000 00	....	....	95,000 00	95,000 00
Fireman's Trust, Brookl'n	150,000 00	....	....	88,000 00	88,000 00
Fulton Fire, New York,	200,000 00	....	7,500 00	123,800 00	131,300 00
Gallatin Fire, New York,	150,000 00	....	....	70,000 00	70,000 00
Gebhard Fire, New York,	200,000 00	....	....	160,000 00	160,000 00
Germania Fire, N. Y.,	500,000 00	....	50,000 00	50,000 00	100,000 00
Glens Falls, Glens Falls,	200,000 00	....	1,800 00	*47,762 00	49,562 00
Globe Fire, New York,	200,000 00	....	....	45,000 00	45,000 00
Greenwich, New York,	200,000 00	....	18,000 00	107,000 00	125,000 00
Grocers' Fire, New York,	200,000 00	....	3,650 00	85,000 00	88,650 00
Guardian Fire, New York,	200,000 00	....	....	97,000 00	97,000 00
Hamilton Fire, New York,	150,000 00	....	24,280 00	52,934 00	77,214 00
Hanover Fire, New York,	400,000 00	....	....	67,000 00	67,000 00
Harmony Fire, New York,	....	....	6,000 00	264,600 00	270,600 00
Hoffman Fire, New York,	200,000 00	....	....	100,000 00	100,000 00
Home, New York,	2,000,000 00	....	....	771,300 00	771,300 00
Hope Fire, New York,	150,000 00	....	....	200,000 00	200,000 00
Howard, New York,	500,000 00	....	65,000 00	120,000 00	185,000 00
Humboldt Fire, N. Y.,	200,000 00	....	....	95,000 00	95,000 00
Imp'rs' & Traders', N. Y.,	200,000 00	....	....	117,000 00	117,000 00
Indemnity Fire, N. Y.,	....	....	....	41,300 00	41,300 00
International, New York,	1,000,000 00	....	....	130,000 00	130,000 00
Irving Fire, New York,	200,000 00	....	....	55,000 00	55,000 00
Jefferson, New York,	200,010 00	....	4,541 00	204,455 00	208,996 00
Kings Co. Fire, Brooklyn,	150,000 00	....	....	120,850 00	120,850 00
Knickerbocker Fire, N. Y.,	280,000 00	....	65,000 00	150,000 00	215,000 00
La Fayette Fire, Brooklyn,	150,000 00	....	....	120,400 00	120,400 00
Lamar Fire, New York,	300,000 ,0	....	....	125,500 00	125,500 00
Lenox Fire, New York,	150,000 00	....	....	50,900 00	50,900 00
Long Island, Brooklyn,	200,000 00	....	12,000 00	175,091 00	187,091 00
Lorillard Fire, New York,	1,000,000 00	....	40,000 00	335,000 00	375,000 00
Manhattan, New York,	500,000 00	....	....	....	....
Market Fire, New York,	200,000 00	....	....	54,600 00	54,600 00
Mechanics' Fire, Brooklyn,	150,000 00	....	....	135,000 00	135,000 00
Mech's'&Trad's'Fire, N.Y.,	200,000 00	....	30,900 00	168,500 00	199,400 00
Mercantile Fire, N. Y.,	200,000 00	....	....	102,000 00	102,000 00
Merchants', New York,	200,000 00	....	....	120,000 00	120,000 00
Metropolitan, New York,	300,000 00	....	....	392,402 00	392,402 00
Montauk Fire, Brooklyn,	150,000 00	....	....	78,000 00	78,000 00
Mutual, Buffalo,	292,650 00	....	7,260 00	225,190 00	232,450 00
Amount carried forward,	$19,189,660 00	....	$602,984 00	$9,681,221 00	$10,284,205 00

* Includes $8,562 bank stock.

Insurance Companies — (Continued).

NEW YORK JOINT STOCK FIRE INSURANCE COMPANIES.	Capital.	Gross Assets.	ASSESSED VALUATION. Amount of real estate.	Amount of stock taxable, deducting real estate.	Total Valuation.
Amount brought forward,	$19,189,660 00	$	$602,984 00	$9,681,221 00	$10,284,205 00
Nassau Fire, Brooklyn,	150,000 00	....	....	138,625 00	138,625 00
National Fire, New York,	200,000 00	....	57,292 00	143,908 00	201,200 00
New Amst'm Fire, N. Y.,	300,000 00	....	....	175,000 00	175,000 00
N. Y. Bowery Fire, N. Y.,	300,000 00	....	8,000 00	148,950 00	156,950 00
N. Y. Cent., Union Springs,	100,000 00	....	....	....	....
New York Equitable, N. Y.,	210,000 00	....	....	210,000 00	210,000 00
New York Fire, N. Y.,	200,000 00	....	36,653 00	122,347 00	159,000 00
Niagara Fire, New York,	1,000,000 00	....	4,000 00	493,500 00	497,500 00
N. American Fire, N. Y.,	500,000 00	....	....	158,000 00	158,000 00
North River, New York,	350,000 00	....	12,300 00	324,799 00	337,099 00
North Western, Oswego,	150,000 00	....	....	....	150,000 00
Pacific Fire, New York,	200,000 00	....	45,488 00	136,511 00	181,999 00
Park Fire, New York,	200,000 00	....	....	60,000 00	60,000 00
People's Fire, New York,	150,000 00	....	....	96,500 00	96,500 00
Peter Cooper Fire, N. Y.,	150,000 00	....	....	70,000 00	70,000 00
Phœnix, Brooklyn,	1,000,000 00	....	700 00	307,219 00	307,919 00
Relief Fire, New York,	200,000 0	....	....	157,500 00	157,500 00
Republic Fire, New York,	300,000 00	....	....	44,665 00	44,665 00
Resolute Fire, New York,	200,000 00	....	....	68,000 00	68,000 00
Rutger's Fire, New York,	200,000 00	....	64,000 00	115,750 00	179,750 00
Schenectady, Schenectady,	50,000 00	....	....	....	....
Security, New York,	1,000 000 00	....	....	764,058 00	764,058 00
St. Marks Fire, New York,	150,000 00	....	....	74,500 00	74,500 00
St. Nicholas, New York,	150,000 00	....	26,654 00	31,306 00	57,960 00
Standard Fire, New York,	200,000 00	....	....	40,000 00	40,000 00
Star Fire, New York,	200,000 00	....	....	44,750 00	44,750 00
Sterling Fire, New York,	200,000 00	....	....	30,000 00	30,000 00
Stuyvesant, New York,	200,000 00	....	7,685 00	85,315 00	93,000 00
Tradesmen's Fire, N. Y.,	150,000 00	....	....	67,000 00	67,000 00
United States Fire, N. Y.,	250,000 00	....	....	249,958 00	249,958 00
Washington, New York,	400,000 00	....	....	159,600 00	159,600 00
Western, Buffalo,	300,000 00	....	....	214,220 00	214,220 00
Will'sb'h City Fire, B'klyn,	150,000 00	....	1,100 00	86,000 00	87,100 00
Yonk's & N. Y. Fire, Yonk's,	500,000 00	....	....	....	190,000 00
	$29,149,660 00		$866,856 00	$14,499,202 00	$15,706,058 00
NEW YORK MUTUAL FIRE INSURANCE COMPANIES.					
Dutchess Co., Poughk'sie,	....	$734,680 56	$3,000 00	$59,855 00	$62,855 00
Farmers', Buffalo	....	7,728 15	....	....	....
Franklin County, Malone,	....	20,150 41	....	....	....
Glen Cove, Glen Cove,	....	321,244 09	....	36,000 00	36,000 00
Huntington, Huntington,	....	13,858 00	....	....	....
Monroe Co., Rochester,	....	1,217 31	....	....	....
Montgom'y Co., Canajoh'e,	....	1,653 29	....	....	....
Mutual, Albany,	....	305,074 24	....	3,490 00	3,490 00
Orange County, Goshen,	....	204,146 24	....	....	....
Richm'd Co., Richm'd Vill.,	....	170,932 71	....	....	....
Suffolk County, Southold,	....	166,422 54	....	....	....
Wayne County, Newark,	....	2,926 09	....	....	....
Westches'r Co., N. Roch'lle,	....	239,202 79	....	....	....
Western Farm's', Batavia,	....	24,621 16	....	....	....
Wyoming Co., Warsaw,	....	28,583 36	....	....	....
		$2,242,440 94	$3,000 00	$99,345 00	$102,345 00
NEW YORK JOINT STOCK MUTUAL MARINE INSURANCE COMPANIES.					
Atlantic Mutual, N. Y.,	....	$12,536,304 46	$251,288 00	$1,856,365 00	$2,107,653 00
Commercial Mutual, N. Y.,	....	1,103,083 96	....	259,267 00	259,267 00
Great Western, New York,	$1,000,000 00	....	241,000 00	759,000 00	1,000,000 00
Mercantile Mutual, N. Y.,	975,400 00	....	....	500,000 00	500,000 00
New York Mutual, N. Y.,	....	753,634 07	41,500 00	200,918 00	242,418 00
Orient Mutual, New York,	....	1,195,964 03	....	250,000 00	250,000 00
Pacific Mutual, New York,	....	1,188,893 54	....	250,000 00	250,000 00
Sun Mutual, New York,	....	1,988,889 39	150,000 00	747,350 00	897,350 00
Union Mutual, New York,	....	1,506,587 56	70,000 00	550,000 00	620,000 00
Washington Marine, N. Y.,	393,700 00	....	24,500 00	305,800 00	330,300 00
	$2,369,100 00	$20,273,357 01	$778,288 00	$5,678,700 00	$6,456.988 00
NEW YORK LIFE INS. COMPANIES.					
American Popular, N. Y.,	$100,000 00	....	....	....	....
Atlantic Mutual, Albany,	110,000 00	....	....	....	....
Brooklyn, Brooklyn,	125,000 00	....	....	....	....
Amount carried forward,	$335,000 00	$	$	$	$

Insurance Companies — (Continued).

NEW YORK LIFE INSURANCE COMPANIES.	Capital.	Gross assets.	Assessed Valuation.		
			Amount of real estate.	Amount of stock taxable, deducting real estate.	Total valuation.
Amount brought forward,	$335,000 00	$	$	$	$
Continental, New York,	100,000 00				
Equitable, New York,	100,000 00			100,000 00	100,000 00
Germania, New York,	200,000 00			100,000 00	100,000 00
Globe Mutual, New York,	100,000 00				
Great Western, New York,	115,000 00				
Guardian, New York,	125,000 00			10,500 00	10,500 00
Home, Brooklyn,	125,000 00				
Knickerbocker, N. Y.,	100,000 00		$4,000 00		4,000 00
Manhattan, New York,	100,000 00		9,300 00		9,300 00
Mutual, New York,		$18,495,507 55	8,600 00		8,600 00
Nat. Life & Trav'rs', N. Y.,	130,000 00			128,600 00	128,600 00
New York, New York,		7,009,092 25			
N. Y. Life & Trust, N. Y.,	1,000,000 00				
New York State, Syracuse,	120,000 00				24,637 50
North America, N. Y.,	100,000 00				
Security, New York,	110,000 00				
United States, New York,	100,000 00			100,000 00	100,000 00
Universal, New York,	200,000 00				
Washington, New York,	125,000 00			50,000 00	50,000 00
Widows' & Orphans', N. Y.,	200,000 00				
	$3,485,000 00	$25,504,599 80	$21,900 00	$489,100 00	$535,637 00
CASUALTY INS. COMPANIES OF THE STATE OF NEW YORK.					
Fidelity, New York,	$100,000 00				
Nat. Travelers', N. Y.,	200,000 00				
U. S. Accident, Syracuse,	200,000 00				$51,200 00
	$500,000 00				$51,200 00

FIRE AND FIRE MARINE INSURANCE COMPANIES OF OTHER STATES.	Capital.	Gross assets.	Amount of real estate.	Amount of stock taxable, deducting real estate.	Total valuation.
Ætna, Hartford, Conn.,	$3,000,000 00				
American, Boston, Mass.,	300,000 00				
American, Provid'e, R. I.,	150,000 00				
American Fire, Pa., Penn.,	400,000 00				
Atlantic Fire and Marine, Providence, R. I.,	200,000 00				
City Fire, Hartford, Conn.,	250,000 00				
Cleveland, Cleveland, O.,	150,000 00				
Conn. Fire, Hartf'd, Conn.,	200,000 00				
Commerc'l Mut., Cleve., O.,		$277,664 19			
Eliot Fire, Boston, Mass.,	200,000 00				
Ent'prise Fire & M., Cin. O.,	200,000 00				
Equit'ble F. & M., Prov. R.I,	200,000 00				
Franklin Fire, Pa., Penn.,	400,000 00				
Girard Elect'l, Gir'd, Penn.,	50,000 00				
Girard F. & M., Pa., Penn.,	200,000 00				
Hartf'd Fire, Hartf., Conn.,	1,000,000 00				
Home, New Haven, Conn.,	1,000,000 00				
Hope, Providence, R. I.,	150,000 00				
Ins. Co. of State of Penn., Philadelphia, Penn.,	200,000 00				
Manufact'rs, Bost'n, Mass.,	400,000 00				
Maryl'd Fire, Baltim., Md.,	200,000 00				
Merchants', Boston, Mass.,	500,000 00				
Merchants', Chicago, Ill.,	432,200 00				
Merchants', Hartf'd, Conn.,	200,000 00				
Merchants', Provid., R. I.,	200,000 00				
Narragansett Fire and Marine, Providence, R. I.,	328,490 00				
National, Boston, Mass.,	300,000 00				
North American Fire, Boston, Mass.,	200,000 00				
North Amer'n Fire, Hartford, Conn.,	300,000 00				
Norw'h Fire, Norw. Conn.,	300,000 00				
New England Mut. Marine, Boston, Mass.,	200,000 00				
Peopl's' Fire, Worc'r, Mass.	200,000 00				
Phœnix, Hartford, Conn.,	600,000 00				
Pres. & Direct's', Pa. Penn.,	500,000 00				
Prov. Wash'ton, Prov. R.I.,	200,000 00				
Putnam Fire, Hart., Conn.,	500,000 00				
Roger Williams, Prov. R.I.,	100,000 00				
Amount carried forward,	$13,910,690 00	$277,664 19	$	$	$

Insurance Companies—(Continued).

FIRE & FIRE MARINE INSURANCE CO'S OF OTHER STATES.	Capital.	Gross assets.	Assessed Valuation. Amount of real estate.	Amount of stock taxable, deducting real estate.	Total valuation.
Amount brought forward.	$13,910,690 00	$277,664 19	$	$	$
Springfield Fire & Marine, Springfield, Mass..	500,000 00	....	....	....	....
Sun, Cleveland, Ohio,	200,000 00	....	....	....	....
	$14,610,690 00	$277,664 19	....	....	....
MARINE INS. COMPANIES OF OTHER STATES.					
Pacific. S. Francisco, Cal.,	$750,000 00	....	....	....	....
Nation'l, S. Francisco, Cal.,	1,000,000 00	....	....	....	....
	$1,750,000 00	....	....	....	....
LIFE INS. CO'S OF OTHER STATES.					
Ætna, Hartford, Conn.,	$60,600 00	....	....	....	....
Berkshire, Pittsfi'd, Mass.,	53,000 00	....	....	....	....
Char. Oak, Hartf'd, Conn.,	100,000 00	....	....	....	....
Conn. Gen., Hartf'd, Conn.,	251,000 00	....	....	....	....
Conn. Mut., Hartf'd, Conn.,	....	$13,316,275 97	....	....	....
Economical Mutual, Providence, R. I.,	100,000 00	....	....	....	....
Hahnemann, Clevel'd, O.,	200,000 00	....	....	....	....
John Hancock, Bos. Mass.,	100,000 00	....	....	....	....
Mass. Mut. Spr'gfi'd, Mass.,	100,000 00	....	....	....	....
Mut. Benefit, Newark, N. J.	....	11,656,728 74	....	....	....
National, Montpelier, Vt.,	25,000 00	....	....	....	....
N. Eng. Mut., Bos., Mass.,	....	5,067,382 84	....	....	....
N. J. Mut., Newark, N. J.,	100,000 00	....	....	....	....
Phœnix Mutual, Hartford, Conn.,	16,000 00	....	....	....	....
Union Mut., Augusta, Me.,	....	2,088,429 20	....	....	....
	$1,105,600 00	$32,128,816 75	....	....	....
CASUALTY INS. CO'S OF OTHER STATES.					
Hartford Accident, Hartford, Conn.,	$125,100 00	....	....	....	....
Hartford Life Stock, Hartford, Conn.,	105,000 00	....	....	....	....
Railway Passengers', Hartford, Conn.,	218,000 00	....	....	....	....
Travelers', Hartf'd, Conn.,	500,000 00	....	....	....	....
Travelers', Provid'ce, R. I.,	106,000 00	....	....	....	....
U. S. Casualty, Trent. N. J.,	100,000 00	....	....	....	....
	$1,154,100 00	....	....	....	....
FOREIGN FIRE INS. CO'S.					
Liverpool and London and Globe, Liverpool, Engl'd,	$1,896,079 68	....	....	....	....
American Branch of same,	....	$1,831,811 45	....	$251,138 00	$251,138 00
North British and Mercantile, London, England,	1,210,000 00	....	....	....	
American Branch,	....	9,444 74	....	....	
Queen, Liverpool, Engl'd,	916,318 48	....	....	....	
United States' Branch,	....	255,610 51	....	....	
Royal, Liverpool, England,	1,395,589 80	....	....	....	
	$5,417,987 96	$2,096,866 70	....	$251,138 00	$251,138 00
FOREIGN LIFE INS. CO'S.					
British Commercial, London, England,	....	....	....	....	....
American Br. of, N. Y. city,	....	$227,735 04	....	$50,000 00	$50,000 00
Intern'l Life, Lond'n, Eng.,	....	....	....	83,500 00	83,500 00
Liverpool and London and Globe, Liverpool, Engl'd,	$1,896,079 68	....	....	....	....
American Br. of, N. Y. city,	....	2,642 72	....	....	....
Royal, Liverpool, England,	1,395,589 80	....	....	....	....
American Br. of, N. Y. city,	....	526,193 49	....	*10,000 00	10,000 00
	$3,291,669 48	$756,571 25	....	$143,500 00	$143,500 00

In the foregoing table the gross assets are given where there is no Capital.
* Assessed to "Royal Life and Fire."

12

GAS LIGHT COMPANIES.

COMPANIES.	Capital stock paid in.	Assessed Valuation. Amount of real estate.	Amount of stock taxable deducting real estate.	Total valuation.
Abbottsford, Hastings, ...	$30,000 00	....	....	....
Albany, ...	250,000 00	$123,850 00	$95,500 00	$219,350 00
Albion, ...	15,000 00	2,000 00	13,000 00	15,000 00
Astoria, ...	14,950 00	....	....	....
Auburn, ...	60,000 00	....	....	....
Ballston Spa, ...	....	2,000 00	....	2,000 00
Batavia, ...	32,500 00	5,000 00	20,000 00	25,000 00
Bath, Steuben county, ...	15,000 00	2,000 00	5,000 00	7,000 00
Binghamton, ...	50,000 00	400 00	30,000 00	30,400 00
Brockport, ...	15,000 00	500 00	....	500 00
Brooklyn, ...	1,500,000 00	338,800 00	1,159,500 00	1,498,300 00
Buffalo, ...	600,000 00	52,780 00	547,220 00	600,000 00
Canandaigua, ...	50,000 00	6,240 00	26,000 00	32,240 00
Chuctanunda, Amsterdam, ..	18,000 00	....	....	....
Citizens, Brooklyn, L. I., ...	1,200,000 00	214,800 00	785,200 00	1,000,000 00
Clyde, ...	10,000 00	....	4,000 00	4,000 00
Cohoes, ...	50,000 00	30,000 00	....	30,000 00
College Point, Flushing, L. I.,	10,000 00	....	....	....
Cold Spring, ...	30,000 00	4,000 00	....	4,000 00
Corning,*	9,000 00	2,000 00	....	2,000 00
Dansville, ...	....	3,000 00	....	3,000 00
East Albany, ...	....	5,000 00	....	5,000 00
Elmira, ...	50,000 00	6,000 00	47,500 00	53,500 00
Fishkill, ...	10,000 00	1,500 00	....	1,500 00
Flushing, ...	20,500 00	15,000 00	....	15,000 00
Fredonia, ...	10,000 00	2,400 00	....	2,400 00
Fulton, ...	15,900 00	....	....	....
Geneva, ...	36,250 00	9,800 00	10,000 00	19,800 00
Geneseo, ...	....	1,000 00	3,500 00	4,500 00
Glens Falls, ...	35,000 00	5,400 00	....	5,400 00
Greenpoint, ...	80,000 00	11,825 00	67,625 00	79,450 00
Harlem, ...	1,000,000 00	125,000 00	524,247 00	649,247 00
Hempstead, ...	17,100 00	....	8,000 00	8,000 00
Homer & Cortland, Cortland,	40,000 00	2,000 00	4,000 00	6,000 00
Hornellsville, ...	20,000 00	2,000 00	....	2,000 00
Hudson,*	50,000 00	10,000 00	40,000 00	50,000 00
Ithaca, ...	72,500 00	35,000 00	....	35,000 00
Jamaica,*	20,000 00	....	10,000 00	10,000 00
Jamestown, ...	27,300 00	2,000 00	....	2,000 00
Johnstown, ...	17,650 00	....	....	....
Lansingburgh, ...	9,000 00	....	....	....
Leroy, ...	20,000 00	6,000 00	....	6,000 00
Little Falls, ...	20,000 00	....	....	....
Lockport, ...	40,000 00	....	17,000 00	17,000 00
Lyons, ...	12,800 00	....	6,500 00	6,500 00
Manhattan, New York city, ..	4,000,000 00	1,785,300 00	2,214,700 00	4,000,000 00
Metropolitan, ...	2,500,000 00	296,260 00	1,003,740 00	1,300,000 00
Mohawk, ...	....	300 00	....	300 00
Newburgh, ...	70,000 00	6,000 00	65,000 00	71,000 00
New York, ...	1,000,000 00	834,000 00	487,374 00	1,321,374 00
Niagara Falls, ...	25,275 00	5,250 00	11,000 00	16,250 00
Norwich, ...	12,000 00	....	....	....
Nyack, ...	14,000 00	....	....	....
Ogdensburgh, ...	75,000 00	18,000 00	....	18,000 00
Oswego, ...	81,250 00	....	....	81,250 00
Owego, ...	30,900 00	7,000 00	13,000 00	20,000 00
Palmyra,*	12,000 00	1,800 00	....	1,800 00
Peekskill, ...	31,000 00	2,000 00	18,000 00	20,000 00
Penn Yan, ...	11,000 00	....	....	....
Peoples, Hunter's Point,*	100,000 00	....	....	....
Plattsburgh, ...	16,000 00	....	....	....
Portchester,*	25,000 00	....	....	....
Port Jervis,*	20,000 00	10,000 00	....	10,000 00
Poughkeepsie, ...	84,000 00	....	84,000 00	84,000 00
Richmond County, S. I.,*	150,000 00	....	....	....
Rochester, ...	300,000 00	81,200 00	151,000 00	232,200 00
Rome, ...	35,000 00	12,500 00	....	12,500 00
Rondout & Kingston, Rond't,	65,000 00	10,000 00	....	10,000 00
Amount carried forward, .	$14,240,875 00	$4,096,905 00	$7,471,606 00	$11,649,761 00

Gas Light Companies — (Continued).

COMPANIES.	Capital stock paid in	ASSESSED VALUATION.		
		Amount of real estate	Amount of stock taxable, deducting real estate.	Total valuation.
Amount brought forward, ..	$14,240,875 00	$4,096,905 00	$7,471,606 00	$11,649,761 00
Sag Harbor, ...	10,000 00	....	....	....
Saratoga Springs, ...	75,000 00	300 00	40,000 00	40,300 00
Saugerties,*	16,000 00	....	....	....
Schenectady, ...	20,000 00	....	....	....
Seneca Falls, ...	80,000 00	....	....	....
Sing Sing, ...	22,500 00	....	....	....
Syracuse, ...	200,000 00	....	....	215,300 00
Tarryt'n & Irv'gton, Tarryt'n,	70,000 00	....	....	....
Troy, ...	200,000 00	102,300 00	100,000 00	202,300 00
Union, East New York, ...	50,000 00	2,160 00	....	2,160 00
Utica, ...	80,000 00	6,900 00	....	6,900 00
Warren, Haverstraw, ...	12,000 00	....	....	....
Waterford, ...	12,000 00	12,000 00	....	12,000 00
Watertown, ...	20,000 00	3,500 00	16,500 00	20,000 00
Westchester county, ...	130,000 00	....	....	....
West Troy, ...	30,000 00	....	....	....
White Plains, ...	11,600 00	....	....	....
Whitehall,*	20,000 00	2,000 00	5,000 00	7,000 00
Williamsburgh, ...	750,000 00	178,800 00	571,200 00	750,000 00
Yonkers, ...	126,092 50	....	....	76,200 00
	$16,176,067 50	$4,404,865 00	$8,204,306 00	$12,981,921 00

* These companies neglected to report to the Inspector of Gas Meters.

RAILROAD COMPANIES.

COMPANIES.	Capital stock paid in.	ASSESSED VALUATION.		
		Amount of real estate.	Amount of stock taxable, deducting real estate.	Total valuation.
Adirondack Company, ...	$4,183,000 00	$50,250 00	....	$50,250 00
Albany Railway, ...	89,850 00	5,000 00	$39,393 00	44,393 00
Albany & Susquehanna, ...	1,675,138 70	332,249 00	4,114 00	336,363 00
Albany & Vermont, ...	600,000 00	17,700 00	....	17,700 00
Albany & West Stockbridge,	1,000,000 00	1,232,376 00	....	1,232,376 00
A. & G. W. in N. Y. (1865), ..	919,265 02	213,140 00	....	413,400 00
Avon, Geneseo & Mt. Morris,	194,250 00	62,500 00	....	62,500 00
Bleecker St. & Fulton Ferry,	900.000 00	110,000 00	90,000 00	200,000 00
Blossburgh & Corning (1865),	250,000 00	170,870 00	....	170,870 00
Boston, Hartford & Erie, ...	....	33,900 00	....	33,900 00
Broadway R. R. of Brooklyn,	200,000 00	25,400 00	144,604 00	170,004 00
Broadway & Seventh Av., ...	2,100,000 00	358,665 00	141,335 00	500,000 00
Brooklyn, Bath & Coney Is., .	99,850 00	26,500 00	6,000 00	32,500 00
Brooklyn & Jamaica, ...	488,100 00	55,485 00	122,046 00	177,531 00
Brooklyn City, ...	1,000,000 00	200,500 00	607,436 00	807,936 00
Brooklyn City & Newtown, ..	399,800 00	....	109,287 00	109,287 00
B'lyn City & Ridgew'd (1865),	164,000 00	....	....	....
B'lyn City & Rockaway (1864),	12,000 00	....	....	....
Brooklyn & Rockaway Beach,	102,150 00	10,000 00	....	10,000 00
Brooklyn, East New York & Rockaway (1864), ...	5,000 00	....	....	....
Buffalo & Allegany Val. (1864),	16,000 00	....	....	....
Buffalo, Bradford & P'burgh,	1,100,000 00	....	....	20,000 00
Buffalo & Lake Huron.	....	44,060 00	....	44,060 00
Buffalo, N. Y & Erie (1863), .	850,000 00	370,375 00	....	370,375 00
Buffalo & State Line, ...	2,200,000 00	1,162,475 00	....	1,162,475 00
Buffalo & Wash. Railway, ...	59,500 00	....	....	....
Buffalo & Oil Cr'k Cross Cut,	344,500 00	1,134 00	....	1,134 00
Amount carried forward, .	$18,952,403 72	$4,482,579 00	$1,264,215 00	$5,967,054 00

Railroad Companies — (Continued).

COMPANIES.	Capital stock paid in.	ASSESSED VALUATION.		
		Amount of real estate.	Amount of stock taxable, deducting real estate.	Total valuation.
Amount brought forward,	$18,952,403 72	$4,482,579 00	$1,264,215 00	$5,967,054 00
Buffalo St. R. R. Co.,	....	5,820 00	20,000 00	25,820 00
Canarsie, Brooklyn & Winfield (1864),	15,000 00	13,000 00	....	13,000 00
Cayuga & Susquehanna,	589,110 00	....	....	....
Central City R R. Co., Syr.,	....	....	....	25,600 00
Central Park, N. & E. River,	970,000 00	142,155 00	227,086 00	369,241 00
Champlain & St. Lawrence,	....	6,150 00	....	6,150 00
Chemung,	380,000 00	81,000 00	....	81,000 00
Chenango Valley R. R. Co.,	....	....	....	....
Cohoes & Waterford, (1865),	500 00	....	....	....
Coney Island & Brooklyn,	500,000 50	45,250 00	363,119 00	408,369 00
Corning & Seneca Lake,	6,000 00	....	....	....
Del., Lack. & W. R. R. Co.,	....	206,800 00	58,000 00	264,800 00
Dry Dock, E. B'dway & Bat.,	1,200,000 00	209,504 00	100,000 00	309,504 00
East & North River,	650 00	....	....	....
E. N. Y. & Jamaica R. R. Co.	....	30,000 00	....	30,000 00
Eighth Avenue,	1,000,000 00	375,630 00	289,000 00	664,630 00
Elmira, Jefferson & Canandaigua (1862),	500,000 00	....	....	....
Elmira & W'msport (1865),	1,000,000 00	230,690 00	....	230,690 00
Erie & N. Y. City (1863),	352,064 85	....	....	....
Erie Railway,	25,105,800 00	4,422,508 00	....	5,404,605 00
Flushing & Woodside R. R.,	....	1,000 00	....	1,000 00
42d St. & Grand St. F'y (1865),	750,000 00	300,000 00	142,000 00	442,000 00
Gen. & W. St. R. R. Co., Syr.,	42,500 00	....	....	8,000 00
Grand St. & Newtown,	....	....	67,400 00	67,400 00
Har. B'ge, Morris'ia & Fd'm,	90,000 00	....	....	....
Harlem River & Tarrytown,	3,550 00	....	....	....
Hicksville & Cold Spring,	....	12,000 00	....	12,000 00
Hudson & Boston,	175,000 00	332,300 00	....	332,300 00
Hudson River,	6,962,971 45	3,135,205 95	90,000 00	3,363,205 95
L. Ontario, Aub. & N. Y. ('64),	77,855 86	....	....	....
Long Island,	1,852,715 00	317,048 00	....	317,048 00
Maine & Ohio St., Buffalo,	....	....	....	....
New York Central,	24,801,000 00	9,566,519 00	....	11,034,566 00
New York & Flushing,	200,000 00	55,600 00	....	55,600 00
New York & Harlem,	6,785,050 00	908,728 00	50,000 00	1,049,588 00
New York & New Haven,	3,982,614 33	148,500 00	....	354,250 00
N. Y., Housatonic & North'n,	110,820 00	....	....	....
N. Y. Northern Central (1865),	2,520 00	....	....	....
Niag. B'ge & Canandaigua ('62),	1,000,000 00	103,000 00	700 00	103,700 00
Niagara St., Buffalo,	80,000 00	....	67,675 00	67,675 00
Ninth Avenue,	797,320 00	432,695 00	252,625 00	685,320 00
Northern of New Jersey,	158,800 00	15,000 00	....	15,000 00
North Shore,	192,945 00	7,000 00	....	7,000 00
Ogdensb'h & L. Champlain,	2,797,000 00	796,058 00	....	796,058 00
Oswego & Rome,	222,987 00	....	....	137,000 00
Oswego & Syracuse,	482,400 00	....	....	422,070 00
Pt Morris & Westch'r (1865),	1,200 00	....	....	....
Plattsburgh & Montreal,	....	57,750 00	....	57,750 00
Rensselaer & Saratoga,	800,000 00	805,029 00	400 00	805,429 00
Rochester City & Brighton,	133,400 00	10,000 00	5,000 00	15,000 00
Rochester & Genesee Valley,	557,560 00	170,925 00	....	170,925 00
Rome, Watert'n & Ogdensb'h,	2,385,500 00	799,227 00	....	913,207 00
Rutland & Wash. R. R. Co.,	....	67,000 00	....	67,000 00
Sac. Har., Rome & N. Y. ('61),	30,889 57	....	....	....
Saratoga & Hud. River ('65),	1,020,000 00	40,475 00	....	40,475 00
Saratoga & Schenectady,	300,000 00	116,000 00	....	116,000 00
Saratoga & Whitehall,	500,000 00	125,000 00	....	125,000 00
Schenectady & Utica,	11,600 00	....	....	....
Second Avenue,	670,000 00	....	....	....
Sixth Avenue,	750,000 00	544,647 00	205,352 00	749,999 00
S. Br'klyn & Berg'n St. R. R. Co.,	....	1,000 00	20,800 00	21,800 00
Sodus Point & Southern, ('63),	31,585 76	....	....	....
South Side Railroad Co.,	....	5,000 00	....	5,000 00
Southern Central,	10,640 00	....	....	....
Amount carried forward,	$109,151,952 52	$29,123,792 95	$3,223,372 00	$36,160,828 95

Railroad Companies — (Continued).

COMPANIES.	Capital stock paid in.	Assessed Valuation.		
		Amount of real estate.	Amount of stock taxable, deducting real estate.	Total valuation.
Amount brought forward,	$109,151,952 52	$29,123,792 95	$3,223,372 00	$36,160,828 95
Staten Island,	660,000 00	24,800 00	100,000 00	*124,800 00
Staten Island Shore (1864),	5,500 00	1,500 00	1,500 00	†3,000 00
Sterling Mountain Railway,	80,000 00	14,000 00	....	14,000 00
Syracuse, Bingamton & N.Y.,	1,200,130 00	270,500 00	....	473,100 00
Syracuse & Geddes,	25,000 00	....	....	17,000 00
Syracuse & Onondaga,	31,000 00	....	....	8,900 00
TenthAv. & G'd St.Ferry('63),	1,420 00	....	....	....
Third Avenue,	1,170,000 00	452,096 00	317,904 00	770,000 00
Third Av. & Fordham (1865),	975 00	....	....	....
Troy & Bennington (1864),	75,400 00	25,000 00	....	25,000 00
Troy & Boston (1865),	607,111 22	299,140 00	....	299,140 00
Troy & Cohoes,	50,000 00	9,000 00	....	9,000 00
Troy & Greenbush,	274,400 00	156,800 00	....	156,800 00
Troy & Lansingburgh,	250,000 00	15,000 00	29,560 00	44,560 00
Troy & Rutland (1864),	325,000 00	30,000 00	....	30,000 00
Troy Union,	30,000 00	30,000 00	....	30,000 00
Utica & Black River,	811,600 00	48,100 00	5,000 00	53,100 00
Utica, Chenango & Sus. Val.,	146,470 00	....	....	....
Utica & Waterville,	124,500 00	....	....	....
Van Brunt St. & Erie Basin,	50,000 00	3,800 00	10,000 00	13,800 00
Warwick Valley,	98,650 00	33,000 00	....	33,000 00
Watervliet T'pike & R. R. Co.	240,000 00	4,500 00	30,172 00	34,672 00
Westchester (1865),	7,370 00	....	....	....
West Shore (1865),	2,200 00	....	....	....
W'burgh & Coney Isl. (1864),	15,000 00	....	....	....
W'towm, Redfield & Forrest,	....	....	....	6,000 00
	$115,433,678 74	$30,541,028 95	$3,717,508 00	$38,306,700 95

* Staten Island Railroad and Ferry Co. † Staten Island Railroad Co.

The year immediately after the name of the company indicates the last official report to the State Engineer's office.

EXPRESS COMPANIES.

COMPANIES.	Amount of real estate.	Amount of stock taxable, deducting real estate.	Total valuation.
Adams,	....	$100,000 00	$100,000 00
American,	$37,400 00	65,000 00	105,400 00
Harndens,	....	5,000 00	5,000 00
Kinsley & Co.,	....	4,000 00	4,000 00
Merchants' Union,	13,000 00	....	13,000 00
National,	....	25,000 00	25,000 00
United States,	4,500 00	51,000 00	57,500 00
Wells, Fargo & Co.,	....	25,000 00	25,000 00
Westcott & Co.,	....	20,000 00	20,000 00
	$54,900 00	$295,000 00	$354,900 00

NAVIGATION COMPANIES.

COMPANIES.	Assessed Valuation.		
	Amount of real estate.	Amount of stock taxable, deducting real estate.	Total valuation.
American and Mexican Mail St'm'p Co.	....	$90,000 00	$90,000 00
Atlantic Coast Mail Steamship Co.,	....	525,000 00	525,000 00
Atlantic Coast Wrecking Co.,	....	15,800 00	15,800 00
Atlantic Navigation Co.,	....	100,000 00	100,000 00
Columbian Wrecking Co	....	87,916 00	87,916 00
Harlem and New York Navigation Co.,	....	55,000 00	55,000 00
New York and Havre Steamship Co.,	....	300,000 00	300,000 00
New York Mail Steamship Co.,	....	532,131 00	532,131 00
N. Y., Nuevitas & Cuba Steamship Co.,	....	110,000 00	110,000 00
New York & Virginia Steamship Co.,	....	250,000 00	250,000 00
New York & Washington Steams'p Co.,	....	110,800 00	110,800 00
North American Lloyd Steamship Co.,	....	600,000 00	600,000 00
Pacific Mail Steamship Co.,	....	3,500,000 00	3,500,000 00
U. S. Brazil Steamship Co.,	....	1,700,000 00	1,700,000 00
	....	$7,976,647 00	$7,976,647 00

MISCELLANEOUS COMPANIES.

COMPANIES.	Amount of real estate.	Amount of stock taxable, deducting real estate.	Total valuation.
Albany County.			
Albany Exchange Company,	$100,000 00	....	$100,000 00
Bailey Manufacturing Co. (now Troy Co.),	30,000 00	....	30,000 00
Clifton Company,	45,000 00	....	45,000 00
Coeymans Plankroad Company,	7,500 00	....	7,500 00
Cohoes Company,	155,750 00	....	155,750 00
Cohoes Water Works,	2,000 00	....	2,000 00
New York & Albany Propeller Line,	....	$40,000 00	40,000 00
Schuyler's Line of Steam Tow-Boats,	....	100,000 00	100,000 00
Swifture Line of Barges,	....	55,000 00	55,000 00
The Harmony Mills Company,	522,246 00	....	522,246 00
Union Turnpike Company (Coeymans),	2,000 00	....	2,000 00
	$864,496 00	$195,000 00	$1,059,496 00
Broome County.			
Barker & Lisle Bridge Company,	$2,700 00	....	$2,700 00
Centreville " "	900 00	....	900 00
Colesville " "	400 00	....	400 00
Conklin " "	600 00	....	600 00
Rock Bottom " "	2,000 00	....	2,000 00
Susquehanna " "	5,000 00	....	5,000 00
Union Paper Mill Company,	5,800 00	....	5,800 00
	$17,400 00	....	$17,400 00
Chautauqua County.			
Fair Ground Corporation,	$220 00	....	$220 00
Chemung County.			
Elmira Main Street Bridge Company,	$2,000 00	....	$2,000 00
" Rolling Mill Company,	80,000 00	....	80,000 00
" & Southport Bridge Company,	3,500 00	....	3,500 00
" Umbrella Company,	7,000 00	$6,000 00	13,000 00
" Water Company,	15,200 00	....	15,200 00
" Woolen Manufacturing Company,	18,612 00	28,041 00	46,653 00
Horseheads Building Association,	3,500 00	....	3,500 00
Junction Canal Company,	30,000 00	....	30,000 00
Lumberman's Bridge Company,	3,000 00	....	3,000 00
Towanda Coal Company,	6,000 00	2,000 00	8,000 00
	$168,812 00	$36,041 00	$204,853 00

Miscellaneous Companies — (Continued).

COMPANIES.	Assessed Valuation.		
	Amount of real estate.	Amount of stock taxable, deducting real estate.	Total valuation.
Clinton County.			
Ausable Horse-Nail Company,	$10,500 00	$69,500 00	$80,000 00
Columbia County.			
Catskill & Albany Steamboat Company,	$7,000 00	$80,000 00	$87,000 00
Columbia Co. Agricultural and Horticultural Association,	3,000 00	....	3,000 00
Columbia County Iron Company,	55,000 00	....	55,000 00
Columbia Turnpike Company,	15,300 00	....	15,300 00
Hudson Aqueduct Company,	2,200 00	11,800 00	14,000 00
Hudson Iron Company,	150,000 00	109,839 00	259,839 00
Union Turnpike Company,	3,500 00	....	3,500 00
	$236,000 00	$201,639 00	$437,639 00
Delaware County.			
Harpersfield Turnpike and Bridge Company,	$50 00	$600 00	$650 00
Sidney Bridge Company,	1,500 00	....	1,500 00
	$1,550 00	$600 00	$2,150 00
Dutchess County.			
Amenia Mining Company,	$12,600 00	....	$12,600 00
Amenia Lead Company,	2,000 00	....	2,000 00
Condensing Milk Factory,	16,000 00	....	16,000 00
Dover Marble Company,	2,000 00	....	2,000 00
Dutchess Company,	84,500 00	$55,000 00	139 500 00
Dutchess County Iron Works,	20,000 00	....	20,000 00
Dutchess Turnpike Company,	17,200 00	....	17,200 00
Fallkill Iron Works,	100,000 00	20,000 00	120,000 00
Fishkill Landing Machine Company,	10,000 00	18,500 00	28,500 00
Fishkill Peat Company,	1,740 00	....	1,740 00
Franklindale Company,	37,950 00	17,300 00	55,250 00
Glenham Company,	60,000 00	180,000 00	240,000 00
Hudson River Slate Company,	10,255 00	....	10,255 00
Landon Iron Company,	950 00	....	950 00
Manchester Paper Company,	15,000 00	15,000 00	30,000 00
Manhattan Iron Company,	13,725 00	....	13,725 00
Millerton Iron Company,	10,000 00	65,000 00	75,000 00
New York Rubber Company,	28,781 00	153,195 00	181,976 00
Pawling & Beekman Turnpike Company,	2,564 00	....	2,564 00
Peekskill Iron Company,	9,000 00	....	9,000 00
Poughkeepsie Iron Works	75,000 00	15,000 00	90,000 00
Poughkeepsie and New Paltz Ferry Co.,	....	13,000 00	13,000 00
Salt Point Turnpike Company,	1,000 00	....	1,000 00
Schenck Machine Company,	....	27,000 00	27,000 00
Seamless Clothing Company,	10,000 00	46,000 00	56,000 00
	$540,265 00	$624,995 00	$1,165,260 00
Erie County.			
Aurora & Buffalo Plankroad Co.,	$3,000 00	....	$3,000 00
Brayton Nut Manufacturing Co.,	1,340 00	....	1,340 00
Buffalo Agricultural Machine Works,	....	$40,000 00	40,000 00
Buffalo Elevating and Storing Co.,	16,000 00	....	16,000 00
Buffalo General Hospital,	180 00	....	180 00
Buffalo & Hamburg Turnpike Co.,	1,200 00	....	1,200 00
Buffalo Iron and Nail Co.,	136,370 00	....	136,370 00
Buffalo Scale Works Co.,	....	15,000 00	15,000 00
Buffalo & Toledo Transportation Co.,	....	100,000 00	100,000 00
Buffalo Water Works Co.,	66,150 00	433,850 00	500,000 00
	$224,240 00	$588,850 00	$813,090 00
Essex County.			
Adirondack Iron and Steel Co.,	$13,760 00	....	$13,760 00
American Graphite Co.,	15,000 00	....	15,000 00
Amount carried forward,	$28,760 00	$	$28,760 00

Miscellaneous Companies — (Continued).

COMPANIES.	ASSESSED VALUATION. Amount of real estate.	Amount of stock taxable, deducting real estate.	Total valuation.
Essex Co. (continued), brought forward,...	$28,760 00	$	$28,760 00
Barton Hill Ore Bed Co, ...	12,400 00	....	12,400 00
Cheever Ore Bed Co.,..........................	200,100 00	....	200,100 00
Crown Point Iron Co.,.........................	19,164 00	....	19,164 00
Essex & Lake Champlain Ore & Iron Co.,....	41,203 00	....	41,203 00
Fisher Iron Co.,..............................	21,000 00	....	21,000 00
Lake Champlain Iron Ore and Furnace, ...	12,000 00	....	12,000 00
Lake Champlain Mining Co.,..................	25,000 00	....	25,000 00
Port Henry Furnaces,.........................	150,025 00	....	150,025 00
Port Henry Iron Ore Co., ...	211,150 00	....	211,150 00
Port Henry Marble Co.,..............	200 00	....	200 00
Ticonderoga Iron Co.,.........................	22,800 00	....	22,800 00
Vulcan Furnace Co., ...	2,200 00	....	2,200 00
	$746,002 00	....	$746,002 00
FRANKLIN COUNTY.			
The Malone Sandstone Co.,............	$400 00	....	$400 00
The Malone Water Works Co., ...	1,000 00	$11,500 00	12,500 00
	$1,400 00	$11,500 00	$12,900 00
GENESEE COUNTY.			
Batavia Peat Co., ...	$1,500 00	....	$1,500 00
GREENE COUNTY.			
Catskill Bridge Co.,.................	....	$5,000 00	$5,000 00
Catskill Steam Transportation Co., ...	....	20,000 00	20,000 00
Maleable Iron Co., ...	$4,000 00	....	*4,000 00
Waterville Manufacturing Co., ...	45,000 00	35,000 00	80,000 00
	$49,000 00	$60,000 00	$109,000 00
HERKIMER COUNTY.			
Ilion Agricultural Works,....	$50,000 00	$50,000 00	$100,000 00
Ilion Protection Store,.....	....	800 00	800 00
Mohawk and Newport Plankroad,........	....	1,500 00	1,500 00
Newport and Herkimer Plankroad Company,	400 00	....	400 00
Utica Water Works Company, ...	1,100 00	....	1,100 00
	$51,500 00	$52,300 00	$103,800 00
JEFFERSON COUNTY.			
Jefferson County Leather Company,........ ..	....	....	$3,300 00
Portable Steam Engine Company,............	$19,500 00	....	19,500 00
Remington Paper Mill Company, ...	18,000 00	....	18,000 00
Watertown Paper Company, ...	6,500 00	....	6,500 00
Watertown River Park Association, ...	2,000 00	....	2,000 00
Watertown and Rutland Plankroad Company,	1,000 00	....	1,000 00
Watertown and Watertown Centre P. R. Co.,	500 00	....	500 00
	$47,500 00	....	$50,800 00
KINGS COUNTY.			
Academy of Music,...........................	$125,000 00	....	$125,000 00
American Oil Company,...................... ...	700 00	....	700 00
American Water Proof Cloth Company,......	9,800 00	$140,200 00	150,000 00
Atlantic Dock Company,......................	1,091,050 00	....	1,091,050 00
Atlantic White Lead Company, ...	92,300 00	....	92,300 00
Brooklyn Athæneum, ...	25,000 00	....	25,000 00
Brooklyn Arms Company, ...	....	104,500 00	104,500 00
Brooklyn Art Association,....................	8,000 00	....	8,000 00
Brooklyn Brass and Copper Company, ...	43,850 00	....	43,850 00
Brooklyn Club.................................	30,000 00	....	30,000 00
Brooklyn Dye Wood Company, ...	10,600 00	....	10,600 00
Brooklyn Ferry Company,....................	219,000 00	....	219,000 00
Brooklyn and Gowanus Toll Bridge Company,	900 00	....	900 00
Amount carried forward, ...	$1,656,200 00	$244,700 00	$1,900,900 00

* Not taxed.

Miscellaneous Companies — (Continued).

COMPANIES.	ASSESSED VALUATION.		
	Amount of real estate.	Amount of stock taxable, deducting real estate.	Total valuation.
Kings Co. (continued), brought forward, ..	$1,656,200 00	$244,700 00	$1,900,900 00
Brooklyn Manufacturing Company, ...	10,000 00	....	10,000 00
City Bank of New Haven, ...	31,200 00	....	31,200 00
Connecticut Banking Company, ...	650 00	....	650 00
Coney Island Shell Road Company	5,000 00	....	5,000 00
Coney Island Turnpike and Bridge Company,	500 00	....	500 00
Empire Building Association, ...	4,800 00	....	4,800 00
Erie Dock Basin Company, ...	10,000 00	....	10,000 00
Franklin Building Association, ...	8,650 00	....	8,650 00
Home Building Company, ...	18,100 00	....	18,100 00
Hudson Ave. and Jackson St. Ferry Co., ...	2,000 00	....	2,000 00
La Fayette Flint Glass Company, ...	4,300 00	....	4,300 00
Manhattan Building Association, ...	1,600 00	....	1,600 00
Mercantile Library Association, ...	12,000 00	....	12,000 00
Merchants Bank of New Haven, ...	25,350 00	....	25,350 00
Nassau Building Association, ...	8,000 00	....	8,000 00
National Arms Co., ...	22,300 00	162,583 00	184,883 00
New Haven Savings Bank, ...	19,550 00	....	19,550 00
New Haven County National Bank, ...	39,125 00	....	39,125 00
New York Building Association, ...	2,600 00	....	2,600 00
New York Warehousing Co., ...	58,000 00	....	58,000 00
North American Trust and Banking Co., ...	600 00	....	600 00
Phœnix Bank of New Haven, ...	17,700 00	....	17,700 00
Phœnix Bank of Hartford, ...	19,150 00	....	19,150 00
Phœnix Oil and Candle Co., ...	24,000 00	....	24,000 00
Second Mechanics' Building Association, ...	2,800 00	....	2,800 00
South Brooklyn Land Association, ...	125 00	....	125 00
Union Ferry Co., ...	360,500 00	314,000 00	674,500 00
Union White Lead Co., ...	45,400 00	....	45,400 00
	$2,410,200 00	$721,283 00	$3,131,483 00
LEWIS COUNTY.			
Martinsburgh Mining Co., ...	....	....	$1,000 00
Port Leyden Iron Co., ...	....	....	10,000 00
Rochester Mining Co., ...	....	....	1,000 00
	....	....	$12,000 00
MONROE COUNTY.			
American Concentrated Malt Co., ...	....	$5,000 00	$5,000 00
East Avenue Plankroad Co., ...	$4,500 00	....	4,500 00
Mech. & Manuf'rers Bank of Rhode Island, ..	1,500 00	....	1,500 00
Osborne Hotel Co., ...	3,500 00	....	3,500 00
Rochester Paper Co., ...	....	23,500 00	23,500 00
Rochester Brick and File Co., ...	20,790 00	....	20,790 00
Rochester and Pittsford Plankroad Co., ...	5,000 00	....	5,000 00
Rochester Transportation Co., ...	500 00	....	500 00
	$35,790 00	$28,500 00	$64,290 00
MONTGOMERY COUNTY.			
Canajoharie Water Works, ...	$335 00	$1,200 00	$1,535 00
St. Johnsville Bridge Co., ...	3 000 00	....	3,000 00
	$3,335 00	$1,200 00	$4,535 00
NEW YORK COUNTY.			
American Agricultural Works, ...	....	$60,000 00	$60,000 00
American Bank Note Co., ...	....	115,000 00	115,000 00
American Bell Co., ...	....	20,000 00	20,000 00
American Coal Co., ...	....	500 00	500 00
American Metre Co., ...	....	175,000 00	175,000 00
American Telegraph Co., ...	....	10,000 00	10,000 00
American Umbrella Frame Co., ...	....	100,000 00	100,000 00
Architectural Iron Works, ...	$176,900 00	27,100 00	204,000 00
Astor Gold and Silver Co., ...	....	1,913 00	1,913 00
Amount carried forward, ...	$176,900 00	$509,513 00	$686,413 00

Miscellaneous Companies — (Continued).

COMPANIES.	Assessed Valuation.		
	Amount of real estate.	Amount of stock taxable, deducting real estate.	Total valuation.
New York Co. (continued), br't forward, ..	$176,900 00	$509,513 00	$686,413 00
Berdan Fire Arms Manufacturing Co.,	....	500 00	500 00
Bergen Oil and Coal Co.,	....	450 00	450 00
Bishop Gutta Percha Co.,	....	10,000 00	10,000 00
Black Heath Coal Co.,	....	500 00	500 00
Burroughs' Gold Co.,	....	5,416 00	5,416 00
Cataract Washing Machine Co.,	....	700 00	700 00
Central Coal Mining and Manufacturing Co.,	....	500 00	500 00
Central Gold Mining Co.,	....	150,000 00	150,000 00
Clark Patent Steam and Fire Regulating Co.,	....	3,500 00	3,500 00
Continental Bank Note Co.,	....	23,225 00	23,225 00
Consolidated Coal Co.,	....	2,000 00	2,000 00
Consolidation Coal Co.,	....	1,050 00	1,050 00
Croton Manufacturing Co.,	19,900 00	5,100 00	25,000 00
Dolphin Manufacturing Co.,	....	250,000 00	250,000 00
Farmers' Loan and Trust Co.,	....	557,820 00	557,820 00
French Self-Fastening Button Co.,	....	5,000 00	5,000 00
Gerner Furnace Co.,	12,000 00	10,000 00	22,000 00
Globe Copper Co.,	....	1,000 00	1,000 00
Goodenough Horse Shoe Co.,	30,000 00	3,000 00	33,000 00
Gutta Percha and Rubber Co.,	....	190,000 00	190,000 00
Hammond Oil Co.,	....	2,500 00	2,500 00
Locomotive Engine Safety Truck Co.,	....	24,000 00	24,000 00
Lawrence Cement Co.,	....	5,000 00	5,000 00
Mackeral and Richardson Manufacturing Co.,	23,750 00	21,250 00	45,000 00
Madison Silver Co.,	....	500 00	500 00
Magic Ruffle Co.,	....	20,000 00	20,000 00
Mammoth Vein Consolidated Coal Co.,	....	500 00	500 00
Manhattan Iron Co.,	....	50,000 00	50,000 00
Manhattan Oil Co.,	2,000 00	48,000 00	50,000 00
Manhattan Piano Manufacturing Co.,	....	3,000 00	3,000 00
Manhattan Soap Co.,	....	10,000 00	10,000 00
Manley Patent Wheel Co.,	....	20,000 00	20,000 00
Masterton, Smith & Sinclair, Stone Dress. Co.,	87,500 00	12,500 00	100,000 00
Methodist Book Concern,	....	250,000 00	250,000 00
Metropolitan Fire Arms Co.,	....	3,284 00	3,284 00
Metropolitan Public Conveyance Co.,	....	18,500 00	18,500 00
National Bank Note Co.,	....	60,000 00	60,000 00
National Leg and Arm Co.,	....	2,000 00	2,000 00
New England Car Spring Co.,	70,000 00	130,000 00	200,000 00
Nevada Star Mining Co.,	....	13,200 00	13,200 00
Newtown Copper Face Type Company,	....	1,000 00	1,000 00
New York Balance Dock Company,	....	200,000 00	200,000 00
New York Cement Company,	....	81,400 00	81,400 00
New York & Brooklyn Ferry Company,	....	499,000 00	499,000 00
New York Floating Dry Dock Company,	....	200,000 00	200,000 00
New York Guaranty and Indemnity Company,	....	2,000,000 00	2,000,000 00
New York Hard Rubber Collar & Cravat Co.,	....	2,000 00	2,000 00
New York Ice Company,	....	50,000 00	50,000 00
New York Lead Company,	....	20,000 00	20,000 00
New York R. R. Chair Works Company,	....	6,000 00	6,000 00
New York Steam Sugar Refining Company,	237,557 00	162,442 00	399,999 00
New York Steam Engine Works,	....	100,000 00	100,000 00
New York Warehouse and Security Company,	....	400,000 00	400,000 00
North River Steam Sugar Refining Company,	140,000 00	35,000 00	175,000 00
Novelty Iron Works,	....	150,000 00	150,000 00
Novelty Rubber Company,	....	5,000 00	5,000 00
Owens' Lake Silver Lead Company,	....	3,000 00	3,000 00
Pontiac Gold Company,	....	1,750 00	1,750 00
Safe Deposit Company,	....	95,500 00	95,500 00
Screw Dock Company,	....	75,000 00	75,000 00
Sheet Metal Screw Company,	....	6,000 00	6,000 00
Silver Slate Company,	....	2,500 00	2,500 00
Singer Manufacturing Company,	....	150,000 00	150,000 00
Standard Gold Mining Company,	....	50,000 00	50,000 00
Steam Stone Cutter Company,	....	15,280 00	15,280 00
Tarrant & Company,	....	25,000 00	25,000 00
Amount carried forward,	$799,607 00	$6,759,380 00	$7,558,987 00

Miscellaneous Companies — (Continued).

COMPANIES.	Assessed Valuation.		
	Amount of real estate.	Amount of stock taxable, deducting real estate.	Total valuation.
New York Co. (continued), br't forward,..	$799,607 00	$6,759,380 00	$7,558,987 00
Union Condensed Milk Company,............	....	3,000 00	3,000 00
Union India Rubber Company, ...	56,000 00	220,702 00	276,702 00
Union White Lead Company.	....	20,000 00	20,000 00
U. S. Bank Note Company, ...	....	250,000 00	250,000 00
U. S. Trust Company,.......	....	1,000,000 00	1,000,000 00
U. S. Trust Co. (in trust for other parties), ...	....	142,000 00	142,000 00
U. S. Warehouse Company, ...	325,000 00	75,000 00	400,000 00
Vulcanite Jewelry Company,...............	....	10,000 00	10,000 00
Warren Chemical Manufacturing Company,..	26,343 00	45,464 00	71,807 00
Warren Roofing Company,.............. ...	....	15,000 00	15,000 00
	$1,206,950 00	$8,540,546 00	$9,747,496 00
Non-resident Companies.			
American Clock Company,..................	....	$15,000 00	$15,000 00
American Whip Company,.....	....	4,000 00	4,000 00
Bigelow Carpet Company,..................	....	20,000 00	20,000 00
Central Express Company,.................	....	5,000 00	5,000 00
Glasgow Thread Company,..................	....	15,000 00	15,000 00
Goodyear India Rubber Glove Manuf. Co.,...	....	10,000 00	10,000 00
Grover & Baker's Sewing Machine Company,	....	20,000 00	20,000 00
Hartford Carpet Company,.................	....	25,000 00	25,000 00
Hoboken Ferry Company,...................	$32,000 00	....	32,000 00
Humphreyville Manufacturing Company,.....	....	1,000 00	1,000 00
Jersey City Ferry Company,...............	33,000 00	....	33,000 00
London Printing and Publishing Company, ..	....	6,400 00	6,400 00
Metropolitan Washing Machine Company,..	....	5,000 00	5,000 00
Meridian Brittania Company,..............	....	5,000 00	5,000 00
New Jersey Transportation Company,.......	8,000 00	....	8,000 00
New Jersey Zinc Company,.................	....	10,000 00	10,000 00
New York Belting and Packing Company, ...	....	50,000 00	50,000 00
Norwalk Lock Company,....................	....	3,000 00	3,000 00
Plant's Manufacturing Company,...........	....	1,000 00	1,000 00
Rockland and New Jersey Milk Company,...	....	1,000 00	1,000 00
Rubber Clothing Company, ...	....	10,000 00	10,000 00
Russell & Irwin Manufacturing Company, ...	....	25,000 00	25,000 00
Scoville Manufacturing Company,..........	....	25,000 00	25,000 00
Stamford Manufacturing Company, ...	....	20,000 00	20,000 00
Stanley Rule and Level Company,..........	....	5,000 00	5,000 00
Waterbury Brass Agency,..................	....	20,000 00	20,000 00
Waterbury Clock Company,.................	....	10,000 00	10,000 00
Wheeler & Wilson Manufacturing Company,.	....	25,000 00	25,000 00
	$73,000 00	$336,400 00	$409,400 00
Niagara County.			
Holly Manufacturing Company, ...	$1,000 00	$10,000 00	$11,000 00
International Bridge Company, ...	1,500 00	150,000 00	151,500 00
Lockport Edge Tool Manufacturing Co., ...	....	15,000 00	15,000 00
Lockport Hydraulic Company, ...	18,000 00	....	18,000 00
Lockport Woolen and Knitting Factory, ...	....	10,000 00	10,000 00
Lockport and Wright's Corn's Plankroad Co.,	5,000 00	....	5,000 00
Manufacturers' Building Company.	8,000 00	....	8,000 00
Merchants Gargling Oil Company, ...	2,000 00	50,950 00	52,950 00
Niagara Falls Paper Manufacturing Co., ...	22,000 00	....	22,000 00
Niagara Manufacturing Company, ...	4,100 00	38,760 00	42,860 00
	$61,600 00	$274,710 00	$336,310 00
Oneida County.			
Empire Woolen Mills,...	$40,000 00	....	$40,000 00
Franklin Iron Works,................	27,800 00	....	27,800 00
Globe Woolen Mills, ...	44,300 00	....	44,300 00
Paris Furnace Company,...................	12,000 00	....	12,000 00
Rome Iron Works,......	2,000 00	....	2,000 00
Rome and Madison Plankroad Company, ...	1,000 00	....	1,000 00
Amount carried forward,..	$127,100 00	$	$127,100 00

Miscellaneous Companies — (Continued).

COMPANIES.	Assessed Valuation.		
	Amount of real estate.	Amount of stock taxable, deducting real estate.	Total valuation.
Oneida Co. (continued), brought forward,.	$127,100 00	$	$127,100 00
Rome and Taberg Plankroad Company,......	1,000 00	....	1,000 00
Utica and Mechanics' Association,.	11,500 00	....	11,500 00
Utica Steam Cotton Mills Company, ...	78,000 00	....	78,000 00
Utica Steam Woolen Mills,..........	41,750 00	....	41,750 00
Utica Water Works Company, ...	5,600 00	12,000 00	17,600 00
	$264,950 00	$12,000 00	$276,950 00
Onondaga County.			
Baldwinsville Woolen Company,.	....	....	$10,000 00
Delano Iron Works,...	....	....	48,000 00
Dryden, Moravia & Groton Telegraph Co.,...	....	....	4,000 00
Hubbard Manufacturing Company, ...	....	....	25,000 00
Lysander Cheese Manufacturing Company, ..	....	....	1,000 00
Onondaga Fire Brick Company,.............	....	....	10,000 00
Salina and Brewerton Plankroad, ...	....	....	3,500 00
Salt Company of Onondaga, ...	....	....	1,488,165 00
Syracuse Company, ...	....	....	200 00
Syracuse City Water Works Company,.......	....	....	50,000 00
Syracuse Distillery Company,................	....	....	20,000 00
Syracuse Glass Manufacturing Company, ...	....	....	42,000 00
Syracuse Iron Works,.........................	....	....	50,000 00
Syracuse Patent Broom Company,............	....	....	12,000 00
Syracuse Peat Company,.....................	....	....	2,600 00
Turks Island Company, ...	....	....	500 00
Union C. Salt Company, ...	....	....	600 00
Vestry of St. James.....................	....	....	1,500 00
	....	....	$1,769,065 00
Ontario County.			
Brigham Hall Asylum, ...	$24,960 00	....	$24,960 00
Clifton Water Cure,..	30,300 00	....	30,300 00
Geneva Water Works Company, ...	....	$2,000 00	2,000 00
Hobart College, ...	3,136 00	....	3,136 00
Hygienic Institute,...........................	4,410 00	....	4,410 00
	$62,806 00	$2,000 00	$64,806 00
Orange County.			
Chester Shoe Manufacturing Company, ...	....	$4,500 00	$4,500 00
Delaware and Minnisink Turnpike Company,	$2,000 00	....	2,000 00
Erie Lead Mining Company, ...	5,000 00	....	5,000 00
Newburgh Steam Mills, ...	80,300 00	50,000 00	130,300 00
New York Knife Company, ...	3,000 00	....	3,000 00
Wallkill Mining Company,....................	2,000 00	....	2,000 00
Washington Iron Works, ...	132,300 00	75,000 00	207,300 00
	$224,600 00	$129,500 00	$354,100 00
Oswego County.			
Brewerton Bridge Company, ...	....	....	$1,000 00
New Hotel Company, ...	....	....	10,000 00
Ontario Iron Works, ...	....	....	5,600 00
Ontario Steam Boat Company,...............	....	....	26,000 00
Oswego Canal Company,.....................	....	....	11,400 00
Oswego Falls Peat Company, ...	....	....	6,000 00
Oswego Falls Plankroad Company, ...	....	....	1,200 00
Oswego Starch Company,....................	....	....	170,000 00
	....	....	$231,200 00
Otsego County.			
Arkwright Manufacturing Company,.........	$8,000 00	$3,000 00	$11,000 00
Centre Bridge Company, ...	1,000 00	....	1,000 00
Cooperstown Aqueduct Association, ...	....	2,500 00	2,500 00
Guilford Bridge Company, ...	400 00	....	400 00
Susquehanna Bridge Company, ...	2,000 00	....	2,000 00
	$11,400 00	$5,500 00	$16,900 00

Miscellaneous Companies — (Continued).

COMPANIES.	Assessed Valuation. Amount of real estate.	Amount of stock taxable, deducting real estate.	Total valuation.
PUTNAM COUNTY.			
Erie Railroad and Steamboat Company,.. ...	....	$200,000 00	$200,000 00
Southeast Temperance Hall, ...	$500 00	... .	500 00
West Point Foundery,........................	100,000 00	100,000 00	200,000 00
	$100,500 00	$300,000 00	$400,500 00
QUEENS COUNTY.			
Brooklyn Ridgewood Water Works,..........	$15,000 00	....	$15,000 00
Brooklyn Water Works, ...	14,600 00	....	14,600 00
Bushwick and Newtown Turnpike Road and Bridge Company, ...	15,000 00	....	15,000 00
Corporation of New York City, ...	10,000 00	....	10,000 00
East River Ferry Company,..................	15,000 00	$25,000 00	40,000 00
Flushing and Jamaica Plankroad Company,..	1,500 00	....	1,500 00
Flushing and Little Neck Plankroad Co.,....	2,000 00	....	2,000 00
Flushing and Newtown Turnpike Road and Bridge Company, ...	12,500 00	....	12,500 00
Flushing Skating Pond Association,..	1,000 00	....	1,000 00
Glen Cove Starch Manufacturing Company, ..	40,000 00	110,000 00	150,000 00
Hebrew United Association Cemetery,.......	500 00	....	500 00
Incorpor'n for Relief of Widows & Children,.	1,700 00	....	1,700 00
Kerosene Oil Co., or Blissville Oil Works,....	50,000 00	....	50,000 00
Long Island and North Shore Passenger and Freight Transportation Company,..........	....	70,000 00	70,000 00
Long Island Oil Company, ...	8,000 00	....	8,000 00
Lutheran Cemetery (Walker St. Church), ...	3,500 00	....	3,500 00
Newtown and Jackson Avenue Company,....	15,000 00	....	15,000 00
North Hempstead Turnpike and Bridge Co., .	1,500 00	....	1,500 00
Quog Lane Dock Company, ...	2,000 00	....	2,000 00
Trustees of Lutheran Cemetery, ...	800 00	....	800 00
Trustees of St. Patrick's Cathedral,..........	2,000 00	....	2,000 00
Trustees of Union College,..................	65,000 00	....	65,000 00
Vestry of St. George's Church,...............	3,000 00	....	3,000 00
Warren Chemical Manufacturing Company,..	13,200 00	....	13,200 00
	$292,800 00	$205,000 00	$497,800 00
RENSSELAER COUNTY.			
Congress Street Methodist Episcopal Church,	$1,000 00	....	$1,000 00
North Second St. Meth. Episcopal Church, ...	2,600 00	....	2,600 00
Rensselaer Iron Works,......................	91,600 00	$80,000 00	171,600 00
Second Presbyterian Church,.................	800 00	....	800 00
Second Street Presbyterian Church,..........	9,500 00	....	9,500 00
State Street Methodist Episcopal Church,....	3,000 00	....	3,000 00
Troy and Greenbush Railroad Association,...	12,000 00	....	12,000 00
Troy Hosiery Company,......................	250 00	60,000 00	60,250 00
Troy House Association,....................	40,000 00	....	40,000 00
Troy Iron Moulders' Association, ...	7,000 00	....	7,000 00
Troy Steamboat, ...	1,000 00	....	1,000 00
Troy Woolen Company,.......................	42,000 00	108,000 00	150,000 00
Trustees of Christ Church, ...	1,500 00	....	1,500 00
Trustees of Lansingburgh Academy,.........	....	4,053 00	4,053 00
Trustees of Leving's Chapel, ...	650 00	....	650 00
Trustees of St. John's Church,......	4,500 00	....	4,500 00
Trustees of St. Paul's Church, ...	7,000 00	....	7,000 00
Trustees of St. Peter's Church, ...	1,600 00	....	1,600 00
Trustees of Universalist Church,.............	600 00	....	600 00
Union Bridge Company,......................	100 00	....	100 00
United States Telegraph Company,...........	500 00	....	500 00
Walter A. Wood Mowing and Reaping Machine Company,.....	....	$200,000 00	200,000 00
	$227,200 00	$452,053 00	$679,253 00
RICHMOND COUNTY.			
Staten Island Warehouse Company,..........	$38,750 00	....	$38,750 00

Miscellaneous Companies — (Continued).

COMPANIES.	Assessed Valuation.		
	Amount of real estate.	Amount of stock taxable, deducting real estate.	Total valuation.
Rockland County.			
Ramapo Manufacturing Company,	$50,000 00	....	$50,000 00
Sloatsburg Manufacturing Company,	60,000 00	....	60,000 00
Tompkins Cove Lime Company,	30,000 00	$5,000 00	35,000 00
	$140,000 00	$5,000 00	$145,000 00
Saratoga County.			
American Linen Thread Company,	$20,000 00	$20,000 00	$40,000 00
Congress & Empire Spring Company,	70,675 00	....	70,675 00
Fort Miller Bridge Company,	....	2,500 00	2,500 00
Gardner Howland Paper Mill Company,	9,000 00	9,000 00	18,000 00
Glens Falls Paper Mill Company,	12,000 00	....	12,000 00
Greenfield Céntre Mercantile Association,	....	700 00	700 00
Half Moon Bridge Company,	5,000 00	....	5,000 00
Ladow & Smith Knitting Mill,	....	1,200 00	1,200 00
Mosher, Haight & Co., Paper Mill Company,	4,000 00	3,000 00	7,000 00
Pioneer Paper Company,	13,000 00	....	13,000 00
Porter's Corners Mercantile Association,	350 00	930 00	1,280 00
Reservoir Company,	5,564 00	....	5,564 00
Round Lake Petroleum Mining Company,	8,000 00	1,200 00	9,200 00
Saratoga A. Spring Company,	4,000 00	....	4,000 00
Saratoga Lake Bridge Company,	....	3,500 00	3,500 00
Saratoga Paper Mill Company,	18,000 00	....	18,000 00
Saratoga Society for the Improvement in Breeds of Horses,	10,000 00	....	10,000 00
Saratoga Star Spring Company,	5,000 00	....	5,000 00
Schuylerville Bridge Company,	300 00	4,500 00	4,800 00
Stephenson & Co., Globe Mill Company,	3,000 00	4,000 00	7,000 00
Stillwater Bridge Company,	2,000 00	....	2,000 00
Union Bridge Company,	1,000 00	30,000 00	31,000 00
Union Store Company,	....	2,800 00	2,800 00
Victory Manufacturing Company,	200,500 00	....	200,500 00
West Greenfield Mercantile Association,	....	630 00	630 00
Wilson & Co. Woolen Factory Company,	4,000 00	4,000 00	8,000 00
	$395,389 00	$87,960 00	$483,349 00
Schenectady County.			
Mohawk Bridge,	$8,000 00	....	$8,000 00
Schoharie County.			
American Hub Factory,	....	$5,000 00	$5,000 00
Blenheim Bridge Company,	....	1,500 00	1,500 00
Bridge Company (Esperance),	$300 00	2,700 00	3,000 00
Central Bridge Company,	....	4,000 00	4,000 00
Middleburgh Bridge Company,	....	1,000 00	1,000 00
Middleburgh and Schoharie Plankroad Co.,	....	1,200 00	1,200 00
	$300 00	$15,400 00	$15,700 00
Schuyler County.			
Morris Run Coal Company,	$36,000 00	....	$36,000 00
Seneca County.			
Downs Manufacturing Company,	$15,000 00	....	$15,000 00
Phœnix Manufacturing Company,	35,000 00	....	35,000 00
Seneca Falls Churn Factory,	10,000 00	....	10,000 00
Seneca Lake Petroleum Company,	....	$500 00	500 00
Seneca Knitting Mills,	30,000 00	....	30,000 00
Waterloo Woolen Manufacturing Company,	79,000 00	71,000 00	150,000 00
	$169,000 00	$71,500 00	$240,500 00
St. Lawrence County.			
Cooper Falls Iron Works,	$14,000 00	....	$14,000 00
Lead Mining Company,	13,000 00	....	13,000 00
Macomb Mining Company,	15,000 00	....	15,000 00
Ogdensburgh and Heuvelton Plankroad Co.,	8,000 00	....	8,000 00
Rossie Iron Works,	18,000 00	....	18,000 00
	$68,000 00	....	$68,000 00

Miscellaneous Companies — (Continued).

COMPANIES.	Assessed Valuation.		
	Amount of real estate.	Amount of stock taxable, deducting real estate.	Total valuation.
Steuben County.			
Addison and Elkland Plankroad Company,...	$2,000 00	....	$2,000 00
Pleasant Valley Wine Company, ...	5,000 00	....	5,000 00
Urbana Wine Company,....................	15,000 00	....	15,000 00
	$22,000 00	....	$22,000 00
Suffolk County.			
Greenport Wharf Company, ...	....	....	$1,800 00
Olympic Club, ...	....	....	2,000 00
Orient Wharf Company, ...	....	....	1,900 00
Sag Harbor Wharf Company, ...	....	....	4,000 00
Southside Club,...........................	....	....	12,000 00
Suffolk Society, ...	....	....	4,900 00
	....	....	$26,600 00
Sullivan County.			
Cohocton Bridge Company, ...	$1,200 00	....	$1,200 00
Continental Zinc and Lead Company, ...	....	$1,500 00	1,500 00
Fallbrook Stone Company,...................	16 00	....	16 00
Narrowsburgh Bridge Company, ...	2,000 00	....	2,000 00
Oakland Oil Company,......................	1,400 00	....	1,400 00
	$4,616 00	$1,500 00	$6,116 00
Tioga County.			
Owego Bridge Company,....................	$6,000 00	....	$6,000 00
Waverly Paper Mill Company, ...	5,000 00	....	5,000 00
	$11,000 00	....	$11,000 00
Tompkins County.			
Freeville Cheese Factory Association, ...	$1,400 00	....	$1,400 00
Groten " " "	1,200 00	....	1,200 00
McLean " " "	3,000 00	....	3,000 00
	$5,600 00	....	$5,600 00
Ulster County.			
Bigelow Blue Stone Company, ...	$45,000 00	$90,000 00	$135,000 00
Eddyville Bridge Company, ...	5,000 00	....	5,000 00
Ellenville Glass Company, ...	20,000 00	5,000 00	25,000 00
Kingston and Rhinebeck Ferry Company,....	7,600 00	....	7,600 00
Laflin Powder Company,.....................	4,275 00	95,000 00	99,275 00
Lawrence Lime and Cement Company,.......	19,850 00	....	19,850 00
Newark " "	70,000 00	....	70,000 00
Rosendale Cement Company, ...	8,600 00	....	8,600 00
Smith & Rand Powder Company, ...	14,400 00	....	14,400 00
Ulster County Lumber Company, ...	9,000 00	2,500 00	11,500 00
Ulster Iron Works,..........................	50,000 00	....	50,000 00
Ulster White Lead Company, ...	20,000 00	18,000 00	38,000 00
	$273,725 00	$210,500 00	$484,225 00
Warren County.			
Glens Falls and Lake George Plankroad Co.,	$4,200 00	....	$4,200 00
Steamer Minnehaha, ...	....	$1,000 00	1,000 00
Warrensburgh and Lake George Plankr'd Co.,	1,000 00	....	1,000 00
	$5,200 00	$1,000 00	$6,200 00
Washington County.			
Battenkill Knitting Company, ...	$10,000 00	....	$10,000 00
Greenwich Boot and Shoe Company,.........	....	$15,000 00	15,000 00
Fort Edward and Argyle Plankroad Company,	2,500 00	....	2,500 00
Fort Edward Blast Furnace Company, ...	25,000 00	45,000 00	70,000 00
Amount carried forward,.................	$37,500 00	$60,000 00	$97,500 00

Miscellaneous Companies — (Continued).

COMPANIES.	ASSESSED VALUATION.		
	Amount of real estate.	Amount of stock taxable, deducting real estate.	Total valuation.
Washington Co. (continued), br't forward,	$37,500 00	$60,000 00	$97,500 00
Fort Edward Water Works Company, ...	1,500 00	1,000 00	2,500 00
Middle Granville Slate Company, ...	8,500 00	....	8,500 00
	$47,500 00	$61,000 00	$108,500 00
WESTCHESTER COUNTY.			
Corporation of New York, ...	....	....	$54,150 00
Empire Sewing Machine Company, ...	$50,000 00	$50,000 00	100,000 00
National Stove Works, ...	15,000 00	....	15,000 00
Peekskill Blast Furnace, ...	18,000 00	....	18,000 00
Peekskill Manufacturing Company, ...	15,000 00	26,000 00	41,000 00
Peekskill Marble Company, ...	2,500 00	....	2,500 00
Peekskill Plow Works, ...	35,000 00	40,000 00	75,000 00
Turnpike Company, Rye, ...	....	... .	800 00
	$135,500 00	$116,000 00	$306,450 00
ASSESSED IN DIFFERENT COUNTIES.			
Brooklyn White Lead Company, ...	$106,500 00	$15,811 00	$122,311 00
Delaware and Hudson Canal Company, ...	1,605,246 00	....	1,605,246 00
Hudson River Bridge Company, ...	293,770 00	....	293,770 00
Knickerbocker Ice Company, ...	119,000 00	68,469 00	187,469 00
New York Dyeing and Print'g Establishment,	72,800 00	161,887 00	234,687 00
Northern Transportation Company, ...	6,900 00	150,000 00	157,300 00
Pennsylvania Coal Company, ...	106,900 00	....	106,900 00
Peru Steel and Iron Company, ...	47,140 00	....	47,140 00
Salina and Central Square Plankroad, ...	....	....	12,000 00
Washington Ice Company, ...	60,881 00	21,398 00	82,279 00
Western Transportation Company, ...	2,000 00	500,000 00	502,000 00
Western Union Telegraph Company, ...	14,500 00	401,500 00	416,000 00
	$2,435,637 00	$1,319,065 00	$3,767,102 00

NOTE.—In some instances the returns of the Supervisors give the assessed valuation in the aggregate only, hence the distributions as given in the foregoing tables of Incorporated Companies do not in all cases agree with the total assessed valuation.

The amount of capital stock paid in, of the Miscellaneous, Express and Navigation Companies, has not been ascertained.

The following counties have neglected to make returns of Incorporated Companies for 1866, viz.: Cayuga, Chenango, New York, in part, Schenectady, Westchester, except the following towns — Bedford, Cortland, Lewisboro, Mamaroneck, Mt. Pleasant, New Castle, North Castle, Pelham, Poundridge, Rye, Somers, Yonkers and Yorktown — Wyoming.

The returns of 1865 have been used for the following counties, viz.: Schenectady, Wyoming, New York, for banks and non-resident companies. No reports from Cayuga, Chenango and Westchester for 1865.

(L.)

*Amount of County, City, Town and Village Debts, so far as returns have been received.**

COUNTIES.	Total debt for bounties and other war expenses.	Total debt for other purposes.	Total county, town, city and village debt.
Albany,	$1,744,250 00	$2,066,100 75	$3,810,350 75
Allegany,	74,548 59	18,948 00	93,496 59
Broome,	266,047 82	161,527 00	427,574 82
Cattaraugus,	15,766 00	21,100 00	36,866 00
Cayuga,	647,989 19	374,916 33	1,022,905 52
Chautauqua,	5,900 00	171,912 92	177,812 92
Chemung,	34,139 66	83,951 52	118,091 18
Chenango,	372,271 17	551,348 51	923,619 68
Clinton,	190,939 15	4,613 29	195,552 44
Columbia,	309,758 95	168,900 00	478,658 95
Cortland,	679,940 00	43,750 00	723,690 00
Delaware,	90,808 45	606,970 00	697,778 45
Dutchess,	825,000 00	146,465 70	971,465 70
Erie,	817,256 91	497,696 00	1,314,952 91
Essex,	187,556 49	501 04	188,057 53
Franklin,	149,307 75	20,675 00	169,982 75
Fulton,	147,326 00	292,409 00	439,735 00
Genesee,	423,347 00	10,500 00	433,847 00
Greene,	527,300 00	11,939 22	539,239 22
Hamilton,	38,721 00	4,530 00	43,251 00
Herkimer,	130,076 98	8,199 99	138,276 97
Jefferson,	1,234,758 48	193,353 49	1,428,111 97
Kings,	3,717,000 00	10,860,419 92	14,577,419 92
Lewis,	67,881 22	196,949,46	264,830 68
Livingston,	154,951 73	100,500 00	255,451 73
Madison,	6,342 75	403,580 30	409,923 05
Monroe,	1,950,339 50	673,897 75	2,624,237 25
Montgomery,	302,157 80	129,018 11	431,175 91
New York,	12,825,600 00	21,132,675 01	33,958,275 01
Niagara,	372,800 00	....	372,800 00
Oneida,	3,550 00	972,928 70	976,478 70
Onondaga,	1,282,120 00	45,149 98	1,327,269 98
Ontario,	498,060 00	300 00	498,360 00
Orange,	721,176 49	8,971 65	730,148 14
Orleans,	239,860 00	2,000 00	241,860 00
Oswego,	814,900 00	85,380 03	900,280 03
Otsego,	100,995 95	701,200 00	802,195 95
Putnam,	46,200 00	....	46,200 00
Queens,	1,159,651 00	8,000 00	1,167,651 00
Rensselaer,	973,473 40	1,015,628 28	1,989,101 68
Richmond,	801,850 00	77,414 28	879,264 28
Rockland,	78,067 08	3,100 00	81,167 08
St. Lawrence,	740,413 85	93,550 00	833,963 85
Saratoga,	178,914 30	985 00	179,899 30
Schenectady,	121,600 00	27,400 00	149,000 00
Schoharie,	90,815 00	180,162 67	270,977 67
Schuyler,	118,379 04	4,958 71	123,337 75
Seneca,	314,545 33	13,487 75	328,033 08
Steuben,	482,568 84	5,464 00	488,032 84
Suffolk,	250,099 94	1,725 00	251,824 94
Sullivan,	323,411 00	111,850 00	435,261 00
Tioga,	154,800 00	67,900 00	222,700 00
Tompkins,	27,134 85	70,923 73	98,058 58
Ulster,	1,585,875 00	1,095,098 15	2,680,973 15
Warren,	37,278 05	3,808 32	41,086 37
Washington,	299,335 00	8,500 00	307,835 00
Wayne,	303,969 00	28,000 00	331,969 00
Westchester,	1,847,509 08	142,000 00	1,989,509 08
Wyoming,	3,840 00	1,200 00	5,040 00
Yates,	17,524 00	13,212 32	30,736 32
	$41,927,998 79	$43,747,645 88	$85,675,645 67

* Returns had not been received from the city of Oswego, nor from 143 towns at the time of printing this table. The summaries following the details given on a subsequent page will be more complete, and will present the specific objects for which these debts were contracted, their rate of interest, and the years when they will become due.

This table embraces returns from the treasurer of every county in the State, and from 16 cities, 785 towns, and 62 villages. It is believed that most of the towns and villages not heard from are free from debt, and that they have not reported because they had no returns to make under the various headings of inquiry embraced in the blanks. Reports are coming in daily from other towns, and will be included in the final summaries.

(M.)

Statement showing the Amounts due for Principal and Interest on Loans from the Common School Fund to Corporations, &c., and Bonds for Lands under Contract, to 30th September, 1866.

Book.	Page.	TO WHAT, OR TO WHOM LOANED.	Principal.	Interest.	Total.
		COUNTIES.			
1	7	Allegany,	$15,000 00	$892 50	$15,892 50
1	8	do	2,000 00	40 00	2,040 00
1	36	Broome,	2,627 55	814 38	3,441 93
1	37	do	2,000 00	770 33	2,770 33
1	38	do	20,000 00	2,883 60	22,883 60
1	39	do	15,000 00	3,268 27	18,268 27
1	40	do	8,000 00	3,642 53	11,642 53
1	92	Chemung,	20,000 00	698 67	20,698 67
1	82	do	2,250 00	67 50	2,317 50
1	83	do	6,000 00	180 00	6,180 00
1	80	Clinton,	1,969 52	....	1,969 52
1	85	Cortland,	326 51	89 79	416 30
1	86	do	130 00	35 75	165 75
1	94	do	3,000 00	87 00	3,087 00
1	193	Franklin,	5,000 00	1,797 50	6,797 50
1	268	Jefferson,	1,000 00	217 83	1,217 83
1	270	do	2,688 44	76 86	2,765 30
1	271	do	3,360 95	177 33	3,538 28
1	273	do	17,500 00	700 00	18,200 00
1	378	Niagara,	1 52	2 56	4 08
1	379	do	7 67	9 84	17 51
1	407	Oswego,	13,045 44	378 32	13,423 76
1	467	Schuyler,	10,000 00	1,180 00	11,180 00
1	594	Warren,	1,624 49	329 77	1,954 26
1	598	do	1,053 50	213 86	1,267 36
1	599	do	1,262 37	256 26	1,518 63
1	602	do	625 78	213 86	839 64
		TOWNS.			
1	10	Aurora,	525 00	35 70	560 70
1	87	Cape Vincent,	575 96	178 54	754 50
1	89	Clayton,	834 41	27 53	861 94
1	272	Jay,	1,467 55	171 70	1,639 25
1	298	Lyme,	302 04	167 30	469 34
1	426	Palmyra,	500 00	17 50	517 50
1	461	Saranac,	5 19	2 25	7 44
1	584	Watertown,	1,000 00	157 50	1,157 50
1	591	do	936 49	162 01	1,098 50
1	590	Wilna,	128 65	7 20	135 85
1	592	Watertown,	1,000 00	277 04	1,277 04
1	593	do	1,500 00	485 07	1,985 07
		INSTITUTIONS AND CORPORATIONS.			
1	9	Antwerp Liberal Literary Institute,	3,000 00	1,312 50	4,312 50
1	318	Board of Education, vil. of Medina,	1,468 18	95 43	1,563 61
6	284	Oswego & Syracuse R. R. Co.,	730 50	321 32	1,051 82
1	427	Penn Yan Union School District.	992 02	50 59	1,042 61
1	428	Port Byron Free School,	5,000 00	1,021 70	6,021 70
7	12	Syr., Binghamton & N. Y. R. R. Co.,	3,250 00	339 63	3,589 63
		INDIVIDUALS.			
8	135	O. Abell, Jr., and H. Glidden,	222 60	11 35	233 95
7	486	Daniel Abrams,	40 00	6 00	46 00
6	426	Benj. W. Adams,	28 76	5 06	33 82
8	200	John Aiken,	185 10	52 09	237 19
8	170	Joshua Aiken,	566 78	132 95	699 73
7	112	W. Ainslee and V. Pratt,	163 58	47 54	211 12
6	124	Albert F. Allen,	27 04	9 30	36 34
4	338	Amos Allen,	196 00	14 59	210 59
6	64	Benj. Allen,	750 00	23 25	773 25
3	42	Geo. W. Allen,	268 02	133 04	401 06
3	424	Seth Allen,	60 00	22 92	82 92
6	220	Solomon Allen,	414 34	396 72	811 06
6	474	T. G. Alvord,	258 75	78 67	337 42
6	475	do	273 75	90 26	364 01

Principal and Interest on School Fund Loans, &c. — (*Continued*).

Book.	Page.	TO WHAT OR TO WHOM LOANED.	Principal.	Interest.	Total.
6	476	T. G. Alvord, ...	$510 00	$155 04	$665 04
4	321	Moody Ames, ...	192 00	4 80	196 80
6	619	Jacob Amos, ...	272 62	52 54	325 16
4	576	Joseph Anderson, ...	155 10	21 24	176 34
4	600	Asa Andrews, ...	196 85	21 96	218 81
3	537	Luther Andrews, ...	66 00	49 89	115 89
8	568	do	127 00	8 10	135 10
4	266	Sam'l W. Andrews, ...	112 00	14 00	126 00
7	52	T. F. Andrews, ...	600 00	10 80	610 80
6	199	Joseph Annin, ...	97 99	6 47	104 46
4	190	John Archibald, ...	36 00	39	36 39
7	185	do	120 00	1 24	121 24
7	186	do	120 00	1 24	121 24
7	189	do	84 50	50	85 00
7	191	do	84 50	48	84 98
7	192	do	90 00	87	90 87
7	206	do	66 00	1 30	67 30
7	207	do	90 00	87	90 87
5	17	Virgil M. Armour, ...	379 00	56 20	435 20
5	18	do	379 00	56 69	435 69
3	431	Wm. Armstrong, ...	750 00	37 88	787 88
5	15	Orriel Austin, ...	249 90	37 01	286 91
5	16	do	79 34	6 18	85 52
4	253	James Averill, 3d, ...	324 66	87 53	412 19
4	254	do	412 00	111 24	523 24
4	255	do	57 34	5 61	62 95
8	49	Zina Austin, ...	67 00	13 50	80 50
3	250	Gardiner Avery, ...	151 92	3 04	154 96
5	442	do	438 76	127 83	566 59
5	443	do	470 00	30 55	500 55
5	448	do	297 83	52 30	350 13
6	286	James L. Bagg, ...	285 00	9 77	294 77
6	287	do	153 00	5 74	•158 74
6	288	do	146 00	5 83	151 83
6	551	Geo. Barnes and D. P. Phelps, ...	487 00	216 59	703 59
5	162	Joel Baker, ...	1,000 00	223 67	1,223 67
4	453	Harvey Baldwin, ...	163 50	....	163 50
6	576	do	232 50	24 38	256 88
4	333	James Baldwin, ...	138 00	7 59	145 59
4	334	do	94 96	6 12	101 08
3	20	T. P. Ballou, ...	558 12	426 96	985 08
3	21	do	787 75	473 03	1,260 78
3	122	do	244 70	141 83	386 53
6	147	Eli T. Bangs, ...	151 57	6 06	157 63
4	465	Freeman Barber, ...	286 04	23 94	309 98
6	118	Thomas Barbour, ...	250 06	17 27	267 33
3	30	J. L. Barnes & H. B. Miller, ...	1,091 25	530 36	1,621 61
3	31	do do	1,132 50	550 39	1,682 89
3	32	do do	1,128 75	548 56	1,677 31
4	491	H. D. Barnes and H. Buck, ...	146 62	48 48	195 10
3	489	L. B. Barnes, ...	88 35	42 25	130 60
3	477	do	93 57	44 73	138 30
3	514	James Barr, ...	47 48	66	48 14
4	525	Oliver Bartholomew, ...	68 34	42 17	110 51
7	169	J. C. Barnum, ...	52 00	66	52 66
7	114	L. Barnum and M. Richardson, ...	131 08	... .	131 08
8	474	L. A. Battershall, ...	795 00	128 79	923 79
3	450	Eli Beebe, Jr., ...	70 00	8 90	78 90
3	440	do	45 00	5 58	50 58
3	457	T. W. Beebe, ...	169 85	16 12	185 97
7	270	Willard Bell, ...	101 71	11 93	113 64
6	94	Lewis Benedict, ...	139 00	22 85	161 85
6	105	Lewis Benedict, ...	75 00	6 28	81 28
4	507	F. N. Benedict, ...	323 13	121 87	445 00
6	122	Jessie Bennett, ...	423 75	209 79	633 54
6	125	do	431 25	213 42	644 67
6	127	do	209 76	109 91	319 67
6	143	do	88 60	43 87	132 47
6	145	do	91 88	45 48	137 36
6	146	do	82 03	40 59	122 62
6	152	do	72 19	3 97	76 16
6	153	do	75 47	4 16	79 63
6	156	do	82 03	4 52	86 55
6	159	do	95 16	5 24	100 40

Principal and Interest on School Fund Loans, &c. — (Continued).

Book.	Page.	TO WHAT OR TO WHOM LOANED.	Principal.	Interest.	Total.
6	160	Jessie Bennett,	$88 59	$4 88	$93 47
6	168	Morris Bennett,	3,899 92	1,531 19	5,431 11
5	492	Nicholas Betzinger,	220 94	5 74	226 68
5	493	do	193 97	47 28	241 25
3	52	Solon Bevins,	90 00	40 77	130 77
7	271	F. A. Bickford and Nahum Darling,	41 39	1 08	42 47
4	15	Lucius Bishop,	47 85	24	48 09
8	626	Noah Bissell,	206 50	87 61	294 11
8	627	do	117 00	49 61	166 61
4	577	Joseph Black,	111 03	6 75	117 78
5	102	Joseph Black, Jr.,	199 66	29 05	228 71
5	26	J. B. Black and Asa Alworth,	203 48	30 36	233 84
4	506	Anson Blake,	1,737 00	964 03	2,701 03
5	10	Lyman Bliss,	279 00	60 06	339 06
5	13	Adonijah Bond,	200 00	34 80	234 80
6	181	J. W. Bonesteele,	14,226 00	23,188 30	37,414 30
4	274	Oliver Botton,	64 54	8 85	73 39
5	568	Frederick Bovee,	130 43	4 56	134 99
5	603	Henry Bovee,	60 14	6 12	66 26
5	556	David Boyer,	121 71	14 27	135 98
7	19	C. C. Bradley,	527 00	49 45	576 45
7	51	do	356 25	43 36	399 61
7	473	Geo. Bradley and David Underwood,	120 00	33 96	153 96
7	474	George Bradley,	145 00	47 85	192 85
7	475	do	188 99	80 13	269 12
7	476	do	171 00	58 43	229 43
3	104	Geo. Bradley and D. Underwood,	672 00	10 75	682 75
3	332	Horace Braman,	110 48	15 68	126 16
4	538	Allen Brewer,	228 05	5 41	233 46
6	633	W. M. Brewster,	500 00	50 50	550 50
5	577	Oliver E. Briant,	100 79	27 74	128 53
8	210	Joseph Briggs,	43 00	44 08	87 08
6	193	Gideon Brockway,	63 37	4 07	67 44
6	194	do	103 60	6 13	109 73
6	173	Alvin Bronson,	248 37	3 22	251 59
6	173	Alvin Bronson and L. B. Crocker,	1,599 67	1,650 35	3,250 02
8	583	Eli Brooks and Cutting Bagley,	196 00	126 02	322 02
7	266	E. J. Brown,	93 53	3 31	96 84
4	213	John Brown,	105 00	5 42	110 42
4	285	Nathaniel Brown (rent due),	....	43 87	43 87
4	545	do do	170 56	43 18	213 74
6	119	Robert Brown,	412 50	55 22	467 72
6	117	do	488 14	31 73	519 87
7	430	Thomas Brown,	45 00	5 61	50 61
7	210	William Brown,	78 50	44	78 94
4	567	Oliver Brownson,	429 81	46 33	476 14
4	588	Simeon Brownson,	86 76	16 10	102 86
8	166	Robert Buchanan,	2 08	82	2 90
4	63	Hiram Buck,	47 00	13 30	60 30
8	16	H. Buck and O. L. Knox,	47 88	13 84	61 72
6	136	C. J. Burckle,	738 28	61 07	799 35
6	165	do	807 19	399 57	1,206 76
7	57	Peter Burns,	322 50	25 73	348 23
8	489	Benj. C. Butler,	108 00	12 67	120 67
8	490	do	90 00	10 53	100 53
8	491	do	138 00	16 15	154 15
5	626	Adam Buyea,	168 47	15 92	184 39
3	254	J. C. and Peter Buyea,	638 23	47 00	685 23
5	96	Elizabeth Byrne,	180 11	21 32	201 43
4	159	Elias Cadwell,	110 71	27 50	138 21
4	161	do	129 62	32 42	162 04
4	162	do	115 42	28 83	144 25
4	163	do	65 24	16 40	81 64
8	309	do	50 00	12 50	62 50
8	312	do	51 09	12 50	63 59
7	172	Isaac Calkin,	33 70	....	33 70
8	488	George Cameron,	102 00	48 69	150 69
4	530	Daniel Campbell,	556 08	20 43	576 51
4	573	do do	114 36	7 28	121 64
8	266	R. A. Campbell,	83 81	29 62	113 43
8	48	E. J. Cannon,	224 02	16 28	240 30
6	320	Charles Carpenter,	105 00	4 60	109 60
5	41	John Carpenter,	94 16	32 64	126 80

Principal and Interest on School Fund Loans, &c. — (*Continued*).

Book.	Page.	TO WHAT OR TO WHOM LOANED.	Principal.	Interest.	Total.
5	89	Michael Carn and Jno. Murray, ...	$131 77	$36 00	$167 77
4	569	Elisha Carrington, ...	258 28	25 60	283 88
4	570	do do	413 77	82 17	495 94
4	575	do do	420 83	28 09	448 92
4	587	do do	44 20	10 32	54 52
6	61	F. T. Carrington and M. Pardee, ...	71 25	24 49	95 74
6	62	do do	75 00	25 77	100 77
6	141	do do	82 03	44 72	126 75
6	142	do do	65 63	35 76	101 39
6	155	do do	82 03	44 72	126 75
6	161	do do	101 97	56 57	158 54
6	138	F. T. Carrington, President of Syracuse and Oswego Railroad Co., ...	4,875 00	1,886 75	6,761 75
6	167	F. T. Carrington and M. Pardee, ...	948 00	521 66	1,469 66
5	167	John Carter, ...	333 00	9 52	342 52
3	432	John Carter, ...	289 66	25 49	315 15
5	165	Nathan Carter, ...	54 86	3 60	58 46
8	214	William Casey, ...	148 40	17 83	166 23
4	322	John Catlin and Moody Ames, ...	249 00	6 22	255 22
8	132	Steptoe Catlin, ...	86 00	31 59	117 59
6	478	Edward Chapman, ...	300 00	27 00	327 00
5	21	Isaac Cheeseman, ...	69 58	7 86	77 44
8	464	Albert N. Cheney, ...	28 00	13 58	41 58
8	447	A. N. Cheney and L. L. Arms, ...	48 00	23 28	71 28
8	448	do do	36 00	15 45	51 45
8	449	do do	30 00	14 55	44 55
8	451	do do	36 00	17 46	53 46
8	454	do do	29 60	14 35	43 95
8	460	do do	54 75	26 57	81 32
8	463	do do	36 00	17 46	53 46
8	466	do do	60 00	29 10	89 10
8	467	do do	89 60	43 45	133 05
8	455	A. N. Chency and Ira A. Paddock, ..	66 00	32 01	98 01
6	33	Eli Clarke, ...	206 66	4 91	211 57
8	202	Harvey Clark, ...	170 25	75 52	245 77
6	634	James W. Clark, ...	582 00	7 30	589 30
6	635	do	600 00	6 60	606 60
7	6	J. A. Clark and Henry Horton, ...	300 00	54 75	354 75
7	7	do do	337 50	44 72	382 22
3	271	Sylvester Clark, ...	185 14	30 24	215 38
3	277	do	185 94	17 66	203 60
6	222	Hiram Clift, ...	226 64	6 57	233 21
7	116	James Colby, ...	408 27	5 31	413 58
7	208	Enoch Colby, ...	88 00	12 50	100 50
5	348	Uri Colgrove, ...	127 40	8 69	136 09
4	221	Isaac Colt, Jr., ...	82 09	4 80	86 89
2	39	J. C. Colton, W. Hunt and J. B. Mead,	140 00	166 93	306 93
6	547	Geo. F. Comstock, ...	375 00	39 37	414 37
4	534	David Cone, ...	106 91	67 64	174 55
5	449	A. Cook and M. Austin, ...	323 00	68 89	391 89
4	109	Obadiah Coolidge, ...	138 13	67 01	205 14
4	497	John Cooper, ...	400 00	6 40	406 40
5	28	David Coe, ...	109 06	19 08	128 14
6	206	Joel Cornish, ...	219 36	....	219 36
1	77	Ashbel Cornwell, ...	852 71	135 35	988 06
4	210	Nelson Cornwell, ...	626 25	298 39	924 64
5	90	James Cowing and David Thompson,	250 39	54 34	304 73
5	606	E R. Crain, ...	423 92	25 46	449 38
8	60	Hunter Craine, ...	64 50	22 16	86 66
3	334	Ransom Cram, ...	56 27	18 08	74 35
5	613	William Cramer, ...	1,741 01	808 66	2,549 67
3	54	Gideon Crandall, ...	94 00	32 55	126 55
6	154	Hunter Crane, ...	82 03	30 78	112 81
4	290	do rent due, ...	... .	642 50	642 50
4	432	Andrew and Ezra Crawford, ...	239 20	78 35	317 55
6	148	J. M. and J. Croleus, ...	71 25	35 37	106 62
6	149	do do	127 50	63 10	190 60
6	392	James Cronkhite, ...	49 76	....	49 76
4	393	Cephas Cross, ...	128 99	12 28	141 27
6	170	Edwin Croswell, ...	322 69	154 25	476 94
6	171	do	215 62	103 07	318 69
6	174	do	376 23	179 84	556 07
6	175	do	215 62	103 07	318 69

Principal and Interest on School Fund Loans, &c. — (*Continued*).

Book.	Page.	TO WHAT, OR TO WHOM LOANED.	Principal.	Interest.	Total.
6	176	Edwin Croswell,	$322 89	$154 34	$477 23
6	177	do	697 42	30 36	727 78
4	288	Nicholas Cummings,	....	61 70	61 70
3	460	Benj. Culver,	124 06	32 35	156 41
4	541	Joseph Curtis,	333 83	95 97	429 80
2	85	Edwin M. Daniel,	5,100 00	10 20	5,110 20
8	581	Henry S. Darby,	195 00	160 98	355 98
4	29	Robert Davis,	35 05	41	35 46
4	330	D. W. Dean,	88 87	23 57	112 44
4	331	Jonathan Dean,	98 23	8 25	106 48
5	247	J. G. Dearstyne,	30 49	15	30 64
1	135	Peter Decker,	299 05	18 21	317 26
5	527	Daniel Dickey and Danforth Armour,	298 00	32 43	330 43
5	528	do do	162 67	7 16	169 83
5	19	Silvester Dickey,	236 00	36 36	272 36
5	20	do	239 00	36 97	275 97
6	549	Henry A. Dillaye,	397 00	41 68	438 68
5	156	Asa Dix,	432 83	40 82	473 65
6	321	John Dodge,	97 36	4 11	101 47
6	322	do	96 34	4 54	100 88
8	600	Ammi Doubleday, Jr.,	145 01	86	145 87
8	415	John Dougherty,	29 13	1 97	31 10
8	547	do	74 16	12 58	86 74
3	276	John Downer,	1,019 00	111 18	1,130 18
4	486	Joseph G. Downer,	75 00	7 19	82 19
4	593	Joel Downer,	474 09	90 93	565 02
4	273	Abial Drake,	67 93	4 76	72 69
8	196	Joseph Driggs,	53 50	1 51	55 01
7	124	S. V. Dubois,	209 36	46 41	255 77
7	126	do	130 00	33 12	163 12
8	216	Jacob Drum and Wm. Stevens,	291 11	198 66	489 77
7	369	John T. Duncan,	138 66	33 98	172 64
4	19	Simeon Durand,	26 95	2 03	28 98
6	20	Calvin Dutton,	218 91	63 27	282 18
5	409	Jonathan Dygert,	145 86	3 87	149 73
3	274	Seneca Eddy,	183 00	25 12	208 12
4	546	Nathan Edson,	190 64	4 00	194 64
5	25	George W. Ellinwood,	467 00	44 13	511 13
5	29	do do	189 00	1 84	190 84
7	469	Joseph Estes,	57 75	4 10	61 85
8	17	William Everest,	209 29	47 13	256 42
6	608	George Everson,	461 00	22 94	483 94
6	629	do	3,975 00	3,188 62	7,163 62
6	499	John Ewen,	157 50	28 94	186 44
6	503	do	112 50	20 66	133 16
6	504	do	176 25	32 39	208 64
5	347	Ann B. Fannan, Elvira Starr and Louisa Smith,	241 02	10 54	251 56
6	462	Marcellus Farmer,	296 25	152 56	448 81
5	530	James Faulkner,	127 27	35 83	163 10
6	218	D. D. Fellows and Jos. Blanchard,	278 38	93 81	372 19
4	606	Thomas and Sam'l Faulkner,	54 89	1 78	56 67
7	495	Joseph Fellows,	28 77	12 11	40 88
7	496	do	80 19	34 00	114 19
7	497	do	26 94	11 42	38 36
7	498	do	21 75	9 32	31 07
7	508	do	86 77	36 79	123 56
7	511	do	20 23	8 58	28 81
7	512	do	20 23	8 58	28 81
7	513	do	19 42	8 23	27 65
7	514	do	25 57	10 84	36 41
7	515	do	21 00	8 90	29 90
7	516	do	28 72	12 18	40 90
7	520	do	24 70	10 47	35 17
7	521	do	67 88	28 78	96 66
7	522	do	51 84	21 98	73 82
7	524	do	92 41	39 18	131 59
7	535	do	44 29	18 78	63 07
7	537	do	24 51	10 39	34 90
7	174	Aaron Felt,	32 75	4 07	36 82
4	340	Daniel Ferguson,	88 00	19 71	107 71
4	344	do	57 00	18 70	75 70
7	125	W. & E. Field,	216 01	68 51	284 52

Principal and Interest on School Fund Loans, &c. — (Continued).

Book.	Page.	TO WHAT, OR TO WHOM LOANED.	Principal.	Interest.	Total.
6	229	Stutely Field,	$59 48	$27 42	$86 90
6	191	Isaac Finch,	500 00	4 27	504 27
6	201	Hurd & Finch,	71 87	82 30	154 17
8	538	J. W. & D. J. Finch,	100 71	40 69	141 40
8	541	do	110 11	44 44	154 55
8	358	Ebenezer Fish,	83 00	19 75	102 75
7	190	Elisha Flagg,	96 36	26 65	123 01
5	420	Friend W. Forbes,	928 00	46 87	974 87
5	497	do	200 09	26 84	226 93
3	266	John Fort and Joseph Randall,	552 60	21 55	574 15
5	133	Susannah Foster,	82 00	5 27	87 27
5	134	do	60 00	4 94	64 94
8	404	Eleanor Foster	50 00	18 52	68 52
7	360	Loring Fowler and C. Calkins,	69 20	25 63	94 83
2	119	Josiah Francis,	347 06	37 75	384 81
4	303	Philip Freeman (rent due),	....	40 41	40 41
5	574	Wm. French,	452 13	47 45	499 58
5	353	Joseph Frisbee,	167 75	8 23	175 98
8	79	R. H. Fuller,	209 00	24 55	233 55
4	339	Walter Gage,	119 00	7 72	126 72
6	557	Thos. Gale,	197 01	20 71	217 72
6	543	do	216 57	22 78	239 35
6	573	do	737 67	77 44	815 11
5	413	H. N. Gardiner,	334 17	32 12	366 29
6	367	Gardiner & Albina Woolson,	157 50	11 67	169 17
6	369	do do	157 50	12 38	169 88
5	417	H. N. Gardiner,	211 83	15 45	227 28
5	202	Willis Gates,	73 00	10 11	83 11
5	205	do	51 00	2 54	53 54
7	20	Wm. F. Gere,	528 75	50 00	578 75
7	21	do	457 50	43 20	500 70
2	132	E. J. Genet,	5,937 48	7,605 91	13,543 39
2	133	Geo. R. Genet,	4,170 66	5,342 61	9,513 27
7	194	Russel Gibbs,	120 00	16 50	136 50
8	313	Henry Gibson,	49 39	36	49 75
5	11	Sumner Gill,	286 00	22 43	308 43
4	257	Watson Gillett,	118 58	13 10	131 68
7	254	John & M. Gilmore,	4 58	31	4 89
5	446	Lyman Goff,	395 84	94 08	489 92
5	429	Matthew Golding,	381 00	56 06	437 06
5	141	Sarah Goodrich,	53 00	2 33	55 33
5	143	do	66 35	2 33	68 68
5	163	Daniel B. Gordon,	506 54	16 21	522 75
7	257	Gilman Graves,	83 00	13 10	96 10
7	204	James Graves, Jr., and G. Graves,	110 00	24 55	134 55
5	313	M. C. Graves,	37 13	13 80	50 93
5	314	do	46 00	15 81	61 81
5	610	John Green,	238 19	13 40	251 59
6	636	John A. Green, Jr.,	825 00	121 00	946 00
3	451	M. Green, R. H. Green & M. Lawyer,	130 00	47 80	177 80
7	60	Squire J. Green,	356 25	28 53	384 78
7	62	do	378 75	30 27	409 02
6	36	Mary Ann Greenman,	103 50	1 32	104 82
5	35	Gregg, Sloan & Parks,	261 21	33 19	294 40
5	583	David Gregg,	562 14	98 84	660 98
5	93	Hannah Gregg,	291 06	186 00	477 06
5	617	W. T. Gregg,	220 50	14 97	235 47
5	501	W. T. N. C. & Hugh M. Gregg,	88 82	8 70	97 52
4	308	Gregg, Hodge & Bronson (rent due),	....	99 26	99 26
6	600	Geo. F. Grinnell,	381 50	33 62	415 12
6	611	John Guilfoyle,	396 56	82 45	479 01
8	137	Frederick Haasz,	47 54	....	47 54
2	151	Robert Hadfield,	675 00	40 02	715 02
3	311	Isaac Hall,	107 10	67 12	174 22
4	100	Munroe Hall,	80 00	33 92	113 92
4	102	do	82 95	10 62	93 57
4	103	do	26 00	3 33	29 33
7	311	do	336 00	45 02	381 02
7	314	do	46 00	19 50	65 50
7	320	do	162 00	19 84	181 84
7	321	do	336 00	40 32	376 32
7	322	do	84 24	10 11	94 35
7	332	do	81 00	34 34	115 34

Principal and Interest on School Fund Loans, &c. — (Continued).

Book.	Page.	TO WHAT, OR TO WHOM LOANED.	Principal.	Interest.	Total.
7	337	Munroe Hall,	$39 00	$16 54	$55 54
7	370	do	66 00	27 98	93 98
7	376	do	58 00	20 65	78 65
7	436	do	36 00	10 94	46 94
7	437	do	47 00	8 65	55 65
7	439	do	82 00	34 77	116 77
7	441	do	32 00	13 57	45 57
3	516	do	50 40	6 00	56 40
3	517	do	37 00	4 40	41 40
3	519	do	61 95	7 37	69 32
3	520	do	46 20	5 50	51 70
7	390	do	26 00	11 02	37 02
5	376	Jeremiah Hallock,	466 59	25 20	491 79
3	256	Giles Harrington,	392 42	44 48	436 90
3	259	do	434 21	49 33	483 54
3	264	do	439 28	50 23	489 51
8	351	Charles Harris,	75 00	41 73	116 73
8	37	James Harris,	20 00	21 55	41 55
4	215	Joel Harris,	75 00	8 31	83 31
6	109	Samuel Hart,	37 50	5 45	42 95
3	270	Sylvanus Hart,	99 81	14 82	114 63
3	272	Sylvanus and Reuben Hart,	194 36	25 43	219 79
7	272	Imla Hartwell,	146 31	2 43	148 74
8	274	Peter Hasbrouck,	69 28	3 71	72 99
2	152	Amos Haskins,	902 10	341 57	1,243 67
7	161	H. D. Hatch,	990 00	158 40	1,148 40
7	162	do	861 00	21 53	882 53
8	486	Albina Hawley,	133 00	27 13	160 13
3	216	Thaddeus Hayes,	254 45	28 13	282 58
7	253	Asa Heald,	198 10	80 83	278 93
8	348	Horace Heath,	175 00	21 24	196 24
8	349	do	91 78	11 57	103 35
8	134	Milo Henry,	33 00	7 45	40 45
8	106	do	36 00	16 90	52 90
8	178	H. A. Herrick,	89 77	28 10	117 87
8	198	do	85 84	22 09	107 93
8	174	W. H. Herrick,	54 23	18 10	72 33
8	199	W. W. Herrick,	121 22	36 57	157 79
5	618	Isaac Hesler,	215 50	39 69	255 19
4	121	Roger Hickok,	262 50	34 07	296 57
5	421	Sands Higinbotham,	590 82	155 94	746 76
4	568	Stephen Hill, Jr.,	201 43	20 08	221 51
3	260	Elisha Hills,	232 66	....	232 66
8	254	John Hilliker	103 77	20 96	124 73
7	187	Squire Kinckley and Jos. Call,	120 00	1 14	121 14
7	188	do do	120 00	2 42	122 42
4	191	Squire Hinckley,	37 56	18 15	55 71
4	526	Moses Hinman,	137 41	2 06	139 47
6	23	A. G. Hitchcock,	402 11	93 27	495 38
8	235	William Hogan,	232 00	11 01	243 01
8	236	do	197 00	9 36	206 36
8	237	do	179 00	8 51	187 51
3	427	W. Hogan and J. Clendening,	432 31	20 70	453 01
7	273	James S. and Harvey Holt,	53 82	55	54 37
4	489	Elizabeth Holmes,	381 84	60 33	442 17
6	7	Robert Hollister,	390 06	41 10	431 16
3	183	Horace Hooker,	530 40	124 53	654 93
6	617	Frederick Horner, Jr.,	225 00	4 17	229 17
6	228	N. & B. Horton,	386 57	6 96	393 53
6	54	Columbia Hoseley,	64 77	60 28	125 05
4	199	Calvin Hotchkiss,	172 50	29 97	202 47
4	201	do	187 50	41 89	229 39
4	222	do	97 50	5 25	102 75
5	296	E Hotchkiss,,	31 00	....	31 00
5	297	do	78 54	33 38	111 92
5	298	do	78 54	33 38	111 92
5	317	do	50 00	21 20	71 20
8	546	Wm. Hotchkiss,	44 40	... ...	44 40
5	173	Henry C. House,	113 42	10 95	124 37
5	586	John A. House,	193 53	102 82	296 35
5	587	do	130 22	62 11	192 33
6	548	A. H. Hovey,	394 00	41 27	435 27
6	556	do	199 00	20 90	219 90

Principal and Interest on School Fund Loans, &c.—(Continued).

Book.	Page.	TO WHAT, OR TO WHOM LOANED.	Principal.	Interest.	Total.
7	75	A. A. Howlett, ...	$1,241 25	$3 70	$1,244 95
4	379	Alden Hull, ...	106 27	50 53	156 80
8	136	W. H. H. Hull and Otis Estes, ...	56 04	14 90	70 94
7	69	James Hunter, ...	1,035 00	163 61	1,198 61
5	126	C. T. Huntington, ...	235 00	99 64	334 64
5	170	Carlos T. Huntington, ...	84 00	35 82	119 82
3	409	Nehemiah Huntington, ...	227 17	24 70	251 87
4	58	John Hutchings, ...	46 28	1 30	47 58
7	259	Ebenezer F. Ingalls, ...	94 83	28 78	123 61
5	445	John J. Ingalls, ...	38 44	3 08	41 52
5	451	James Ingalls, Jr., ...	324 51	32 36	356 87
5	454	do	122 00	26 17	148 17
1	264	Israel Jackson, ...	376 27	17 65	393 92
1	265	do	97 15	5 19	102 34
2	183	Joseph James, ...	1,000 00	164 00	1,164 00
6	639	J. M. Jaycox, ...	690 00	213 50	903 50
5	500	H. T. Jenkins, ...	73 95	12 87	86 82
2	182	James Jenner, ...	286 15	91 85	378 00
4	632	Joseph Jennings, ...	437 74	29 62	467 36
6	422	William Jerome, ...	74 87	2 23	77 10
1	266	Ezekiel Jewell, ...	350 00	41 59	391 59
5	405	Franklin Johnson, ...	459 28	22 99	482 27
8	276	George Johnson, ...	60 89	6 86	67 75
3	223	Abram Johnston, ...	247 68	19 86	267 54
3	224	do	229 10	19 53	248 63
6	374	James Johnson, ...	69 40	5 55	74 95
6	383	do	149 31	27 24	176 55
7	341	do	750 00	37 50	787 50
5	354	Ezekiel Jones, ...	480 12	36 39	516 51
8	378	Leonard Jones, ...	496 52	21 85	518 37
3	329	Russell Jones, ...	398 43	43 21	441 64
6	2	Silas Judd, ...	43 75	8 26	52 01
4	535	Elijah Kellogg, ...	286 68	10 89	297 57
8	1	Isaac Kellogg, ...	103 92	3 31	107 23
8	105	Michael Kelly, ...	41 00	20 33	61 33
5	359	Freeman R. Kelly, ...	140 11	19 68	159 79
4	214	Patrick Kelly, ...	75 00	8 31	83 31
4	307	L. J. Kendall, rent due, ...	....	10 16	10 16
7	104	Hansell Kenney, ...	104 37	9 29	113 66
7	364	John Kenrick, ...	13 38	2 48	15 86
3	487	Clayton L. Kenyon, ...	59 00	4 00	63 00
3	466	Geo. W. Kenyon, ...	30 57	10 35	40 92
8	380	H. & S. Kenyon, ...	3,046 88	1,048 13	4,095 01
6	150	Angus Kerr, ...	120 00	7 50	127 50
6	151	do	86 00	5 37	91 37
5	453	Peter Kelts, ...	232 18	....	232 18
6	180	Edmund Knower, ...	807 26	7,034 38	7,841 64
4	302	James C. Knox, ...	709 66	4 97	714 63
4	524	John Knox, ...	245 44	57 69	303 13
5	115	Russell Knox, ...	63 26	3 80	67 06
5	116	do	55 23	2 76	57 99
6	627	Charles Kruger, ...	497 64	26 37	524 01
8	265	George Lamping, ...	76 80	24 44	101 24
7	367	B. P. Lamson, ...	120 00	10 84	130 84
3	392	Frederick Lansing, ...	100 00	12 48	112 48
4	345	Benj. Latham, ...	124 72	27 94	152 66
4	383	Asa Lawrence, ...	137 74	32 42	170 16
6	501	Grove Lawrence, ...	183 75	11 79	195 54
6	502	do	157 50	19 94	177 44
6	630	do	840 00	163 82	1,003 82
6	616	James R. Lawrence, ...	637 00	241 67	878 67
6	641	do	1,200 00	455 50	1,655 50
3	105	John D. Lawyer, ...	12 00	6 42	18 42
3	106	do	12 00	6 42	18 42
3	119	do	12 00	4 12	16 12
3	120	do	12 00	4 12	16 12
3	462	J. B. Leavens, ...	100 00	23 71	123 71
5	532	Joseph Leffingwell, ...	1,563 34	187 54	1,750 88
7	22	Peter Leinhart, ...	412 50	7 25	419 75
6	106	Geo. F. Leitch and Jas. L. Voorhees,	68 00	5 19	73 19
5	337	Elihu Lewis, ...	91 14	1 56	92 70
4	328	Robert Lewis, ...	4 23	08	4 31
6	157	Samuel Lewis, ...	135 00	10 11	145 11

Principal and Interest on School Fund Loans, &c.—(Continued).

Book.	Page.	TO WHAT, OR TO WHOM LOANED.	Principal.	Interest.	Total.
6	158	Samuel Lewis,..........	$115 00	$6 33	$121 33
7	8	Alexander Leyns,.............	400 00	30 40	430 40
3	265	Jacob W. Link,.....................	435 69	47 59	483 28
8	201	Henry Loughley,...........	137 78	58 86	196 64
7	106	Norman Luce, ...	186 30	12 33	198 63
4	423	Lyman R. Lyon, ...	1,800 00	63 00	1,863 00
5	155	Asa McDoel, ...	717 93	52 66	770 59
6	447	Thos. McCarty,.....	100 00	48 59	148 59
4	150	Nicholas McIntosh,................	169 00	82 75	251 75
5	100	Ezra Mack,.........................	294 00	36 75	330 75
1	465	John Mack and W. M. Waterman,...	7,825 63	70 42	7,896 05
6	614	Alex. McKinstry, ...	98 25	9 80	108 05
6	625	do	393 98	10 64	404 62
1	311	John McKinlay, ...	371 32	....	371 32
3	434	R. McKnight,.......................	1,050 00	283 25	1,333 25
7	221	John McLane, ...	88 09	10 03	98 12
7	308	James McLeod,......................	105 52	31 06	136 58
4	313	Catherine McLoughlin, rent due,....	....	5 27	5 27
4	110	R. S. McMurdy,....	131 61	3 16	134 77
4	574	J. W. Macomber and A. Taylor, ...	49 15	6 06	55 21
6	163	John Mahon,........................	262 50	127 93	390 43
8	308	John Main, ...	87 00	23 40	110 40
5	360	John Mambrute,.....................	184 97	7 55	192 52
8	168	Alrice Man,............	65 62	22 32	87 94
7	165	Laurien W. Marsh, ...	1,350 00	148 50	1,498 50
4	108	Nathan B. Markham, ...	180 00	11 25	191 25
4	115	do	71 92	20 82	92 74
8	493	James M. Marvin,...........	90 00	52 24	142 24
8	494	do	101 00	42 83	143 83
8	495	do	83 00	16 15	99 15
6	140	Henry H. Martin, ...	1,848 66	1,691 49	3,540 15
8	30	Sewell Martin,..	58 22	1 28	59 50
6	507	H. G. Matteson,........	169 50	7 31	176 81
6	376	John Matthews, ...	123 75	1 85	125 60
6	391	do	75 00	7 88	82 88
6	482	John Maynard, ...	109 00	1 42	110 42
8	171	H. B. Mears,...........	95 00	11 79	106 79
5	567	Robert Menzie,.....................	91 62	9 38	101 00
3	258	Solomon Merrill,...................	106 17	17 24	123 41
7	202	Philip S. Miller, ...	96 33	2 47	98 80
2	220	Samuel Miller,.....................	1,425 00	46 05	1,471 05
8	11	Samuel Mills,......................	87 00	32 55	119 55
2	218	William T. Miller, ...	9,478 15	3,501 81	12,979 96
3	515	Alexander Milne,.	98 87	14 14	113 01
1	315	Richard S. Mooers, ...	96 96	4 99	101 95
5	554	William H. Moat,...................	47 48	8 14	55 62
7	264	Thomas Mooney, ...	132 00	13 88	145 88
5	158	Eli G. Moore,...........	279 03	8 93	287 96
3	221	H. Moore and Abram Johnston, ...	167 70	14 08	181 78
5	609	James Mooers,......................	271 94	62 84	334 78
4	314	John Moore (rent due), ...	....	6 00	6 00
4	218	T. S. Morgan,......	82 50	30 21	112 71
4	219	do	78 75	28 74	107 49
4	247	do	97 50	35 59	133 09
4	248	do	101 25	6 73	107 98
4	249	do	150 00	9 75	159 75
6	172	do	2,511 02	2,840 80	5,351 82
3	229	Clark Morrison,..........	186 46	9 31	195 77
8	50	Job Mosher, ...	37 00	7 45	44 45
5	38	Jared Moss,........................	360 20	17 24	377 44
3	534	Samuel Mower, ...	459 10	44 43	503 53
3	333	Samuel Muzzy,......................	49 87	10 43	60 30
3	211	William W. Mumford, ...	147 00	34 05	181 05
4	610	Ephraim Munger, Jr., ...	173 74	....	173 74
4	605	Jotham Munger,.....................	273 24	114 81	388 05
7	342	Jerome J. Munger, ...	750 00	18 75	768 75
6	137	Allen Munroe and J. W. Barker,....	1,064 00	110 65	1,174 65
5	537	George Murray,.....................	123 28	45 78	169 06
5	147	L. Myrick and L. S. Hart,........ ..	201 67	... .	201 67
7	422	T. S. Nash, ...	34 00	8 60	42 60
7	423	do	55 57	4 92	60 49
4	123	Miles Neal, ...	41 69	22 61	64 30
4	107	Benj. C. Needham,...	44 63	....	44 63

Principal and Interest on School Fund Loans, &c.,— (Continued).

Book.	Page	TO WHAT, OR TO WHOM LOANED.	Principal.	Interest.	Total.
4	434	Barnhardt Nellis,...	$350 21	$33 46	$383 67
5	523	do	1,125 00	251 19	1,376 19
4	64	Robert Nelson, ...	16 50	....	16 50
4	346	Shadrach Newton, ...	22 35	1 22	23 57
5	559	N. B. Ney,..............	1,126 25	220 53	1,346 78
5	560	do	1,237 12	313 32	1,550 44
7	184	Charles Noble,......................	65 15	6 96	72 11
7	198	Charles and H. R. Noble, ...	86 40	21 57	107 97
3	321	Henry R. Noble, ...	39 02	40	39 42
8	117	H. R. Noble and E. F. Williams,....	57 80	19 88	77 68
8	118	do do	77 00	26 46	103 46
6	139	T. W. Olcott, ...	7,000 00	4,012 17	11,012 17
6	164	Loveland Paddock, ...	834 07	531 73	1,365 80
2	315	Nathaniel Page, ...	112 50	49 29	161 79
5	160	Wm. Page, John Sergent & R. Carpenter, ...	810 00	11 66	821 66
8	70	Geo. Palmer,..	127 37	9 40	136 77
6	169	Myron, Pardee, ...	5,617 13	2,734 34	8,351 47
6	179	do	2,000 00	970 00	2,970 00
3	484	Marvin Parker, ...	48 00	4 83	52 83
5	602	C. G. Parker,........................	152 81	16 66	169 47
3	486	Leonard Pasko, ...	48 00	1 86	49 86
4	275	Jasper W. Parmlee,............... ..	17 39	1 27	18 66
5	293	Albert Patten, ...	38 00	17 49	55 49
5	581	Hiram Parsons,......	169 06	82 28	251 34
5	321	E. Willard and A. Patton,...........	67 00	3 35	70 35
7	217	James O. Pattrige,..................	150 00	34 43	184 43
8	175	Ezekiel Payne,........................	18 73	2 90	21 63
5	294	Joh. Peck, ...	111 17	26 27	137 44
8	631	Lucien T. Peckham, ...	128 00	21 89	149 89
2	317	Miles W. Perry,.......................	300 00	136 80	436 80
7	218	James Perry, ...	30 00	2 35	32 35
7	316	M. P. Perry and W. Cressy, ...	146 82	32 87	179 69
7	317	do do	117 24	25 96	143 20
5	531	Elisha Pettibone, ...	836 66	56 59	893 25
6	368	Isaac R. Pharis, ...	120 00	18 96	138 96
6	319	Charles E. Pharis, ...	46 50	2 38	48 88
6	362	Mills P. Pharis, ...	124 00	8 62	132 62
6	363	do	87 00	6 05	93 05
6	446	Bishop Phelps, ...	187 78	13 87	201 65
4	197	Geo. P. Philes, ...	393 75	213 41	607 16
4	200	do	668 25	362 86	1,031 11
6	202	do	255 75	138 87	394 62
4	107	Asa Phillips, ...	75 00	6 28	81 28
6	108	do	64 00	4 49	68 49
6	110	do	75 00	....	75 00
6	612	Jefferson Phillips, ...	232 06	32 95	265 01
6	59	James Platt, Mayor of Oswego, ...	376 50	232 30	608 80
8	523	Starr Platt,......	196 01	14 50	210 51
5	382	Grove Pomeroy, ...	400 00	54 06	454 06
6	30	James Porter, ...	324 50	29 19	353 69
5	4	John Porter,..........	411 83	175 65	587 48
6	235	do	117 33	14 40	131 73
5	192	Nathan Porter, ...	312 91	44 54	357 45
2	314	Homer Pratt and Jno. Foote, ...	375 00	5 02	380 02
8	346	Stephen Pratt and Layton Wells, ...	109 49	42 92	152 41
4	584	Ormond Pray, ...	110 59	24 16	134 75
4	542	James Gregg, Jr.,...................	167 79	15 77	183 56
8	487	Henry Pulver,..........	119 70	17 36	137 06
8	133	H. A. Putnam. C. N. Williams, and O. Abell, Jr., ...	136 50	14 06	150 56
8	134	H. A, Putnam, C. N. Williams, and O. Abell, Jr., ...	136 50	14 06	150 56
8	130	H. A. Putnam, C. N. Williams, and O. Abell, Jr., ...	149 00	15 35	164 35
8	122	H. A. Putnam,.......................	252 00	27 97	279 97
5	210	H. A. Putnam, C. N. Williams, and O. Abell, Jr., ...	134 40	13 17	147 57
6	562	Hiram Putnam,.......................	251 34	24 16	275 50
3	542	Jonas Putnam, ...	94 55	11 44	105 99
3	194	Nelson Randall, ...	350 00	7 16	357 16
3	195	do	350 00	7 16	357 16
1	445	Nicholas P. Randall, ...	786 17	2 05	788 22

Principal and Interest on School Fund Loans, &c. — (Continued).

Book.	Page.	TO WHAT, OR TO WHOM LOANED.	Principal.	Interest.	Total.
4	537	Matthew Rankin,	$111 43	$4 85	$116 28
6	205	Isaac Rann,	376 02	46 55	422 57
5	607	Justin W. Ranney,	125 57	2 35	127 92
5	166	James H. Ransom,	139 69	19 42	159 11
6	4	Acors Rathbun,	400 00	68 40	468 40
4	527	Elias Rawson,	338 15	9 77	347 92
7	164	Richard Raynor,	1,200 00	36 00	1,236 00
7	122	Willett and Henry Raynor,	180 33	41 91	222 24
5	244	Philip Reilly,	40 00	14 20	54 20
4	23	Richard Remington,	82 00	4 34	86 34
6	534	Steuben Rexford,	225 00	193 08	418 08
7	121	John Rich,	562 58	14 44	577 02
8	521	H. S. Richards,	72 00	40 86	112 86
4	492	Daniel Richmond and J. W. Smith,	652 50	249 25	901 75
3	540	Charles Roberts,	84 00	30 66	114 66
5	264	do	86 50	12 33	98 83
6	530	William Roberts,	328 48	44 98	373 46
5	401	Seneca Robinson,	150 00	47 30	197 30
8	532	William W. Rockwell,	76 00	11 35	87 35
5	3	H. H. Rodmore,	236 88	25 11	261 99
3	192	Peter Rohe, Jr.,	400 00	2 40	402 40
6	638	Hugh Rogers,	667 00	54 80	721 80
5	518	Wm. Root,	1,042 00	189 40	1,231 40
7	178	Daniel Ross,	92 00	14 72	106 72
4	1	Henry H. Ross,	69 34	29 50	98 84
8	115	do	110 90	47 02	157 92
8	120	do	141 96	23 69	165 65
8	121	do	147 62	26 10	173 72
8	126	do	146 94	62 30	209 24
8	127	do	201 54	36 97	238 51
8	124	Leonard G. Ross,	84 00	28 81	112 81
6	120	R. L. Ross,	339 30	109 60	448 90
7	269	do	88 00	3 42	91 42
7	328	do	16 00	6 30	22 30
7	329	do	16 00	6 30	22 30
7	333	do	18 00	1 72	19 72
7	334	do	16 00	6 30	22 30
7	335	do	16 00	6 30	22 30
8	272	do	338 51	59 93	398 44
8	565	do	202 00	48 43	250 43
8	584	do	110 46	38 00	148 46
8	590	do	158 54	54 54	213 08
5	220	W. D. Ross,	125 00	42 96	167 96
8	290	do and Jonathan Steele,	291 15	123 53	414 68
8	291	do and H. H. Ross,	121 00	51 30	172 30
6	86	Clinton H. Sage,	156 00	6 44	162 44
8	213	Benjamin Sanborn,	251 14	8 80	259 94
8	169	do	66 67	20 32	86 99
2	438	Alexander Sanderson,	400 00	16 40	416 40
4	392	Reuben Sanford,	347 32	22 83	370 15
3	209	Jonathan Scoby,	120 00	23 10	143 10
4	232	Seymour Scovell,	135 00	49 47	184 47
1	452	Billy Seymour,	941 76	155 39	1,097 15
5	601	John Shaver and Lydia Shaver, administrator and administratrix of David Buyea, deceased,	585 36	327 31	912 67
6	224	Theodore Sheldon,	40 00	19 40	59 40
4	207	Leonard Shepard,	86 25	3 76	90 01
4	245	do	67 50	14 56	82 06
5	414	Isaac Sherman,	631 74	109 70	741 44
5	608	John C. Sherwood,	56 88	5 01	61 89
5	623	do	275 50	24 63	300 13
5	533	Jno. P. Sherwood,	432 74	95 58	528 32
5	534	do	470 00	70 19	540 19
7	13	C. Shirley, A. P. Granger and D. O. Salmon,	2,000 00	382 66	2,382 66
5	36	W. Sloan, Jr.,	106 07	14 20	120 27
8	9	Abijah Smith, Jr.,	110 00	30 84	140 84
8	524	do	72 71	13 50	86 21
8	520	do	43 00	14 37	57 37
8	526	do	45 10	6 49	51 59
5	538	Francis Smith,	547 09	71 00	618 09
8	38	Isaac Smith,	30 00	11 31	41 31

Principal and Interest on School Fund Loans, &c. — (*Continued*).

Book.	Page.	TO WHAT, OR TO WHOM LOANED.	Principal.	Interest.	Total.
8	39	Isaac Smith,	$34 50	$11 86	$46 36
8	40	do	54 00	18 58	72 58
8	41	do	60 00	20 62	80 62
8	42	do	60 00	20 62	80 62
8	43	do	30 00	10 31	40 31
8	44	do	18 00	6 21	24 21
8	45	do	54 00	18 58	72 58
4	35	J. Moreau Smith,	568 16	204 27	772 43
4	118	Luke Smith,	53 01	6 23	59 24
4	613	Nehemiah Smith,	166 75	8 54	175 29
3	212	Peggy Smith,	575 60	175 94	751 54
6	506	S. F. Smith,	86 25	30 88	117 13
7	115	Asa Snow,	131 09	23 71	154 80
3	4	Ebenezer Spears,	204 00	33 45	237 45
3	5	do	204 00	33 45	237 45
2	439	P P. Spear and A. Carter,	400 00	83 86	483 86
6	500	Thomas Spencer,	251 25	46 17	297 42
3	304	Isaac O. Sperry,	73 00	5 73	78 73
3	218	William Spinning,	146 95	4 30	151 25
3	322	Norman B. Squires,	41 51	18 05	59 56
5	148	Joseph Starn,	882 28	28 00	910 28
7	113	John Stanton,	474 62	81 03	555 65
7	105	Benjamin A. Stearns,	214 35	....	214 35
4	160	Samuel Stearns,	120 00	6 12	126 12
7	481	Samuel Stevens,	34 85	14 75	49 60
8	306	Thomas Stevens, Jr.,	49 00	14 25	63 25
7	478	William Stevens, 2d,	47 00	10 42	57 42
8	275	do	45 02	3 61	48 63
8	307	do	34 47	7 72	42 19
8	310	do	100 77	9 99	110 76
8	311	do	136 43	7 32	143 75
8	564	do	84 00	4 79	88 79
8	566	do	84 00	12 35	96 35
8	570	do	132 00	28 43	160 43
8	500	James Stevenson, Jr.,	101 00	35 11	136 11
5	605	John L. Stevenson,	278 54	50 59	329 13
5	159	Almon Stewart,	383 18	59 31	442 49
4	585	George Stewart,	320 19	56 00	376 19
5	486	do	136 40	29 37	165 77
5	487	do	334 20	79 36	413 56
5	490	do	296 78	61 92	358 70
7	361	Joseph Stickney,	88 64	2 22	90 86
1	457	Abner Stone,	400 00	25 55	425 55
5	177	Frederick Stone,	448 22	57 89	506 11
4	18	James Strong,	42 00	14 44	56 44
6	225	O. R. Strong,	8 41	42	8 83
1	459	Gerrit H. Stryker, Jr.,	4,532 35	7,133 19	11,665 54
3	338	Ira Sumner,	29 66	4 45	34 11
6	609	Charles Tallman,	375 00	24 25	399 25
7	15	do	375 00	35 75	410 75
7	18	do	375 00	30 69	405 69
4	316	J. J. Talmadge and Saml. Bell (rent),	....	94 17	94 17
3	210	Ashael Taylor,	144 62	41 21	185 83
3	214	do	265 87	160 31	426 18
4	377	Daniel Taylor,	329 10	27 64	356 74
6	18	John Taylor,	101 41	30 81	132 22
6	19	do	130 71	6 09	136 80
4	292	J. B. Taylor & O. W. Brennan (rent),	....	43,221 93	43,221 93
3	185	Enoch Tefft,	74 34	3 83	78 17
7	343	A. A. Thayer,	900 00	25 50	925 50
4	324	Delight Thayer,	118 77	29 99	148 76
4	325	do	281 90	79 76	361 66
4	323	Gardner Thayer, Jr.,	277 56	22 69	300 25
5	375	Henry Thomas,	213 03	107 54	320 57
5	378	John Thomas,	294 89	96 14	391 03
3	391	James and Ann Thompson,	355 00	32 01	387 01
7	181	James E. Thompson,	58 60	8 50	67 10
7	208	John M. Thompson,	75 00	16 80	91 80
7	219	R. Thompson, A. L. Rice & R. P. Rice	68 00	43 01	111 01
7	391	Roswell Thompson,	57 50	15 89	73 39
5	49	William F. Tiffany,	96 12	43 87	139 99
4	341	Thomas Tifford,	46 45	7 75	54 20
4	342	do	37 07	6 23	43 30

Principal and Interest on School Fund Loans, &c. — (Continued).

Book.	Page.	TO WHAT, OR TO WHOM LOANED.	Principal.	Interest.	Total.
5	575	John Tipple,	$153 49	$33 38	$186 87
5	579	do	121 09	41 64	162 73
7	340	C. S. Totman,	675 00	58 05	733 05
6	121	A. Tovey,	457 50	412 00	869 50
7	324	T. A. Tomlinson,	60 00	48	60 48
7	327	do	32 00	22 05	54 05
4	385	do	150 59	1 05	151 64
4	391	do	387 94	2 74	390 68
7	76	Edward Townsend	515 53	13 40	528 93
5	614	Henry Truax,	528 06	92 67	620 73
7	268	T. D. Trumbull,	110 00	24 64	134 64
4	208	Amos B. Tryon,	108 75	51 78	160 53
4	209	do	101 25	48 29	149 54
4	212	do	150 00	71 47	221 47
8	221	Benjamin Tryon,	100 00	50 30	150 30
5	342	Zebina Tryon,	83 62	6 94	90 56
3	433	John Turner,	539 75	22 65	562 40
5	309	Phineas Tuttle,	70 00	13 30	83 30
5	310	do	56 00	10 69	66 69
5	320	do	296 00	14 80	310 80
4	611	Alpheus Twist,	86 19	11 13	97 32
5	468	Daniel Twogood,	287 44	4 89	292 33
3	290	Joseph Tyler,	70 00	8 70	78 70
1	544	Josiah Tyler,	421 07	48 30	469 37
8	326	Rila Tyrrell,	138 61	11 56	150 17
8	527	Wolcott Tyrrell,	95 00	53 87	148 87
8	518	do	18 70	2 98	21 68
3	207	Amos and Cyrus Underwood,	598 87	153 75	752 62
8	525	Barent Van Benthuysen,	35 00	3 97	38 97
8	528	do	86 00	17 02	103 02
3	442	do	81 00	21 26	102 26
3	448	do	94 32	40 06	134 38
8	396	J. H. Van Benthuysen,	120 00	59 00	179 00
5	496	Garret Van Brocklin,	259 47	28 36	287 83
6	133	John Van Buren,	5,315 73	330 75	5,646 48
6	134	James Vanderpool,	2,957 86	2,062 99	5,020 85
5	604	Joshua Van Loon,	60 14	6 12	66 26
3	215	Nelson Van Ness,	448 91	45 34	494 25
6	162	P. J. Van Patten,	105 00	45 24	150 24
1	573	George Van Santvoord,	567 39	59 40	626 79
5	520	George W. Van Swall,	924 00	90 79	1,014 79
1	572	Ashael Vaughn,	500 00	65 06	565 06
6	34	Rufus Vaughn,	340 04	15 13	355 17
5	385	Howard Vinton,	70 50	44 40	114 90
6	207	John A. Wadsworth,	334 26	133 40	467 66
3	293	John Wagar,	60 00	26 30	86 30
7	53	George H. and Peter Waggoner	600 00	298 80	898 80
7	54	do	577 50	287 59	865 09
7	61	G. B. Waters, C. Tallman and Joseph B. Dunlop,	525 00	72 45	597 45
6	208	Roderick Ward,	200 00	15 24	215 24
6	213	do	200 00	28 94	228 94
3	543	William Ward,	104 00	29 68	133 68
3	273	Sylvanus Watson,	412 00	71 85	483 85
3	275	do	168 00	....	168 00
5	423	John H. Webster,	108 81	39 90	148 71
5	263	Jacob R. Weeks,	80 00	....	80 00
3	9	George W. Welsh,	630 00	53 55	683 55
3	10	do	600 00	51 00	651 00
3	11	do	600 00	51 00	651 00
7	389	A. Weldin,	75 51	33 79	109 30
7	193	Darius Westcott,	108 00	87	108 87
7	195	do	94 50	....	94 50
7	183	Selah Westcott,	73 73	1 94	75 67
7	182	John Westcott,	103 51	21	103 72
6	626	Louis Westphall,	475 00	25 18	500 18
6	135	J. P. Wetmore,	600 00	38 99	638 99
6	195	William Wheadon,	251 02	9 66	260 68
8	332	Melancton Wheeler,	140 00	69	140 69
8	335	do	65 00	33	65 33
8	336	do	63 00	32	63 32
8	336	do	52 85	1 62	54 47
3	527	Preston S. Whitcomb,	27 00	3 42	30 42

Principal and Interest on School Fund Loans, &c. — (Continued).

Book.	Page.	TO WHAT OR TO WHOM LOANED.	Principal.	Interest.	Total.
5	83	John Whitehead,..................	$315 55	$31 34	$346 89
6	334	John Whiting,......................	75 00	11 14	86 14
6	335	do	98 25	24 30	122 55
8	569	Peter Whitney,....................	150 00	3 55	153 55
3	213	E. Whittlesy, A. Taylor and J. Scoby,	247 35	114 77	362 12
3	317	Alanson Wilder,....................	82 00	39 77	121 77
4	194	do	90 00	43 65	133 65
4	195	do	68 00	32 98	100 98
5	291	Erastus Willard,....................	116 00	39 88	155 88
5	384	do	326 96	173 65	500 61
5	386	do	210 24	115 75	325 99
5	391	do	269 64	39 86	309 50
6	233	William Willett,....................	100 00	....	100 00
4	455	Daniel D. Williams,.................	177 23	7 97	185 20
5	381	Joseph L. Williams,.................	536 99	107 65	644 64
5	416	do	211 84	15 45	227 29
5	418	J. L. Williams and Erastus Willard,	676 62	58 77	735 39
6	640	Lucy A. Williams,..................	975 00	23 40	998 40
3	123	David Wilson,...........	51 00	21 62	72 62
5	219	do	113 00	38 87	151 87
8	114	do	69 00	29 26	98 26
8	116	do	96 00	40 70	136 70
5	387	Elijah Wilson,.............	443 50	112 38	555 88
4	601	Thomas Wilson,.....................	185 31	6 63	191 94
3	110	Harvilla Winchell..................	28 80	31 15	59 95
2	542	Jonathan K. Wing,..................	953 11	151 54	1,104 65
3	29	Henry Weisser and F. C. Brunck,...	1,162 50	346 18	1,508 68
3	33	do do ...	1,016 25	320 53	1,336 78
4	439	N. Wisner. D. Beach and E. Goodell,	616 47	25 03	641 50
4	438	M. Wisner, W. Rook and D. Beach,.	559 03	21 17	580 20
7	56	D. P. Wood and M. F. Graves,......	311 25	61 48	372 73
7	58	do do	386 25	229 28	615 53
7	59	do do	352 50	204 00	556 50
6	202	T. M. Wood,.......................	115 70	5 18	120 88
6	628	Augusta J. Woodruff,............ ..	620 00	47 74	667 74
6	336	Albina and Gardner Woolson,.......	92 25	1 81	94 06
6	361	do do ,......	210 00	15 44	225 44
7	109	Samuel Worden,....................	494 73	118 17	612 90
7	76	A. M. Wright,......................	757 20	22 41	779 61
6	131	Luther Wright's Bank,.............	2,544 18	502 14	3,046 32
6	544	John F. Wyman,....................	300 00	51 50	351 50
6	550	do	431 16	45 49	476 65
6	552	do	412 00	304 12	716 12
6	553	do	385 00	13 48	398 48
6	554	do	585 00	211 88	796 88
6	560	do	270 00	215 51	485 51
6	561	do	236 00	215 51	451 51
6	585	do	93 75	75 81	169 56
5	422	Henry B. Young,....................	42 00	14 57	56 57
		Total,........	$491,765 82	$188,256 71	$680,022 53

STATE TREASURER.

Under the present Constitution the Treasurer is elected for two years, and gives bonds for $50,000. He receives all moneys of the State, and disburses upon the warrants of the Comptroller, Auditor, Superintendent of Banking Department, and Superintendent of Public Instruction. Pursuant to chapter 103, Laws of 1857, he countersigns all securities withdrawn from the Bank Department.

The Treasurer is a member of the Canal Board and of the Board of State Canvassers, a Commissioner of the Canal Fund and of the Land Office, and a Trustee of Union College. He receives a salary of $2,500, and is allowed a deputy, cashier, book-keeper and clerk.

Receipts, from the year 1847 *to* 1866, *both inclusive.*

YEARS.	General Fund.	U. S. Deposit Fund.	Literature Fund.	Common School Fund.	Canal Fund.
1847, ...	$1,177,383 01	$302,178 84	$44,363 92	$461,183 05	$3,380,913 87
1848, ...	1,085,230 51	331,263 99	45,308 61	446,196 89	3,133,084 78
1849, ...	1,325,122 16	273,252 39	42,129 96	388,254 15	7,348,181 53
1850, ...	1,158,211 00	386,614 08	39,439 16	745,491 51	4,066,601 18
1851, ...	859,175 48	425,268 32	40,455 24	448,879 70	4,835,979 60
1852, ...	1,122,714 13	263,747 66	52,292 23	395,716 88	3,975,534 37
1853, ...	769,278 53	292,542 97	43,461 80	399,404 11	3,174,894 84
1854, ...	1,949,590 27	265,560 35	43,661 80	404,552 31	6,297,844 38
1855, ...	1,684,110 22	390,371 38	81,381 80	504,954 45	7,160,940 67
1856, ...	2,343,306 16	259,108 89	44,827 63	407,547 86	10,381,653 84
1857, ...	1,988,347 61	249,858 99	81,892 13	373,495 72	6,057,853 78
1858, ...	3,471,064 82	247,179 18	91,112 30	358,932 09	6,133,354 98
1859, ...	3,413,527 27	244,815 24	11,802 00	225,916 75	3,145,917 88
1860, ...	3,234,798 68	251,856 28	39,802 96	391,892 50	8,033,552 74
1861, ...	5,346,070 72	262,971 69	39,853 88	379,967 84	5,653,008 52
1862, ...	7,936,648 79	259,741 18	42,481 31	385,876 82	7,912,717 85
1863, ...	7,820,009 06	329,781 70	42,767 02	415,908 28	6,709,318 47
1864, ...	7,785,069 51	429,321 54	142,667 02	425,703 23	5,097,364 61
1865, ...	11,911,635 82	350,942 02	36,637 02	399,727 38	6,786,477 30
1866, ...	7,489,042 09	255,074 79	126,041 12	731,975 48	7,708,314 78
	$73,870,335 84	$6,071,451 48	$1,132,378 91	$8,691,577 00	$116,993,509 97

Receipts, from the year 1846 *to* 1866, *both inclusive.*

YEARS.	Mariners' Fund, Gospel Fund for Stockbri'e Indians, and Soldiers' Allotment Fund.	Bank Fund.	Hudson & Berkshire Railroad Sinking Fund, and Metropolitan Police Fund.	Tioga Iron, Coal and Railroad Sinking Fund.	General Fund Debt Sinking Fund.
1847, ...	*$66,660 70	$110,514 09	§$999 88	$54 29	....
1848, ...	*64,196 94	107,304 11	§7,869 88	52 27	....
1849, ...	*68,721 48	136,596 06	§651 08	52 27	....
1850, ...	....	181,756 56	§5,737 93	52 27	....
1851, ...	....	132,418 23	§6,545 75	52 27	$354,005 20
1852, ...	†18,000 00	126,389 15	....	52 27	354,005 20
1853, ...	....	121,770 49	....	52 27	822,975 20
1854, ...	....	99,650 66	....	52 27	364,009 20
1855, ...	....	81,873 63	....	52 27	701,116 20
1856, ...	....	71,200 92	....	52 27	365,435 50
1857, ...	....	62,230 48	‖183,190 38	52 27	301,835 92
1858, ...	....	165,494 38	‖1,319,595 02	52 27	102,911 54
1859, ...	....	57,912 32	‖1,367,827 18	52 27	1,193,881 71
1860, ...	....	44,111 00	‖1,532,132 00	1,516 77	602,455 99
1861, ...	....	42,471 25	‖1,805,731 00	863 67	2,312,126 67
1862, ...	‡15,657 87	43,030 70	‖1,910,100 00	2,946 27	1,233,870 20
1863, ...	‡7,477 00	34,730 61	‖1,848,962 50	1,546 27	350,000 00
1864, ...	‡36 00	33,509 86	‖2,067,629 95	1,546 27	350,000 00
1865, ...	....	29,170 96	‖2,537,322 43	9,984 13	950,000 00
1866, ...	....	44,403 72	‖2,528,709 14	....	782,961 04
Total,..	*$199,579 12 †18,000 00 ‡23,170 87	$1,726,539 18	§$21,798 52 ‖17,101,199 60	$19,084 91	$11,141,589 57

* Mariners' Fund.
† Gospel Fund for Stockbridge Indians.
‡ Soldiers' Allotment Fund.
§ Hudson and Berkshire Railroad Sinking Fund.
‖ Metropolitan Police Fund.

Receipts, from the years 1847 *to* 1866, *both inclusive.*

YEARS.	Tonawanda Railroad Sinking Fund.	Free School Fund.	Long Island Railroad Sinking Fund.	Auburn and Rochester Railroad Sinking Fund and Col'ge Land Scrip Fund.	Total receipts.
1847, ...	$2,064 74	....	$289 87	*$5,643 71	$5,552,243 97
1848, ...	2,123 76	....	1,289 87	*5,803 37	5,229,724 98
1849, ...	2,211 26	....	289 87	*6,040 87	9,591,503 08
1850, ...	9,604 09	....	2,289 87	*6,157 83	6,601,955 48
1851, ...	2,492 22	....	4,804 12	*26,855 39	7,136,931 52
1852, ...	2,824 39	....	687 00	*6,984 32	6,318,947 60
1853, ...	4,201 00	....	4,147 00	*20,595 32	5,653,323 53
1854, ...	1,328 50	$37,434 21	1,891 00	*8,250 32	9,473,825 27
1855, ...	8,357 61	775,443 65	1,959 64	*22,517 32	11,413,078 84
1856.	6,388 07	739,500 26	10,685 89	*47,482 82	14,677,190 11
1857, ...	3,861 25	921,220 78	2,166 64	*10,641 92	10,236,647 87
1858, ...	3,685 00	1,207,401 40	17,571 64	*31,339 00	13,149,693 62
1859, ...	4,305 00	1,152,853 75	2,334 00	*14,817 32	10,835,962 69
1860, ...	9,245 00	1,199,219 38	1,427 14	*196,252 65	15,538,263 09
1861, ...	6,617 75	1,064,473 06	28,641 48	*180 00	16,942,977 53
1862, ...	13,852 01	1,081,890 11	2,100 09	....	20,840,913 20
1863, ...	2,851 80	1,087,332 46	2,000 00	....	18,652,685 17
1864, ...	2,839 20	1,120,968 99	....	†64,762 40	17,521,418 58
1865, ...	70,238 88	1,076,522 08	4,000 00	†2,618 21	24,165,306 23
1866, ...	....	1,369,066 29	17 27	†8,416 94	‡21,606,583 47
Total,.	$159,091 53	$12,833,356 42	$88,592 49	*$409,562 16 †75,797 55	$251,139,175 83

* Auburn and Rochester Railroad Sinking Fund.
† College Land Scrip Fund.
‡ Includes Military Record Fund, $1,713.75. Metropolitan Fire Department Fund, $500,000, and Metropolitan Board of Health Fund, $60,847.06, which are not embraced in the preceding columns.

Payments from the year 1847 *to* 1866, *both inclusive.*

YEARS.	General Fund.	Common School Fund.	U. S. Deposit Fund.	Literature Fund.	Bank Fund.
1847, ...	$1,170,187 30	$298,076 41	$274,578 08	$47,195 60	$69,533 49
1848, ...	1,241,864 81	454,227 72	381,156 62	43,532 66	106,553 72
1849, ...	1,163,599 15	420,107 14	268,993 58	43,436 64	174,303 04
1850, ...	1,166,983 94	685,738 21	402,891 36	43,869 59	179,864 52
1851, ...	890,734 49	438,593 16	427,799 89	44,181 97	135,346 14
1852, ...	1,271,532 56	394,252 92	279,074 67	44,786 02	128,169 82
1853, ...	999,081 66	315,198 11	245,375 51	44,688 94	91,662 44
1854, ...	1,782,976 35	381,686 40	249,780 77	55,280 87	74,212 76
1855, ...	1,755,904 39	521,850 78	398,578 00	80,120 40	27,779 43
1856, ...	1,765,363 61	353,000 00	257,590 44	42,701 93	186,826 71
1857, ...	2,247,517 92	449,330 57	267,240 21	44,194 78	50,671 98
1858, ...	3,054,204 55	451,164 00	262,767 99	44,321 20	161,305 17
1859, ...	3,707,029 73	402,195 16	44,689 95	44,177 79	67,661 45
1860, ...	3,104,028 59	361,696 05	277,672 17	46,234 00	8,586 09
1861, ...	5,345,599 59	614,470 47	350,691 45	101,946 30	81,768 66
1862, ...	7,146,843 99	354,118 98	231,865 00	42,776 58	28,467 44
1863, ...	9,782,267 33	334,272 70	254,492 93	45,189 53	47,592 44
1864, ...	7,417,312 80	325,485 76	370,201 20	41,243 91	37,683 44
1865, ...	12,175,968 67	326,560 79	431,446 44	44,071 52	27,686 44
1866, ...	8,854,074 32	358,142 58	369,266 76	43,233 18	46,378 68
Total,.	$76,043,075 75	$8,240,167 91	$6,046,153 02	$987,183 41	$1,732,053 86

Payments from the year 1847 *to* 1866, *both inclusive*—(*Continued*).

YEARS.	Canal Fund.	Mariners' and Metropolitan Police Fund.	Free School Fund.	Long Island Railroad.	Tonawanda Railroad.
1847, ...	$3,380,913 87	*$34,679 34	....	....	....
1848, ...	3,133,084 78	*89,486 08	....	....	$3,500 00
1849, ...	5,623,044 85	*6,166 13	....	....	....
1850, ...	4,974,254 47	....	....	....	5,800 00
1851, ...	4,242,354 55	....	....	$8,950 00	8,750 00
1852, ...	4,067,902 43	*142,232 83	....	....	....
1853, ...	3,360,101 11	*571 86	....	3,430 00	....
1854, ...	4,209,380 53	*84 53	$35,285 38	1,153 11	8,062 50
1855, ...	7,532,291 63	....	777,048 17	....	9,006 72
1856, ...	10,797,169 43	....	739,515 06	12,400 00	6,000 00
1857, ...	5,653,371 65	†183,190 38	921,278 08	....	4,105 00
1858, ...	7,459,799 91	†1,319,595 02	1,207,015 75	....	4,000 00
1859, ...	3,439,750 57	†1,367,827 18	1,152,366 83	....	4,037 90
1860, ...	6,982,788 11	†1,515,132 00	1,199,014 04	22,923 22	7,000 00
1861, ...	5,480,548 53	†1,822,731 00	1,064,535 52	31,155 00	....
1862, ...	5,972,776 84	†1,910,100 00	1,081,823 28	1,005 00	....
1863, ...	6,857,015 74	†1,848,962 50	1,087,652 85	....	....
1864, ...	5,833,855 34	†2,067,629 95	1,117,906 65	....	....
1865, ...	8,165,658 64	†2,360,106 59	1,079,408 07	....	94,000 00
1866, ...	5,550,640 46	†2,705,924 98	1,333,566 91	....	6,000 00
Total,.	$112,719,703 44	*$273,220 77 †17,101,199 60	$12,796,416 59	$81,016 33	$160,262 12

* Mariners' Fund. † Metropolitan Police Fund.

Payments from the year 1847 *to* 1866, *both inclusive*—(*Continued*).

YEARS.	Auburn and Roch'ter Railroad Sinking Fund.	Hudson and Berksh'e Railroad Sinking Fund.	Soldiers' Allotment Fund.	General Fund & Sinking Fund.	Total payments.
1847, ...	....	....	....	....	$5,275,164 09
1848, ...	....	$9,500 00	....	....	§5,462,906 39
1849, ...	....	....	....	....	7,699,650 53
1850, ...	$13,000 00	....	....	....	7,472,402 09
1851, ...	21,200 00	5,298 52	....	$339,374 69	¶6,562,583 41
1852, ...	4,000 00	....	....	366,896 71	*6,716,847 96
1853, ...	17,179 50	....	....	834,485 54	5,911,774 67
1854, ...	6,245 00	....	....	366,247 63	7,170,395 83
1855, ...	24,401 53	....	....	702,713 00	11,829,694 05
1856, ...	48,000 00	....	....	354,543 50	14,563,110 68
1857, ...	8,779 57	....	....	347,259 56	10,176,939 70
1858, ...	32,000 00	....	....	362,041 22	14,358,214 81
1859, ...	16,104 24	....	....	772,957 24	11,018,798 04
1860, ...	....	....	....	621,480 99	14,148,667 64
1861, ...	200,000 00	....	....	2,071,126 65	17,167,573 17
1862, ...	....	....	$15,546 91	1,379,909 84	18,165,233 86
1863, ...	....	....	7,533 00	438,606 82	20,703,585 84
1864, ...	....	....	36 00	598,380 11	17,809,735 16
1865, ...	....	....	....	581,378 33	†25,370,285 49
1866, ...	....	....	....	752,837 34	‡20,580,912 27
Total,..	$390,909 84	$14,798 52	$23,115 91	$10,890,239 17	$248,164,475 68

* Includes $18,000 School and Gospel fund, Stockbridge Indians, not embraced in the preceding columns.

† Includes $64,000 on account of College Land Scrip fund, and $22,100.12 Tioga Coal, Iron and Railroad Co., not included in the preceding columns.

‡ Includes $60,847.06 on account of Metropolitan Board of Health, and $500,000 on account of the Metropolitan Fire Department, which are not embraced in the preceding columns.

Recapitulation.

FUNDS.	Receipts.	Payments.	Excess of Receipts.	Excess of Payments.
General Fund,...............	$73,870,335 84	$76,043,075 75	....	$2,172,739 91
Common School Fund, ...	8,691,577 00	8,240,167 91	$451,409 09	....
U. S. Deposit Fund, ...	6,071,451 48	6,046,153 02	25,298 46	....
Literature Fund,.............	1,132,378 91	987,183 41	145,195 50	....
Bank Fund,...................	1,726,539 18	1,732,053 86	....	5,514 68
Canal Fund,..................	116,993,509 97	112,719,703 44	4,273,806 53	....
Mariners' Fund,.............	199,579 12	273,220 77	....	73,641 65
Metropolitan Police Fund,...	17,101,199 60	17,101,199 60	....	....
Free School Fund,...........	12,833,356 42	12,796,416 59	36,939 83	....
Long Island Railroad Fund,..	88,592 39	81,016 33	7,576 06	....
Tonawanda Railroad Fund,..	159,091 53	160,262 12	....	1,170 59
Auburn & Roch'r R. R. Fund,	409,562 16	390,909 84	18,652 32	....
Hud. & Berkshire R. R. Fund,	21,798 52	14,798 52	7,000 00	....
General Sinking Fund, ...	11,141,589 57	10,890,239 17	251,350 40	....
Soldiers' Allotment Fund,...	23,170 87	23,115 91	54 96	....
Gospel and School Fund, Stockbridge Indians, ...	18,000 00	18,000 00	....	....
Metropolitan Board of Health Fund,..................	60,847 06	60,847 06	....	....
Metropolitan Fire Dep. Fund,	500,000 00	500,000 00	....	....
College Land Scrip Fund,....	75,797 55	64,000 00	11,797 55	....
Tioga, Coal, Iron & R. R. Co.,	19,084 91	22,112 38	....	3,027 47
Military Record Fund,.......	1,713 75	....	1,713 75	....
Total, ...	$251,139,175 83	$248,164,475 68	$5,230,794 45	$2,256,094 30

Excess of receipts over payments, $2,974,700.15.

STATE ASSESSORS.

The State Board of Equalization was created by chapter 312, Laws of 1859, and consists of the Commissioners of the Land Office, and three State Assessors appointed by the Governor and Senate.

The Assessors are appointed for three years, and required to "visit officially every county in the State at least once in two years, and prepare a written digest of such facts as they may deem most important for aiding the Board of Equalization in the discharge of its duties."

The duties of the board are confined to the equalization of the real estate, and it may "increase or diminish the aggregate valuations of the real estate of any county so as to produce a just relation between all the valuations of real estate in the State," but shall not reduce the aggregate valuations of all the counties below the total amount returned to the Comptroller. Supervisors may appeal to the Comptroller.

The State Assessors in the performance of their duties, have submitted, to the Board of Equalization annually, between the first Tuesday in September, and the tenth of October in each year, the digested results of their labors in a detailed written equalization or plan of equalization for consideration, and upon the final written action of the board thereon the State taxes are equalized, upon the filing of a duly certified copy of such written action in the office of the Comptroller.

Tables of returned and equalized valuations are published in the annual reports of the Comptroller from 1860 to 1867, both inclusive.

COMMISSIONERS FOR EXAMINING THE TREASURER'S ACCOUNTS.

From an early period the Legislature has provided for the revision of the Treasurer's accounts, from time to time, by commissioners named by law. In 1828, on the revision of the statutes, it was ordered that a committee of both houses should be annually appointed to perform this duty, and report the result of their labors to the Legislature. The number of this committee was not to be less than three nor more than five, and, in practice, it was composed of one member from the Senate, and two from the Assembly. By an act passed April 14th, 1862, the Governor and Senate appoint three commissioners, who hold for three years, and are so classified that one is appointed annually. Under a section in chapter 612, of the Laws of 1865, they were required to inspect, audit, and compare the vouchers for the disbursement of all military or bounty moneys. The commissioners report annually to the Governor, for the information of the Legislature, the results of their labors.

CANAL DEPARTMENT.

The Canals were originally constructed under the direction of Commissioners appointed by law. Any vacancies that might occur in the Board were to be filled by the Legislature, in the same manner as Senators in Congress are appointed. The number appointed in 1816 was five, but by an act passed May 6, 1844, they were reduced to four, and by the Constitution of 1846 to three.

The financial affairs of the Canals were managed by the Comptroller until, by an act passed March 11, 1833, the office of Second Deputy Comptroller was created for this duty, and the person appointed was allowed to perform all the duties of the Comptroller in relation to Canals, except as a Commissioner of the Canal Fund. This office was continued until May 13, 1840, when it was abolished, and these Commissioners were empowered to appoint a Chief Clerk, who filled the place of the former officer until 1848, when the office of Auditor of the Canal Department was created, and it has been since continued. This officer is Secretary of the Canal Board and of the Commissioners of the Canal Fund, and is a member of the Contracting Board. He has a seal of office, and issues warrants for all payments from the canal fund. He publishes annually a financial report and a report of the trade, tolls and tonnage of the Canals. He instructs collecting and disbursing agents, keeps a register of boats built and of changes in the names of boats, and has general charge of affairs relating to the finance of the Canals.

The powers and duties of the office were increased by chapter 177 of the Laws of 1861.

The following tables, numbered from I to XV, have been prepared for this Manual by the Auditor, and present the operations and business of the New York State Canals collectively, and each one separately, in regard to the receipts from tolls and the cost or expense of collection, superintendence and ordinary repairs, from 1846 to the close of the fiscal year on the 30th of September, 1866.

In reference to these tables the Auditor says:

"After seeing what the annual receipts from tolls and the payments on account of the support and maintenance have been during the period named in the tables, the Convention may desire further information; what that may be, I cannot anticipate.

"That subject was voluminously presented to, and elaborately discussed in the convention of 1846, and the fruits of that examination we have in the 7th, or financial article of the Constitution then framed, and subsequently approved by the people. The fiscal accounts between the canals and the treasury, or general fund, were by that article settled and adjusted; the award was final, and we may say conclusive, and no longer open to discussion in legislative debate. The finances of the canals were divorced from the other finances of the State, as a necessary measure, in order to carry into effect the objects and designs contemplated in creating the canal debt sinking funds. Those objects and designs have, thus far, been realized and accomplished, though not, perhaps, as rapidly as was anticipated. The tables submitted will show that what remains to be done in that direction, in reference to existing obligations, may be confidently anticipated, if no hostile interventions are placed in the way.

"Statement A, shows the progress of the canal debt, the amount paid for interest on loans, to the general fund debt sinking fund and to the treasury, for the support of Government, with the surpluses under article VIIth in each fiscal year, from 1846 to 1866.

"Statements B, C and D, show the operations of the sinking funds under sections 1, 3, and 12, of article VII, from 1846 to May 1st, 1867.

"Statement E, is a general exhibit of the description of the canal stock debt on the 1st of May, 1867, and the date of maturity, with the rate of interest.

"Statement F, gives the amount of moneys raised by taxes and paid into the treasury on account of the canals, and their debt, which are to be repaid to the treasury, with interest, out of the canal revenues, as directed by the 5th section of the VIIth article.

"Statement G, and the following, relate to the cost of the several State canals. The canals have no accounts to settle with the treasury or general fund, behind or anterior to 1846. When the general fund debt of 1846 is liquidated, in accordance with the provisions of the present 2d section of the VIIth article, and the moneys received from taxes repaid into the treasury, the commands of the Constitution, in respect to the treasury or general fund debt, will have been obeyed."

TABLE NO. 1.

All the Canals.

STATEMENT showing: 1. *The tolls on all the canals in the State (including rents from surplus waters), received in each fiscal year from* 1846 *to* 1866. 2. *The cost of repairs and collection of tolls.* 3. *The percentage which the cost of repairs and maintenance of all the canals bears to the gross amount of tolls.* 4. *The surplus revenues each year after paying the cost of maintenance.* 5. *The aggregate of the total movement on all the canals from* 1846 *to, and including,* 1866.

YEARS.	(1) Tolls collected.	(2) Expenses of collection and repairs.	(3) Per cent. of cost of maintenance on tolls.	(4) Surplus revenues in each.	(5) Tonnage of all the canals.
1847	$3,463,710 26	$641,650 08	18.52	$2,822,060 18	2,869,810
1848	3,156,968 38	855,850 64	27.11	2,301,117 74	2,796,230
1849	3,378,920 18	685,803 91	20.30	2,693,116 27	2,894,732
1850	3,393,081 37	835,965 81	24.64	2,557,115 56	3,076,617
1851	3,703,999 34	907,730 20	24.50	2,796,269 14	3,582,733
1852	3,174,857 49	1,049,045 92	33.04	2,125,811 57	3,863,441
1853	3,162,190 14	1,098,476 92	34.73	2,063,713 22	4,247,853
1854	2,982,114 97	1,237,866 20	41.51	1,744,248 77	4,165,862
1855	2,632,906 11	989,792 12	37.59	1,643,113 99	4,022,617
1856	2,721,740 63	786,633 40	28.90	1,935,107 23	4,116,082
1857	2,531,804 38	970,453 46	38.33	1,561,350 92	3,344,061
1858	2,047,391 01	1,078,878 91	52.69	968,512 10	3,665,192
1859	1,814,362 47	897,878 96	49.49	916,483 51	3,781,684
1860	2,381,301 28	746,976 78	31.33	1,634,324 50	4,650,214
1861	3,358,033 97	706,786 14	21.05	2 651,247 83	4,507,635
1862	4,797,283 09	773,398 32	16.12	4,023,884 77	5,598,785
1863	5,029,596 32	770,882 52	15.33	4,258,713 80	5,557,692
1864	4,310,293 02	1,028,909 46	23.87	3,281,383 56	4,852,941
1865	3,521,631 63	1,927,373 59	54.73	1,594,258 04	4,729,654
1866	4,253,224 92	1,434,989 73	33.74	2,818,235 19	5,775,220
	$65,815,410 96	$19,425,343 07	.....	$46,390,067 89	....

Yearly average of gross tolls $3,290,770 54
Yearly average of cost of maintenance 971,267 15
Yearly average of surplus revenues 2,319,503 39

Note.—The above table is a twenty years' exhibit of the receipts from tolls and cost of maintenance of all the canals in the State since the constitution of 1846 went into effect, as well as the annual surpluses of revenue carried to the capital of the sinking funds, and used in the payment of the interest and principal of the debt charged by the constitution upon the canal revenues. In these tables no account is made of moneys received from taxes, or other sources of revenue than those derived from the canals. Separate statements of these taxes will be given in the proper tables. The expenditures for collection, superintendence and repairs have been largely in excess of the estimates of 1846—see Table No. XV.

TABLE NO. II.

Erie and Champlain Canals.

STATEMENT showing: 1. *The tolls received in each fiscal year from* 1846 *to* 1866. 2. *Cost of collection, superintendence and ordinary repairs each year during the same time.* 3. *Per cent. of cost of maintenance on tolls.* 4. *Surplus revenues in each.* 5. *The tonnage of the Erie and Champlain Canals each year.* 6. *Contributed yearly to the lateral Canals.* 7. *Surplus tolls from lateral Canals each year:*

Year	(1) Tolls collected.	(2) Expenses of collection and repairs.	(3) Per cent. of cost of maintenance on tolls.	(4) Surplus revenues in each year.	(5) Tonnage of Erie and Champlain Canals.	(6) Contributed yearly to the lateral canals.	(7) Surplus tolls from lateral canals.
1847,..	$3,235,270 89	$425,847 02	13.15	$2,809,423 87	1,974,699	$65,403 00	$49,617 16
1848,..	2,915,215 56	594,474 16	18.85	2,320,741 40	1,893,854	88,062 07	20,064 17
1849,..	3,127,839 71	475,665 20	15.53	2,652,174 51	1,983,789	74,593 52	50,989 59
1850,..	3,150,749 32	507,658 63	16.11	2,643,090 69	2,095,308	142,497 72	15,579 22
1851,..	3,328,671 54	614,441 93	18.46	2,714,229 61	2,469,058	95,661 55	27,057 57
1852,..	2,920,810 88	703,267 83	24.08	2,217,543 05	2,660,335	167,255 68	24,794 59
1853,..	2,931,429 96	692,764 25	23.63	2,238,665 71	2,804,662	202,456 32	33,860 20
1854,..	2,762,901 42	836,189 97	30.26	1,926,711 45	2,826,921	211,278 98	35,366 54
1855,..	2,446,218 34	696,891 77	28.49	1,749,326 57	2,739,571	130,382 11	31,055 54
1856,..	2,527,572 77	597,107 58	23.62	1,930,465 19	2,719,288	38,839 41	70,874 22
1857,..	2,340,139 34	622,765 82	26.61	1,717,373 52	2,113,860	158,643 73	30,285 81
1858,..	1,908,388 60	572,953 93	30.02	1,335,434 67	2,375,922	343,231 40	1,122 70
1859,..	1,690,679 92	629,648 17	37.24	1,061,031 75	2,505,000	115,538 34	16,507 26
1860,..	2,205,665 46	484,051 78	21.95	1,721,613 68	2,934,690	125,169 27	73,167 20
1861,..	3,173,858 09	449,198 99	14.15	2,724,659 10	3,046,712	127,122 13	98,305 19
1862,..	4,587,583 28	418,575 01	9.12	4,169,008 27	3,851,595	178,577 20	91,160 28
1863,..	4,854,422 26	468,547 87	9.65	4,385,874 39	3,834,222	146,865 87	108,610 31
1864,..	4,079,285 93	601,166 49	14.74	3,478,119 44	3,382,582	278,903 73	118,140 35
1865,..	3,361,523 50	978,629 91	29.11	2,382,893 59	3,338,801	734,673 88	1,872 15
1866,..	4,057,413 15	903,831 40	22.28	3,153,581 75	3,897,520	299,569 82	20,744 46
	$61,605,639 92	$12,273,677 71	19.92	$49,331,962 21	55,448,389	$3,724,725 73	$919,172 51

Yearly average of gross tolls on the whole period,.. $3,080,282 00
Yearly average of cost maintenance,.. 613,683 89
Yearly average of surplus revenues,.. 2,466,598 11

Note.—This table shows the twenty years' operations of the Erie and Champlain Canals, and that, without the aids contributed from the tolls of these canals, the lateral canals, as a whole, would have failed from their own revenues to pay the expenses of their maintenance, superintendence and repairs, laying aside and entirely out of view all repayment of the debt for the cost of their construction and the interest paid on that debt. The aggregate of these contributions to the lateral canals, in excess of their own surpluses, is $2,804,753.73, or a yearly average of $140,237.69. This is the simple financial view of this question, without any reference to the increased receipts of the Erie and Champlain Canals from the tonnage contributed by the lateral canals, which will be presented in the following tables.

TABLE NO. III.

OSWEGO CANAL.

STATEMENT showing: 1. The tolls received in each fiscal year from 1846 to 1866. 2. Toll paid on the Erie Canal by the tonnage received from the Oswego Canal during the same period. 3. Cost of collection, superintendence and ordinary repairs each year during the same time. 4. Per cent. of cost on the receipts of Oswego alone. 5. Paid by Erie and Champlain Canal tolls to support the Oswego. 6. Contributed by the Oswego Canal to the Erie and Champlain Canal Fund. 7. The tons shipped on the Oswego Canal each year.

YEAR.	(1) Tolls on Oswego Canal proper.	(2) Tolls on Erie from tonnage of Oswego.	(3) Cost of collection, superintendence and repairs.	(4) Per cent. of cost on receipts of Oswego alone.	(5) Paid by Erie and Champlain tolls to support Oswego.	(6) Paid by Oswego to Erie and Champlain Canals.	(7) Tonnage of Oswego Canal.
1847,...	$67,610 71	$183,067 21	$40,239 86	59.52	....	$27,370 85	441,096
1848,...	69,832 76	176,078 96	76,063 95	108.92	$6,231 19	....	490,147
1849,...	86,139 66	219,584 58	42,265 96	49.07	....	43,873 70	557,637
1850,...	94,549 17	239,586 66	115,737 49	122.41	21,188 32	....	583,346
1851,...	104,366 58	241,678 67	99,459 38	95.30	....	4,907 20	676,321
1852,...	83,036 22	236,571 72	110,197 74	132.71	27,161 52	....	684,191
1853,...	93,194 79	293,504 65	197,245 36	211.65	104,050 57	....	761,276
1854,...	81,266 00	169,755 18	181,266 00	253.08	100,000 00	....	611,533
1855,...	65,124 48	216,955 66	100,407 00	154.18	35,282 52	....	654,399
1856,...	96,136 22	322,633 09	65,540 01	68.17	....	30,596 21	657,381
1857,...	105,141 39	226,928 55	89,499 44	85.12	....	15,641 95	605,218
1858,...	84,027 09	169,517 31	104,234 16	124.05	20,207 07	....	688,960
1859,...	69,423 07	196,177 04	62,283 38	89.71	....	7,139 69	612,390
1860,...	110,012 54	430,417 86	49,465 38	44.96	....	60,547 16	1,080,076
1861,...	131,604 64	448,799 80	33,563 81	25.50	....	98,040 83	852,920
1862,...	155,589 92	491,799 08	69,060 51	44.39	....	86,529 41	1,063,413
1863,...	143,773 75	445,023 24	47,834 43	33.27	....	95,939 32	992,173
1864,...	142,561 87	344,319 79	39,776 80	27.90	....	102,785 07	765,097
1865,...	120,891 65	411,281 57	314,909 40	260.48	194,017 75	....	825,649
1866,...	143,920 84	453,724 49	163,118 95	113.06	19,198 11	....	990,809
	$2,048,203 35	$5,917,405 11	$2,002,169 01	97.75	$527,337 05	$573,371 39	14,594,032

NOTE.—The excess of tolls on this Canal over the cost of superintendence and repairs, $46,034.34, and the contributions to the Erie and Champlain Canal Fund exceed the amount paid from the tolls of those Canals for the support of the Oswego is $44,034.34, making an aggregate of $90,068.68. It is claimed for this Canal that the tolls on the Erie paid by the tonnage from the Oswego during the twenty years has been $5,917,405.11, and that this is a creditor Canal in the same light as the Erie and Champlain. Others aver that most of this tonnage was from the West and diverted from the Erie at Buffalo, through the Welland Canal. Since 1846 there has been paid for principal and interest on loans made for original construction, $779,357; on account of enlargement, $2,945,787; paid by the General Fund and Erie and Champlain tolls before 1846, $341,618.86; making a total of $4,067,762.86, stating an interest account up to 1866 might not leave this Canal greatly in advance.

TABLE NO. IV.

Cayuga and Seneca Canal.

STATEMENT showing: 1. *The tolls received each fiscal year from* 1846 *to* 1866. 2. *The tolls paid on the Erie by the tonnage received from the Cayuga and Seneca Canal during the same period.* 3. *Cost of collection, superintendence and repairs each year during the same time.* 4. *Per cent. of cost on the receipts of the Cayuga and Seneca alone.* 5. *Paid by Erie and Champlain Canal tolls to support the Cayuga and Seneca.* 6. *Contributed by the Cayuga and Seneca Canal to the Erie and Champlain Canal Fund.* 7. *The tons shipped on the Cayuga and Seneca Canal each year.*

YEAR	(1)	(2)	(3)	(4)	(5)	(6)	(7)
	Tolls on Cayuga and Seneca Canal proper.	Tolls on Erie from tonnage of Cayuga and Seneca.	Cost of collection, superintendence, and repairs.	Per cent. of cost on receipts of Cayuga and Seneca alone.	Paid by Erie and Champlain tolls to support Cayuga and Seneca.	Paid by Cayuga and Seneca to Erie and Champlain Canals.	Tonnage of Cayuga and Seneca Canal.
1847,	$25,382 27	$54,695 80	$15,005 05	59.11	....	$10,377 25	58,204
1848,	27,773 29	51,680 22	14,230 07	51.23	....	13,543 22	46,252
1849,	27,735 44	41,556 55	65,238 14	235.21	$37,502 70	....	40,440
1850,	27,589 59	41,218 23	63,847 68	231.42	36,258 09	....	42,379
1851,	26,258 40	32,426 42	22,520 82	85.76	....	3,737 58	37,084
1852,	22,524 38	31,104 34	31,023 71	137.73	8,499 33	....	47,275
1853,	25,169 84	40,422 30	27,820 85	110.53	2,651 01	....	58,973
1854,	24,808 90	39,174 74	18,738 01	75.53	....	6,070 89	72,995
1855,	23,915 81	36,593 84	12,728 48	53.22	....	11,187 33	76,744
1856,	20,919 78	42,901 22	12,641 13	60.42	....	8,278 65	131,908
1857,	19,457 35	34,330 97	15,723 12	80.80	....	3,734 23	120,435
1858,	14,401 16	32,499 44	33,983 32	235.97	19,582 16	....	75,968
1859,	25,763 12	33,778 02	17,486 61	67.88	....	8,276 51	80,602
1860,	20,287 94	38,786 99	8,718 90	42.97	....	11,569 04	98,678
1861,	18,778 32	31,871 02	22,357 01	119.06	3,578 69	....	100,992
1862,	26,146 30	36,383 11	22,946 25	87.76	....	3,200 05	125,659
1863,	25,243 93	38,070 11	17,640 78	69.88	....	7,603 15	119,704
1864,	28,040 29	56,624 52	16,901 47	60.27	....	11,138 82	185 161
1865,	23,802 22	68,029 04	26,768 27	112.46	2,966 05	....	192,312
1866,	34,151 25	68,745 58	16,511 98	48.35	....	17,639 27	368,233
	$488,149 58	$850,892 46	$482,831 62	98.91	$111,038 03	$116,355 99	2,079,998

NOTE.—The tolls proper on this canal, and the cost of superintendence and repairs, very nearly balance; and the payments to and advances from the Erie and Champlain Canal tolls hold the same relation. It remains to dispose of the $850,892.46 tolls received on the Erie, from the tonnage brought to it from this canal.

There has been paid for principal and interest on loans made for orignal construction, $474,-404.83; by general fund for deficiencies prior to 1846, $146,497.44; and expended for enlargement since 1853, $1,121,552.11, making a total of $1,742,454.38, which more than balances the tolls paid on the Erie by the tonnage from this canal.

TABLE NO. V.

CHEMUNG CANAL.

STATEMENT showing: 1. The tolls received in each fiscal year from 1846 *to* 1866. 2. *Tolls paid on Erie Canal by tonnage received from the Chemung Canal during the same period.* 3. *The cost of collection, superintendence and ordinary repairs each year during the same time.* 4. *Per cent. of cost on receipts of Chemung Canal alone.* 5. *Paid by Erie and Champlain Canal tolls, to support the Chemung.* 6. *Contributed by the Chemung Canal to the Erie and Champlain Canal Fund.* 7. *The tons shipped on the Chemung Canal each year.*

YEAR	(1) Tolls on Chemung Canal proper.	(2) Tolls on Erie from tonnage of Chemung Canal.	(3) Cost of collection, superintendence, and repairs.	(4) Per cent. of cost on receipts of Chemung C'n'l alone.	(5) Paid by Erie and Champlain Canals to support Chemung.	(6) Paid by Chemung to Erie and Champlain C'nls.	(7) Tonnage of Chemung Canal.
1847,	$12,116 13	$66,674 54	$19,846 25	163.80	$7,730 12	......	189,165
1848,	15,921 58	59,842 01	28,711 34	180.33	12,789 76	......	150,697
1849,	16,048 96	50,388 20	39,089 28	243.55	23,040 32	......	135,867
1850,	16,276 54	66,989 90	70,430 64	432.71	54,154 10	......	128,263
1851,	15,986 04	66,752 91	53,412 23	334.12	37,426 19	......	159,563
1852,	15,683 31	60,981 26	37,364 79	238.24	21,681 48	......	187,577
1853,	20,810 23	83,029 85	39,436 51	189.50	18,626 28	......	249,980
1854,	19,635 35	89,734 50	38,598 88	196.57	18,963 53	......	270,978
1855,	19,771 91	80,406 85	25,432 76	128.63	5,660 85	......	223,271
1856,	17,224 45	62,969 12	20,648 57	119.88	3,424 12	......	245,621
1857,	17,101 71	49,318 29	108,281 14	633.16	91,179 43	......	188,201
1858,	13,347 95	50,440 87	192,658 72	1,443.36	179,310 77	......	205,168
1859,	17,474 93	55,395 28	64,673 30	370.09	47,198 37	......	256,323
1860,	18,615 24	52,648 01	85,854 38	461.29	67,239 14	......	226,051
1861,	15,319 76	39,442 30	48,755 90	318.25	33,436 14	......	208,792
1862,	22,361 38	55,789 95	112,461 91	502.93	90,100 53	......	243,628
1863,	21,628 77	54,147 03	104,682 40	483.99	83,053 63	......	307,151
1864,	23,430 05	42,874 98	73,212 99	312.47	49,782 94	......	280,834
1865,	16,745 91	24,912 86	104,103 49	621.66	87,357 58	......	164,796
1866,	18,252 04	41,166 70	63,563 73	348.25	45,311 69	......	226,510
	$353,752 24	$1,153,905 40	$1,331,219 21	376.31	$977,466 97	......	4,248,436

NOTE.—This canal has not paid the cost of superintendence, collection and repairs the last twenty years, into $977,466.97. It never contributed a dollar toward the payment of the principal and interest on the cost of its construction; and since 1846 there has been paid from the sinking fund $883,161.14, on the principal and interest of the debt contracted for the construction of the canal. These two sums quite overbalance the tolls paid on the Erie from the tonnage of the Chemung. The increasing and extended trade in anthracite coal may help the revenues of this canal, but not very materially at the present low rates of toll.

TABLE NO. VI.

CROOKED LAKE CANAL.

STATEMENT showing: 1. *The tolls received in each fiscal year from* 1846 *to* 1866. 2. *Tolls paid on the Erie Canal by the tonnage received from the Crooked Lake Canal during the same period.* 3. *The cost of collection, superintendence and ordinary repairs each year during the same time.* 4. *Per cent. of costs on the receipts of the Crooked Lake alone.* 5. *Paid by Erie and Champlain tolls to support the Crooked Lake Canal.* 6. *Contributed by the Crooked Lake Canal to the Erie and Champlain Canal fund.* 7. *The tons shipped on the Crooked Lake Canal each year.*

YEAR.	(1) Tolls on Crooked Lake proper.	(2) Tolls on Erie from tonnage of Crooked Lake.	(3) Cost of collection, superintendence and repairs.	(4) Per cent. of cost on receipts of Crooked Lake alone.	(5) Paid by Erie and Champlain Canals to support Crooked Lake.	(6) Paid by Crooked Lake to Erie and Champl'n Canals.	(7) Tonnage of Crooked Lake.
1847,	$899 55	$24,318 31	$52,696 65	5,857.85	$51,797 10	....	36,318
1848,	1,452 44	22,908 97	66,528 93	4,580.48	65,076 49	....	34,155
1849,	1,819 17	26,363 97	13,160 43	723.43	11,341 26	....	36,317
1850,	1,796 17	26,182 49	15,022 01	836.33	13,225 84	....	38,797
1851,	1,714 34	19,546 38	13,488 02	786.78	11,773 68	....	29,309
1852,	1,246 02	23,197 03	8,900 54	714.32	7,654 52	....	35,757
1853,	1,656 75	22,411 33	6,308 50	380.77	4,651 75	....	53,985
1854,	1,303 69	12,274 11	6,044 12	463.62	4,740 43	....	25,349
1855,	837 48	15,939 I8	6,208 84	741.30	5,371 36	....	25,850
1856,	1,154 48	16,161 82	5,602 26	485.26	4,447 78	....	28,559
1857,	879 26	7,430 54	12,691 91	1,443.48	11,812 65	....	16,571
1858,	520 82	8,364 77	10,929 91	2,098.60	10,409 09	....	16,318
1859,	715 06	6,422 48	5,650 55	790.22	4,935 49	....	17,933
1860,	683 34	8,543 19	6,300 12	921.96	5,616 78	....	14,723
1861,	699 94	7,073 42	7,034 21	1,012.40	6,384 27	....	12,239
1862,	712 70	11,064 42	8,081 91	1,133.98	7,369 21	....	19,632
1863,	746 40	5,690 58	5,877 16	787.40	5,130 76	....	11,230
1864,	585 88	3,826 40	34,021 90	5,806.97	33,436 02	....	6,316
1865,	290 65	5,505 67	37,088 85	12,760.65	36,798 20	....	9,376
1866,	534 96	8,680 37	7,904 12	1,477.51	7,369 16	....	12,189
	$20,249 10	$281,905 43	$329,590 94	1,632.51	$309,341 84	....	480,932

NOTE.—The tolls on this canal proper, and the tolls on the Erie from the tonnage of the Crooked Lake Canal, have not paid the expenses of superintendence and repairs into $27,436.41. The tolls on the canal proper do not pay the cost of collection, leaving the expense of repairs a charge upon the Erie and Champlain Canal tolls. The deficiencies upon this canal, amounting to $472,721.06, have been paid by the general fund and the Erie and Champlain Canal tolls. It is estimated that the rebuilding of the locks on this canal, originally of wood, will cost $300,000.

TABLE NO. VII.

CHENANGO CANAL.

STATEMENT showing: 1. *The tolls received in each fiscal year from* 1846 *to* 1866. 2. *Tolls paid on the Erie Canal by the tonnage received from the Chenango Canal during the same period.* 3. *The cost of collection, superintendence and ordinary repairs each year during the same time.* 4. *Per cent. of cost on the receipts of the Chenango alone.* 5. *Paid by Erie and Champlain Canal tolls to support the Chenango.* 6. *Contributed by the Chenango Canal to the Erie and Champlain Canal Fund.* 7. *The tons shipped on the Chenango Canal each year.*

YEAR.	(1) Tolls on Chenango Canal proper.	(2) Tolls on Erie from tonnage of Chenango.	(3) Cost of collection, superintendence and repairs.	(4) Per cent. of cost on receipts of Chenango alone.	(5) Paid by Erie and Champlain tolls to support Chenango.	(6) Paid by Chenango to Erie & Champlain Canals.	(7) Tonnage of Chenango Canal.
1847,.	$24,394 01	$10,940 10	$20,410 04	83.66	....	$3,983 97	44,051
1848,.	27,353 62	5,853 87	21,455 77	78.44	....	5,897 85	35,207
1849,.	28,028 98	4,426 97	29,290 33	104.50	$1,261 35	....	36,557
1850,.	20,343 65	4,718 43	26,381 25	129.68	6,037 60	....	41,892
1851,.	19,732 35	3,793 82	32,708 27	165.76	12,975 92	....	40,307
1852,.	16,921 86	2,287 87	42,158 20	249.13	25,236 34	....	44,939
1853,.	18,107 89	2,211 00	39,251 51	216.76	21,143 62	....	76,538
1854,.	19,496 15	1,529 53	50,879 57	260.97	31,383 42	....	77,142
1855,.	20,304 08	1,794 58	45,807 04	225.60	25,502 96	....	89,390
1856,.	18,839 28	1,567 68	24,848 75	131.89	6,009 47	....	105,502
1857,.	22,969 47	707 14	30,166 07	131.33	7,196 60	....	96,722
1858,.	15,433 07	1,028 63	47,444 15	307.42	32,011 08	....	72,526
1859,.	17,801 72	1,614 18	27,879 11	156.61	10,077 39	....	89,691
1860,.	22,214 37	1,499 13	30,834 26	138.80	8,619 89	....	83,035
1861,.	23,438 70	1,089 97	63,484 70	270.85	40,046 00	....	91,661
1862,.	22,155 94	914 78	43,720 19	197.28	21,564 25	....	79,442
1863,.	24,415 18	853 48	37,889 46	155.19	13,474 28	....	90,215
1864,.	30,034 43	638 74	81,096 63	270.08	51,062 20	....	89,021
1865,.	21,710 98	283 46	139,308 55	641.50	117,597 57	....	68,822
1866,.	35,465 80	274 05	124,581 98	351.27	89,116 18	....	107,402
	$449,161 53	$48,027 41	$959,595 83	213.64	$520,316 12	$9,881 82	1,460,062

NOTE.—The tolls on this canal and the tolls on the Erie from the Chenango tonnage, $497,188.94, have not paid the cost of superintendence and repairs, $959,595.83, into $462,406.89. The principal of the loans contracted for the construction of this canal, with the interest, amounting in all to $3,682,792.12, have been paid by contributions from the Erie and Champlain Canal tolls, with the exception of the $9,881.82. The tolls of this canal now pay about 50 per cent. of the cost of superintendence, collection, and ordinary repairs, without reference to the cost of amending breaks. The locks of wood will, in the course of a very short time, be replaced with wood and stone locks, at an expense of not less than $1,000,000, which charge must be borne by the Erie and Champlain Canal tolls.

TABLE NO. VIII.

Black River Canal.

STATEMENT showing: 1. *The tolls received in each fiscal year from* 1846 *to* 1866. 2. *Tolls paid on the Erie Canal by tonnage received from the Black River Canal during the same period.* 3. *The cost of collection, superintendence and repairs in each year during the same time.* 4. *Per cent. of cost on the receipts of the Black River Canal alone.* 5. *Paid by Erie and Champlain Canal tolls to support the Black River.* 6. *The tons shipped on the Black River Canal each year.*

YEARS.	(1) Tolls on Black River Canal proper.	(2) Tolls on Erie from tonnage of Black River.	(3) Cost of collection, superintendence and repairs.	(4) Per cent. of cost on receipts of Black River alone.	(5) Paid by Erie and Champlain tolls to support the Black River.	(6) Tonnage of Black River Canal.
1847.	....	....	....	....	....	....
1848,	....	....	....	....	....	....
1849,	....	....	....	....	....	....
1850,	$1,115 73	....	$10,014 52	897.58	$8,898 79	....
1851,	3,834 73	$2,312 42	26,071 26	679.87	22,236 53	25,320
1852,	4,230 28	3,164 05	29,934 50	707.62	25,704 22	36,497
1853,	5,546 32	5,548 06	24,969 85	450.21	19,423 53	41,924
1854,	5,843 42	7,462 88	37,451 81	640.92	31,608 39	55,525
1855,	6,808 05	7,550 45	36,424 35	535.02	29,616 30	51,347
1856,	5,594 10	5,310 69	17,785 43	317.93	12,191 33	68,126
1857,	6,575 22	6,458 11	14,998 37	228.10	8,423 15	69,135
1858,	5,170 61	5,276 34	19,293 76	373.14	14,123 15	62,352
1859,	5,963 01	7,504 45	27,570 05	462.35	21,607 03	75,946
1860.	6,330 71	8,997 24	24,977 25	394.54	18,646 54	70,687
1861,	9,590 38	7,424 02	26,782 43	279.26	17,192 05	69,930
1862,	8,741 17	8,542 86	23,676 44	270.06	14,935 27	85,442
1863,	10,172 66	10,779 19	20,868 84	205.15	10,696 18	90,448
1864,	10,078 30	11,344 99	23,643 42	234.60	13,565 12	72,519
1865,	10,985 87	9,861 31	59,898 57	545.23	48,912 70	73,317
1866,	13,449 82	14,449 21	51,313 21	381.52	37,863 39	85,908
	$120,030 39	$121,986 27	$475,674 06	396.29	$355,643 67	1,034,423

Note.—Here the tolls proper and the Erie tolls on the Black River Canal tonnage have failed to pay the cost of superintendence and repairs into $233,657.40. This is one of the Canals whose completion was secured by the Constitution of 1846. The principal and interest of the loans contracted for this Canal prior to 1846, amounting to $3,017,337.37, have been paid from other sources than the income of the Canal, and the payments by the Canal Commissioners since 1854 of $623,940.78 for completion, make this an expensive feeder for the Erie Canal. The last mentioned sum is covered by the new enlargement and completion loans yet to be paid. The extension of this Canal to Carthage by the improvement of the Black River has not yet brought out a very large increase in tolls, although it has done so in the cost of maintenance.

TABLE NO. IX.

Genesee Valley Canal.

STATEMENT showing: 1. *The tolls received in each fiscal year, from* 1846 *to* 1866. 2. *Tolls paid on Erie Canal by tonnage received from the Genesee Valley Canal during the same period.* 3. *The cost of collection, superintendence and ordinary repairs each year during the same time.* 4. *Per cent. of cost on the receipts of Genesee Valley Canal alone.* 5. *Paid by Erie and Champlain Canal tolls to support the Genesee Valley Canal.* 6. *Contributed by the Genesee Valley Canal to the Erie and Champlain Canal Fund.* 7. *The tons shipped on the Genesee Valley Canal each year.*

YEARS.	(1) Tolls on Genesee Valley Canal proper.	(2) Tolls on Erie from tonnage of Genesee Valley.	(3) Cost of collection, superintendence and repairs.	(4) Per cent. of cost on receipts of Genesee Valley alone.	(5) Paid by Erie and Champlain tolls to support the Genesee Valley.	(6) Paid by Genesee Valley to Erie and Champlain canals.	(7) Tonnage of Genesee Valley Canal.
1847,.....	$23,549 19	$39,040 38	$15,782 32	67.02	....	$7,766 87	95,632
1848,.....	25,293 01	37,737 37	27,813 47	109.96	$2,520 46	....	98,467
1849,.....	25,234 04	39,362 95	18,791 26	74.47	....	6,442 78	84,674
1850,.....	28,821 98	38,357 08	18,737 15	65.01	....	10,084 83	89,804
1851,.....	25,451 36	32,867 70	36,700 59	144.19	11,249 23	....	100,722
1852,.....	25,064 39	24,344 97	76,382 66	304.71	51,318 27	....	122,901
1853,.....	30,183 73	33,564 99	62,093 29	205.72	31,909 56	....	157,164
1854,.....	30,662 08	30,857 89	49,883 03	162.69	19,220 95	....	158,942
1855,.....	28,390 12	22,808 50	54,294 76	191.24	25,904 64	....	102,321
1856,.....	23,365 84	17,442 43	35,405 53	151.53	12,039 69	....	113,731
1857,.....	26,044 97	25,007 19	64,590 53	247.99	38,545 56	....	114,576
1858,.....	25,651 07	37,025 82	87,240 42	340.10	61,589 35	....	118,303
1859,.....	28,948 94	35,364 59	55,257 27	190.88	26,308 33	....	124,263
1860,.....	31,131 82	40,005 92	51,261 77	164.66	20,129 95	....	123,602
1861,.....	29,702 31	20,715 69	36,162 13	121.76	6,459 82	....	94,329
1862,.....	28,797 27	30,246 61	70,580 04	245.09	41,782 77	....	129,974
1863,.....	32,747 98	29,685 26	64,123 61	195.81	31,375 63	....	112,549
1864,.....	27,830 57	20,303 44	152,887 30	549.35	125,056 73	....	71,411
1865,,....	18,410 41	7,653 59	257,143 23	1,396.72	238,732 82	....	55,581
1866,.....	17,772 82	14,442 21	110,883 40	623.89	93,110 58	....	86,578
	$533,053 90	$576,834 58	$1,346,013 76	252.51	$837,254 34	$24,294 48	2,156,524

NOTE.—It is hardly necessary to repeat that the tolls on this canal, with the tolls on the Erie from the tonnage contributed by this canal, have fallen short of paying the cost of repairs and maintenance $237,125.28. This canal was not well built, and will require large annual outlays, as it has done heretofore, to keep it in running order. The principal loans contracted before 1846 for this canal, with the interest, amounting to $8,185,267.20, have been paid from funds other than those derived from its revenues. Since 1853, the Canal Commissioners have paid $855,580.45 on account of completion, which sum was raised on the enlargement and completion loans that remain to be paid. A large number of locks on this canal must soon be rebuilt at a heavy cost.

TABLE NO. X.

ONEIDA LAKE CANAL.

STATEMENT showing: 1. *The tolls received in each fiscal year from* 1846 *to* 1866. 2. *Tolls paid on the Erie Canal by the tonnage received from the Oneida Lake during the same period.* 3. *Cost of collection, superintendence and ordinary repairs each year during the same time.* 4. *Per cent. of cost on receipts of Oneida Lake Canal alone.* 5. *Paid by Erie and Champlain Canal tolls to support the Oneida Lake Canal.* 6. *Contributed by the Oneida Lake Canal to the Erie and Champlain Canal Fund.* 7. *The tons shipped on the Oneida Lake Canal each year.*

YEARS	(1) Tolls on Oneida Lake Canal proper.	(2) Tolls on Erie from tonnage of Oneida Lake Canal.	(3) Cost of collection, superintendence, and repairs.	(4) Per cent. of cost on receipts of Oneida Lake Canal.	(5) Paid by Erie and Champlain Canals to support Oneida Lake Canal.	(6) Paid by Oneida Lake Canal to Erie and Champlain Canals.	(7) Tonnage of Oneida Lake Canal.
1847,.	$254 24	....	$6,130 02	2,411.11	$5,875 78	....	30,642
1848,.	560 76	$124 68	2,004 93	357.54	1,444 17	....	47,451
1849,.	794 67	463 94	2,242 56	282.20	1,447 89	....	59,451
1850,.	2,513 19	409 65	5,248 17	208.82	2,734 98	....	56,828
1851,.	6,178 57	153 40	4,315 62	69.85	....	$1,862 95	45,049
1852,.	7,795 05	50 01	6,052 15	77.64	....	1,742 90	43,969
1853,.	10,282 18	24 16	6,584 05	64.03	....	3,698 13	43,351
1854,.	9,802 11	6,994 44	12,789 15	130.47	2,987 04	....	34,532
1855,.	7,340 81	6,642 62	7,512 64	102.37	171 83	....	27,116
1856,.	8,639 04	6,302 41	3,608 31	41.77	....	5,030 73	18,485
1857,.	4.849 34	4,832 27	4,803 25	99.05	....	46 09	19,343
1858,.	1,235 32	4,450 17	4,866 56	393.95	3,631 24	....	19,675
1859,.	701 41	4,293 22	5,725 87	816.34	5,024 46	....	19.536
1860,.	290 33	3,227 78	5,207 30	1,793.58	4,916 97	....	18,672
1861,.	218 86	2,399 27	5,061 27	2,312.56	4,842 41	....	30,060
1862,.	121 83	....	2,804 16	2,301.70	2,682 33	....	....
1863,.	45 21	....	3,147 44	6,961.82	3,102 23	....	....
1864,.	5 00	....	5,077 87	101,557.40	5,072 87	....	....
1865,.	....	....	7,792 21	....	7,792 21	....	....
1866,.	....	....	4,166 72	....	4,166 72	....	... ...
	$61,627 92	$40,368 02	$105,140 25	170.60	$55,893 13	$12,380 80	514,160

NOTE.—This canal was purchased by the State in 1841, of the Oneida Lake Canal Company, at a cost of $50,000, and a stock loan was made for that amount, which, with $11,250, has, since 1846, been paid out of the canal debt sinking fund. No part of this debt and interest has been paid from the revenues of this canal. The tolls of the canal proper are less the cost of collection, superintendence and repairs by $43,512.32, and the excess of payments by the Erie and Champlain canals to support this canal exceed the supposed tolls received on the Erie from the tonnage derived from the Oneida Lake Canal by $3,512.33. This canal is not now in navigable order, and is awaiting repairs, or reconstrnction and enlargement.

TABLE NO. XI.

Baldwinsville Canal.

STATEMENT showing: 1. *The tolls received in each fiscal year from* 1846 *to* 1866. 2. *Tolls paid on the Erie Canal by the tonnage received from the Baldwinsville Canal during the same period.* 3. *Cost of collection, superintendence and ordinary repairs each year during the same time.* 4. *Per cent. of cost on the receipts of Baldwinsville Canal alone.* 5. *Paid by Erie and Champlain Canal tolls to support the Baldwinsville.* 6. *Contributed by the Baldwinsville Canal to the Erie and Champlain Canal fund.* 7. *The tons shipped on the Baldwinsville Canal each year.*

YEARS.	(1) Tolls on Baldwinsville Canal proper.	(2) Tolls on Erie from tonnage of Baldwinsville Canal.	(3) Cost of collection, superintendence and repairs.	(4) Per cent. of cost on receipts of Baldwinsville Canal alone.	(5) Paid by Erie and Champlain Canals to support Baldwinsville Canal.	(6) Paid by Baldwinsville to Erie and Champl'n Canals.	(7) Tonnage of Baldwinsville Canal.
1847,......	....	....	....	....	....	....	....
1848,......	....	....	....	....	....	....	....
1849,......	....	....	....	....	....	....	....
1850,......	....	....	....	....	....	....	....
1851,......	....	....	....	....	....	....	....
1852,......	....	....	....	....	....	....	....
1853,......	$472 06	....	$159 46	33.78	....	$312 60	....
1854,......	429 86	$707 39	2,805 08	652.55	$2,375 22	....	31,945
1855,......	76 01	150 74	2,947 66	3,877.99	2,871 65	....	32,608
1856,......	73 02	191 55	800 04	1,095.64	727 02	....	27,481
1857,......	32,81	....	1,519 15	4,628.31	1,486 34	....	....
1858,......	14 13	....	2,381 62	16,855.06	2,367 49	....	....
1859,......	26 03	....	413 30	1,587.78	387 27	....	....
1860,......	23 17	....	....	....	....	23 17	....
1861,......	22 57	....	1,069 60	4,739.03	1,047 03	....	....
1862,......	31 83	....	174 67	548.76	142 84	....	....
1863,......	39 17	....	72 33	184.66	33 16	....	....
1864,......	20 82	....	948 67	4,556.53	927 85	....	....
1865,......	....	....	499 00	....	499 00	....	....
1866,......	....	....	2,646 68	....	2,646 68	....	....
	$1,261 48	$1,049 68	$16,437 26	1,303.01	$15,511 55	$335 77	92,034

Note.—This canal (so called) was purchased by the State in 1850, of an individual, for which he was paid $9,519.16 out of the general fund. It was not a State canal in 1846. This canal, from the Mud Lock to Jack's Reefs, including the Seneca River towing-path and Seneca River improvement, is twelve miles long, and has been kept up and maintained by the levy of taxes and by contributions from the Erie and Champlain Canal tolls. The general fund has some charges against this canal.

TABLE NO. XII.

Oneida River Improvement.

STATEMENT showing: 1. *The tolls received in each fiscal year from* 1846 *to* 1866. 2. *Tolls paid on the Erie Canal by the tonnage received from the Oneida River Improvement during the same period.* 3. *The cost of collection, superintendence and ordinary repairs each year during the same time.* 4. *Per cent. of cost on the receipts of Oneida River Improvement alone.* 5. *Paid by Erie and Champlain Canal tolls to support the Oneida River Improvement.* 6. *Contributed by the Oneida River Improvement to the Erie and Champlain Canal Fund.*

YEARS.	(1) Tolls on Oneida River Improvement.	(2) Tolls on Erie from tonnage of Oneida River Improvement.	(3) Cost of collection, superintendence and repairs.	(4) Per cent. of cost on receipts of Oneida River Improvement.	(5) Paid by Erie and Champlain to support Oneida River Improvement.	(6) Paid by Oneida River to Erie and Champlain Canals.	(4) Tonnage of Oneida River Improvement.
1847,.......	$118 22	....	....	....	....	$118 22	......
1848,.......	200 50	....	....	....	....	200 50	......
1849,.......	230 71	....	....	....	....	230 71	......
1850,.......	5,555 63	....	$394 67	7.10	....	5,160 96	......
1851,.......	18,409 56	....	2,249 61	12.22	....	16,159 95	......
1852,.......	24,540 54	....	1,765 37	7.19	....	22,775 17	......
1853,.......	31,275 36	....	1,707 40	5.46	....	29,567 96	......
1854,.......	31,992 92	....	3,047 37	9.53	....	28,945 55	......
1855,.......	24,004 94	....	4,543 22	18.93	....	19,461 72	......
1856,.......	29,035 78	....	2,481 73	8.55	....	26,554 05	......
1857,.......	15,758 42	....	5,299 02	33.62	....	10,459 40	......
1858,.......	3,725 19	....	2,797 27	75.09	....	927 92	......
1859,.......	2,044 64	....	1,204 38	58.90	....	840 26	......
1860,.......	1,015 98	....	218 92	21.54	....	797 06	......
1861,.......	919 63	....	15,055 35	1,637.11	$14,135 72	....	......
1862,.......	2,311 06	....	1,375 76	59.53	....	935 30	......
1863,.......	4,399 07	....	5 00	.11	....	4,394 07	......
1864,.......	3,572 36	....	....	....	....	3,572 36	......
1865,.......	2,489 87	....	1,097 09	44.06	....	1,392 78	......
1866,.......	2,688 53	....	....	....	....	2,688 53	......
	$204,288 91	....	$43,242 16	21.16	$14,135 72	$175,182 47	......

Note.—This is one item in our system of internal improvements which has not only paid the cost of superintendence and repairs the last twenty years, but has also paid by its overplus tolls, the principal and interest of the loans contracted for its improvement.

TABLE NO. XIII.

SENECA RIVER TOWING PATH.

STATEMENT showing: 1. *The tolls received in each fiscal year from* 1846 *to* 1866. 2. *Tolls paid on the Erie Canal by tonnage received from the Seneca River Towing Path during the same period.* 3. *The cost of collection, superintendence and ordinary repairs each year during the same time.* 4. *Per cent. of cost on the receipts of the Seneca River Towing Path alone.* 5. *Paid by Erie and Champlain Canal tolls to support the Seneca River Towing Path.* 6. *Contributed by the Seneca River Towing Path to the Erie and Champlain Canal funds.*

YEARS.	(1) Tolls on Seneca River Towing Path proper.	(2) Tolls on Erie from tonnage of Seneca River Towing Path.	(3) Cost of collection, superintendence and repairs.	(4) Per cent. of cost on receipts of Seneca Towing Path alone.	(5) Paid by Erie and Champlain canals to support Seneca River Towing Path.	(6) Paid by Seneca River Towing Path to Erie and Champlain canals.	(7) Tonnage of Seneca River Towing Path.
1847,.....	....	....	....	....	....	....	....
1848,.....	$422 60	....	....	....	....	$422 60	....
1849,.....	379 65	....	....	....	....	379 65	....
1850,.....	230 45	....	....	....	....	230 45	....
1851,.....	314 22	....	$19 54	....	....	294 68	....
1852,.....	161 45	....	....	....	....	161 45	....
1853,.....	145 62	....	....	....	....	145 62	....
1854,.....	212 15	....	....	....	....	212 15	....
1855,.....	242 56	....	....	....	....	242 56	....
1856,.....	250 51	....	....	....	....	250 51	....
1857,.....	210 23	....	....	....	....	210 23	....
1858,.....	99 69	....	....	....	....	99 69	....
1859,.....	163 82	....	....	....	....	163 82	....
1860,.....	144 05	....	....	....	....	144 05	....
1861,.....	190 38	....	....	....	....	190 38	....
1862,.....	374 55	....	....	....	....	374 55	....
1863,.....	480 57	....	....	....	....	480 57	....
1864,.....	468 17	....	....	....	....	468 17	....
1865,.....	344 36	....	....	....	....	344 36	....
1866,.....	416 66	....	....	....	....	416 66	....
	$5,251 69	....	$19 54	....	....	$5,232 15	....

NOTE.—This improvement first came into use as a State work in 1841. All the tolls received, except $19.54, since 1847, have been paid to the Erie and Champlain Canal Fund. These are not charged with any cost for collection, superintendence and repairs.

TABLE NO. XIV.

Cayuga Inlet.

STATEMENT showing: 1. *The tolls received in each year, from* 1846 *to* 1866. 2. *Tolls paid on Erie Canal by tonnage received from the Cayuga Inlet during the same period.* 3. *The cost of collection, superintendence and ordinary repairs each year during the same time.* 4. *Per cent. of cost on the receipts of the Cayuga Inlet alone.* 5. *Paid by Erie and Champlain Canal tolls to support the Cayuga Inlet.* 6. *Contributed by the Cayuga Inlet to the Erie and Champlain Canal Fund.*

YEARS.	(1) Tolls on Cayuga Inlet.	(2) Tolls on Erie from tonnage of Cayuga Inlet.	(3) Cost of collection, superintendence and repairs.	(4) Per cent. of cost on receipts of Cayuga Inlet.	(5) Paid by Erie and Champlain tolls to support Cayuga Inlet.	(6) Paid by Cayuga Inlet to Erie and Champlain Canals.
1847,	....	....	....	....	....	....
1848,	....	....	....	....	....	....
1849,	$121 50	....	$60 75	50.00	....	$60 75
1850,	205 96	....	102 98	50.00	....	102 98
1851,	190 41	....	95 20	50.00	....	95 21
1852,	230 14	....	115 07	50.00	....	115 07
1853,	271 78	....	135 89	50.00	....	135 89
1854,	311 16	....	173 21	55.66	....	137 95
1855,	327 86	....	163 93	50.00	....	163 93
1856,	328 13	....	164 06	50.00	....	164 07
1857,	387 82	....	193 91	50.00	....	193 91
1858,	190 18	....	95 09	50.00	....	95 09
1859,	173 95	....	86 97	50.00	....	86 98
1860,	173 44	....	86 72	50.00	....	86 72
1861,	147 97	....	73 99	50.00	....	73 98
1862,	241 94	....	120 97	50.00	....	120 97
1863,	386 40	....	193 20	50.00	....	193 20
1864,	351 85	....	175 92	50.00	....	175 93
1865,	270 03	....	135 02	50.00	....	135 01
1866,	286 44	....	1,073 75	374.86	$787 31	....
	$4,596 96	....	$3,246 63	72.81	$787 31	$2,137 64

Note.—This is an improvement brought into use since 1845, and the expense of making it was paid out of the General Fund. As one-half of the annual receipts from tolls are, by the conditions of the law authorizing the improvement, payable to the General Fund as a compensation for advances, the revenues to the Canal Fund do not pay the cost of repairs and superintendence.

TABLE NO. XV.

Estimated and actual results Compared.

STATEMENT showing: 1. *The estimated increase of the tolls of* 1846. 2. *The estimated ordinary annual expenses of maintenance.* 3. *The estimated net annual revenue.* 4. *The actual receipts from Canal tolls from* 1846 *to* 1866, *inclusive.* 5. *The actual annual expenses; and* 6. *The actual surplus revenues each year.*

YEARS.	ESTIMATED RECEIPTS OF CANAL TOLLS FOR TWENTY YEARS, COST OF REPAIRS AND MAINTENANCE OF THE CANALS AND NET REVENUE.		
	(1)	(2)	(3)
	Tolls of 1846 increased at 3.02 per cent. annually.	Estimated ordinary annual expenses.	Estimated net revenue.
1846,	$2,757,178 08	$600,000 00	$2,157,178 08
1847,	2,840,444 86	600,000 00	2,240,444 86
1848,	2,923,711 64	600,000 00	2,323,711 64
1849,	3,006,978 42	600,000 00	2,406,978 42
1850,	3,090,245 20	600,000 00	2,490,245 20
1851,	3,173,511 98	600,000 00	2,573,511 98
1852,	3,256,778 76	600,000 00	2,656,778 76
1853,	3,340,045 54	600,000 00	2,740,045 54
1854,	3,423,312 32	600,000 00	2,823,312 32
1855,	3,506,579 10	600,000 00	2,906,579 10
1856,	3,589,845 88	600,000 00	2,989,845 88
1857,	3,673,112 66	600,000 00	3,073,112 66
1858,	3,756,379 43	600,000 00	3,156,379 43
1859,	3,839,646 21	600,000 00	3,239,646 21
1860,	3,922,912 99	600,000 00	3,322,912 99
1861,	4,006,179 77	600,000 00	3,406,179 77
1862,	4,089,446 55	600,000 00	3,489,446 55
1863,	4,172,713 33	600,000 00	3,572,713 33
1864,	4,255,980 11	600,000 00	3,655,980 11
1865,	4,339,246 89	600,000 00	3,739,246 89
1866,	4,422,513 67	600,000 00	3,822,513 67
	$75,386,763 39	$12,600,000 00	$62,786,763 39

Note.—The estimated columns of figures 1, 2 and 3, down to and including 1855, were laid before the Convention in 1846, and have been continued to the year 1866, in order to institute a comparison between the estimated and actual results. The aggregate of the estimated receipts exceed the real by $6,772,502.17, and the ascertained expenses exceed the estimated by $7,466,-813.12, which shows a difference of $14,239,314.30, a sum nearly equal to the whole Canal debt, chargeable to the Canal revenues at this time.

These estimates were made upon the assumed fact that the rates of toll in 1846 would not be reduced, at least until 1856, and the 3.2 per cent. annual increase was based upon an anticipated increase in the Canal tonnage, and it did increase gradually from 2,268,662 in 1846 to 5,775,220 in 1866, more than 150 per cent, while upon the rates of 1846 the estimates only called for an increase of 60.4 per cent. But the rates of 1846 were materially reduced in 1852, to meet anticipated railway competition, and again a further reduction in the rates was made in 1858 and 1859. An examination of the tables will show that from 1846 to 1852, when the first reduction took place, the actual exceeded the estimated gross receipts every year, and from that time onward until 1862, with a largely increasing tonnage, the actual receipts of tolls were annually below the estimated. In 1859 when the actual receipts were $2,000,000 below the estimated, the Canal tonnage exceeded that of 1846 by 1,513,022 tons. In 1860, 1861 and 1862 the rates of toll were gradually raised and restored to the rates before the reduction in 1858, and this, with the increased tonnage very nearly equalized the actual and estimated receipts from 1861 to 1866, including both dates. Assuming there had been no increase on the tonnage and traffic of 1846, there has been an aggregate loss in tolls of more than $10,000,000, caused by the reduction in rates, during the ten years, and more than double that sum if the increased traffic had been subjected to the rates of 1846.

Table No. XV—(Continued).

YEARS.	ASCERTAINED RECEIPTS OF CANAL TOLLS FOR TWENTY YEARS, COST OF REPAIRS AND MAINTENANCE OF THE CANALS, AND NET OR SURPLUS REVENUE.		
	(4)	(5)	(6)
	Actual receipts from tolls.	Actual annual expenses.	Actual surplus revenues in each year.
1846,	$2,798,849 76	$639,353 01	$2,159,496 75
1847,	3,463,710 26	643,766 08	2,819,944 18
1848,	3,156,968 38	855,850 64	2,301,117 74
1849,	3,378,920 18	685,803 91	2,693,116 27
1850,	3,393,081 87	835,965 81	2,557,116 06
1851,	3,703,999 34	907,730 20	2,796,269 14
1852,	3,174,857 49	1,049,045 92	2,125,811 57
1853,	3,162,190 14	1,098,476 97	2,063,713 17
1854,	2,982,114 97	1,237,866 20	1,744,248 77
1855,	2,632,906 11	989,792 12	1,643,113 99
1856,	2,721,740 63	786,633 40	1,935,107 23
1857,	2,531,804 38	970,453 46	1,561,350 92
1858,	2,047,391 01	1,078,878 91	968,512 10
1859,	1,814,362 47	897,878 96	916,483 51
1860,	2,381,301 28	746,976 78	1,634,324 50
1861,	3,358,033 97	706,786 14	2,651,247 83
1862,	4,797,283 09	773,398 32	4,023,884 77
1863,	5,029,596 32	770,882 52	4,258,713 80
1864,	4,310,293 02	1,028,909 46	3,281,383 56
1865,	3,521,631 63	1,927,373 59	1,594,258 04
1866,	4,253,224 92	1,434,989 73	2,818,235 19
	$68,614,261 22	$20,066,812 13	$48,547,449 09

STATEMENT A,

Showing the progress of the Canal Debt, the amount paid for interest on loans, to General Fund for support of Government, and to General Fund Debt Sinking Fund, in each fiscal year, from 1846 to May 1, 1867, and also the surplus revenues of each fiscal year.

FISCAL YEAR.	PROGRESS OF THE CANAL DEBT.			PAID.			
	Borrowed.	Redeemed.	Canal debt at close of each fiscal year.	Interest on loans.	General Fund for support of Government.	General Fund Debt Sinking Fund.	Surplus revenues.
1846,	$300,000 00	$2,961,780 64	$17,028,240 13	$976,552 48	....	....	$2,202,861 12
1847,	....	284,490 54	16,743,749 57	937,205 64	$200,000 00	$471,916 66	2,831,834 52
1848,	1,314,819 34	1,344,919 00	16,713,649 91	911,736 05	200,000 00	350,000 00	2,348,219 52
1849,	1,889,024 76	2,097,392 00	16,505,345 67	898,599 05	200,000 00	350,000 00	2,757,102 71
1850,	192,595 49	482,786 64	16,215,144 52	868,873 74	200,000 00	350,000 00	2,650,206 49
1851,	1,000,000 00	573,609 91	16,641,534 61	835,064 66	200,000 00	350,000 00	2,814,432 91
1852,	700,000 00	340,265 45	17,001,269 16	843,795 62	200,000 00	350,000 00	2,130,099 86
1853,	....	....	17,001,269 16	960,790 28	200,000 00	350,000 00	2,070,069 59
1854,	2,250,000 00	479,025 00	18,772,244 16	926,231 51	200,000 00	350,000 00	1,750,799 01
1855,	3,750,000 00	2,240,911 00	20,281,333 16	1,076,573 17	....	350,000 00	1,650,000 00
1856,	6,750,000 00	4,489,266 34	22,542,066 82	1,194,306 62	....	350,000 00	1,962,500 00
1857,	2,750,000 00	102,285 00	25,189,781 82	1,361,736 93	....	262,500 00	1,589,015 60
1858,	2,200,000 00	2,929,767 34	24,460,014 48	1,406,120 80	....	....	993,325 97
1859,	....	152,170 00	24,307,844 48	1,358,892 32	....	....	962,000 67
1860,	3,900,000 00	1,100,523 00	27,107,321 48	1,472,745 78	....	....	1,669,611 61
1861,	1,200,000 00	2,175,551 23	26,131,770 25	1,505,304 64	....	....	2,695,842 16
1862,	....	2,120,000 00	24,011,770 25	1,429,859 36	....	350,000 00	4,081,591 35
1863,	....	733,300 00	23,278,470 25	1,381,995 76	200,000 00	350,000 00	4,347,618 83
1864,	....	836,700 00	22,441,770 25	1,321,440 26	200,000 00	350,000 00	3,317,356 06
1865,	....	2,844,374 76	19,597,395 49	1,176,289 39	151,113 40	950,000 00	1,650,091 86
1866,	....	1,348,935 49	18,248,460 00	1,081,875 38	....	782,961 04	2,874,756 39
1867, to 1st May,	....	2,465,400 00	15,783,060 00	504,632 50	....	363,000 00	....
	$28,196,439 59	$32,103,453 34	....	$24,430,621 94	$2,151,113 40	$7,030,377 70	$49,349,336 23

May 1, 1867.—Balance of Canal debt, less $1,700,000, floating debt loan,	$14,083,060 00
Deduct Canal revenue balances in Sinking Funds,	1,975,752 33
Balance of Canal debt chargeable upon revenue,	$12,107,207 67

NOTE.—Since 1860, when the debt was the largest $11,324,261.48 has been paid on it, leaving the above balance in the Sinking Funds applicable to the payment of interest and principal. In this operation the canal revenues have been aided by the levy of taxes to the amount of $4,734,072.92, to pay interest and deficiency loans on the enlargement and completion debt of 1854, and the principal and interest of the Floating Debt Loan. After the payment of the remaining debt of 1846, $3,276,060, the General Fund debt of 1846 is next in order of payment. The aggregate of the surplus revenue in this table will be found larger than the aggregate in some of the other tables, because the miscellaneous receipts are included in this statement and omitted in the others.

STATEMENT B.

Of the Operation of the Sinking Fund for the Canal Debt, under Art. 7, Sec. 1 of the Constitution.

YEARS.	RECEIVED.								
	Loans to supply deficiencies.	Premiums on Loans.	Proceeds of Taxes.	From tolls.	Interest on deposits and investments.	Reimbursement of temporary investments in taxes to be levied, and interest thereon.	Sale of stock investments.	Miscellaneous.	Total.
1846,	....	....	....	$433,333 33	....	....	....	....	$433,333 33
1847,	....	....	....	1,300,000 00	....	....	....	....	1,300,000 00
1848,	$825,000 00	$16,858 94	$119,410 30	1,300,000 00	$1,899 71	....	....	....	2,263,168 95
1849,	1,739,024 76	....	....	1,300,000 00	7,774 28	....	....	$760 00	3,047,559 04
1850,	....	215,610 76	....	1,300,000 00	....	....	....	42,869 93	1,558,480 69
1851,	....	....	....	1,300,000 00	....	....	....	....	1,300,000 00
1852,	....	....	....	1,300,000 00	3,250 00	....	....	....	1,303,250 00
1853,	....	....	....	1,300,000 00	23,335 79	....	....	....	1,323,335 79
1854,	....	....	....	1,300,000 00	10,000 00	$657,145 86	....	....	1,967,145 86
1855,	....	....	....	1,300,000 00	28,000 00	....	....	....	1,328,000 00
1856,	4,000,000 00	....	....	1,700,000 00	14,000 00	....	....	....	5,714,000 00
1857,	....	28,427 73	....	1,589,015 60	34,714 11	....	....	1,989 94	1,654,147 38
1858,	1,500,000 00	24,300 00	40,500 00	993,325 97	65,674 74	....	$121,938 00	112 65	2,745,851 36
1859,	....	....	47,000 00	962,000 67	18,705 32	....	....	....	1,027,705 99
1860,	....	....	....	1,669,611 61	36,258 18	835,663 75	....	....	2,541,533 54
1861,	1,200,000 00	16,883 50	....	1,700,000 00	14,650 48	....	....	....	2,931,533 98
1862,	....	....	....	1,700,000 00	22,942 24	....	....	....	1,722,942 24
1863,	....	....	....	1,700,000 00	54,000 00	582,113 76	....	....	2,336,113 76
1864,	....	....	....	1,700,000 00	68,227 00	....	....	....	1,768,227 00
1865,	....	....	....	1,650,091 86	99,232 25	9,731 68	....	....	1,759,055 79
1866,	....	....	....	1,700,000 00	59,992 22	468,000 00	....	....	2,227,992 22
1867, to 1st of May,	....	....	....	991,666 67	16,147 50	....	....	49,600 00	1,057,414 17
	$9,264,024 76	$302,080 93	$206,910 30	$30,189,045 71	$578,803 82	$2,552,655 05	$121,938 00	$95,332 52	$43,310,791 09

Statement B—(Continued).

YEARS.	PAID.											
	Principal of debt.	Interest on debt.	Claims prior to 1st June, 1846.	Prem. on stocks purchased.	Accrued interest on stocks purchased.	Tempor'y investments in taxes to be collected.	Investments in stocks.	Certificat's, plates and agency in New York.	Premium on coin purchas'd to pay interest.	General fund for deferred contributions, under art. 7, sec. 2 of the Constitut'n, and int. thereon.	Miscellaneous.	Total.
1846,	$433,333 33											$433,333 33
1847,	205,256 00	$937,205 64		$5,131 40				$2,116 00				1,149,709 04
1848,	1,341,489 00	911,736 05		3,829 25	$9 21			2,452 00				2,259,515 51
1849,	2,097,329 00	898,599 05			2,101 38			2,597 00				3,000,626 43
1850,	482,786 64	861,211 00	$84,715 52		1,636 34			2,185 00				1,432,534 50
1851,	573,609 91	822,435 38	34,829 53		177 05			2,257 50				1,433,309 37
1852,	340,265 45	801,161 00			278 53			2,170 75				1,143,875 73
1853,		801,161 00				$621,467 47		2,087 50				1,424,715 97
1854,	479,025 00	792,911 00	10,936 86					2,229 66				1,285,102 52
1855,	1,111,911 00	750,669 07	25,177 03					2,411 05				1,890,168 15
1856,	4,118,266 34	692,193 28	12,113 37					2,908 13				4,825,481 12
1857,	102,285 00	692,193 28	32,377 93		267 95		$72,938 00	2,391 63				902,453 79
1858,	2,929,767 34	672,710 72	217 39		82 22		49,000 00	3,001 38			$338 35	3,655,117 40
1859,	152,170 00	614,263 04	180 00			600,000 00		2,358 00			4,156 28	1,373,127 32
1860,	900,523 00	600,116 50	318 00			200,000 00		2,381 25				1,703,338 75
1861,	2,175,551 23	538 675 36						2,412 00			156 31	2,716,794 90
1862,	920,000 00	517,230 08	220 00	22 49		559,724 77		2,212 00				1,999,409 34
1863,	431,300 00	487,366 48	11 01	36,304 75	3,212 08			2,184 00	$80,715 93		406 77	1,041,501 02
1864,	457,700 00	457,105 98	50 00	8,391 25	363 60	9,268 27		2,307 25	31,418 47			966,604 82
1865,	2,644,374 76	325,462 61		8,308 50	1,617 42	450,000 00		2,191 50		$600,000 00		4,031,954 79
1866,	415,750 00	251,565 00			576 92	600,000 00		2,239 00		782,961 04		2,053,091 96
1867 to 1st of May,	1,644,000 00	119,582 50		500 00	7,539 82			1,378 00		363,125 00		2,136,125 32
	$23,956,693 00	$13,545,554 02	$201,146 64	$62,487 64	$17,862 52	$3,040,460 51	$121,938 00	$48,470 60	$112,134 40	$1,746,086 04	$5,057 71	$42,857,891 08
Balance on hand 1st May, 1867,												452,900 01
												$43,310,791 09
In addition to the above balance of,												$452,900 01
There will be reimbursed from the taxes of 1866, when collected, say 30th September, 1867, the temporary loan made thereon in 1866, under Act, Chapter 219, Laws of 1866, together with one year's interest,												624,000 00
												$1,076,900 01
Debt under article 7, section 1, May 1st, 1867,												$3,276,060 00

STATEMENT C.

Of the operation of the Sinking Fund for the Canal Debt, under Art. 7, Sec. 3 of the Constitution.

YEARS.	RECEIVED.						
	Loans to supply deficiencies.	Premiums on Loans.	Proceeds of Taxes	From tolls.	Interest on deposits and investments.	Miscellaneous.	Total.
1854,	....	....	....	$94,861 72	....	....	$94,861 72
1855,	....	....	....	....	$3,809 00	....	3,809 00
1856,	$500,000 00	....	$ 232,500 00	....	8,426 92	....	740,926 92
1857,	500,000 00	$10,450 47	....	....	4,420 32	$310 92	515,181 71
1858,	500,000 00	31,025 50	....	....	4,408 84	....	535,434 34
1859,	....	....	680,000 00	....	4,629 29	....	684,629 29
1860,	1,200,000 00	15,178 50	....	....	4,860 75	....	1,220,039 25
1861,	....	....	....	645,842 16	5,103 79	....	650,945,95
1862,	....	....	1,580,742 61	1,146,242 66	....	41,086 77	2,768,072 04
1863,	....	....	198,534 00	1,116,242 66	37,178 76	....	1,351,955 42
1864,	....	....	....	1,116,242 66	40,998 54	....	1,157,241 20
1865,	....	....	....	....	40,443 25	....	40,443 25
1866,	....	....	690,000 00	824,756 39	32,766 75	....	1,547,523 14
1867, to 1st of May,	....	....	....	....	20,262 90	25,000 00	45,262 90
	$2,700,000 00	$56,654 47	$3,381,776 61	$4,944,188 25	$207,309 11	$66,397 69	$11,356,326 13

Statement C—(Continued).

YEARS.	PAID.							
	Principal of debt.	Interest on debt.	Premium on stocks purchased.	Accrued interest on stocks purchased.	Interest on temporary advances.	Premium on coin purchased to pay interest.	Miscellaneous.	Total.
1854,	....	$18,691 23	....	....	....	....	....	$18,691 23
1855,	....	211,274 82	....	....	....	....	....	211,274 82
1856,	....	477,484 11	....	....	....	....	....	477,484 11
1857,	....	644,914 37	....	....	....	....	....	644,914 37
1858,	....	706,280 80	....	....	....	....	....	706,280 80
1859,	....	710,000 00	....	....	....	....	....	710,000 00
1860,	....	728,000 00	....	....	$40,614 02	....	$431 29	769,045 31
1861,	....	782,000 00	$498 13	$745 35	....	....	132 53	783,376 01
1862,	$1,200,000 00	728,000 00	....	....	....	....	....	1,928,000 00
1863,	60,000 00	710,000 00	6,982 50	288 75	....	$117,593 75	....	894,865 00
1864,	204,000 00	704,450 00	22,737 50	1,038 50	....	10,735 55	....	942,961 55
1865,	69,000 00	694,212 50	8,990 00	188 47	....	....	....	772,390 97
1866,	100,000 00	690,850 00	....	249 42	....	....	....	791,099 42
1867, to 1st of May,	760,000 00	334,050 00	....	3,040 21	....	....	....	1,097,090 21
	$2,393,000 00	$8,140,207 83	$39,208 13	$5,550 70	$40,614 02	$128,329 30	$563 82	$10,747,473 80
Balance on hand May 1st, 1867,								608,852 33
								$11,356,326 13
Debt under art. 7, sec. 3, May 1st, 1867,								$10,807,000 00

STATEMENT D.

Statement of the operation of the Sinking Fund for the Canal Debt, under Art. VII, Sec. 12, of the Constitution.

YEARS.	RECEIVED.				PAID.							
	Proceeds of taxes.	Interest on deposits and investments.	Temporary loan to pay interest.	Total.	Principal of debt.	Interest on debt.	Premium on stocks purchased.	Accrued interest on stocks purchased.	Temporary Loan.	Premium on coin purchased to pay interest.	Stock debt under art. 7, sec. 10, of the Constitution.	Total.
1860,	....	....	$187,500 00	$187,500 00	....	$112,500 00	....	....	....	....	....	$112,500 00
1861,	$350,000 00	....	....	350,000 00	....	150,000 00	....	....	$187,500 00	....	....	337,500 00
1862,	475,205 60	$18,045 69	....	493,251 29	....	150,000 00	$3,469 85	$526 68	....	....	....	153,996 53
1863,	355,040 28	5,764 58	....	360,804 86	$242,000 00	150,000 00	14,200 00	1,283 00	....	$24,843 75	....	432,326 75
1864,	535,373 94	21,101 64	....	556,475 58	15,000 00	135,255 00	3,700 00	197 43	....	605 59	....	154,758 02
1865,	367,744 97	18,989 58	....	386,734 55	41,000 00	132,735 00	1,993 75	419 69	....	....	....	176,148 44
1866,	379,965 52	35,097 36	....	415,062 88	459,000 00	123,765 00	270 00	316 50	....	....	$392,585 49	975,936 99
1867, to 1st of May	....	12,319 59	....	12,319 59	43,000 00	51,000 00	....	....	....	....	....	94,000 00
	$2,463,330 31	$111,318 44	$187,500 00	$2,762,148 75	$800,000 00	$1,005,255 00	$23,633 60	$2,743 30	$187,500 00	$25,449 34	$392,585 49	$2,437,166 73
Balance on hand May 1, 1867,												324,982 02
												$2,762,148 75
Debt under article 7, section 12, May 1, 1867,												$1,700,000 00

STATEMENT E.

Canal Debt 1st May, 1867, under Article 7, Section 1, of the Constitution.

Erie and Champlain Canals:		
Stock not bearing interest,........		$160 00
Redeemable as follows, viz.:		
Six per cent., 1st July, 1837,........	$160 00	
Genesee Valley Canal:		
Stock not bearing interest,........		10,000 00
Redeemable as follows, viz.:		
Five per cent. after 1860,........	10,000 00	
To supply deficiencies:		
Stock bearing five per cent. interest,........		3,265.900 00
Redeemable as follows, viz.:		
Five per cent., 1st October, 1868,........	$257,900 00	
Five per cent., 1st January, 1874,........	3,008,000 00	
	$3,265,900 00	
Total Canal Debt under article 7, section 1, of the Constitution,........		$3,276,060 00
Of which there pays no interest,........		10,160 00
Canal Debt under section 1, paying interest,........		$3,265,900 00
(*Under article 7, section 3 of the Constitution.*)		
For the enlargement of the Erie, the Oswego, etc., viz.:		
Stock bearing six per cent. interest,........		$8,750,000 00
Redeemable as follows, viz.:		
Six per cent., 1st July, 1872,........	$2,000,000 00	
Six do 1st January, 1873,........	1,000,000 00	
Six do 1st July, 1873,........	1,250,000 00	
Six do 1st November, 1873,........	2,250,000 00	
Six do 1st October, 1874,........	2,250,000 00	
	$8,750,000 00	
For payment of canal revenue certificates:		
Stock bearing six per cent. interest,........		$1,500,000 00
Redeemable as follows, viz.:		
Six per cent., 1st July, 1873,........	$1,500,000 00	
To supply deficiencies:		
Stock bearing five per cent. interest,........	57,000 00	
do do six do do	500,000 00	
		557,000 00
Redeemable as follows, viz.:		
Five per cent., 1st January, 1871,........	$57,000 00	
Six per cent., 1st October, 1875,........	500,000 00	
	$557,000 00	
Total Canal Debt under article 7, section 3 of the Constitution, paying interest,........		$10,807,000 00
Under article 7, section 12 of the Constitution:		
For the payment of the floating debt:		
Stock bearing six per cent. interest,........		$1,700,000 00
Redeemable as follows, viz:		
Six per cent., 1st July, 1872,........	$800,000 00	
Six do 1st December, 1877,........	900,000 00	
	$1,700,000 00	
Total Canal Debt under article 7, section 12 of the Constitution, paying interest,........		$1,700,000 00
Recapitulation of the foregoing statement of the Canal Debt, paying interest on the 1st May, 1867:		
Under article 7, section 1 of the Constitution,........		$3,265,900 00
Under article 7, section 3 of the Constitution,........		10,807,000 00
Under article 7, section 12 of the Constitution,........		1,700,000 00
		$15,772,900 00

STATEMENT of the Canal Debt, 1st *May,* 1867, *showing each description of stock, the amount redeemable in each year, and the annual interest on the same.*

WHEN DUE.	6 per cent.	5 per cent.	Total.
1837,	$160 00	....	$160 00
1860,	....	$10,000 00	10,000 00
Pays no interest,	$160 00	$10,000 00	$10,160 00
1868,	....	$257,900 00	$257,900 00
1871,	....	57,000 00	57,000 00
1872,	$2,800,000 00	....	2,800,000 00
1873,	6,000,000 00	....	6,000,000 00
1874,	2,250,000 00	3,008,000 00	5,258,000 00
1875,	500,000 00	....	500,000 00
1877,	900,000 00	....	900,000 00
Debt paying interest,	$12,450,000 00	$3,322,900 00	$15,772,900 00
Debt not paying interest,	160 00	10,000 00	10,160 00
Total debt,	$12,450,160 00	$3,332,900 00	$15,783,060 00
Annual interest,	$747,000 00	$166,145 00	$913,145 00

An Analysis of the foregoing Table.

Principal of debt and sections of article 7 of the Constitution.		Annual interest of the debt.	
Section 1, 5s,	$3,265,900 00	....	$163,295 00
Section 3, 6s,	10,750,000 00	$645,000 00	....
Section 3, 5s,	57,000 00	2,850 00	647,850 00
Section 12, 6s,	1,700,000 00	....	$102,000 00
	$15,772,900 00	....	$913,145 00

STATEMENT F.

Showing the amount of taxes paid into the Treasury for account of the Canal Fund under the present Constitution.

YEARS.	For redemption of Cayuga and Seneca Canal stock.	For Sinking Fund under art. 7, sec. 1.	For Sinking Fund under art. 7, sec. 3.	For Sinking Fund under art. 7, sec. 12.	For General Fund debt, Sinking Fund.	For damages prior to 1st June, 1846, and sundry objects and works.	For enlargem't and completion of the Canals, under art. 7, sec. 3.	For improvem't of the Champlain Canal.	For extension of the Chenango Canal.	For improvem't of the Genesee Valley Canal.	Total.
1846,	$56,503 47										$56,503 47
1847,		$119,410 30									119,410 30
1854,						$621,467 47					621,467 47
1856,			$232,500 00		$87,500 00						320,000 00
1857,					262,500 00						262,500 00
1858,		40,500 00					$1,200,000 00				1,240,500 00
1859,		47,000 00	680,000 00				163,567 66				890,567 66
1860,							869,515 70				869,515 70
1861,				$350,000 00			490,552 28				840,552 28
1862,			1,580,742 61	475,205 60			713,674 88				2,769,623 09
1863,			198,534 00	355,040 28			866,614 17				1,420,188 45
1864,				535,373 94							535,373 94
1865,				367,744 97				$147,097 99	$275,000 00	$91,936 24	881,779 20
1866,			690,000 00	379,965 52			586,330 00	151,986 21	285,782 86		2,094,064 59
	$56,503 47	$206,910 30	$3,381,776 61	$2,463,330 31	$350,000 00	$621,467 47	$4,890,254 69	$299,084 20	$560,782 86	$91,936 24	$12,922,046 15
Tax of 1866 in course of collection but not paid to Canal Fund,				189,489 66			663,213,83	284,234 50	284,234 50		1,421,172 49
	$56,503 47	$206,910 30	$3,381,776 61	$2,652,819 97	$350,000 00	$621,467 47	$5,553,468 52	$583,318 70	$845,017 36	$91,936 24	$14,343,218 64
Balance of tax collected in 1866 on hand unappropriated,											53,549 33
											$14,396,767 97

NOTE.—These taxes must be repaid to the treasury out of the Canal revenues, as charged by the 5th section of the present 7th article, with quarterly interest as soon as it can be done consistently with the just rights of the creditors holding the Canal stock debt.

CANAL APPRAISERS.

The Board of Canal Appraisers was first created in 1817 by an act of April 17th of that year, which conferred upon the Supreme Court the power of appointing not less than three nor more than five Appraisers on the application of the Canal Commissioners. A law passed April 3, 1821, made it a part of the duties of the Canal Commissioners to appraise damages growing out of the construction of the canals. In 1836, the system was changed to the appointment by the Governor and Senate of three Appraisers to hold for two years. On the 15th of April, 1857, their term of office was extended to three years, and this tenure and term still continues.

Their duties consist chiefly in estimating the damages from permanent appropriation of lands or waters in the construction of canals, damages arising from the building of dams, and setting water back upon adjacent lands, and such other estimates and appraisals as are, from time to time, referred to them through special acts of the Legislature, and all cases which come under the jurisdiction of the Canal Commissioners, where they are unable to effect a settlement and think proper to refer to the Board of Appraisers.

A complete record is kept in the office of the Appraisers (with suitable indexes), of the awards made by them; maps upon which is delineated each particular piece or parcel of land appropriated by the State for the use of the canals, with an abstract of claimants' title, are also recorded in this office.

A peculiar feature of the jurisdiction of this board is, that they are required by law to personally examine the premises for which damages or compensation is claimed, and to decide the case upon the evidence obtained from such examination, as well as that derived from witnesses.

Appeals can be taken from the decisions of this board, on behalf of the State by the Canal Commissioner in charge, or by the claimant to the Canal Board, whose decision is final and conclusive.

The annexed tables furnish the number of claims filed each year since 1847, together with amount awarded on the different canals of the State, and the gross amount claimed and allowed.

STATEMENT showing the number of Claims filed in the Canal Appraiser's Office, on the Canals of the State, from 1847 *to* 1866 *(inclusive), and the number decided on each of the Canals, and the amount awarded, together with the total amount awarded and total claimed.*

YEARS.	No. of claims filed each year since 1847.	ERIE CANAL ENLARGEMENT.		ERIE AND CHAMPLAIN CANALS.*		CHENANGO CANAL.	
		No. of awards.	Amount awarded.	No. of awards.	Amount awarded.	No. of awards.	Amount awarded.
1847,	108	88	$27,757 60	14	$2,525 64	2	$357 06
1848,	147	40	17,513 05	1	1,760 67	4	8,349 47
1849,	217	41	26,664 02	6	5,002 19	2	379 80
1850,	341	306	182,216 89	2	982 57	2	602 13
1851,	364	146	70,028 00	....	....	....	....
1852,	326	152	79,208 63	....	....	....	....
1853,	177	81	57,933 12	....	....	....	....
1854,	135	25	16,234 75	....	....	....	....
1855,	588	88	61,724 18	....	....	....	....
1856,	568	109	66,745 46	....	....	....	....
1857,	617	113	100,378 33	....	....	....	....
1858,	655	133	68,230 30	....	....	2	8,255 00
1859,	295	316	156,835 88	....	....	....	....
1860,	235	446	230,712 72	....	....	....	....
1861,†	103	227	271,670 63	....	....	....	....
1862,	152	292	178,471 79	....	....	....	....
1863,	149	158	116,183 46	....	....	....	....
1864,	141	77	81,033 09	....	....	....	....
1865,	177	118	104,600 55	....	....	....	....
1866,	232	110	98,953 38	....	....	....	....
Total,	5,726	3,066	$2,013,095 83	23	$10,270 87	12	$17,943 46

YEARS.	BLACK RIVER CANAL.		OSWEGO CANAL.		CAYUGA & SENECA CANAL.		CHEMUNG CANAL.	
	No. of awards.	Amount awarded.	No. of awards.	Amount awarded.	No. of awards.	Amount awarded.	No. of awards.	Amount awarded.
1847,	9	$1,100 00	1	$137 47	1	$756 00	....	....
1848,	1	570 31	....	....	1	4,296 48	1	$795 00
1849,	....	....	....	....	2	6,045 25	3	2,609 39
1850,	15	4,780 00	....	....	....	....	....	....
1851,	9	2,608 60	17	11,206 53	2	2,070 00	9	1,259 74
1852,	31	13,375 00	10	24,588 33	3	7,248 25	....	....
1853,	6	4,949 09	....	....	....	....	1	858 10
1854,	14	897 50	....	....	....	....	1	447 28
1855,	16	2,037 73	10	4,844 66	....	....	6	3,306 79
1856,	6	1,066 81	6	27,119 70	4	2,620 59	....	....
1857,	12	5,030 75	14	23,425 98	3	5,474 59	3	4,239 74
1858,	62	104,664 55	4	4,610 47	....	....	1	....
1859,	5	4,788 74	27	45,034 00	48	39,005 57	....	....
1860,	....	....	5	510 50	18	13,656 93	....	....
1861,	....	....	....	....	1	640 00	....	....
1862,	....	....	8	2,734 38	9	7,307 00	....	....
1863,	32	21,367 67	1	85 00	41	35,281 10	....	....
1864,	1	2,460 00	41	23,571 06	37	50,955 09	11	9,343 49
1865,	7	3,509 33	23	85,432 88	5	1,015 00	1	....
1866,	56	22,479 59	26	60,280 10	21	14,830 94	11	11,288 69
Total,	282	$195,685 67	193	$313,381 06	196	$191,203 25	48	$34,148 22

* Prior to 1852 the awards made on either the Erie or Champlain canal were charged in one item to "Erie and Champlain canals;" since that time the awards have been charged separately, thus: "Erie canal," "Champlain canal."

† Nine months.

Statement showing the number of claims filed in Canal Appraisers, &c. — (Continued).

YEARS.	GENESEE VALLEY CANAL AND EXTENSION.		SENECA RIVER IMPROVEMENT AND TOWING PATH.		ERIE CANAL.		CHAMPLAIN CANAL.	
	No. of awards.	Amount awarded.	No. of awards.	Amount awarded.	No. of awards.	Amount awarded.	No. of awards.	Amount awarded.
1847,......	63	$9,189 77	....	....	....	....	....	....
1848,......	35	7,445 28	....	....	....	....	....	....
1849,......	6	927 31	....	....	....	....	....	....
1850,......	4	583 52	....	....	....	....	....	....
1851,......	1	1,285 00	....	....	....	....	....	....
1852,......	....	....	16	$10,219 16	....	....	10	$10,568 48
1853,......	28	8,080 27	....	....	3	$7,472 41	1	305 12
1854,......	4	11,759 81	....	....	29	11,032 46	10	40,996 29
1855,......	6	1,648 27	1	600 00	3	1,163 44	17	15,746 81
1856,......	....	....	....	....	12	11,355 92	2	1,794 06
1857,......	51	43,336 35	....	....	3	1,688 40	1	247 89
1858,......	4	6,592 48	....	....	17	1,285 50	1	400 00
1859,......	18	3,336 18	....	....	4	609 50	24	9,388 90
1860,......	6	7,419 00	....	....	1	....	7	2,761 25
1861,......	1	2,500 00	....	....	...	....	....	....
1862,......	....	....	....	....	....	....	....	....
1863,......	64	64,494 90	1	1,031 83	....	....	12	7,869 00
1864,......	46	46,011 30	....	....	....	....	59	20,062 74
1865,......	2	1,600 69	....	....	....	....	3	12,955 20
1866,......	14	30,481 15	....	....	....	....	3	1,227 00
Total, ...	353	$202,691 28	18	$11,850 99	72	$34,607 63	150	$124,322 74

YEARS.	ONEIDA RIVER IMPROVEMENT.		TOTAL AWARDED.	TOTAL CLAIMED.
	No. of awards.	Amount awarded.		
1847,..........................	....	....	$41,823 54	$178,321 00
1848,..........................	....	....	40,730 26	197,306 21
1849,..........................	....	....	41,628 42	230,060 26
1850,..........................	....	....	189,164 91	451,377 13
1851,..........................	....	....	88,257 87	215,529 98
1852,..........................	....	....	145,207 85	337,994 31
1853,..........................	....	....	79,598 11	159,024 75
1854,..........................	22	$1,473 75	82,841 84	296,390 49
1855,..........................	....	....	91,071 88	208,571 62
1856,..........................	....	... .	*136,271 62	522,938 37
1857,..........................	1	4,200 00	188,022 03	543,617 44
1858,..........................	....	....	194,038 30	845,207 78
1859,..........................	52	16,651 60	275,650 37	942,583 82
1860,..........................	....	....	255,060 40	779,161 34
1861,..........................	....	....	274,810 63	612,946 51
1862,..........................	21	13,923 64	202,436 81	563,038 23
1863,..........................	2	1,300 00	227,612 96	676,938 00
1864,..........................	....	....	†209,738 02	505,659 00
1865,..........................	28	29,810 75	238,924 40	521,088 57
1866,..........................	....	....	239,540 85	491,700 52
Total,........................	126	$67,359 74	$3,242,431 07	$9,279,455 35

* Includes $25,569.08 awarded on fifty-three claims for damages on Erie and Genesee Valley Canals (Rochester Millers' claims), in 1856.

† Includes $301.25 awarded on one claim for damages on Onondaga Lake Outlet, in 1864.

CANAL COMMISSIONERS.

The Canal Commissioners are elected under the provisions of Section 3, Article V., of the present Constitution, and are classified so that one vacancy occurs every year. They have the general supervision of the State canals, which are divided into three Divisions, one of which is under the immediate care of each Commissioner.

The Eastern Division includes the Erie Canal as far west as to the east bank of the Oneida Lake Canal, 136 miles; the Champlain Canal, 66 miles; the Glens Falls Feeder, 12 miles; the pond above the Troy dam, 3 miles, and the Black River Canal and river improvement, 98 miles. Total, 315 miles.

The Middle Division includes the Erie Canal from the east bank of the Oneida Lake Canal, to the county line between Seneca and Wayne counties, with the several feeders and reservoirs, 76 miles; the Chenango Canal, feeders and reservoirs, 97 miles; Chenango Canal extension, now under construction, 30 miles; the Oswego Canal, 38 miles; the Oneida Lake Canal, 7 miles; the Oneida river improvement, 20 miles; the Seneca river towing path, 5¾ miles; the Cayuga and Seneca Canal, 23 miles; the Cayuga inlet, 2 miles; the Crooked Lake Canal, 8 miles; the Chemung Canal, 23 miles; the Chemung Canal feeder, 16 miles, and the Seneca river improvement, 12¼ miles. Total, 358 miles.

The Western Division includes the remainder of the Erie Canal, 155 miles; the Genesee Valley Canal, 118 miles, and the extension of the Genesee Valley Canal, 7 miles. Total, 280 miles.

The annual reports of the Canal Commissioners exhibit statements of the expenditures for construction and repairs, an account of improvements made and recommended, and such general or special statements as the Commissioners deem important.

Under authority of an act passed March 14th, 1857, the Contracting Board, consisting of the Canal Commissioners, the Comptroller, and the State Engineer and Surveyor, were authorized and required to let by contract, under such regulations as they might prescribe, to the lowest bidder or bidders who could give adequate security, the contract for keeping in repair all completed sections of the canals of the State, and all feeders and reservoirs connected therewith, and also to let all or any uncompleted portions of said canals and other improvements, upon which, in the opinion of the Board, the repairs may be made by contract more thoroughly and economically than they were then done by the Superintendents of Repairs.

The report made in 1867, for the year ending with the fiscal year in 1866, shows that 89 proposals had been accepted, of which 34 had been abandoned, 3 did not enter into contract, 7 were to expire in January, 1867, 23 had expired, and 22 were to continue after the year 1867.

The following table, prepared from the reports of the Canal Commissioners, shows the total number of boats, with their tonnage, that have been built and registered in each year, and for the whole period.

Number and tonnage of boats built and registered annually since 1846, *and total from beginning, on canals:*

TONS.	Prior to 1847.	1847.	1848.	1849.	1850.	1851.	1852.	1853.	1854.	1855.	1856.	1857.	1858.
300,...	......	....	....	....	....	....	....	....	....	....	....	....	....
280,...	......	....	....	....	....	....	....	....	....	....	....	....	....
250,...	......	....	....	....	....	....	....	3	2	....	1	1	1
240,...	......	...	....	.. .	....	....	....	1	....	1	2	....	....
230,...	......	....	....	....	....	....	....	....	....	....	....	....	....
225,...	......	....	....	....	....	....	....	....	....	....	....	....	...
220,...	......	....	....	...	...	....	....	1	1	....	....	....	....
210,...	......	....	....	....	....	....	....	....	....	....	....	....	....
200,...	......	....	....	....	...	....	....	5	3	4	....	3	3
195,...	......	....	....	....	....	.. .	....	....	....	....	....	....	....
190,...	......	....	....	....	....	....	....	....	....	....	....	....	....
180,...	......	....	....	....	....	....	....	....	....	....	4	....	7
175,...	......	....	....	....	....	....	....	....	....	....	....	....	....
170,...	......	....	....	....	....	1	....	....	1	....	....	....	15
160,...	......	....	....	....	....	....	....	....	....	....	....	....	....
150,...	......	....	....	...	2	....	1	6	13	2	2	51	46
145,...	......	....	....	....	....	....	....	....	....	....	....	....	....
140,...	......	....	....	....	....	....	....	....	....	....	4	15	5
135,...	......	....	....	....	....	....	....	....	....	....	5	2	...
130,...	......	....	....	1	....	1	2	7	9	43	22	16	4
125,...	......	....	....	...	....	1	....	18	105	18	14	21	15
120,...	......	....	....	1	....	2	....	16	143	125	118	84	13
118,...,	......	....	....	....	....	...	....	10	34	17	13	4	....
115,...	......	....	....	....	....	....	....	....	....	....	....	....	....
110,...	......	....	....	....	....	....	....	16	87	13	10	6	3
105,...	......	....	....	....	....	....	....	....	....	....	1	2	....
100,...	......	....	....	2	13	27	34	79	83	28	28	8	25
95,...	5	6	....	4	6	33	63	180	69	40	38	18	15
90,...	10	27	10	4	25	72	90	164	95	58	69	43	16
85,...	9	45	20	13	16	11	22	22	20	16	3	16	5
80,...	125	560	148	78	38	28	26	33	44	28	6	15	22
75,...	293	553	158	75	17	22	10	15	32	43	17	14	14
70,...	529	162	59	20	20	18	9	6	10	23	4	3	7
65,...	469	44	13	2	4	1	4	3	1	2	....	1	3
60,...	639	30	25	7	3	2	2	2	2	4	....	3	18
55,...	312	13	8	....	....	....	....	....	....	....	....	....	....
50,...	479	4	2	2	4	1	6	3	1	3	1	....	7
45,...	162	3	4	....	...	1	....	....	1	....	....	....	1
40,...	151	4	1	....	3	1	....	....	1	....	1	1	3
35,...	35	3	....	....	....	1	...	....	....	....	....	....	....
30,...	48	3	6	4	....	...	....	....	....	....	....	1	....
25,...	17	3	....	....	....	....	...	....	1	1	....	...	3
20,...	14	2	..	2	....	....	....	....	....	1	1	.. .	....
15,...	4	1	1	....	....	....	....	.. .	2	1	1	....	1
10,...	7	2	1	....	....	....	....	....	....	....	1	1	1
5,...	4	....	....	....	1	....	....	....	....	....	....	....	1
2,...	3	....	...	....	...	....	....	....	...	...	....	....	....
Total,	3,315	1,465	456	215	152	223	269	590	760	471	366	329	254

TONS.	1859.	1860.	1861.	1862.	1863.	1864.	1865.	1866.	Total number.	Total tonnage.
300,...	.....	.....	1	.....	.....	....	....	....	1	300
280,...	.....	.....	.....	2	.....	....	....	....	2	560
250,...	2	2	15	3	.....	....	4	8	42	10,500
240,...	.....	.....	5	1	.....	1	3	40	54	12,960
230,...	.....	.....	2	2	3	3	4	28	42	9,660
225,...	.....	.....	12	28	2	11	4	24	81	18,225
220,...	.....	3	41	87	69	30	19	43	294	64,680
210,...	.....	.....	5	16	.....	....	....	....	21	4,410
200,...	4	33	169	298	254	98	45	68	987	197,400
195,...	.....	.....	1	2	.....	...	.. .	....	3	585
190,...	.....	.....	16	6	25	3	....	...	50	9,500
180,...	12	60	36	11	70	7	4	4	215	38,700
175,,..	.....	.....	5	22	.....	....	....	....	27	4,725
170,,..	7	17	3	.....	8	....	3	....	55	9,350
160,...	.....	.....	1	4	9	2	....	4	20	3,200

Number and Tonnage of Boats, &c. — (Continued).

TONS.	1859.	1860.	1861.	1862.	1863.	1864.	1865.	1866.	Total number.	Total tonnage,
150,...	11	14	27	88	24	24	8	11	330	49,500
145,...	.....	.....	1	.....	.....	....	....	....	1	145
140,...	1	2	19	13	14	15	3	5	96	13,440
135,...	.....	2	1	2	.....	....	....	....	12	1,620
130,...	2	2	3	4	16	3	2	7	144	18,720
125,...	1	5	8	1	3	5	2	4	221	27,625
120,...	9	22	15	12	15	6	6	21	608	72,960
118,...	.....	.....	.....	7	.....	....	....	....	85	10,030
115,...	.....	5	.....	4	3	4	4	12	32	3,740
110,...	1	4	5	5	5	2	6	2	165	18,150
105....	2	.....	1	.....	.....	....	....	....	6	630
100,...	14	55	67	194	61	38	11	75	862	86,200
95,...	5	13	19	21	14	38	5	21	613	58,235
90,...	38	42	41	51	102	66	37	65	1,125	101,250
85,...	8	35	25	1	8	4	2	2	303	25,755
80,...	25	49	43	4	18	19	8	6	1,323	105,840
75,...	21	19	10	2	7	1	6	4	1,333	99,975
70,...	16	4	5	1	10	7	6	4	923	64,610
65,...	4	2	2	.....	.....	....	....	....	555	36,075
60,...	8	3	6	.....	6	6	3	4	773	46,380
55,...	10	.....	.....	.....	.....	....	....	....	343	18,920
50,...	1	2	2	2	5	1	1	1	528	26,400
45,...	3	2	.....	1	6	3	....	....	187	8,415
40,...	.....	1	1	.....	.....	....	....	....	168	6,720
35,...	.....	1	.....	1	.....	....	....	....	41	1,437
30,...	.....	.....	.....	1	9	....	1	....	73	2,190
25,...	.....	.....	1	3	.....	1	....	....	30	750
20,...	.....	2	1	1	4	1	1	1	31	620
15,...	1	.....	.....	.....	.....	....	....	....	12	180
10,...	1	2	.....	.....	.....	....	....	....	16	160
5,...	1	1	.....	2	1	....	....	1	12	60
2,...	.....	.....	.....	.....	.....	....	2	....	5	10
	208	404	615	903	771	399	200	485	12,850	1,291,497

BANKING DEPARTMENT.*

The first bank charter granted by the legislature of the State of New York was in 1782, to the Bank of North America, which had already been incorporated by the Continental Congress, with a recommendation that the several States should likewise grant charters to the institution.

Though this recommendation was favorably considered by the Legislature of New York, the bank never transacted business under this State charter.

The history of banking under the laws of this State begins, therefore, practically, with the incorporation of the Bank of New York, in 1791.

Prior to 1804, banking corporations had no powers not enjoyed in common with private individuals or associations. All alike could issue and discount notes and receive deposits. The sole, though not inconsiderable advantage of the former, was, that they were "not liable beyond their corporate property, while the latter were accountable in their persons and to the full extent of their private estate."

But this common privilege of banking, till then enjoyed and pursued under the common law, ceased upon the passage of an act April 11, 1804, "to restrain unincorporated banking associations."

This act prohibited persons or companies not duly incorporated by law from "issuing notes, receiving deposits, making discounts, or transacting any other business which incorporated banks may or do transact by virtue of their respective acts of incorporation." Thereupon banking in the State of New York became a monopoly, a franchise to be enjoyed only by those who, through political subserviency, or the more disreputable influence of bribery, could gain favor with the Legislature; and this feature of monopoly, with its incidents of corruption, characterized our banking system until superseded by the free banking system of 1838.

Another distinguishing feature of this period was, that prior to 1825, banking powers were not enumerated in the charters issued, which merely contained certain restrictive clauses against dealing in State stocks, goods, wares and merchandise, as not pertaining to legitimate banking, but, in 1825, and thereafter, the charters granted by the Legislature specifically enumerated the powers conferred thereby, and expressly prohibited the exercise of any powers not thus enumerated.

The most important and notable feature of our incorporated banking system was introduced in 1829, by the passage of what is commonly

---

* This historical statement was prepared by Mr. E. W. Keyes, Deputy Superintendent.

known as the Safety Fund Act. This was the first measure of legislation that looked toward the securing of creditors of banking corporations against improvidence, recklessness, or fraud in their management, resulting in insolvency. This act provided for an annual contribution by all incorporated banks of one-half per cent. upon their capital, until three per cent. had been thus contributed to a common or Safety Fund, to be held in trust by the State Treasurer, and to be applied to the payment of the debts of any insolvent bank whose assets should be found insufficient for that purpose. Provision was also made for replenishing the fund by further contributions, whenever it should be reduced by the payment of such debts. The banks were thus required, in effect, to insure each other, for the benefit of the public having dealings with them, as holders of their circulating notes or otherwise.

This act further, for the first time, imposed limitations upon the amount of notes which any bank might issue, and upon the amount of their discounts, both being required to bear a certain ratio to the capital of the bank.

The salutary purpose of these limitations was, however, defeated by leaving the issue of notes within the personal supervision and control of the officers of the bank, who, as experience sadly demonstrated, were too frequently restrained neither by the unlawfulness of the act, nor by their own solemn oaths and sworn testimony, from issuing notes to an amount many times exceeding that authorized by law.

In the redemption of these fraudulent issues of notes, the safety fund was exhausted, and its resources from future contributions wholly pledged, within less than fifteen years from its institution.

The provision to apply the fund to the payment of the *debts* of any insolvent bank, instead of restricting it to the redemption of their *notes*, added to the burden which broke down the Safety Fund system, and though this feature was changed in 1842, it was not until the mischief was fully wrought, and the fund, both present and prospective, was hopelessly exhausted.

The abuses growing out of the monopoly of banking, and the inadequacy of the measures theretofore adopted to protect the public from loss in the use and employment of bank notes, as revealed by the disasters of the period, after protracted discussion and much careful investigation and earnest thought on the part of the ablest minds in the State, resulted in the enactment of the Free Banking Law of 1838.

The distinguishing features of the banking system thus inaugurated were:

First. The monopoly in banking was destroyed, the business being left open for any person or association to engage in at pleasure.

Second. The issue department was separated from the general banking business, and was intrusted to a State officer [first the Comptroller, and later, in 1851,* the Superintendent of the Banking Department], who had sole charge and custody of the plates, and who furnished notes duly

* The Banking Department was organized under an act passed April 12th, 1851.

countersigned and registered in his office, to bank officers, only in amount and upon terms prescribed by law. Thus the motive for fraud and the opportunity for fraud were no longer, as under the former system, concentrated in the same individual. The State officer was without motive, the bank officer was deprived of all opportunity for the unlawful issue of notes.*

Third. The issue of notes, instead of being proportioned to the capital of the bank (which, in the control of the bank, as under the former system, afforded no certain security to bill holders), was made to depend upon the deposit with the State officer of an equal amount of value in the available form of bonds and mortgages and State or government stocks, to be by him converted and applied to the redemption of the notes issued, whenever the bank should fail to redeem the same. Thus each bank was made to insure its own circulation in full for the benefit of the public.

The losses upon circulation under this system have been but trifling, and have resulted from the admission, in the earlier years of its operation, of securities of doubtful value, as stocks of the different States; or of those not readily convertible into the value expressed upon their face. But with the growth of the system these errors have been eliminated, until now it is scarcely possible for a bank to fail, without leaving in the hands of the superintendent ample means for the redemption of its notes at par.

No banks were incorporated by special charter after the passage of the act of 1838, and the successful operation of the system was attested by the constitutional convention of 1846, which incorporated into the instrument adopted by it and ratified by the people, a provision prohibiting the special incorporation of banks thereafter.

The last of the limited charters of incorporated banks expired January 1, 1866. The charters of the Bank of the Manhattan Company, and of the New York Dry Dock Company are unlimited, but the latter is now voluntarily closing its banking business.

Within the last few years the national banking system, embracing the principle of security, but devoid of the principle of freedom that characterized the free banking system of this State, has, to a great extent, supplanted the latter. The distinguishing features of the New York system are for the time obliterated. We no longer have any banks of issue under the laws of this State. Such as remain to us, and retain their corporate rights, do so as banks of discount and deposit only. The State circulation under the free banking law has been reduced from the highest amount, $43,962,535, in 1854, to $3,378,953, on the first of April, 1867.

Shrewd and sagacious financiers are of the opinion still, that the banking system of the State of New York has not outlived its usefulness, but is destined to a revival, and to a long and prosperous career.

---

* This feature was applied to incorporated banks in 1843.

Statistics of Incorporated Banks, from 1791 *to* 1838.

1791 TO 1804, BOTH INCLUSIVE.

No. of banks incorporated, 6; aggregate capital,.................... $4,230,000

1805 TO 1825, BOTH INCLUSIVE.

No. of banks incorporated, 36; aggregate capital,.................. $24,940,000

1825 TO 1828, BOTH INCLUSIVE.

No. of banks incorporated, none.

1829 TO 1838,

No. of banks incorporated, 64; aggregate capital,.................. $17,350,000
No. of banks re-chartered during the entire period above named, 25; aggregate capital,.. $18,160,000

RECAPITULATION.

Whole number of banks chartered from 1791 to 1838, ...	106
do do re-chartered,.............	25

No banks were re-chartered prior to 1829. Many banks whose charters expired subsequent to 1838, re-organized under the general banking of that year.

Statistics of Banking Associations and Individual Bankers, under the Banking Law of 1838.

YEARS.	Filed certificates of organization.	Never went into operation.	Have since failed.	Have closed or are now closing.	YEARS.	Filed certificates of organization.	Never went into operation.	Have since failed.	Have closed or are now closing.
1838,................	45	15	15	5	1854,...............	26	....	3	2
1839,...	97	48	18	5	1855,.................	19	....	4	1
1840,................	25	15	3	3	1856,................	34	1	3	3
1841,................	2	1	....	....	1857,................	9	2	2	....
1842,...............	4	2	....	1	1858,...............	7	1	2	....
1843,................	5	1	1	2	1859,.........	15	1	1	1
1844,.............. .	10	....	2	5	1860,................	8	....	1	2
1845,..	5	....	....	3	1861,................	11	1	...	. ..
1846,................	8	1	1	5	1862,................	18	....	1	...
1847,...............	20	1	3	3	1863,...........	11	....	....	....
1848,................	11	....	1	7	1864,................	3	....	....	1
1849,................	13	1	....	4	1865,................	1	1	....	....
1850,................	20	....	2	8	1856,...	1	....	....	....
1851,........	34	3	2	8	1867,................	3	1	....	....
1852,........	56	2	5	12					
1853,........	58	7	4	4	Total, ...	579	105	74	85

Leaving 315 banks that are still organized and doing business under the State or National law. Of these 201 have become National banks, and of the remaining 114, a large number are practically closing, without having made a deposit of cash to return circulation, which is the final act of official notice, still retaining their organization for use when found practicable. But 71 now report to the Bank Department.

Savings Banks in the State of New York.

These institutions are all incorporated by special acts of the Legislature, and since 1857, have been required to report their condition annually, to the Superintendent of the Banking Department. The subjoined tables present the summaries of the reports made in each year since 1857, and the statistics embraced in the report of 1867 concerning each separate institution. To the latter list, we have added in their places the names of those Savings Banks that have been recently incorporated, and of which no financial statements have yet been made. The number incorporated in each year has been as follows: One in 1819; one in 1820; one in 1821; one in 1823; one in 1827; one in 1829; one in 1830; two in 1831; one in 1833; two in 1834; one in 1836; one in 1839; one in 1841; two in 1842; one in 1846; four in 1848; two in 1849; seven in 1850; twelve in 1851; four in 1852; five in 1853; nine in 1854; six in 1855; two in 1858; seven in 1859; twelve in 1860; four in 1861; six in 1863; two in 1865; thirteen in 1866, and six in 1867. Total, one hundred and thirty-five, of which thirty-five failed to organize; six closed voluntarily; two closed through insolvency; three are now closing, and the remainder are now in active operation.

Annual Statistics of Savings Banks since 1857.

YEARS.	Number of Institutions in operation.	Number of open accounts.	Average to each depositor.	Invested in bonds and mortgages.	Estimated value of mortgaged premises.	Stock investments.
1858,............	54	$203,804	$203 24	$20.234,586	$48,668,888	$17,349,300
1859,............	57	230,074	209 47 1-2	21,014,211	51,352	22,365,172
1860,............	64	273,697	208 91	20,844,594	55,872.318	29,597,774
1861,............	71	300.693	224 28	26,455,007	64,288,421	33,550,918
1862,............	74	300,511	213 21	25,643,014	59,594,466	30,821,821
1863,............	71	347,184	220 45	25,511,312	60,958,741	40,305,743
1864,............	71	400,194	234 35 2-10	23,922,202	56,402,975	59,287,019
1865,............	73	456,403	244 82 2-10	23,138,760	54,730,966	78,383,151
1866,............	75	465,001	248 33	24,271,577	56,486,558	84.679,321
1867,............	86	488,501	270 10	31,112,153	76,030,243	89,415,351

YEARS.	Par value of stock.	Estimated value of stock.	Stocks upon which money has been loan'd, par value.	Am't loaned on stocks at par value.	Am't loaned on personal securities.	Amount invested in real estate.
1858,....	$17,818,700	$17,029,242	$1,582,227	$1,123,961	$21,046	$947,165
1859,....	22,470,773	22,613,414	969,929	735,394	50,945	1,072,845
1860,....	29,703,128	28,932,740	1,762,581	1,233,904	55,237	1,101,791
1861,....	33,726,985	32,542,376	1,749,410	1,429,153	49,177	1,042,305
1862,....	31,025,582	27,469,299	1,562,788	1,073,899	135,718	1,010,295
1863,....	40,550,360	40,518,354	2,789,838	2,314,816	174,717	1,111,470
1864,....	59,348,834	59,993,360	3,988,747	3,409,219	372,926	1,237,532
1865,....	78,757,671	81,578,551	4,311,943	3,333,983	559,132	1,314,498
1866,....	85,219,601	83,983,201	4,548,391	3,411,684	449,602	1,452,805
1867,....	90,982,271	....	....	5,525,337	491,120	1,737,020

Annual Statistics of Savings Banks — (Continued).

YEARS.	Cash on deposit in banks.	Cash on h'nd not deposited in bks.	Am't loaned or deposited not included in the preceding col'ms.	Miscellaneous resources.	Total resources.	Am't due depositors.
1858, ...	$3,287,441	$854,770	$54,462	$17,260	$43,885,991	$41,422,672
1859,....	4,353,280	1,010,752	57,862	25,869	50,686,331	48,194,847
1860,....	4,845,890	919,961	120,945	33,300	60,753,396	58,178,160
1861,....	6,485,130	1,197,169	152,256	48,637	70,409,752	67,441,397
1862,....	6,251,410	1,937,385	177,155	93,536	67,144,233	64,083,119
1863,....	8,345,406	1,824,964	643,782	160,856	80,393,066	76,538,183
1864,....	8,080,862	1,644,955	692,522	233,934	98,881,171	93,786,384
1865,....	7,453,930	1,712,216	2,189,968	255,755	119,341,383	111,737,763
1866,....	6,202,348	2,455,370	1,364,418	177,336	124,464,461	115,472,566
1867,....	8,635,037	3,187,351	1,321,436	231,708	141,659,513	131,769,074

YEARS.	Miscellaneous liabilities.	Excess of assets over liabilities.	Total amount deposited during the last calendar year.	Total am't withdrawn during the last calendar year.	Total amount received for interest during the last calendar year.	Total amount of interest credited depositors during the last calendar year.
1858,....	$25,696	$2,437,623	$24,830,443	$26,541,682	$2,643,615	$2,070,851
1859,....	20.098	2,472,658	26,514,144	21,789,493	2,595,489	2,197,787
1860,....	23,157	2,552,085	30,808,383	23,308,109	3,049,924	2,610,912
1861,....	20,160	2,949,195	34,934,271	28,308,414	3,682,158	2.834.249
1862,....	5,048	3,056,066	27,439,855	33,678,073	3,954,724	3,088,921
1863,...	8,781	3,846,102	39,096,308	28,897,495	4,167,005	3,079,302
1864,....	9,204	5,085,583	54,257,096	40,257,953	5,074,759	3,760,524
1865,...	13,456	7,590,174	81.429,749	67,423,482	6,718,217	4,593,901
1866,....	27,327	8,964,885	77,431,751	78,692,433	7,436,877	5,647,505
1867,....	25,058	9,865,441	84.765,054	73,393,905	8,054,271	5,678,453

Name and location, date of incorporation, amount of resources, amount due to depositors, and number of open accounts of Savings Banks.

NAME AND LOCATION.	Date of incorporation.	Amount of resources.	Amount due to depositors.	No. of open accounts.
ALBANY CITY.				
Albany Savings Bank,..................	Mar. 24, 1820	$2,185,278	$2,082,870	6,486
Albany City Savings Institution,......	Mar. 29, 1850	333,394	333,394	911
Albany Exchange Savings Bank,.......	Apr. 18, 1856	133,394	132,726	317
Hope Savings Bank of Albany,........	Apr. 28, 1866	....	....	....
Mechanics' and Farmers' Savings Bank,	Apr. 12, 1855	1,039,151	1,022,264	2,378
AUBURN CITY.				
Auburn Savings Institution, ...	Mar. 12, 1849	866,958	820,428	3,928
Mutual Savings Bank of Auburn,......	Apr. 16, 1862	246,027	242,373	748
BROOKLYN CITY.				
Brooklyn Savings Bank,...............	Apr. 7, 1827	6,140,530	5,730,886	19,736
Dime Savings Bank of Brooklyn,......	Apr. 12, 1859	2,546,200	2,419,181	15,314
Dime Savings Bank of Williamsburgh,	Apr. 19, 1864	400,747	391,988	3,335
East Brooklyn Savings Bank,..........	Apr. 17, 1860	265,792	257,192	1.950
Emigrant Savings Bank of Brooklyn,..	Apr. 25, 1863	100,520	99,876	334
German Savings Bank of Brooklyn,...	Apr, 20, 1866	141,128	140,258	629
Germania Savings Bank of Kings Co.,	Apr. 19, 1867	....	....	....
Hamilton Savings Bank of Brooklyn,..	Mar. 20, 1867	....	....	....
Kings County Savings Institution,....	Apr. 10, 1860	727,471	686,798	2,101
Long Island Savings Bank of Brooklyn,	Apr. 15, 1865	130,660	129,288	450
Mutual Savings Bank of Brooklyn,....	Apr. 15, 1867	....	....	....
South Brooklyn Savings Institution,...	Apr. 10, 1850	2,043,827	1,889,074	8,760
Williamsburgh Savings Bank,.........	Apr. 9, 1851	5,920,742	5,415,933	16,804

Names and Locations of Savings Banks, &c.—(Continued).

NAME AND LOCATION.	Date of incorporation.	Amount of resources.	Amount due to depositors.	No. of open accounts.
BUFFALO CITY.				
Buffalo Savings Bank,	May 9, 1846	$2,680,479	$2,495,032	14,334
Emigrant Savings Bank of Buffalo,	Apr. 17, 1848	159,324	159,105	810
Erie County Savings Bank,	Apr. 10, 1854	3,350,876	3,132,627	15,387
National Savings Bank of Buffalo,	Jan. 23, 1867	....	....	....
Western Savings Bank of Buffalo,	July 9, 1851	612,386	581,414	1.630
NEW YORK CITY.				
Atlantic Savings Bank,	Apr. 11, 1860	$1,533,337	$1,450,975	4,436
Bank for Savings in the City of N. Y.,	Mar. 26, 1819	15,481,137	14,238,471	55,307
Bowery Savings Bank,	May 1, 1834	17,257,865	15,598,769	50,242
Broadway Savings Institution,	June 20, 1851	1,466,714	1,330,033	4,058
Central Park Savings Bank,	Apr. 19, 1867	....	....	....
Citizen's Savings Bank,	Apr. 5, 1860	3,355,947	3,189,587	8,968
Dry Dock Savings Institution,	Apr. 12, 1848	5,775,294	5,445,685	14,285
East River Savings Institution,	Apr. 11, 1848	2,171,985	1,939,014	7,064
Emigrant Industrial Savings Bank,	Apr. 10, 1850	5,752,782	5,428,402	16,853
Franklin Savings Institution,	Apr. 14, 1860	249,692	243,264	1,414
Germans' Savings Bank of New York,	Apr. 9, 1859	4,251,233	4,110,877	14,312
Greenwich Savings Bank,	Apr. 24, 1833	5,159,190	4,748,119	17,756
Harlem Savings Bank,	Apr. 17, 1863	76,444	75,537	545
Inst. for Savings of Merchants' Clerks,	Apr. 12, 1848	2,038,530	1,815,073	6,742
Irving Savings Institution,	July 1, 1851	1,690,582	1,578,536	5,846
Manhattan Savings Institution,	Apr. 10, 1850	4,812,252	4,604,161	15,824
Market Savings Bank,	May 5, 1863	596,602	584,828	1,932
Mechanics' and Traders' Savings Inst.,	Apr. 16, 1852	2,430,583	2,288,521	5,695
Metropolitan Savings Bank,*	Apr. 16, 1852	2,146,785	2,001,288	6,103
New York Savings Bank,†	Apr. 17, 1854	650,449	613,247	2,738
North River Savings Bank,	Apr. 20, 1866	11,627	11,627	75
Seamen's Bank for Savings,	Jan. 31, 1829	9,271,882	8,358,538	25,574
Sixpenny S. Bank of the Empire City,	June 4, 1853	446,641	438,577	13,749
Third Avenue Savings Bank,‡	Apr. 17, 1854	4,034,415	3,884,345	11,807
Union Dime Savings Institution,	Apr. 12, 1859	2,642,261	2,482,151	15,409
Up Town Savings Bank,	Apr. 7, 1866	114,718	114,718	459
ROCHESTER CITY.				
Monroe County Savings Bank,	Apr. 8, 1850	2,087,641	1,960,035	4,930
Rochester Savings Bank,	Apr. 21, 1831	2,454,359	2,251,844	7,908
SYRACUSE CITY.				
Onondaga County Savings Bank,	Apr. 10, 1855	1,670,022	1,543,169	6,118
Syracuse Savings Institution,	Mar. 30, 1849	972,528	904,555	3,595
TROY CITY.				
Central Savings Bank of Troy,	Apr. 15, 1857	56,303	56,303	210
Manufacturers' Savings Bank of Troy,	Apr. 15, 1857	22,714	22,714	128
Mutual Savings Bank of Troy,	Apr. 15, 1857	131,110	131,110	478
State Savings Bank of Troy,	Apr. 18, 1856	153,521	153,277	792
Troy Savings Bank,	Apr. 23, 1823	1,892,425	1,837,653	5,484
UTICA CITY.				
Central City Savings Institution,	June 20, 1851	130,377	128,774	515
National Savings Bank of Utica,	Mar. 22, 1865	320,476	319,349	1,232
Savings Bank of Utica,	Apr. 26, 1839	1,619,189	1,475,321	5,267
OTHER LOCALITIES.				
Amsterdam Savings Bank, Amsterdam,	Mar. 5, 1866	....	....	....
Carthage Savings Bank, Carthage,	Apr. 17, 1867	....	....	....
Chautauqua Co. Sav. Bank, Fredonia,	Apr. 18, 1866	25,436	25,430	118
Chenango Val. Sav. Bank, Binghamton,	§Apr. 15, 1867	....	....	....
Chenango Co. Savings Bank, Norwich,	Mar. 17, 1860	80,842	80,157	252
Cohoes Savings Institution, Cohoes,	Apr. 11, 1851	209,261	209,261	913
Corning Sav'gs Bank, Corning (clos'g),	Apr. 5, 1860	322	382	24
Cortland Savings Bank, Cortland,	Apr. 13, 1866	21,228	21,128	79
Elmira Savings Bank, Elmira (closing),	Apr. 17, 1854	9,000	7,250	....
Fishkill Savings Institute, Fishkill,	Feb. 25, 1857	181,172	152,711	618
Hudson City Sav. Institution, Hudson,	Apr. 4, 1850	326,357	297,070	1,483
Jamaica Savings Bank, Jamaica,	Apr. 20, 1866	....	....	....
Jefferson Co. Sav'gs Bank, Watertown,	Apr. 5, 1859	112,064	104,964	682
Mech. S. B'k of Fishkill on the Hudson,	Apr. 20, 1866	39,024	38,525	233

* Formerly "Mariners' Savings Institution." Name Changed April 28th, 1865.
† Formerly "Rose Hill Savings Bank." Name changed April 17th, 1862.
‡ Formerly "Bloomingdale Savings Bank." Name Changed April 1st, 1865.
§ Charter revived April 20, 1857.

Names and Locations of Savings Banks, &c. — (Continued).

NAME AND LOCATION.	Date of incorporation.	Amount of resources.	Amount due to depositors.	No. of open accounts,
OTHER LOCALITIES (Continued).				
Middletown Savings Bank, Middletown	Mar. 5, 1866	....	....	....
Newburgh Savings Bank, Newburgh, .	Apr. 13, 1852	$857,356	$775,336	3,488
New Rochelle Sav. B'k, New Rochelle,	Apr. 24, 1865	9,773	9,339	105
Niagara Co. Savings Bank, Lockport, .	Apr. 10, 1851	5,541	5,293	46
Oneida Savings Bank, Oneida, ...	Feb. 19, 1866	76,493	75,939	235
Oswego City Savings Bank, Oswego,..	Mar. 4, 1859	307,196	292,967	1,519
Peekskill Savings Bank, Peekskill, ...	Apr. 18, 1859	305,520	282,620	1,366
People's Savings Bank, Yonkers, ...	Apr. 5, 1866	....	....	....
Port Chester Sav. Bank, Port Chester,	Mar. 14, 1865	64,917	64,323	446
Poughkeepsie Sav. B'k, Poughkeepsie,	Apr. 16, 1831	1,182,053	1,074,036	4,712
Queens Co. Savings Bank, Flushing, ..	Apr. 14, 1859	175,219	162,559	1,287
Rhinebeck Savings Bank, Rhinebeck,.	Apr. 12, 1860	56,229	54,911	305
Rome Savings Bank, Rome,...........	June 30, 1851	387,081	362,365	1,070
Sag Harbor Savings Bank, Sag Harbor,	Apr, 12, 1860	105,832	101,419	884
Saratoga Sav. Bank, Saratoga Springs,	Apr. 19, 1867	....	....	....
Schenectady Sav. Bank, Schenectady,.	Apr. 29, 1834	363,007	352,317	1,169
Skaneateles Savings B'k, Skaneateles,	Apr. 16, 1866	53,261	52,229	276
Sing Sing Savings Bank, Sing Sing, ...	Mar. 9, 1854	191,051	176,584	722
Southold Savings Bank, Southold,.....	Apr. 7, 1858	268,937	255,252	1,082
Ulster Co. Sav. Institution, Kingston, .	Apr. 12, 1851	557,330	522,150	2,002
Westchester Co. Sav. B'k, Tarrytown,	July 21, 1853	383,112	363,149	1,339
Yonkers Savings Bank, Yonkers, ...	Apr. 13, 1854	350,465	328,515	1,855
RECAPITULATION.				
Albany, 4, ...	....	3,691,217	3,571,254	10,092
Auburn, 2,............................	....	1,112,985	1,062,801	4,676
Brooklyn, 10, ...	....	18,417,617	17,160,474	69,413
Buffalo, 4, ...	....	6,803,065	6,368,088	32,161
New York, 25,........................	....	93,418,947	86,574,343	307,192
Rochester, 2, ...	....	4,542,000	4,211,879	12,838
Syracuse, 2, ...	....	2,642,550	2,447,724	9,713
Troy, 5,...............................	....	2,256,073	2,201,057	7,092
Utica, 3,..............................	....	2,070,042	1,923,444	7,014
Other localities, 29,..................	....	6,704,979	6,248,010	28,310
Grand Totals, ...	....	$141,659,475	$131,769,074	488,501

INSURANCE DEPARTMENT.

This Department was established and charged with the execution of the laws relating to Insurance, by the act of April 15th, 1859, chap. 366, and all the powers vested in and duties imposed upon the Comptroller in relation to Insurance Companies, their formation and regulation, were transferred by that act to the Superintendent of this Department. This law went into effect on the first day of January, 1860. The Superintendent was appointed on the eleventh day of January, 1860, and on the twelfth day of the same month and year, that officer, on complying with the requirements of the statute creating the Department, entered upon the discharge of his official duties.

Under and by virtue of the provisions of the act, the books, documents, stocks, bonds, mortgages, securities and other papers in the offices of the Comptroller and Secretary of State, were transferred and delivered to the Superintendent.

The Superintendent, with the approval of His Excellency, Governor Morgan, devised an official seal, selecting the motto, "*Alter alterius onera portate,*" (Bear ye one another's burdens,) as being the best expression of the scope, object and philosophy of Insurance.

Experience had demonstrated the need of such a Department, for the organization, regulation and examination of Insurance Companies existing in this State, and for the management of such companies of other States and countries, as desired to transact business in this State.

Prior to the Constitution of 1846, Insurance Corporations were created by special acts of the Legislature, and there was no Department in this State having special cognizance of matters relating to these corporations. Article 8 of that instrument prohibited *sub modo* the creation of corporations by special act of the Legislature, and on the 10th day of April, 1849, in obedience to the Constitution, the Legislature passed a general act providing for the incorporation of Insurance Companies. By this act, the Comptroller was charged with the duty of organizing and regulating Fire and Inland Navigation, Marine, and Life and Health Insurance Companies in this State, and of regulating such companies of other States and countries as were transacting or desired to transact business in this State.

By the act of June 25, 1853 (chap. 466), the general act of 1849, so far as it related to the organization and regulation of Fire and Inland Navigation Insurance Companies, was repealed, and that act which provides for and regulates the incorporation of Fire Insurance Companies became a law.

On the 24th day of June, 1853, the general act (chap. 463), providing for the incorporation of Life and Health Insurance Companies was passed, repealing so much of the act of April 10, 1849, as relates to Life Insurance.

By chap. 328, of the Laws of 1865, the general Life and Health act was so amended as to embrace within its provisions, all Casualty Insurance Companies. Under existing laws the Superintendent is vested with jurisdiction, among other things:

I. Over the formation of Fire and Inland Navigation Insurance Companies in this State; the increase of their capital stock; the reduction of their capital stock; the extension of their charters; the change of mutual into joint stock companies; the examination into their affairs; their regulation in the State; their annual statements and prescribing the manner of making the same; their compulsory retirement from business, in certain cases, in connection with the Attorney-General and the Supreme Court; the admission into the State, issuing of certificates of authority to agents in the State, and the examination and exclusion from the State of such companies of other States and countries, and the deposit of securities by foreign companies in the Insurance Department, for the protection of their fire policy-holders in the United States.

II. Over the organization of Marine Insurance Companies in this State; the increase and reduction of their capital stock; the extension of their charters; the conversion of mutual into joint stock companies; the examination into their affairs; their regulation in the State; their annual statements, and prescribing the manner of making the same; their compulsory retirement from business in certain cases, in connection with the Attorney-General and the Supreme Court; the admission into the State, the issuing of certificates of authority to agents in the State, and the examination and exclusion from the State of such companies of other States and countries.

III. Over the organization of Life, Health, and Casualty Insurance Companies in this State; their deposit of securities in the Insurance Department for the protection of their policy holders; their annual statements, and prescribing the manner of making the same; the examination into their affairs; their regulation in the State; the registration of policies in the Insurance Department, and the making of special deposits of securities in said department for the protection of their registered policy holders; the admission into the State, the issuing of certificates of authority to agents in the State, and the examination and exclusion from the State of such companies of other States and countries; and the deposit by foreign companies of securities in the Insurance Department, for the protection of their life policy holders in the United States.

Under the laws requiring deposits of securities in the Insurance Department, the total amount of stocks and mortgages now held by the department for the security of the policy holders of Life and Casualty and Foreign Fire Insurance Companies is $4,439,035.57, credited to the various companies at the sum of $4,406,838.38.

Of this aggregate, New York companies have deposited $2,958,350, credited for $2,929,692, and foreign companies $1,480,685.57, credited for $1,477,146.38.

The following table contains the names, dates of establishment, incorporation or organization, location, capitals, and gross assets of all the insurance companies of the State of New York, and of other States and countries transacting business in said State, and over which the superintendent has supervision.

New York Joint Stock Fire Insurance Companies.

NAME.	Date of incorporation or organization.	Location.	Capital.	Gross Assets.
Ætna Fire,	Mar. 31, 1824	N. Y. City,	$300,000	$364,136 56
Adriatic Fire,	Nov. 24, 1858	N. Y. City,	200,000	206,166 01
Agricultural,	Feb. 17, 1853	Watertown,	100,000	302,059 94
Albany,	Mar. 8, 1811	Albany,	150,000	210,405 04
Albany City,	Dec. 8, 1860	Albany,	200,000	208,501 75
American Fire,	April 30, 1857	New York,	200,000	578,517 47
American Exchange Fire,	Mar. 1, 1859	New York,	200,000	249,581 25
Arctic Fire,	July 28, 1853	New York,	250,000	530,077 73
Astor Fire,	July 15, 1851	New York,	250,000	329,009 23
Atlantic Fire,	Feb. 20, 1851	Brooklyn,	300,000	496,468 09
Baltic Fire,	June 28, 1864	New York,	200,000	264,193 99
Beekman Fire,	Sept. 7, 1853	New York,	200,000	237,415 67
Broadway,	Dec. 17, 1849	New York,	200,000	291,883 08
Brooklyn Fire,	April 3, 1824	Brooklyn,	153,000	298,916 99
Buffalo German,	Feb. 15, 1867	Buffalo,	100,000	100,000 00
Buffalo City,	April 27, 1867	Buffalo,	200,000	200,000 00
Capital City,	Feb. 1, 1865	Albany,	200,000	244,624 99
Citizen's,	April 28, 1836	Brooklyn,	300,000	537,485 43
City Fire,	April 26, 1833	New York,	210,000	371,819 80
Clinton Fire,	July 9, 1850	New York,	250,000	318,028 53
Columbia Fire,	Mar. 24, 1853	New York,	250,000	379,119 71
Commerce,	May 31, 1859	Albany,	400,000	532,701 29
Commerce Fire,	April 13, 1859	New York,	200,000	230,521 41
Commercial Fire,	May 14, 1850	New York,	200,000	281,767 97
Commonwealth Fire,	Sept. 5, 1853	New York,	250,000	296,120 20
Continental,	Jan. 6, 1853	New York,	500,000	1,668,136 57
Corn Exchange,	Feb. 6, 1853	New York,	400,000	501,095 79
Eagle Fire,	April 4, 1806	New York,	300,000	460,748 36
Empire City Fire,	Oct. 3, 1850	New York,	200,000	251,853 35
Excelsior Fire,	Dec. 14, 1853	New York,	200,000	335,129 79
Exchange Fire,	May 14, 1853	New York,	150,000	197,612 21
Farmers' Joint Stock,	April 9, 1861	Meridian,	100,000	125,933 14
Fireman's,	April 18, 1825	New York,	204,000	298,388 47
Fireman's Fund,	May 1, 1858	New York,	150,000	196,329 58
Fireman's Trust,	Mar. 15, 1859	Brooklyn,	150,000	193,285 45
Fulton Fire,	Mar. 23, 1853	New York,	200,000	276,942 65
Franklin Fire,	April 8, 1867	New York,	250,000	250,000 00
Gallatin Fire,	Aug. 26, 1857	New York,	150,000	161,389 90
Gebhard Fire,	Oct. 7, 1857	New York,	200,000	253,622 26
Germania Fire,	Mar. 2, 1859	New York,	500,000	740,482 43
Glens Falls,	May 4, 1850	Glens Falls,	200,000	273,637 66
Globe Fire,	Mar. 2, 1863	New York,	200,000	247,878 97
Greenwich,	May 5, 1834	New York,	200,000	324,899 47
Grocers' Fire,	Feb. 15, 1850	New York,	200,000	182,614 61
Guardian Fire,	Feb. 2, 1865	New York,	200,000	199,392 20
Hamilton Fire,	May 22, 1852	New York,	150,000	214,633 73
Hanover Fire,	April 15, 1852	New York,	400,000	561,331 61
Hoffman Fire,	May 4, 1864	New York,	200,000	193,676 60
Home,	April 13, 1853	New York,	2,000,000	3,645,388 87
Hope Fire,	July 19, 1856	New York,	150,000	227,548 28
Howard,	Mar. 9, 1825	New York,	500,000	618,468 89
Humboldt Fire,	April 24, 1857	New York,	200,000	252,317 06
Importers' and Traders',	Mar. 31, 1859	New York,	200,000	208,895 58
International,	Jan. 5, 1864	New York,	1,000,000	1,444,936 17
Irving Fire,	Jan. 30, 1852	New York,	200,000	279,627 00
Jefferson,	Mar. 4, 1824	New York,	200,010	287,901 59
Kings County Fire,	Oct. 21, 1858	Brooklyn,	150,000	209,963 94
Knickerbocker Fire,	April 3, 1787	New York,	280,000	373,652 58
La Fayette Fire,	Dec. 22, 1856	Brooklyn,	150,000	191,978 12
Lamar Fire,	Dec. 9, 1856	New York,	300,000	433,321 13
Carried forward,			$16,197,010	$24,342,536 14

New York Joint Stock Fire Ins. Companies — (Continued).

NAME.	Date of incorporation or organization.	Location.	Capital.	Gross assets.
Brought forward, ...	....	....	$16,197,010	$24,342,536 14
Lenox Fire,	April 25, 1853	New York, ...	150,000	190,824 36
Long Island,	April 26, 1833	Brooklyn, ...	200,000	307,149 06
Lorillard Fire,	Feb. 3, 1852	New York, ...	1,000,000	1,436,540 27
Manhattan,	Mar. 23, 1821	New York, ...	500,000	1,052,128 10
Market Fire,	Feb. 14, 1853	New York, ...	200,000	418,450 84
Mechanics' Fire,	May 7, 1857	Brooklyn, ...	150,000	186,236 27
Mechanics' and Traders' Fire,	April 18, 1853	New York, ...	200,000	263,237 48
Mercantile Fire,	Jan. 15, 1852	New York, ...	200,000	230,750 61
Merchants',	April 20, 1850	New York, ...	200,000	330,530 73
Metropolitan,	April 30, 1854	New York, ...	300,000	1,502,873 98
Montauk Fire,	May 22, 1857	Brooklyn, ...	150,000	205,533 30
Mutual,	April 18, 1843	Buffalo, ...	292,650	459,091 32
Nassau Fire,	Feb. 3, 1852	Brooklyn, ...	150,000	282,250 67
National Fire,	April 9, 1838	New York, ...	200,000	251,973 18
New Amsterdam Fire,	April 13, 1853	New York, ...	300,000	385,141 45
New York Bowery Fire,	April 24, 1833	New York, ...	300,000	403,290 52
New York Central,	Jan. 9, 1863	Union Springs,	100,000	155,909 53
New York Equitable,	April 23, 1823	New York, ...	210,000	315,250 50
New York Fire,	April 18, 1832	New York, ...	200,000	308,122 43
Niagara Fire,	July 31, 1850	New York, ...	1,000,000	1,278,405 98
North American Fire,	Mar. 29, 1823	New York, ...	500,000	755,057 77
North River,	Feb. 6, 1822	New York, ...	350,000	408,395 75
North Western,	April 26, 1832	Oswego, ...	150,000	168,794 85
Pacific Fire,	April 29, 1851	New York, ...	200,000	303,908 81
Park Fire,	Mar. 30, 1853	New York, ...	200,000	253,835 62
People's Fire,	April 22, 1851	New York, ...	150,000	178,830 10
Peter Cooper Fire,	April 7, 1853	New York, .	150,000	204,115 34
Phœnix,	Sept. 10, 1853	Brooklyn, ...	1,000,000	1,663,085 13
Relief Fire,	Dec. 17, 1855	New York, ...	200,000	255,867 66
Republic Fire,	April 12, 1852	New York, ...	300,000	584,737 76
Resolute Fire,	July 18, 1857	New York, ...	200,000	275,918 48
Rutger's Fire,	Oct. 1, 1853	New York, ...	200,000	260,223 61
Schenectady,	May 26, 1841	Schenectady, .	50,000	82,215 45
Security,	June 13, 1856	New York, ...	1,000,000	1,421,325 39
St. Marks Fire,	July 14, 1853	New York, ...	150,000	196,369 84
St. Nicholas,	July 31, 1852	New York, ...	150,000	195,429 37
Standard Fire,	Mar. 26, 1859	New York, ...	200,000	291,736 15
Star Fire	Dec. 2, 1864	New York, ...	200,000	243,615 67
Sterling Fire,	Jan. 18, 1864	New York, ...	200,000	228,566 65
Stuyvesant,	Jan. 28, 1851	New York, ...	200,000	258,439 70
Tradesmen's Fire,	Dec. 14, 1858	New York, ...	150,000	242,377 97
United States Fire,	Mar. 31, 1824	New York, ...	250,000	368,079 12
Washington,	Dec. 14, 1850	New York, ...	400,000	749,184 21
Western,	May 26, 1862	Buffalo, ...	300,000	502,026 06
Williamsburgh City Fire,	Mar. 22, 1853	Brooklyn, ...	150,000	248,155 52
Yonkers and New York Fire,	Mar. 12, 1863	Yonkers, ...	500,000	619,945 24
Total,			$29,699,660	$45,266,463 94

New York Mutual Fire Insurance Companies.

NAME.	Date of incorporation or organization.	Location.	Gross assets.
Dutchess County,	April 12, 1836,	Poughkeepsie,	$734,680 56
Farmers',*	May 14, 1845,	Buffalo,	7,728 15
Franklin County,	May 12, 1836,	Malone,	20,150 41
Glen Cove,	Mar. 29, 1837,	Glen Cove,	321,244 09
Huntington,	April 2, 1838,	Huntington	13,858 00
Monroe County,*	Mar. 21, 1836,	Rochester	1,217 31
Montgomery County,*	Mar. 30, 1836,	Canajoharie,	1,653 29
Mutual,	May 3, 1836,	Albany,	305,074 24
Carried forward,			$1,405,606 05

* These companies are closing up business.

New York Mutual Fire Ins. Companies — (Continued).

NAME.	Date of incorporation or organization.	Location.	Gross assets.
Brought forward,			$1,405,606 05
Orange County,	March 15, 1837	Goshen,	204,146 24
Richmond County,	March 30, 1836	Richmond Village,	170,932 71
Suffolk County,	April 30, 1836	Southold,	166,422 54
Wayne County,*	May 12, 1836	Newark,	2,926 09
Westchester County,	March 14, 1837	New Rochelle,	239,202 79
Western Farmers',*	April 23, 1844	Batavia,	24,621 16
Wyoming County,*	January 2, 1852	Warsaw,	28,583 36
Total,			$2,242,440 94

* These companies are closing up business.

Fire and Fire Marine Insurance Companies of other States.

NAME.	Date of incorporation.	Location.	Capital.	Gross assets.
Ætna,	June 5, 1819	Hartford, Conn.,	$3,000,000	$4,478,100 74
American,	June 12, 1818	Boston, Mass.,	300,000	802,756 12
American,	June, 1831	Providence, R. I.,	150,000	244,200 90
American Fire	Feb. 28, 1810	Philadelphia, Penn.,	400,000	901,531 75
Atlantic Fire and Marine,	May, 1852	Providence, R. I.,	200,000	277,441 84
City Fire,	May, 1847	Hartford, Conn.,	250,000	399,977 12
Cleveland,	1830	Cleveland, O.,	150,000	196,610 56
Connecticut Fire,	May, 1850	Hartford, Conn.,	200,000	277,319 03
Commercial Mutual,	1851	Cleveland, O.,	Mutual.	277,664 19
Eliot Fire,	Feb. 16, 1849	Boston, Mass.,	200,000	435,718 96
Enterprise Fire & Marine,	Nov. 24, 1865	Cincinnati, O.,	200,000	363,158 17
Equitable Fire & Marine	May, 1859	Providence, R. I.,	200,000	225,639 26
Franklin Fire,	Apr. 22, 1829	Philadelphia, Penn.,	400,000	2,553,146 13
Girard Electrical	Mar. 2, 1866	Girard, Penn.,	50,000	50,000 00
Girard Fire and Marine,	Mar. 1853	Philadelphia, Penn.	200,000	322,927 96
Hartford Fire,	May, 1810	Hartford, Conn.,	1,000,000	1,788,153 82
Home,	May, 1857	New Haven, Conn.,	1,000,000	1,438,491 60
Hope,	May, 1858	Providence. R. I.,	150,000	192,134 42
Independent.	Mar. 9, 1867	Boston, Mass.,	300,000	300,000 00
Ins. Co. of the State of Pa.	Apr. 18, 1794	Philadelphia, Penn.,	200,000	586,525 81
Manufacturers',	Feb. 23, 1822	Boston, Mass.,	400,000	1,122,569 70
Maryland Fire,	1858	Baltimore, Md.,	200,000	301,030 10
Merchants',	Dec. 5, 1816	Boston, Mass.,	500,000	894,758 06
Merchants',	Feb. 18, 1861	Chicago, Ill.,	432,200	519,753 30
Merchants',	May, 1857	Hartford, Conn.,	200,000	350,422 87
Merchants',	May, 1851	Providence, R. I.,	200,000	281,084 70
Narragansett Fire & Mar.,	July 8, 1859	Providence, R. I.,	328,490	480,708 04
National,	June 13, 1825	Boston, Mass.,	300,000	687,713 20
North American Fire,	Feb. 28, 1851	Boston, Mass.,	200,000	503,010 95
North American Fire,	May, 1857	Hartford, Conn.,	300,000	392,048 46
Norwich Fire,	May, 1803	Norwich, Conn.,	300,000	416,973 21
New England Mutual Mar.	Apr. 8, 1839	Boston, Mass.,	200,000	1,109,310 75
People's Fire,	Mar. 23, 1847	Worcester, Mass.,	200,000	433,877 51
Phœnix,	May, 1854	Hartford, Conn.,	600,000	1,103,468 35
President & Directors, etc.	Apr. 14, 1794	Philadelphia, Penn.	500,000	1,763,267 23
Providence Washington,	Feb. 1820	Providence, R. I.,	200,000	343,575 00
Putnam Fire,	June, 1864	Hartford, Conn.,	500,000	617,478 86
Roger Williams,	May, 1848	Providence, R. I.,	100,000	165,925 06
Springfield Fire & Marine,	Apr. 24, 1849	Springfield, Mass.,	500,000	710,519 44
Sun,	Jan. 18, 1865	Cleveland, O.,	200,000	208,371 24
Total,			$14,910,690	$28,517,364 41

Foreign Fire Insurance Companies.

NAME.	Date of establishment or incorporation.	Location.	Capital.	Gross assets.
Liverpool, London and Globe,.	May 21, 1836	Liverpool, Eng.	$1,896,079 68	$16,542,719 87
American Branch of same,....	....	New York,....	....	1,831,811 45
North British and Mercantile,..	1809	London, Eng...	1,210,000 00	12,829,373 19
American Branch of same, ...	....	New York,....	....	9,444 74
Queen, ...	Aug. 7, 1858	Liverpool, Eng.	916,318 48	1,779,241 21
United States Branch of same,	....	New York,....	....	255,610 51
Royal, ...	May 31, 1845	Liverpool, Eng.	1,395,589 80	6,217,711 00
Total,			$5,417,987 96	$39,465,911 97

New York Joint Stock and Mutual Marine Insurance Companies.

NAME.	Date of incorporation or organization.	Location.	Capital.	Gross assets.
Atlantic Mutual,...............	Apr. 11, 1842	New York,...	*	$12,536,304 46
Commercial Mutual,...........	Apr. 12, 1842	New York,...	*	1,103,083 96
Great Western,................	Sep. 27, 1855	New York,..,	† $1,000.000	2,869,378 79
Mercantile Mutual,............	Apr. 12, 1842	New York,...	† 975,400	1,298,764 89
New York Mutual, ...	Apr. 12, 1842	New York,...	*	753,634 07
Orient Mutual, ...	Feb., 1854	New York,...	*	1,195,964 03
Pacific Mutual,................	Jan. 6, 1855	New York,...	*	1,188,893 54
Sun Mutual,...................	May 22, 1841	New York,...	*	1,988,889 39
Union Mutual,.................	May 14, 1845	New York,...	*	1,506,587 56
Washington Marine,...........	Dec. 27, 1859	New York,...	† 393,700	707,569 07
Total,			$2,369,100	$25,149,069 76

* Mutual. † Capital.

Marine Insurance Companies of other States.

NAME.	Date of incorporation.	Location.	Capital.	Gross assets.
Pacific,........................	July, 1863	San Francisco,	$750,000	$1,624,389 13
National,......................	Dec. 29, 1865	San Francisco,	1,000,000	1,143,131 92
Total,			$1,750 000	$2,767,521 05

New York Life Insurance Companies.

NAME.	Date of incorporation or organization.	Location.	Capital.	Gross assets.
American Popular,.	May 24, 1866	New York,...	$100,000	$149,676 85
Atlantic Mutual,............	May 3, 1866	Albany,.......	110,000	175,532 49
Brooklyn,.................	July 26, 1864	Brooklyn,.....	125,000	404,411 52
Continental,.....................	May 3, 1866	New York,...	100,000	295,848 07
Excelsior,.......................	May 7, 1867	New York,...	125,000	125,000 00
Carried forward,			$560,000	$1,150,468 93

New York Life Insurance Companies — (Continued).

NAME.	Date of incorporation or organization.	Location.	Capital.	Gross assets.
Brought forward,	....	....	$560,000	$1,150,468 93
Equitable,	July 25, 1859	New York,	100,000	3,077,788 30
Germania,	July 1, 1860	New York,	200,000	1,240,299 65
Globe Mutual,	June 7, 1864	New York,	100,000	800,129 10
Great Western,	Dec. 30, 1865	New York,	115,000	179,633 90
Guardian,	Aug. 11, 1859	New York,	125,000	740,413 66
Home,	Apr. 30, 1860	Brooklyn,	125,000	1,231,678 50
Knickerbocker,	Apr. 18, 1853	New York,	100,000	1,579,245 88
Manhattan,	July 16, 1850	New York,	100,000	3,525,827 64
Mutual,	Apr. 12, 1842	New York,	Mutual.	18,495,507 55
National,	Apr. 25, 1863	New York,	130,000	206,707 47
New York,	May 21, 1841	New York,	....	7,009,092 25
New York Life and Trust,	Mar. 9, 1830	New York,	1,000,000	1,921,272 64
New York State,	June 4, 1866	Syracuse,	120,000	155,767 15
North America,	Oct. 22, 1862	New York,	100,000	1,566,405 82
Security,	Jan. 17, 1862	New York,	110,000	757,398 56
United States,	Feb. 25, 1850	New York,	100,000	2,005,702 64
Universal,	Feb. 1, 1865	New York,	200,000	314,028 32
Washington,	Jan. 31, 1860	New York,	125,000	727,129 99
Widows' and Orphans'	Sept. 16, 1864	New York,	200,000	530,839 70
World Mutual,	Nov. 19, 1866	New York,	200,000	213,668 55
Total,			$3,810,000	$47,429,006 20

Life Insurance Companies of other States.

NAME.	Date of incorporation or organization.	Location.	Capital.	Gross assets.
Ætna,	1820	Hartford, Conn.,	$60,600	$4,312,433 86
Berkshire,	May, 1851	Pittsfield, Mass.,	53,000	677,898 03
Charter Oak,	May, 1850	Hartford, Conn.,	100,000	2,480,049 17
Connecticut General,	July, 1865	Hartford, Conn.,	251,000	543,424 86
Connecticut Mutual,	June 12, 1846	Hartford, Conn.,	Mutual.	13,316,275 97
Economical Mutual,	May, 1866	Providence, R. I.,	100,000	141,443 78
Hahnemann,	Sept. 14, 1865	Cleveland, O.,	200,000	247,316 32
John Hancock,	Apr. 21, 1862	Boston, Mass.,	100,000	524,874 97
Massachusetts Mutual,	May 15, 1851	Springfield, Mass.,	100,000	1,509,585 48
Mutual Benefit,	Jan. 21, 1845	Newark, N. J.,	Mutual.	11,656,728 74
National,	Nov. 13, 1848	Montpelier, Vt.,	25,000	571,707 50
New England Mutual,	Apr. 1, 1835	Boston, Mass.,	Mutual.	5,067,382 84
New Jersey Mutual,	Mar. 19, 1863	Newark, N. J.,	100,000	163,967 95
Phœnix Mutual,	May, 1851	Hartford, Conn.,	16,000	1,457,314 95
Union Mutual,	July 17, 1848	Augusta, Me.,	Mutual.	2,088,429 20
Total,			$1,105,600	$44,758,833 62

Foreign Life Insurance Companies.

NAME.	Date of establishment or incorporation.	Location.	Capital.	Gross assets.
British Commercial,	1820	London, Eng.,	....	....
American Branch,	....	New York,	....	$227,735 04
Liverpool, London and Globe,	May 21, 1836	Liverpool, Eng	$1,896,079 68	16,542,719 87
American Branch,	....	New York,	....	2,642 72
Royal,	June 13, 1845	Liverpool, Eng	1,395,589 80	6,217,711 00
American Branch,	....	New York,	....	526,193 49
Total,			$3,291,669 48	$23,517,002 12

Casualty Insurance Companies of the State of New York.

Name.	Date incorpor'n or organization.	Location.	Capital.	Gross assets.
Fidelity, *	April 7, 1865	New York,	$100,000	$107,571 40
National Travelers',	May 5, 1866	New York,	200,000	247,300 74
United States Accident,*	January 25, 1866	Syracuse,	200,000	195,994 86
Total,			$500,000	$550,867 00

* These Companies retiring from business.

Casualty Insurance Companies of other States.

Name.	Date of incorporation.	Location.	Capital.	Gross Assets.
Hartford Accident,	May 2, 1866	Hartford, Conn.	$125,100	$119,810 54
Hartford Live Stock,	May 2, 1866	Hartford, Conn.	105,000	170,728 62
Railway Passengers,	May, 1865	Hartford, Conn.	218,000	294,101 06
Travelers,	June 17, 1863	Hartford, Conn.	500,000	840,980 22
Travelers,*	January, 1865	Providence, R. I.	106,000	125,065 65
United States Casualty,	Feb. 13, 1866	Trenton, N. J.	100,000	152,786 56
Total,			$1,154,100	$1,703,472 65

* This Company retiring from business.

The following table shows the number of the existing Insurance Companies in this State, as follows: 1st. The number incorporated by special Acts of the Legislature, before the general Act of 1849. 2d. The number incorporated by special Acts of the Legislature since the said Act of 1849. 3d. The number organized under the general Act of April 10 1849. 4th. The number organized under the general Acts of June 24, 1853, and June 25, 1853.

CLASSES.	Incorporated by special act before 1849.	Incorporated by spec'l act since 1849.	Organized under act of 1849.	Organized under acts of June 24 and June 25, 1853.	Total.
Joint Stock Fire Insurance Companies,	21	..	40	45	106
Mutual Fire Insurance Companies,	14	..	1	..	15
Joint Stock and Mutual Marine Insurance Companies,	6	..	4	..	10
Life Insurance Companies,	3	1	3	18	25
Casualty Insurance Companies,	..	1	..	2	3
Total,	44	2	48	65	159

The number and kind of Insurance Companies under the supervision of this department are as follows:

	FIRE INS'NCE. Joint Stock.	FIRE INS'NCE. Mutual.	Marine Insurance.	Life Insurance.	Casualty Insurance.	Total.
New York companies,	106	15	10	25	3	159
Other State companies,	40	..	2	15	6	63
Foreign companies,	4	..	..	3	..	7
Total,	150	15	12	43	9	229

The following is a synopsis of the annual statements, for the year 1865, of the New York Fire, Marine, Life and Casualty Insurance Companies and of those of other States transacting business in this State:

New York Insurance Companies.

	FIRE INSURANCE COMPANIES.		Marine Insurance Companies.
	Joint Stock.	Mutual.	
Premiums in cash,	$19,620,068 09	$97,970 12	$11,096,058 29
Losses,	13,991,996 54	66,920 77	7,955,258 14
Gross assets,	45,360,887 90	2,435,180 70	26,925,769 52
All liabilities,	43,116,788 30	214,427 75	22,867,127 85
Gross income in cash,	22,522,436 40	132,978 44	12,173,717 15
Gross expenditures,	23,301,239 22	109,869 14	13,632,026 96
Risks in force,	1,812,894,739 22	46,930,485 75	241,409,023 00

	Life Insurance Companies.	Casualty Insurance Companies.	Aggregate.
Premiums in cash,	$8,993,717 65	$59,143 84	$39,866,957 99
Losses,	2,120,410 92	6,499 67	24,141,086 04
Gross assets,	33,296,832 03	268,777 78	108,287,447 93
All liabilities,	30,007,864 48	278,086 36	96,484,294 74
Gross income in cash,	10,797,297 89	68,773 84	45,695,203 72
Gross expenditures,	5,036,946 38	49,317 31	42,129,399 01
Risks in force,	289,846,316 50	12,224,140 00	2,403,304,704 47

Insurance Companies of other States.

	FIRE INSURANCE COMPANIES.		Marine Insurance Companies.
	Joint Stock.	Mutual.	
Premiums in cash,	$9,899,024 19	....	....
Losses,	6,619,587 01	....	....
Gross assets,	25,005,891 32	....	....
All liabilities,	20,170,898 19	....	....
Gross income in cash,	11,876,325 92	....	....
Gross expenditures,	11,393,539 12	....	....
Risks in force,	820,894,705 82	....	....

Insurance Companies of other States — (Continued).

	Life Insurance Companies.	Casualty Insurance Companies.	Aggregate.
Premiums in cash,	$6,282,134 34	$493,325 38	$16,674,483 91
Losses,	2,085,608 60	93,230 29	8,798,425 90
Gross assets,	31,061,283 24	730,057 01	56,797,231 57
All liabilities.	22,795,164 59	754,161 38	43,720,224 16
Gross income in cash,	7,777,256 80	530,281 13	20,183,863 85
Gross expenditures,	4,550,768 19	370,450 37	16,314,757 68
Risks in force,	291,035,936 96	87,411,500 00	1,199,342,142 78

The following is the grand aggregate of the New York Companies and of those of other States transacting business in the State of New York:

Premiums in cash,	$56,541,441 90
Losses,	32,939,511 94
Gross assets,	165,084,679 50
All liabilities,	140,204,518 90
Gross income in cash,	65,879,067 57
Gross expenditures,	58,444,156 69
Risks in force,	3,602,646,847 25

STATE ENGINEER AND SURVEYOR.

The office of State Engineer and Surveyor was created by Section 2, Article V., of the Constitution of 1846, and replaces that of "Surveyor-General," which had existed from an early period of the State government.

The Section defining his duties is as follows:

"A State Engineer and Surveyor shall be chosen at a general election, and shall hold his office two years, but no person shall be elected to said office who is not a practical engineer."

Act, chapter 72, Laws of 1848, provides as follows:

"§ 2. The State Engineer and Surveyor shall possess all the powers and discharge all the duties prescribed or required by law to be discharged by the Surveyor-General prior to the first day of January, eighteen hundred and forty-eight, except his powers and duties as a Commissioner of the Canal Fund."

"§ 3. The State Engineer and Surveyor shall have the general supervision of the engineer department, and shall perform all such duties in relation to the canals as shall be required by the canal board, and shall visit and inspect the public works of this State as often as, in his judgment, it shall be necessary."

By act, chapter 140, Laws of 1848; act, chapter 434, Laws of 1849, and act, chapter 140, Laws of 1850, it was provided that every railroad corporation in this State should make a detailed annual report of its operations to the State Engineer and Surveyor, and that this officer should "arrange the information contained in such reports in a tabular form, and prepare the same, together with the said reports, in a single document for printing, for the use of the Legislature."

The State Engineer and Surveyor is a member of the Canal Board, the Contracting Board, and one of the Commissioners of the Land Office.

State Canals.

There are in the State 893 70-100 miles of completed, navigable canals and feeders, as follows:

Erie canal,	350.66	miles.
Albany basin,	.77	"
Port Schuyler and West Troy side-cut,	.35	"
Pond above Troy dam,	3	"
Champlain canal and Waterford side-cut,	66	"
Glens Falls feeder and pond above,	12	"
Black River canal,	35.33	"

Black River feeder and pond above dam,	12.09 miles.
Delta feeder,	1.38 "
Black River improvement,	42.50 "
Oneida Lake canal,	6 "
Oswego canal,	38 "
Cayuga and Seneca canal,	22.77 "
Crooked Lake canal,	8 "
Chemung canal and feeder,	39 "
Chenango canal,	97 "
Oneida River improvement,	20 "
Seneca River towing path,	5 "
Baldwinsville canal,	1 "
Cayuga Inlet,	2 "
Limestone feeder,	.80 "
Butternut feeder,	1.55 "
Camillus feeder,	1 "
Genesee Valley canal,	113.50 "
Dansville Branch of Genesee Valley canal,	11 "
Genesee River feeder at Rochester,	2.75 "
Genesee River feeder at Oramel,	.75 "
Total,	893.70 miles.

Of the above, the Erie, Oswego, Cayuga and Seneca canals have been enlarged to the following dimensions:

Width of bottom,	52½ feet.
Width of surface,	70 "
Depth of water,	7 "

Locks 110 feet long and 18 feet wide; capacity of boats about 250 tons.

The Champlain canal has been partially enlarged, to enable boats drawing five feet of water to navigate it. The remaining canals are of the following general dimensions:

Width at bottom,	28 feet.
Width at surface,	40 "
Depth of water,	4 "

Locks 96 feet long and 14 feet wide; capacity of boats about 60 tons.

Of the twenty-one locks upon the Champlain canal, fifteen have been enlarged to the size of those upon the Erie, while six remain of the original size.

The locks upon the Erie canal are double, except thirteen locks between Clyde and Rochester, upon the Western Division.

Those upon all the other State canals are single.

The canals are divided into the Eastern, Middle and Western Divisions, to each of which is assigned one division engineer and one resident engineer. A resident engineer is also in especial charge of the Chenango canal extension, which is now in process of construction, extending from its junction with the Chenango canal at Binghamton, to the Pennsylvania State line, 40¼ miles.

The divisions are as follows:

Eastern Division.

Erie canal from Albany to the east bank of Oneida Lake canal,	133.58	miles.
Albany basin,	.77	"
Port Schuyler and West Troy side-cut,	.35	"
Pond above Troy dam,	3	"
Champlain canal and Waterford side-cut,	66	"
Glens Falls feeder and pond above,	12	"
Black River canal,	35.33	"
Black River feeder and pond above dam,	12.09	"
Delta feeder,	1.38	"
Black River improvement,	42.50	"
	307	miles.

Middle Division.

Erie canal from east side of Oneida Lake canal to east line of Wayne county,	68.58	miles.
Oneida Lake canal,	6	"
Oswego canal,	38	"
Cayuga and Seneca canal,	22.77	"
Crooked Lake canal,	8	"
Chemung canal and feeder,	39	"
Chenango canal,	97	"
Oneida River improvement,	20	"
Seneca River towing path,	5	"
Baldwinsville canal,	1	"
Cayuga Inlet,	2	"
Limestone feeder,	.80	"
Butternut feeder,	1.55	"
Camillus feeder,	1	"
	310.70	miles.

Western Division.

Erie canal from east line of Wayne county to Buffalo,	148.50	miles.
Genesee Valley canal from Rochester to Millgrove,	113.50	"
Dansville branch of this canal from junction at Spraker's to Dansville,	11	"
Genesee River feeder at Rochester,	2.25	"
Genesee River feeder at Oramel,	.75	"
	276	miles.

Railroads.

There are within the State about 3,000 miles of railroads, which are operated by steam, all of which, together with the horse or street railroads are required by law to report annually to this department, and the State Engineer and Surveyor is required to tabulate the results and submit the same, with the reports themselves, in a single document to the Legislature at the commencement of each session.

STATEMENT showing the date when construction was authorized, date of completion, length, number of locks, aggregate feet of lockage, and cost of construction of the New York State Canals.

NAME OF CANAL.	WHEN AUTHORIZED.		WHEN COMPLETED.		LENGTH, MILES.		NO. OF LOCKS.		Total lockage in feet.	COST OF CONSTRUCT'N	
	Original.	Enlargement.	Original.	Enlarge-ment.	Original.	Enlarged.	Single.	Double.		Original.	Enlarge-ment.
Erie Canal,	Apr. 15, 1817	May 11, 1835,	Oct. 26, 1825,	Sept. 1862,	363.	350.50	56	15	654.80	$7,143,789	$32,008,851
Champl'n Canal and	Apr. 15, 1817		1822,		66.		20		179.50	921,011	
Glens Falls feeder,	Apr. —, 1822				7.		13		132.	91,944	
Oswego Canal,	Apr. 20, 1825	April 15, 1854,	Dec. 10, 1828,	Sept. 1862,	38.	38.	17		154.85	565,437	2,511,992
Cayuga & Sen. Can. and Cayuga inlet,	Apr. 20, 1825	May 25, 1836, & April 15, 1854,	Nov. 15, 1828,	Sept. 1862,	24.75	24.75	11		76.64	214,000	1,133,149
Chemung Can. & f'der,	Apr. 15, 1829		Sept. 1831,		23. F'der 16.		49 Feeder 4		491.12	314,395	
Crooked Lake Canal,	Apr. 11, 1829		Oct. 10, 1833,		8.		27		277.83	156,766	
Chenango Canal,	Feb. 23, 1833		Oct. —, 1836,		97.		116		1,015.33	2,316,186	
Black River Canal and feeder,	Apr. 19, 1836		1849,		Canal 35. Fe'd'r 15. River 42½		109		1,082.25	3,157,296	
Gen. Val. Canal and Dansville Branch,	May 6, 1836		To Dansville, Nov. 1, 1842 To Olean, Nov. 1856 To Millgrove, Dec. 1861		124.75		112		1,123.60	5,663,183	
Oneida Lake Canal,	Mar. 22, 1832		1836,		7.		7		60.25	*50,000 78,829	
Oneida River Improvement,	Apr. 29, 1839		1850,		20.		2		6.25	79,346	
Chenango Canal Extension,	Apr. 9, 1863		Incomplete,		40.11		11		81.	Incomp'te	

* Cost by purchase.

Summary of Steam Railroads.

NAME.	Points connected.	Length in miles when completed.	Length in miles built.	When completed.	Amount of capital stock authorized by law.	Amount of capital stock paid in.	Total amount of funded debt.	Total amount of funded and floating debt.
Adirondack Company,	Saratoga and North Woods,	....	25.	......	$5,000,000	$4,183,000 00	$915,000 00	$1,333,711 92
Albany and Susquehanna,	Albany and Binghamton,	140.	98.52	......	1,400,000	1,675,138 70	2,114,000 00	2,133,643 28
Albany and Vermont,	Albany and Waterford Junction,	12	12.	......	600,000	600,000 00	....	....
Albany and West Stockbridge,	Greenbush and State Line,	38.	38.	1842	1,000,000	1,000,000 00	1,389,559 22	1,389,559 22
Atlantic and Great Western,*	Salamanca and Pa. State Line,	49.10	49.10	1860	3,450,000	919,265 02	1,777,665 00	1,951,461 34
Avon, Geneseo and Mount Morris,	Avon and Mount Morris,	15.50	15.50	1859	200,000	194,250 00	23,500 00	23,500 00
Blossburgh and Corning,*	Corning to Pa. State Line,	14.83	14.83	......	250,000	250,000 00	50,000 00	65,302 77
Brooklyn and Jamaica,	Brooklyn and Jamaica,	14.50	14.50	1860	500,000	488,100 00	498,110 00	530,295 52
Brooklyn and Rockaway Beach,	East N. Y.. and Canarsie Land'g,	3.50	3.50	1866	150,000	102,150 00	35,000 00	35,000 00
Buffalo, Bradford and Pittsburgh,	Carrolton, N. Y., to Pa. State line (to Lafayette, Pa. 26 miles)	8.	8.	......	1,100,000	1,100,000 00	1,766,000 00	1,766,000 00
Buffalo, New York and Erie,†	Buffalo and Corning,	142.	142.	1858	....	....	....	....
Buffalo and State Line,	Buffalo and Erie, Pa.,	68.34	68.34	1852	1,900,000	2,200,000 00	1,018,000 00	1,018,000 00
Buffalo and Oil Creek Cross Cut,	....	36.31	....	......	600,000	344,500 00	600,000 00	600,000 00
Buffalo and Washington,	....	110.	....	......	3,500,000	59,500 00	....	....
Cayuga and Susquehanna,	Oswego and Ithaca,	34.61	34.61	1834	1,500,000	589,110 00	....	....
Chemung,	Elmira to head of Seneca Lake,	17.36	17.36	1849	380,000	380,000 00	....	....
Corning and Seneca Lake,	....	....	....	......	600,000	6,000 00	....	....
Elmira, Jefferson and Canandaigua,†	Elmira and Canandaigua,	46.84	46.84	1851	500,000	500,000 00	....	....
Elmira and Williamsport,*	Elmira to Pa. State line (to Williamsport, Pa.. 78 miles),	9.	9.	......	1,000,000	1,000,000 00	1,570,000 00	1,570,000 00
Erie Railway,	New York, Dunkirk and Buffalo,	446.	446.	1851	Not fixed.	25,105,800 00	22,368,834 94	26,007,450 23
Erie Railway, Buffalo Branch,	Hornellsville and Attica,	60.	60.	......	....	....	....	....
Harlem River and Tarrytown,	Harlem River & Tarryt'n Junc'n,	19.	....	......	3,000,000	3,550 00	....	....
Hudson and Boston,	Hudson and Chatham,	17.33	17.33	1839	175,000	175,000 00	....	....
Hudson River,	New York and Albany,	144.	144.	1850	4,000,000	6,962,971 45	7,227,460 00	7,228,627 00
Hicksville and Cold Spring,	(Branch of Hudson River),	4.	4.	......	....	....	....	....
Long Island,	Brooklyn and Greenport,	107.	107.	1844	3,000,000	1,852,715 00	932,000 00	932,000 00
New York Central (main line),	Albany and Buffalo,	297.75	297.75	1843	24,801,000	24,801,000 00	14,095,804 34	14,095,804 34
Branches of New York Central,	Troy to Schenectady,	21.	21.	......	....	....	....	....
	Syracuse to Rochester (Auburn),	104.	104.	......	....	....	....	....
	Batavia to Attica,	11.	11.	......	....	....	....	....
	Rochester to Suspension Bridge,	74.75	74.75	......	....	....	....	....
	Lockport Junction to Tonawanda,	12.25	12.25	......	....	....	....	....
	Rochester to Charlotte,	6.88	6.88	......	....	....	....	....
	Buffalo to Lewiston,	28 25	28.25	......	....	....	....	....
New York and Flushing,	Flushing and Hunter's Point,	8.	8.	1854	200,000	200,000 00	125,000 00	145,000 00
New York and Harlem,	New York and Chatham,	130.75	130.75	1852	8,000,000	6,785,050 00	6,152,365 00	6,152,365 00
New York and New Haven,	N. York and Conn. State Line, (to New Haven, 62.25 miles),	14.14	14.14	1850	5,000,000	3,982,614 33	2,000,000 00	2,123,783 06

New York, Housatonic and Northern,	White Plains & Brookfield, Conn.,	39.	24.	......	1,000,000	110,820 00	....	19,200 00
Niagara Bridge and Canandaigua,‖	Canandaigua and Tonawanda,	98.46	98.46	1853	1,000,000	1,000,000 00	....	....
North Shore,	....	12.	6.25	......	200,000	192,945 00	$99,600 00	101,100 00
Northern,	Piermont, N. Y., and Bergen, N. J.	21.25	21.25	......	1,000,000	158,800 00	280,000 00	354,740 02
Ogdensburgh and Lake Champlain,	Ogdensburgh and Rouse's Point,	118.	118.	1850	3,077,000	2,797,000 00	1,494,900 00	1,494,900 00
Oswego and Rome,	Oswego and Richland Station,	28.58	28.58	1866	300,000	222,987 00	678,400 00	706,541 46
Oswego and Syracuse,	Oswego and Syracuse,	36.30	36.30	1848	482,400	482,400 00	386,000 00	405,875 00
Plattsburgh and Montreal,	Plattsburgh and Canada line,	23.17	23.17	1852	No report.	....	....	....
Rensselaer and Saratoga,	Troy and Ballston,	25.22	25.22	1835	800,000	800,000 00	498,750 00	498,750 00
Rochester and Genesee Valley,	Rochester and Avon,	18.45	18.45	......	800,000	557,560 00	109,000 00	110,500 00
Rome, Watertown and Ogdensburgh,	Rome and Ogdensburgh,	141.11	141.11	1862	2,400,000	2,385,500 00	1,575,793 66	1,631,781 35
Branches of the same,	....	48.52	48.52	......	....	....	....	....
Rutland and Whitehall,	Whitehall to Vermont State Line,	7.	7.	......	No report.	....	....	....
Sackett's Harbor, Rome and New York,§	Pierrepont Manor and Sackett's H.	18.	18.	1853	100,000	30,889 57	....	57,262 60
Saratoga and Hudson,	Schenectady and Athens,	37.87	37.87	1866	No report.	....	....	....
Saratoga and Schenectady,	Schenectady and Saratoga Springs	21.	21.	......	300,000	300,000 00	40,000 00	40,000 00
Saratoga and Whitehall,	Whitehall and Saratoga Springs,	40.86	40.86	1848	500,000	500,000 00	400,000 00	400,000 00
Schenectady and Utica,	Not commenced,	78.	....	......	2,400,000	11,600 00	....	....
Staten Island,	Tottenville and Vanderbilt's Land.	13.	13.	1860	800,000	660,000 00	200,000 00	295,000 00
Sterling Mountain,	Sterling Mine and Erie Railway,	7.60	7.60	......	80,000	80,000 00	350,000 00	350,000 00
Southern Central,	Fairhaven, Auburn and Ithaca,	115.	....	......	3,000,000	10,640 00	....	....
Syracuse, Binghamton and New York,	Syracuse and Binghamton,	81.	81.	1854	1,201,300	1,200,130 00	1,635,470 43	1,688,602 92
Troy and Boston,*	Troy to Vermont State Line,	34.91	34.91	1852	1,000,000	607,111 22	1,452,000 00	1,734,216 18
Troy and Bennington,¶	Eagle Bridge to Vermont State L.	5.	5.	1853	80,000	75,400 00	116,104 19	116,804 19
Troy and Greenfield,	Eagle Bridge to Vermont State L.	7.	7.	......	No report.	....	....	....
Troy and Greenbush,	Troy and Greenbush,	6.	6.	1845	275,000	274,400 00	....	....
Troy and Rutland,¶	....	62.	62.	......	325,000	325,000 00	60,000 00	60,000 00
Troy Union,	....	2.14	2.14	1853	30,000	30,000 00	680,000 00	680,000 00
Utica and Black River,	Utica and Philadelphia, N. Y.,	86.25	34.94	......	860,000	811,600 00	....	....
Utica, Chenango and Susquehanna Valley,	Utica and Binghamton,	82.	....	......	2,500,000	146,470 00	....	....
Warwick Valley,	Warwick and Greycourt,	10.33	10.33	1862	150,000	98,650 00	85,000 00	85,600 00
		3,591.01	3,062.16	......	$96,466,700	$99,333,617 29	$74,799,316 78	$79,932,377 40

* Report of 1865. † Leased to Erie Railway Company for 490 years, from May 1, 1863. ‡ Report of 1862.
‖ Leased in perpetuity to New York Central Railroad Company from May 1, 1858. § Report of 1861. ¶ Report of 1864.

LANDS OF THE STATE.

The Lieutenant-Governor, Speaker of the Assembly, Secretary of State, Comptroller, Treasurer, Attorney-General, and State Engineer and Surveyor are, by the Constitution, made the Commissioners of the Land Office. The Deputy Secretary of State is by law made, *ex officio*, Clerk of the Board, and their records are kept in the office of the Secretary of State. Their mode of selling land is as follows:

The Commissioners of the Land Office order the lands of the State to be surveyed into lots, and valuations made, and minimum prices set on them. They are then advertised and exposed for sale by auction. The lots unsold are liable to be taken by the first applicant on paying the one-fourth part of the prices set on them, and giving bonds for the residue, as required by law; and if any lots remain for a time unsold, the Commissioners order a re-appraisement to be made and re-exposure for sale by auction.

By chapter 230, Laws of 1827, the Commissioners of the Land Office may sell any unappropriated lands (counties of Saratoga, Montgomery, Hamilton, Washington, Warren, Clinton, Essex, Franklin, and St. Lawrence), not less than one hundred and sixty acres, if already surveyed, at such price as they shall ascertain to be their cash value, and if application be made for any quantity not less than one thousand acres not already surveyed, the Commissioners may cause surveys and estimates to be made, and sell the same at their cost value.

Under these provisions the Commissioners have made sales, and authorized the State Engineer and Surveyor, until otherwise directed, to sell the wild lands at sums not less than seventy cents per acre.

STATEMENT of the unsold lands belonging to the people of this State, specifying the counties where situated, the number of acres, and the funds to which they belong, viz.:

GENERAL FUND.

COUNTIES.	ACRES.	COUNTIES.	ACRES.
Clinton,	12,481	Seneca,	175
Delaware,	1,147	Sullivan,	116
Essex,	4,317	Ulster,	6,138
Erie,	1,544	Warren,	1,511
Franklin,	1,497	Washington,	57
Hamilton,	12,116		
Herkimer,	780		41,879

SCHOOL FUND.

COUNTIES.	ACRES.	COUNTIES.	ACRES.
Clinton,	3,027	Oneida,	28
Columbia (city of Hudson).		Onondaga,	43
Dutchess,	6	Oswego (city lots).	
Essex,	10,512	St. Lawrence,	75
Fulton,	25	Schoharie,	105
Hamilton,	6,987	Washington,	160
Herkimer,	12	Warren,	2,844
Montgomery,	16		
Niagara (village lots).			23,840

FIFTY ACRES. That part of East Oswego which is the subject of litigation, in regard to the bounds of the reservation, is not included in this statement.

SALT FUND LANDS.

Reserved lands leased for salt purposes, see Appendix F, in Senate Journal of 1829, page 52.

	ACRES.
Estimated about,	550.00
Lands purchased or exchanged since the adoption of the Constitution, in 1846,	543.12
	1,093.12
Lands sold since 1848,	114.85
	978.27
Reclaimed by the lowering of Onondaga Lake,	209.00
Total,	1,187.27

LITERATURE FUND.

COUNTY.		ACRES.
Hamilton,	Benson Township,	640

UNITED STATES DEPOSIT FUND.

Premises bid in for the State, under foreclosure of mortgages and remaining unsold

COUNTIES.			COUNTIES.		EST. VAL.
Chemung,	1 piece.		Queens,	1 piece.	
Clinton,	2 do	24 ac.	Rensselaer,	7 do	
Erie,	3 do		Richmond,	1 do	
Herkimer,	1 do		Tompkins,	1 do	
Monroe,	3 do		Warren,	1 do	
Oswego,	1 do		Westchester,	1 do	$5,200 00

NOTE.—Mostly city out lots, &c.

Summary.

Arranged according to the Funds to which they belong.

FUNDS.	ACRES UNSOLD.
General Fund,	41,879
School Fund,	23,840
Salt Fund,	1,187
Literature Fund,	640
United States Deposit Fund,	......
Total,	67,546

For a detailed statement of the lands belonging to the State, see State Engineer and Surveyor's Report, Assembly Document No. 38, of 1866, pages 95 to 132, inclusive.

Premises bid in for the State, under Foreclosure of Mortgages belonging to the United States Deposit Fund, remaining unsold.

COUNTY.	Number of mortgage.	When bid in.	Description.	Principal due.
Chemung,	175	1857	Village lot.	$256 00
Erie,	353	1860	25 acres.	400 00
Erie,	437, 3 city lots	1860	1 acre.	500 00
Erie,	466	1862	20 acres.	1,000 00
Herkimer,	264	1866	Village lot.	250 00
Monroe,	410	1865	2¾ acres.	1,800 00
Monroe,	443	1856	75 x 130 feet.	900 00
Monroe,	475	1865	66 x 130 feet.	300 00
Oswego,	271	1841	....	300 00
Queens,	19 and 37	1852	40 acres.	850 00
Rensselaer,	49	1846	156 acres.	348 00
Rensselaer,	203	1858	111 acres.	2,000 00
Rensselaer,	181	1859	194 acres.	850 00
Rensselaer,	222	1862	50 acres.	375 00
Rensselaer,	258	1863	171 acres.	600 00
Rensselaer,	286	1863	Unknown.	896 00
Rensselaer,	259	1866	....	1,000 00
Richmond,	41	1861	....	2,000 00
Tompkins,	417	1862	72 acres.	400 00
Warren,	112	1866	67 acres.	300 00
Westchester,	122	1862	27½ acres.	250 00

ONONDAGA SALT SPRINGS.

These springs are reserved and owned by the State, and are under the direction of a Superintendent appointed by the Governor and Senate. The State, by its officers and agents, sinks the wells for salt water, which are generally over three hundred feet deep, pumps the salt water, and distributes to the manufacturers, receiving therefor one cent a bushel. All the salt is made and inspected and weighed under the direction of the State officers. This is to protect the consumer against fraud in quality and quantity.

All the salt is manufactured by individuals or companies, in their own works, which are nearly all on lands owned by the State and leased to the manufacturers. The manufacturers have constructed works far beyond the ability of the salt wells to supply with water, so that it is necessary to divide them into classes and supply such classes in their order. During the best weather for making salt, not more than one-half of all the works can be supplied with salt water; sometimes less than that proportion.

There are three hundred and sixteen blocks for boiling salt that are equally entitled to water; and could these blocks be fully supplied with water for the eight months they are allowed by law to make salt, they could produce 12,640,000 bushels of 56 lbs. each. There are over 41,000 vats for making coarse or solar salt, which have a capacity of manufacturing over 2,000,000 bushels. Could the water be furnished, the salt works could easily produce 15,000,000 of bushels per annum.

STATEMENT of the number of bushels of salt made at the Onondaga Salt Springs since June 20, 1797, which is the date of the first leases of the lots.

Date.	Number of bushels.	Date.	Number of bushels.	Date.	Number of bushels.	Date,	Number of bushels.
1797,....	25,474	1815,....	322,058	1833,....	1,838,646	1851,....	4,614,117
1798,....	59,928	1816, ...	348,665	1834,....	1,943,252	1852,...	4,922,533
1799,....	42,704	1817,....	408,665	1835,....	2,209,867	1853,...	5,404,524
1800,....	50,000	1818,....	406,540	1836,....	1,912,858	1854,....	5,803,347
1801,....	62,000	1819,....	548,374	1837,....	2,167,287	1855,....	6,082,885
1802,....	75,000	1820,....	558,329	1838,....	2,575,033	1856,....	5,966,810
1803,....	90,000	1821,....	526,049	1839,....	2,864,718	1857,....	4,312,126
1804,....	100,000	1822,....	481,562	1840,....	2,622,305	1858,....	7,033,219
1805,....	154.071	1823,....	726,988	1841,....	3,340,767	1859,....	6,894,272
1806,....	122,577	1824,....	816,634	1842, ...	2,291,903	1860,....	5,593,247
1807,....	165,448	1825, ...	757,203	1843,....	3,127,500	1861,...	7,200,391
1808,....	319,618	1826,..	811,023	1844,....	4,300,554	1862,...	9,053,874
1809,....	128,282	1827,....	983,410	1845,....	3,762,358	1863,....	7,942,383
1810,....	450,000	1828,....	1,160,888	1846.....	3,838,851	1864,....	7,378,834
1811,....	200,000	1829,....	1,129,280	1847,...	3,951,355	1865,....	6,385,930
1812,....	221,011	1830, ...	1,435,446	1848,....	4,737 126	1866,....	7.158,503
1813,....	226,000	1831,....	1,514,037	1849,....	5,083,569	....	....
1814,....	295,000	1832,....	1,652,985	1850,....	4,268,919	....	....
Total,......							175,857,072

TABLE showing the net revenue derived from the manufacture of salt, and paid into the general fund, since the duties were reduced to one cent per bushel.

YEAR.	Amount.	YEAR.	Amount.
1846,	$7,705 48	1857,	....
1847,	9,717 63	1858,	$19,766 93
1848,	21,491 46	1859,	27,306 38
1849,	20,153 69	1860,	12,342 50
1850,	15,104 87	1861,	26,761 28
1851,	13,337 55	1862,	49,696 21
1852,	19,284 61	1863,	38,064 94
1853,	29,557 19	1864,	29,906 96
1854,	23,711 57	1865,	18,620 59
1855,	10,867 46	1866,	24,557 48
1856,	9,690 79		....
			$427,645 56
Deduct deficit in 1857,			6,063 01
Total net revenue above expenditures,			$421,582 55

INDIAN TRIBES.

A few remnants of the native races still reside in the State, mostly occupying Reservations of lands in common, and receiving annuities under treaties by which their original territory was ceded to the State. The Reservations are as follows:

Allegany Reservation, chiefly of Senecas, lying in the towns of South Valley, Cold Spring, Bucktooth, Great Valley and Carrolton, in Cattaraugus county. The tract extends 35 miles along both sides of the Allegany river, is about half a mile wide, and contains about 42 square miles, or 26,680 acres. Population, in 1865, 825, being an increase of 71 in ten years.

Cattaraugus Reservation, on both sides of Cattaraugus creek, in the towns of Perrysburgh, Cattaraugus county, Collins, Erie county, and Hanover, Chautauqua county, including 21,680 acres of excellent land, and mostly under improvement. A council house is owned by the tribe, and three churches are maintained. Population, in 1865, 1,347, being an increase of 168 in ten years. The Thomas Orphan Asylum, hitherto aided by the State, is located here.

The *Cayugas* have no Reservation. Many have removed west of the Mississippi river, and 64 persons, in 1865, received $1,093.50 annuities from the sale of their former Reservation. Others have received the principal of their annuities, and a few reside among the Senecas at Cattaraugus.

The *Oneidas*, now reduced to 155 persons (in 1865), reside on farms owned as individual freeholds, in the towns of Lenox, Madison county, and Vernon, Oneida county. The greater part of these people emigrated, over thirty years since, to the neighborhood of Green Bay, Wisconsin, where they own about 800 acres of land, and now reside.

Onondaga Reservation, on Onondaga creek, in the towns of Fayette and Onondaga, in Onondaga county. Population, in 1865, 360, an increase of 11 in ten years. They receive annuities from the State amounting to about $1,550 annually. About two-thirds of their lands are leased to the State.

St. Regis Reservation, bordering upon the St. Lawrence river and the Province line of Canada. The tribe were originally Mohawks and other tribes of the Five Nations, who were induced to emigrate in the French Colonial period of Canada, and who settled at their present location about 1760. Population living south of the boundary line, in 1865, 426, being an increase of 13 in ten years. The number of this tribe living on the Canada side is about 760. Some of these draw annuities from this State by virtue of treaties of cession. In 1864, the number who shared in the State annuities was 648, and the amount paid was $2,396.60.

The division of this tribe into British and American parties, which determines from which government they shall receive their annuities or presents, originated in the war of 1812–'15, and according as they or their ancestors declared their preferences at that time. The distinction is kept up by inheritance from mother to child, according to the Indian custom. Each party is governed by a separate class of trustees or chiefs, and their domestic affairs are generally managed harmoniously. Although tenants in common, it is customary for them to buy and sell improvements among themselves, and the conventional titles thus acquired are respected by common consent.

Shinnecock Reservation. This is a tract of land held in common by a remnant of the native tribes of Long Island, numbering, in 1865, 147 persons. Many of these people show traces of African blood. They have lost all traces of their native language and customs, are generally industrious, and support one or two small churches. They receive no annuities from the State.

Tonawanda Reservation, in Alabama and Pembroke, in Genesee county, Newstead, Erie county, and Royalton, Niagara county. This reservation lies on the Tonawanda creek, and contains about 45,440 acres. Population, in 1865, 509, a decrease of 93 in ten years.

Tuscarora Reservation, in Lewiston, Niagara county, embracing 6,249 acres of land purchased with moneys received from the sale of lands in North Carolina, and given by the Holland Land Company and the Senecas. They receive no annuities. Population, in 1865, 370, an increase of 54 in ten years.

These people anciently emigrated from North Carolina and settled near the Oneidas. They were removed to their present location through the influence of British agents, during the revolutionary war.

On all the Indian Reservations, schools are maintained by the State. The number of schools, by latest reports, was 25; children between 5 and 16, 1,175; number of children attending schools, 866. These schools are under the immediate care of the Superintendent of Public Instruction.

WEIGHTS AND MEASURES

The office of Superintendent of Weights and Measures was created in 1851, soon after the receipt of a full set of the standard weights and measures transmitted to the State by order of Congress.* The standards previously owned by the State were in the custody of the Secretary of State. Sets of less elaborate construction are furnished to the several counties and towns, and these are replaced, when lost by fire or otherwise, at the expense of the corporation requiring them. The Superintendent is expected to answer inquiries relative to disputed questions of measurement, and appeals from County and Town Sealers of Weights and Measures. He furnishes sets upon the order of Supervisors, to be repaid by tax. The expense is at present between two and three hundred dollars. It is understood that a series of decimal measures is under construction by order of the Federal Government, for the several States, and this subject will probably before long engage the attention of our Legislature. Public opinion would in this case demand that the change in common business transactions should be at first optional rather than imperative.

By an act passed April 15, 1857, the following weights were established for a legal bushel, in the absence of agreement to the contrary, between the parties: "Whenever wheat, rye, Indian corn, buckwheat, barley, oats, beans, peas, clover seed, timothy seed, flax seed, or potatoes, shall be sold by the bushel, and no special agreement shall be made by the parties as to the mode of measuring, the bushel shall consist of sixty-two pounds of beans, sixty pounds of wheat, peas, clover seed, or potatoes; fifty-eight pounds of Indian corn, fifty-six pounds of rye, fifty-five pounds of flax seed, forty-eight pounds of buckwheat or barley, forty-four pounds of timothy seed, and thirty-two pounds of oats."

* These standards were furnished pursuant to a joint resolution of Congress, approved June 14, 1836, and consist of one standard yard, one set of standard weights of one, two, three, four, five, ten, twenty, twenty-five and fifty pounds respectively; one set of standard Troy ounce weights, divided decimally from ten ounces to the one ten-thousandth of an ounce; one set of standard liquid capacity measures, consisting of one wine gallon of two hundred and thirty-one cubic inches, one half gallon, one quart, one pint, and one half pint measure, and one standard half bushel, containing 1,075.21 cubic inches. These are, by the statute of 1851 (chap, 134), declared the standards of weights and measures throughout the State.

MILITARY DEPARTMENT.*

The necessity of a well-organized militia is apparent to every thoughtful and reflecting mind. It is the great arm of our strength, and the bulwark of our safety and support. It is the powerful lever that maintains and gives character and permanency to the civil structure of government, and opposes every effort to disturb and despoil the fair fabric, both National and State, so firmly established, and so well secured by the fathers of the Revolution.

The framers of the Constitution of 1789 recognized this principle, and they incorporated the same in the following article: "A well-regulated Militia being necessary to the security of a free State, the right of the people to keep and bear arms shall not be infringed."

And so the people of this State, from an early day, have cherished this same principle, and have fostered and sustained it to the present time.

The history of all governments has proven a conflict with the established civil powers to be inevitable, and that to support the honor and will of the people, a resort to arms is necessary; to this end the people must be educated in the school of military.

The laws of this State provide that every person between the ages of eighteen and forty-five shall be amenable to military duty. A portion of this large army is incorporated into the "National Guard," and armed and equipped for service at the expense of the State. The balance are known as the "Reserve Militia," and are required to parade, armed and equipped at their own expense, on one day in each year; in default of this duty they are subjected to a fine which is appropriated to the support of the active militia. Or, in lieu of this duty, are privileged to pay the sum of one dollar as a commutation fee for the service required. To reach the persons liable to this duty, it is provided that an annual enrollment of the persons so liable be made. The principle governing this system is eminently correct. Surely, every man within the ages prescribed should be willing, and at all times in readiness, to defend his State and his country. The security of a republican form of government depends upon a fulfillment of this requirement, and to make it practicable, a prescribed number of the men liable should be constantly engaged in the exercise of arms, and the other duties conveyed through the necessity of this education.

In our State the militia has been sustained and kept up for more than half a century, and while it has had much opposition at times strewn in

---

* This summary was prepared by Gen. SELDEN E. MARVIN, Adjutant-General.—ED.

its way, it has continued to prosper, and its fruits have been apparent in the manner in which it has, at all times, and under all circumstances, and in all emergencies, discharged its duties.

Prior to the late terrible conflict, very many of the people of the State looked upon the existence of the militia with eyes of disrespect, and laughed at the efforts that were being made for its support, pouring out invectives of contumely and contempt, and, like many of the most important institutions of society and government, the inestimable importance of a well-organized militia was ignored by the great mass, and it was only in the consideration of its entire abolition, or in the exercise of its fullest authority and influence in the hour of need, that its indispensable functions were recognized and appreciated. So much opposition was engendered that those who saw clearly the necessity of maintaining the organization, found many obstacles to encounter and difficulties to overcome, much self-sacrifice was demanded, and the reproaches of the many well nigh stifled the efforts of the few. But manfully and heroically the battle was fought, the war came, and the labor of years was crowned with success.

The importance of the militia as a strictly military force, cannot be too highly estimated. It constitutes the true military strength of the republic, in which the people retain all the power, as in its co-ordinate branch, the civil authority. It is organized in accordance with the spirit of the Constitution of the United States, and is made applicable to the condition of the country in its growing capacity and extended relations. Its governance is under constitution and laws prescribed and regulated by the people, and for the support of the government created by and sustained for the people.

In a time when taxation is grievous, and falls with heaviness upon the people, the militia, in its relations to political economy, is of the greatest importance. The cost of the maintenance of the entire force of the National Guard in this State in a high state of efficiency, would not support a single regiment of the regular army, including all contingent expenses, and yet, as has been proved, the militia would be as serviceable as the forces whose business is war.

And again, the National Guard, as an auxiliary to the police force of the State, is indispensable. It is the only reliance the people have in the suppression of riots and the wiping out of local insurrections. To think of maintaining a constabulary force for such emergencies would be absurd. The cost for a force sufficiently large for all such emergencies, especially in large centers of population, would be immense and insupportable.

The militia, in its well conceived organization and with liberal support, exerts a moral influence upon the evil disposed, and thereby prevents the inception of plots or designs of organized resistance to the laws. It is, in times of such danger, the sole resource of the people, and gives to legislative and judicial decisions their force and influence. Without such a reliable resource it is possible, and even probable, that laws, and the decisions and verdicts of constituted authority would be nugatory and despised. A small proportion of the people, if evil disposed, could, by concerted and well organized action, defy the large majority of peaceable and law-abiding citizens. Such a successful resistance of law, if even for a very limited period, would demoralize society, and the loss of life inevitable in such collisions would be terrible, and the value of the property which might be jeopardized would support an adequate militia for centuries.

In this connection, permit me to furnish a brief *resume* of the services of the National Guard.

Whenever it has been necessary in various localities to call upon the military authorities for aid and support, the response has always been attended with promptness, and the service effectually performed. The police force has always found in the military a sure and reliable body for its support, and it has ever proved effective in the suppression of riots, and in upholding the civil frame of government. In the Astor Place riots, the police difficulties, the bread riots of '57, the quarantine riots, and the anti-rent troubles, the militia has ever faithfully discharged all duties imposed upon them by the civil authorities. In the late war its services have been largely felt, and its influences have been spread over a large extent of the success that attended our armies.

A brief synopsis of the service in the late war, I trust will not be regarded as tedious, or out of place.

In April, 1861, immediately after the rebellion had been actively inaugurated, and the safety of the National Capitol was threatened, the State of New York furnished and forwarded to the points of danger eleven regiments, comprising 7,334 officers and men, whose presence undoubtedly saved the nation from a great and almost fatal calamity at the very outbreak of actual hostilities. That the State, after so long a period of profound peace, should have been enabled to promptly furnish this force for the national exigency, is a marked and undeniable indication of the natural and innate martial spirit of its citizens. This martial spirit, nobly evinced during the great revolution, and rekindled by the war of 1812, has never been quenched in this State, and ever since this last named epoch, a military organization, more or less efficient, has been sustained under exclusive State influences and authority, without assistance or encouragement from the General Government; and during long years of peace, when the martial profession was deemed the most useless office of man, the New York militia, at its own expense, and despite every discouragement, retained that organization and schooled officers and soldiers for the nation's greatest need.

In addition to the force above named, six complete regiments of the State militia volunteered during the first months of the war, and were mustered into the service for and served three years. Over five thousand (5,000) officers for volunteer regiments were furnished by the militia of the State.

The rebellion having revived in all a military ardor, and the advance in military science, and the unexpected draft upon the national resources having exhibited defects and suggested their remedies, the Legislature of the State, after consideration, enacted, April 23d, 1862, an amended law, which provided for the enrollment of the arms-bearing population, and the organization of an active force, entitled the "National Guard," with a maximum since fixed at 50,000 men. Whilst this body was in process of organization, the State was enabled to furnish from its incomplete ranks twelve regiments, comprising 8,588 men, who were mustered into the United States service for three months in May, 1862, and again, after the active volunteering and drafts for the general service had depleted their ranks, twenty-six regiments, comprising 13,971 men, marched, in 1863, to the defense of Pennsylvania and Maryland. Again, in 1864, ten regiments of the National Guard were mustered into the United States service for one hundred days. During the years of 1864 and 1865, when threatened raids from Canada harassed and distracted the Government, the National Guard, ordered on duty at exposed points of the frontier, relieved the apprehensions of our citizens, saved the detaching of troops from the armies in front of Richmond, and frustrated the designs of our enemies.

This hasty sketch of the service of the militia of this State displays their efficiency and usefulness at a period when the demands of the general government, by volunteering or forced drafts from their ranks, constantly tended to impair and disorganize them, and exhibits a vitality and zeal under every discouragement, which deserves and should receive the respect and consideration of all.

After the close of the war had returned to the State its hundreds of thousands of veterans scarred in every great battle-field, the organization of the National Guard was resumed and completed, until it now comprises one hundred and ten (110) regiments of infantry, artillery, and cavalry, and fifty-two thousand (52,000) officers and men, most of them armed, uniformed and equipped in the most complete manner—an army of disciplined citizens representing every class of society, intelligent, brave and ardent, bound by every relation of life to sustain social and political order, and prepared at a moment's notice to vindicate the enforcement of the laws, National or State, or repel invasions from abroad.

The Governor, by virtue of his office, is Commander-in-Chief of the National Guard. The labor connected with its sustenance is apportioned to the members of his staff representing various departments.

The Adjutant-General is the chief of the staff, and has general supervision of all matters appertaining to the militia. He acts for the Commander-in-Chief, and by his orders. Through him the Commander-in-Chief communicates to the various departments, and to the officers and soldiers comprising the organizations of the National Guard. It is his duty to keep a complete roster of all the officers of the military forces of the State, and under the direction of the Commander-in-Chief, to issue such orders to the National Guard as may be necessary.

The Inspector-General is generally charged with all matters appertaining to the inspection of troops, their condition, the state of their arms and uniform, their discipline and efficiency; he is also to inspect the various armories, arsenals and other State property, and report in full to the Commander-in-Chief.

The Commissary-General of Ordnance has charge of all the arsenals and armories, together with all ordnance and ordnance stores in the State; he makes issues of property upon the orders of the Commander-in-Chief, and reports to him, in detail, the operations of his department.

The Quartermaster-General issues all clothing and other articles belonging to his department, in the same manner as the Commissary-General of Ordnance.

The Judge-Advocate-General is charged with all matters relating to the administration of justice among the military force of the State He examines carefully all matters relating to appeals from the decisions of courts-martial, and is the legal adviser of the several staff departments.

The Paymaster-General is charged with all matters relating to the disbursements of moneys to the officers and soldiers of the National Guard. During the war, the duties of the office were particularly onerous, as the large sums of money appropriated by the State, as bounties to its soldiers, were disbursed in this department.

The Surgeon-General is charged with the administrative details of the medical department, and general oversight and charge of the officers connected with it.

The duties of the other staff departments are confined to such labor as may be specially assigned them by the Commander-in-Chief.

The labor attached to the several staff departments during the war cannot be too highly estimated. The State furnished the army of the General Government with 473,443 men. The work connected with the organization, equipment and forwarding to the front, this large body of men, was performed under the direction of the Commander-in-Chief, by the heads of the several staff departments, and the promptitude and alacrity displayed by the State in filling its quota attest the magnitude of the work, and the faithfulness of those to whom its performance was specially assigned.

The following tables exhibit:

1. The strength of the uniformed militia for the years 1857 to 1866, inclusive.

2. A statement of persons liable to military duty and not performing the same for the years from 1847 to 1866, inclusive.

3. A statement of moneys received for commutation for the years 1849 to 1853, inclusive.

RESERVE MILITIA.

STATEMENT of number of persons, between the prescribed ages, liable to military duty in the State in each year, from 1847 to 1866 inclusive, taken from enrollments made according to law.

YEAR.	No. of Reserve Militia.	YEAR.	No. of Reserve Militia.
1847,	177,606	1856,	337,235
1848,	178,549	1857,	350,000
1849,	201,452	1858,	350,000
1850,	224,665	1859,	224,479
1851,	267,433	1860,	450,000
1852,	289,306	1861,	480,000
1853,	313,313	1862,	350,000
1854,	317,706	1864,	360,866
1855,	333,368	1866,	361,505

UNIFORMED MILITIA.

STATEMENT of the strength of the Organized Militia (National Guard), officers, musicians and privates, in each year, from 1857 to 1866 inclusive.

YEAR.	Strength.	YEAR.	Strength.
1857,	16,434	1862,	23,684
1858,	18,107	1863,	32,435
1859,	18,466	1864,	44,185
1860,	19,189	1865,	50,246
1861,	19,613	1866,	52,247

COMMUTATION FEES.

Amount of Commutation Fees received in each year, from 1849 to 1853 inclusive.

YEAR.	Amount received.	Amount paid.	Balance.
1849,	$41,121 32	$25,808 96	$15,312 36
1850,	39,422 06	28,109 07	11,314 99
1851,	13,492 47	12,835 53	2,113 26
1852,	14,751 32	12,030 10	2,721 22
1853,	13,579 72	10,431 12	3,364 54

Showing disbursements in the Paymaster-General's Office, State of New York, for Bounties and Militia for following years:

1862.

Bounties, Gov. Morgan's proclamation,			$3,436,300 00

1863.

Bounties, Gov. Morgan's proclamation and chap. 184, Laws 1863,			1,507,460 00

1864.

Bounties, Gov. Morgan's proclamation and chap. 184, Laws 1863,	$4,046,910 00	$4,046,910 00	
"National Guard" services in 1862,	$7,711 46		
do do 1863,	10,393 51	18,104 97	
			4,065,014 97
Carried forward,			$9,008,774 97

1865.				
Brought forward, ...				$9,008,774 97
Bounties, Gov. Morgan's proclamation, ...		$18,000 00		
do chap. 184, Laws 1863, ...		293,605 00		
do chap. 29, Laws 1865:				
Bonds, ...	$21,495,000 00			
Money, ...	4,254,243 96			
		25,730,343 96		
			$26,041,948 96	
"National Guard" services in 1862, ...		$3,069 96		
do do 1863, ...		2,461 32		
do do 1864, ...		25,383 25		
do do 1865, ...		6,438 71		
			37,358 24	
				26,079,302 20
1866.				
Bounties, Gov. Morgan's proclamation, ...		$2,625 00		
do chap. 184, Laws 1863, ...		36,780 00		
do chap. 29, Laws 1865:				
Bonds, ...	$640,000 00			
Money, ...	338,505 41			
		978,505 41		
			$1,017,910 41	
Militia services in 1861, ...		$4,075 60		
"National Guard" services in 1862, ...		473 79		
do do 1863, ...		926 73		
do do 1865, ...		1,841 15		
do do 1866, ...		840 98		
			8,158 25	
				1,026,068 66
1867, to May 1st.				
Bounties, Gov. Morgan's proclamation, ...		$225 00		
do chap. 184, Laws 1863, ...		4,675 00		
do chap. 29, Laws 1865, ...		9,700 00		
			$14,600 00	
"National Guard" services in 1866, ...			860 00	
				15,460 00
				$36,129,605 83

A Summary of the different laws passed since 1846, *is furnished herewith, for easy reference.*

CHAP. 290, LAWS OF 1847,

Provides that all able-bodied white male citizens between the ages of eighteen and forty-five, residing in this State and not exempted by the laws of the United States, shall be subject to military duty, except officers in the army of the United States, ministers and preachers of the Gospel, persons who have been or hereafter shall be regularly discharged in consequence of the performance of military duty in pursuance of any law of this State, and such firemen as are now exempted by law, commissioned officers honorably discharged from the militia after four (4) years service, and non-commissioned officers and privates honorably discharged after seven (7) years service.

All persons subject to military duty, except members of regularly organized military companies, shall be exempt from the performance of military duty by paying, on or before the first day of August in each year, to the receiver or collector of taxes, seventy-five cents.

The State shall be divided into division, brigade, regimental and company districts.

All able-bodied white male citizens not belonging to uniform companies, those not exempt, and who have not commuted, shall constitute the ununiformed militia, and be attached to the uniform companies in whose bounds or company district they shall reside. Such militia to be under command of company officers as herein provided, until a uniformed company shall be organized in the district.

The officers of uniformed companies shall take command of a company district; the Commander-in-Chief shall designate the company district and the officer who shall take command.

Members of uniformed companies shall parade four days in each year, and the ununiformed militia one day in each year.

The penalty for non-attendance at parades shall be two dollars for each and every day, and forfeiture of per diem allowance.

In districts where there are no company commandants, the Commander-in-Chief shall designate a captain, first lieutenant and second lieutenant from officers who were in commission in 1846, for each of such districts, to command until organization of company and election of officers, and then their duties shall cease.

The commanding officer of company districts shall, from time to time, enroll all persons liable to military duty. He shall file copy of enrollment with the Adjutant-General, and deliver one copy, certified under oath, to the collector of town or receiver of taxes, who shall deliver moneys collected by him to the county treasurer, and receive seven per cent. compensation therefor.

Every officer (line or staff) shall provide himself with a uniform complete, such as the Commander-in-Chief shall prescribe.

Every officer, non-commissioned officer and private shall be exempt from jury duty, and shall be allowed two days' deduction from their assessment of highway labor.

Line and field officers and brigadier-generals shall be elected by ballot.

County treasurers shall make a return annually to the Adjutant-General of all moneys received as fines or commutation money. The money thus received and collected shall be the military fund of the regiment, and be applied exclusively to military purposes.

The field officers of each regiment and the brigade commander shall constitute a board of officers whose duty it shall be to fix the compensation of company commandants for making complete enrollment of the militia in their respective districts, direct payment of per diem allowance to officers and men for actual duty performed, order such printing, etc., as may be necessary, and determine whether regiments shall parade one day for review and inspection or by encampment.

Whenever eight companies are organized in any regimental district a suitable armory shall be erected or rented within such regimental district, but no armory shall be erected unless the lands shall be ceded to the State free and clear from all incumbrances, and $400 shall be appropriated out of the regimental fund. In case an armory is not erected, a room or building shall be rented, and annual rent paid out of regimental fund.

Arms shall be furnished by the Commissary-General to duly organized companies on the order of the Commander-in-Chief, provided the prescribed bonds are executed and delivered, and armory provided for their safe keeping.

There shall be paid for services rendered at any regimental parade or encampment,

To all non-commissioned officers, musicians and privates, ...	$1 25 per day.
To all non-commissioned officers of line below captain, ...	1 25 do
To all commanding officers of companies,......	1 50 do
To all field officers below colonel, ...	2 00 do
To all commanding officers of regiments, ...	2 50 do
To all regimental staff officers, ...	1 50 do
To all non-commissioned staff officers,...	1 50 do
To all Brigadier-Generals, ...	4 00 do

Each company shall consist of not less than 32 nor more than 42 men.

The First Division shall be excepted from the provisions of this act.

CHAP. 307, LAWS of 1849,

Makes more effective the provisions of law for making the enrollment, and the payment and collection of fines, &c.

CHAP. 166, LAWS OF 1851,

Authorizes the Commander-in-Chief, at his discretion, to organize a "Hussar Brigade" in the First Division.

CHAP. 180, LAWS OF 1851,

Provides that the Commander-in-Chief is to appoint and commission brigade, regimental and company officers necessary to complete the organization of all military districts not now organized.

The Assessors in each city, village, town or ward, shall prepare a roll of all persons liable to military duty.

Notice shall be put up in three public places that a roll has been prepared, and specifying the place where it may be seen.

Persons exempt must file affidavit of the fact with the Assessors.

Assessors shall subsequently meet and complete the roll by determining who are exempt, and strike such names from the roll.

The Board of Supervisors shall compare the military roll with the assessment roll, and, in a column prepared for that purpose on said assessment roll, set opposite the name of every person liable to such commutation the sum of fifty cents. The said sum of fifty cents to be collected at the same time and in the same manner as other taxes are collected.

All moneys so collected shall be paid over to the County Treasurer, to the credit of the military fund. Assessors shall receive one dollar and twenty-five cents for every day employed in the discharge of this duty.

All fines for non-performance of military duty by the ununiformed militia are abolished, and all persons liable to military duty in the ununiformed militia shall pay the commutation tax.

There shall be an Inspector-General and an Assistant Adjutant-General appointed.

CHAP. 204, LAWS OF 1852,

Authorizes the organization of a regiment of artillery and cavalry in the county of Kings, to be attached to the Fifth Brigade.

CHAP. 7, LAWS OF 1853,

Authorizes the organization of an additional regiment of infantry in the Fifth Brigade district.

CHAP. 371, LAWS OF 1853,

Authorizes the organization of the surviving members of the First Regiment New York Volunteers (Mexican War) into a Battalion to be known as the First Regiment New York Volunteers.

JOINT RESOLUTION OF FEBRUARY 3, 1853,

Authorizes the Governor to appoint Commissioners to codify the Militia Laws.

CHAP. 398, LAWS OF 1854,

Provides that all able-bodied white male citizens between the ages of eighteen and forty-five residing in this State, and not exempted by the laws of the United States, shall be subject to military duty, except persons in the army and navy of the United States. (Other exemptions same as Law of 1847.)

Major-Generals and the Commissary-General shall be appointed by the Governor, with the consent of the Senate.

Captains, subalterns and non-commissioned officers shall be elected by the written or printed votes of members of their respective companies. Brigadier-Generals and Brigade Inspectors by the field officers of their respective brigades.

Major-Generals, Brigadier-Generals and regimental commanders shall appoint their staff officers.

The Commander-in-Chief shall appoint and commission the brigade, regimental and company officers necessary to facilitate the organization of districts not sufficiently organized to authorize an election.

Assessors, at the same time they are engaged in taking the assessment of real and personal property, shall include in their assessment rolls the names of all persons liable to military duty, adding thereto an additional column headed "Military Roll;" in such column opposite the name of every person not exempt insert "fifty," and notify such person that they are so enrolled.

Persons claiming to be exempt shall file affidavit, stating disability or other reason, with city or town clerk.

Every citizen enrolled shall perform at least one day's duty armed and equipped.

Boards of Supervisors shall in a corrected assessment roll, in a column to be provided for that purpose, enter the sum of fifty cents opposite the names of all persons not marked exempt, or shall have been armed and equipped, and performed one day's duty.

The commutation fee shall be collected at the same time and in the same manner as other taxes are collected.

Collectors shall pay over all such moneys to County Treasurer.

The County Treasurer shall, in books to be provided for that purpose, keep an account of all moneys received and paid out.

The fund thus created shall be applied exclusively to military purposes. No money shall be paid from this fund except on the order of regimental board of officers, countersigned by the commandant of the brigade.

Assessors shall be compensated for their services under this act, at the same rate and in like manner as they are compensated for making the annual assessment of property.

Treasurers to whom any fines or commutation money shall be paid, may retain therefrom one per cent. as fees for receipt and disbursement thereof. Collectors shall be entitled to add double the fees for the commutations as are by law allowed them for collection of taxes.

Each company shall consist of not less than 32 nor more than 50 men. Each regiment shall consist of eight battalion companies and two flank companies, at the discretion of the Commander-in-Chief.

Whenever six uniform companies are organized in any regimental district, an election for field officers may be ordered. When field officers in any brigade district are elected and commissioned, an election for Brigadier-General may be ordered.

The staff of the Commander-in-Chief shall consist of an Adjutant-General, Inspector-General, Engineer-in-Chief, Quartermaster-General, Paymaster-General, Commissary-General, Surgeon-General, three Aids-de-Camp and a Military Secretary.

Armories shall be erected or rented as soon as regimental organizations are completed.

Arms and equipments shall be issued on the order of the Commander-in-Chief, but shall not be furnished unless at the date of application they are in some armory of the State, nor until armory or place for security is provided, and bonds for their safe keeping are filed.

The uniformed militia shall parade annually by regiment, battalion or company, or, in lieu of said annual parade, the commanding officer may order his regiment to parade and encamp, not to exceed six days in any one year, twenty days' notice to be given in either case.

Compensation for military service same as in law of 1847.

In case of riots, tumults, breaches of the peace, or resistance to process, it shall be lawful for the Sheriff of any county, or the Mayor of any city, to call for aid from any brigade, regiment, battalion or company, and the commanding officer to whom such order is given, shall order out in aid of the civil authorities the military force or any part thereof under his command. Expenses and pay of officers and men shall be a county charge.

Drafts of the militia, when ordered by the President of the United States, shall be made by companies, regiments or brigades. In case the whole number called for shall exceed the whole force of the brigade, such additional number shall he taken from the military roll of the ununiformed milita, to be in all cases determined by lot.

Makes general provision for courts-martial and courts of inquiry.

Regimental boards of audit to consist of the field officers of regiments, and the Brigadier-General shall audit claims against the regimental fund for contingent expenses, and per diem allowance for services and duty performed, and make order on the County Treasurer for payment.

County Treasurers shall report annually to the Brigadier-General the amount of money received by him and the balance remaining in his hands.

CHAP. 228, LAWS OF 1865,

Provides that the pay of officers and men while on duty in pursuance of the order of the Sheriff of any county or Mayor of any city shall be audited and paid by the Board of Supervisors, and shall be a county charge.

CHAP. 391, LAWS OF 1857,

Authorizes the Governor to confer the brevet rank of colonel on officers who have served as commandant of company continuously for twenty years.

CHAP. 129, LAWS OF 1858,

Authorizes the appointment of military instructors, with rank of colonel, in each division district.

Makes it the duty of the Inspector-General to visit arsenals and armories at least once in two years, and report their condition and property therein contained.

CHAP. 292, LAWS OF 1861,

Appropriates $500,000 for the purpose of arming the militia of the State, &c., &c.

CHAP. 477, LAWS OF 1862,

Provides that all able-bodied white male citizens between the ages of eighteen and forty-five years residing in this State, and not exempted by the laws of the United States, shall be subject to military duty, excepting the same as in law of 1854, with the following additions: The Lieutenant-Governor, members and officers of the Legislature, Comptroller, Secretary of State, Attorney-General, State Engineer and Surveyor, State Treasurer, and clerks and employees in their offices, judicial officers, including Justices of the Peace, Sheriffs, Coroners and Constables, Shakers, Quakers, professors, teachers and students in all colleges, academies and common schools, officers, non-commissioned officers, musicians and privates in the militia of this State after seven (7) years service.

Idiots, lunatics, paupers, habitual drunkards and persons convicted of infamous crimes, shall not be subject to military duty.

The enrollment of persons liable to military duty shall be made by commandants of companies, or where there is no company commandant, by an officer detailed by the regimental commander, or appointed by Commander-in-Chief. One or more persons may be appointed to assist. Compensation $1.50 per day, not to exceed ten days.

The ununiformed militia shall assemble for parade and inspection, armed and equipped, on the first Monday in September in each year. Company commandants shall file in the office of the Adjutant-General, a roster of all such as attend such parade, properly armed and equipped.

All who shall neglect to attend such parade, will be subject to a fine of one dollar, to be paid to the County Treasurer on or before the first of December. If not paid by that day, the Supervisors shall issue warrants, directed to the collector or receiver of taxes, for the collection of the same.

County Treasurers shall pay to the Comptroller the sum of one dollar for each person enrolled who does not parade on the day specified. If, on presentation of Comptroller's draft, he has not received all or any of the money so directed to be collected and paid, said County Treasurer is authorized and directed to borrow an amount sufficient to pay said draft, upon the credit of the county, to be a county charge.

The organized militia shall be known as the "National Guard of the State of New York," and shall consist of eight divisions, thirty-two brigades, and one hundred and twenty-eight regiments; the regimental districts, except in cities, shall conform as nearly as possible to the assembly districts of the State. The Commander-in-Chief shall have power in case of insurrection or invasion to increase the number of organizations.

The Commander-in-Chief may, in the first instance, when necessary to complete the organization, commission the brigade, regimental and company officers. In all other cases officers, except Major-Generals, shall be elected.

Major-Generals and the Commissary-General shall be appointed by the Governor, by and with the advice and consent of the Senate.

Companies shall consist of not less than 32 nor more than 100 men.

In case companies do not reach or should fall below the minimum, the Commander-in-Chief may, in his discretion, order a draft from the ununiformed militia.

Uniforms shall be furnished by the State to all companies duly organized.

Uniforms shall be manufactured under the direction of the Quartermaster-General in the regimental district in which the organization is located.

The Commander-in-Chief may appoint a board of officers to examine into the qualifications and general fitness for the service of such commissioned officers as may be ordered before it. If the decision of the board is unfavorable, the commission of such officer shall be vacated. He may appoint a similar board, one of whom shall be of the medical staff, to examine officers who may, from physical or other disability, seem to be unfit for service. If such officers as appear before it, are found to be incapacitated for actual service, they will be rendered supernumerary.

The organization of the staff departments shall be same as in law of 1854, with the addition of a Commissary-General of Subsistence with rank of colonel.

Whenever any company of the National Guard is duly organized, the Supervisors of the county in which it is located shall, on the demand of the captain and certificate of the Adjutant-General that the company is duly organized, erect or rent a suitable armory, drill-room and place of deposit for safe keeping of arms, the expense to be a county charge. In case of failure of Supervisors to build or rent, the captain may, with the approval of Inspector-General, hire a building, the rent thereof not to exceed $250, and shall be a county charge.

The Commissary-General shall, on the order of the Commander-in-Chief, issue the necessary arms and equipments to all duly organized companies, provided, a suitable armory is erected or rented, and bonds given for their safe keeping.

The National Guard shall parade annually for review and inspection, and in addition there shall be six drills or parades, three of which shall be by regiment.

All officers, non-commissioned officers and privates shall be exempt from jury duty, and from the payment of highway taxes not exceeding six days in any one year, and persons not assessed for highway taxes shall be entitled to a deduction in assessment of real and personal estate to the amount of $500, and on honorable discharge, shall forever be entitled to the same exemption.

The Commander-in-Chief may order once in each year, in each division district, a camp of instruction, to continue ten days, to the extent of 10,000 men in one year.

The military forces of the State, when in the actual service of the State in time of war, insurrection or rebellion, receive the same pay as allowed to the army of the United States. In all other cases, they shall receive the pay allowed by law of 1864.

In case of war, insurrection or rebellion, when the military forces of the State are in the actual service of the United States, the Commander-in-Chief shall fix the pay of his staff, the assistants and clerks in the several departments at such sum as he may deem proper, not to exceed the pay and allowances of officers of the same rank in the regular army. The pay of clerks not to exceed $100 per month.

The Comptroller shall annually draw his warrant on the Treasurer in favor of the County Treasurer of each county for the sum of five hundred dollars for each regiment or battalion, certified by the Adjutant-General, to be organized within his county, which, with the fines collected, shall constitute the military fund.

A board of officers shall be appointed who shall audit all just claims on the military fund for contingent expenses of regiments. The County Treasurers shall pay the same on order of said board.

County Treasurers shall report annually to the Brigadier-General the amount paid by them, and the amount on hand.

No property now exempt by law shall be exempt from payment of fines imposed by courts-martial, &c. In case the goods and chattels of delinquents, or goods and chattels of parents or guardians of delinquents who are minors, shall not be sufficient to satisfy the claim, the officer empowered to collect shall take the body of delinquent and convey him to the county jail.

Officers issuing warrant for collection of fines may renew it at any time within two years if necessary.

In case of insurrection or invasion, the Commander-in-Chief may, by proclamation, require companies to be filled to the maximum by volunteers, or if sufficient number do not offer, then a sufficient number may be drafted from the reserve militia.

In case of riot, tumult, or breach of the peace, it shall be lawful for the Sheriff of any county or the Mayor of any city to call for such aid as may be required from any brigade, regiment or company.

Officers not responding to such call shall be fined not less than $100 or more than $500, and imprisonment for not exceeding six months.

Whenever the President or Commander-in-Chief shall order a draft, it shall be by company, regiment or brigade. If the number called for shall exceed the force of the whole brigade, the deficiency shall be supplied by draft from the reserve militia.

CHAP. 425, LAWS OF 1863,

Adds to the class of persons subject to military duty: All persons of foreign birth who shall have declared their intention to become citizens of the United States, and who are between the ages of eighteen and forty-five years.

Strikes from the class of persons exempt, the Lieutenant-Governor, members and officers of the Legislature, Secretary of State, Attorney-General, Comptroller, State Engineer and Surveyor, State Treasurer, and their clerks and employees, judicial officers, including Justices of the Peace, Sheriffs, Coroners, Constables, Shakers and Quakers, and professors, teachers and students in all colleges, academies and common schools.

Makes the power discretionary with Supervisors as to providing armories.

Provides that persons drafted who, from scruples of conscience, may be averse to bearing arms, shall be excused on paying to the clerk of the county $300.

Remits all fines against persons for neglecting to attend the annual parade of the ununiformed militia which have not been paid at passage of this act. All money, however, which has been collected, shall be paid to the Comptroller.

Provides that the ununiformed militia shall not be required to assemble on the first day of September in 1863, and the provisions of law so far as relates to fines for neglect to attend such parade are suspended for the year 1863

CHAP. 334 LAWS OF 1864,

Authorizes the appointment of Assistant Quartermaster-General.

Prohibits the Governor from commissioning any officers of the National Guard, except Major-Generals, unless such officer shall have been duly elected, and directs that an election shall be ordered within one hundred days in all regiments sufficiently organized for that purpose.

Appropriates $100,000 for replacing uniforms worn out or destroyed while in the service of the United States, and constitutes the Comptroller, Secretary of State, State Treasurer, Inspector-General and Quartermaster-General a board to determine what regiments or companies are entitled to receive such uniforms.

Appropriates $350,000 for the purchase of uniforms and arms for the National Guard.

CHAP. 612, LAWS OF 1865,

Provides that it shall be lawful for the Governor to order a draft from the reserve militia in any company which shall not have reached the number of 64 men.

The Quartermaster-General, with the approval of the Commander-in-Chief, shall have authority to purchase such uniforms as may from time to time be required for the National Guard, without regard to location of regiment.

The Military Secretary shall have the rank of colonel.

Authorizes the appointment of an Assistant Paymaster-General.

Empowers the Governor, in time of war, to appoint three additional aids with the rank of colonel, and such assistants in the several military departments as he may judge necessary, to be selected from persons who have served in the volunteer forces of this State.

Appropriates $500,000 for military purposes.

CHAP. 809, LAWS OF 1866,

Fixes the maximum of the National Guard which shall be fully armed and equipped at 50,000 non-commissioned officers and privates, and fixes the minimum of company organizations at 64 men.

Directs that an election of field officers shall be held whenever six uniformed companies shall be organized, the colonel not to be commissioned, however, until eight companies of sixty-four men each shall be fully completed.

Provides that all officers who have become or who shall hereafter become incapable of discharging the duties of his office, and any commissioned officer who has served continuously in the same grade for ten years, may be placed on the supernumerary list, and retired from active service and command.

The staff of the Commander-in-Chief, the assistants and clerks in the several military departments, in lieu of all compensation and allowances now authorized by law, in time of peace when on actual duty, etc., shall receive such compensation as the Commander-in-Chief shall deem proper, not exceeding the full pay and allowances of officers of the same rank in the regular army; in no event to exceed the sum of $2,500 per annum, together with necessary expenses, and those of their departments.

Department of Commissary-General of Ordnance.

The office of Commissary-General was formed under the Constitution of the State of New York, adopted November 3d, 1846. See section 3, article 11, which says: "The Governor shall nominate, and with the consent of the Senate, appoint the Commissary-General. The Commissary-General shall hold his office for two years. He shall give security for the faithful execution of the duties of his office in such manner and amount as shall be prescribed by law.

By sections 52 and 104, chapter 477, Laws of 1862, the office of Commissary-General was changed to Commissary-General of Ordnance.

The duties of the Commissary-General of Ordnance are as follows:

To purchase all ordnance and ordnance stores.

To furnish, on the order of the Commander-in-Chief, all necessary arms and equipments, and all ordnance and ordnance stores of every description to all regular military organizations of the State.

To keep in good repair the arsenals, armories and magazines of the State, and attend to the due preservation, safe keeping, cleaning and repairing of the ordnance, arms, accoutrements, ammunition and munitions of war, the property of the State; to dispose, to the best advantage, of all damaged ordnance and ordnance stores that shall be deemed unsuitable for the use of the State.

To keep true accounts of all expenses necessarily incurred in his department, including all purchases of ordnance and ordnance stores, all repairs to arsenals, armories and ordnance and ordnance stores, transportation of ordnance and ordnance stores, &c., &c.

To render accounts of all sales of unserviceable ordnance and ordnance stores.

To collect all ordnance and ordnance stores, the property of the State, in the possession of persons or corporations not authorized to hold the same.

To report annually to the Commander-in-Chief the amount of purchases, receipts and issues of ordnance and ordnance stores; the amount of expenditures; the condition of the arsenals, armories and ordnance and ordnance stores under his control; the repairs to arsenals and armories, and the actual situation and condition of his department in every respect.

Previous to the commencement of the late rebellion, the Commissary-General had sole charge of all the military property of the State, including such articles as properly belong to the department of Quartermaster-General, but at the commencement of the war, and on the re-organization of the militia of the State, it was found that the duties devolving upon this department were too onerous, and the department of the Quartermaster-General was re-organized, and all property and business pertaining to that department was turned over to it, since which time the operations of the two departments have been distinctive.

Prior to the organization of the National Guard under the laws of 1862, there was comparatively but a small quantity of ordnance and ordnance stores in possession of the military organizations of the State, but during the years of 1862, 1863, 1864, 1865 and 1866, large quantities have been purchased and issued to the organizations. It is impossible at present to give the precise number of arms and accoutrements issued to the National Guard alone during the years of 1862, 1863 and 1864, as in the multiplicity of issues to the Volunteers and to the National Guard acting as Volunteers, and in turning in the same to this department and to the general government, some errors have necessarily been made, and can only be made clear when a final settlement is made between the State and the general government.

Quartermaster-General's Department.

The Quartermaster-General, previous to April, 1861, was not at the head of an active department, and the care and issue of property properly belonging to his department constituted a portion of the duties of the Commissary-General; and the exigency of 1861 found the State without a department through which to economically and efficiently equip and transport the troops which the patriotism of the people furnished for the defense of the government. But the military operations then undertaken by the State required the complete organization of the Quartermaster General's Department, which was effected under the direction of the Commander-in-Chief.

"An Act to provide for the enrollment of the militia, the organization and discipline of the National Guard of the State of New York, and for the public defense," passed April 23d, 1862, provides that: "In the Quartermaster-General's Department there shall be a Quartermaster-General, with the rank of Brigadier-General; an Asssistant Quartermaster-General with the rank of Colonel; to each division a Division Quartermaster-General with the rank of Lieutenant-Colonel; to each Brigade a Brigade Quartermaster with the rank of Captain; and to each regiment or battalion a Quartermaster with the rank of Lieutenant." And since the passage of the above act, authority has been conferred upon the Commander-in-Chief to assign to the several staff departments such number of Acting Assistants as he may deem necessary. (Act of April 29th, 1865.)

The duties of the department have been made to conform as nearly as practicable to the regulations governing the Quartermaster's Department of the United States Army.

Since its organization the department has supplied the militia, furnished necessary clothing, equipments, quarters, transportation and subsistence to volunteers called into the United States service, and through the department was purchased much of the material required for the placing in the field of the military forces of the State.

The Soldiers' Homes, maintained in the cities of New York and Albany during the late rebellion, and while troops were passing to and from the State, were, during the last years of the war, under the supervision of this department, and all expenses incurred on that account were audited and paid by the Quartermaster-General.

At present the duties of the department are sufficient to employ the official and clerical force connected with it, and must so continue so long as an efficient militia organization is maintained, and the institutions provided for disabled soldiers continued.

The Quartermaster-General is required to cause to be manufactured and issued to the National Guard such uniforms and equipments as are named in this connection in the "Act to provide for the militia," &c., passed April 23, 1862, and acts passed subsequent thereto; the care of all quartermaster's stores of the State; and the department still exercises the same supervisory control over the Soldiers' Home at Albany and military agencies as during the war.

To this department has also been assigned by the Governor the duty of settling the claims of the State against the United States for expenses incurred in furnishing troops for the general service.

The annexed statement will show the amount of business which has been transacted by the department, and the cost to the State of performing it:

1863.	
Services and expenditures, other than for uniforms, during the year 1863,	$23,245 52
Expenditures for uniforms,	60,566 80
1864.	
Services and expenditures, other than for uniforms, during the year 1864,	18,494 36
Expenditures for uniforms,	163,608 74
Expenditures under chapter 421, Laws of 1862,	18,310 69
1865.	
Services and expenditures, other than for uniforms, during the year 1865,	18,490 13
Expenditures for uniforms for National Guard,	158,285 92
1866.	
Services and expenditures, other than for uniforms, during the year 1866,	16,020 26
Expenditures for uniforms,	151,514 29

Aid afforded by the Legislature of New York, to Soldiers from the State during the late war.

On the 7th of January, 1862, an association was organized at Washington, D. C., for the purpose of affording relief to the sick, wounded and destituted soldiers from the State of New York, who might then be in the army and hospitals in the vicinity, or within reach of the city of Washington, having for its President Hon. IRA HARRIS, and for its Vice-President Hon. R. E. FENTON, who was afterward made President, with Treasurer, Secretary, Executive Committee and Finance Committee. This timely and useful association received its supplies from the voluntary contributions of patriotic citizens, and continued until September of that year, when it turned over its supplies to the New York State agency.

On the 23d day of April, 1862, the Legislature passed an act (chap. 458, Laws of 1862), appropriating $30,000 for expenses incident to the transportation, care and supplies of hospital for sick and wounded soldiers belonging to this State, &c. Under the authority of this act, Governor MORGAN appointed S. H. SWETLAND, Esq., agent, who disbursed the sum of $15,179.47.

On the 31st day of March, 1863, Governor SEYMOUR directed an order to be issued from the office of the Adjutant-General of the State (being Special Order No. 151), creating a board of managers of an institution to be established in the city of New York, as a temporary home or resting place for soldiers, consisting of four members of his staff, who met April 9th, 1863, and proceeded to locate the institution they were authorized to estabish, at the premises in that city known as Nos. 50 and 52 Howard street, and 16 Mercer street, rented the same for two years at an annual rent of $6,000, and gave it the official name of "The New York State Soldiers' Depot."

On the 24th day of April, 1863, the Legislature of the State passed an act (chap. 224, Laws of 1863) entitled "An act to provide additional means of relief for the sick and wounded soldiers of the State of New York in the United States service," which act appropriated for that purpose the sum of $200,000, to be paid on the order and disbursed under the direction of the Governor.

For the purpose of carrying out the provisions of this act, Governor SEYMOUR directed the issue, from the office of the Adjutant-General, of Special Orders No. 204, bearing date May 8, 1863, transferring to the Board of Managers of the N. Y. State Soldiers' Depot the duty of controlling and directing the disbursement of the sum of $200,000 thus appropriated, who thereupon appointed JOHN F. SEYMOUR, Esq., General Agent of the State of New York for the relief of the soldiers of the State.

Under the authority conferred upon him, Mr. SEYMOUR appointed agents at various localities, whose duty it was:

1. To visit all the hospitals within the bounds of their respective agencies; to ascertain the treatment of the sick or wounded New York soldiers; to supply clothing and such other reasonable wants as are not supplied by the hospitals, and to correspond, when desired, with the friends or relatives of the soldier.

2. To ascertain and forward to the central office at New York, the names of the soldiers from this State in hospitals, with the proper designation of their respective regiments, and describing the character of their wounds or sickness.

3. To keep an office where our soldiers or their friends might always apply for assistance in obtaining furloughs or discharge from service for good cause, transportation home, back pay, and such other assistance as their case might warrant.

The New York Soldiers' Depot was opened for the reception of soldiers on the 18th day of May, 1863, with a superintendent, an assistant superintendent and twenty-seven employees. The number of men received, registered and directly relieved up to January 1st, 1864, was 15,727, and the number treated in the hospital during the same period was 1,101.

The total expenditure to January 1, 1864, embracing the expenses of the New York Soldiers' Depot and all the agencies outside the State, was $64,335.89, of which amount the sum of $14,820.53 was the unexpended balance from 1862, and $49,515.36 from the appropriation of 1863, leaving a balance available for future operations of $150,484.64. In the amounts expended are included the sum of $2,000, donated to the Elmira Soldiers' Home, and about $18,000, the cost of fitting and furnishing the buildings of the State Depot.

During the year 1864 the labor and usefulness both of the agencies and depot were increased. Local agents were stationed at Washington, Alexandria, Fredericksburg, Norfolk, Baltimore, Harrisburg, Philadelphia, New Orleans, Buffalo, Louisville and Nashville. Temporary agencies were established at Belle Plain and in the valley of the Shenandoah, and supplies were sent to our armies at Harper's Ferry, Hilton Head, and at City Point. The Depot at New York city provided for more than 70,000 soldiers of our own and other States.

The amount expended on account of the Soldiers' Depot was $51,225.99, and on account of the Agencies $106,581.46, there having been overdrawn the sum of $7,322.81. Included in the expenses of this year are $7,000 contributed for the support of the Soldiers' Home at Elmira, and $500 to the Soldiers' Rest at Buffalo.

On the 4th day of January, 1865, Governor FENTON directed Col. D. G. MORGAN to investigate the condition of the military agencies. A very brief examination showed that the fund had been overdrawn, and that the frauds and abuses alleged to have been perpetrated in some of them had created distrust on the part of the public authorities, and seriously affected their usefulness.

On the 2d of February, the Legislature passed an act (chapter 15, Laws of 1865) appropriating $200,000 for the continuance of the agencies and the depot at New York city. On the 1st of March, Col. MORGAN was appointed superintendent of the agencies. He immediately proceeded to appoint new agents, discontinue useless agencies, collect supplies, and re-organize the whole system of business. The fall of Richmond and surrender of LEE'S army soon closed operations in the field. Early in May, Col. MORGAN commenced a tour to investigate the causes of complaints, which were rapidly multiplying, of New York soldiers in hospitals in the west and south-west, and upon his representations, Governor FENTON obtained an order from the Surgeon-General U. S. A., directing that all eastern soldiers in western hospitals should be immediately transferred east of the mountains, and it was so arranged that nearly all the soldiers of our own State were brought within our own limits.

At this time a new and extensive field of usefulness was opened to the agencies. The accounts of more than 100,000 New York soldiers in the field were to be finally settled. These accounts kept by the officers on company books, which were subject to all the contingencies of an active campaign, were in great confusion, and the soldier would have been subjected to much delay and expense, if not ultimate loss, had it not been for the aid afforded by the agencies. The business of the agencies during the year may be briefly summed up as follows:

Number of officers' accounts made out and forwarded to the department, ...	482
Number of officers' certificates of non-indebtedness obtained, ...	1,600
Amount collected for soldiers from office of Paymaster-General, U. S. A., ...	$86,803 27
Amount of State Bounty collected, ...	11,605 00
Number of letters written, ...	19,820

The Soldiers' Depot at New York city, at the commencement of the administration of Governor FENTON, was under the superintendence of Col. JOHN S. NEVILL, who was continued in that position until the end of February following, and was succeeded by Col. VINCENT COLYER, who remained in charge until September 1st, after which date Hon. T. L. PREVOST, was acting superintendent of the institution.

The lease of the premises occupied by it expired on the 1st of May. A new lease could not be effected at less than $16,000 per year, an increase of $10,000 upon the rental of the previous year. After a careful consideration of all the circumstances attending a removal and consequent temporary discontinuance of the depot, at a time when it was so much needed, it was deemed advantageous to the State, to accede to the demand.

So great was the number of troops passing through New York about the 1st of June, that the capacity of the depot was found to be inadequate to the accommodation of all who desired to avail themselves of its benefits. Increased accommodations were therefore sought, and the use of the armories of the 6th, 8th and 71st Regiments of the National Guard were procured and fitted up at an expense of $2,500.

The whole number of soldiers received into the depot during the year was 82,304.

Amount deposited by soldiers for safe keeping,	$244,902 87
Amount of transportation sold at government rates,	23,250 00
Amount free transportation issued,	857 94
Number of volumes in library,	1.200
Number of volumes issued and returned,	8,850
Number of sick and wounded soldiers received in hospital,	2,649
Number of deaths,	39

The expenses of agencies and depot for the year were as follows:

Agencies,	$69,867 71
Depot,	54,596 69
Total,	$124,464 40

Included in expenses of agencies are $5,000 paid to Relief Association in Albany and Syracuse, and $2,078.70 employed in discharging obligations incurred under former administration.

The amount of voluntary contributions received and disbursed by Col. COLYER was $14,929.99.

On the 22d of March, 1866, the Legislature passed an act (chap. 185, Laws of 1866) which authorized the Governor to establish a temporary Soldiers' Home at Albany, N. Y., and to continue military agencies at Albany and Washington, and appropriated $70,000 for these purposes. Major WILLIAM W. POST was appointed agent at Albany, and Lieut. Col. J. E. LEE agent at Washington, both gentlemen having been connected with their respective agencies since the early part of 1865. The number of employees in each agency was limited to five. The business of these officers was exclusively that of prosecuting claims of soldiers, and the heirs of those deceased, against the U. S. Government. The following is a report of the business of the agencies during the year:

Total number of claims settled,	5,059
Total number of claims filed and unsettled Dec. 31, 1866,	14,638
Total amount of money collected and paid claimants,	$475,398 89
Number of letters received,	34,734
Number of letters written,	35,516

The expenses were as follows:

Washington agency,	$15,975 23
Albany agency,	13,727 19

The Soldiers' Depot at New York was closed March 31st, a portion of the property having been sold, and the balance transferred to the Soldiers' Home in Albany.

The number of persons admitted into the depot from January 1st until it was closed, was 6,423. The number of inmates who received medical treatment was 174. Number of deaths, 5. The expenditures of the depot during this period, including the repairing of damages to the building, were $18,433.17.

On the 1st of January a temporary home was established at Albany, until provision for the same could be made by the Legislature, in the Industrial School building belonging to the city, which had been occupied by the United States as a hospital. Surgeon-General POMFRET had charge of the same until December 1st, when Colonel E. A. LUDWICK was appointed superintendent.

Total number of persons admitted to the Home during the year, was,	630
Total number discharged,	393
Total number of deaths,	19
Number of inmates, Dec. 31,	259
Number under medical treatment, Dec. 31,	65
Number who have lost limbs,	213
Average number of employees,	33
Whole number of rations issued,	73,939
Expenses for the year,	$55,435 59

Recapitulation of the condition of the Fund appropriated for Military Agencies, Soldiers' Depot, and Soldiers' Home.

Balance of fund on hand Dec. 31, 1865,		$69,303 59
Appropriated by chapter 185, Laws of 1866,		70,000 00
Total available January 1, 1866,		$139,303 59
Expenditures Soldiers' Home,	$55,435 59	
Expenditures Soldiers' Depot,	18,433 17	
Expenditures Washington Agency,	15,975 23	
Expenditures Albany Agency,	13,727 19	
		103,571 18
Balance unexpended December 31, 1866,		$35,732 41

By act of the Legislature passed April 3d, 1867 (chapter 255, Laws of 1867), $100,000 was appropriated for the continuance of the agencies at Albany and Washington, and also the Soldiers' Home.

From January 1st to May 1st, 1867, the number of claims received by the agencies, in excess of the number settled, was 3,338, making the whole number of claims remaining unsettled, 17,796. The number of letters written during the same period was 17,442. Number received, 16,881.

The average number of inmates, employees, and amount of expenditures of the Soldiers' Home for the same period has been about the same as during the year 1866.

The whole amount appropriated by the Legislature, for the relief and assistance of the soldiers of the State, is $600,000.

Bureau of Military Record.

This office was created by Governor MORGAN, under authority of chapter 477 of the Laws of 1862, under the name of the Bureau of Military Statistics, and its operations have since been modified by special enactments, especially in 1864, when it was made a department of record. Its design was to collect, in permanent form, an authentic sketch of every person from this State who had volunteered into the service of the government during the then existing war; to obtain the history of the services of regiments and other organizations from this State, and to collect an account of the aid afforded by the several towns and counties of the State in the prosecution of the war.

From the first, the collection of relics and memorials of the war, and especially the preservation of the worn-out flags of New York regiments, was regarded as a matter of prime importance. The return of regiments to the State, in 1863 and 1864, after the expiration of their terms of enlistment, and especially in 1865, at the close of the war, and the collection of the banners which were returned under military orders to the custody of the State, indicated the necessity of providing for the permanent preservation of these interesting memorials. A temporary structure in the rear of the State Library was built, and in a few months filled to the extent of capacity, and the collection has since increased by voluntary donations, until it has become an object of much public interest, and a prominent place of daily resort.

By an act passed in 1865, trustees were appointed with authority to erect a fire proof structure, to be called the Hall of Military Record, provided the sum of $75,000 should be voluntarily contributed by the people for this purpose. This Hall was to be located in the city of Albany, provided that that city should convey an acceptable site for the purpose, but in case of their neglect to do this, the trustees were at liberty to accept a site from the city of New York or other municipality. In June, 1865, the Mayor and Council of Albany resolved to accept the proposition, and after due discussion the site occupied as a reservoir north of the State Hall was offered and accepted for this purpose.

The original design of relying upon voluntary contributions, was further modified the year following, by giving to the Boards of Supervisors discretionary power to levy and collect the amount assessed to their towns, and on the 4th day of March, 1867, the receipts from town supervisors and individual subscriptions had amounted to $31,950.05. These payments as they come in are deposited in the State treasury, until needed for use.

The results of inquiry into the expenditures and indebtedness of towns on account of the war, made by this office, are as follows:

STATEMENT showing the amount of moneys paid by the several counties, cities and towns in the State of New York, during the war, for bounties, fees and expenses, interest on loans, support of soldiers' families; the amount of voluntary contributions for objects connected with the war, as shown by reports from Treasurers of counties, Treasurers or Chamberlains of cities, and Supervisors of towns; also the amount of loans outstanding and to be paid.

	Bounties paid.	Loans outstanding.
Amount paid for bounties by 46 counties, to Dec. 31, 1865, as shown by complete reports from treasurers of counties,............	$43,099,912 21	
Amount paid for fees and expenses, to Dec. 31, 1865, as shown by complete reports from treasurers of counties,...............	2,748,778 93	
Amount paid for interest on county loans, to Dec. 31, 1865, as shown by complete reports from treasurers of counties,,.....	3,834,075 79	
Carried forward,..	$49,682,766 93	

	Bounties paid	Loans outstanding.
Brought forward,	$49,682,766 93	
Amount paid for support of soldiers' families, to Dec. 31, 1865, as shown by complete reports from treasurers of counties,	7,141,343 66	
Amount of outstanding county loans to be paid,	....	$34,786,358 69
Amount paid for bounties by 13 counties (leaving Monroe still to report), as shown by partial returns, down to and including the year 1864,	7,404,447 50	
Amount paid for bounties by 513 towns complete, as shown by reports from Supervisors, to December 21, 1865,	19,530,138 09	
Amount paid for fees and expenses, as shown by reports from Supervisors, to December 31, 1865,	622,096 02	
Amount paid for interest on town loans, as shown by reports from Supervisors, to December 31, 1865,	1,076,257 68	
Amount paid for support of soldiers' families, as shown by reports from Supervisors, to December 31, 1865,	367,558 01	
Amount of town loans outstanding and to be paid,	....	6,301,060 03
Amount paid for bounties by 92 towns, partial returns, as shown by reports from Supervisors, to December 31, 1865,	4,455,755 57	
Amount paid for fees and expenses, as shown by reports from Supervisors, to December 31, 1865,	90,444 60	
Amount paid for interest on town loans, as shown by reports from Supervisors, to December 31, 1865,	189,342 96	
Amount paid for support of soldiers' families, as shown by reports from Supervisors, to December 31, 1865,	116,621 09	
Amount of town loans outstanding and to be paid,	....	1,098,462 08
Amount paid for bounties by 251 towns (leaving 76 towns still to report), as shown by partial returns down to and including the year 1864,	83,374,222 37	
Amount paid for bounties by six cities, as shown by reports from treasurers or chamberlains, down to and including the year 1864,	2,888,321 82	254,699 09
Amount paid for recruiting fees, support of soldiers' families, interest on loans, by two cities, down to and including the year 1865,	261,948 61	
Amount paid by the State for bounties, in the years 1862, 1863 and 1864,	9,181,373 44	
Total amount paid as above	$186,382,638 35	
Amount raised by voluntary subscription in 535 towns, to promote enlistments, aid to families of volunteers, aid to soldiers in hospitals, and for sanitary purposes, part taken from former reports,	1,757,184 17	
	$188,139,822 52	
Amount of county and town loans, from 46 counties and 605 towns, outstanding and to be paid, as shown by the above,		$42,440,579 89

These figures are yet to be swelled by the returns from 76 towns, which have not reported, and from 251 from which only partial returns have been received, and by such other additional expenditures for war purposes after the close of 1864 as may have been incurred.

The number of flags of New York regiments that have been deposited in the collections of this office is eight hundred and four. The number of rebel ensigns captured in the war is twenty-eight. The collections in other departments are thus summed up in the report of the chief of the department, now in press:

Of individual military histories, 24,377; of regimental reports, 201; of financial returns from towns, cities and counties there are registered, 573 of towns, 4 of cities, and 34 of counties; of personal narratives of soldiers and sailors confined in rebel prisons, 309, exclusive of filled up blanks of personal naval histories, 135; of photographic likenesses of soldiers, about 3,000; of newspapers and pamphlets, about 2,000 volumes; of volumes on military matters and statistics, 2,000 sets; of general orders, bound and unbound, the files represent 31 military departments, during and subsequent to the years of active operations.

THE UNIVERSITY OF THE STATE OF NEW YORK.

The Legislature of the State, at its session in 1784, the first after the termination of our revolutionary struggle, passed an act entitled "An act for granting certain privileges to the college heretofore called King's College, for altering the name and charter thereof, and erecting an university within this State." This act was amended on the 26th of November, 1784, and was superseded by an act passed April 13, 1787, entitled "An act to institute an university within this State, and for other purposes therein mentioned."* The draft of this act is generally believed to have been prepared by Alexander Hamilton, then a member of the Assembly, and, with some modifications, still continues in force as the fundamental law of the State on this subject. This act provides "that an university be and is hereby instituted within this State, to be called and known by the name or style of the Regents of the University of the State of New York." It also prescribes the mode of appointment, the tenure of office, and the powers and duties of the said regents; and provides for the incorporation by them of colleges and academies within the State, as component parts of the university established by the act.

The Regents of the University.

The Board, as now constituted, consists of the Governor, the Lieutenant-Governor, the Secretary of State, and the Superintendent of Public Instruction as *ex officio* members, and of nineteen other persons chosen by the Legislature in the same manner as Senators in Congress. They may be removed by a concurrent resolution of the Senate and Assembly. The actual and necessary expenses incurred by members of the Board in the discharge of official duties are paid, but no compensation, is allowed for services.

The officers of the Regents are a Chancellor, a Vice-Chancellor, a Treasurer, a Secretary and an Assistant Secretary, who are appointed by the Board, and who hold their offices at its pleasure. The Secretary and the Assistant Secretary receive salaries, for which annual appropriations are made by the Legislature.

The annual meeting of the Board is held, pursuant to law, at the Senate Chamber, on the evening of the second Thursday of January in each year, and other meetings at the rooms of the Regents, from time to time, as the business of the Board may require. Six members constitute a quorum.

---

* These acts are reprinted in the Manual of the Regents, pages 126–154.

The leading duties with which the Regents are charged, are the incorporation of colleges, academies and other institutions of learning, under such general rules and regulations as they may from time to time establish; the visitation and general supervision of all colleges and academies; the preparation of suitable forms for the annual reports of such institutions, and the examination and analysis of such reports; the equitable distribution of general appropriations for the benefit of incorporated academies; and the preparation of an annual report to the Legislature on the condition of the various institutions subject to their visitation.

The Regents have the right of conferring, by diplomas under their common seal, on any person whom they may think worthy thereof, such degrees above that of Master of Arts, as are known to and usually granted by any college or university in Europe. This right has been rarely exercised, the degree of Doctor of Laws having been conferred upon eleven persons only, that of Doctor of Philosophy upon three persons, and that of Doctor of Literature upon the same number, at various times since 1787.

The Legislature has from time to time assigned to the Regents certain other important trusts, among which are the following:

In 1844, the Regents were constituted the Trustees of the State Library, in the place of certain State officers. The Library at that time contained only about ten thousand volumes, deposited in two small rooms in the upper part of the Capitol. It has since increased to about seventy-four thousand volumes, and includes a law department second to none in this country in American law; a very extensive and rare collection of works illustrative of American history; standard authors in almost every department of literature and science, together with a large number of maps, charts, prints, manuscripts, coins and medals, the aggregate of which has nearly outgrown the spacious building erected in 1852 for its reception.

In 1845, the Regents were also made the Trustees of the State Cabinet of Natural History, and the Historical and Antiquarian Collection connected therewith. Under their supervision, the Cabinet has also greatly increased in the extent and scientific value of its collections, and in its attractions for general visitors, and for investigators in special branches of scientific research.

The State Normal School, established at Albany in 1844, is under the supervision, management and government of the Superintendent of Public Instruction and the Regents of the University. They appoint an Executive Committee, of whom the Superintendent is one, and make an annual report to the Legislature.

The Regents have been charged with the management, on behalf of the State, of an extended system of international and State exchanges, by which means the official publications of other States and countries, and also to some extent of learned societies abroad, are regularly secured to the State Library, and the public documents and law reports of this State are in return transmitted to other governments. They also receive annual reports from the law libraries established by the State at Brooklyn, Schenectady, Syracuse, Rochester and Buffalo.

For many years the Regents conducted a system of meteorological observations, under the authority of the Legislature. This system has recently been abandoned, as the Smithsonian Institution includes this State within its field of operations.

The Regents have likewise had charge of a limited series of longitude determinations within the State, under acts of the Legislature, passed in 1857 and 1858. Most of the results reached in regard to both meteorology and longitude have already been published by the Legislature.

Under authority of a resolution of the Senate, the Regents expect to prepare a history of the several boundary lines of the State, and to examine into the condition of the various monuments erected to designate such lines, some of which it is highly important to renew and replace. The history of the southern and western boundaries has already been investigated, and that of the western boundary has proved to be a subject of special historic interest.

Under the appointment of the Regents, a meeting of the officers of colleges and academies, subject to the visitation of the board, was convened in August, 1863, which resulted in an organization called "The University Convocation of the State of New York," which holds an annual session at Albany, commencing on the first Tuesday of August. These meetings have thus far been of marked interest, and are already attracting much attention abroad, through the published proceedings which have been issued each year as an appendix to the annual report of the Regents.

In 1865, the Regents instituted in the academies under their visitation, an uniform system of written examinations, to determine what pupils are justly entitled to be included in the annual *pro rata* distribution of the income of the Literature Fund. Three examinations are held during each year, under the immediate supervision of an examining committee appointed by the trustees of each academy, who make a full report to the Regents of the results of such examinations, and certify the observance of the instructions required to be followed in the use of the sets of questions prepared by the Regents. On the basis of these returns the Regents issue formal certificates of academic scholarship to such pupils as are duly certified to have attained a certain standard of proficiency. The effect of these examinations has already been very marked in stimulating attention to the elementary branches, and in promoting thoroughness in all the departments of academic instruction.

The regents annually apportion among the academies the sum of $40,000 from the income of the Literature Fund, on the basis of the number of strictly academic pupils reported by each academy; also the sum of $18,000, or thereabouts, to academies appointed by them to instruct classes in the science of common-school teaching; and $3,000, at the rate of not more than two hundred and fifty dollars each, to academies which shall have raised equal amounts, apart from their corporate funds, for the purchase of books and philosophical and chemical apparatus.

The various services required of the Board are in part performed by the Standing Committees, eight in number, some of which are frequently in session; that on the State Library every Monday morning.

Annual reports on the several matters under the supervision of the Regents are submitted to the Legislature, and published as documents of standard interest and value. The eightieth annual general report on Colleges and Academies, the forty-ninth on the State Library (since its establishment), and the twentieth on the State Cabinet, were submitted at the session of 1867.

The Regents have from time to time issued "instructions" to the numerous institutions under their care, the last of which was published in 1864, under the title of the "Manual of the Regents of the University."

Regular minutes have been kept of the meetings of the board since its organization in 1784. Those since the beginning of 1853 have been printed, making about seven hundred octavo pages. These minutes, together with the annual reports of the colleges and the academies, form a complete and voluminous official record of all the institutions subject to the visitation of the Regents.

The names of the present members of the board are given below. A full catalogue of all the Regents since 1784, arranged in the regular order of succession, and of the officers of the board, is given in the Regents' Manual, pages 155–165.

Lists are also given below of the colleges and academies which have been incorporated within the State, both by the Regents — by whom this power was exclusively exercised until 1813 in the case of academies, and 1831 in respect to colleges — and by the Legislature, together with the location and the date of the incorporation of each, and the time when certain academies chartered by the Legislature were received under the visitation of the Regents. A statement is also given of those institutions which are known or supposed to have failed to organize under their respective charters, or to have ceased to exist.

It is proper to add that, although the Regents have been charged with the care of colleges and academies only, they were the first to propose, in their annual report in 1793, "the institution of schools in various parts of the State, for the purpose of instructing children in the lower branches of education," and that this suggestion, renewed by Governor CLINTON in his annual message, was followed, in 1795, by the passage of a temporary "act for the encouragement of schools," and, in 1812, by "An act for the establishment of common schools," from which has grown the present common school system of the State. It is also worthy of note that a venerable, and, for more than twenty years, a most active member of the present Board of Regents, who was also for more than twenty-five years its efficient Secretary, was the first Superintendent of Common Schools; of whom it has been officially said that "to no individual in the State are the friends of common school education more deeply indebted for the impetus given to the cause of elementary instruction in its infancy, than to GIDEON HAWLEY." (S. S. RANDALL'S Common School System of New York.)

Regents of the University.

JOHN V. L. PRUYN, *Chancellor of the University;* appointed Regent May 4, 1844; residence, Albany.

GULIAN C. VERPLANCK, *Vice Chancellor;* appointed Regent January 26, 1826; residence, New York.

The Governor (REUBEN E. FENTON), *ex officio.*

The Lieutenant-Governor (STEWART L. WOODFORD), *ex officio.*

The Secretary of State (FRANCIS C. BARLOW), *ex officio.*

The Sup't of Public Instruction (VICTOR M. RICE), *ex officio.*

NAME.	Date of appointment.	Residence.
Erastus Corning,	1833, February 5,	Albany.
Prosper M. Wetmore,	1833, April 4,	New York.
Gideon Hawley,	1842, February 1,	Albany.
Robert Campbell,	1846, February 2,	Bath.
Samuel Luckey,	1847, May 6,	Rochester.
Robert G. Rankin,	1847, September 22,	Newburgh.
Erastus C. Benedict,	1855, March 22,	New York.
George W. Clinton,	1856, March 6,	Buffalo.
Isaac Parks,	1857, April 7,	Whitehall.
Lorenzo Burrows,	1858, February 16,	Albion.
Robert S. Hale,	1859, March 29,	Elizabethtown.
Elias W. Leavenworth,	1861, February 5,	Syracuse.
J. Carson Brevoort,	1861, February 5.	Brooklyn.
George R. Perkins,	1863, January 30,	Utica.
Alexander S. Johnson,	1864. April 12,	Albany.
George W. Curtis,	1864, April 12,	North Shore, S. I.
William H. Goodwin,	1865, January 24,	Geneva.

SAMUEL B. WOOLWORTH, *Secretary of the Board.*
DANIEL J. PRATT, *Assistant Secretary.*

Officers of State Library and State Cabinet of Natural History.

Alfred B. Street, *Librarian, Law Library.*
Henry A. Homes, *Librarian, General Library.*
Norman S. Curtis, *Assistant Librarian.*

James Hall, *Curator of the State Cabinet of Natural History.*

I. *Existing Literary and Scientific Colleges.*

No.	NAME.	Location.	Date of Charter.	Incorporated by.	Remarks.
1	Alfred University,	Alfred, Allegany Co.,	Mar. 28, 1857	Legislature.	
2	College of the City of New York,	New York city,	Mar. 30, 1866	Legislature,..	Formerly the New York Free Academy.
3	College of St. Francis Xavier,	New York city,	Jan. 10, 1861	Regents.	
4	Columbia College,	New York city,	Oct. 31, 1754	Col. Gov't, ..	Incorporated as "The Governors of the College of the Province of New York," and commonly known as King's College, until May 1, 1784, at which time the name was changed to Columbia College.
5	Cornell University,	Ithaca, Tompkins Co.,	Apr. 27, 1865	Legislature.	
6	Elmira Female College,	Elmira, Chemung Co.,	Apr. 13, 1855	Legislature.	
7	Genesee College,	Lima, Livingston Co.,	Feb. 27, 1849	Legislature.	
8	Hamilton College,	Clinton, Oneida Co.,	May 26, 1812	Regents.	
9	Hobart College,	Geneva, Ontario Co.,	Apr. 5, 1824	Regents, ...	Incorp'ed as Geneva College; name changed to Hobart Free College, April 10, 1852, and to Hobart College, March 27, 1860.
10	Ingham University,	Le Roy, Genesee Co.,	Apr. 3, 1857	Legislature,..	Formerly the Ingham Collegiate Institute.
11	Madison University,	Hamilton, Madison Co.,	Mar. 26, 1846	Legislature.	
12	Manhattan College,	New York city,	Apr. 2, 1863	Regents.	
13	Place College,	....	Apr. 22. 1867	Legislature,..	In the act of incorporation no location is fixed.
14	Rutgers Female College,	New York city,	Apr. 11, 1867	Legislature,..	Lately Rutger's Female Institute.
15	St. John's College,	Fordham, Westchester Co.,	Apr. 10, 1840	Legislature.	
16	St. Lawrence University,	Canton, St. Lawrence Co.,	Apr. 3, 1856	Legislature.	
17	St. Stephen's College,	Red Hook, Dutchess Co.,	Mar. 20, 1860	Legislature.	
18	Union College,	Schenectady, Schenectady Co.,	Feb. 25, 1795	Regents.	
19	University of Albany,	Albany, Albany Co.,	Apr. 17, 1851	Legislature,..	Only Law Department organized.
20	University of the City of New York,	New York city,	Apr. 18, 1831	Legislature,..	Literary, Scientific, Law and Medical Departments organized.
21	University of Rochester,	Rochester, Monroe Co.,	May 8, 1846	Legislature.	
22	University of Buffalo,	Buffalo, Erie Co.,	May 11, 1846	Legislature,..	Only Medical Department organized.
23	Vassar College,	Poughkeepsie, Dutchess Co.,	Jan. 11, 1861	Legislature,..	Incorporated as Vassar Female College; name changed February 1, 1867.

Whole number, 23; incorporated by the Regents, 5; by the Legislature, 17; by the Colonial Government, and reincorporated by the Legislature, 1 (Columbia College)

II. *Existing Medical Colleges, etc.*

No.	NAME.	Location.	Date of Charter.	Incorporated by.	Remarks.
24	Albany Medical College,	Albany, Albany Co.,	Feb. 16, 1839	Legislature.	
25	Bellevue Hospital Med. Col. of the city of N. Y.,	New York city,	Apr. 3, 1861	Legislature.	
26	College of Pharmacy of the city of New York,	New York city,	Apr. 25, 1831	Legislature,	For the education of druggists; does not report.
27	Col. of Physicians and Surg. of the city of N. Y.,	New York city,	Mar. 10, 1807	Regents,	Degrees conferred by Columbia College.
28	Eclectic Medical College,	New York city,	Apr. 22, 1865	Legislature.	
29	Geneva Medical College,	Geneva, Ontario Co.,	Mar. 27, 1835	Legislature,	Organized as Medical Institution of Geneva College, and afterward known for a time as Medical Department of Hobart College. Present name fixed by act of March 15, 1861.
30	Homœopathic Med. College of the State of N. Y.,	New York city,	Apr. 12, 1860	Legislature.	
31	Long Island College Hosp. of the city of Brooklyn,	Brooklyn, Kings Co.,	Mar. 6, 1858	Legislature.	
32	New York Medical College and Hosp. for Women,	New York city,	Apr. 14, 1863	Legislature,	Incorporated as the New York Medical College for Women. Name changed to New York Medical College for Women, and Hospital for Women and Children, April 19, 1864, and to New York Medical College and Hospital for Women, June 12, 1866,
33	Medical Department of the University of Buffalo,	Buffalo, Erie Co.,	May 11, 1846	Legislature.	
34	Med. Dep't. of the University of the city of N. Y,	New York city,	Feb. 11, 1837	Legislature.	
35	New York College of Dentistry,	New York city,	Mar. 31, 1865	Legislature.	

Whole number, 12; incorporated by the Regents, 1; by the Legislature, 11.

III. Extinct Colleges.

The following colleges have been incorporated, but have not been organized, or have ceased to exist, or have failed to make any report of their condition to the Regents for some time past.

No.	NAME.	Location.	Date of Charter.	Incorporated by.	REMARKS.
36	American College of Medical Science,	New York city,	Apr. 2, 1858	Legislature.	
37	Auburn College,	Auburn, Cayuga Co.,	Feb. 26, 1836	Regents,	Conditions of provisional charter not fulfilled.
38	Auburn Female University,	Auburn, Cayuga Co.,	Jan. 29, 1852	Regents,	Not organized.
39	Brockport College,	Brockport, Monroe Co.,	Mar. 4, 1836	Regents,	Conditions of provisional charter not fulfilled.
40	Buffalo College,	Buffalo, Erie Co.,	Apr. 18, 1859	Legislature,	Not organized.
41	Clinton College,	Fairfield, Herkimer Co.,	Mar. 25, 1816	Regents,	Conditions of provisional charter not fulfilled.
42	College of Physicians and Surgeons of the Western district,	Fairfield, Herkimer Co.,	June 12, 1812	Regents,	Commonly known as the Fairfield Medical College, and highly flourishing for many years.
43	Excelsior Medical College,	New York city,	Apr. 16, 1857	Legislature,	Not organized.
44	Flushing Female College,	Flushing, Queens Co.,	Apr. 6, 1857	Legislature,	Formerly St. Thomas' Hall.
45	Ithaca College,	Ithaca, Tompkins Co.,	Apr. 10, 1822	Regents,	Conditions of provisional charter not fulfilled.
46	Medical Department of Columbia College,	New York city,	1792	....	Organized under the College charter, and merged in the College of Physicians and Surgeons of the city of New York.
47	Metropolitan Medical College,	New York city,	Mar. 28, 1857	Legislature,	Charter repealed, April 12, 1862.
48	New York Central College Association,	McGrawville, Cortland Co.,	Apr. 17, 1851	Legislature,	Property now owned and occupied by the New York Central Academy.
49	New York College of Dental Surgery,	Syracuse, Onondaga Co.,	Apr. 13, 1852	Legislature.	
50	New York Law College,	New York city,	Mar. 30, 1858	Legislature.	
51	New York State Agricultural College,	Ovid, Seneca Co.,	Apr. 15, 1853	Legislature,	Property now occupied as "The Willard Insane Asylum."
52	People's College,	Havana, Schuyler Co.,	Apr. 12, 1853	Legislature.	
53	Richmond College,	——, Richmond Co.,	Apr. 18, 1838	Legislature,	Not organized.
54	St. Paul's College, Proprietors of,	Flushing, Queens Co.,	May 9, 1840	Legislature.	
55	Troy University,	Troy, Rensselaer Co.,	Apr. 12, 1855	Regents,	Conditions of provisional charter not fulfilled.
56	University of Western New York,	Buffalo, Erie Co.,	Apr. 8, 1836	Legislature,	Not organized.
57	Washington College,	——, Richmond Co.,	Jan. 27, 1817	Regents,	Conditions of provisional charter not fulfilled.
58	Westminster College,	Buffalo, Erie Co.,	Apr. 17, 1851	Legislature,	Not organized.

Whole number (in addition to Medical Department of Columbia College), 22; incorporated by the Regents, 8 (of which seven were provisional); by the Legislature, 14.

Condensed Summary.

Whole number of incorporated Literary and Medical Colleges (in addition to number 46), 57; by the Regents, 14; by the Legislature, 43.

"An act to incorporate the De Veaux College for orphan and destitute children," was passed April 15, 1853, and an institution adopting that name (which is found only in the title of the act), has been established at Suspension Bridge, in Niagara county. It reports annually to the Legislature, but holds none of the special rights and privileges usually conferred upon incorporated colleges.

Several corporations claiming to be academic or collegiate organizations have filed certificates in the office of the Secretary of State, under the provisions of chapter 319, of the Laws of 1848, entitled "An act for the incorporation of benevolent, charitable, scientific and missionary societies," but none of these have reported to the Regents.

The following is a list of these institutions:

American College of Pharmacy, Syracuse, January 22, 1851.
Brooklyn Academy of Medicine, Brooklyn, May 30, 1861.
Buffalo College of St. Joseph, Buffalo, March 12, 1851.
Central Medical College Association, Rochester, March 20, 1850.
German Martin Luther College, Buffalo, July 1, 1853.
Hahneman Academy of Medicine, New York, December 8, 1849.
Metropolitan Medical College, New York, July 2, 1852.
New York Central College, McGrawville, December 6, 1848.
Randolph Eclectic Medical Institute, Randolph, August 21, 1848.
Syracuse Medical College Association, Syracuse, December 5, 1850.
St. Paul's College, New York, November 12, 1851.
Union Homœpathic Medical College Academy of the State of New York, Dundee, Nov. 26, 1852.
Western Medical College, Jamestown, April 17, 1851.
Woman's College of Physicians and Surgeons, New York, July 14, 1865.
Brownville Literary and Educational Association, Brownville, August 1, 1860.
Penn Yan Female Academy, Penn Yan, April 29, 1853.
Rochester Christian Brothers Academy and Seminary, Rochester, July 18, 1857.
Seminary of Our Lady of the Angels, Niagara county, February 27, 1861.

Academies incorporated since the organization of the State.

I. BY THE REGENTS OF THE UNIVERSITY.

No.	NAME.	Location.	Date of incorporation.	REMARKS.
1	Adams Collegiate Institute,	Adams, Jefferson county,	April 22, 1855	
2	Addison Academy,	Addison, Steuben county,	February 8, 1849	
3	Albany Academy,	Albany, Albany county,	March 4, 1813	
4	Alfred Academy,	Alfred, Allegany county,	January 31, 1843	
5	Amenia Seminary,	Amenia, Dutchess county,	March 29, 1836	Now conducted as a private school.
6	Andes Collegiate Institute,	Andes, Delaware county,	July 3, 1862	
7	Angelica Academy,	Angelica, Allegany county,	October 31, 1859	
8	Antwerp Liberal Literary Institute,	Antwerp, Jefferson county,	February 1, 1856	
9	Arcade Academy,	Arcade, Wyoming county,	February 20, 1862	
10	Argyle Academy,	Argyle, Washington county,	May 4, 1841	
11	Astoria Institute,*	Astoria, Queens county,	February 13, 1844	
12	Attica Union School,	Attica, Wyoming county,	January 10, 1867	
13	Auburn Academy,	Auburn, Cayuga county,	February 14, 1815	
14	Augusta Academy,	Augusta, Oneida county,	February 28, 1842	
15	Baldwinsville Academy,	Baldwinsville, Onondaga county,	July 27, 1864	
16	Ball Seminary,	Hoosick Falls, Rensselaer county,	April 11, 1843	Merged in Hoosick Falls Union School.
17	Ballston Academy,*	Ballston, Saratoga county,	March 21, 1808	
18	Batavia Union School,	Batavia, Genesee county,	February 26, 1861	Organized under act of June 18, 1853.
19	Binghamton Academy,	Binghamton, Broome county,	August 23, 1842	
20	Blooming Grove Academy,*	Blooming Grove, Oneida county,	April 1, 1811	
21	Brockport Collegiate Institute,	Brockport, Monroe county,	February 15, 1842	
22	Brookfield Academy,	Brookfield, Madison county,	April 17, 1847	
23	Brooklyn Collegiate and Polytechnic Institute,	Brooklyn, Kings county,	April 7, 1854	
24	Brownville Female Seminary,*	Brownville, Jefferson county,	January 10, 1860	
25	Buffalo Central School,	Buffalo, Erie county,	January 9, 1862	Organized under act of April 16, 1861.
26	Buffalo Female Academy,	Buffalo, Erie county,	October 14, 1851	
27	Cambridge Washington Academy,	Cambridge, Washington county,	March 30, 1815	
28	Canandaigua Academy,	Canandaigua, Ontario county,	March 4, 1795	
29	Carlisle Seminary,	Carlisle, Schoharie county,	October 20, 1853	
30	Cary Collegiate Seminary,	Oakfield, Genesee county,	May 16, 1845	
31	Catskill Academy,*	Catskill, Greene county,	March 12, 1804	
32	Cayuga Academy,	Aurora, Cayuga county,	March 23, 1801	Name changed to Cayuga Lake Acad., Jan. 13, '60.
33	Cayuga Lake Academy,	Aurora, Cayuga county,	March 23, 1801	Name changed from Cayuga Academy, Jan. 13, '60.
34	Chamberlain Institute,	Randolph, Cattaraugus county,	January 24, 1851	Name ch'd from Randolph Acad. Asso. April 11, '66.
35	Champlain Academy,	Champlain, Clinton county,	August 23, 1842	
36	Chautauqua Collegiate Institute,	Stockton, Chautauqua county,	April 21, 1857	Never organized.
37	Cherry Valley Academy,*	Cherry Valley, Otsego county,	February 8, 1796	
38	Chester Academy,	Chester, Orange county,	February 27, 1844	

39	Cincinnatus Academy,	Cincinnatus, Cortland county,	April	21, 1857	
40	Clarence Academy,	Clarence, Erie county,	October	12, 1854	
41	Clarkson Academy,*	Clarkson, Monroe county,	March	17, 1835	
42	Claverack Academy and Hudson River Institute,	Claverack, Columbia county,	June	14, 1854	
43	Clinton Academy,	East Hampton, Suffolk county,	November	17, 1787	Oldest Academy in the State.
44	Clinton Seminary,*	Clinton, Oneida county,	February	15, 1842	
45	Columbia Academy,*	Kinderhook, Columbia county,	March	13, 1797	
46	Cooperstown Sem'y and Female Collegiate Inst.*	Cooperstown, Otsego county,	June	14, 1854	
47	Corning Free Academy,	Corning, Steuben county,	March	1, 1860	Organized under act of April 13, 1859.
48	Cortland Academy,	Homer, Cortland county,	February	2, 1819	
49	Cortlandville Academy,	Cortlandville, Cortland county,	January	31, 1843	
50	Coxsackie Academy,	Coxsackie, Greene county,	April	2, 1863	
51	Dansville Seminary,	Dansville, Livingston county,	January	14, 1858	
52	De Lancey Institute,*	Hampton, Oneida county,	April	13, 1842	
53	Delaware Academy,	Delhi, Delaware county,	February	2, 1820	
54	Deposit Academy,	Deposit, Broome county,	April	9, 1867	
55	De Ruyter Institute,	De Ruyter, Madison county,	December	3, 1847	
56	Dundee Academy,	Dundee, Yates county,	March	22, 1855	
57	Dutchess County Academy,*	Poughkeepsie, Dutchess county,	February	1, 1792	
58	East Genesee Conference Seminary,	Ovid, Seneca county,	February	11, 1864	
59	Ellington Academy,	Ellington, Chautauqua county,	February	11, 1853	
60	Elmira Academy,*	Elmira, Chemung county,	March	31, 1840	
61	Elmira Academy,	Elmira, Chemung county,	January	9, 1863	Organized under act of April 4, 1859.
62	Elmira Collegiate Seminary,	Elmira, Chemung county,	October	20, 1853	
63	Erasmus Hall,	Flatbush, Kings county,	November	17, 1787	
64	Evans Academy,	Peterboro', Madison county,	January	28, 1853	Name changed from Peterboro' Acad., Dec. 1, 1864.
65	Fairfield Academy,	Fairfield, Herkimer county,	March	15, 1803	
66	Falley Seminary,	Fulton, Oswego county,	March	5, 1857	
67	Farmers' Hall,	Goshen, Orange county,	March	26, 1790	
68	Fayetteville Seminary,*	Fayetteville, Onondaga county,	April	21, 1857	
69	Forestville Union School,	Forestville, Chautauqua county,	January	10, 1867	Organized under general act of June 18, 1853.
70	Fort Edward Collegiate Institute,	Fort Edward, Washington county,	July	6, 1854	Name changed from Washington County Seminary and Collegiate Institute, Jan. 13, 1865.
71	Fort Plain Seminary and Female Col. Inst.,	Fort Plain, Montgomery county,	October	20, 1853	
72	Franklin Academy,	Malone, Franklin county,	April	28, 1831	
73	Franklin Academy,	Prattsburgh, Steuben county,	February	23, 1824	
74	Friends' Academy,	Union Springs, Cayuga county,	January	13, 1860	
75	Friendship Academy,	Friendship, Allegany county,	February	8, 1849	
76	Galway Academy,*	Galway, Saratoga county,	October	11, 1845	
77	Genesee Conference Seminary,	Pike, Wyoming county,	February	1, 1856	Name changed to Pike Seminary Oct. 13, 1859.
78	Genesee Valley Seminary,	Belfast, Allegany county,	January	8, 1857	
79	Genesee and Wyoming Seminary,	Alexander, Genesee county,	March	27, 1845	
80	Geneva Academy,*	Geneva, Ontario county,	March	29, 1813	Merged in Geneva College, 1824.
81	Genoa Academy,	Genoa, Cayuga county,	February	4, 1847	
82	German American School of Morrisania,	Morrisania, Westchester county,	March	2, 1865	
83	Gilbertsville Academy and Collegiate Institute,	Gilbertsville, Otsego county,	May	4, 1841	

* Academies which have become extinct, or which have failed to make any report for some time past, and are believed to have suspended operations, if not already extinct.

Academies incorporated since the organization of the State — (Continued).

No.	NAME.	Location.	Date of incorporation by regents.	REMARKS.
84	Glen's Falls Academy,	Glen's Falls, Warren county,	January 12, 1842	
85	Gloversville Union Seminary,	Gloversville, Fulton county,	January 11, 1855	
86	Grammar School of Columbia College,	New York city,	April 17, 1838	
87	Grammar School of Madison University,	Hamilton, Madison county,	June, 17, 1853	
88	Grammar School of New York Central College,*	McGrawville, Cortland county,	January 14, 1858	
89	Grammar School of University of City of N. Y.,	New York city,	April 17, 1838	
90	Greenville Academy,	Greenville, Greene county,	February 27, 1816	
91	Half Moon Academy,	Halfmoon, Saratoga county,	February 14, 1851	
92	Hamilton Academy,	Hamilton, Madison county,	February 23, 1824	
93	Hamilton Female Seminary,	Hamilton, Madison county,	January 17, 1856	Now conducted as a private school.
94	Hamilton Oneida Academy,	Kirkland, Oneida county,	January 29, 1793	Merged in Hamilton College, 1812.
95	Hartford Academy,	South Hartford, Washington Co.,	January 12, 1866	
96	Hartwick Seminary,	Hartwick, Otsego county,	August 13, 1816	
97	Hedding Literary Institute,*	Ashland, Greene county,	October 12, 1854	
98	Hempstead Institute,*	Hempstead, Queens county,	January 14, 1858	
99	Herkimer County Academy,*	Herkimer, Herkimer county,	February 11, 1840	
100	Holley Academy,	Holley, Orleans county,	March 28, 1850	
101	Hubbardsville Academy,*	Hubbard's Corners, Madison Co.,	February 14, 1850	
102	Hudson Academy,	Hudson, Columbia county,	March 3, 1807	
103	Hungerford Collegiate Institute,	Adams, Jefferson county,	March 24, 1864	
104	Huntington Union School,	Huntington, Suffolk county,	January 9, 1863	Organized under act of April 22, 1862.
105	Johnstown Academy,	Johnstown, Montgomery county,	January 27, 1794	
106	Jordan Academy,	Jordan, Onondaga county,	January 12, 1842	
107	Kingsborough Academy,	Kingsborough, Fulton county,	February 5, 1839	
108	Kingston Academy,	Kingston, Ulster county,	February 3, 1795	
109	Kingston Academy,	Kingston, Ulster county,	January 12, 1866	
110	Lancaster Academy,*	Lancaster, Erie county,	January 22, 1846	
111	Lansingburgh Academy,	Lansingburgh, Rensselaer county,	February 8, 1796	
112	Laurel Bank Seminary,	Deposit, Broome county,	March 17, 1854	
113	Lawrenceville Academy,	Lawrenceville, St. Lawrence Co.,	April 8, 1861	
114	Leavenworth Institute,	Wolcott, Wayne county,	July 14, 1859	
115	Le Roy Academic Institute,	Le Roy, Genesee county,	February 11, 1864	
116	Le Roy Female Seminary,	Le Roy, Genesee county,	February 16, 1841	Merged in Ingham Collegiate Institute, 1853.
117	Lewiston High School Academy,	Lewiston, Niagara county,	April 16, 1828	
118	Little Falls Academy,	Little Falls, Herkimer county,	October 17, 1844	
119	Lowville Academy,	Lowville, Lewis county,	March 21, 1808	
120	Lyons Union School,	Lyons, Wayne county,	January 8, 1857	Organized under act of April 19, 1855.
121	Marathon Academy,	Marathon, Cortland county,	March 2, 1866	
122	Marion Collegiate Institute,	Marion, Wayne county,	July 6, 1855	
123	Marshall Seminary of Easton,	Easton, Washington county,	December 1, 1863	
124	Mechanicville Academy,	Mechanicville, Saratoga county,	July 11, 1861	

125	Middlebury Academy,	Wyoming, Wyoming county,	January	26, 1819	
126	Monroe Academy, *	Henrietta, Monroe county,	July	2, 1827	
127	Monroe Academy,	Henrietta, Monroe county,	February	7, 1843	
128	Montgomery Academy,	Montgomery, Orange county,	January	21, 1791	
129	Monticello Academy,	Monticello, Sullivan county,	April	1, 1852	
130	Moravia Institute,	Moravia, Cayuga county,	January	23, 1840	
131	Moriah Academy, *	Moriah, Essex county,	February	16, 1841	
132	Mount Morris Union School,	Mount Morris, Livingston county,	January	13, 1859	Organized under act of June 18, 1853.
133	Mount Pleasant Academy,	Mount Pleasant, Westchester Co.,	March	27, 1827	
134	Mount Pleasant Female Seminary, *	Sing Sing, Westchester county,	May	10, 1836	
135	Munro Academy,	Elbridge, Onondaga county,	April	23, 1839	Name changed to Munro Collegiate Institute April 12, 1855.
136	Munro Collegiate Institu e,	Elbridge, Onondaga county,	April	23, 1839	Name changed from Munro Academy April 12, 1855.
137	Naples Academy,	Naples, Ontario county,	March	10, 1859	
138	Newark Union Free School,	Newark, Wayne county,	February	5, 1863	Organized under general act of June 18, 1853.
139	New Berlin Academy,	New Berlin, Chenango county,	February	13, 1844	
140	Newburgh Academy, *	Newburgh, Orange county,	March	3, 1806	
141	New Paltz Academy,	New Paltz, Ulster county.	October	11, 1845	
142	New York Central Academy,	McGrawville, Cortland county,	May	4, 1864	
143	New York Conference Seminary,*	Charlotteville, Schoharie county,	October	26, 1850	
144	N. Y. Conference Seminary and Collegiate Inst.	Charlotteville, Schoharie county,	March	5, 1857	
145	North Granville Female Seminary,	North Granville, Washington Co.	February	10, 1854	
146	North Granville Ladies' Seminary,*	North Granville, Washington Co.	December	2, 1862	
147	North Hebron Institute,	North Hebron, Washington Co.	March	17, 1854	
148	North Salem Academy,	North Salem, Westchester county,	February	19, 1790	
149	Norwich Academy,	Norwich, Chenango county,	February	14, 1843	
150	Nunda Literary Institute,*	Nunda, Livingston county,	January	30, 1845	
151	Olean Academy Association,	Olean, Cattaraugus county,	April	11, 1853	Name changed to Olean Academy, June 3, 1853.
152	Olean Academy,	Olean, Cattaraugus county,	April	11, 1853	Name changed from Olean Acad. Ass., June 3, 1853.
153	Oneida Institute of Science and Industry,*	Whitesboro', Oneida county,	March	24, 1829	
154	Oneida Seminary,	Oneida, Madison county,	July	9, 1857	
155	Onondaga Academy,	Onondaga Valley, Onondaga Co.	April	10, 1813	
156	Orleans Academy,*	Orleans, Jefferson county,	February	5, 1851	
157	Oswego High School,	Oswego, Oswego county,	January	13, 1859	Organized under general act of June 18, 1853.
158	Otsego Academy,*	Cooperstown, Otsego county,	February	8, 1796	
159	Owego Academy,	Owego, Tioga county,	April	16, 1828	
160	Oxford Academy,	Oxford, Chenango county,	January	27, 1794	
161	Oyster Bay Academy,*	Oyster Bay, Queens county,	March	15, 1803	
162	Palatine Bridge Union Free School,	Palatine Bridge, Montgomery Co.	January	10, 1861	Organized under general act of June 18, 1853.
163	Parma Institute,	Parma, Monroe county,	March	10, 1859	
164	Penfield Seminary,	Penfield, Monroe county,	October	8, 1857	
165	Penn Yan Academy,	Penn Yan, Yates county,	January	13, 1860	
166	Perry Academy,	Perry, Wyoming county,	April	7, 1854	
167	Perry Center Institute,*	Perry Center, Wyoming county,	January	31, 1843	
168	Peterboro' Academy,	Peterboro', Madison county,	January	28, 1853	Name changed to Evans Academy, Dec. 1, 1864.

* Academies which have become extinct. or which have failed to make any report for some time past, and are believed to have suspended operations, if not already extinct.

Academies incorporated since the organization of the State — (Continued).

No.	NAME.	Location.	Date of incorporation by regents.	REMARKS.
169	Phipps Union Seminary,	Albion, Orleans county,	February 11, 1840	
170	Pike Seminary,	Pike, Wyoming county,	February 1, 1856	Name changed from Genesee Conference Seminary Oct. 13, 1859.
171	Piermont Academy,*	Piermont, Rockland county,	March 15, 1842	
172	Pompey Academy,	Pompey, Onondaga county,	March 11, 1811	
173	Port Byron Free School and Academy,	Port Byron, Cayuga county,	January 30, 1860	Organized under act of April 7, 1857.
174	Prattsville Academy,*	Prattsville, Greene county,	January 30, 1850	
175	Princetown Academy,*	Princetown, Schenectady county,	October 20, 1853	
176	Prospect Academy,	Prospect, Oneida county,	January 24, 1851	
177	Randolph Academy Association,	Randolph, Cattaraugus county,	January 24, 1851	Name changed to Chamberlain Inst. April 11, 1866.
178	Raymond Collegiate Institute,*	Carmel, Putnam county,	March 30, 1859	
179	Red Creek Union Seminary,	Red Creek, Wayne county,	January 10, 1867	
180	Rensselaerville Academy,	Rensselaerville, Albany county,	January 30, 1845	
181	Rhinebeck Academy,*	Rhinebeck, Dutchess county,	February 23, 1841	
182	Richburgh Academy,	Richburgh, Allegany county,	April 12, 1850	
183	Richmondville Union Seminary and Female Collegiate Institute,*	Richmondville, Schoharie county,	February 10, 1854	
184	Riga Academy,	Riga, Monroe county,	May 11, 1846	
185	Riverdale Institute,	Yonkers, Westchester county,	April 10, 1863	
186	Rochester Collegiate Institute (No. 1),*	Rochester, Monroe county,	February 26, 1839	
187	Rochester Collegiate Institute (No. 2),	Rochester, Monroe county,	January 13, 1865	
188	Rochester Free Academy,	Rochester, Monroe county,	July 3, 1862	Same as Rochester High School (No. 2).
189	Rochester High School (No. 1),	Rochester, Monroe county,	July 3, 1862	Organized under act of April 8, 1861.
190	Rockland County Female Institute,*	Orangetown, Rockland county,	October 12, 1855	
191	Rogersville Union Seminary,	Rogersville, Steuben county,	January 28, 1853	
192	Rural Academy,	Montgomery, Orange county,	April 1, 1852	Not organized.
193	Rural Seminary,	East Pembroke, Genesee county,	April 17, 1856	
194	Rush Academy of the M. E. Zion connection,	Twelfth Township, Essex county,	December 1, 1864	
195	Rushford Academy,	Rushford, Allegany county,	March 4, 1852	
196	Sag Harbor Institute,*	Sag Harbor, Suffolk county,	January 20, 1848	
197	St. Lawrence Academy,	Potsdam, St. Lawrence county,	March 25, 1816	
198	Sand Lake Academy,	Sand Lake, Rensselaer county,	February 19, 1846	
199	Sans Souci Seminary,	Ballston, Saratoga county,	December 1, 1864	
200	Saugerties Academy,*	Saugerties, Ulster county,	April 7, 1854	
201	Sauquoit Academy,	Sauquoit, Oneida county,	April 6, 1849	
202	Schenectady Academy,*	Schenectady, Schenectady county.	January 29, 1793	Merged into Union College, 1795.
203	Schuylerville Academy,*	Schuylerville, Saratoga county,	January 23, 1840	
204	Sherburne Union Academy,*	Sherburne, Chenango county,	January 23, 1840	
205	Sodus Academy,	Sodus, Wayne county,	January 11, 1855	
206	Spring Mills Academy,	Spring Mills, Allegany county,	April 8, 1861	
207	Starkey Seminary,	Starkey, Yates county,	February 25, 1848	
208	Stillwater Academy,*	Stillwater, Saratoga county,	January 29, 1839	

No.	Name	Location	Date		Remarks
209	Stillwater Seminary,*	Stillwater, Saratoga county,	February	25, 1848	
210	Susquehanna Seminary,	Binghamton, Broome county,	April	7, 1854	Property sold on foreclosure of mortgage, 1862.
211	Syracuse High School,	Syracuse, Onondaga county,	January	9, 1862	Organized under act of April 13, 1860.
212	Ticonderoga Academy,	Ticonderoga, Essex county,	April	8, 1858	
213	Troupsburgh Academy,	Troupsburgh, Steuben county,	October	17, 1861	
214	Troy High School,	Troy, Rensselaer county,	January	9, 1863	Organized under act of April 22, 1862.
215	Trumansburgh Academy,	Trumansburgh, Tompkins county,	July	6, 1854	
216	Unadilla Academy,	Unadilla, Otsego county,	April	1, 1852	
217	Union Academy,*	Stone Arabia, Montgomery Co.,	March	31, 1795	
218	Union Academy,*	Granger, Allegany county,	January	11, 1855	
219	Union Academy of Belleville,	Belleville, Jefferson county,	January	5, 1830	Name changed from Union Literary Society, Oct. 13, 1859.
220	Union Hall,	Jamaica, Queens county,	February	29, 1792	
221	Union Village Academy,	Union Village, Washington Co.,	January	23, 1840	
222	Utica Academy,	Utica, Oneida county,	March	14, 1814	Made one of the common schools of the city, by act of May 26, 1853, but still subject to Regents.
223	Walton Academy,	Walton, Delaware county,	February	10, 1854	
224	Warnerville Union Sem. and Female Institute,	Warnerville, Schoharie county,	January	27, 1854	
225	Warrensburgh Academy,	Warrensburgh, Warren county,	May	4, 1860	
226	Warsaw Union School,	Warsaw, Wyoming county,	January	11, 1855	Organized under general act of June 18, 1853.
227	Warwick Institute,	Warwick, Orange county,	March	17, 1854	
228	Washington Academy, *	Salem, Washington county,	February	15, 1791	
229	Washington Academy,	Warwick, Orange county,	March	25, 1811	
230	Washington Co. Seminary and Collegiate Inst.,	Fort Edward, Washington county,	July	6, 1854	Name changed to Fort Edward Collegiate Institute January 13, 1865.
231	Waterford Female Academy, *	Waterford, Saratoga county,	March	19, 1819	
232	Waterloo Union School,	Waterloo, Seneca county,	October	11, 1855	Organized under act of April 10, 1855.
233	Watertown High School,	Watertown, Jefferson county,	January	12, 1866	Organized under act of April 21, 1865.
234	Watkins Academy,	Watkins, Schuyler county;	January	13, 1860	
235	Waverly Institute,	Waverly, Tioga county,	January	21, 1858	
236	Wayne County Collegiate Institute,	Newark, Wayne county,	July	6, 1855	Name changed to Wayne and Ontario Collegiate Institute January 13, 1860.
237	Wayne and Ontario Collegiate Institute,	Newark, Wayne county	July	6, 1850	Name changed from Wayne County Collegiate Institute January 13, 1860.
238	Webster Academy,	Webster, Monroe county,	April	17, 1850	
239	West Hebron Classical School,	West Hebron, Washington county,	March	22, 1855	
240	Westport Union Free School,	Westport, Essex county,	January	10, 1867	Organized under act of May 2, 1864.
241	West Winfield Academy,	West Winfield, Herkimer county.	February	14, 1851	
242	Whitehall Academy,	Whitehall, Washington county,	October	27, 1848	
243	Whitesboro' Academy,*	Whitesboro', Oneida county,	March	23, 1813	
244	Whitestown Seminary,	Whitestown, Oneida county,	March	27, 1845	
245	Williamsville Academy,	Williamsville, Erie county,	January	10, 1867	
246	Wilson Collegiate Institute,	Wilson, Niagara county,	February	19, 1846	
247	Windsor Academy,	Windsor, Broome county,	March	15, 1849	
248	Yates Academy.	Yates, Orleans county,	August	23, 1842	
249	Yates Polytechnic Institute,	Chittenango, Madison county,	April	11, 1853	

* Academies which have become extinct, or which have failed to make any report for some time past, and are believed to have suspended operations, if not already extinct.

Academies incorporated since the organization of the State — (Continued).

II. BY THE LEGISLATURE.

No.	NAME.	Location.	Date of incorporation by legislature.	Time when they became subject to the regents.	REMARKS.
1	Academy of our Lady of the Cataract,	Niagara Falls, Niagara county,	Apr. 10, 1866		
2	Academy of the Sacred Heart,	Rochester, Monroe county,	Apr. 11, 1849		
3	Albany Female Academy,	Albany, Albany county,	Feb. 16. 1821	Jan. 29, 1828	
4	Albany Female Seminary,	Albany, Albany country,	Apr. 9, 1828	Apr. 16, 1828	
5	Albany Pearl Street Academy,*	Albany, Albany county,	Apr. 23, 1836		
6	Albion Academy,	Albion, Orleans county,	May 1, 1837	Feb. 27, 1841	
7	Alexander Classical School,*	Alexander, Genesee county,	May 6, 1834	Feb. 5, 1839	
8	Ames Academy,	Ames, Montgomery county,	Apr. 22. 1837	Feb. 5, 1839	
9	Amsterdam Academy,	Amsterdam, Montgomery Co.,	Mar. 29, 1839	Feb. 16, 1841	Name changed from Amsterdam Female Seminary, April 27, 1865.
10	Amsterdam Female Seminary,	Amsterdam, Montgomery Co.,	Mar. 29, 1839	Feb. 16, 1841	Name changed to Amsterdam Academy, April 27, 1865.
11	Angelica Academy,	Angelica, Allegany county,	May 12, 1836		
12	Auburn Academic High School,	Auburn, Cayuga county,	Mar. 19, 1866		
13	Auburn Female Seminary,*	Auburn, Cayuga county,	Apr. 18, 1838	Feb. 11, 1840	
14	Aurora Academy,	East Aurora, Erie county,	Apr. 16. 1838	Jan. 29, 1839	Name changed from Aurora Manual Labor Seminary, April 16, 1838.
15	Aurora Manual Labor Seminary,	Aurora, Erie county,	Apr. 30, 1833	Jan. 29, 1839	Name changed to Aurora Academy, April 16, 1838.
16	Avon Academy,*	Avon, Livingston county,	Apr. 30, 1836	Feb. 27, 1841	
17	Batavia Female Academy,*	Batavia, Genesee county,	Mar. 5, 1838	Feb. 5, 1839	
18	Bedford Academy,*	Bedford, Westchester county,	Apr. 8, 1826		
19	Berneville Academy and Female Seminary,*	Berne, Albany county,	Mar. 8, 1833		
20	Bethany Academy,	Bethany, Genesee county,	Mar. 29, 1841	Feb. 28, 1842	
21	Black River Literary and Religious Institute,	Watertown, Jefferson county,	May 25, 1836	Jan. 30, 1838	Name changed to Jefferson County Institute, May 12, 1846.
22	Bridgewater Academy,*	Bridgewater, Oneida county,	Apr. 8, 1826	Apr. 16, 1828	
23	Brooklyn Collegiate Institute for Young Ladies,	Brooklyn, Kings county,	Apr. 23, 1829		
24	Brooklyn Female Academy,	Brooklyn, Kings county,	May 8. 1845	Jan. 14, 1847	Now Packer Collegiate Institute.
25	Broome Academy,	Union, Broome county,	Apr. 30, 1839	....	Not organized.
26	Buffalo Female Seminary,*	Buffalo, Erie county,	Apr. 23, 1831		
27	Buffalo High School Association,*	Buffalo, Erie county,	Apr. 17, 1827	....	Name changed to Buffalo Literary and Scientific Academy, Feb. 12, 1830.
28	Buffalo Literary and Scientific Academy,	Buffalo, Erie county,	Apr. 17, 1827	....	Name changed from Buffalo High School Association, Feb. 12, 1830.
29	Canajoharie Academy,	Canajoharie, Montgomery Co.,	Apr. 13, 1826	Feb. 26, 1828	Dissolved by act of April 21, 1846.
30	Canton Academy,	Canton, St. Lawrence county,	Apr. 24, 1837	Jan. 23, 1840	
31	Catskill Classical School,	Catskill, Greene county,	Apr. 25, 1832		
32	Catskill Female Seminary,	Catskill, Greene county,	Mar. 24, 1820	....	Not organized.

33	Clarkson High School,	Clarkson, Monroe county,	Apr. 6, 1859		
34	Claverack Academy,*	Claverack, Columbia county,	Apr. 25, 1831	Feb. 5, 1839	
35	Clermont Academy,*	Clermont, Columbia county,	Apr. 26, 1834	Feb. 26, 1839	
36	Clinton Grammar School,	Clinton, Oneida county,	Mar. 28, 1817	Feb. 26, 1828	
37	Clinton Liberal Institute,	Clinton, Oneida, county,	Apr. 29, 1834	Mar. 29, 1836	
38	Clover Street Seminary,*	Brighton, Monroe county,	Apr. 7, 1848	Feb. 23, 1849	
39	Collegiate Institute of the City of New York,	New York city,	July 10, 1851	....	Not organized.
40	Collinsville Institute,*	West Turin, Lewis county,	May 2, 1837		
41	Cooper Institute,	New York city,	Feb. 15, 1857		
42	Cooperstown Female Academy,*	Cooperstown, Otsego county,	Apr. 15, 1822		
43	Cortland Female Seminary,*	Cortlandville, Cortland Co.,	Apr. 18, 1828		
44	Coxsackie Academy,*	Coxsackie, Greene county,	May 5, 1837	Feb. 5, 1839	
45	Delaware Literary Institute,	Franklin, Delaware county,	Apr. 23, 1835	Jan. 29, 1839	
46	De Ruyter Institute,*	De Ruyter, Madison county,	Mar. 30, 1836	Jan. 30, 1838	
47	Dover Academy,*	Dover, Dutchess county,	May 9, 1835		
48	Dunkirk Academy,*	Dunkirk, Chautauqua county,	May 1, 1837		
49	East Bloomfield Academy,	East Bloomfield, Ontario Co.,	Apr. 9, 1838	Jan. 23, 1840	
50	Eastern Collegiate Inst. of the City of New York,*	New York city,	May 7, 1844		
51	Egberts Institute,	Cohoes, Albany county,	May 2, 1864		
52	Essex County Academy,*	Westport, Essex county,	May 1, 1834	Mar. 6, 1838	
53	Falley Seminary of the Black River Conference,	Fulton, Oswego county,	May 25, 1836	Feb. 5, 1839	Name changed from Fulton Academy April
54	Fayetteville Academy,*	Fayetteville, Onondaga Co.,	May 4, 1837	Feb. 5, 1839	11, 1849. Merged in Falley Seminary.
55	Female Academy of the Sacred Heart,	New York city,	July 9, 1851		
56	Female Academy of the Sacred Heart,	Albany, Albany county,	Mar. 19, 1861		
57	Female Academy of the Sacred Heart,	Rochester, Monroe county,	Apr. 15, 1858		
58	Fishkill Education Society,*	Fishkill, Dutchess county,	May 11, 1835		
59	Fishkill Female Semin'y and Collegiate Institute,*	Fishkill, Dutchess county,	Apr. 15, 1857		
60	Flushing Institute,*	Flushing, Queens county,	Apr. 16, 1827		
61	Fonda Academy,*	Fonda, Montgomery county,	May 13, 1845	Oct. 11, 1845	
62	Fort Covington Academy,	Fort Covington, Franklin Co.,	Apr. 21, 1831	Apr. 21, 1831	Re-organized by act of April 11, 1853, ch. 755.
63	Fredonia Academy,	Fredonia, Chautauqua county,	Nov. 25, 1824	Feb. 23, 1830	
64	Fulton Academy,	Fulton, Oswego county,	May 25, 1836	Feb. 5, 1839	Name changed from Fulton Female Sem'y, April 11, 1842, and to Falley Seminary of the Black River Conference, Apr. 11, 1849.
65	Fulton Female Seminary,	Fulton, Oswego county,	May 25, 1836	Feb. 5, 1839	Name changed to Fulton Acad. Apr. 11, '42.
66	Gaines Academy,*	Gaines, Orleans county,	Apr. 14, 1827	Jan. 26, 1830	
67	Galway Academy,*	Galway, Saratoga county,	May 26, 1836	Jan. 29, 1839	
68	Genesee Seminary,*	Batavia, Genesee county,	May 11, 1835		
69	Genesee Manual Labor Seminary,*	Bethany, Genesee county,	Apr. 13, 1832 Mar. 27, 1834		
70	Genesee Wesleyan Seminary,	Lima, Livingston county,	Apr. 30, 1833	Mar. 9, 1836	
71	Geneseo Academy,	Geneseo, Livingston county,	Mar. 10, 1827	Feb. 7, 1829	Name ch'ged from Livingston High School Association, May 13, 1846.
72	Geneva Classical and Union School,	Geneva, Ontario county,	Apr. 15, 1853	Feb. 10, 1854	
73	Gouverneur High School,	Gouverneur, St. Lawrence Co.,	Apr. 5, 1828	Feb. 19, 1829	Name changed to Gouverneur Wesleyan Seminary, April 24, 1840.

* Academies which have become extinct, or which have failed to make any report for some time past, and are believed to have suspended operations, if not already extinct.

Academies incorporated since the organization of the State — (Continued).

No.	NAME.	Location.	Date of incorporation by legislature.	Time when they became subject to the regents.	REMARKS.
74	Gouverneur Wesleyan Seminary,	Gouverneur, St. Lawrence Co.,	Apr. 5, 1828	Feb. 19, 1829	Name changed from Gouverneur High School, April 24, 1840.
75	Gowanda Union School,	Gowanda, Cattaraugus county,	Apr. 29, 1863		
76	Granville Academy,*	Granville, Washington county,	Mar. 31, 1828	Apr. 16, 1830	
77	Greenbush and Schodack Academy,*	East Greenbush, Renssel'r Co.,	Apr. 25, 1831	Feb. 27, 1841	
78	Griffith Academy, } (Identical),	Springville, Erie county,	Mar. 19, 1827	Jan. 26, 1830	Name changed by the Regents from Springville Academy, March 2, 1866.
79	Griffith Institute, }	Springville, Erie county,	Mar. 19, 1827	Jan. 26, 1830	Name changed by the Legislature from Springville Academy, March 16, 1866.
80	Groton Academy,	Groton, Tompkins county,	May 6, 1837	Jan. 29, 1829	
81	Harlem Literary and Scientific Academy,*	New York city,	Jan. 24, 1829		
82	Hempstead Seminary,*	Hempstead, Queens county,	May 2, 1836	Jan. 29, 1839	
83	Highland Grove Gymnasium,*	Fishkill, Dutchess county,	Apr. 11, 1831		
84	Hobart Hall,*	Holland Patent, Oneida Co.,	Mar. 16, 1839	Jan. 23, 1840	
85	Holland Patent Academy,*	Trenton, Oneida county,	Apr. 24, 1834		
86	Hudson River Agricultural Seminary,*	Stockport, Columbia county,	May 6, 1837		
87	Ingham Collegiate Institute,	Le Roy, Genesee county,	Apr. 6, 1852	Jan. 28, 1853	Merged in Ingham University.
88	Ingham University, Academical Department,	Le Roy, Genesee county,	Apr. 3, 1857		
89	Ithaca Academy,	Ithaca, Tompkins county,	Mar. 24, 1823	Apr. 17, 1826	
90	Jamestown Academy,	Jamestown, Chautauqua Co.,	Apr. 16, 1836	Feb. 5, 1839	Merged in Jamestown Union School, 1866.
91	Jamestown Union School,	Jamestown, Chautauqua Co.,	....	....	Organized under act of May 2, 1864.
92	Jefferson Academy,*	Jefferson, Schoharie county,	Nov. 27, 1824	Jan. 22, 1833	
93	Jefferson County Institute,	Watertown, Jefferson county,	May 25, 1836	Jan. 30, 1838	Name changed from Black River Literary and Religious Institute, May 12, 1846.
94	Jonesville Academy,	Jonesville, Saratoga county,	Apr. 1, 1850	Oct. 26, 1850	
95	Keeseville Academy,	Keeseville, Clinton Co.,	May 4, 1835	Feb. 5, 1839	
96	Kinderhook Academy,	Kinderhook, Columbia county,	Apr. 3, 1824	Feb. 19, 1828	
97	Knoxville Academy,	Knox, Albany county,	May 9, 1837	Feb. 15, 1842	
98	La Fayette High School,	La Fayette, Onondaga county,	Apr. 23, 1836		
99	Liberty Normal Institute,	Liberty, Sullivan county,	Apr. 10, 1849	Sept 20, 1849	
100	Literary and Scientific Institute of York,*	York, Livingston county,	Mar. 27, 1839		
101	Livingston County High School Association,	Geneseo, Livingston county,	Mar. 10, 1827	Feb. 7, 1829	Name changed to Genesee Academy, May 13, 1846.
102	Lockport Academy,	Lockport, Niagara county,	May 26, 1841		
103	Lockport Union School,	Lockport, Niagara county,	Mar. 18, 1850	Oct. 26, 1850	
104	Lyons Academy,	Lyons, Wayne county,	Mar. 29, 1837		
105	Lyons Academy,	Lyons, Wayne county,	May 7, 1840		
106	Macedon Academy,	Macedon, Wayne county,	Apr. 11, 1842	Jan. 30, 1845	
107	Manlius Academy,	Manlius, Onondaga county,	Apr. 13, 1835	Jan. 29, 1839	
108	Mansion Square Female Seminary,	Poughkeepsie, Dutchess Co.,	Mar. 15, 1849	....	Private School.

109	Marion Academy,*	Marion, Wayne county,	Mar. 27, 1830		
110	Mayville Academy,	Mayville, Chautauqua county,	Apr. 24, 1839	Feb. 5, 1839	
111	Medina Academy,	Medina, Orleans county,	Apr. 10, 1854	Apr. 25, 1851	
112	Mendon Academy,	Mendon, Monroe county,	Apr. 20, 1830	Feb. 5, 1839	
113	Mexico Academy,	Mexico, Oswego county,	Apr. 13, 1826	Feb. 26, 1828	Name changed from Rensselaer Oswego Academy, May 14, 1845.
114	Millville Academy,*	Millville, Orleans county,	Apr. 25, 1840	Feb. 16, 1841	
115	Monticello Academy,	Monticello, Sullivan county,	May 1, 1865		
116	Mount Pleasant Academy,*	Mt. Pleasant, Westchester Co.	Mar. 24, 1820		
117	Nassau Academy,	Nassau, Rensselaer county,	May 11, 1835		
118	New Paltz Academy,*	New Paltz, Ulster county,	Apr. 12, 1833	Apr. 29, 1836	
119	New Rochelle Academy,*	New Rochelle, Westch'ter Co.	Apr. 13, 1826		
120	Newtown Female Academy,*	Newtown, Queens county,	Mar. 15, 1822		
121	New Woodstock Academy,*	Cazenovia, Madison county,	May 2, 1834		
122	New York Free Academy,	New York city,	May 7, 1847	Oct. 31, 1849	Merged in College of city of New York.
123	New York High School,*	New York city,	April 4, 1825		
124	New York Institution for the Deaf and Dumb,	New York city,	Apr. 15, 1817	Apr. 15, 1830	
125	New York Law Institute,	New York city,	Feb. 22, 1830	....	Conducted as a Library, but authorized to give instruction.
126	New York State Agricultural School,*	....	May 4, 1844		
127	Norwich Union Seminary,*	Norwich, Chenango county,	Mar. 16, 1837		
128	Ogdensburgh Academy,	Ogdensb'gh, St. Lawrence Co.	Apr. 20, 1838	Feb. 5, 1839	Merged in Ogdensburgh Educational Institute.
129	Ogdensburgh Educational Institute,	Ogdensb'gh, St. Lawrence Co.	Apr. 20, 1835	Feb. 5, 1839	See Act of April 13, 1857.
130	Oneida Conference Seminary,	Cazenovia, Madison county,	April 6, 1825	Jan. 29, 1828	Name changed from Seminary of the Genesee and Oneida Conference, May 8, 1835.
131	Ontario Female Seminary,	Canandaigua, Ontario county,	Apr. 14, 1825	Jan. 29, 1828	
132	Ontario High School,*	Victor, Ontario county,	Apr. 6, 1830		
133	Oswegatchie Academy,*	Ogdensb'gh, St Lawrence Co.	Apr. 26, 1813		
134	Oswego Academy,*	West Oswego, Oswego county,	Apr. 25, 1833		
135	Ovid Academy,*	Ovid, Seneca county,	Apr. 13, 1826	Jan. 26, 1830	
136	Packer Collegiate Institute,	Brooklyn, Kings county,	Mar. 19, 1853	Jan. 11, 1855	
137	Palmyra Academy,*	Palmyra, Wayne county,	Apr. 11, 1842		
138	Palmyra High School,*	Palmyra, Wayne county,	Mar. 28, 1829	July 2, 1833	
139	Palmyra Classical Union School,	Palmyra, Wayne county,	April 7, 1857	Jan. 14, 1858	
140	Peekskill Academy,	Peekskill, Westchester county	Apr. 16, 1838	Feb. 5, 1839	
141	Pembroke and Darien Classical School,*	Pembroke, Darien, Genesee Co.	April 6, 1838		
142	Phelps Union and Classical School,	Phelps, Ontario county,	Apr. 19, 1855	Jan. 8, 1847	
143	Plattsburgh Academy,	Plattsburgh, Clinton county,	Apr. 21, 1828	Mar. 4, 1829	
144	Poughkeepsie Collegiate School,*	Poughkeepsie, Dutchess Co.,	May 26, 1836	Feb. 5, 1839	
145	Poughkeepsie Female Academy,	Poughkeepsie, Dutchess Co.,	May 10, 1836	Feb. 28, 1837	
146	Poughkeepsie Female Seminary,*	Poughkeepsie, Dutchess Co.,	Mar. 19, 1834		
147	Preble High School,	Preble, Cortland county,	Apr. 24, 1834	....	Not organized.
148	Pulaski Academy,	Pulaski, Oswego county,	June 4, 1853	July 6, 1855	
149	Red Creek Union Academy,	Red Creek, Wayne county,	Mar. 27, 1839	Feb. 5, 1846	Sold on mortgage, 1866.
150	Red Hook Academy,*	Red Hook, Dutchess county,	Apr. 23, 1823	Feb. 23, 1829	
151	Rensselaer Oswego Academy,*	Mexico, Oswego county,	Apr. 13, 1826	Jan. 4, 1833	Name changed to Mexico Acad. May 14, '45.

* Academies which have become extinct, or which have failed to make any report for some time past, and are believed to have suspended operations, if not already extinct.

Academies incorporated since the organization of the State — (Continued).

No.	NAME.	Location.	Date of incorporation by legislature.	Time when they became subject to the regents.	REMARKS.
152	Rensselaer Polytechnic Institute,	Troy, Rensselaer county,	Mar. 8, 1837	Feb. 5, 1846	
153	Ridgebury Academy,*	Minisink, Orange county,	Apr. 30, 1839	Feb. 11, 1840	
154	Rochester Academy of Music and Art,	Rochester, Monroe county,	Apr. 16, 1860		
155	Rochester Female Academy,	Rochester, Monroe county,	Apr. 21, 1837	Feb. 5, 1839	
156	Rochester High School (No. 2),	Rochester, Monroe county,	Mar 15, 1827	Apr. 19, 1831	Merged in Rochester Collegiate Institute, (No. 1).
157	Rochester Institute of General Education,*	Rochester, Monroe county,	Apr. 19, 1828		
158	Rochester Institute of Practical Education,*	Rochester, Monroe county,	Apr. 14, 1832		
159	Rome Academy,	Rome, Oneida county,	Apr. 28, '35 / Jan. 28, '48	Mar. 15, 1849	
160	Royalton Center Academy,	Royalton, Niagara county,	Apr. 9, 1839		
161	Rutgers Female Institute,	New York city,	Apr. 10, 1838	Jan. 23, 1840	Merged in Rutgers Female College, 1867.
162	Rye Academy,*	Rye, Westchester county,	Apr. 13, 1826		
163	St. Joseph's Academy and Industrial Female School of Lockport,	Lockport, Niagara county,	Feb. 19, 1866		
164	St. Mary's Academy and Female Industrial School of Buffalo,	Buffalo, Erie county,	Apr. 29, 1863	....	Under supervision of Common Council of Buffalo.
165	Sandy Hill Academy,*	Sandy Hill, Washington Co.,	May 26, 1836		
166	Saratoga Academy and Scientific Institute,*	Saratoga Springs, Saratoga Co.	Apr. 28, 1835		
167	Schaghticoke Seminary,*	Schaghticoke, Renssalaer Co.	May 4, 1836		
168	Schenectady Lyceum and Academy,*	Schenectady, Schenectady Co.	Mar. 21, 1837	Feb. 5, 1839	
169	Schenectady Union School,	Schenectady, Schenectady Co.	Apr. 9, 1856	Oct. 13, 1856	
170	Schenectady Young Ladies' Seminary,*	Schenectady, Schenectady Co.	Mar. 22, 1837	Feb. 5, 1839	
171	Schoharie Academy,	Schoharie, Schoharie county,	Apr. 28, 1837	Feb. 5, 1839	
172	Scientific and Military Acad. of the West. Dist.,*	Whitesboro', Oneida county,	Apr. 17, 1826	Jan. 9, 1829	
173	Seminary of the Genesee Conference,	Cazenovia, Madison county,	Apr. 6, 1825	Jan. 29, 1828	Name changed to Seminary of Genesee and Oneida Conference, March 24, 1829.
174	Seminary of the Genesee and Oneida Conference,	Cazenovia, Madison county,	Apr. 6, 1825	Jan. 29, 1828	Name changed to Oneida Conference Seminary, May 8, 1835.
175	Seminary of Our Lady of Angels,	——, Niagara county,	Apr. 20, 1863		
176	Seneca Falls Academy,	Seneca Falls, Seneca county,	Apr. 27, 1837	Feb. 5, 1839	
177	Seward Female Seminary of Rochester,*	Rochester, Monroe county,	Apr. 5, 1839	Feb. 11, 1840	
178	Skaneateles Academy,*	Skaneateles, Onondaga Co.,	Apr. 14, 1829		
179	Southold Academy,*	Southold, Suffolk county,	Apr. 21, 1837		
180	Spencertown Academy,	Spencertown, Columbia Co.,	May 13, 1845	Dec. 3, 1847	
181	Springville Academy,	Springville, Erie county,	Mar. 19, 1827	Jan. 26, 1830	Name changed by Legislature to Griffith Institute, March 16, 1866; by the Regents, to Griffith Academy, March 2, 1866.
182	S. S. Seward Institute	Florida, Orange county,	May 7, 1847	Feb. 4, 1848	

182	Steuben Academy,*	Steuben, Oneida county,	Apr. 17, 1826	Jan. 29, 1828	
183	Sullivan County Academy,*	Bloomingburgh, Sullivan Co.,	Apr. 5, 1828	Mar. 31, 1831	
184	Syracuse Academy,*	Syracuse, Onondaga county,	Apr. 28, 1835	Feb. 5, 1839	
185	Ten Broeck Free Academy,*	Franklinville, Cattaraugus Co.	Apr. 19, 1862	Apr. 19, 1862	
186	Tracy Female Institute,*	Rochester, Monroe county,	Apr. 17, 1857		
187	Troy Academy,	Troy, Rensselaer county,	May 5, 1834	Feb. 5, 1839	
188	Troy Episcopal Institute,*	Troy, Rensselaer county,	Apr. 13, 1839		
189	Troy Female Seminary,	Troy, Rensselaer county,	May 6, 1837	Jan. 30, 1838	
190	Turin Academy,	Turin, Lewis county,	Apr. 30, 1839		
191	Union Literary Society,	Belleville, Jefferson county,	Apr, 13, 1826	Jan. 5, 1830	Name changed to Union Academy of Belleville, October 13, 1859.
192	Utica Female Academy,*	Utica, Oneida county,	Apr. 28, 1837	Feb. 5, 1839	
193	Vernon Academy,	Vernon, Oneida county,	Apr, 18, 1838	Feb. 5, 1839	
194	Victory Academy,*	Victory, Cayuga county,	May 21, 1836		
195	Wallabout Select Gram. Sch., 7th ward, Brooklyn,*	Brooklyn, Kings county,	May 4, 1839		
196	Wallkill Academy,	Wallkill, Orange county,	May 26, 1841	Feb. 13, 1842	
197	Walworth Academy,	Walworth, Wayne county,	May 12, 1841	Apr. 19, 1843	
198	Waterford Academy,*	Waterford, Saratoga county,	Apr. 28, 1834	Feb. 6, 1839	
199	Waterloo Academy,*	Waterloo, Seneca county,	Apr. 11, 1842	Aug. 23, 1842	
200	Watertown Academy.	Watertown, Jefferson county,	May 2, 1835	....	Charter repealed February 19, 1841.
201	Weedsport Academy,*	Weedsport, Cayuga county,	Apr. 18, 1838		
202	Westfield Academy,	Westfield, Chautauqua county,	May 5, 1837	Feb, 5, 1839	
203	Westtown Academy,*	Westtown, Orange county,	Apr. 18, 1839	Jan. 30, 1840	
204	Whitehall Academy,*	Whitehall, Washington Co.,	Apr. 20. 1839		
205	White Plains Academy,*	White Plains, Westchest'r Co.,	Apr. 19, 1828	Jan. 26, 1830	
206	Windsor Academy,*	Windsor, Broome county,	May 16, 1837		
207	Wyomanock Female Seminary,*	New Lebanon, Columbia Co.,	Apr. 13, 1865		
208	Yates County Academy and Female Seminary,*	Penn Yan, Yates county,	Apr. 17, 1828	Jan. 25, 1830	

Summary of Academies.

Incorporated by Regents (excepting duplicate names),	222
Incorporated by Legislature (excepting duplicate names,	213
	435

Extinct.

Incorporated by Regents,	61
Incorporated by Legislature,	104
	165

[A number of other academies, incorporated by the Legislature, have never been received under the visitation of the Regents, and they have no direct means of determining whether they are extinct or not. The number actually reported to the Regents in each year, is a little more than two hundred.]

* Academies which have become extinct, or which have failed to make any report for some time past, and are believed to have suspended operations, if not already extinct.

DEPARTMENT OF PUBLIC INSTRUCTION.

The common school system of New York, dates from the year 1812, when the Legislature passed the first act on the subject. This act created the office of trustee, clerk and collector, for school-districts, which were to be formed by the division of towns into convenient districts. Each town was required to elect three Commissioners of Common Schools, whose first business was to form the school-districts. They were the financial officers of the schools, to whom was paid the public money for distribution to the districts, and to whom the trustees were required to report. In every town also there was to be elected from one to six Inspectors of Schools, who, together with the said Commissioners, had the supervision of schools, and the examination of teachers. The law imposed certain duties relating to the distribution of public money, of blanks and documents, and the making and collating of reports, upon Town Clerks, County Clerks, and County Treasurers. The office of State Superintendent of Common Schools was also created, and the Council of Appointment bestowed it upon GIDEON HAWLEY, who served until 1821.

Mr. HAWLEY prepared the forms and instructions, and set the system into practical operation. He found the law defective in some particulars, and especially in its administrative features, and in 1814 he submitted the draft of a law, creating no new officers, but amending the defects which impeded its easy and effective working. Among the amendments was one requiring the Boards of Supervisors to levy upon each of the towns a sum of money equal to the amount distributed to it from the income of the school fund. The law of 1812 had left it discretionary with the inhabitants of the towns to vote such sum, or not, as they pleased. The act of 1805, creating the school fund, had provided that no distribution of income should be made until it amounted to $50,000 annually. The law of 1814 made it compulsory on the Boards of Supervisors to levy on each town a sum equal to its distributive share of the school moneys, and also authorized the levy of a like sum, in addition thereto, if voted by the town. The trustees were required to have a school kept for three months at least, by the original act, and by the amended act, the failure to levy such sum of money worked a forfeiture of the school money for the county.

The original act was framed on the belief that the income of the school fund, and the tax for the same amount would maintain a school in each district for three months, and no provision was made for raising any money by district taxation or rate bill, to make up deficiencies, or support a school for a longer time. The amended law required the trustees to cause a school to be kept three months, to apply the school moneys to the payment of teachers' wages, and if there should be a deficiency, to collect it from the patrons of the schools, in proportion to the attendance of their children. The school age was between five and fifteen years. The income of the school fund amounted to $50,000 in 1813, but no distribution was made until 1815. The first annual report was made in 1813, but the first report that contained an abstract of the reports of the trustees and commissioners was made in 1816. Mr. HAWLEY was superseded in 1821 by the appointment of WELCOME ESLEECK in his place, but the Legislature the same year abolished the office of Superintendent, and made the Secretary of State, *ex officio*, Superintendent of Common Schools.

The most important amendment to the school law for several subsequent years was in 1822, when the right of appeal to the Superintendent in all questions arising under the school laws was given in terms not since materially changed. This provision was made on the suggestion of JOHN V. N. YATES, and it has prevented litigation, which would probably have overwhelmed the courts, and destroyed the school system. The school laws were revised in 1827, and form a chapter in the Revised Statutes. They remained substantially unaltered until 1841, when an act drawn by JOHN C. SPENCER was passed, creating the office of County Superintendent of Schools, to whom all appeals were to be first made, subject to revision by the State Superintendent. In 1843 the offices of Town Commissioner and Inspector were abolished, and a single officer called a Town Superintendent was substituted. In this year Teachers' Institutes, which have now become a part of the school system, were first held, although their legislative recognition was not made until 1847. The Legislature in 1847 abolished the office of County Superintendent, and required appeals to be brought directly to the State Superintendent, and the returns of the Town Superintendents to be made to County Clerks.

In 1849 the Legislature passed an act establishing Free Schools. The main feature of this act was the abolition of the rate bill, leaving the deficiency, after applying the public money to the payment of teachers' wages, to be made up by district taxation. The act was submitted to the people and approved by a vote of 249,872 in its favor, to 91,951 against it. Its opponents procured, in 1850, the passage of a law to repeal the Free School act, which being submitted to the people was defeated by a vote of 209,616 against repeal, and 184,308 for repeal. In 1851 the controversy was settled by a repeal of the law, and levying a State tax of $800,000, to be distributed with the school moneys in support of schools, instead of the county tax equal to the annual distribution from the school fund.

In 1854 the Legislature created a Department of Public Instruction, and placed at its head a Superintendent, elected by joint ballot of the Senate and Assembly. The school laws remained substantially as they were left by the revision of 1847, until 1856, when the office of School Commissioner was created, the office of Town Superintendent was abolished, and the Supervisors of the several towns were made the financial agents, to hold and pay out the school moneys apportioned by the School Commissioners, to the towns and districts for the support of schools. The School Commissioner districts were originally, and are now nearly the same as the assembly districts, but since 1856 some counties entitled to one member of Assembly have formed two commissioner districts, and other counties have more School Commissioners than Assemblymen. The number of Commissioners is 112, besides the Superintendents of city schools.

The general revision of the school law, in 1864, was an arrangement of the various existing statutes under proper titles and chapters, with such alterations and amendments as experience and the increased demand for educational privileges seemed imperatively to demand.

In 1866 the Legislature passed an act authorizing the taking of land for school-houses by right of eminent domain. The same thing had been done for many years in Massachusetts and other States.

In 1844 the State Normal School was established at Albany. It was organized during the summer, and opened on the 18th December. In 1863, the Oswego Training School was taken under the patronage of the State, and has been, by the Laws of 1866 and 1867, erected into a Normal School. Under chapter 466 of the Laws of 1866, four Normal Schools have been authorized, one at Fredonia, one at Brockport, one at Cortland, and one at Potsdam. The Legislature has also, by special acts in 1867, authorized the establishment of one at Geneseo and another at Buffalo.

In 1834 an act of the Legislature required the Regents of the University to apply the surplus income of the Literature Fund, beyond the sum of $12,000, to the education of common school teachers, by the distribution of it to such academies as should undertake their instruction.

In 1838 the income of the United States Deposit Fund was appropriated as follows, viz.: $110,000 to the payment of teachers' wages; $55,000 to the purchase of books for district libraries; to the Literature Fund, $28,000, to be expended for the education of common school teachers; to colleges, $15,000. It was supposed that the income would amount to $260,000, and that the residue would be $50,000, which was directed to be annually added to the capital of the School Fund. For several years the importunity of local institutions extracted from the Legislature appropriations so large that no surplus was left to be added to the capital of the School Fund. The Constitutional Convention of 1846 ordained that $25,000 annually should be set apart from the income of the United States Deposit Fund, and become a part of the capital of the School Fund. In 1840 Governor SEWARD estimated that the capital would be $3,000,000 by the year 1850. But it had increased from 1840 to 1846 only from $1,932,421.99 to $2,090,632.41, or $58,210.42. From 1846 to 1866, it increased to $2,799,630.04, or $708,997.63 in twenty years, being at the rate of $35,449.88. It will be seen that the $25,000 set apart by this Constitution from the income of the United States Deposit Fund has been the chief accretion of the Common School Fund, and that without it, the fund in 1866 would have reached only $2,299,630.04.

The Legislature of 1856 also substituted for the $800,000 State tax a levy of three-fourths of a mill upon every dollar of the valuation of real and personal estate. This law graduated the tax so that it would increase yearly with the increased valuation of the State. It made growing wealth contribute to educate the growing population.

By the law of 1812, the public money was paid to those districts only that should maintain a school for three months in the year, kept by a qualified teacher. In 1841 the time was increased to four months, in 1851 to six months, and in 1864 to twenty-eight weeks.

The law of the present year, abolishing rate bills and establishing free schools, has done away with that feature in the system which has been most prolific of dispute and controversy; which has imposed the heaviest and most perplexing duties upon trustees; which has been burdensome and odious to the poor; which has imposed an unequal and unjust tax upon the families more blessed in their children than in their basket and store; and which has been the great cause of irregular attendance and absenteeism. The following table exhibits the sums levied annually by rate bill since the year 1828:

Year.	Amount.	Year.	Amount.	Year.	Amount.
1828,...........	$297,048 49	1841,...........	$468,688 22	1854,............	$382,359 08
1829,...........	346,807 20	1842,...........	509,376 97	1855,............	461,779 13
1830,...........	374,001 54	1843,...........	447,565 97	1856,............	427,956 07
1831,...........	358,320 17	1844,...........	458,127 78	1857,............	390 515 50
1832,...........	369,696 36	1845,...........	460,764 78	1858 (9 months),.	318,353 41
1833,...........	398,137 04	1846,...........	462,840 74	1858–59,..........	414,062 72
1834,...........	419,878 69	1847,...........	466,674 85	1859–60,..........	420,257 98
1835,...........	425,643 61	1848,...........	489,696 63	1860–61,..........	397,215 87
1836,...........	436,346 46	1849,...........	508,724 56	1861–62,..........	407,009 57
1837,...........	477,875 27	1850,...........	136,949 59	1862–63,..........	363,741 05
1838,...........	521,477 49	1851,...........	224,971 71	1863–64,..........	429,892 52
1839,...........	476,443 27	1852,..........	308,851 30	1864–65,..........	655,158 78
1840,...........	475,000 00	1853,...........	330,190 93	1865–66,..........	709,025 36
Total,..........					$16,427,426 66

The average sum yearly collected by rate bill for the forty years, included in the table, is $410,685.66.

For the fourteen years prior to 1828, it is probable that the amount collected by rate bill was $250,000 a year; and we may reasonably suppose that the sum for the year ending September 30, 1867, will be $700,000. The aggregate will be, therefore, increased to $20,627,426.66 for fifty-four years, and the yearly average will be $381,989.38.

It will be observed that the sum raised by rate bill has uniformly exceeded, and generally quadrupled the amount distributed from the income of the Common School Fund. It has as regularly exceeded the whole public money apportioned from the School Fund, and the United States Deposit Fund, added to the county and town taxes, until the imposition of the State tax in 1851. The years to be excepted from these statements are 1850–1–2, the years of the free school controversy. The rate bill has been the special tax upon the patrons of the common schools. It may justly be styled a tax upon knowledge. The present law has merely transferred this burden from the fathers of families to the taxable property of the whole State.

The rate bill having been abolished, the common schools will hereafter be supported from the following sources:

1. The income of the Common School Fund.
2. The amount that the Legislature may annually set apart from the income of the United States Deposit Fund.
3. The General State Tax.
4. District, Village and City Taxation.
5. The income of Local Funds.

(1.) The revenue of the Common School Fund is about $170,000 a year. The distribution from it is at present $155,000 yearly.

(2.) The appropriation from the income of the United States Deposit Fund, is $165,000 annually; but it depends upon the Legislature, which may, at any time, divert the income to some other object.

(3.) The main dependence of the schools, so far as relates to the payment of teachers' wages, must be upon the State tax, which being now fixed at one and a quarter mills upon each dollar of valuation, will probably yield about two millions of dollars a year. The income of the two funds is about one-eighth of the sum annually needed to pay teachers.

(4.) District, village and city taxation is voluntary, and the amount raised annually varies with the exigencies of the year. The purchase of sites, the building of school-houses, and the furnishing of them with seats, desks, chairs, stoves, fuel and apparatus are all done by local taxation. No money has ever been appropriated for these objects from the income of the State funds, or the avails of the State tax.

(5.) The income of local funds, chiefly gospel and school lands, was last year $19,182.60. It does not vary much from year to year.

Apportionment.

The public moneys apportioned annually, are the income of the School Fund, and the United States Deposit Fund, and the proceeds of the State tax.

The Superintendent of Public Instruction, after ascertaining the amount to be apportioned—

(1.) Sets apart from the income of the United States Deposit Fund the amount necessary to pay the salaries of the School Commissioners.

(2.) To *each* city 'having a Superintendent of Common Schools, or clerk doing the duty of supervision, the sum of five hundred dollars for each member of Assembly to which the city is entitled.

(3.) The library money appropriated by the Legislature.

(4.) He then sets apart from the *Free School Fund* two thousand dollars for a contingent fund.

(5.) He then sets apart for the support of Indian schools an equitable sum, the same in proportion to their numbers that is apportioned to schools for white children.

(6.) He then ascertains the total of the sums so apportioned, and deducts it from the aggregate of school moneys appropriated, and divides the remainder into two parts, one equal to one-third thereof, and one to two-thirds.

(7.) The one-third thereof is distributed to the districts, each district in which a school has been taught twenty-eight weeks by a qualified teacher to have one share, and an additional share for every additional qualified teacher who has taught the said term; and the term may be completed by a succession of qualified teachers.

(8.) He then apportions the remaining two-thirds, and also the library money, among the several counties according to their population, excluding Indians, as it appears from the State or United States census, last previously made; but in counties where there are cities having special school acts, separate apportionments are made, the one to the city and the other to the rest of the county.

(9.) There are four separate neighborhoods to which he apportions a sum, deemed equitable, out of the contingent fund.

When the apportionment is completed he certifies to the County Clerk, County Treasurer and to the School Commissioners, and to City Chamberlains or Treasurers, the amount apportioned to each county and city. The apportionment is payable on the first day of February after it is made.

The School Commissioners of a county, having received such certificate, meet and proceed to apportion the money to the several districts.

(1.) They set apart to each district the "district quotas" allowed by the State Superintendent.

(2.) They set apart any sums of money assigned to any districts as equitable allowances.

(3.) Deducting the above sums from the money applicable to the payment of teachers' wages, they divide the remainder into two equal parts, one of which is apportioned to the districts in proportion to the number of children residing in them between the ages of 5 and 21 years. The other half is then apportioned to the districts according to the average daily attendance of resident pupils.

(4.) They also apportion the library money according to the number of resident children between 5 and 21 years.

Having then signed their apportionment in duplicate, they deliver one copy to the County Treasurer, and send one to the Superintendent of Public Instruction.

They also certify to the Supervisor of each town the amount of school money apportioned to his town, the portions thereof to be paid by him for library money and for teachers' wages, to each district and separate neighborhood.

Organization.

The school-district is the smallest territorial subdivision of the State. It is formed by the School Commissioner, who makes an order defining its boundaries, and files it in the office of the Town Clerk of the town or towns in which it is situated. The Commissioner may alter a district by a similar order, a copy of which must be served on the trustees of the districts affected. If they give their written assent, the order takes effect immediately, or on any day named therein, not between October 1st and April 1st, thereafter. If they withhold their assent, it may take effect on any day named therein, not less than three months from its date, but not between October 1st and April 1st, thereafter. But the trustees, on receiving notice of the order, and of a day and place when their objections may be heard, may request the Supervisor and Town Clerk of the town or towns within which the district is situated to be present. The decision of this joint meeting is final unless appealed from, and must either confirm or vacate the Commissioner's order. The decision must be filed in the Town Clerk's office.

A joint district is one that lies partly in two or more counties.

A neighborhood is a small subdivision whose inhabitants are permitted to send their children to a school in an adjoining State.

Union free school-districts are formed under the law that authorizes the inhabitants, lawfully assembled in district meeting, to organize in a district comprising more territory and inhabitants, and possessing more enlarged powers than an ordinary district.

About 100 districts have been formed by act of the Legislature, granting special powers and privileges.

The inhabitants, at the annual district meeting to be held on the second Tuesday of October in each year, have power to elect a chairman, one or three Trustees, a District Clerk, a Collector and Librarian. They have the power to designate a site for a school-house, to vote taxes to pay for a site, and to build and repair school-houses, and to furnish them with fuel and appendages, and to make up deficiencies for previous taxes. They may also vote taxes not exceeding $25, for apparatus and text-books, $10 for library, $25 for contingent expenses, and any sum necessary to insure the school-house, furniture, books and apparatus, and to pay the costs of prosecuting and defending suits in which the district is interested, and the reasonable expenses incurred therein by district officers. By chapter 406, of the Laws of 1867, the money necessary to support the schools, after the public school moneys have been applied, is to be raised by district taxation.

The Librarian is elected for one year, and has charge of the district library.

The Collector serves for a year, gives a bond for the faithful discharge of his duties, which consist in collecting the moneys due on tax lists, and holding them subject to the order of the trustees.

The Clerk holds office for a year. It is his duty to keep a record of the district meetings; to call annual and special meetings; to attend the meetings of trustees, and keep a record of their proceedings; to notify persons of their election to office; to report to the Town Clerk the names and post-office address of district officers; to give trustees notice of every resignation accepted by the Supervisor; and to keep and preserve all the records, books and papers belonging to the office.

The district may elect one or three trustees. If it decide to have but one, he is elected for one year, and thenceforth the district can elect but one trustee. If it decide to have three trustees, their term of office is three years, one to be elected annually. The three trustees act as a board. The sole trustee has the same power as a board of three. The sole trustee, or the board, holds the property of the district as a corporation.

The powers and duties of trustees are to call meetings; to make out tax lists and warrants; to purchase sites, and build or hire school-houses; to insure district property; to have the custody and safe keeping of the school-house and other property; to contract with and employ teachers, and pay them; and generally to attend to all the business of the district.

All children between the ages of five and twenty-one years residing in the district may attend school; and non-residents, by the written consent of the trustees, may attend on such terms as may be prescribed by the trustees.

None but a qualified teacher can receive public money in payment for his wages. A qualified teacher is one who holds a diploma from a State Normal School, a certificate from the Superintendent of Public Instruction, or from a School Commissioner, or from the city or village officer empowered to grant one. Such certificates and diplomas are good for the time, and for the grade named therein, but may be canceled and annulled, and thus rendered invalid.

Teachers are required to keep school lists of all pupils, showing their daily attendance in the schools.

The trustees of each school-district are required, between the first and fifteenth days of October, in every year, to make and direct to the School Commissioner a report in writing, dated on the first day of October of the year in which it is made, and to sign and certify it, and deliver it to the clerk of the town in which the school-house of the district is situate; and every such report must certify:

1. The whole time any school has been kept in their district during the year ending on the day previous to the date of such report, and distinguishing what portion of the time such school has been kept by qualified teachers, and the whole number of days, including holidays, in which the school was taught by qualified teachers.

2. The amount of their drafts upon the Supervisor, for the payment of teachers' wages during such year, and the amount of their drafts upon him for the purchase of books and school apparatus during such year, and the manner in which such moneys have been expended.

3. The number of children taught in the district school or schools during such year by qualified teachers, and the sum of the days' attendance of all such children upon the school.

4. The number of children residing in the district on the last day of September previous to the making of such report, between the ages of five and twenty-one, and the names of the parents or other persons with whom such children respectively reside, and the number of children residing with each.

5. The amount of money paid for teachers' wages, in addition to the public money paid therefor, the amount of taxes levied in said district for purchasing school-house sites, for building, hiring, purchasing, repairing and insuring school-houses, for fuel for district libraries, or for any other purposes allowed by law, and such other information in relation to the schools and the district as the Superintendent of Public Instruction may from time require.

The Town Clerk is required to keep in his office all books, maps, papers and records touching schools; to record in a book the certificate of apportionment of school moneys; to notify the Trustees of the filing of such certificate; to obtain from Trustees their annual reports; to furnish the School Commissioner with the names and post-office address of all district officers; to distribute to trustees all books and blanks forwarded to him for their use; to file and record the final accounts of Supervisors; to preserve the Supervisor's bond; to file and keep the description of district boundaries; and when called upon, to take part in the erection or alteration of a school-district.

The Supervisor is vested with the powers formerly possessed by the Trustees of Gospel and School Lots, and with the powers imposed by the act of 1829, in relation to moneys in the hands of the Overseers of the Poor. The school moneys apportioned to the several towns are paid over by the County Treasurer to the Supervisor, who gives a bond, with two sureties, in the penalty of double the amount of money set apart to the town, for the safe keeping, disbursement, and accounting for of such moneys, and all other school moneys that may come into his hands.

The school moneys apportioned to a county are paid by the State Treasurer on the warrant of the Superintendent of Public Instruction; the Treasurer's check on the bank in which the money is deposited is countersigned by the Superintendent and made payable to the order of the Country Treasurer.

The School Commissioners are elected in separate districts originally formed by the Boards of Supervisors, but now established by law. The number of Commissioners is one hundred and twelve. Their term of office is three years.

They have power, and it is their duty, to see that the boundaries of districts are correctly described; to visit and examine the schools; to advise with and counsel the trustees; to look after the condition of the school-houses, and condemn such as are entirely unfit for use; to recommend studies and text-books; to examine and license teachers; to examine charges against teachers, and, on sufficient proof, annul their certificates; and, when required by the Superintendent, to take and report testimony in cases of appeal. It is also their duty, annually, to apportion and divide among the districts the school moneys apportioned to their respective counties by the Superintendent of Public Instruction.

The Superintendent of Public Instruction is elected by joint ballot of the Senate and Assembly. He holds office for three years; has general superintendence of the public schools, visits them, inquires into their management, and advises and directs in regard to their course of instruction and discipline. He apportions and distributes the public moneys appropriated by the State for the support of schools; examines the supplementary apportionments made to all the districts by the School Commissioners, and sees that to each district is set apart its proportionate share, and that the same is expended by the trustees, and paid by the Supervisors of towns, according to law. He gives advice and direction to school officers, teachers and inhabitants upon all questions arising under the school laws. He establishes rules and regulations concerning appeals. He hears and decides all appeals, involving school controversies, that are brought before him, and his decision is final. He is charged with the general control and management of Teachers' Institutes in the several counties of the State; is authorized to employ teachers and lecturers for the Institutes, and to pay them, and to certify the accounts for expenses incurred by the Commisioners in conducting the same. He is required by the law to visit the Institutes and to advise and direct concerning their proper management. He establishes rules and regulations concerning district school libraries; he makes appointments of State pupils to the institutions for the instruction of the deaf and dumb and for the blind, upon the certificate of the proper local officers; and he visits and examines into the condition and management of these institutions. He is chairman of the executive committee of the State Normal School at Albany, and apportions among the counties the number of pupils to which each is entitled. He is one of the board for the selection of the places in which to establish four additional normal schools. After the schools are established he has general supervision and direction of them; he appoints the local board to manage them; he approves the rules for their government; he directs the form of their reports; and all payments for their support are paid upon his certificate. He approves the course of study; the number of teachers and their wages are subject to his approval; he can cause one or more of the schools to be composed of males, and one or more of females, in his discretion; and he decides upon the manner in which pupils shall be admitted from the several parts of the State. He has similar powers over the Oswego, the Buffalo and Geneseo Normal Schools. He has charge of all the Indian Schools in the State, employs local agents to superintend them, visits them, and directs concerning the erection and repair of their school-houses, and determines the branches of instruction to be pursued in the schools. He is, *ex officio*, a Regent of the University and chairman of the committee on teachers' classes in academies. He is also, *ex officio*, a member of the Board of Trustees of the Idiot Asylum, the People's College, and the Cornell University. He receives and compiles the abstracts of the reports from all the school-districts in the State, setting forth their condition and proceedings, and the account of receipts and expenditures for each year. He makes annually to the Legislature a report of the condition of all the schools and institutions under his supervision, and recommends such measures as in his judgment will contribute to their welfare and efficiency.

Attendance.

The following table exhibits the attendance of pupils at the Academies and Common Schools since 1839. The second column shows the number of pupils pursuing classical studies at the several dates; the third column shows the number instructed in the Common Schools:

DATE.	Classical pupils in Academies.	Pupils attending Common Schools.	DATE.	Classical pupils in Academies.	Pupils attending Common Schools.
1839,	7,070	572,995	1853,	20,977	844,186
1840,	8,842	603,583	1854,	22,675	856,512
1841,	10,186	598,749	1855,	22,788	830,491
1842,	10,560	657,782	1856,	18,051	832,735
1843,	11,277	709,156	1857,	20,860	842,137
1844,	11,699	736,045	1858,	21,633	599,229
1845,	12,257	742,433	1859,	20,571	851,533
1846,	13,481	748,387	1860,	21,125	867,388
1847,	13,998	775,723	1861,	22,335	872,854
1848,	14,262	778,309	1862,	22,685	892,550
1849,	15,043	794,500	1863,	21,314	886,815
1850,	16,514	726,291	1864,	21,548	881,184
1851,	17,912	832,481	1865,	21,947	916,617
1852,	19,552	622,268	1866,	23,035	919,309

The whole number of pupils under instruction in the State during the year 1866 was 1,019,069, of whom 1,541 were in the colleges, 36,465 in the academies, 61,754 in private schools, and 919,309 in the common schools. The per cent which each number bears to the aggregate is as follows:

In the colleges,	.00151
In the academies,	.03578
In the private schools,	.06060
In the common schools,	.90211
	1.0000

Nothing could more conclusively show the paramount importance of the common schools.

The number of different teachers employed in 1866 was 26,494, of whom 5,062 were males, and 21,432 females. The number actually necessary to supply all the schools, if each teacher should teach throughout the year, is 15,666.

The schools were in session on an average during the year, in the cities, forty-three weeks, and in the rural districts, thirty-two weeks and two days.

Progress of the School System.

The following table exhibits a comparative statement of the progress of the State in population, wealth and education for the past fifty years, by decades, from 1815, when the school system went into practical operation. The population has nearly quadrupled. The assessed valuation of property is nearly seven times as great; and doubtless the actual value of property is ten times as much. The number of school-districts is five times as many; and the whole surface of the State, with the exception of the northern wilderness, which roads and canals have not yet opened to settlement and cultivation, has been mapped into districts.

The first four decades show more children taught than were enumerated. The cause of this apparent anomaly is that the school age was between four and sixteen until 1851, when it was changed from four to twenty-one.

The gross expenditures for the support of common schools cannot be accurately stated for the time prior to 1854, because the trustees had not been required to make returns of the cost of sites and school-houses; of the expense of fuel, repairs and furniture; of the amount of local taxation; and of the salaries and fees of school officers.

YEAR.	Population.	Valuation of real and personal estate.	Number of school districts.	Number of children of school age.	Number of children taught.	School fund income distributed.	Money raised by State and county taxation, and distributed.	Gross expenditures of all kinds for the support of schools.	Number of volumes in the district school libraries.
1815,.....	1,035,910	$292,388,827	2,631	176,449	140,106	$60,000	....	....	....
1825,.....	1,614,458	299,197,721	7,642	395,586	402,940	80,000	$80,000	....	....
1835,.....	2,174,517	527,531,634	10,207	538,398	541,401	100,000	100,000	$739,020	....
1845,.....	2,604,495	605,646,095	11,018	703,399	742,433	110,000	193,503	1,191,697	1,203,139
1855,.....	3,466,212	1,402,849,304	11,798	1,214,113	945,087	155,000	800,000	4,679,815	1,418,100
1865,.....	3,831,777	1,550,879,685	11,780	1,398,757	916,617	155,000	1,148,422	7,383,606	1,181,811

An item small in each case, but large in the aggregate, does not appear. Every pupil must be supplied with text-books. The expense of supplying all the pupils in the common schools, cannot fall short of one million of dollars a year.

The value of the school-houses and school-house sites is reported as follows:

YEARS.	Cities.	Rural Districts.	Total.
In 1866,...	$6,720,535	$5,534,422	$12,254,957
In 1865,...	5,041,061	4,904,862	9,945,923

The difference between the valuation of 1865 and 1866, is not due to an actual increase in the number and value of the houses and sites, but to the incomplete returns of 1865. The valuation of 1866 is not quite complete.

The burden of local taxation for buying sites, building houses, for repairing, furnishing and insuring, for fencing and out-houses, will appear from the fact that in 1866 the amount expended for such purpose was $970,224.68; and that the amount thus expended for the last ten years was $6,980,743.40.

The number of school-houses in 1866 was reported as 181 log-houses, 9,815 frame houses, 1,021 brick houses, and 530 stone houses. The value of the sites and the houses, was reported at $6,720,535 in the cities, and $5,534,422 in the rural districts, a total of $12,254,957.

What is a Common School?

The law of 1812, although entitled "An act for the establishment of Common Schools," did not contain any definition of "common school." Nor has any subsequent act given a statutory definition.

The term is found in Gov. GEORGE CLINTON'S message to the Legislature in 1795. He says, "While it is evident that the general establishment and liberal endowment of academies are highly to be commended, and are attended with the most beneficial consequences, yet it cannot be denied that they are principally confined to the children of the opulent, and that a great proportion of the community is excluded from their immediate advantages. The establishment of common schools throughout the State is happily calculated to remedy this inconvenince, and will therefore re-engage your early and decided consideration."

In pursuance of this recommendation, an act was passed April 9, 1795, entitled "An act for the encouragment of Schools," which appropriated $50,000 annually for five years, "for the purpose of encouraging and maintaining schools in the several cities and towns in this State, in which the children of the inhabitants residing in the State, shall be instructed in the English language, or be taught English grammar, arithmetic, mathematics, and such other branches of knowledge as are most useful and necessary to complete a good English education." This act was enforced for three years, and no longer, and was not re-enacted. It will be observed that the only limitation is "a good English education," without confining the range of studies.

The act of 1814 copies substantially the language of the act of 1812, and all we can learn as to the meaning of "Common School" must be gathered from the context, and from a comparison of subsequent acts with them and with each other.

The two acts of 1812 and 1814 recognized the Lancaster School of Albany as a common school. All the Lancaster Schools in the State subsequently incorporated were also recognized as common schools.

The general school law of 1812 and 1814 did not include the city of New York. A supplementary act, passed March 12, 1813 (chapter 52), permitted the city to share in the distribution of the School Fund, providing for the appointment of commissioners to distribute the school moneys, and to make reports of the condition of the schools to the Superintendent of Common Schools. The school moneys were required to be distributed and paid "to the trustees of the Free School Society of the city of New York, and the trustees or treasurers of the Orphans' Asylum Society, the Society of the Economical School in the city of New York, the African Free School, and of such incorporated religious societies in said city as now support or hereafter shall establish charity schools within the said city, who may apply for the same." It must be held, therefore, that the Legislature considered these and similar schools, especially the Lancaster

Schools and the schools kept in orphan asylums, common schools, although outside of the common school system.

In the city of New York the public money was given to the Free School Society and the other schools, on the condition that gratuitous education should be given to pupils for nine months in the year. But the theory on which such education was given in New York was that only the children of the poor should be received into such schools. In fact, gratuitous education was given in all the schools to all comers. The act of 1842, chapter 150, that embraced in the general system the city of New York, did not deprive the public school society, nor any of the incorporated societies, of any rights or privileges previously granted or possessed, but continued to them the same share in the bounty of the State. The common schools — or more strictly, the ward schools — were made free schools like the schools of the public school society. The rate bill never was applied to the support of the New York city schools. They were always common schools, and substantially free schools. The charter of the Free School Society was altered in 1826, and the society was required to provide for the education of all children without regard to the sect or denomination to which their parents might belong. As this change would admit pupils who could not be classed among indigent persons, the society was permitted to charge a "moderate compensation adapted to the abilities of the parents of the children." The prices charged for a few years ranged from twenty-five cents to two dollars per quarter. In 1831–32 the last money was collected, being $839. After that date a city tax yielded money enough, together with the moneys received from the State, to make them entirely free. Other cities, one after another, established free schools.

But the common schools of the State, under the general law, were never free, except for the short time that the law of 1849 continued in force.

The act of April 12, 1851, entitled "An act to establish Free Schools throughout the State," was falsely so entitled. Its only difference from the system of 1812 and 1814 was in the substitution of a State tax for county and town taxation. The evidence in proof of the misnomer of the title may be seen in the collections by rate bill, from which it appears that from $300,000 to $700,000 annually have been drawn from the fathers of families, the patrons of the schools, by the pressure of the rate bill screw.

The range of studies in the common schools has been gradually enlarged, as the system has grown and expanded, until it includes the ancient and modern languages, and all the sciences.

The idea of a common school, as expressed in the law of 1795, and as intended in the law of 1812 and 1814, has its only expression now in our ordinary district schools in the country, and in the primary schools of the cities and villages. The union free schools in many of our villages, the graded schools, and high schools in villages and cities, take rank with the very best academies, and excel them in the good scholarship of the pupils. This is especially true of the high schools to which only the best scholars from the primary and graded schools are admitted. In the city of New York the common school system extends over the whole field of instruction, from the primary school to the college of the city of New York, including every department of human knowledge. The common school is no longer a school for teaching merely "those branches of knowledge most useful and necessary to complete a good English education," unless a good English education embraces everything that can fit a man for any station or employment in life. A common school must therefore be whatever school the Legislature by law may include in the general system of schools.

The Supreme Court, in 1851, at the October term, in Kings county, undertook to do what the Legislature had never done. The judicial definition of a common school is as follows: "The word 'common,' as applied to our schools, bears the broadest and most comprehensive signification. It is equivalent to *public, universal, open to all;* for such is their character, subject only to such general statutory regulations as are prescribed by the Legislature. They are common to all children, in the sense that public highways are common to all persons who may choose to ride or drive thereon, observing only the law of the road. Thus have they been treated by the Legislature in the various enactments on the subject. They have been always kept distinct from academies, colleges, and private seminaries of learning; and especially have they been kept free from everything savoring of sectarian influence or control."

This definition is in the main correct, although not strictly true. The school moneys have been paid since 1814 to the trustees of Erasmus Hall, an academy in Flatbush, Kings county, on condition that the trustees should apply them to the education of such poor children in that part called the "Old Town," as in their opinion were entitled to gratuitous education. The trustees of Montgomery Academy, in the town of Montgomery, Orange county, also received, from the year 1815, the school moneys which were apportioned to district number seven, and the law does not appear to have been repealed. The Lancastrian schools, until they surrrendered their charters, and were superseded by free schools, were treated as common schools, and shared in the distribution of the school fund. Many incorporated schools and orphan asylums, from the beginning, were regarded as common schools, received, and still participate in, the school moneys.

In 1834, also, the Legislature, by chapter 241, of the Session Laws, ordered the revenue of the Literature Fund then in the treasury, and the excess of the annual revenue thereafter, over the sum of twelve thousand dollars, to be expended in educating teachers of common schools in the academies, in such manner and under such regulations as the Regents of the University might prescribe. In 1838, $28,000 from the United States Deposit Fund was ordered to be distributed annually with the revenue of the Literature Fund, partly with a view to the education of common school teachers. In 1849, a further appropriation was made to the academies for the purpose of educating common school teachers, and the appropriation has been continued yearly ever since, amounting to sums varying from $14,000 to $19,000 a year. Hence it appears that the Court was not strictly correct in its statement that the common schools have been kept distinct from the academies. It has been gravely questioned whether the connection has been beneficial either to the academies or to the common schools, and whether it would not have been better if Normal and training schools had been established as a part of the common school system.

The Court was equally unhappy in its illustration. The schools were not "common to all children in the sense that public highways are common to all persons who may choose to ride or drive thereon, observing only the law of the road;" but were common to all children in the sense that turnpikes and railroads are common to all persons who pay the toll or fare.

And they have never been common to all children, for, although sectarianism has been excluded, they have been shut against colored children, who have always and uniformly been provided with separate schools from which white children are excluded. For fifty years, also, the Legislature has directed the establishment of schools for the children of the Indians on their several reservations, and has partly supported them from the revenue of the School Fund, and yet they are for Indian children exclusively, and white children are not permitted to attend them.

QUARANTINE.

The administration of this department is now by law vested in a Health Officer and three Commissioners of Quarantine.

They are each appointed by the Governor and Senate, and the term of office of the former is two years, and that of the latter three years. (Laws of 1863, p. 573.)

Quarantine in this port existed under the Colonial Government by legislative authority, and was established by State authority as early as 1784. (Act of May 4, 1784, 1 Greenleaf, 117.)

It has been a subject of frequent legislation since that time, as a reference to the following acts will show:

Act of	March	27, 1794,	3 Greenleaf,	144.
do	April	1, 1796,	do	305.
do	February	10, 1797,	do	367.
do	March	28, 1797,	do	433.
do	March	30, 1797,	do	450.
do	April	1, 1800,	1 W. and S.,	171.
do	March	30, 1801,	do	371.
do	February	28, 1804,	3 W., 471, Stat.,	17.
do	April	8, 1811,	6 W. and S.,	247.
do	April	14, 1820,	Statutes,	208.
do	March	23, 1821,	do	126.
do	March	21, 1823,	do	64.

Revised Statutes concerning, 1 R. S., 427.

Act of	May	7, 1839,	Statutes,	331.
do	December	15, 1847,	do	716.
do	April	10, 1850,	do	597.
do	April	9, 1856,	do	230.
do	March	6, 1857,	do	163.
do	April	29, 1863,	do	573.
do	April	25, 1864,	do	899.
do	April	28, 1865,	do	1205.
do	April	21, 1866,	do	1625.
do	April	22, 1867.		

The act of April 21, 1796 created the Health Officer *eo nomine*, and the office has existed ever since that time.

The same act authorized the appointment of *seven* Commissioners of Health of the city of New York, who in conjunction with the Health Officer constituted the executive officers of quarantine, the latter being the chief executive officer.

By the act of February 10, 1797, the number of Commissioners was reduced to *three*.

The act of March 30, 1801, declared that there should continue to be a Health Officer in the city of New York, under the superintendence of *three* Commissioners, to consist of the Health Officer, a Physician to be styled the Resident Physician, and one other person.

The duties of the Commissioners under the above acts, related mainly to the general care and management of the quarantine hospital, and to the receipts and expenditures of the moneys appropriated or authorized to be received for quarantine purposes.

The act of April 8, 1811, made a change in the management of quarantine by placing the health office under the superintendence of the Board of Health of the city, and *three* Health Commissioners, who were made *ex officio* members of the Board. The Commissioners were to consist of the Health Officer, who was to reside on Staten Island, a Resident Physician, to reside in the city, and a Health Commissioner, who was to take charge of the receipt and disbursement of all moneys appropriated to the use of the Marine Hospital.

The duties of the Health Officer under this act were substantially the same as under previous acts. He was the chief sanitary officer at quarantine, and attended to the boarding and examination of vessels, and determining the period of quarantine and sanitary measures to which a vessel should be subject.

The control and management of quarantine continued to be vested in the above-mentioned officers without any substantial change, except in the manner of organizing the Board of Health, and except that certain powers were conferred upon the Commissioners of Health to be exercised by them in conjunction with the Mayor of the city, when the Board of Health were not in session, down to 1847.

By the act of December 15th of that year, the entire custody and control of the Marine Hospital was vested in the Commissioners of Emigration, and it continued under their control down to the time of its destruction by fire in September, 1858. The transfer of the control of the Marine Hospital to the Commissioners of Emigration did not, however, deprive the Board of Health, or the Mayor and Commissioners of Health, of the powers they exercised in reference to quarantine, except so far as they related to the Marine Hospital.

The act of 1856 made a slight change in the supervision or control to be exercised by the Mayor and Commissioners over the acts of the Health Officer. Acts which before that time could be performed by him only, with the concurrence of the Mayor *and* Commissioners of Health, could, under that act, be performed with the consent either of the Mayor *or* Commissioners of Health.

By the act of 1863, the entire management of quarantine was placed under the control of the Health Officer and *three* Commissioners of Quarantine, and it has ever since continued under their control.

COMMISSIONERS OF EMIGRATION.

The Board of Emigration, called the Commissioners of Emigration of the State of New York, was organized in pursuance of an act passed May 5, 1847, entitled "An act concerning passengers in vessels coming to the city of New York, and intended for the greater protection of alien emigrants arriving at this port." Under the provisions of that act the board was made to consist of ten members, six appointed by the Governor, by and with the consent of the Senate, to hold office for six years, and four *ex officio* members, consisting of the Mayors of New York and Brooklyn, and the Presidents of the German and Irish Emigrant Societies. It is made the duty of this Commission to provide for the care and maintenance of all sick and destitute alien passengers, for whom commutation has been paid, during a period of five years after their arrival. The funds for the purpose are furnished by the aforesaid commutation, which is a *per capita* tax on every alien passenger, in lieu of an indemnity bond, by act of May 5, 1847, of $1; afterward, by act of July 11, 1851, increased to $1.50; again, by act of April 13, 1863, increased to $2; and finally, by act of April, 1867, fixed at $2.50. Within twenty-four hours after arrival, the master of every vessel carrying emigrant passengers is required to report in writing, on oath, a list of all such passengers, together with the name, birthplace, last legal residence, age and occupation of each, and within the same period the amount of commutation must be paid to the Chamberlain of the City of New York, or bonds executed.

Furthermore, for a certain class of emigrants, such as lunatics, idiots, deaf and dumb, blind, infirm persons, or persons liable from attending circumstances to become a public charge, a special bond of $500 must be given by said master, with two sufficient securities, conditioned to indemnify every city, town and county in the State for the support of said passengers during a period of five years after arrival, which bond may also be commuted in the discretion of the Commissioners. The Commission is also required to indemnify the several counties of the State for the support of all emigrants for whom commutation has been paid during a period of five years after arrival. Under this law, they have disbursed to the several counties since 1847 over $1,000,000. The whole number of emigrants landed at the port of New York since the creation of the Commission is 3,640,000, of whom over 1,040,000 have received the assistance and protection of the Commission.

The buildings under the charge of the Commission consist of the receiving depot at Castle Garden, held under lease from the city of New York, and the hospitals and refuge buildings, asylum for lunatics, &c., on Ward's Island, about one-half of which is land, *i. e.*, one hundred and ten acres are held by the Commissioners in fee as trustees for the State. These buildings furnish accommodations for about eight hundred sick and a like number of destitute emigrants. At Castle Garden all emigrants are required by law to be landed, nor is any communication with them permitted until after they are so landed and have been properly examined and recorded by the officers of the Commission.

In Castle Garden the emigrant is afforded all needful information and facilities for procuring suitable employment. Their baggage is received and cared for, and opportunity is afforded them of exchanging their money at the current rates. Responsible railroad agents, representing the Trunk lines as follows: New York Central Railroad, New York and Erie Railway, Pennsylvania and New Jersey Central Railroad Companies, are admitted, to furnish them transportation to their several places of destination; and a limited number of boarding-house keepers, under such checks and safeguards as have secured the emigrant from the frauds and extortions to which in all these matters he was formerly exposed.

The accompanying table will furnish all the desired statistical information.

The following is a list of the present members of the Board:

Commissioners of Emigration.	Ex officio Commissioners of Emigration.
Gulian C. Verplanck, President. Wilson G. Hunt, Vice President. Frederick S. Winston, Cyrus H. Lourtrel, Isaac T. Smith. Frederick Kapp.	Richard O'Gorman, Pres. Irish Em. Society. Philip Bessinger, President German Society. John T. Hoffman, Mayor New York city. Samuel Booth, Mayor Brooklyn city.

Statistics of the Commissioners of the Board of Emigration, from 1847 to 1866 inclusive.

YEARS.	*NUMBER OF VESSELS ARRIVED.			Number of emigrants arrived.	NUMBER OF PERSONS TREATED, CARED FOR, FORWARDED, ETC., CLASSIFIED UNDER DIFFERENT HEADS.			
	Sailing vessels.	Steam-ships.	Total.		Number treated and cared for at Emigrant Refuge and Hospital, &c., Ward's Island.	Number treated at Marine Hospital, Staten Island.	Number supplied temporarily in New York city with board and lodging.	Number temporarily relieved with money, &c., in New York city.
1847,......	......	.....	......	129,062	1,629	6,474	†	503
1848,......	1,041	.....	1,041	189,176	4,057	8,661	†	6,640
1849,......	1,651	.....	1,651	220,603	8,320	6,159	†	16,854
1850,......	1,912	.....	1,912	212,796	10,156	3,411	27,314	†
1851,......	1,712	.....	1,712	289,601	14,939	6,343	23,941	†
1852,......	1,662	.....	1,662	300,992	15,182	8,887	117,568	†
1853,......	1,618	.....	1,618	284,945	14,365	4,796	24.317	20,197
1854,......	1,566	.....	1,566	319,223	15,950	4,762	51,569	17,516
1855,......	1,626	.....	1,626	136,233	12,901	2,402	59,520	34,405
1856,......	552	22	574	142,342	7,610	1,648	11,093	79
1857,......	588	69	657	183,773	8,539	1,856	5,108	303
1858,......	367	84	451	78,589	6,906	1,204	5,731	413
1859,......	332	105	437	79,322	4,361	‡274	3,860	722
1860,......	373	109	482	105,162	4,729	......	5,115	122
1861,......	358	95	453	65,539	5,079	......	6,084	93
1862,......	370	100	470	76,306	3,247	......	3,649	......
1863,......	371	170	541	156,844	4,911	......	6,660	......
1864,......	349	197	546	182,296	7,363	......	4,317	......
1865,......	302	257	559	196,352	7,425	......	5,860	......
1866,......	349	401	750	233,418	10,306	......	12,487	......
	17,099	1,609	18,708	3,582,574	167,975	56,877	372,193	97,847

* In the annual report for 1866 will be found statistics of the relative proportions of passengers on sailing and steam vessels since 1856 (table C, p. 74), and relative mortality on sailing and steam vessels (table F, p. 82) of the report cited. The total number of arrivals of steamers under different flags, from 1856 to 1866, both inclusive, was: United States, 50; Great Britain, 1.048; Bremen, 162; Hamburgh, 241; Belgium, 11, and France 6.

During the year 1866, 27,507 emigrants arrived in steamers, as cabin, and 156,931 as steerage passengers. In sailing vessels, there were 636 of the former, and 74,898 of the latter. The number of births on the passage was 245, and of deaths 1,667.

The percentage of deaths from different ports was:

From	Antwerp,	55 deaths	among	2,117	steerage passengers,	or about	2	1-2	per cent.
do	Bremen,	129 do	do	21,548	do	do	do	5-8	do
do	Havre,	99 do	do	6,280	do	do	do 1	3-5	do
do	Hamburgh,	387 do	do	14,335	do	do	do 2	5-7	do
do	London,	46 do	do	4,335	do	do	do	11-16	do
do	Liverpool,	116 do	do	24,167	do	do	do	1-2	do
do	Rotterdam	18 do	do	1,042	do	do	do 1	5-7	do

† During the years marked thus (†) no statistics were kept.

‡ In the year 1859 the buildings ceased to be used for hospital purposes.

Statistics of the Com'rs of the Board of Emigration — (Continued).

YEARS.	NUMBER OF PERSONS TREATED, CARED FOR, FORWARDED, ETC., CLASSIFIED UNDER DIFFERENT HEADS.					REPORT OF MORTALITY AMONG EMIGRANTS AFTER ADMISSION TO INSTITUTIONS ON WARD'S ISLAND AND TO MARINE HOSPITAL, STATEN ISLAND, AND DURING THE VOYAGE.				
	Number provided at labor exchange of Com'rs of Emigration with employment.	Number of persons forwarded to destinat'n inland and to Europe.	Number treated in other institutions of this city at expense of this commission.	Number relieved in the counties of the State, and chargeable to this commission.	Grand total of persons treated, cared for, relieved, forwarded, etc., by and at expense of the Com'rs of Emig.	Ward's Island report. Average daily number of inmates.	Marine Hospital report. Average daily number of inmates.	Sailing vessels.*	Steamships.	Total number of deaths.
1847, ..	†......	798	1,190	†......	10,594	214	874	†....	†....	1,088
1848, ..	†......	2,102	694	5,369	27,523	305	1,181	1,002	†....	2,488
1849, ..	†......	2,999	1,360	5,566	41,258	1,230	923	2,357	†....	4,510
1850, ..	8,000	2,301	267	5,937	57,386	894	391	†....	†....	1,285
1851, ..	18,204	7,391	1,658	12,550	85,026	1,654	894	1,879	†....	4,427
1852, ..	14,971	4,601	1,364	18,432	181,005	1,543	1,561	†....	†....	3,104
1853, ..	14,334	3,262	1,152	9,351	91,774	1,108	731	†....	†....	1,839
1854, ..	13,964	4,608	2,021	10,504	120,894	1,707	909	†....	†....	2,616
1855, ..	15,151	4,996	807	12,175	142,357	1,278	312	†....	†....	1,590
1856, ..	9,378	589	1,081	5,346	36,824	526	203	180	3	912
1857, ..	10,933	529	864	4,523	32,385	519	209	849	17	1,594
1858, ..	9,346	515	245	4,200	26,560	487	50	263	11	811
1859, ..	7,150	176	485	2,407	19,435	262	‡25	168	23	478
1860, ..	7,717	401	527	2,104	20,615	226	.....	192	22	440
1861, ..	6,023	537	695	1,950	20,461	293	.....	160	27	480
1862, ..	6,636	178	405	2,343	16,458	231	.....	272	17	520
1863, ..	13,425	254	612	4,583	30,445	374	.....	420	43	837
1864, ..	11,190	146	1,265	4,556	28,837	709	.....	725	84	1,518
1865, ..	10,361	178	627	4,946	29,397	634	.....	526	113	1,273
1866, ..	10,771	272	316	4,567	38,719	871	.....	884	§816	2,259
	187,554	36,733	17,635	121,139	1,057,953	15,067	8,263	9,877	1,176	34,069

STATE LUNATIC ASYLUMS.

State Lunatic Asylum at Utica.

By an act passed March 10, 1836, three Commissioners were appointed to select and purchase a site, and to contract for the building of a Lunatic Asylum. In 1837 a farm of one hundred and thirty acres was bought in the western part of the city of Utica, at the joint expense of the city and State. The first plans embraced four buildings, each 550 feet, facing outward and connected by verandahs, but after the foundations were laid, this plan was abandoned, and the present one adopted. The Institution opened in 1842, and has since been in successful operation. The following tables present the general statistics of the asylum during the last twenty years:

* In the annexed report for 1866 will be found statistics of the relative proportion of passengers on sailing and steam vessels since 1856 (Table C, p. 74), and relative mortality on sailing and steam vessels (Table F, p. 82).

† During the years marked thus (†) no statistics were kept.

‡ In the year 1859 the buildings ceased to be used for hospital purposes.

§ Cholera broke out during the voyage on several steamers.

General Statistics of the New York State Lunatic Asylum at Utica, from 1846 *to* 1866 *inclusive.*

YEARS.	Admitted.	Discharged.	Recovered.	Improved.	Unimproved.	Died.
1847,	428	330	187	70	25	48
1848,	405	382	174	84	38	86
1849,	362	408	203	66	70	69
1850,	367	387	171	57	108	51
1851,	366	360	112	56	134	48
1852,	390	400	156	53	152	39
1853,	424	403	169	66	129	39
1854,	390	386	164	42	115	65
1855,	275	270	128	15	95	32
1856,	242	236	100	33	73	30
1857,	235	245	95	25	93	32
1858,	333	282	114	33	104	31
1859,	312	295	114	57	89	35
1860,	337	339	105	56	136	42
1861,	295	280	83	58	108	31
1862,	287	305	106	51	118	30
1863,	287	267	80	38	107	42
1864,	319	289	109	44	88	48
1865,	356	305	113	35	100	57
1866,	388	362	164	39	115	44
Total,	6,798	6,531	2,647	978	1,997	899

For Officers' Salaries, Wages of Attendants, Assistants, Laborers, &c., Provisions and Household Stores, Furniture of all kinds, additions, alterations and repairs, Farm, Barn, Garden and Grounds, Fuel and Gas and Oil Lights, Books, Stationery, Printing, &c., Medicines and Medical Stores, and all miscellaneous expenses.

YEARS.	Sums.	YEARS.	Sums.
1847,	$33,932 48	1857,	$95,387 61
1848,	68,655 49	1858,	103,834 05
1849,	62,672 09	1859,	109,465 46
1850,	65,028 25	1860,	105,865 44
1851,	77,978 71	1861,	114,116 64
1852,	80,001 35	1862,	99,949 81
1853,	78,558 81	1863,	116,506 51
1854,	87,451 68	1864,	150,045 34
1855,	98,689 12	1865,	157,927 75
1856,	100,432 53	1866,	185,382 34
			$1,991,881 46

Expenses of heating and ventilation during the period from 1853 to 1860, and of remodeling the building, ... $151,137 44
Expense of rebuilding the parts destroyed by fire in July, 1857, ... 80,392 58

State Lunatic Asylum for Insane Convicts.

This establishment was organized under an act passed April 8, 1858, for the purposes indicated in its name. It is located on the grounds of the Auburn State Prison, and is under the care of the State Prison Inspectors, who appoint a Medical Superintendent, and provide the necessary arrangements for its support.

Willard Lunatic Asylum.

The Legislature of 1865 provided for the erection of a second general Lunatic Asylum, to be named in honor of Dr. SYLVESTER D. WILLARD, of Albany, who had been chiefly instrumental in collecting and presenting statistics that indicated the need of additional provisions for insane paupers. The Institution has been located at Ovid, Seneca county, where the buildings begun for an Agricultural College have been purchased, and others are in course of erection. In relation to the origin, intention and progress of this enterprise, the following statement has been prepared by one of the Commissioners in charge:

"The general statute now makes it the duty of all county officers, on taking charge of insane poor, to send them to the State Lunatic Asylum at Utica. The overcrowded state of the Asylum at Utica renders it necessary, if these patients do not recover in a few months, that they be sent back to the county houses from whence they came. Under this system the county houses of the State, according to the official report of the late Dr. WILLARD to the Legislature of 1865, contain 1,500 insane persons, many of whom are in the most loathsome condition, without a single provision to mitigate the sufferings consequent upon their unfortunate mental condition.

"It is a well-settled fact, that a much larger percentage of the chronic insane are orderly and inclined to labor, than of recent cases; hence larger numbers of the former may be congregated together than of the latter; many of them needing little or no treatment, simply something to do — mechanical or farm labor under proper surveillance.

"The statute of 1865, organizing the Willard Asylum for the chronic insane, directs that these rejected cases, or cases of over one year's standing, shall be sent to the Willard Asylum at Ovid, and, so far as practical, that those now in the county poor-houses, shall also be removed to the same place. Thus it will be seen that the object of the "Willard Asylum for the chronic insane" is to break up the system above described, of consigning these *unfortunates* to the loathsome cells of our county poor-houses, and to send them where they can have the benefit of a curative institution, with ample provisions for employment for those who are inclined to labor; hence rendering the Asylum, as far as possible, self-supporting.

"The Willard Asylum for the 'chronic insane' is located on the east shore of the Seneca Lake, and embraces the farm known as the "State Agricultural Farm," which contains about five hundred acres of good land, well watered and abounding in beautiful scenery. The hospital building now in course of construction is located on a bluff sixty feet above the level of the lake, and three hundred feet from the shore, with beautiful ravines on either side, thickly wooded with oaks and pines. Two first-class steamboats make four landings each week day during the year, at the dock in front of the hospital, on their respective trips from Geneva to Watkins and return, and from Watkins to Geneva and return. Of the three hundred and forty lineal feet by forty feet width of the hospital building, now in course of construction, one hundred and seventy feet is nearly ready for receiving the roof, and the balance is rapidly progressing and will likewise be ready for the roof in the course of three or four weeks. The foundation and basement story of a center building sixty by seventy feet, designed for superintendent's department and offices, &c., are completed. The excavation is made, and a portion of the foundation walls laid for the rear building designed for chapel, workshop, culinary purposes, engine-house, &c.

Three appropriations have been made by the Legislature:

First, 1865,		$75,000
Second, 1866,		50,000
Third, 1867,		100,000
Whole amount,		$225,000
There has been expended in the purchase of the farm, including the Agricultural College Building,*	$36,800	
For work and material for hospital building,	88,206	$125,000
The balance,		$100,000

It is estimated will inclose the work begun, and furnish the material for its completion."

Hudson River Asylum for the Insane.

The Legislature, by an act passed April 18, 1866, directed the appointment of three Commissioners to select a site for another Insane Asylum on the Hudson below Albany. They have selected a site in the city of Poughkeepsie, and the Legislature, by an act passed March 16, 1867, appropriated the sum of $100,000 toward the erection of suitable buildings thereon. The site was purchased at the expense of Dutchess county, at a cost of $32,000, and the city of Poughkeepsie has become pledged for $48,000 toward the erection of buildings.

ASYLUM FOR IDIOTS.

The New York Asylum for Idiots was founded by an act passed at the extra session of the Legislature, in 1851.

The institution was opened in buildings leased for the purpose near Albany, in October of the same year. At the end of four years, it was removed to new buildings erected for its use at Syracuse. These are capable of accommodating 145 pupils.

The total cost of buildings, grounds and furniture to this date has been $100,300, distributed in this manner:

Grounds (49 acres),	$13,200
Building (gas and water apparatus, heating, &c.),	68,300
Out-buildings, wall and fence,	7,800
Furniture, farm and stable stock,	11,000
	$100,300

Provision was made at the outset for 20 State pupils. This number was increased the second year to 30. This number was gradually

* This building will accommodate two hundred quiet patients, but cannot be used for violent cases. Patients will be put into it as soon as some portion of the hospital building can be put in condition to receive violent cases, thus enabling a proper classification.

increased to 120, at the end of six years, or, in 1859, where it remained till a year ago, when it was increased to 130.

Besides the State pupils, there have usually been some 20 pay pupils under its care. The annual appropriation has been gradually increased from $6,000 to $25,200, the present amount. Till 1863, the average annual cost per pupil was a little more than $150; since then it has averaged about $200 per pupil. The total number of pupils that have received its benefits have been 431, of whom 145 are still connected with it.

NEW YORK INSTITUTION FOR THE INSTRUCTION OF THE DEAF AND DUMB.

Historical Sketch and Statistics — Foundation of the Institution.

This Institution was the second on this side of the Atlantic, and was founded just half a century ago. By the act of incorporation, passed April 15th, 1817, the management of the Institution was intrusted to a Board of Directors, consisting of a President, two Vice-Presidents, a Treasurer, a Secretary, and twenty other members. This Board is directed to be elected annually by the "members of the Institution, but it is left to our own by-laws to fix the time and place of election, and designate those who are the "members of the Institution." At first, and till within a few years, this membership and right of voting for Directors were restricted to those who had made donations of a prescribed amount to the funds of the Institution. The present rule is that the existing members of the Institution simply admit other members by vote.

Though the Institution is thus nominally independent of the State, still, as it is entirely dependent for its means of support from year to year on the annual appropriations of the Legislature, which, moreover, as long ago as March, 1827, especially stipulated for a right of visitation and examination into all its affairs, educational, domestic, and financial, by the State Superintendent of Common Schools (now of Public Instruction), a right extended to the newly created Board of Commissioners of Public Charities, — as, further, the State Superintendent decides in all selections of pupils; and as the Board of Directors submit to the Legislature every year a full and minute report of their transactions, — the Institution is in every essential respect a State institution, the only effect of the mode of election of its Board of Directors being to remove its government entirely out of the turmoils and changes of politics, and vest it in a body of citizens drawn together by philanthropic interest in the education of the deaf and dumb. The Directors, as such, receive no compensation for their services. For many years only one member of the Board, the Principal, has been a salaried officer of the Institution.

No location is prescribed for the Institution by law. It is, however, in effect, restricted to New York city, or its vicinity, by the provision in the act of incorporation, which requires at least two-thirds of the Directors to be residents of that city and county.

The school was opened in May, 1818, with only four pupils. At the date of the first Annual Report, January 1, 1820, they had increased to fifty-six. The annexed table shows the admissions, dismissions, and number remaining for each year, to the end of the year 1866:

Statistics of the Institution for the Deaf and Dumb.

YEARS.	Admissions.	Dismissions.	Remaining in school.	YEARS.	Admissions.	Dismissions.	Remaining in school.
1818, } 1819, }	67	11	56	1844,	40	45	168
1820,	8	12	52	1845,	66	34	200
1821,	15	15	52	1846,	45	37	208
1822,	19	18	53	1847,	54	37	225
1823,	11	14	50	1848,	36	41	220
1824,	16	13	53	1849,	44	42	222
1825,	18	15	56	1850,	45	40	227
1826,	23	15	64	1851,	50	34	243
1827,	14	15	63	1852,	61	44	270
1828,	19	17	65	1853,	62	44	278
1829,	30	27	68	1854,	44	43	279
1830,	37	20	85	1855,	49	38	290
1831,	15	11	89	1856,	56	31	315
1832,	15	17	87	1857,	39	52	302
1833,	58	11	134	1858,	56	53	305
1834,	23	20	137	1859,	52	59	298
1835,	43	40	140	1860,	50	48	300
1836,	57	37	160	1861,	52	42	310
1837,	24	34	150	1862,	51	42	319
1838,	37	32	155	1863,	73	55	337
1839,	37	23	169	1864,	81	61	357
1840,	35	52	152	1865,	93	44	406
1841,	36	26	162	1866,	73	45	434
1842,	28	36	154	Total admissions....	2,003		
1843,	46	27	173				

Of these 2,003 admissions, 187 were re-admissions, leaving 1,816 as the actual number of deaf mutes who have shared in the benefits of the institution.

At the date of the last annual report, Dec. 31, 1866, the pupils were classified as follows, according to their means of support:

	Males.	Females.	Total.
Supported by the State of New York,	164	117	281
Supported by the counties of New York,	63	28	91
Supported by the State of New Jersey,	9	12	21
Supported by their friends,	26	14	40
Supported by the institution,	1	....	1
Total,	263	171	434

State Pupils.

The first appropriations from the State Treasury to the institution were made in April, 1819. The first specific appropriation for State pupils in April, 1822. Only thirty-two beneficiencies were provided for by that law. The following table shows the subsequent slow and guarded increase in this number:

YEARS.	No. of State pupils.	YEARS.	No. of State pupils.
1822,	32	1838,	128
1830,	56	1845,	160
1833,	96	1852,	192
1836,	120		

As often as the number was increased it was speedily filled up, leaving applicants to wait, and sometimes to lose the precious opportunity of education, who were equally deserving with the fortunate ones admitted. This consideration finally prevailed with the Legislature of 1854 to remove this unjust limit to the number of State beneficiencies, and since that year the Superintendent of Public Instruction is authorized to admit on the State list all whom that high officer should, by the requisite proofs furnished him, find to be deserving and eligible applicants. This number has gradually increased since 1854, partly by the increase of deaf mutes with the increase of population, partly by the more general diffusion of information among their natural guardians, who are now less apt to keep them at home in degrading ignorance, partly by extensions of the term of instruction.

The term for education allowed to the State beneficiencies by the act of 1822 was only three years, a limitation which, in the present state of our knowledge, seems almost incredible. On this, as on other points, the progress of public opinion has been slow but sure. In 1826, the term was extended to four years; in 1830, to five. In 1838, two years more were granted to such as should be judged likely to profit by the extension, usually more than half of the whole. These two years were extended to three in 1864, a provision reaffirmed by the General School Law of 1866. Finally, and as the crowning act of legislative beneficence toward the unfortunate deaf and dumb, the Legislature, by act passed April 5th, 1853, allowed three years more for such of its beneficiaries as should be selected by the State Superintendent, on the recommendation of the Directors, for the purpose of pursuing a course of studies in the higher branches of learning. Chapter 272 of the Laws of 1856, reaffirming this provision, limited the number of State pupils in the high class to twelve. This class has proved very valuable as a nursery for teachers.

To sum up, the first selections of State pupils are made for five years, at the end of which the State Superintendent, at his discretion, allows, on the recommendation of the Board, three years more. A select number of the most worthy, capable and diligent, not to exceed twelve, are retained for a course of higher studies. The period allowed to the generalty of the pupils is about equal to that enjoyed by the pupils blessed with all their faculties, in the common schools of the State, while the high class offers to the more gifted, advantages analogous to those of the free academies for youths who hear.

The age of admission was at first between ten and twenty-five years. At the representation of the Directors and Principal that twelve years was, in most cases, the most advantageous time for deaf mutes to begin a course of instruction, that age was, by chapter 244, of the Laws of 1838, fixed as the lower limit. The State Superintendent of Public Instruction has discretionary power to prescribe what portion of the annual expense shall be paid by parents or guardians who may be judged able to pay in part.

Since 1838 the counties are required to furnish clothing to those deaf mutes whose parents or guardians are unable to furnish them with suitable clothing. The charge for this purpose was not to exceed twenty dollars for each pupil, but since the great advance of prices, this allowance has been increased to thirty dollars.

County Pupils.

As early as 1822, the Supervisors of the counties were authorized, at their discretion, to support in the institution a number of deaf mutes equal to the number of their members of Assembly. This provision was regularly carried out by the Supervisors of the city and county of New York, down to the year 1859, but was very rarely acted on by any other county, except that Montgomery, for several years, supported the authorized number of pupils in the Central Asylum at Canajoharie, in that county, united in 1836 to the New York institution. By chapter 325, of the Laws of 1863, the Overseers of the Poor of any town, or the Supervisors of any county, were required to place in the institution such deaf mute children, under twelve years, as are, or are liable to become a town or county charge, and also such other deaf mute children, between the years of six and twelve, whose health, morals or comfort may be endangered through the want of a home, and the extreme indigence of its parents or guardians. Under this law the number of pupils in the institution was thirty in 1863, fifty-one in 1864, seventy-eight in 1865, and ninety-one in 1866. On reaching the age of twelve, these county pupils are transferred to the State list.

Buildings and Grounds.

The school was kept in rooms provided by the city of New York, the pupils being boarded in hired houses, till 1829. From 1829 to 1857, it occupied buildings on Fiftieth street, the cost of erecting which was defrayed in part by donations from the State, and in part by the donations of benevolent citizens of New York. The rapid growth of the city in that direction, and the opening of streets through the grounds of the institution, made the site too restricted for the health and comfort of the pupils. The buildings and grounds were sold, and a new site was purchased on Washington Heights, about nine miles north of the City Hall, four times as large, and every way more suitable for such an institution, and leave a considerable building fund. The grounds embrace thirty-seven and a half acres, with a valuable river front, in which is a dock where coal and other bulky articles for the institution can be landed by the cargo. The grounds are kept in cultivation by the labor of some of the older pupils, who thus gain skill and practice in the best modes of horticulture. The buildings were planned to accommodate four hundred and fifty pupils; that they were not made too large is proved by the fact that already, within ten years of the removal to them, they are beginning to be crowded, and additional buildings will probably be required in a year or two. A full detail of the arrangement and of the cost of the grounds and buildings is given in a report by CHARLES KING, HORATIO SEYMOUR and CHRISTOPHER MORGAN, Commissioners (Senate Document 107, for 1858).

From this document it appears that the actual cost of the grounds was..	$115,000 00
Of the buildings and improvements, ...	358,256 13
Interest, insurance, and incidental expenses while building and before occupied,.	62,256 53
Total expenditure to 1858,...........	$535,512 66

Several thousand dollars have recently been expended on permanent improvements, such as laying pipes for a supply of water from the Croton Aqueduct and for a new wash-house. A new building for workshops is urgently needed, it being a very important part of the system to give the pupils instruction in some trade by which they can support themselves after they leave school.

Of the above sum of $535,512.66, there was realized from the sale of the Fiftieth street property, after paying off mortgages, $272,040. The Legislature made special appropriations amounting to $48,750, about twenty thousand dollars were borrowed from funds donated to the Institution by private benefactors, and the balance was borrowed.

Debt of the Institution.

The debt incurred in the erection of the buildings now amounts to $196,000. The State makes a special appropriation each year to meet the interest of this debt.

Method of Instruction.

The method is substantially the same that prevails in all the other American institutions for deaf mutes, except one or two small private schools, and in the greater number of those in Continental Europe, out of Germany. It was brought by the present principal, Dr. PEET, from the asylum at Hartford in 1831, but has been improved by the diligent labors of Dr. PEET and his assistants, especially of his son, the present vice-principal. It employs an expanded and improved language of gestures as the principal *means*, while written language and the acquisition of general and religious knowledge are the great *ends* of instruction.

The most thorough and careful investigation having demonstrated that the attempt to teach articulation to deaf mutes (except the small number who learned to speak before deaf, or who are are only partially deaf), does not produce results of any practical value to the pupil, and while it exacts a heavy sacrifice of time and labor, to the great detriment of his progress in general knowledge, this instruction has no place in the method of the New York Institution.

Financial Condition.

The Institution has no permanent funds, except its large investments in grounds and buildings. The annexed statements condensed from the last annual report, will show the sources of its income, and the amount received last year.

I. Appropriations from the State Treasury:		
1. For board and tuition of State pupils,	$49,630 00	
2. For interest on the debt,	12,065 00	
3. A special appropriation to meet deficiencies,	22,500 00	
		$84,195 00
II. Payments from the counties:		
1. For support and clothing of county pupils,	$11,893 46	
2. For clothing of the more indigent State pupils,	5,762 16	
3. Arrears from the county of New York,	3,000 00	
		20,655 62
III. From the State of New Jersey, for her State pupils,		4,612 69
IV. From the friends of the pupils:		
1. From paying pupils for board and tuition,	$5,967 79	
2. From pupils clothed by friends, for clothing furnished and cash advances,	563 67	
		6,533 46
V. From the Regents of the University for distributive share of the literature fund,		849 19
VI. From proceeds of place,		485 59
VII. Money borrowed to supply deficiencies,		15,515 20
Total for the year 1866,		$132,846 75

Of this amount $10,393.69 was employed to pay the unpaid bills of the preceding year 1865, leaving the amount used for the expenses of 1866, $122,553.06.

The large sums to supply deficiencies were made necessary by the omission of the Legislature for some years past, to raise the regular annual compensation for State and county pupils in proportion to the greatly increased prices of all the necessaries of life. Twenty years ago, one hundred and fifty dollars for each pupil was an allowance about as ample as two hundred and fifty would be now, and this enhancement of prices as a result of an inflated currency and other causes, has not perhaps yet reached its limit, certainly has not begun to decline. The cost per capita on the number of the pupils, for provisions and groceries, was:

YEARS.	Amount.	YEARS.	Amount.
1861,	$50 32	1864,	$84 07
1862,	51 53	1865,	90 00
1863,	62 43	1866,	100 00

There is a corresponding increase in all the items of expenditure, except interest and the salaries of teachers.

NEW YORK INSTITUTION FOR THE BLIND.

In the early part of 1831, a society was organized for the purpose of founding an Institution for the education of the blind. A petition, signed by many of the most eminent citizens of New York, was prepared and presented to the Legislature, and on the 21st of April, 1831, an act was passed incorporating "The New York Institution for the Blind."

Although the New York Institution was the second school for the blind incorporated in America, it was the first to go into actual operation, which it did March 15th, 1832. The Institution is located on the west side of the city, on the Ninth Avenue, between Thirty-third and Thirty-fourth streets. It is eligibly situated in one of the best portions of the city, and is easily accessible from any point. The building is a substantial structure, built of Sing Sing marble, and is three stories high. There is a main or center building 125 feet front by 60 feet deep, and a north and south wing each 25 feet wide by 125 feet long. The Institution has capacity to accommodate properly from 140 to 150 pupils, together with the officers, teachers and domestics, who are required to carry out its purposes. The object of the Institution was not to provide a home or asylum, where those who entered might remain permanently, nor to establish a "hospital" for the treatment of diseases of the eye, but it was to educate the blind, and to train them in such branches as are adapted to their condition, with a view to their future usefulness. To accomplish this end, the instruction given is three-fold in its character, viz.: Intellectual, musical and mechanical. In the first department, the pupils are taught reading, writing, spelling, geography, grammar, arithmetic, algebra, geometry, history, natural philosphy, civil polity, and mental and moral science. The course of instruction is graded and regular, and each pupil advances year by year, from one class to another, until the whole is completed. When this is done, the pupil is prepared to attend to any business pursuit he may choose to follow, and also to meet the duties and responsibilities of citizenship. The musical department combines utility with pleasure, the beautiful with the useful. In this department, the pupils are instructed in the rudiments, in chorus singing, the voice, piano, organ, and the more advanced, in harmony.

In the mechanical department those branches of handicraft are taught which are most available to the blind, and by which many are enabled to provide for themselves. The branches taught are mat, broom and mattress making.

For the past thirty-six years the institution has steadily advanced in usefulness and prosperity. Its success is shown by the fact that many of its pupils are now occupying useful, responsible, and in some cases lucrative positions. Among them may be found merchants, manufacturers, life and fire insurance agents, piano tuners, organists, teachers and clergymen. The institution is under the charge of a Board of twenty managers. The Board is subdivided in four committees, as follows:

Committee on Finance, Committee on Supplies,
Committee on Music and Instruction, Committee on Manufactures.

Each Committee has special charge of the department indicated by its name. The Board of Managers meet at the institution once in each month, while the committee hold meetings weekly for the transaction of business, and for the purpose of inspecting all departments of the institution.

STATEMENT of Receipts and Expenditures of the New York Institution for the Blind for each year since 1846.

YEARS.	Receipts.	Expenditures.	YEARS.	Receipts.	Expenditures.
1847, ...	$28,548 28	$27,416 39	1858, ...	$61,702 08	$60,430 01
1848, ...	29,490 67	29,782 92	1859, ...	51,731 63	55,050 34
1849, ...	44,278 21	43,451 19	1860, ...	148,510 29	148,038 17
1850, ...	34,830 35	36,285 90	1861, ...	71,460 05	71,274 20
1851, ...	34,924 77	30,919 25	1862, ...	61,610 53	61,455 40
1852, ...	40,596 12	51,186 32	1863, ...	228,894 23	228,221 21
1853, ...	48,354 66	51,658 68	1864, ...	56,581 55	55,649 68
1854, ...	118,318 64	114,766 12	1865, ...	80,105 06	79,412 24
1855, ...	67,691 60	54,920 73	1866, ...	178,585 93	175,315 14
1856, ...	52,412 17	58,641 25			
1857, ...	49,287 75	48,440 36		$1,487,914 57	$1,482,315 50

The following statement shows the number of pupils instructed in the Institution for each year since 1846:

YEARS.	No.	YEARS.	No.	YEARS.	No.	YEARS.	No.
1847, ...	116	1852, ...	104	1857, ...	143	1862, ...	158
1848, ...	115	1853, ...	116	1858, ...	147	1863, ...	145
1849, ...	103	1854, ...	125	1859, ...	157	1864, ...	138
1850, ...	105	1855, ...	133	1860, ...	157	1865, ...	132
1851, ...	102	1856, ...	132	1861, ...	169	1866	155

Total expenditures since first establishment.

Total expenditures from 1832 to 1866 inclusive, for all purposes, ... $1,873,466 45
Average attendance per year:
New York State pupils,.......... 112
New Jersey and pay pupils,.. 6
Proportion of New York pupils,...................................... 94 per cent.
Amount expended for all purposes, in 35 years, for (6) New Jersey and pay pupils,.. 95,260 29
Amount expended for all purposes in 35 years for New York State pupils,........... 1,778,205 47
Total amount received from State of New York since 1832,......................... 647,621 82
Amount of moneys expended by the Institution for all purposes since 1832, for New York State pupils, over and above the amounts appropriated by the Legislature, 1,130,583 65
Average amount paid yearly by New York State, for all purposes, since 1832,.... ... 18,503 48
Average amount per pupil paid yearly by New York State,................. $165 21
Average amount of Institution resources paid per year for New York State pupils since 1832,.. 32,302 39

Average amount per pupil paid yearly by the Institution,.................. $288 41
Proportion of whole expense borne by the State of New York for the blind under the care of the Institution since 1832,.......................... .... 36 per cent.
Proportion borne by the Institution,.................................. 64 per cent.
The estimated value of property owned by the Institution is $313,699 04

This amount arises almost entirely from the enhanced value of the real estate held by the institution.

STATE PRISONS.

There are three State Prisons in this State, one Asylum for insane convicts, and one Female Prison, all of which are under the control of three Inspectors of State Prisons elected by the people, one of which is elected each year. The duties of the Board of Inspectors are to meet on the first Wednesday in January next after said election, at Sing Sing Prison, and then organize by selecting of a President of their Board. They assign to each Inspector the special charge of one of the Prisons for four months, and make a similar assignment and designation at the commencement of each four months in the year.

The Board of Inspectors of State Prisons are required by law to visit jointly each of the State Prisons at least four times each year, and at such meeting to inquire and examine into all matters connected with the government, discipline and police of each Prison, the punishment and employment of the convicts therein confined, the money concerns, and all contracts for work, or the employment of said convicts on the part of the State.

They require reports from the agent and warden of each of the Prisons, in relation to any or all of the preceding matter, and make such general regulations for the government and discipline of each Prison as they may deem expedient, and from time to time to alter and amend the same as, in their judgment, shall best conduce to the reformation of convicts. They inquire into all matters in relation to improper conduct which may be alleged to have been committed by the agent and warden, or other officers of the Prison. They are bound to keep regular minutes of each of their meetings, and to make a report to the Legislature on or before the 15th day of January in each year. They appoint all officers connected with said Prisons, namely: One agent and warden for each of the Prisons, one principal keeper, one chaplain, one clerk, one store-keeper, one physician and surgeon, superintendent of the asylum, clerk and six attendants, one principal matron and one assistant for every twenty-four convicts (except at Clinton Prison), one kitchen keeper, one yard keeper, and one keeper for every twenty-four convicts confined in our Prisons, besides guards.

It shall be the duty of each Inspector having charge of a Prison assigned to him, to spend at least seven days, once in each month, at the Prison, to examine and inquire into the condition of the Prison, as to its discipline, government and its financial condition, examine all vouchers of the agent, examine the books of the store-keeper and kitchen keeper, certify the same to the Comptroller, and examine and certify to the estimate of the agent each month; to suspend all officers for neglect of duty until the next meeting of the Board, and fill such vacancies until the Board convenes, and to have a general supervision of the Prison while under his charge, subject to the approval of the Board.

The following is the statistical and financial statement of all the Prisons and Asylums for insane convicts:

New York State Prison at Sing Sing.

Located on the alluvial margin of the Hudson, at the point where it widens into the Tappan Zee. The main building, 350 feet from the river, is 484 feet long, running north and south, 42 feet wide, and 50 feet high.

It contains 6 tiers of cells on each side, each tier comprising 100 cells; total of the building, 1,200.

The structure was commenced in May, 1825, by convicts drafted from Auburn Prison. Two stories have been subsequently added, at different periods, as the increase of receptions demanded.

The workshops, situated at right angles with the main prison, are 40 feet wide, from two to three stories high. An iron foundry at the south end of the yard employs, on contract, 100 convicts; a whip contract in upper story of same building, 50; the cabinet contract, 100; the shoe contract, 190; the buckle, brass foundry and saddle contracts, collectively, 130; the auger contract, 115; the Westchester Marble and Lime Company, who work the adjacent quarries, and burn the stone into lime, 100 convicts; and the hame contract, 25. In the female department 100 women are employed by contract in making clothing. The male convict Prison receives commitments from the First and Second Judicial Districts, with the addition of Ulster, Greene and Sullivan counties, also United States prisoners at large. The female convict Prison contains 108 cells; is located east of the male convict building, on elevated ground, and was commenced in 1835. It receives commitments from all Judicial Districts save the Seventh and Eighth. Both buildings are constructed of the white limestone from the contiguous quarries. The total number of male convicts now confined is 1,319; females, 156.

ANNUAL EXHIBIT

Of the Total Earnings and Expenditures, with balance against the State Prison for females at Sing Sing, at the close of each year, for the twenty years ending September 30, 1866.

YEARS.	Total Earnings.	Total Expenditures.	Balance.
1847, September 30,	$1,564 81	....	....
1848, do 30,	2,363 66	$11,790 54	$9,426 88
1849, do 30,	2,373 30	10,411 70	8,038 40
1850, do 30,	3,165 13	10,930 50	7,765 37
1851, do 30,	4,185 29	8,677 65	4,492 36
1852, do 30,	4,029 76	7,669 10	3,639 34
1853, do 30,	5,557 40	8,636 10	3,078 60
1854, do 30,	5,960 59	10,899 91	4,939 32
1855, do 30,	2,747 33	10,000 91	7,253 32
1856, do 30,	1,667 75	8,028 74	6,360 99
1857, do 30,	3,273 90	7,225 07	3,951 17
1858, do 30,	2,965 60	7,630 64	4,665 04
1859, do 30,	2,651 64	9,023 87	6,372 23
1860, do 30,	3,124 56	11,270 92	8,146 36
1861, do 30,	2,958 50	13,657 58	10,699 08
1862, do 30,	2,153 35	14,205 92	12,052 57
1863, do 30,	2,164 61	15,031 25	12,866 64
1864, do 30,	2,487 36	21,838 47	18,351 11
1865, do 30,	5,236 08	29,949 36	24,713 28
1866, do 30,	4,829 01	27,149 13	22,320 12

ANNUAL EXHIBIT

Of the Total Earnings, Expenditures and Balance of the State Prison for Males at Sing Sing, at the close of each year, for the twenty years, ending September 30, 1866.

YEARS.	Total Earnings.	Total Expenditures.	Dr. Balance	Cr. Balance.
1847, September 30,	$61,738 06	$73,303 59	$11,565 53	....
1848, do 30,	51,652 77	97,221 41	45,568 64	....
1849, do 30,	63,052 83	81,850 28	18,797 45	....
1850, do 30,	70,234 99	99,539 70	29,304 71	....
1851, do 30,	87,755 08	79,506 82	8,248 26	....
1852, do 30,	98,580 62	85,414 42	13,166 20	....
1853, do 30,	97,752 64	120,818 73	23,066 09	....
1854, do 30,	93,845 34	136,142 24	42,296 90	....
1855, do 30,	90,904 71	116,774 37	25,869 66	....
1856, do 30,	86,440 89	100,529 77	14,088 88	....
1857, do 30,	94,946 97	109,586 53	14,639 56	....
1858, do 30,	75,916 48	119,900 14	43,983 66	....
1859, do 30,	96,649 13	128,439 94	31,790 81	....
1860, do 30,	111,640 92	130,226 50	18,585 58	....
1861, do 30,	125.530 96	123,622 87	....	$1,908 09
1862, do 30,	84,808 73	130,022 31	45,213 58	....
1863, do 30,	86,637 35	128,191 58	41,554 23	....
1864, do 30,	100,440 13	154,802 09	54,361 96	....
1865, do 30,	94,666 33	181,132 03	86,465 70	....
1866, do 30,	125,704 32	220,259 36	94,555 04	....

ANNUAL EXHIBIT

Of the number of prisoners received at and discharged from the State Prison at Sing Sing, with nativity, color and sex, for the twenty years ending September 30, 1866.

DATE.	Received.	DISCHARGED.				Escaped.	Captured.	TRANS-FERRED.		Died.	IN PRISON AT END OF YEAR.					
		Expiration.	Commutation.	Pardon.	Appellate Court.			To Lunatic Asylum.	To other prison.		White.	Black.	Native.	Foreign.	Sex.	Total.
1847, Sept. 30,...	194	159	.....	30	1	...	1	4	1	32	588	137	491	234	Male,......	725
1847, Sept. 30,...	45	18	.....	2	...	2	...	.....	.....	2	67	22	31	58	Female,..	89
1848, Sept. 30,...	169	204	.....	44	2	3	1	7	.....	31	481	129	402	208	Male,......	604
1848, Sept. 30....	24	19	.....	7	...	...	...	.....	.....	4	65	19	34	50	Female,..	84
1849, Sept. 30,...	246	133	.....	11	1	3	...	.....	15	22	503	162	415	250	Male,......	665
1849, Sept. 30,...	29	32	.....	2	...	...	...	.....	.....	...	57	22	27	52	Female,..	79
1850, Sept. 30,...	246	153	.....	15	1	1	...	1	17	20	568	126	434	260	Male,......	703
1850, Sept. 30,...	29	28	.....	3	...	1	...	1	....	3	53	19	28	44	Female,..	72
1851, Sept. 30,...	280	156	.....	42	1	1	...	1	.....	19	587	145	450	282	Male,......	763
1851, Sept. 30,...	38	29	.....	1	...	...	...	2	.....	3	61	14	30	45	Female,..	75
1852, Sept. 30,...	320	172	.....	42	2	...	...	3	.....	23	678	163	550	291	Male,......	841
1852, Sept. 30,...	44	21	.....	3	...	...	...	.....	.....	3	80	12	32	60	Female,..	92
1853, Sept. 30,...	314	168	.....	47	...	...	...	3	1	14	737	185	487	435	Male,......	922
1853, Sept. 30,...	48	27	.....	5	...	2	...	.....	1	3	84	18	37	65	Female,..	102
1854, Sept. 30,...	312	203	2	54	...	...	...	4	.....	34	789	148	478	459	Male,......	937
1854, Sept. 30,...	54	30	.....	3	...	1	..	1	1	4	96	20	34	82	Female,..	116
1855, Sept. 30,...	247	221	30	59	1	3	...	.....	18	11	732	109	412	429	Male,......	841
1855, Sept. 30,..	35	39	.....	2	...	...	...	.....	.....	5	92	13	33	72	Female,..	105
1856, Sept. 30,...	346	216	33	34	...	2	...	.....	.....	6	766	119	464	421	Male,......	885
1856, Sept. 30,...	29	43	.....	4	...	...	...	.....	.....	2	67	18	31	54	Female,..	85
1857, Sept. 30,...	347	252	16	53	1	5	...	.....	.....	11	791	103	424	470	Male,......	894
1857, Sept. 30,...	31	34	1	1	...	...	...	.....	.....	1	61	18	32	47	Female,..	79
1858, Sept. 30,...	399	239	.....	43	...	4	...	.....	15	24	845	123	473	495	Male,......	968
1858, Sept. 30,...	55	28	.....	2	...	...	...	.....	...	...	75	29	40	64	Female,..	104
1859, Sept. 30,...	383	187	1	33	...	4	...	.....	22	12	986	106	604	488	Male,......	1,092
1859, Sept. 30,...	59	21	.....	2	1	...	...	.....	.....	3	116	20	48	88	Female,..	136
1860, Sept. 30,...	438	255	1	5	2	5	...	7	.....	17	1,089	149	677	561	Male,......	1,238
1860, Sept. 30,...	49	39	.....	5	...	...	...	.....	.....	4	118	19	43	94	Female,..	137
1861, Sept. 30,...	452	264	1	23	27	2	...	9	100	26	1,143	95	680	558	Male,......	1,238
1861, Sept. 30,...	42	39	.....	1	...	...	...	.....	.....	2	121	16	60	77	Female,..	137
1862, Sept. 30,...	246	359	3	17	3	6	...	11	101	15	893	76	571	398	Male,......	969
1862, Sept. 30,...	28	48	.....	2	...	...	...	1	.....	1	104	9	55	58	Female,..	113
1863, Sept. 30,...	279	121	232	28	1	9	2	4	.....	16	764	73	493	344	Male,......	837
1863, Sept. 30,...	76	22	29	5	1	...	...	1	.....	1	119	11	64	66	Female,..	130
1864, Sept. 30,...	241	28	280	47	1	6	4	3	16	10	626	57	372	311	Male,......	683
1864, Sept. 30,...	91	52	.....	6	...	1	...	1	.....	3	148	10	66	92	Female,..	158
1865, Sept. 30,...	443	13	237	62	1	10	2	2	.....	13	742	42	409	375	Male,......	784
1865, Sept. 30,...	107	65	.....	6	...	1	...	1	29	4	149	10	69	90	Female,..	159
1866, Sept. 30,...	717	4	149	68	1	17	6	.....	50	16	1,123	79	648	554	Male,......	1,202
1866, Sept. 30,...	71	13	50	.....	2	...	...	.....	....	1	146	18	73	91	Female,..	164

ABSTRACT

Of the Total Earnings and Cash Receipts, and the total Cash Expenditures, with the average number of all the Convicts, per day, per month, at the Sing Sing Prison, from October 1st, 1846, to September 30th, 1866.

YEARS.	Contract earnings.	Miscellaneous earnings.	Total earnings.	Deposits in bank.
1847	$57,961 04	$3,777 02	$61,738 06	....
1848	....	....	51,652 77	....
1849	53 479 39	9,573 44	63,052 83	....
1850	45,947 57	27,452 55	73,400 12	....
1851	71,437 27	16,948 00	88,385 27	....
1852	75,542 25	23,837 87	99,380 12	....
1853	81,609 84	17,473 05	99,082 89	....
1854	71,210 61	24,134 73	95,345 34	$32,501 34
1855	....	....	90,904 71	....
1856	81,194 32	5,246 57	86,440 89	87,964 94
1857	87,576 29	7,370 68	94,946 97	81,692 33
1858	64,397 87	11,518 61	75,916 48	38,985 94
1859	83,022 65	12,726 48	†96,649 13	93,630 13
1860	89,342 99	22,297 93	111,640 92	97,582 84
1861	94,813 34	30,717 62	125,530 96	27,433 75
1862	65,986 32	20,975 76	86,962 08	58,744 63
1863	65,413 96	23,438 00	88,851 96	112,173 20
1864	67,627 98	36,299 51	103,927 49	110,451 05
1865	61,696 14	38,206 27	99,902 41	102,012 94
1866	94,329 63	36,203 70	130,533 33	129,476 23
Totals,	$1,312,589 46	$368,197 79	*$1,824,244 73	$972,649 32

* Including the sums for 1848 and 1855, which are not embraced in the preceding columns.
† Thus in "copy." It will be noticed that the sum of the two preceding items is $95,749.13, a probable error of $900 in one or the other column. — ED.

YEARS.	Treasurer's draft.	Salaries of officers.	Expenditures for ordinary support.	Expenditures for building, repairs, &c.
1847	....	....	....	....
1848	....	....	$91,930 57	$5,290 84
1849	....	....	79,320 00	2,530 28
1850	....	$37,085 63	51,870 88	17,674 06
1851	....	....	76,843 62	2,663 20
1852	....	40,214 17	43,276 29	1,923 96
1853	....	....	114,106 17	6,712 56
1854	$58,448 05	44,723 11	87,799 81	3,617 72
1855	....	37,564 46	77,040 54	2,099 81
1856	100,464 87	38,975 52	58,805 04	2,742 83
1857	109,975 81	42,350 57	56,984 69	10,251 27
1858	119,387 74	47,991 42	61,960 62	9,948 10
1859	128,075 32	51,692 08	66,948 19	9,799 67
1860	132,044 71	52,574 71	73,019 39	4,632 40
1861	122,902 29	55,151 22	81,417 07	712 16
1862	143,683 04	55,498 59	84,139 77	4,589 87
1863	144,420 98	52,250 66	85,270 27	5,702 08
1864	174,408 56	56,392 19	112,260 67	7,988 10
1865	211,844 37	59,357 60	135,323 63	9,989 91
1866	247,075 33	63,844 70	167,882 46	12,234 53
Totals,	$1,692,821 07	$735,665 63	$1,606,199 68	$121,103 35

NOTE.—Wherever blanks occur in the above, reliable data could not be obtained.

Total Earnings and Cash Receipts, &c., — (*Continued*).

YEARS.	Convict deposit refunded.	Total expenditures.	Number convicts on contract.	Number not on contract.	Total number of convicts.
1847,	....	$73,303 59	......	......	......
1848,	....	97,221 41	411	333	744
1849,	....	81,850 28	436	277	713
1850,	$128 57	106,759 14	495	270	765
1851,	....	79,506 82	628	168	796
1852,	205 75	85,414 42	667	227	894
1853,	....	120,818 73	733	228	961
1854,	1 60	136,142 24	758	283	1,041
1855,	....	116,704 81	752	274	1,026
1856,	....	100,523 39	702	261	963
1857,	....	109 586 53	776	205	981
1858,	....	119,900 14	589	470	1,059
1859,	....	128,439 94	795	384	1,179
1860,	....	130,226 50	1,021	354	1,375
1861,	....	137,280 45	764	611	1,375
1862,	....	144,228 23	633	449	1,082
1863,	....	143,222 83	648	319	967
1864,	....	176,640 56	530	311	841
1865,	6,410 25	211,081 29	569	374	943
1866,	3,446 80	247,408 49	897	469	1,366
Totals,	....	$2,546,259 89	......	......	......

The Auburn State Prison is situated in the city of Auburn, on the outlet of Owasco Lake. This prison was begun in 1817. It is constructed upon the plan of an oblong square, inclosed by a wall of 3,000 feet in extent, the east and west walls being 500 feet, and the north and south walls 1,000 feet long. The front of the prison on State street is 387 feet long, the wings extend back 242 feet. The main building is 56 feet high, wings 45 feet high. The north wing is L shaped, 350 feet by 45 feet; contains 550 cells and 5 dungeons. The south wing is 203 feet by 53 feet; contains 442 cells. Total number of cells, 992. The cells are five stories high in north wing, and six stories, part of the way, in south wing. The north wing was finished in 1823. The extension to the south wing, the chapel, hospital and mess room was built in 1860. The prison wall was originally 500 feet on each side, but in 1834 it was extended to its present dimensions. The Owasco river flows along the south wall, furnishing water for prison use, and also power to drive part of the machinery. The shops are all within the prison walls. Between the north wing and the north wall is the sash and blind shop, 240 feet by 39 feet, employing 60 convicts. The shop is one story high, and 32 feet from the wall. Joining the end of the sash and blind shop, and running west, is a brick shop, 582 feet by 34 feet, formerly used as a tool shop. It runs back of the tool and hame shops, and is now used partly by the hame contractors, and partly as a store-room. The shop is one story high, parallel to and 46 feet from the north wall. Extending west from the end of the north wing is the tool shop, 214 feet by 37 feet, two stories

NOTE.—Wherever blanks occur in the above, reliable data could not be obtained.

high, employing 93 convicts. Joining the tool shop and running west is the hame shop, 222 feet by 40 feet, employing 97 convicts. Across the west end of the yard, and 39 feet from the west wall, is the shoe shop, 240 feet by 50 feet, three stories high, employing 206 convicts. Between the south wing and the south wall is the axle-tree shop, 194 feet by 64 feet, employing 96 convicts. The shop is two stories high, and 30 feet from the wall. Joining the end of the south wing is the machine shop, 230 feet by 60 feet, two stories high, employing 97 convicts. Between the machine shop and south wall is the foundry, 118 feet by 52 feet, one story high. The convicts here are included in the machine contract. Joining the machine shop, and running west, is the cabinet shop, 330 feet by 50 feet, employing 68 convicts. Shop two stories high and basement. In the west end of the same building is the State tailor shop, washroom, etc.

ABSTRACT

Of the Total Earnings and Cash Receipts, and the Total Cash Expenditures, with the average number of all the Convicts, per day, per month, at the Auburn Prison, from October 1st, 1846, to September 30th, 1866.

YEARS.	Contract earnings.	Miscellaneous earnings.	Total earnings.	Deposits in bank.
1847,	$46,515 08	$6.544 71	$53,059 79	....
1848,	....	....	53,456 71	....
1849,	....	....	63,021 54	....
1850,	64,190 20	4,547 11	68,737 31	....
1851,	....	....	73,494 91	....
1852,	58,934 22	6,052 07	64,986 29	....
1853,	....	....	81,150 24	....
1854,	71,252 80	6,405 85	77,658 65	....
1855,	70,212 79	4,740 61	74,953 40	$65,785 95
1856,	67,746 91	5,216 57	72,763 48	75,185 26
1857,	63,999 53	5,954 55	69,954 08	62,643 78
1858,	47,263 07	5,325 60	52,588 67	34,990 77
1859,	64,512 09	8,171 24	72,683 33	77,783 59
1860,	88,211 11	12,134 61	100,345 72	103,879 62
1861,	92,144 32	9,857 51	102,001 83	42,849 82
1862,	92,885 86	9,638 04	102,523 90	107,690 54
1863,	87,179 49	12,746 57	99,926 06	104,784 16
1864,	74,940 22	41,850 74	116,790 96	119,312 74
1865,	74,601 39	5,671 29	80,272 68	80,712 50
1866,	89,323 94	8,410 97	97,734 91	95,839 17
Totals,	$1,153,913 02	$153,268 04	$1,578,104 46	$971,457 90

NOTE. — Wherever blanks occur in the above, reliable data could not be obtained.

Total Earnings and Cash Receipts, &c., — (Continued).

YEARS.	Treasurer's draft.	Salaries of officers.	Expenditures for ordinary support.	Expenditures for building, repairs, &c.
1847,	....	$22,965 00	$24,426 66	$5,138 60
1848,	....	....	56,057 29	10,912 12
1849,	....	....	51,451 85	5,326 14
1850,	....	24,828 96	30,894 32	15,440 79
1851,	....	....	69,107 11	19,439 14
1852,	....	28,201 44	39,288 94	18,801 35
1853,	....	....	66,047 43	14,468 94
1854,	$28,972 37	21,780 54	50,570 17	2,831 33
1855,	66,666 67	....	65,441 49	2,345 17
1856,	70,030 19	26,399 54	40,760 04	2,755 88
1857,	74,492 00	29,378 02	42,522 38	2,279 95
1858,	77,213 98	32,147 85	40,166 88	5,359 39
1859,	79,496 69	33,144 51	39,493 10	7,237 46
1860,	81,167 60	32,166 08	43,025 81	5,719 66
1861,	87,096 94	32,544 06	44,278 53	10,428 07
1862,	88,745 56	33,832 02	43,561 52	11,009 81
1863,	86,172 74	34,341 95	45,757 46	6,195 23
1864,	104,425 50	36,140 57	51,177 11	4,539 17
1865,	106,927 85	37,637 74	57,578 33	2,572 73
1866,	136,526 90	41,907 04	84,139 61	4,737 21
Totals,	$1,087,934 99	$467,415 32	$985,746 03	$157,538 14

YEARS.	Convict deposit refunded.	Total expenditures.	Number convicts on contract.	Number not on contract.	Total number of convicts.
1847,	....	$52,530 26	427	80	507
1848,	....	66,969 41	381	116	497
1849,	....	56,777 99	413	99	512
1850,	....	71,164 07	599	133	732
1851,	....	88,546 25	620	132	752
1852,	....	86,291 73	597	155	752
1853,	....	80,516 37	609	144	753
1854,	....	75,182 04	628	104	732
1855,	....	67,786 66	618	112	730
1856,	....	69,915 46	579	107	686
1857,	....	74,180 35	469	174	643
1858,	....	77,674 12	455	241	696
1859.	....	79,875 07	595	193	788
1860,	....	80,911 55	723	132	855
1861,	....	87,250 66	729	127	856
1862,	....	88,403 35	744	115	859
1863,	....	86,294 64	671	101	772
1864,	$12,016 85	103,873 70	553	99	652
1865,	8,201 14	105,989 94	417	110	527
1866,	3,197 67	134,001 73	517	171	688
Totals,	$23,415 66	$1,634,135 35	11,344	2,645	13,989

NOTE.—Wherever blanks occur in the above, reliable data could not be obtained.

ANNUAL EXHIBIT

Of the number of Prisoners received at, and discharged from, the State Prison at Auburn, with nativity and color, for the twenty years ending September 30, 1866.

YEARS.	Received.	DISCHARGED.				Escaped.	Captured.	TRANS-FERRED.		Died.	Total.	IN PRISON AT END OF THE YEAR.				
		Expiration.	Commutation.	Pardon.	Appellate Court.			To Lunatic Asy.	To other Prisons.			White.	Black.	Native.	Foreign.	Total.
1847,.	107	154	....	38	2	2	..	3	..	26	225	433	59	349	143	492
1848,.	179	133	....	55	2	2	..	3	..	3	198	414	59	393	80	473
1849,.	312	141	....	15	..	1	1	2	..	7	167	558	60	518	100	618
1850,.	304	133	....	22	3	4	..	8	2	9	181	668	64	527	205	732
1851,.	298	182	....	55	1	3	..	6	..	12	259	703	68	561	210	771
1852,.	293	172	....	85	1	3	..	4	36	11	312	. ..	..	540	212	752
1853,.	290	175	....	64	4	..	..	..	..	23	266	675	73	....	....	748
1854,.	237	165	....	62	3	1	..	1	4	17	253	672	60	....	....	732
1855,.	259	183	....	87	1	4	..	..	27	16	318	639	48	....	....	687
1856,.	201	164	8	47	..	1	..	..	..	6	226	610	52	....	....	662
1857,.	238	183	....	50	..	1	..	..	..	6	240	579	64	433	210	643
1858,.	297	172	....	53	1	4	..	..	..	14	244	633	63	457	239	696
1859,.	339	147	....	39	2	2	..	21	1	12	224	757	54	558	253	811
1860,.	283	194	...	25	..	2	..	7	..	13	241	780	73	600	253	853
1861,.	229	221	....	39	5	3	..	4	..	13	285	729	68	552	245	797
1862,.	300	238	....	29	7	2	..	10	..	18	304	735	58	503	290	793
1863,.	205	229	....	17	3	4	..	5	..	18	276	666	56	470	252	722
1864,.	168	267	....	50	2	3	..	3	..	15	340	511	39	370	180	550
1865,.	205	4	170	54	..	4	..	4	..	4	240	475	40	350	165	515
1866,.	469	4	156	61	3	..	..	3	..	3	230	708	45	506	247	753

Clinton State Prison.

This prison is located at Dannemora, in Clinton county, sixteen miles north-westerly from Plattsburg, on Lake Champlain, and on an elevation of seventeen hundred feet above the level of the lake. In addition to the prison inclosure, the State owns considerable real estate in the vicinity, from which timber is supplied for the use of the forges and other iron works connected with the prison.

The labor performed by the convicts is exclusively the manufacture of iron, procured from mines either belonging to or leased by the State, the ore being mined, separated, smelted, rolled into plates, and cut into nails of assorted sizes, all by convict labor, under the supervision of skilled foremen. The kegs for transportation are made from lumber sawed and seasoned on the premises, and the whole manufacture is carried on by the State, which realizes all the profits accruing from sales, the contract system having been abandoned about two years since. About 38,500 kegs of nails are annually manufactured.

The prison grounds, as inclosed within the pickets, comprise an area of about thirty-seven acres, and contain the following buildings:

1. The prison proper, consisting of a T shaped building, the central part containing cells, and the wings being used for the kitchen, eating, and guard-rooms, and other purposes. The prison dormitory, which contains the cells, is a stone edifice 500 feet in length, and 50

feet in width, in the clear, facing north and south, containing on each side three blocks of cells, one on the lower floor, which is paved with stone, and two above, fronted by wooden galleries, each block containing ninety cells, or five hundred and forty in all, three of which have solid iron doors instead of gratings, and are devoted exclusively to punishment by solitary confinement in darkness. Adjoining the dormitory, and forming part of the same structure, is a building three stories in height, facing westward, one hundred and sixty feet in length and forty-five feet in breadth, the lower floor of which is used as an eating-room for convicts, cook-room, kitchen, bake-house, and meat cellar. Above, and on a level with the lower floor of the dormitory, are the guard-room, keepers' mess-room, and chapel. The third story is used for hospital purposes, and contains also a dry-room and one or two smaller apartments.

2. The offices of the agent and warden, manufacturing department, and chaplain, which latter office also contains the prison library, and two dwelling-houses, one occupied by the agent, and the other rented to the clerk and chaplain, all frame buildings of moderate size, two stories in height.

3. The buildings and premises used for the manufacture of iron, as follows: A forge building, 132 feet by 64 feet, containing five steam boilers, two steam engines, with power sufficient to run ten forge fires, and turn out ten tons of iron per day. Two boiler rooms attached, each 35 feet by 26 feet, and engine room 51 feet by 56 feet. Rolling mill attached to forge, 71 feet by 30 feet, with boiler room 23 feet by 50 feet. Rolling mill, 107 feet by 72 feet, with three boilers and double engine of 30-horse power, with capacity of rolling twenty tons of plate iron per day. Nail factory number one, 70 feet by 36 feet. Nail factory number two, 42 feet by 33 feet, containing 48 nail machines, and capable of turning out 250 kegs of nails per day. Machine shop, 108 feet long by 40 feet, with boiler room attached, 51 feet by 18 feet. Blacksmith shop, under nail factory number one, 36 feet by 24 feet. Separator building, 150 feet long by 50 feet wide, with steam power and machinery attached for running eighteen stampers and eight sieves. Wood shed, 171 feet long by 33 feet wide. Ore house attached to separator, 63 feet long by 32 feet wide. Two coal houses for the accommodation of the forge, one 40 feet by 120 feet, and the other 40 feet by 100 feet, and yard room sufficient for piling 5,000 cords of wood. Five coal kilns, 43 feet by 16 feet. Office, near the forge, 26 feet by 18 feet. Horse barn, 40 feet by 20 feet. Saw-mill, 50 feet by 60 feet, containing one English gate of two or more saws, and one stock gang of 24 saws, capable of being increased to 42 saws, which machinery is propelled by a steam engine of 30-horse power, the basement being used as a stave factory. A dry house for staves, 23 feet square. (For valuation see Synopsis, page 318, 19th Annual Report.)

4. A three-story wooden building with cupola, now unoccupied, 150 feet long and 50 feet wide, formerly used as a contract shoe shop.

5. Tailor shop, 70 feet by 20 feet, with wash-house attached.

6. Barns, outhouses, &c.

Annexed will be found statistics of the prison, in a tabular form, since 1847.

TABLE of the number of Prisoners received at, and discharged from, Clinton Prison since 1847, *giving their color and nativity.*

YEARS.	Received during year.	DISCHARGED.				TRANS-FERRED.		Escaped.	REMAINING AT THE CLOSE OF THE YEAR.					
		By expiration and commutation.	Pardon.	Died.	By order of court.	To Insane Asylum.	To other prisons.		Total.	White.	Black.	Indian.	Native of United States.	Foreigners.
1847 *														
Dec. 31, 1848,.	85	33	10	4	..	1	....	2	181	...	..	..	....	...
do 1, 1849,.	†47	33	4	4	..	1	62	..	124	118	6	..	83	41
do 1, 1850,.	39	38	5	3	..	....	....	3	114	109	5	.	79	35
do 1, 1851,.	42	33	9	..	..	....	....	1	113	103	8	2	72	41
do 1, 1852,.	96	28	12	2	..	....	....	..	167	‡	‡	‡	‡	‡
do 1 1853,.	77	41	10	2	..	....	....	1	190	165	25	..	§	...
do 1, 1854,.	99	47	15	6	..	1	....	..	220	192	28	..	148	72
do 1, 1855,.	147	53	24	4	..	1	....	4	281	251	30	..	§	§
do 1, 1856,.	111	49	33	4	..	....	‖51	1	254	235	19	..	151	103
Oct. 1, 1857,.	¶121	62	35	1	3	....	....	..	274	258	16	..	169	105
do 1, 1858,.	171	67	18	1	1	....	....	..	358	335	23	..	117	141
do 1, 1859,.	185	63	16	2	1	12	...	2	447	414	30	..	262	185
do 1, 1860,.	114	**107	16	2	1	....	....	4	431	394	37	..	264	167
do 1, 1861,.	226	134	17	3	..	1	....	..	502	460	42	..	309	193
do 1, 1862,.	86	106	15	5	3	5	....	..	454	412	42	..	284	170
do 1, 1863..	129	166	18	4	1	1	1	..	392	347	44	1	253	139
do 1, 1864,.	103	130	13	12	..	....	....	..	340	307	31	2	219	121
do 1, 1865,.	††423	49	364	7	..	3	....	2	338	312	24	2	211	127
do 1, 1866,.	270	91	‡‡65	3	..	1	....	8	440	408	31	1	284	156

* No official report made during the year.
† Received since December 1, 1848, and partly embraced in preceding report.
‡ No report of color, &c.
§ No report.
‖ Transferred in November 1856, and therefore embraced in preceding report.
¶ Received since September 30, 1856, and therefore partly embraced in preceding report.
** Excess from report of preceding year.
†† Part United States prisoners.
‡‡ Pardoned by order of Secretary of War.

Account current of Clinton Prison (predicated upon Earnings and Expenditures) for 1865 *and* 1866.

1865.		1865.	
To total expenditures,..........	$110,829 15	By total earnings, ...	$38,275 71
		By manufacturing profit (statement 3), ...	49,617 85
		By due from U. S. for subsistence U. S. convicts, ...	20,150 40
		By cash on hand, ...	823 73
		By balance against prison,......	1,961 46
	$110,829 15		$110,829 51
1866.		1866.	
To total expenditure,...........	$93,797 22	By total earnings, ...	$27,956 05
To balance in favor of Prison,..	1,737 29	By manufacturing profit (statement 3), ...	67,576 23
		By cash on hand,................	1 63
	$95,534 51		$95,534 15

CONSOLIDATION, 1855 AND 1856.

1865.		1866.	
To balance brought down,.... .	$1,961 46	By balance brought down,......	$1,739 29
		By balance against prison, ...	224 17
	$1,961 46		$1,961 46
To balance against Prison brought down,................	$224 17		

NOTE.—The balance of $1,961.46 is the correct balance. In the annual report of this year, page 133, the available earnings should have been printed $27,557.56. See page 134.

Account Current of Clinton Prison (predicated upon the cash receipts from Comptroller), for years 1865 *and* 1866.

1865.		1865.	
To cash on hand,...............	$569 68	By deposited to credit of the State Treasurer, ...	$29,229 05
To cash received from Comptroller,...	111,083 20	By unavailable earnings,........	10,718 15
		By due from U. S. for subsistence of U. S. convicts,.............	20,150 40
		By net profits on manufacturing account (per statement No. 3),	49,617 85
		By balance, cash, carried down,.	823 73
		By balance against Prison, carried down,...................	1,113 70
	$111,652 88		$111,652 88
1866.		1866.	
To cash balance down,.........	$823 73	By deposited to credit of State Treasurer, ...	$5,974 60
To balance against Prison brought down, ...	1,113 70	By unavailable earnings,........	21,982 05
To cash received from Comptroller, ...	92,975 12	By net profit on manufacturing account (per statement No. 3),	67,576 23
To balance in favor of Prison,..	621 96	By balance cash on hand,.......	1 63
	$95,534 51		$95,534 51
1866.		1866.	
To balance on hand, cash,......	$1 63	By balance in favor of Prison,..	$621 96

Upon reference to the official annual reports of 1865 and 1866, it will be found that the deficit for the year 1865 was shown by a comparison between the earnings and expenditures, without taking in consideration the balance cash on hand remaining September, 1864; but the balance or deficit for the year 1866 was adduced by an analysis of cash received and expenditures, with balance of cash on hand. The above account current shows cash balances and total cash received, against which is placed the cash deposits, available earnings, and net profits of the manufacturing account.

MANUFACTURING BRANCH, CLINTON PRISON, N. Y.

ABSTRACT from the books and vouchers of the Manufacturing Department of Clinton Prison (and compared with the official annual reports), from the 1st April, 1865, to 1st October, 1866, showing the amount of cash received from all sources, the total expenditures, total cash deposits, stock on hand, with a consolidation of Prison and Manufacturing accounts.

PERIOD.	Cash rec'd from Comptroller.	Cash rec'd from sale of nails, ore, etc.	Total cash receipts.	Total cash expenditures.	Total cash deposited to credit of State Treasur'r.	Stock on hand.*
1865,.........	$48,473 85	$28,994 50	$77,468 35	$57,853 90	$17,333 84	$78,477 25
1866,.........	123,101 10	147,315 73	270,416 83	191,640 90	80,412 36	†$190,378 65
	$171,574 95	$176,310 23	$347,885 18	$249,494 80	$97,746 20	$190,378 65
Total cash deposited as above,.........				97,746 20		
Cash balance, 30th September, 1866,.........				644 18		
				$347,885 18		

STATEMENT SHOWING NET PROFIT.

To stock on hand, 30th September, 1866,.........			$190,378 65
By received from Comptroller,.........		$171,574 95	
Deduct amount paid Comptroller,.........	$97,746 20		
Deduct amount cash on hand,.........	644 18		
		98,390 38	
Actual net profits of the manufacturing account,.........			73,184 57
			$117,194 08

‡ RECAPITULATION.—Net profit, 1865,.........	$49,617 85	
Net profit, 1866,.........	67,576 23	
		$117,194 08

* Upon reference to the official reports of the years 1865 and 1866, it will be found that the "stock on hand" herein given are distinct and separate from the general Prison stock. These amounts have been earned by the manufacturing branch of the Prison, and therefore the manufacturing account has been credited with them. This report, therefore, shows a net profit to manufacturing account as follows: $117.194.08. (See statement per other side, showing that the amount paid into the treasury is less than the amount received from the Comptroller by $73,184.57; consequently, that amount deducted from the "stock on hand" leaves the actual net profit, as every other indebtedness has been adjusted.)

† This amount ($190,378.65) embraces "stock on hand," $182,028.65, and "new machinery," $8,370, both of which amounts are shown on page 294, in Manufacturing Statement, 19th Official Annual Report.

‡ See Account Current.

ABSTRACT

Of the Books and Vouchers (and compared with annual reports) of Clinton Prison, from September 30th, 1854, to September 30th, 1866, giving Cash Receipts from Treasury and other sources, available and unavailable Earnings, &c.

PERIOD.	Cash received from Comptroller.	Miscellaneous earnings received and deposited.	Contract earnings.	Unavailable earnings.	Total earnings.	Total expenditures.	Total receipts deposited to the credit of State Treasurer.
1855,	$49,403 82	$980 05	$28,120 91	$8,226 60	$37,327 56	$48,844 56	$980 05
1856,	55,039 30	1,188 11	28,675 25	16,855 21	46,718 57	55,032 74	7,497 26
1857,	47,651 41	1,339 55	24,502 59	12,462 55	38,304 69	47,947 30	24,884 66
1858,	55,825 43	1,087 86	20,333 02	31,505 00	52,925 88	55,782 25	6,994 91
1859,	71,126 32	374 20	20,129 86	24,897 50	45,401 56	71,018 67	16,263 95
1860,	63,144 61	519 36	26,121 56	17,178 07	43,818 99	63,115 14	27,515 81
1861,	63,769 15	1,180 00	36,921 64	12,669 12	50,770 76	63,857 38	14,533 27
1862,	63,663 70	797 36	40,351 52	11,567 23	52,716 11	63,585 92	33,330 05
1863,	65,430 74	2,832 77	38,930 56	7,205 69	48,969 02	64,694 51	41,479 34
1864,	69,719 64	2,371 66	36,355 06	8,731 63	47,458 35	70,176 58	38,256 58
1865,	111,083 20	5,564 41	21,993 15	10,718 15	38,275 71	110,829 15	29,229 05
1866,	92,975 12	5,974 60	....	21,982 05	27,956 65	93,797 22	5,974 60
	$808,832 44	$24,209 93	$322,435 12	$183,998 80	$530,643 85	$808,681 42	$246,939 53
Balance due Mr. Hull, agent, September, 1854,						149 39	
Balance on hand 30th September, 1866,						1 63	
						$808,832 44	

The books of Mr. Hull, agent, show a balance at the end of the fiscal year 1854 of $149.39 in favor of the Prison.

Several typographical errors have been discovered in the printed official reports, which have been corrected in this statement.

For statistics of the manufacture of iron, see Appendix ——, the figures contained in the columns of the years 1865 and 1866 are from the books of the Prison proper, and have no connection with the accounts of the manufacturing department.

Total value of State property 30th September, 1866, including real estate, Prison buildings, &c., &c., $678,606.21. (See Annual Report, 1867.)

LEGISLATIVE APPROPRIATIONS.

ABSTRACT of the books and vouchers of Clinton Prison, from 30th September, 1847, *to* 30*th September*, 1854, *showing cash appropriations, total cash earnings, total receipts, total expenditures, with cash balances, &c., &c.*

YEARS.	Cash received from appropriations.	Total cash earnings.	Total cash receipts.	Total expenditures.	CASH BALANCES. Dr. Due by prison.	CASH BALANCES. Cr. Due to prison.	REMARKS.
1847, cash balance on hand, $801.20,	....	....	....	....	$801 20	....	No official report was made for the year 1847.
1848,	$40,487 47	$1,049 46	$41,536 93	$41,510 16	827 97	....	
1849,	40,330 12	9,210 97	49,541 09	50,126 47	242 59	....	
1850,	19,723 01	12,601 95	32,324 96	32,693 97	....	$126 42	
1851,	13,500 00	12,364 10	25,864 10	25,958 13	....	220 45	
1852,	30,000 00	10,029 79	40,029 79	39,825 20	....	15 86	
1853,	21,000 00	21,847 26	42,847 26	44,483 14	....	1,651 74	This statement includes all the cash appropriations received to the 30th Sept., 1854.
1854,	26,816 64	14,819 40	41,636 04	39,983 96	34	....	
	$191,857 24	$81,922 93	$274,581 37	$274,581 03	The succeeding statement commences with cash received from Comptroller, from 1st October, 1854.		
Cash balance on hand, September 30, 1854,				34			
				$274,581 37			

ABSTRACT

Of the Total Earnings and Cash Receipts, and the total Cash Expenditures, with the average number of all the Convicts, per day, per month, at the Clinton Prison, from October 1st, 1846, *to September 30th,* 1866.

YEARS.	Contract earnings.	Miscellaneous earnings.	Total earnings.	Deposits in bank.	Treasurer's draft.	Salaries of officers.
1847,........	....	....	$62, 23	....	....	....
1848,.......	....	....	5, 549 46	....	....	....
1849,........	....	....	13,210 97	....	....	....
1850,........	....	....	18,451 95	....	....	....
1851,........	....	....	17, 664 10	....	....	....
1852,........	....	....	29, 736 20	....	$30, 000 00	$14,145 82
1853,........	$22,188 02	$15,019 75	37,207 77	....	....	....
1854,........	23,182 04	18, 492 00	41,674 04	....	26,816 84	15,344 02
1855,........	28,120 91	4, 251 27	32 372 18	....	....	18,734 77
1856,...	28,675 20	9,225 56	37,900 76	$7,651 04	55, 039 30	20,302 95
1857,........	24, 553 03	2, 329 55	26, 882 58	24,882 66	47,651 41	22,753 16
1858,........	20,333 02	335 61	20,668 63	6,994 91	55,825 43	25,630 26
1859,........	20, 129 86	374 20	20 504 06	16,263 95	71,126 32	28,996 89
1860,........	26,121 56	519 36	26,640 92	27,515 81	63,144 61	29,048 06
1861,........	36,921 64	1,098 35	38,019 99	14,533 27	63,769 15	29,360 28
1862,........	40,351 52	797 36	41,148 88	33, 330 05	63,663 70	29,683 10
1863,........	38,930 56	2, 836 77	41,767 33	41,479 34	65, 430 74	28,898 67
1864,........	36,355 06	2,371 66	38,726 72	38, 256 58	69,719 64	30,157 72
1865,........	21,993 15	5,564 41	27,567 56	29,229 05	111,083 20	34,683 61
1866,........	....	5,974 60	5,974 60	5,794 60	92,975 12	34,061 24
Totals, ...	....	....	$521,730 93	....	....	....

YEARS.	Expenditures for ordinary support.	Expenditures for building, repairs, &c.	Convict deposit refunded.	Total expenditures.	No. of convicts on contract.	No. not on contract.	Total number of convicts.
1847,...............	....	....	....	$45,000 00	....	....	....
1848,...............	$30,807 82	$9,093 16	....	39,900 98	....	....	146
1849,...............	30,620 96	19,505 51	....	50,126 47	....	....	157
1850,...............	24,895 66	12,798 31	....	37,693 97	....	....	114
1851,...............	29,843 12	8,115 01	....	37,958 13	....	....	119
1852,...............	16,447 22	9,452 61	....	40,045 65	....	....	167
1853,...............	29,307 86	20,175 28	....	49,483 14	....	....	186
1854,...............	42,833 30	2,911 43	....	61,088 75	72	127	199
1855,...............	25,321 26	4,778 53	....	48,844 56	161	84	249
1856,...............	29,484 06	5,245 75	....	55,032 76	184	119	303
1857,...............	23,734 39	1,459 74	....	47,947 29	193	84	277
1858,...............	28,523 51	1,627 99	....	55,781 76	184	140	324
1859,...............	38,065 42	3,956 36	....	71,018 67	237	210	447
1860,...............	32,857 80	1,209 28	....	63,115 14	243	206	449
1861,...............	31,824 86	2,672 24	....	63,857 38	336	149	485
1862,...............	31,643 04	2,259 76	....	63,585 90	346	108	454
1863,...............	34,425 83	1,370 01	....	64,694 51	329	106	435
1864,...............	38,028 83	1,990 03	....	70,176 58	283	88	371
1865,...............	75,492 63	625 71	....	110,892 15	155	292	447
1866,...............	59,521 59	214 13	....	93,797 22	....	....	393
Totals,...	....	....	....	$1,169,978 01	....	....	....

NOTE.—Wherever blanks occur in the above, reliable data could not be obtained.

State Asylum for Insane Convicts.

The State Asylum for Insane Convicts is situated immediately in the rear of Auburn State Prison. The grounds of the institution form a square, surrounded by a substantial stone wall measuring 12 feet high and 500 feet in length on either side. The main structure is of stone, and consists of a central building 44 feet wide and 60 feet deep; a wing on either side, 100 feet wide and 27 feet deep; a transept on either end, 25 feet wide and 66 feet deep—the whole presenting an entire front of 294 feet.

In the rear are several other buildings for purposes immediately relating to the care of the insane. One, comprising a chapel, sewing-room, apothecary shop, bakery, cook-room and dining-room, &c., 90 feet long and 40 feet wide; carpenter shop and blacksmith shop, 45 feet long and 18 feet wide; ice-house, soup-house and tool-room, 47 feet long and 18 feet wide; barn, with vegetable cellar, 33 feet long and 34 feet wide; wash-house, boiler-house and ironing-room, 40 feet long and 28 feet wide.

A great portion of the stone, tin-roofing, window sash and frames, iron grating, and other building materials of which the Asylum was constructed, was taken from a building formerly standing within the prison walls, and which was taken down for that purpose.

The institution was first opened for the reception of patients on February 2, 1859, since which time the number of inmates received and discharged has been as follows:

	Received.	Discharged.
During fiscal year ending September 30, 1859,	55	4
do do do 1860,	14	10
do do do 1861,	30	16
do do do 1862,	27	15
do do do 1863,	10	12
do do do 1864,	6	14
do do do 1865,	9	7
do do do 1866,	4	7
To June 1, 1867,	9	3
Whole since opening of Asylum,	164	88

Of the whole number received, there were of those born in the United States (white 55, colored 17),	72	In Italy,	2
In Canada,	8	In Turkey,	1
In Ireland,	45	In France,	2
In England,	10	In Cuba,	1
In Germany,	21	In Denmark,	1
In Switzerland,	1		164

Since the opening of the Asylum the number of deaths has been 12. These are enumerated in the list of those discharged.

The annexed tables, taken from the last Annual Report, will give an exhibit of the yearly expenses of the Asylum from its opening until the close of the fiscal year ending September 30, 1866:

TABLE NO. 9.

Showing the current expenses of each year since the opening of the Asylum.

YEARS.	Amount.
For the eleven months ending September 30, 1859,	$16,387 07
do year ending September 30, 1860,	17,491 50
do do do 1861,	14,173 85
do do do 1862,	12,674 01
do do do 1863,	12,035 80
do do do 1864,	13,942 07
do do do 1865,	16,699 18
do do do 1866,	15,937 15
	$119,340 63

TABLE NO. 10.

Showing the average number of patients in the Asylum each year since its opening.

YEARS.	Average.
During the eleven months ending September 30, 1859,	27 1-73
do year ending September 30, 1860,	48 1-2
do do do 1861,	62
do do do 1862,	78 2-3
do do do 1863,	80 1-10
do do do 1864,	79 1-12
do do do 1865,	72 3-4
do do do 1866,	70 1-5

TABLE NO. 11.

Showing the average total cost per week for each patient during the several years since the opening of the Asylum.

YEARS.	Average.
For the eleven months ending September 30, 1859,	$11 66 1-2
do year ending September 30, 1860,	5 80 3-4
do do do 1861,	4 38
do do do 1862,	3 10
do do do 1863,	2 89
do do do 1864,	3 39
do do do 1865,	4 41 1-2
do do do 1866,	4 36 3-5

Table showing the nativity of all the inmates of our prisons, including the Asylum for Insane Convicts, at the close of the year ending September 30, 1866.

PRISONS.	NATIVES OF THE U. S.		FOREIGNERS.		TOTAL.	
	Male.	Female.	Male.	Female.	Male.	Female.
Auburn,	506	....	247	....	753	....
Sing Sing,	648	73	554	91	1,202	164
Clinton,	295	....	145	....	440	....
Insane Asylum,	40	....	30	....	70	....
Totals,	1,489	73	976	91	2,465	164

Table exhibiting the total number of convicts remaining in the several prisons on the 30th September, 1866, and the nature of their conditions.

PRISONS.	Crimes against person.	Crimes against property.	Crimes against both.	Crimes against United States.	Total.	Temperate.	Moderate.	Intemperate.	Total.
Sing Sing,..........................	160	959	81	2	1,202	221	434	547	1,202
Sing Sing, Female,........	20	144	....	....	164	61	29	74	164
Auburn,............................	130	591	....	32	753	165	201	387	753
Clinton,............................	81	354	....	5	440	107	185	148	440
Asylum,.....	19	44	6	1	70	....	....	....	70
Totals,..........................	410	2,092	87	40	2,629	554	849	1,156	2,629

Table showing the number of white and colored convicts remaining in all the prisons, September 30, 1866; also, the number of cells in each of the prisons.

PRISONS.	White.	Colored.	Indian.	Total convicts.	Cells.
Sing Sing, ...	1,123	79	....	1,202	1,191
Sing Sing, Female,..	146	18	....	164	117
Auburn,..	708	45	....	753	992
Clinton,...	408	31	1	440	544
Asylum, ...	57	12	1	70	....
Totals,...	2,442	185	2	2,629	2,844

Exhibit of the real and personal property at the several State Prisons in this State, including the Asylum for Insane Convicts, for the year ending September 30, 1866.

PRISONS.	Real estate.	Personal property.	Total.
Sing Sing,................................	$548,918 80	$105,553 28	$654,472 08
Female Prison,.....................	122,825 00	9,619 41	132,444 41
Auburn,...................................	559,210 00	49,150 23	608,360 23
Clinton,..................................	....	....	678,006 21
Convict Asylum,..........................	82,291 00	11,395 24	93,686 24
Totals,...................................	$1,313,244 80	$175,718 16	$2,166,969 17

NEW YORK PRISON ASSOCIATION.

The Prison Association was organized in 1844, and chartered by the Legislature in 1846. It was formed on the suggestion of the Board of State Prison Inspectors, and many leading citizens took part in its organization. The first President was the Hon. WILLIAM T. McCOUN, Vice-Chancellor of the State.

The officers of the society are a President, Vice-President, Recording Secretary, Corresponding Secretary, and Treasurer, who, together with an Executive Committee of twenty-five, constitute a Board of Management. The objects of the Association, as stated in its charter of incorporation, are three, viz.: 1. The amelioration of the condition of prisoners, whether detained for trial, or finally convicted, or as witnesses. 2. The improvement of prison discipline, and the government of prisons, whether for cities, counties, or States. 3. The support and encouragement of reformed convicts after their discharge, by affording them the means of obtaining an honest livelihood, and sustaining them in their efforts at reform.

The act of incorporation imposes on the Association important duties, and confers high powers. Among its duties is that of visiting, inspecting and examining all the prisons in the State, and annually reporting to the Legislature their state and condition, and all such other things in regard to them as may enable the Legislature to perfect their government and discipline. To enable it to discharge this duty, by obtaining the necessary information and making the required report, it is clothed with the power and authority to examine, on oath, any of the officers of the prisons visited and inspected, and to converse with the prisoners confined therein, without the presence of the keepers thereof, or any of them; and it is made the duty of the keepers to admit the members of the Association as inspectors, or any of them, into every part of the prisons; to exhibit to them all the books, papers, documents, and accounts pertaining to the prison or to the detention of the persons confined therein, and to render them every other facility in their power, to enable them to discharge the duties above described.

To aid itself in carrying into effect the first and third of the objects named in its charter, the Society employs a general agent, who visits the various detention prisons in New York and Brooklyn, looking into the cases of persons held in them for examination or trial, and gives such relief and assistance as they may seem severally to require. He also seeks situations for discharged prisoners, and aids them in such other ways as may appear proper.

The second object named in the charter is reached through the action of special committees of visitation, annually appointed by the executive committee, who make the examinations of the prisons required. By such committees all the prisons in the State, of every class and grade, have been repeatedly examined and full reports made thereupon, as directed by law.

In addition to the labors of the agents of the Association in New York and Kings counties, there are local committees appointed in each county of the State, who exercise a general supervision on behalf of the Association over the jails and penitentiaries in their several districts, and report annually to the central office. The organization in Erie county has been particularly efficient and satisfactory. These committees serve without pay.

It is thus seen that the Prison Association is in part a State and in part a voluntary organization. It expends annually on its work about

$12,000, a part of which is drawn from State and city appropriations, and a part is contributed by private benevolence.

The Association has been twenty-two years in existence, and has just issued its twenty-second annual report. The general results of the labors of these twenty-two years are therein thus summed up: 78,664 persons visited in prisons; 22,881 complaints examined; 6,233 complaints withdrawn; 6,970 prisoners discharged from custody; 12,881 released prisoners aided with board, clothing, tools, railroad tickets or money; and 3,677 discharged convicts provided with situatious — giving a total of 130,108 cases in which relief, moral and material, or both, has been extended to persons who, justly or unjustly, have been subjected to criminal arrest, prosecution or imprisonment; besides which, assistance more or less extensive, has been afforded to thousands connected with the families so relieved.

STATE AGRICULTURAL SOCIETY.

The Society for the Promotion of Agricultural Arts and Manufactures was instituted February 26, 1791, and incorporated March 12, 1793. For more efficient action this Society, in 1801, divided the State into as many districts as there were counties, and in each district there was appointed a Secretary, with power to convene the members of the Society within his district, inquire into the state of agriculture and manufactures, receive communications, and arrange and transmit them to the President of the Society. Its transactions were printed by the State, and the organization numbered among its members persons of eminence throughout the State. Their labors were highly valuable to the cause of science, and contributed largely toward inspiring a laudable emulation in the several departments of practical knowledge that came within their sphere of operation. In 1791 the Society issued circulars for the purpose of collecting information upon a wide range of subjects, and although no general summaries were published, they had a most beneficial influence upon the public. It may be remarked that this movement was prior to the formation of the "Board of Agriculture" in England, and that it anticipated most of the ideas which subsequently entered into the plans of that organization.

The charter of the Society for the Promotion of Agriculture, Arts and Manufactures, expired by its own limitation in 1804, and was continued under a new act as the "Society for the Promotion of the Useful Arts," in which the affairs of the Society were managed by a board of nine members, and the State patronage in the printing of its transactions was continued. This, like the former, was a State society, and continued to engage the interest of prominent citizens throughout the State. In 1808-12, during the international difficulties which preceded the war, and while the importation of foreign fabrics was forbidden by embargo laws, the Legislature invested this society with powers to award, alone or in conjunction with the judges of county courts, such discretionary premiums upon woolen cloths manufactured in families as they might deem proper within certain limits. The samples upon which these awards were made are still preserved in the library of the Albany Institute, and form an authentic and interesting record of the progress of the domestic arts at that period.

On the 7th of April, 1819, the Legislature passed "An act to improve the agriculture of the State" which appropriated $10,000 a year for two years for the promotion of agriculture and family domestic manufactures within the State, specified the amount due to each county, encouraged the formation of county agricultural societies, and provided that the Presidents of these societies, or a delegate to be chosen for the purpose should constitute a "Board of Agriculture." This Board was to meet in the Capitol on the first Monday after the meeting of the Legislature, organize, receive and examine papers and essays, with power to publish annually, at the expense of the State, a volume to be distributed by means of the county societies throughout the State.

The Board of Agriculture, in the more essential features of its operations, superceded the Society for the promotion of Useful Arts, although the latter continued to exist as a local institution until 1829, when it was merged with the "Albany Lyceum of Natural History," in the "Albany Institute." The latter has, in its library and cabinet, at its rooms in the Albany Male Academy, all the collections of the societies that preceded it, holds stated meetings throughout the winter months, and publishes its transactions.

The Board of Agriculture existed but a short period, and published three volumes of its Memoirs. The societies formed under this impulse in the several counties, continued in active existence a few years, but they gradually declined in interest and were abandoned, one after another, until, it is believed, all except that in Jefferson county were extinct. The premiums awarded under the patronage of the act of 1819 were mostly in plate, and there is scarcely a county in the State in which there may not be found more or less of these mementoes of successful competition in household manufactures or agricultural products.

The State Agricultural Society now in existence was organized in 1832, under the presidency of JAMES D. LE RAY DE CHAUMONT, an early and wealthy landholder of Jefferson county. It received nothing from the Legislature but a corporate existence, with power to take and hold real and personal estate (the former to the amount of $25,000), and was limited in its existence to twenty years. Under this impulse, the effort of maintaining county societies was renewed to some extent. The State Society held a cattle show and fair in 1833, but want of funds prevented for several years the continuation of this practice. In 1841 an act was passed for the encouragement of agriculture, by appropriating $8,000 annually for five years, to be divided among the County Agricultural Societies, according to a rate specified in the act, and this appropriation has been since continued. The State Society was re-organized the same year, and a fair held with great success, and these fairs have since been held annually in various parts of the State, increasing in interest, utility and importance each year. The statements which follow exhibit the financial results of these fairs and other items of interest relating to them. The State Society had no rooms of its own for its meetings until 1844, when the Commissioners of the Land Office assigned for its use the rooms formerly occupied by the Comptroller in the old State Hall. These were occupied until December of that year, when the rooms formerly used by the Treasurer, in the rear of the wing, were assigned for this use. In 1848 more ample accommodations were allowed, and upon rebuilding the premises in 1855 the present accommodations for the Society were provided.

The library was commenced by Judge BUEL, and has been increased by exchanges and donations until it amounts to about 3,000 volumes, besides pamphlets. It is constantly receiving the publications of other societies in this and other countries, and most of the periodicals and publications having especial reference to agriculture or the sciences that relate thereto. Its museum now embraces a large collection of agricultural implements and articles of historical and practical interest. A lecture-room affords ample facilities for the meetings of the Society, and the plans embrace a laboratory for such chemical analyses as might be needed, although this feature of the institution has never been carried into effect.

The Society holds an annual meeting on the second Wednesday of February, at its rooms in Albany, for the election of officers, and on this occasion there is held an exhibition of grains, fruits and agricultural products, upon which premiums are awarded, although the principal display of these articles is made at the autumnal fairs.

By an act to facilitate the formation of agricultural and horticultural societies, passed June 8, 1853, and amended April 13, 1855, any ten or more persons of full age, citizens of the United States, and a majority of them citizens of this State, may form a society and file their articles in the office of the Secretary of State, and also in the office of the County Clerk of the county in which their business is held. These articles must state the name and title by which the society shall be known in law, the particular business and objects of the society, the number of trustees, directors or managers, and the names of those chosen for the first year of its existence.

The societies thus formed may acquire real estate for their use, not exceeding $25,000 in value if a county, or $10,000 if a town, village or city society. The personal estates of the former are limited to $1,000, and of the latter to $3,000. There can be but one county society in a county, nor but one town society in a town, but two or more towns may unite in forming a society without infringing this regulation. They are required to report annually to the State Agricultural Society a duly certified statement of receipts and expenditures, and a list of premiums awarded, and they possess the ordinary powers and liabilities of corporations. The act of 1855 provided that any person paying into the treasury of the society a sum to be fixed by the by-laws, and not less than $10, should become life members, with all the privileges of annual members, and gave to those who should contribute annually a given sum the rights and immunities of stockholders in such societies. The general results of transactions under these laws are stated on pages 39 and 40 of this volume. Their reports are usually published in the annual reports of the State Agricultural Society.

Record of New York State Fairs, from 1841 *to* 1867.

LOCATIONS.	Years.	DATES.		Fair receipts.	Other receipts.	PRESIDENTS.
Syracuse, ...	1841	September	29, 30	$349 00	$1,707 87	Joel B. Nott.
Albany,.......	1842	do	27, 28, 29	876 70	1,473 22	Jas. S. Wadsworth.*
Rochester,....	1843	do	19, 20, 21	2,479 88	1,756 79	do do
Poughkeepsie,	1844	do	17, 18, 19	3,723 80	1,142 00	John P. Beekman.*
Utica, ...	1845	do	16, 17, 18	4,450 18	940 00	B. P. Johnson.
Auburn, ...	1846	do	15, 16, 17	4,530 17	1,105 00	John W. Sherwood.
Saratoga, ...	1847	do	14, 15, 16	4,187 22	1,735 97	George Vail.
Buffalo, ...	1848	do	5, 6, 7	6,417 80	1,917 25	Lewis F. Allen.
Syracuse, ...	1849	do	11, 12, 13	8,287 55	1,793 28	John A. King.
Albany,.......	1850	do	3, 4, 5, 6	10,855 61	1,590 00	Ezra P. Prentice.
Rochester,...	1851	do	16, 17, 18, 19	12,396 25	2,179 53	John Delafield.*
Utica, ...	1852	do	7, 8, 9, 10	8,336 16	1,147 06	Henry Wager.*
Saratoga,.....	1853	do	20, 21, 23, 24	6,411 39	1,190 38	Lewis G. Morris.
New York, ...	1854	October	3, 4, 5, 6	9,538 70	204 75	William Kelly.
Elmira, ...	1855	do	2, 3, 4, 5	11,527 25	....	Samuel Cheever.
Watertown, ..	1856	Sept. 30, Oct.	1, 2, 3	8,536 00	1,300 00	Theodore S. Faxton.
Buffalo, ...	1857	October	6, 7, 8, 9	15,585 34	2,500 00	Alonzo S. Upham.
Syracuse, ...	1858	do	5, 6, 7, 8	10,970 28	3,290 73	Wm. T. McCoun.
Albany,.......	1859	do	4, 5, 6, 7	18,819 33	2,940 00	A. B. Conger.
Elmira, ...	1860	do	2, 3, 4, 5	9,345 95	3,031 80	B. N. Huntington.
Watertown, ..	1861	September	17, 18, 19, 20	8,018 40	2,511 12	George Geddes.
Rochester,....	1862	Sept. 30, Oct.	1, 2, 3	11,559 45	2,008 69	Ezra Cornell.
Utica, ...	1863	September	15, 16, 17, 18	11,619 78	2,161 67	Edwin G. Faile.*
Rochester,....	1864	do	20, 21, 22, 23	15,487 94	2,064 00	James O. Sheldon.
Utica, ...	1865	do	12, 13, 14, 15	11,471 76	3,505 36	Theodore C. Peters.
Saratoga, ...	1866	do	11, 12, 13, 14	11,226 45	1,994 17	J. Stanton Gould.

Secretaries — 1841, H. S. RANDALL; 1842-3-5, LUTHER TUCKER; 1844, HENRY O'REILLY; 1846, JOEL B. NOTT; 1847, and since, B. P. JOHNSON.

AMERICAN INSTITUTE.

This corporation was created by special act, May 2, 1829, "for the purpose of encouraging and promoting domestic industry in this State and the United States, in Agriculture, Manufactures and the Arts, and any improvements made therein, by bestowing rewards," &c. The Institute has since continued in active operation, and by means of annual fairs, discussions and publications, has pursued the objects of its organization with much success. The act of 1841 allowed it to share in the appropriations for the encouragement of Agriculture made in that year and which have been continued. Its annual reports have, since 1841, been printed with the legislative documents. With the exception of one or two years, in which they formed a part of the volume of Transactions of the State Agricultural Society, they have been published separately, and like the report of the State Society, in large editions, for use as premiums by county agricultural societies throughout the State.

* Deceased.

JUDICIAL DEPARTMENT.

Office of the Clerk of the Court of Appeals.

In addition to the records of the Court of Appeals, since its organization, this office contains the records of the Colonial Courts of the State, the records of the late Courts of Chancery and Supreme Courts, the records of the Court for the trial of Impeachments and the Correction of Errors, and also the records of wills admitted to probate in said Courts of Chancery and the Supreme Court prior to 1847, except such records as were turned over by the Register in Chancery and the Clerk of the late Supreme Court to the Clerk of the city and county of New York, pursuant to chapter 280 of the Laws of 1847, entitled "An act in relation to the Judiciary."

Since the organization of the Court of Appeals, in 1847, to the 1st of January, 1867, six thousand five hundred and fifty-five (6,555) causes have been brought up from inferior courts by appeal or writ of error, of which four thousand five hundred and fifty (4,550) have been disposed of, as set forth in Schedule "A." This excludes the causes which have been decided since January 1st, 1867, and those which have been disposed of by settlement between the parties. The number of the latter class it has been impossible to ascertain, although a circular was issued to the members of the bar for the purpose of eliciting definite information on that point. The entire number of causes now remaining upon the yearly calendar for future argument is 894.

The fees received at this office and paid over to the State Treasurer, pursuant to section 10 of chapter 280 of the Laws of 1847, amounted in the aggregate to the sum of $12,665.25. The schedule marked "B" shows the amount received and paid over in each year respectively.

The fund known as the Library Fund came into the hands of the Clerk of this Court on the 4th day of January, 1849, and amounted to the sum of fifty thousand six hundred and fifty-seven dollars and fifty-six cents ($50,657.56), which said sum has not nominally increased or diminished since that time, the whole being invested in bond and mortgage or United States Government securities, the interest accruing therefrom only being subject to draft, and appropriated as follows: One-fourth to the completion and replenishment of the law libraries of the four Judges of this Court, elected directly as such; the balance to the support of the law libraries of this Court located at Binghamton, Rochester and Syracuse. The amounts received by the Clerk of this Court from the interest of said fund, and disbursed by him for the purposes aforesaid, are embraced in Schedule "C."

The amount which passed into the hands of the Clerk of the Court of Appeals, belonging to the Chancery Fund at the time of the organization of this Court in 1847, was ninety-three thousand eight hundred and eight dollars and seventy-three cents ($93,808.73). On the 1st day of August, 1854, an additional sum amounting to three thousand six hundred and twenty-two dollars and two cents ($3,622.02), was paid in by the Life Insurance and Trust Company, and was incorporated with this fund.

The Chancery Fund being held in trust for infants, idiots, lunatics, &c., wards of the court, the principal, as well as interest of the said fund, is at any time liable to be withdrawn upon the order of the court. This fund has, therefore, been reduced actually as well as nominally, schedule "D," being a condensed statement or transcript from the books of the office, shows the amount of receipts and disbursements in gross relating to the fund.

Schedule "E"contains a list of the parcels of land, the title to which is in the Clerk of the Court of Appeals, such title having been acquired under decrees of foreclosure and sale upon mortgages held by him and belonging to said Trust Fund, the said parcels of land being bid in by the clerk upon the sale, no other bidders being present and offering a sum adequate to the value of the premises, or equal to the amount of the mortgage held by him. Schedule "F" contains a list of judgments for the deficiency upon said sales, the names of the judgment debtors, the amount of said judgments, and when the same were docketed.

SCHEDULE A.

Number of causes disposed of in the Court of Appeals since its organization to January 1, 1867; *also, number of causes brought into Court by appeal or writ of error during said time, and number of days in each year during which the Court was in session.*

YEARS.	Dismissed.	Affirmed.	Reversed.	Miscellaneous.	Total.	No. of causes brought into Court.	No. of days in session.
1847,	6	23	4	2	35	119	43
1848,	17	86	25	9	137	268	97
1849,	31	121	36	5	193	275	101
1850,	29	121	29	8	187	228	94
1851,	18	111	46	4	179	257	102
1852,	43	98	65	4	210	260	100
1853,	15	128	45	7	195	207	106
1854,	20	131	63	4	218	265	104
1855,	19	137	61	4	221	239	102
1856,	25	105	49	10	189	301	108
1857,	17	111	45	5	178	362	103
1858,	22	188	108	6	324	479	124
1859,	27	186	78	33	324	457	123
1860,	25	169	57	11	262	447	106
1861,	27	132	55	14	228	446	111
1862,	20	188	75	4	287	497	95
1863,	18	176	83	10	287	383	98
1864,	20	188	59	6	273	361	92
1865,	21	177	61	37	296	317	88
1866,	35	210	63	19	327	387	78
	455	2,786	1,107	202	4,550	6,555	1,978

SCHEDULE B.

Amount of fees received by the Clerk of the Court of Appeals, and paid over to the State Treasurer.

YEARS.	Name of Clerk.	Amount.
1848,	Charles S. Benton,	$697 97
1849,	do do	1,534 60
1850.	do do	556 15
1851,	do do	1,114 87
1852,	do do	1,021 15
1853,	do do	506 60
1854,	Benjamin F. Harwood,	461 86
1855,	do do	227 24
1856,	do do	261 26
1857,	Russell F. Hicks,	506 73
1858,	do do	195 69
1859,	do do	532 09
1860,	Charles Hughes,	200 00
1861,	do do	400 00
1862,	do do	407 20
1863,	Frederick A. Tallmadge,	None.
1864,	do do	599 91
1865,	do do	1,317 90
1866,	Patrick H. Jones,	1,123 94
		$11,665 25

SCHEDULE C.

Statement of the Library Fund of the Court of Appeals.

1849.

Dr.	Amount.	Amount.
To securities discharged and deducted,	$32,649 43	....
To amount paid for new securities,	....	$26,100 00
To amount to librarians,	....	633 32
To amount to libraries,	....	315 00
To amount to judges,	....	5,250 00
To balance of securities,	44,108 23	....
To balance of cash,	....	8,535 37
	$76,757 66	$40,833 69

Cr.	Amount.	Amount.
By amount of securities on hand,	$50,657 66	....
By amount of cash on hand, principal,	....	....
By amount of cash on hand, interest,	....	$5,685 21
By amount received for discharged securities,	....	32,311 93
By amount of interest received,	....	2,836 55
By new securities added,	26,100 00	....
	$76,757 66	$40,833 69

Schedule C — (Continued).

1850.

Dr.	Amount.	Amount.
To securities discharged and deducted,	$16,710 86	....
To amount paid for new securities,	....	$21,900 00
To amount disbursed to librarians,	....	502 06
To amount disbursed to libraries,	....	107 97
To amount disbursed to judges,	....	3,645 13
To balance of securities,	49,297 37	....
To balance of cash,	....	3,239 39
	$66,098 23	$29,394 55

Cr.	Amount.	Amount.
By balance of securities brought down,	$44,108 23	....
By balance of cash brought down,	....	$8,535 37
By amount received for discharged securities,	....	6,710 86
By amount of interest received,	....	4,148 32
By new securities added,	21,900 00	....
	$66,008 23	$29,394 55

1851.

Dr.	Amount.	Amount.
To securities discharged and deducted,	$1,550 00	....
To amount paid for new securities,	....	$2,400 00
To amount disbursed to librarians,	....	379 75
To amount disbursed to libraries,	....	50 35
To amount disbursed to judges,	....	2,056 70
To balance securities,	50,147 37	....
To balance cash,	....	2,135 62
	$51,916 37	$7,022 42

Cr.	Amount.	Amount.
By balance of securities brought down,	$49,297 37	....
By balance of cash brought down,	....	$3,239 39
By amount received for discharged securities,	....	1,550 00
By amount of interest received,	....	2,233 03
By new securities added,	2,400 00	....
	$51,697 37	$7,022 42

1852.

Dr.	Amount.	Amount.
To securities discharged and deducted,	$7,097 37	....
To amount paid for new securities,	....	$4,030 00
To amount disbursed to librarians,	....	626 00
To amount disbursed to libraries,	....	2,235 52
To amount disbursed to judges,	....	3,247 29
To balance securities,	47,080 00	....
To balance cash,	....	3,447 13
	$54,177 37	$13,585 94

Schedule C — (Continued).

1852.

Cr.	Amount.	Amount.
By balance of securities brought down,	$50,147 37	....
By balance of cash brought down,	....	$2,135 62
By amount received for discharged securities,	....	7,097 37
By amount of interest received,	....	4,352 95
By new securities added,	4,030 00	....
	$54,177 37	$13,585 94

1853.

Dr.	Amount.	Amount.
To securities discharged and deducted,	$2,600 00	....
To amount paid for new securities,	....	$2,450 00
To amount disbursed to librarians,	....	612 75
To amount disbursed to libraries,	....	592 31
To amount disbursed to judges,	....	1,915 83
To balance securities,	46,930 00	....
To balance cash,	....	2,991 12
	$49,530 00	$8,562 01

Cr.	Amount.	Amount.
By balance of securities brought down,	$47,080 00	....
By balance of cash brought down,	....	$3,447 13
By amount received for discharged securities,	....	2,600 00
By amount of interest received,	....	2,514 88
By new securities added,	2,450 00	....
	$49,530 00	$8,562 01

1854.

Dr.	Amount.	Amount.
To securities discharged and deducted,	$9,530 75	....
To amount paid for new securities,	....	11,102 53
To amount disbursed to librarians,	....	619 62
To amount disbursed to libraries,	....	1,080 26
To amount disbursed to judges,	....	595 56
To balance securities,	48,501 78	....
To balance cash,	....	2,752 75
	$58,032 53	$16,150 72

Cr.	Amount.	Amount.
By balance of securities brought down,	$46,930 00	....
By balance of cash brought down,	....	$2,991 12
By amount received for discharged securities,	....	9,530 75
By amount of interest received,	....	3,628 85
By new securities added,	11,102 53	....
	$58,032 53	$16,150 72

Schedule C — (Continued).

1855-56.

Dr.	Amount.	Amount.
To securities discharged and deducted,	$6,419 45	....
To amount paid for new securities,	....	$5,586 27
To amount disbursed to librarians,	....	3,047 31
To amount disbursed to libraries,	....	1,758 10
To amount disbursed to judges,	....	641 00
To balance securities,	47,668 60	....
To balance cash,	....	2,588 94
	$54,088 05	$13,621 62

Cr.	Amount.	Amount.
By balance securities brought down,	$48,501 78	....
By balance cash brought down,	....	$2,752 75
By amount received for dicharged securities,	....	6,419 45
By amount of interest received,	....	4,449 42
By new securities added,	5,586 27	....
	$54,088 05	$13,621 62

1857.

Dr.	Amount.	Amount.
To securities discharged and deducted,	$8,252 33	....
To amount paid for new securities,	....	$5,942 31
To amount disbursed to librarians,	....	390 25
To amount disbursed to libraries,	....	798 91
To amount disbursed to judges,	....	658 27
To balance securities,	45,358 58	....
To balance cash,	....	5,357 95
	$53,610 91	$13,147 69

Cr.	Amount.	Amount.
By balance securities brought down,	$47,668 60	....
By balance cash brought down,	....	$5,588 94
By amount received for discharged securities,	....	8,252 33
By amount of interest received,	....	2,306 42
By new securities added,	5,942 31	....
	$53,610 91	$13,147 69

1858.

Dr.	Amount.	Amount.
To securities discharged and deducted,	$11,132 91	....
To amount paid for new securities,	....	$14,524 33
To amount disbursed to librarians,	....	370 25
To amount disbursed to libraries,	....	1,471 75
To amount disbursed to judges,	....	845 53
To balance securities,	48,750 00	....
To balance cash,	....	874 53
To expenses for search, foreclosure, etc.,	....	667 65
	$59,882 91	$18,754 04

Schedule C—(Continued).

1858.

Cr.	Amount.	Amount.
By balance of securities brought down,	$45,358 58	....
By balance of cash brought down,	....	$5,357 95
By amount received for discharged securities,	11,132 91	....
By amount of interest received,	....	2,263 18
By new securities added,	14,524 33	....
	$59,882 91	$18,754 04

1859.

Dr.	Amount.	Amount.
To securities discharged and deducted,	$13,350 00	....
To amount paid for new securities,	....	$5,500 00
To amount disbursed to librarians,	....	673 41
To amount disbursed to libraries,	....	949 23
To amount disbursed to judges.,	....	191 98
To disbursements for costs of search, &c.,	....	431 52
To balance securities,	52,598 33	....
To balance cash,	....	247 07
	$65,948 33	$7,993 16

Cr.	Amount.	Amount.
By balance of securities brought down,	$48,750 00	....
By balance of cash brought down,	....	$874 53
By amount received for discharged securities,	....	5,380 00
By amount of interest received,	....	1,690 40
By new securities added,	17,198 33	....
By extra charge,	....	48 23
	$65,948 33	$7,993 16

1860.

Dr.	Amount.	Amount.
To securities discharged and deducted,	$3,441 60	....
To amount paid for new securities,	....	$3,100 00
To amount disbursed to librarians,	....	790 63
To amount disbursed to libraries,	....	1,518 16
To amount disbursed to judges,	....	404 23
To balance securities,	52,256 73	....
To balance cash,	....	2,103 64
	$55,698 33	$7,916 66

Cr.	Amount.	Amount.
By balance of securities brought down,	$52,598 33	....
By balance of cash brought down,	....	$247 07
By amount received for discharged securities,	....	3,441 60
By amount of interest received,	....	4,227 99
By new securities added,	3,100 00	....
	$55,698 33	$7,916 66

Schedule C — (Continued).

1861.

DR.	Amount.	Amount.
To securities discharged and deducted,	$4,605 00	....
To amount paid for new securities,	....	$1,400 00
To amount disbursed to librarians,	....	703 25
To amount disbursed to libraries,	....	1,636 13
To amount disbursed to judges,	....	664 06
To disbursements for costs of search, &c.,	....	299,67
To balance securities,	50,004 14	....
To balance cash,	....	3,252 26
	$54,609 14	$7,955 37

CR.	Amount.	Amount.
By balance of securities brought down,	$52,256 73	....
By balance of cash brought down,	....	$2,103 64
By amount received for discharged securities,	....	2,605 00
By amount of interest received,	....	3,246 73
By new securities added,	2,352 41	....
	$54,609 14	$7,955 37

1862.

DR.	Amount.	Amount.
To securities discharged and deducted,	$4,205 00	....
To amount paid for new securities,	....	$2,400 00
To amount disbursed to librarians,	....	438 75
To amount disbursed to libraries,	....	1,225 56
To amount disbursed to judges,	....	418 07
To disbursements for costs of search, &c.,	....	46 88
To balance securities,	49,719 34	....
To balance cash,	....	6,023 68
	$53,924 34	$10,552 94

CR.	Amount.	Amount.
By balance of securities brought down,	$50,004 14	....
By balance of cash brought down,	....	$3,252 26
By amount received for discharged securities,	....	4,200 00
By amount of interest received,	....	3,100 68
By new securities added,	3,915 20	....
	$53,919 34	$10,552 94

Schedule C — (Continued).

1863.

Dr.	Amount.	Amount.
To securities discharged and deducted,	$9,650 00	....
To amount paid for new securities,	....	$11,087 75
To amount disbursed to librarians,	....	792 75
To amount disbursed to libraries,	....	697 51
To amount disbursed to judges,	....	530 60
To disbursements for costs of search, &c.,	....	54 65
To balance of securities,	51,157 09	....
To balance of cash,	....	5,193 61
	$60,807 09	$18,356 87

Cr.	Amount.	Amount.
By balance of securities brought down,	$49,719 34	....
By balance of cash brought down,	....	$6,023 68
By amount received for discharged securities,	....	9,650 00
By amount of interest received,	....	2,683 19
By new securities added,	11,087 75	....
	$60,807 09	$18,356 87

1864.

Dr.	Amount.	Amount.
To securities discharged and deducted,	$9,220 00	....
To amount paid for new securities,	....	$12,400 00
To amount disbursed to librarians,	....	789 25
To amount disbursed to libraries,	....	1,121 18
To amount disbursed to judges,	....	259 16
To balance securities,	54,339 09	....
To balance cash,	....	3,183 24
	$63,557 09	$17,752 83

Cr.	Amount.	Amount.
By balance of securities brought down,	$5,157 09	....
By balance of cash brought down,	....	$5,193 61
By amount received for discharged securities,	....	9,220 00
By amount of interest received,	....	3,339 22
By new securities added,	12,400 00	....
	$63,557 09	$17,752 83

1865.

Dr.	Amount.	Amount.
To securities discharged and deducted,	$4,766 00	....
To amount paid for new securities,	....	$4,388 48
To amount disbursed to librarians,	....	617 50
To amount disbursed to libraries,	....	376 15
To amount disbursed to judges,	....	471 75
To deficit securities,	672 48	....
To deficit cash,	....	....
To balance securities,	53,287 09	....
To balance cash,	....	3,350 64
	$58,725 57	$9,204 52

Schedule C — (Continued).

1865.

Cr.	Amount.	Amount.
By balance of securities brought down,	$54,337 09	....
By balance of cash brought down,	....	$3,183 22
By amount received for discharged securities,	....	4,766 00
By amount of interest received,	....	1,255 28
By new securities added,	4,388 48	....
	$58,725 57	$9,204 52

1866.

Dr.	Amount.	Amount.
To securities discharged and deducted,	$8,241 30	....
To amount paid for new securities,	....	$10,350 00
To amount paid to librarians,	....	702 89
To amount paid to libraries,	....	1,489 50
To amount paid to judges,	....	1,901 66
To miscellaneous disbursements,	....	629 29
To balance securities,	55,395 79	....
To balance cash,	....	3,279 71
	$63,637 09	$18,353 05

Cr.	Amount.	Amount.
By balance securities brought down,	$53,287 09	....
By balance cash brought down,	....	3,350 64
By amount received for discharged securities,	....	8,913 78
By amount of interest received,	....	6,088 63
By new securities added,	10,350 00	....
	$63,637 09	$18,353 05

SCHEDULE D.

Statement of the Chancery Fund of the Court of Appeals.

Dr.	Amount.	Amount.
To accounts paid on order of the Court from 1841 to Aug. 1, 1858,	$53,324 63	....
To balance on hand August 1, 1858,	70,448 14	....
	$123,772 77	

Cr.	Amount.	Amount.
By amount in Court at its organization,	$93,808, 73	....
By interest on this sum to August 1, 1858,	25,652 25	....
By moneys of litigants received in 1854,	....	$3,622 02
By interest to August 1, 1858,	....	689 77
	$123,772 77	....

Schedule D — (Continued).

1858.

Dr.	Amount.	Amount.
To balance on hand,	$70,501 49	....

Cr.	Amount.	Amount.
By balance on hand brought down,	$70,448 14	....
By interest received,	53 35	....
	$70,501 49	....

1859.

Dr.	Amount.	Amount,
To disbursements on order of court,	$4,460 92	....
To balance on hand,	69,005 88	....
	$73,466 80	....

Cr.	Amount.	Amount.
By balance on hand brought down,	$70,501 49	....
By interest received,	2,965 31	....
	$73,466 80	....

1860.

Dr.	Amount.	Amount.
To disbursements on order of court,	$12,954 30	....
To balance on hand,	60,526 66	....
	$73,480 96	....

Cr.	Amount.	Amount.
By balance brought down,	$69,005 88	....
By interest received,	4,475 08	....
	$73,480 96	....

1861.

Dr.	Amount.	Amount.
To disbursements on order of the court,	....	$300 00
To balance on hand, securities,	$60,526 66	....
To balance on hand, cash,	....	854 52
	$60,526 66	$1,154 52

Schedule D— (Continued).

1861.

Cr.	Amount.	Amount.
By balance on hand brought down,	$60,526 66	......
By interest received,	......	$1,154 52
	$60,526 66	$1,154 52

1862.

Dr.	Amount.	Amount.
To securities discharged and deducted,	$6,666 00	......
To disbursements on order of the court,	......	$2,688 23
To amount paid for new securities,	......	2,672 11
To balance on hand, securities,	66,789 74	......
To balance on hand, cash,	......	1,730 25
	$73,455 74	$7,090 59

Cr.	Amount.	Amount.
By balance securities brought down,	$60,526 66	......
By balance cash brought down,	......	$854 52
By amount received for discharged securities,	......	2,400 00
By interest received,	......	3,836 07
By new securities added,	12,929 08	......
	$73,455 74	$7,090 59

1863.

Dr.	Amount.	Amount.
To securities discharged and deducted,	$3,234 11	......
To amount paid for new securities,	......	$6,000 00
To balance on hand, securities,	69,628 44	......
To balance on hand, cash,	......	834 17
	$72,862 55	$6,834 17

Cr.	Amount.	Amount.
By balance securities brought down	$66,789 74	......
By balance cash brought down,	......	$1,730 25
By amount received for discharged securities,	......	2,400 00
By interest received,	......	2,703 92
By new securities added,	6,072 81	......
	$72,862 55	$6,834 17

Schedule D — (Continued).

1864.

Dr.	Amount.	Amount.
To securities discharged and deducted,	$12,481 65	....
To disbursements on order of the court,,	....	$126 48
To amount paid for new securities,	....	14,000 00
To balance on hand, securities,	71,146 79	....
To balance on hand, cash,	....	1,626 15
	$83,628 44	$15,752 63

Cr.	Amount.	Amount.
By balance securities on hand,	$69,628 44	....
By balance cash on hand,	....	$834 17
By amount received for discharged securities,	....	12,050 00
By interest received,	....	2,868 46
By new securities added,	14,000 00	....
	$83,628 44	$15,752 63

1865.

Dr.	Amount.	Amount.
To securities discharged and deducted,	$830 00	....
To disbursements on order of court,	....	$153 30
To amount paid for new securities,	....	5,500 00
To balance on hand, securities,	75,986 79	....
To balance on hand, cash,	....	263 97
	$76,816 79	$5,916 27

Cr.	Amount.	Amount.
By balance securities on hand,	$71,146 79	....
By balance cash on hand,	....	$1,626 15
By amount received for discharged securities,	....	800 00
By interest received,	....	3,490 12
By new securities added,	5,670 00	....
	$76,816 79	$5,916 27

1866.

Dr.	Amount.	Amount.
To securities discharged and deducted,	$11,919 99	....
To disbursements on order of court,	....	$4,642 96
To amount paid for new securities,	....	2,200 00
To balance on hand, securities,	70,134 20	....
To balance on hand, cash,	....	2,037 98
	$82,054 19	$8,880 94

Schedule D — (Continued).

1866.

CR.	Amount.	Amount.
By balance of securities on hand,	$75,986 79	....
By balance of cash on hand,	....	$263 97
By amount received for discharged securities,	....	5,936 73
By amount of interest received,	....	2,680 24
By new securities added,	6,067 40	....
	$82,054 19	$8,880 94

SCHEDULE E.

List of the several pieces of land, the title to which is in the Clerk of the Court of Appeals.

No. 1. Lots Nos. 40 and 41, in French's village of Bath, in the town of North Greenbush, in the county of Rensselaer, N. Y. Acquired by foreclosure of mortgage No. 39, schedule B, and sale under decree.

No. 2. Lots Nos. 48, 49 and 50, in French's village of Bath, in the town of North Greenbush, in the county of Rensselaer, N. Y. Acquired by foreclosure of mortgage No. 43, schedule B, and sale under decree.

No. 3. Lots Nos. 339, 340, 341, 355, 356 and 357, in French's village of Bath, in the town of North Greenbush, in the county of Rensselaer, N. Y. Acquired by foreclosure of mortgage No. 43, schedule B, and sale under decree.

No. 4. Lots Nos. 67, 68 and 69, in the Burt farm, in the 10th ward, in the city of Albany. Acquired by the foreclosure of mortgage No. 37, schedule B, and sale under the decree.

No. 5. Lots Nos. 153 and 154, in the Burt farm, in the 10th ward in the city of Albany. Acquired by foreclosure of mortgage No. 51, schedule B, and sale under the decree.

No. 6. Lot No. 106, in French's village of Bath, in the town of North Greenbush, in the county of Rensselaer, N. Y. Acquired by foreclosure of mortgage No. 33, schedule B, and sale under decree.

No. 7. Lot No. 157, in French's village of Bath, in the town of North Greenbush, in the county of Rensselaer, N. Y. Acquired by foreclosure of mortgage No. 27, schedule B, and sale under decree.

No. 8. Lot No. 231, in French's village of Bath, in the town of North Greenbush, in the county of Rensselaer, N. Y. Acquired by the foreclosure of mortgage No. 28, schedule B, and sale under decree.

No. 10. The following piece or parcel of land in Ulster county, New York:

Sixty (60) acres in north-west corner subdivision two (2), of lot three (3), Great Transport, Rochester patent.

Ninety-eight (98) acres of lot forty-three (43), Connecticut tract in great lot six (6), Hardenburgh patent.

Eighty acres (80) north-west corner lot seventy-one (71), Connecticut tract in great lot six (6), Hardenburgh patent.

Thirty-three and eighty-nine one-hundredth acres south-west corner lot eighty-eight Connecticut tract in great lot six, Hardenburgh patent.

Fifty acres north-west corner lot one hundred and thirty-four in Garretson's tract, great lot seven, Hardenburgh patent.

Six acres, being what remains of lot seventy-two of Connecticut tract in great lot No. six, Hardenburgh patent, after deducting ninety acres from the north-west part of said lot.

Lot No. 238, Robinson's tract, division three, Hardenburgh patent, containing one hundred and forty-three acres.

Acquired by sale under judgment No. 45, schedule B.

SCHEDULE F.

Name of judgment debtor.	Amount of judgment.	Judgment when docketed.
CHANCERY FUND.		
Ballou, William P.,	$481 58	March 27, 1867
Ballou, William P.,	453 36	March 27, 1867
Ballou, William,	725 95	March 27, 1867
Eldred, Eldred D.,	1,351 92	July 19, 1861
French, Samuel,	789 62	March 27, 1866
Klump, John,	2,284 78	Sept. 26, 1865
Moore, Sarah J.,	423 96	April 24, 1866
Smith, F. and A.,	5,142 65	March 29, 1865
Straight, W. C.,	5,551 25	July 31, 1862
Swayne, W. D.,	692 93	May 29, 1866
LIBRARY FUND.		
Lozier, E. V.,	1,215 69	April 24, 1866
	$19,113 69	

Statistics of the business of the Supreme Court in the several counties.

Circulars were addressed, in May last, to the several county clerks, calling for a return of the following items of information concerning the business of these courts in the several counties for each year since 1846, viz.:

CIVIL CAUSES.

Number of causes brought before the Court by summons and complaint (or other original process) during each year.

Number of causes tried and decided in each year.

Number of causes tried by jury.

Number of causes tried by Court without a jury.

Number of causes referred.

Number of causes brought before Supreme Court on appeal or certiorari from inferior courts.

Number of causes brought from Special Terms, Circuit, Oyer and Terminer, &c., to General Term on appeal.

CRIMINAL CAUSES.

Number of causes brought before the Court in each year.

Number of causes tried in each year.

Number of causes brought to Supreme Court from Surrogate Courts.

Number of Referees' reports confirmed.

Number of Referees' reports not confirmed.

Returns more or less complete have been received in answer to these inquiries from thirty counties, representing a population of 1,498,939, and to this extent, they exhibit the actual and relative amount of litigation in the State. Embracing, as they do, counties scattered throughout every part of the State, several of which have large cities within their borders, they may perhaps be regarded as showing a fair average of the amount of business in counties during the last twenty years, excepting in the Metropolitan District.

To afford a convenient basis for comparison between different periods and localities, we have placed the population at intervals of five years under the head of each county.

The labor involved in these inquiries was found, in many cases, very great, owing to imperfect indexes of records, and the voluminous mass of documents which it was necessary to examine. No reports have been received from several of the larger counties — in several it was declared impossible, within the time allowed, to digest and prepare this information for its present use.*

As allusion is made to judicial districts in the following tables, their present organization is here given, as established by act of May 8, 1847:

DIST.

I. — City and county of New York.

II. — Counties of Richmond, Suffolk, Queens, Kings, Westchester, Orange, Rockland, Putnam and Dutchess.

III. — Counties of Columbia, Sullivan, Ulster, Greene, Albany, Schoharie and Rensselaer.

IV. — Counties of Warren, Saratoga, Washington, Essex, Franklin, St. Lawrence, Clinton, Montgomery, Hamilton, Fulton and Schenectady.

V. — Counties of Onondaga, Oneida, Oswego, Herkimer, Jefferson and Lewis.

VI. — Counties of Otsego, Delaware, Madison, Chenango, Broome, Tioga, Chemung, Tompkins, Cortland and Schuyler.

VII. — Counties of Livingston, Wayne, Seneca, Yates, Ontario, Steuben, Monroe and Cayuga.

VIII. — Counties of Erie, Chautauqua, Cattaraugus, Orleans, Niagara, Genesee, Allegany and Wyoming.

---

* In reference to the amount of labor which the examination would require, the Clerk of Kings county says:

"The business of this office within the last twenty years (the time covered by your requisition) has been very heavy, and a great mass of papers has been filed, all of which will have to be examined in order to get at the information you require. Your schedule does not occupy much space on the paper, but the labor of filling it would be immense. Thousands of complaints, orders, reports and judgment rolls have been filed, all of which would have to be examined, in addition to which the minutes of the Courts, both Civil and Criminal (in both of which a very great amount of business has been done), would have to be carefully gone over to get the facts desired by you. Indeed, it would take the whole force employed in my office a long time to get together the information required. Without entirely shutting our office to all other business, it is very nearly impossible to do it within the time allowed."

ALBANY COUNTY.

Population in 1845, 77,268; in 1850, 93,279; in 1855, 103,681; in 1860, 113,917; and in 1865, 115,504.

YEAR.	CIVIL CAUSES.							CRIMINAL CAUSES.		Number of causes brought to Supreme Court from Surrogates' Courts.	Number of referees' reports confirmed.	Number of referees' reports not confirmed.
	Number of causes brought before the court by summons and complaint (or other original process), during each year.	Number of causes tried and decided in each year.	Number of causes tried by jury.	Number of causes tried by court without a jury.*	Number of causes referred.	Number of causes brought before Supreme Court on appeal or certiorari from inferior courts.	Number of causes brought from Special Terms, Circuit, Oyer and Terminer, &c., to General Term on appeal.	Number of causes brought before the court in each year.	Number tried in each year.			
1847,.	1,755	98	83	3	12	5	27	40	20	....	11	1
1848,.	2,172	113	77	23	13	9	33	150	29	1	10	3
1849,.	2,132	120	42	51	27	10	35	83	20	1	24	3
1850,.	2,230	188	40	83	65	13	37	51	19	2	57	8
1851,.	2,294	181	39	60	82	12	45	32	13	....	70	12
1852,.	2,502	253	69	96	88	10	40	39	13	....	80	8
1853,.	2,497	164	24	77	63	17	39	52	12	1	63	....
1854,.	2,513	285	44	121	120	15	44	61	22	2	110	10
1855,.	2,564	267	30	167	70	12	51	48	34	....	64	6
1856,.	2,597	222	45	102	75	13	53	75	33	1	72	3
1857,.	2,582	257	42	130	85	17	63	141	42	2	81	4
1858,.	2,561	246	25	110	111	10	65	147	48	2	101	10
1859..	2,579	342	50	130	162	9	47	153	36	1	162	....
1860,.	2,581	154	37	61	56	16	67	157	19	1	47	9
1861,.	2,576	253	31	117	105	18	59	139	25	1	100	5
1862,	2,231	230	41	93	96	12	47	87	18	2	93	3
1863,.	2,217	175	23	69	83	15	41	104	29	2	83	....
1854,.	2,211	120	16	32	72	11	39	73	18	1	65	7
1865,.	2,297	133	17	65	51	9	37	187	18	1	43	8
1866,.	2,321	190	50	55	85	13	35	108	29	1	75	10
	47,412	3,991	725	1,645	1,521	246	904	1,927	497	22	1,411	110

ALLEGANY COUNTY.

Population in 1845, 40,084; in 1850, 37,808; in 1855, 42,910; in 1860, 41,881; and in 1865, 40,285.

YEAR.												
1847,.	102	102	6	93	2	1	1	24	19	....	2	....
1848,.	177	177	17	160	3	1	1	35	23	...	3	...
1849,.	191	191	16	175	6	7	2	33	23	....	6	....
1850,.	186	186	10	176	10	2	3	70	30	....	10	....
1851,.	174	174	12	162	5	1	1	69	28	....	5	...
1852,.	290	290	10	280	16	1	1	64	27	....	16	....
1853,.	314	314	9	305	22	4	3	88	34	....	22	....
1854,.	346	346	19	327	25	2	6	177	46	....	25	...
1855,.	521	521	6	515	51	3	11	163	66	....	51	....
1856,.	373	373	7	366	41	4	8	44	22	....	41	....
1857,.	567	567	16	551	54	9	11	27	10	....	54	....
1858,.	507	507	18	489	54	1	10	54	19	....	54	....
1859,.	379	379	15	364	53	1	11	77	29	....	53	....
1860,.	337	337	20	317	54	1	6	108	30	....	54	...
1861,.	465	465	15	450	57	....	9	66	17	....	57	....
1862,.	266	266	10	255	42	....	10	52	20	....	42	....
1863,.	154	154	6	148	27	1	3	60	33	....	27	....
1864,.	104	104	9	95	26	2	7	31	17	....	26	....
1865,.	149	149	6	143	33	...	7	21	8	....	33	....
1866,.	172	172	7	165	26	1	9	43	24	....	26	....
	5,774	5,774	234	5,531	607	42	120	1,306	525	....	607	...

* In Allegany county this includes defaults.

CATTARAUGUS COUNTY.

Population in 1845, 30,169; in 1850, 38,950; in 1855, 39,530; in 1860, 43,886; and in 1865, 42,205.

YEAR.	CIVIL CAUSES.							CRIMINAL CAUSES.				
	Number of causes brought before the court by summons and complaint (or other original process), during each year.	Number of causes tried and decided in each year.	Number of causes tried by jury.	Number of causes tried by court without a jury.	Number of causes referred.	Number of causes brought before Supreme Court on appeal or certiorari from inferior courts.	Number of causes brought from Special Terms, Circuit, Oyer and Terminer, &c., to General Term on appeal.	Number of causes brought before the court in each year.	Number tried in each year.	Number of causes brought to Supreme Court from Surrogates' Courts.	Number of referees' reports confirmed.	Number of referees' reports not confirmed.
1847,.	.....	9	9	....	1	.....	.....	.....	1	....	.....	....
1848,.	.....	29	24	....	6	.....	.....	.....	4	....	.....	....
1849,.	.....	31	25	9	9	.....	.....	.....	1	....	.....	....
1850,.	.....	50	40	10	18	.....	.....	.....	13	....	.....	....
1851,.	.....	65	38	25	34	.....	.....	.....	12	....	.....	....
1852,.	.....	62	23	8	25	.....	.....	.....	4	....	.....	....
1853,.	.....	43	24	2	14	.....	.....	.....	6	....	.....	....
1854,.	.....	36	18	6	15	.....	.....	.....	5	....	.....	....
1855,.	.....	40	32	10	30	.....	.....	.....	10	....	.....	....
1856,.	.....	63	25	13	33	.....	.....	.....	10	....	.....	....
1857,.	.....	75	40	20	57	.....	.....	.....	3	....	.....	....
1858,.	.....	39	31	13	41	.....	.....	.....	6	....	.....	....
1859,.	.....	50	25	13	40	.....	.....	.....	16	....	.....	....
1860,.	.....	63	29	15	42	.....	.....	.....	14	....	.....	....
1861,.	.....	67	50	21	44	.....	.....	.....	7	....	.....	....
1862,.	.....	30	21	10	12	.....	.....	.....	5	....	.....	....
1863,.	.....	38	12	15	14	.....	.....	.....	7	....	.....	....
1864,.	.....	34	14	18	18	.....	.....	.....	8	....	.....	....
1865,.	.....	36	31	5	14	.....	.....	.....	8	....	.....	....
1866,.	.....	60	52	19	55	.....	.....	.....	6	....	.....	....
	.....	920	563	232	522	.....	.....	.....	146	....	.....	....

CAYUGA COUNTY.

Population in 1845, 49,663; in 1850, 55,458; in 1855, 53,571; in 1860, 55,767, and in 1865, 55,730.

YEAR.	Brought before the court	Tried and decided	Tried by jury	Tried by court without a jury	Referred	On appeal or certiorari from inferior courts	To General Term on appeal	Criminal: brought before the court	Criminal: tried	From Surrogates' Courts	Referees' reports confirmed	Referees' reports not confirmed
1847,.	107	17	7	10	3	1	.....	34	2	....	.....	....
1848,.	199	50	32	18	15	3	1	37	7	....	3	12
1849,.	154	38	25	13	25	4	7	18	5	....	10	15
1850,.	300	28	23	5	27	5	4	32	3	....	24	3
1851,.	216	37	32	5	35	11	11	46	7	....	29	6
1852,.	249	38	25	13	26	12	16	23	1	1	24	2
1853,.	347	28	14	14	47	12	15	57	10	1	28	19
1854,.	294	34	20	14	54	11	16	36	4	....	42	12
1855,.	194	51	32	19	55	21	14	49	5	2	52	3
1856,.	437	38	18	20	74	32	19	61	4	....	55	19
1857,.	295	37	11	26	85	4	18	46	7	....	56	29
1858,.	442	82	19	63	83	5	60	65	2	....	55	28
1859,.	357	38	20	18	56	7	31	110	2	....	49	7
1860,.	390	40	23	17	57	2	27	48	6	2	31	26
1861,.	296	51	26	25	49	2	10	45	1	....	31	18
1862,.	158	15	7	8	42	5	8	58	4	1	38	4
1863,.	168	32	20	12	52	4	23	29	3	1	33	19
1864,.	173	28	16	12	29	2	12	38	1	1	21	8
1865,.	269	36	20	16	35	2	6	35	1	....	27	8
1866,.	351	46	36	10	55	1	16	52	5	....	43	12
	5,306	764	426	338	904	146	314	919	80	9	651	250

COLUMBIA COUNTY.

Population, in 1845, 41,976; in 1850, 43,073; in 1855, 44,391; in 1860, 47,172; and in 1865, 44,905.

YEAR.	CIVIL CAUSES.							CRIMINAL CAUSES.		Number of causes brought to Supreme Court from Surrogates' Courts.	Number of referees' reports confirmed.	Number of referees' reports not confirmed.
	Number of causes brought before the court by summons and complaint (or other original process), during each year.	Number of causes tried and decided in each year.	Number of causes tried by jury.	Number of causes tried by court without a jury.	Number of causes referred.	Number of causes brought before Supreme Court on appeal or certiorari from inferior courts.	Number of causes brought from Special Terms, Circuit, Oyer and Terminer, &c., to General Term on appeal.	Number of causes brought before the court in each year.	Number tried in each year.			
1847,	82	38	38	.. .	8	......	.. . .	15	5	....	.....	....
1848,	96	39	34	5	17	......	......	28	10	.. .	.....	....
1849,	114	47	42	5	26	......	......	38	5	....	.....	....
1850,	98	51	45	6	55	......	......	13	2	....	.....	....
1851,	91	37	23	14	27	......	......	22	11	....	.....	....
1852,	87	33	20	13	36	.....	......	30	6	...	.....	....
1853,	106	40	27	13	24	......	......	43	3	....	.....	....
1854,	92	48	31	17	37	......	......	21	...	....	.....	....
1855,	112	40	26	14	36	......	......	27	4	....	.....	....
1856,	95	30	12	18	32	......	......	16	4	....	.. ..	....
1857,	154	45	18	27	38	......	......	27	2	....	....	....
1858,	204	63	20	43	47	......	......	18	....	....	.....	. ..
1859,	150	50	30	20	22	......	......	29	1	. ..	.....	....
1860,	154	55	30	25	42	......	......	26	1	....	.....	....
1861,	112	55	27	28	16	......	......	19	....	....	.....	....
1862,	160	58	24	34	40	......	......	22	3	....	.....	....
1863,	86	50	26	24	38	......	......	19	3	....	.....	....
1864,	105	30	20	10	28	......	.. ...	9	1	....	.....	....
1865,	117	34	25	9	21	......	......	15	1	....	.....	....
1866,	190	36	25	11	30	......	......	36	7	...	.....	....
	2,905	879	543	336	620	......	......	473	69	....	.....	....

DELAWARE COUNTY.

Population in 1845, 36,990; in 1850, 39,834; in 1855, 39,749; in 1860, 42,465, and in 1865, 41,638.

YEAR.	Brought before the court	Tried and decided	Tried by jury	Tried by court without a jury	Referred	Brought on appeal or certiorari	Brought to General Term on appeal	Criminal: brought before the court	Criminal: tried	Brought from Surrogates' Courts	Referees' reports confirmed	Referees' reports not confirmed
1847,	48	.....	18	2	1	......		19	5	....	.....	....
1848,	56	.....	32	9	8	......	......	8	5	....	.....	....
1849,	78	.....	36	9	10	......	......	† 483	7	...	.....	....
1850,	69	.....	27	20	10	......	......	25	1	....	.....	....
1851,	88	.....	23	14	26	......	......	30	6	....	.....	1
1852,	112	.....	32	44	13	1	......	12	4	....	.....	2
1853,	111	.....	25	32	18	......	......	11	5	....	.....	4
1854,	98	.....	36	22	32	2	......	6	3	....	.....	....
1855,	117	.....	32	22	15	3	......	7	2	....	.....	3
1856.	112	.....	29	27	24	2	......	13	1	....	.....	....
1857,	123	.....	32	21	37	......	......	18	1	....	.....	1
1858,	135	.....	18	18	22	......	......	10	5	....	.....	2
1859,	157	.....	39	32	41	1	......	12	2	....	.....	5
1860,	173	.....	28	26	30	1	......	28	7	....	.....	2
1861,	115	.....	23	32	35	......	......	10	2	....	.....	3
1862,	97	.....	10	32	34	9	......	25	....	....	.....	5
1863,	86	.....	10	26	21	2	......	14	3	....	.....	4
1864,	102	.....	16	25	20	......	......	16	....	....	.....	1
1865,	137	.....	23	22	30	......	......	9	1	....	.....	4
1866,	186	.....	17	35	46	3	......	19	3	....	.....	7
	2,200	.....	506	470	473	24	......	775	63	....	.....	44

* The General Terms of this district are held at Binghamton, Broome county.
† These were mostly anti-rent cases that originated in 1845. The prisoners were discharged.

ERIE COUNTY.

Population in 1845, 78,635; in 1850, 100,993; in 1855, 132,331; in 1860, 141,971; and in 1850 157,158.

YEAR.	CIVIL CAUSES. Number of causes brought before the court by summons and complaint (or other original process), during each year.	Number of causes tried and decided in each year.	Number of causes tried by jury.	Number of causes tried by court without a jury.	Number of causes referred.	Number of causes brought before Supreme Court on appeal or certiorari from inferior courts.	Number of causes brought from Special Terms, Circuit, Oyer and Terminer, &c., to General Term on appeal.	CRIMINAL CAUSES. Number of causes brought before the court each year.	Number of causes tried.	Number of causes brought to Supreme Court to Surrogates' Courts.	Number of referees' reports confirmed.	Number of referees' reports not confirmed.
1847,.	81	88	60	1	13	5	34	116	52	....	1	....
1848,.	105	94	58	4	27	26	23	165	66	....	....	2
1849,.	213	114	56	8	34	6	40	209	80	....	26	1
1850,.	241	147	95	25	127	21	50	181	89	....	4	1
1851,.	275	189	62	40	139	11	27	178	119	....	27	1
1852,.	272	200	100	28	123	20	33	199	63	....	10	....
1853,.	261	219	66	29	128	7	43	268	81	....	8	1
1854,.	352	288	57	64	232	37	130	257	53	1	56	1
1855,.	376	347	98	86	175	14	52	390	57	....	68	....
1856,.	372	348	49	80	230	16	149	169	50	1	84	...
1857,.	474	444	77	98	280	21	84	182	53	3	117	1
1858,.	557	488	107	89	333	27	138	217	69	....	177	1
1859,.	531	512	82	102	347	35	146	191	68	1	190	1
1860,.	435	412	78	98	256	44	144	128	48	1	138	...
1861,.	368	436	38	90	185	35	143	175	44	3	152	....
1862,.	314	353	60	94	163	34	103	126	30	3	90	2
1863,,	216	295	60	69	133	17	96	162	81	2	78	1
1864,.	240	237	67	63	126	26	110	158	55	3	71	2
1865,.	233	197	84	34	105	12	76	232	61	3	44	1
1866,.	226	211	76	33	133	13	111	566	40	5	70	1
	6,142	5,619	1,430	1,135	3,289	427	1,732	4,269	1,257	26	1,411	18

FULTON COUNTY.

Population in 1845, 18,579; in 1850, 20,171; in 1855, 23,284; in 1860, 24, 162; and in 1865, 24,512.

YEAR.	CIVIL CAUSES. Number of causes brought before the court by summons and complaint (or other original process), during each year.	Number of causes tried and decided in each year.	Number of causes tried by jury.	Number of causes tried by court without a jury.	Number of causes referred.	Number of causes brought before Supreme Court on appeal or certiorari from inferior courts.	Number of causes brought from Special Terms, Circuit, Oyer and Terminer, &c., to General Term on appeal.	CRIMINAL CAUSES. Number of causes brought before the court each year.	Number of causes tried.	Number of causes brought to Supreme Court to Surrogates' Courts.	Number of referees' reports confirmed.	Number of referees' reports not confirmed.
1847..	......	....	5	1	4	......	......	12	3	....	....	....
1848,.	......	....	19	....	3	......	......	22	7	....	....	....
1849,.	......	....	12	9	....	......	......	16	12	....	....	....
1850,.	......	....	8	7	....	......	......	5	5	....	....	....
1851,.	......	....	15	10	7	......	......	11	8	....	....	....
1852,.	......	....	5	20	15	......	......	3	6	....	....	....
1853,.	......	....	16	10	23	......	......	12	8	....	....	....
1854,.	......	....	4	8	6	......	......	10	5	....	....	....
1855,.	......	....	15	15	19	......	......	13	4	....	....	....
1856,.	......	....	15	14	10	......	......	9	2	....	....	...
1857,.	......	....	15	8	28	......	......	7	4	....	....	....
1858,.	......	....	17	13	24	......	......	5	9	....	....	....
1859,.	......	....	10	10	26	......	......	6	5	....	....	...
1860,.	......	....	13	12	19	......	......	8	7	....	....	....
1861,.	.....	....	5	1	14	......	......	6	4	....	....	....
1862,.	......	....	19	9	8	......	......	1	1	....	....	...
1863,.	......	....	12	2	5	......	......	6	2	....	....	....
1864,.	......	....	10	4	24	......	......	1	2	....	....	.....
1865,.	.....	....	8	3	10	......	......	6	1	....	....	....
1866,.	......	....	7	4	10	......	......	8	4	....	....	....
	......	...	230	160	255	......	......	167	99	....	....	....

GREENE COUNTY.

Population in 1845, 31,957; in 1850, 33,126; in 1855, 31,137; in 1860, 31,930; and in 1865, 31,710.

YEAR.	CIVIL CAUSES.							CRIMINAL CAUSES.				
	Number of causes brought before the court by summons and complaint, (or other original process), during each year.	Number of causes tried and decided in each year.	Number of causes tried by jury.	Number of causes tried by court without a jury.	Number of causes referred.	Number of causes brought before Supreme Court on appeal or certiorari from inferior courts.*	Number of causes brought from Special Terms, Circuit, Oyer and Terminer, &c., to General Term on appeal.	Number of causes brought before the court in each year.	Number tried in each year.	Number of causes brought to Supreme Court from Surrogates' Courts.	Number of referees' reports confirmed.	Number of referees' reports not confirmed.
1847,.	....	17	16	1	5	....	....	8	6	....	....	....
1848,.	....	32	22	10	12	....	....	39	5	....	....	....
1849,.	....	36	21	15	12	....	....	19	4	....	....	....
1850,.	. ..	25	15	10	21	....	....	20	11	...	...	....
1851,.	....	24	12	12	26	....	....	9	4	....	....	....
1852,.	....	23	12	11	18	....	....	8	4	....	....	....
1853,.	....	23	11	12	17	....	...	9	1	....	....	....
1854,.	....	33	13	20	10	....	....	6	2	....	...	...
1855,.	....	21	11	10	10	....	....	5	3	....	....	....
1856,.	....	42	15	27	13	....	....	14	2	....	....	....
1857,.	....	27	16	11	16	...	....	17	5	....	....	....
1858,.	....	36	13	23	21	....	....	12	9	....	....	....
1859,.	....	38	22	16	5	....	....	10	4	....	....	....
1860,.	...	43	19	24	20	....	....	9	5	. ..	....	..
1861,.	....	26	12	14	7	....	....	10	2	....	....	....
1862,.	99	56	21	35	15	....	....	11	3	....	....	....
1863,.	92	33	13	20	6	....	....	16	3	...	....	....
1864,.	91	24	9	15	15	....	....	20	1	....	....	....
1865,.	95	37	19	18	17	....	....	25	3	....	....	....
1866,.	98	41	22	19	17	....	....	22	4	....	....	....
	475	637	314	323	283	...	....	289	81	....	....	....

JEFFERSON COUNTY.

Population in 1845, 64,999; in 1850, 68,153; in 1855, 65,420; in 1860, 69,825; and in 1865, 66,448.

YEAR.	Number of causes brought before the court by summons and complaint, (or other original process), during each year.	Number of causes tried and decided in each year.	Number of causes tried by jury.	Number of causes tried by court without a jury.	Number of causes referred.	Number of causes brought before Supreme Court on appeal or certiorari from inferior courts.*	Number of causes brought from Special Terms, Circuit, Oyer and Terminer, &c., to General Term on appeal.	Number of causes brought before the court in each year.	Number tried in each year.	Number of causes brought to Supreme Court from Surrogates' Courts.	Number of referees' reports confirmed.	Number of referees' reports not confirmed.
1847,	81	57	17	27	13		24	20	5	....	10	3
1848,	64	40	25	11	7	......	45	25	10	...	5	2
1849,	139	95	47	29	21	......	24	31	16	....	19	2
1850,	114	80	28	24	31	......	20	24	10	...	28	3
1851,	142	79	36	22	27	... ..	20	35	21	....	24	3
1852,	161	81	27	27	31	......	38	41	20	....	30	1
1853,	165	74	23	20	31	......	31	45	22	....	31	1
1854,	280	122	31	43	56	... ..	52	39	19	....	50	6
1855,	186	80	21	30	38	... ..	64	28	24	....	35	3
1856,	189	94	18	36	45	......	55	46	21	....	40	5
1857,	188	100	21	26	58	.... .	47	49	25	....	53	5
1858,	226	134	27	40	72	......	50	41	18	....	67	5
1859,	250	125	32	50	45	......	61	39	20	....	47	2
1860,	254	144	44	50	55	......	72	46	17	....	51	4
1861,	292	159	30	57	80	......	62	39	19	....	75	5
1862,	350	178	42	62	77	......	57	40	9	....	74	3
1863,	300	141	38	54	58	......	65	41	14	....	54	4
1864,	298	125	30	49	50	......	... ..	44	13	....	47	3
1865,	331	159	23	57	79	......	......	45	17	....	75	4
1866,	402	179	39	70	73	......	......	42	10	....	70	3
	4,445	2,246	599	784	947	......	787	760	330	....	885	67

* Not over five cases a year.

LEWIS COUNTY.

Population in 1845, 20,218; in 1850, 24,564; in 1855, 25,229; in 1860, 28,580; and in 1865, 27,840.

YEAR.	CIVIL CAUSES.							CRIMINAL CAUSES.		Number of causes brought to Supreme Court from Surrogates' Courts.	Number of referees' reports confirmed.	Number of referees' reports not confirmed.
	Number of causes brought before the court by summons and complaint, (or other original process), during each year.	Number of causes tried and decided in each year.	Number of causes tried by jury.	Number of causes tried by court without a jury.	Number of causes referred.	Number of causes brought before Supreme Court on appeal or certiorari from inferior courts.	Number of causes brought from Special Terms, Circuit, Oyer and Terminer, &c., to General Term on appeal.	Number of causes brought before the court in each year.	Number tried in each year.			
1847,	10	9	9	.....	1	......	......	5	3	1	1	....
1848,	13	11	10	1	.....	......	......	4	4	....	....	...
1849,	16	16	13	2	1	......	1	7	4	2	1	....
1850,	27	14	8	4	2	1	......	9	4	....	1	1
1851,	18	7	3	4	2	......	......	11	5	2	2	....
1852,	32	12	10	2	6	1	1	8	6	1	4	2
1853,	23	15	9	6	9	......	......	10	6	....	7	2
1854,	61	17	4	13	12	2	......	9	7	....	11	....
1855,	52	21	13	8	11	3	4	6	3	1	7	1
1856,	61	25	11	14	7	......	......	7	5	1	5	....
1857,	100	46	23	23	8	......	3	9	6	....	8	....
1858,	81	24	13	11	5	......	1	3	2	....	6	....
1859,	98	27	12	15	7	......	2	4	1	1	6	1
1860,	96	35	19	16	5	1	3	6	2	....	3	2
1861,	104	30	14	16	9	......	1	9	....	....	1	2
1862,	61	16	9	7	6	......	......	1	....	....	4	....
1863,	77	35	22	13	7	......	2	10	1	1	5	1
1864,	60	16	14	2	10	......	1	7	...	....	10	....
1865,	74	18	11	7	11	......	......	7	2	....	7	2
1866,	101	20	13	7	4	......	......	8	3	....	4	....
	1,165	414	240	171	123	8	19	140	64	10	98	14

LIVINGSTON COUNTY.

Population in 1845, 33,198; in 1850, 40,875; in 1855, 37,943; in 1860, 39,546; and in 1865, 37,555.

YEAR.	Number of causes brought before the court by summons and complaint, (or other original process), during each year.	Number of causes tried and decided in each year.	Number of causes tried by jury.	Number of causes tried by court without a jury.	Number of causes referred.	Number of causes brought before Supreme Court on appeal or certiorari from inferior courts.	Number of causes brought from Special Terms, Circuit, Oyer and Terminer, &c., to General Term on appeal.	Number of causes brought before the court in each year.	Number tried in each year.	Number of causes brought to Supreme Court from Surrogates' Courts.	Number of referees' reports confirmed.	Number of referees' reports not confirmed.
1847,	*238	....	....	....	...	......	......	....	....	....	....	....
1848,	600	37	22	15	26	3	......	....	....	....	....	....
1849,	680	37	24	13	29	9	......	....	....	....	....	....
1850,	478	14	7	7	25	14	......	....	....	....	....	....
1851,	463	60	41	19	45	19	......	....	....	....	....	....
1852,	451	56	27	20	80	22	......	....	....	....	....	....
1853,	431	43	21	22	44	23	......	....	....	....	....	....
1854,	478	45	9	36	81	26	43	....	....	....	....	....
1855,	391	39	18	21	39	30	52	....	....	....	....	....
1856,	620	61	32	29	75	35	30	....	....	....	....	....
1857,	877	76	31	45	116	37	34	....	....	....	....	....
1858,	860	66	17	49	100	35	31	....	....	....	....	....
1859,	625	69	26	43	104	44	52	....	....	....	....	....
1860,	463	64	35	29	67	27	42	....	....	....	....	...
1861,	524	63	19	44	71	40	28	....	....	....	....	....
1862,	355	68	38	30	42	12	22	....	....	....	....	...
1863,	249	52	20	32	36	13	38	....	....	....	....	....
1864,	182	46	24	22	40	17	21	....	....	....	....	....
1865,	190	26	16	14	45	7	20	....	....	....	....	....
1866,	266	45	21	24	36	20	26	...	....	....	....	....
	9,236	967	448	523	1,101	433	439	....	....	....	....	....

* This column includes 254 causes that were dismissed, viz.: in 1848, 3; in 1849, 5; in 1850, 6; in 1851, 8; in 1852, 8; in 1853, 8; in 1854, 11; in 1855, 11; in 1856, 9; in 1857, 11; in 1858, 18; in 1859, 16; in 1860, 16; in 1861, 23; in 1862, 15; in 1863, 12; in 1864, 11; in 1865, 8; and in 1866, 26.

MONROE COUNTY.

Population in 1845, 70,899; in 1850, 87,650; in 1855, 96,324; in 1860, 100,648, and in 1865, 104,235.

YEAR.	CIVIL CAUSES.							CRIMINAL CAUSES.				
	Number of causes brought before the court by summons and complaint (or other original process) during each year.	Number of causes tried and decided in each year.	Number of causes tried by jury.	Number of causes tried by court, without a jury.	Number of causes referred.	Number of causes brought before Supreme Court on appeal or certiorari from inferior courts.*	Number of causes brought from Special Terms, Circuit, Oyer and Terminer, &c., to General Term on appeal.†	Number of causes brought before the court in each year.	Number tried in each year.	Number of causes brought to Supreme Court from Surrogates' Courts.‡	Number of referees' reports confirmed.‡	Number of referees' reports not confirmed.‡
1847,	......	37	37	.....	19	......	160	101	15	...	.....	....
1848,	520	111	100	11	78	......	348	183	50	....	.....	....
1849,	480	75	57	18	72	......	330	164	57	....	.....	....
1850,	678	64	52	12	73	......	370	115	68	....	.....	....
1851,	947	48	29	19	56	......	317	234	54	....	.....	....
1852,	1,466	190	92	98	136	......	364	216	77	....	.....	....
1853,	1,221	87	38	49	68	......	313	145	80	....	.....	....
1854,	1,477	112	50	62	76	......	320	148	64	....	.....	....
1855,	1,837	93	38	55	59	......	459	230	56	....	.....	....
1856,	1,568	278	91	187	129	......	602	220	56	....	.....	....
1857,	1,261	86	34	52	54	......	536	168	64	....	.....	....
1858,	1,886	143	51	92	95	......	547	135	60	....	.....	....
1859,	1,531	226	98	128	126	......	478	240	65	....	.....	....
1860,	962	160	68	92	101	......	409	182	64	....	.....	....
1861,	969	90	58	32	58	......	398	139	50	....	.....	....
1862,	1,103	74	41	33	28	......	537	107	40	....	.....	....
1863,	1,247	98	61	37	34	......	321	57	25	....	.....	....
1864,	1,128	86	48	38	36	......	262	52	11	....	.....	....
1865,	965	104	57	47	27	......	286	87	22	....	.....	....
1866,	1,209	81	49	32	40	......	281	137	45	....	.....	....
	22,405	2,243	1,149	1,094	1,365	......	7,638	3,060	1,023	....	.....	....

ONEIDA COUNTY.

Population in 1845, 84,776; in 1850, 99,566; in 1855, 107,749; in 1860, 105,202; and in 1865, 102.713.

YEAR.												
1847,	651	167	....	....	52	......	......	....	....	....	....	....
1848,	816	116	....	....	....	......	......	....	....	....	....	....
1849,	1,039	188	....	....	....	......	......	....	....	....	....	....
1850,	1,111	82	....	....	....	......	......	....	....	....	....	....
1851,	1,324	88	....	....	....	......	......	....	....	....	....	....
1852,	1,529	124	....	....	....	......	......	....	....	....	....	....
1853,	1,305	27	....	....	....	......	......	....	....	....	....	....
1854,	1,851	136	....	....	....	......	......	....	....	....	....	....
1855,	2,222	170	....	....	....	......	......	....	....	....	....	....
1856,	2,191	120	....	....	....	......	......	....	....	....	....	....
1857,	2,808	144	....	....	....	......	......	....	....	....	....	....
1858,	2,267	101	....	....	....	......	......	....	....	....	....	....
1859,	1,507	52	....	....	....	......	......	....	....	....	....	....
1860,	1,355	37	....	....	....	......	......	....	....	....	....	....
1861,	1,825	48	....	....	....	......	......	....	....	....	....	....
1862,	948	39	....	....	....	......	......	....	....	....	....	....
1863,	778	40	....	....	....	......	......	....	....	....	....	....
1864,	832	38	....	....	....	......	......	....	....	....	....	....
1865,	939	78	....	....	....	......	......	....	....	....	....	....
1866,	1,105	55	....	....	....	......	......	....	....	....	....	....
	28,403	1,850	....	....	52	......	......	....	....	....	....	....

* The clerk reported that he could not fill this column with any accuracy.

† This column includes all appeals to the General Term for the whole Seventh Judicial District, except the appeals noticed for the June Term for the said court, from 1852 to 1862, which term was held at Auburn. The Seventh Judicial District comprises Livingston, Wayne, Seneca, Yates, Ontario, Steuben, Monroe and Cayuga counties.

‡ These cannot be determined.

ONTARIO COUNTY.

Population in 1845, 42,592; in 1850, 43,929; in 1855, 42,672; in 1860, 44,563; and in 1865, 43,316.

YEAR.	CIVIL CAUSES. Number of causes brought before the court by summons and complaint (or other original process), during each year.	Number of causes tried and decided in each year.	Number of causes tried by jury.	Number of causes tried by court without a jury.	Number of causes referred.	Number of causes brought before Supreme Court on appeal or certiorari from inferior courts.	Number of causes brought from Special Terms, Circuit, Oyer and Terminer, &c., to General Term on appeal.	CRIMINAL CAUSES. Number of causes brought before the court in each year.	Number tried in each year.	Number of causes brought to Supreme Court from Surrogates' Courts.	Number of referees' reports confirmed.	Number of referees' reports not confirmed.
1847,		10	7	2	1	†	‡	95	15	§	‖	‖
1848,	......	45	22	9	14	....	....	44	28	....	....	....
1849,	......	32	16	8	8	....	....	62	39	....	....	....
1850,	......	76	22	25	29	....	....	77	41	....	....	...
1851,	......	74	16	26	32	....	....	70	38	....	....	....
1852,	......	91	25	33	33	....	....	45	18	....	....	....
1853,	......	122	30	33	59	....	....	59	31	....	....	....
1854,	......	105	26	39	40	....	....	57	32	....	....	....
1855,	......	117	20	41	56	....	....	61	26	....	....	....
1856,	......	125	25	37	63	....	....	72	11	....	....	....
1857,	......	142	21	45	76	....	....	58	28	....	....	....
1858,	......	145	21	44	80	....	....	65	21	....	....	....
1859,	......	105	18	21	66	....	....	86	26	....	....	....
1860,	......	123	27	28	68	...	....	44	25	....	....	...
1861,	......	90	21	19	50	....	....	44	27	....	....	....
1862,	......	81	13	7	61	....	....	40	6	....	....	....
1863,	......	124	23	27	74	....	....	50	12	....	....	....
1864,	......	94	18	20	56	....	....	57	18	....	....	....
1865,	......	64	13	10	41	....	....	46	11	....	....	....
1866,	......	102	15	27	60	....	....	63	42	....	....	....
	......	1,867	399	501	967	....	....	1,195	495	....	....	....

OTSEGO COUNTY.

Population in 1845, 50,509; in 1850, 48,638; in 1855, 49,735; in 1860, 50,157; and in 1865, 48,616.

YEAR.	Brought before court	Tried and decided	Tried by jury	Tried by court without jury	Referred	On appeal from inferior courts	To General Term on appeal	Criminal: brought before court	Criminal: tried	From Surrogates' Courts	Referees' reports confirmed	Referees' reports not confirmed
1847,	73	5	5	.....	2	¶14	**58	37	2	††	1	....
1848,	118	45	38	7	8	......	110	44	17	1	2	....
1849,	138	70	60	10	13	......	21	29	14	2	.....	....
1850,	101	54	39	15	42	......	49	22	7	....	7	....
1851,	116	4	3	1	18	......	63	16	4	....	3	....
1852,	59	22	19	3	18	......	57	16	3	....	4	....
1853,	213	42	27	15	27	......	80	6	2	....	.....	....
1854,	135	40	26	14	35	......	......	12	1	....	2	....
1855,	213	33	25	8	44	......	......	7	1	....	5	....
1856,	192	57	38	19	30	......	......	11	....	....	2	....
1857,	205	43	28	15	35	......	52	20	1	....	4	....
1858,	230	39	20	19	35	......	......	22	5	....	2	....
1859,	265	53	37	16	24	......	61	13	2	....	.....	....
1860,	209	30	25	5	33	......	......	13	3	....	3	....
1861,	292	69	59	10	39	......	......	6	2	....	5	....
1862,	237	26	21	5	22	......	......	2	1	....	5	....
1863,	171	19	15	4	42	......	......	11	1	....	2	....
1864,	233	33	23	10	44	......	......	7	2	....	3	....
1865,	244	18	16	2	31	......	......	14	4	....	3	....
1866,	231	30	23	7	39	......	......	8	....	....	2	....
	3,675	732	547	185	581	14	551	316	72	3	55	....

* This column would vary but little from the next. Want of time prevented the clerk from preparing the data for this report.

† These would not exceed 24 since 1847. ‡ No General Term is held in this county.

§ None worth returning. ‖ Want of time prevented the clerk from giving these items.

¶ The Clerk reported that there was nothing in his office giving further light under this head.

** These returns are all that could be found under this head.

†† Nothing was found under this head.

QUEENS COUNTY.

Population in 1845, 31,849; in 1850, 36,833; in 1855, 46,266; in 1860, 57,391; and in 1865, 57,997.

YEAR.	CIVIL CAUSES.							CRIMINAL CAUSES.		Number of causes brought to Supreme Court from Surrogates' Courts.	Number of referees' reports confirmed.	Number of referees' reports not confirmed.
	Number of causes brought before the court by summons and complaint (or other original process), during each year.	Number of causes tried and decided in each year.	Number of causes tried by jury.	Number of causes tried by court without a jury.	Number of cases referred.	Number of causes brought before Supreme Court on appeal or certiorari from inferior courts.	Number of causes brought from Special Terms, Circuit, Oyer and Terminer, &c., to General Term on appeal.	Number of causes brought before the court in each year.	Number tried in each year.			
1847,	58	30	10	2	18	3	2	25	11	....	18	....
1848,	60	30	12	....	19	4	3	30	16	....	19	....
1849,	62	31	14	....	17	3	1	32	15	....	17	....
1850,	65	33	15	2	16	4	3	36	18	....	16	....
1851,	70	38	17	3	18	5	2	40	19	....	18	....
1852,	72	40	20	4	16	6	4	43	21	....	16	....
1853,	75	41	23	5	13	5	2	46	24	....	13	....
1854,	73	38	19	3	16	3	1	50	26	...	16	....
1855,	76	40	22	1	17	2	....	56	24	....	17	....
1856,	80	44	24	4	16	2	1	60	21	....	16	....
1857,	85	48	25	5	18	1	....	61	33	....	18	....
1858,	87	50	27	3	20	2	....	65	29	....	20	....
1859,	95	60	36	5	19	1	....	68	34	....	19	....
1860,	101	62	38	8	16	3	1	72	38	2	15	1
1861,	99	61	36	10	15	4	....	69	37	1	14	1
1862,	108	66	38	11	15	3	....	78	35	....	13	2
1863,	114	64	34	6	24	3	....	84	43	1	24	....
1864,	128	68	36	15	17	4	....	90	46	....	15	2
1865,	138	74	42	8	24	2	....	96	45	....	24	....
1866,	147	77	40	11	16	1	....	101	38	....	16	....
	1,793	995	528	106	350	60	20	1,102	583	4	345	6

RENSSELAER COUNTY.

Population in 1845, 62,338; in 1850, 73,363; in 1855, 79,234; in 1860, 86,326; and in 1865, 88,215.

YEAR.	Brought before court	Tried and decided	Tried by jury	Tried by court without jury	Referred	On appeal from inferior courts	To General Term on appeal	Criminal: brought	Criminal: tried	From Surrogates' Courts	Reports confirmed	Reports not confirmed
1847,	518	59	41	3	15	......	......	45	11	2	14	1
1848,	601	111	39	11	61	......	......	110	39	4	58	3
1849,	723	193	59	64	70	......	......	79	43	3	65	5
1850,	828	139	27	63	49	......	......	72	32	1	63	6
1851,	834	175	29	61	85	......	......	103	43	5	81	4
1852,	759	230	33	98	99	......	......	80	31	2	97	2
1853,	675	227	31	86	110	......	......	53	18	3	105	5
1854,	891	190	14	80	96	......	......	113	37	1	94	2
1855,	1,050	199	32	112	55	......	......	83	23	6	52	3
1856,	801	208	21	119	68	......	......	85	26	2	67	1
1857,	1,041	209	27	109	73	......	......	61	24	1	66	6
1858,	1,047	371	35	185	151	......	......	101	39	3	167	6
1859,	705	257	22	105	130	......	......	97	36	2	128	2
1860,	798	361	44	145	172	......	......	93	33	1	169	3
1861,	1,071	337	70	134	133	......	......	93	41	2	129	6
1862,	639	245	19	84	142	......	......	85	22	1	140	2
1863,	495	245	24	70	151	......	......	157	36	3	146	5
1864,	402	148	14	51	83	......	......	140	37	2	79	6
1865,	432	88	21	29	28	......	......	152	68	2	26	2
1866,	923	146	23	44	79	......	......	91	66	3	76	3
	15,233	4,138	625	1,663	1,850	......	.....	1,893	685	47	1,782	67

SARATOGA COUNTY.

Population in 1845, 41,447; in 1850, 45,646; in 1855, 49,379; in 1860, 51,729; and in 1865, 49,892.

YEAR.	CIVIL CAUSES.							CRIMINAL CAUSES.		Number of cases brought to Supreme Court from Surrogates' Courts.	Number of referees' reports confirmed.	Number of referees' reports not confirmed.
	Number of causes brought before the court by summons and complaint (or other original process), during each year.	Number of causes tried and decided in each year.	Number of causes tried by jury.	Number of causes tried by court without a jury.	Number of causes referred.	Number of causes brought before Supreme Court on appeal or certiorari from inferior courts.	Number of causes brought from Special Terms, Circuit, Oyer and Terminer, &c., to General Term on appeal.	Number of causes brought before the court in each year.	Number tried in each year.			
1847,	128	30	23	7	21	10	8	15	10	....	*	*
1848,	144	28	26	2	20	12	8	44	9	....	.....	....
1849,	199	38	27	11	21	5	8	47	9	....	.....	....
1850,	200	30	15	15	20	5	15	12	9	....	.....	....
1851,	210	39	30	9	21	6	13	20	7	....	.....	....
1852,	195	33	21	12	28	5	23	36	4	....	.....	....
1853,	176	27	14	13	26	3	14	25	13	2	.....	....
1854,	255	30	16	14	30	10	31	31	7	....	.....	....
1855,	200	29	16	13	31	6	17	32	15	....	....	....
1856,	195	44	22	20	15	3	23	27	9	9	.....	....
1857,	191	45	15	30	10	5	35	36	12	....	.....	....
1858,	168	36	12	24	17	6	38	60	10	3	.....	....
1859,	130	48	20	28	35	2	32	40	17	2	.....	....
1860,	175	33	29	4	31	2	31	44	9	1	.....	....
1861,	191	30	20	10	25	5	5	9	7	....	.....	....
1862,	200	36	14	22	20	3	30	29	6	3	.....	....
1863,	170	30	16	14	9	4	30	22	5	3	.....	....
1864,	174	19	13	6	15	4	36	63	7	2	.....	....
1865,	200	29	16	13	10	3	33	77	6	1	.....	....
1866,	209	28	18	10	17	4	22	73	14	1	.....	....
	3,710	662	383	277	402	103	452	742	185	27	.....	....

SCHENECTADY COUNTY.

Population, in 1845, 16,630; in 1850, 20,054; in 1855, 19,572; in 1860, 20,002; and in 1865, 20,888.

YEAR.	Brought	Tried and decided	By jury	By court	Referred	On appeal from inferior courts	To General Term on appeal	Criminal brought	Criminal tried	From Surrogates' Courts	Reports confirmed	Reports not confirmed
1847,	16	16	16	.....	.....		......	4	2	....	.....	....
1848,	21	13	13	2	6	......	......	9	3	....	.....	....
1849,	22	11	10	1	8	......	......	17	11	....	. ...	....
1850,	24	7	2	11	11	......	......	13	7	....	.....	....
1851,	24	10	7	9	8	......	......	7	5	....	.....	....
1852,	49	21	7	20	22	......	......	14	8	....	....	....
1853,	36	9	4	14	18	......	3	11	9	....	5	....
1854,	33	15	6	15	17	......	4	8	4	....	6	....
1855,	54	19	8	16	30	......	6	6	3	....	4	....
1856,	44	26	11	22	11	......	5	4	3	...	3	....
1857,	35	9	8	9	18	......	13	12	8	....	4	....
1858,	63	22	9	26	28	.... .	16	5	3	....	7	....
1859,	50	19	5	24	21	......	10	11	9	....	3	....
1860,	49	24	12	19	18	......	8	14	11	....	4	...
1861,	32	10	12	4	16	......	6	9	6	....	6	....
1862,	33	9	6	6	26	......	10	4	1	...	12	....
1863,	25	11	12	9	4	......	30	8	6	....	7	....
1864,	23	9	7	8	8	......	6	7	2	....	5	....
1865,	28	14	10	7	11	......	11	11	5	...	7	....
1866,	36	12	11	12	13	......	6	22	9	....	8	....
	707	286	176	234	294	......	134	196	115	....	81	....

* Information could not be procured under these heads. Entire correctness is not claimed in the returns of this county, but they are as nearly complete as they could be made.

† No record.

SCHOHARIE COUNTY.

Population in 1845, 32,488; in 1850, 33,548; in 1855, 33,519; in 1860, 34,469, and in 1865, 33,353.

YEAR.	CIVIL CAUSES.							CRIMINAL CAUSES.				
	Number of causes brought before the court by summons and complaint (or other original process), during each year.	Number of causes tried and decided in each year.	Number of causes tried by jury.	Number of causes tried by court without a jury.	Number of causes referred.	Number of causes brought before Supreme Court on appeal or certiorari from inferior courts.	Number of causes brought from Special Terms, Circuit, Oyer and Terminer, &c., to General Term on appeal.	Number of causes brought before the court in each year.	Number tried in each year.	Number of causes brought to Supreme Court from Surrogates' Courts.	Number of referees' reports confirmed.	Number of referees' reports not confirmed.
1847,	15	15	15	.....	.....	......	......	15	15	....	.....	....
1848,	32	22	22	1	5	......	......	32	27	....	5	....
1849,	49	32	15	6	11	......	......	49	38	....	11	....
1850.	43	15	12	3	14	......	......	43	15	....	14	....
1851,	54	19	15	2	18	1	......	54	36	....	18	....
1852,	66	32	17	15	19	1	......	66	32	....	19	....
1853,	67	32	17	15	15	2	......	67	32	....	15	....
1854,	54	19	10	9	9	......	......	54	38	....	9	....
1855,	66	29	12	18	12	......	......	66	29	....	12	....
1856,	53	17	10	7	19	......	......	53	17	....	19	....
1857,	69	54	16	18	20	......	......	69	35	....	20	....
1858,	51	25	15	10	19	1	......	51	25	....	19	....
1859,	59	27	10	17	29	......	......	59	27	....	29	....
1860,	58	36	18	18	14	1	......	58	36	....	14	....
1861,	57	44	21	23	8	......	......	57	44	....	8	....
1862,	46	26	13	13	16	......	......	46	26	....	16	....
1863,	40	21	15	6	9	......	......	40	21	....	9	....
1864,	42	25	11	14	15	1	......	42	25	....	15	....
1865,	48	21	15	6	18	1	......	48	21	....	18	....
1866,	65	27	21	6	28	......	......	65	27	....	28	....
	1,034	538	300	207	298	8	......	1,034	566	....	298	....

SCHUYLER COUNTY.

Population in 1855, 18,777; in 1860, 18,840; and in 1865, 18,841.

YEAR.												
1847,	......	.....	....	.....	.....	......	......	.....	....	....	.....	....
1848,	......	.....	....	.....	.....	......	......	.....	....	....	.....	....
1849,	......	.....	....	.....	.....	......	......	.....	....	....	.....	....
1850,	......	.....	....	.....	.....	......	......	.....	....	....	.....	....
1851,	......	.....	....	.....	.....	......	......	.....	....	....	.....	....
1852,	......	.....	....	.....	.....	......	......	.....	....	....	.....	....
1853,	......	.....	....	.....	.....	......	......	.....	....	....	.....	....
1854,	......	.....	....	.....	.....	......	......	.....	....	....	.....	....
1855,	......	.....	....	.....	.....	......	......	.....	....	....	.....	....
1856,	......	.....	....	.....	.....	......	......	.....	....	....	.....	....
1857,	......	.....	....	.....	.....	......	......	.....	....	....	.....	....
1858,	......	.....	....	.....	.....	......	......	.....	....	....	.....	....
1859,	34	1	....	1	3	......	......	34	11	....	.....	....
1860,	74	37	20	17	15	......	......	43	23	....	4	....
1861,	62	42	17	25	14	......	......	37	19	2	1	...
1862,	56	22	9	13	15	......	......	28	13	....	3	....
1863,	56	21	18	3	5	......	......	33	9	1	2	....
1864,	80	25	23	2	16	......	......	21	11	1	.....	....
1865,	102	18	12	6	9	......	......	27	7	....	.....	....
1866,	130	23	18	5	21	......	......	41	14	....	.....	....
	594	189	117	72	98	......	......	264	107	4	10	....

SENECA COUNTY.

Population in 1845, 24,972; in 1850, 25,441; in 1855, 25,358; in 1860, 28,138; and in 1865, 27,653.

YEAR.	CIVIL CAUSES. Number of causes brought before the court by summons and complaint (or other original process), during each year.	Number of causes tried and decided in each year.	Number of causes tried by jury.	Number of causes tried by court without a jury.	Number of causes referred.	Number of causes brought before Supreme Court on appeal or certiorari from inferior courts.*	Number of causes brought from Special Terms, Circuit, Oyer and Terminer, &c., to General Term on appeal.	CRIMINAL CAUSES. Number of causes brought before the court each year.	Number tried in each year.	Number of causes brought to Supreme Court from Surrogates' Courts.	Number of referees' reports confirmed.	Number of referees' reports not confirmed.
1847,.	32	18	7	11	....	....	....	17	1	....	....	....
1848,.	65	26	20	2	4	....	....	20	9	....	....	....
1849,.	114	16	6	2	8	....	....	24	4	....	....	....
1850,.	103	26	6	10	10	2	3	21	3	....	....	....
1851,.	128	35	9	14	12	1	2	12	1	....	....	....
1852,.	120	32	15	8	9	1	3	5	....	....	....	....
1853,.	170	34	7	16	11	2	1	8	1	....	....	....
1854,.	164	33	3	17	13	2	2	11	....	....	....	....
1855,.	155	33	3	15	15	1	2	12	1	....	....	....
1856,.	175	34	4	16	14	3	6	7	....	....	....	....
1857,.	212	55	7	21	27	1	2	13	1	....	....	....
1858,.	272	52	3	16	33	1	1	7	....	....	....	....
1859,.	231	52	7	14	31	....	6	9	....	....	....	....
1860,.	183	46	4	8	34	1	3	5	....	....	....	....
1861,.	347	75	6	18	51	1	1	3	....	....	....	....
1862,.	157	51	4	14	33	1	1	4	1	....	....	....
1863,,	81	37	7	10	20	....	8	13	....	....	....	....
1864,.	90	30	3	9	18	2	1	5	....	....	....	....
1865,.	85	43	14	17	12	2	2	4	....	....	....	....
1866,.	150	54	13	20	21	5	4	12	....	....	....	....
	3,034	782	148	258	376	26	48	212	52	....	....	....

SUFFOLK COUNTY.

Population in 1845, 34,579; in 1850, 36,922; in 1855, 41,066; in 1860, 43,275; and in 1865, 42,867.

YEAR.	Number of causes brought before the court by summons and complaint (or other original process), during each year.	Number of causes tried and decided in each year.	Number of causes tried by jury.	Number of causes tried by court without a jury.	Number of causes referred.	Number of causes brought before Supreme Court on appeal or certiorari from inferior courts.*	Number of causes brought from Special Terms, Circuit, Oyer and Terminer, &c., to General Term on appeal.	Number of causes brought before the court each year.	Number tried in each year.	Number of causes brought to Supreme Court from Surrogates' Courts.	Number of referees' reports confirmed.	Number of referees' reports not confirmed.
1847..	†	‡	‡	‡	....	....	....	9	4	....	....	....
1848,.	....	....	....	....	....	....	....	6	2	....	....	....
1849,.	....	....	....	....	....	....	....	14	8	....	....	....
1850,.	....	....	....	....	....	....	....	10	5	....	....	....
1851,.	....	....	....	....	....	....	....	12	7	....	....	....
1852,.	....	....	....	....	....	....	....	12	6	....	....	....
1853,.	37	16	6	10	....	....	....	47	11	....	....	....
1854,.	51	12	7	5	....	....	....	39	17	....	....	....
1855,.	48	21	13	8	....	....	....	19	10	....	....	....
1856,.	49	17	11	6	....	....	....	7	5	....	....	....
1857,.	47	21	9	12	....	....	....	20	11	....	....	....
1858,.	78	16	10	6	....	....	....	17	14	....	....	....
1859,.	100	23	14	9	....	....	....	36	20	....	....	....
1860,.	56	14	12	2	....	....	....	29	22	....	....	....
1861,.	81	22	6	16	....	....	....	39	23	....	....	....
1862,.	73	27	12	15	....	....	....	20	6	....	....	....
1863,.	50	17	7	10	....	....	....	19	5	....	....	....
1864,.	67	32	21	11	....	....	....	20	8	....	....	....
1865,.	51	22	16	6	....	....	....	17	7	....	....	....
1866,.	77	25	17	8	....	....	....	23	3	....	....	....
	865	285	161	124	....	....	....	415	194	....	....	....

* Includes causes brought from Surrogate's court.

† Taken from the calendars. ‡ Taken from the court minutes.

TIOGA COUNTY.

Population in 1845, 22,456; in 1850, 24,880; in 1855, 26,962; in 1860, 28,748; and in 1865, 28,163.

YEAR.	CIVIL CAUSES.							CRIMINAL CAUSES.‡		Number of causes brought to Supreme Court from Surrogates' Courts.	Number of referees' reports confirmed.	Number of referees' reports not confirmed.
	Number of causes brought before the court by summons and complaint (or other original process), during each year.	Number of causes tried and decided in each year.	Number of causes tried by jury.	Number of causes tried by court without a jury.	Number of causes referred.	Number of causes brought before Supreme Court on appeal or certiorari from inferior courts.	Number of causes brought from Special Terms, Circuit, Oyer and Terminer, &c., to General Term on appeal.	Number of causes brought before the court in each year.	Number tried in each year.			
1847,.	10	9	9	.....	1	......	1	1	...	....	3	....
1848,.	18	14	12	2	2	......	......	5	2	....	5	....
1849,.	22	18	17	1	3	......	......	15	10	....	6	....
1850,.	14	11	4	7	2	......	......	14	8	....	6	....
1851,.	15	8	5	3	6	1	......	14	5	1	11	....
1852,.	32	19	11	8	11	2	5	10	4	....	18	....
1853,.	27	18	12	6	8	2	1	7	4	....	15	....
1854,.	25	15	7	10	3	2	......	2	....	....	5	....
1855,.	27	13	7	6	5	5	4	2	1	....	9	....
1856,.	27	10	4	6	11	1	......	3	1	....	16	....
1857,.	60	24	15	14	22	4	......	4	2	....	29	....
1858,.	86	40	23	20	29	1	2	.....	....	....	37	....
1859,.	51	27	10	17	15	3	......	7	....	....	24	....
1860,.	61	34	15	19	19	8	3	8	1	....	26	....
1861,.	71	40	20	20	20	2	1	4	....	....	31	....
1862,.	46	22	8	15	16	1	1	4	1	1	23	....
1863,.	19	3	....	3	9	2	......	3	....	....	17	....
1864,.	34	18	6	12	13	1	1	2	....	....	22	....
1865,.	28	19	3	17	6	......	2	3	....	....	12	....
1866,.	41	12	8	6	21	......	3	4	....	....	31	....
	*714	†374	196	192	222	35	24	§112	39	2	‖346	....

ULSTER COUNTY.

Population in 1845, 49,907; in 1850, 53,384; in 1855, 67,933; in 1860, 76,331; and in 1865, 75,609.

1847,.	148	12	12	.....	12	2	8	20	1	1	12	....
1848,.	143	53	45	8	20	1	7	28	9	...	19	1
1849,.	126	30	29	1	12	4	9	38	12	1	12	....
1850,.	242	47	20	27	28	3	5	5	11	....	27	1
1851,.	195	56	33	23	12	1	7	20	5	....	11	1
1852,.	182	45	23	22	2	2	11	26	9	1	2	....
1853,.	244	72	48	24	2	1	10	27	5	....	2	....
1854,.	275	58	21	37	5	4	8	24	10	1	5	...
1855,.	337	114	44	70	10	3	6	27	7	....	9	1
1856,.	482	114	54	60	1	2	7	47	4	....	1	....
1857,.	468	70	37	33	1	1	7	43	9	1	1	....
1858,.	258	98	47	51	6	3	15	35	6	1	6	....
1859,.	529	79	44	35	31	2	16	39	1	1	30	1
1860,.	559	41	20	21	1	4	19	48	2	....	1	...
1861,.	494	68	18	50	23	1	11	62	9	....	21	2
1862,.	430	90	27	63	21	1	23	37	5	1	20	1
1863,.	329	87	42	45	24	1	20	34	....	1	23	1
1864,.	343	29	15	14	16	2	14	32	1	....	16	...
1865,.	608	88	47	41	21	3	11	39	9	1	21	....
1866,.	443	25	16	9	18	3	28	33	....	....	17	1
	6,835	1,276	642	634	266	44	242	664	115	10	256	10

* Not including causes in which judgments are entered on default, out of term or on confession.
† Causes referred not included.
‡ In Tioga county Oyer and Terminer.
§ The mere presenting of indictments not included.
‖ Including trials of causes.

WARREN COUNTY.

Population in 1845, 14,908; in 1850, 17,199; in 1855, 19,669; in 1860, 21,434; and in 1865, 21,128.

YEAR.	CIVIL CAUSES.							CRIMINAL CAUSES.				
	Number of causes brought before the court by summons and complaint or other original process), during each year.	Number of causes tried and decided in each year.	Number of causes tried by jury.	Number of causes tried by court without a jury.	Number of causes referred.	Number of causes brought before Supreme Court on appeal or certiorari from inferior courts.	Number of causes brought from Special Terms, Circuit, Oyer and Terminer, &c., to General Term on appeal.	Number of causes brought before the court in each year.	Number tried in each year.	Number of causes brought to Supreme Court from Surrogates' Courts.	Number of referees' reports confirmed.	Number of referees' reports not confirmed.
1847,.	11	7	2	5	3	....	....	11	7	1	....	....
1848,.	41	17	15	2	6	....	....	41	17	....	....	....
1849,,	32	5	3	....	9	....	...	32	5	...	2	....
1850,.	62	17	12	1	8	2	....	64	17	....	2	....
1851,.	66	24	6	4	7	12	...	78	24	....	2	....
1852,.	65	31	14	3	7	7	42	72	31	...	8	....
1853,.	45	29	5	3	7	16	....	61	29	...	7	....
1854,.	95	35	8	12	16	9	....	104	35	....	6	1
1855,.	85	22	5	1	10	11	....	96	22	....	6	....
1856,.	64	18	5	4	6	5	....	69	18	...	4	....
1857,.	62	29	4	3	9	17	....	79	29	....	6	....
1858,.	96	30	5	9	9	12	38	109	30	....	4	1
1859,.	46	25	6	5	4	10	22	56	25	....	6	....
1860,.	71	26	6	5	6	13	40	84	26	....	3	....
1861,.	94	12	3	1	2	5	21	99	12	....	3	....
1862,.	77	43	9	8	2	24	29	101	43	....	2	....
1863,.	27	9	....	5	....	3	57	30	9	....	1	....
1864,.	27	3	....	2	2	....	....	27	3	....	1	...
1865,.	38	8	3	2	13	1	....	39	8	....	3	....
1866,.	52	20	5	1	12	7	....	59	20	....	7	....
	1,156	410	116	76	138	154	249	1,311	410	1	73	2

WASHINGTON COUNTY.

Population in 1845, 40,554; in 1850, 44,750; in 1855, 44,405; in 1860, 45,904, and in 1865, 46,244.

YEAR.	Number of causes brought before the court by summons and complaint or other original process), during each year.	Number of causes tried and decided in each year.	Number of causes tried by jury.	Number of causes tried by court without a jury.	Number of causes referred.	Number of causes brought before Supreme Court on appeal or certiorari from inferior courts.	Number of causes brought from Special Terms, Circuit, Oyer and Terminer, &c., to General Term on appeal.	Number of causes brought before the court in each year.	Number tried in each year.	Number of causes brought to Supreme Court from Surrogates' Courts.	Number of referees' reports confirmed.	Number of referees' reports not confirmed.
1847,.	94	....	....	....	6	*	*	12	7	1	†	†
1848,.	380	....	....	....	4	......	......	36	11	...	.....	....
1849,.	334	....	....	....	7	......	......	25	6	....	.....	....
1850,.	351	....	....	....	7	......	......	38	13	....	....	....
1851,.	301	....	....	....	2	......	......	35	6	....	.....	....
1852,.	258	....	....	....	6	......	......	31	12	....	.....	....
1853,.	219	30	22	5	7	......	......	66	2	....	.....	....
1854,.	374	30	12	11	15	......	......	46	4	....	.....	....
1855,.	450	50	18	22	27	......	......	71	13	1	.....	....
1856,.	394	55	16	26	28	......	......	44	7	....	.....	....
1857,.	438	52	8	25	30	......	......	53	4	....	.....	....
1858,.	351	40	11	18	25	......	......	52	9	....	.....	....
1859,.	296	30	13	12	13	......	......	100	5	....	.....	...
1860,.	243	29	12	12	11	......	......	78	9	....	.....	....
1861,.	448	40	13	21	15	......	.....	50	3	....	.....	....
1862,.	289	36	9	17	20	......	......	39	1	1	.....	....
1863,.	185	20	13	5	6	......	......	43	3	...	.....	....
1864,.	213	12	9	....	12	......	......	33	7	1	.....	....
1865,.	143	26	17	4	13	......	......	36	8	....	.....	....
1866,.	207	28	16	7	13	......	......	32	4	....	.....	....
	5,968	478	189	185	267	......	......	920	134	4	.....	....

* Probably two a year on an average.

† It is estimated that not more than four or five cases have occurred within twenty years, that would come under this head.

WYOMING COUNTY.

Population, in 1845, 27,205; in 1850, 31,981; in 1855, 32,140; in 1860, 31,968; and in 1865, 30,033.

YEAR.	CIVIL CAUSES. Number of causes brought before the court by summons and complaint, (or other original process), during each year.	Number of causes tried and decided in each year.	Number of causes tried by jury.	Number of causes tried by court without a jury.	Number of causes referred.	Number of causes brought before Supreme Court on appeal or certiorari from inferior courts.	Number of causes brought from Special Terms, Circuit, Oyer and Terminer, &c., to General Term on appeal.	CRIMINAL CAUSES. Number of causes brought before the court in each year.	Number tried in each year.	Number of causes brought to Supreme Court from Surrogates' Courts.	Number of referees' reports confirmed.	Number of referees' reports not confirmed.
1847,	23	12	6	6	4	4	1	47	23	....	2	....
1848,	54	32	18	14	7	11	3	34	19	....	3	....
1849,	13	16	9	7	9	12	2	38	25	....	6	1
1850,	12	18	7	8	6	5	4	42	31	...	5	1
1851,	17	16	12	4	9	8	5	29	20	....	9	....
1852,	21	14	8	6	7	3	2	37	28	....	7	....
1853,	16	16	10	6	3	2	6	31	19	....	3	....
1854,	17	11	5	4	5	4	1	28	16	....	5	....
1855,	22	15	10	3	3	2	2	29	20	....	3	....
1856,	19	11	6	5	4	3	1	34	23	....	4	....
1857,	25	18	12	6	3	2	3	33	21	....	3	....
1858,	18	15	11	4	6	4	2	39	30	....	6	....
1859,	29	21	17	4	3	2	3	42	31	....	3	....
1860,	31	23	18	5	2	3	1	31	19	...	4	...
1861,	23	19	11	7	4	2	2	21	15	....	2	....
1862,	16	14	10	3	2	5	2	17	12	....	4	....
1863,	18	13	10	2	2	3	1	14	10	...	2	1
1864,	20	17	9	7	2	2	3	16	11	....	2	....
1865,	22	18	11	7	6	1	....	19	15	....	6	....
1866,	27	21	15	4	5	6	2	22	17	....	5	....
	443	340	215	112	92	84	46	603	405	....	84	3

YATES COUNTY.

Population in 1845, 20,777; in 1850, 20,590; in 1855, 19,812; in 1860, 20,290; and in 1865, 19,338.

YEAR.	Number of causes brought before the court by summons and complaint, (or other original process), during each year.	Number of causes tried and decided in each year.	Number of causes tried by jury.	Number of causes tried by court without a jury.	Number of causes referred.	Number of causes brought before Supreme Court on appeal or certiorari from inferior courts. *	Number of causes brought from Special Terms, Circuit, Oyer and Terminer, &c., to General Term on appeal. †	Number of causes brought before the court in each year. ‡	Number tried in each year.	Number of causes brought to Supreme Court from Surrogates' Courts.	Number of referees' reports confirmed.	Number of referees' reports not confirmed.
1847,	31	16	11	3	1	......	1	10	7	....	....	....
1848,	32	12	7	5	4	......	......	7	4	...	....	....
1849,	58	28	18	10	4	......	1	9	8	....	....	....
1850,	57	19	13	6	5	......	......	12	3	....	....	....
1851,	108	19	13	6	3	......	......	21	9	....	....	....
1852,	120	46	16	30	7	......	2	11	14	....	....	....
1853,	115	46	20	16	14	......	1	10	10	....	....	....
1854,	117	27	16	11	1	......	1	29	8	....	....	....
1855,	120	37	16	20	10	......	2	16	7	....	....	....
1856,	106	46	20	26	16	......	2	23	13	....	....	....
1857,	97	31	15	16	31	......	1	22	15	....	....	....
1858,	119	36	18	18	33	......	1	16	13	....	....	....
1859,	105	27	17	10	22	......	4	39	26	....	....	....
1860,	92	41	20	21	19	......	......	20	13	....	....	....
1861,	81	24	16	8	9	......	2	33	18	....	....	....
1862,	123	40	12	28	13	......	......	11	5	....	....	....
1863,	83	30	11	19	3	......	1	24	20	....	....	....
1864,	100	25	9	16	5	......	......	19	8	....	....	....
1865,	167	60	19	41	6	......	4	27	22	....	....	....
1866,	78	21	9	12	8	......	......	16	19	....	....	....
	1,909	631	306	322	231	......	23	375	242	....	....	....

* No General Term being held in this county, the clerk had no means of obtaining information for this column.

† These are all the criminal causes returned in this column. No civil causes are returned; nor does the column include the causes brought from Special Terms or Circuits.

‡ This comprises cases in Oyer and Terminer and Courts of Sessions. No criminal causes have come before the Supreme Court to be tried.

FINANCIAL CONDITION OF CITIES.

ALBANY.

Summary of Taxes during the last five years.

	1862.	1863.	1864.	1865.	1866.
Contingents, ...	$84,500 00	$79,500 00	$100,000 00	$138,470 00	$186,000 00
Lamps, ...	22,000 00	23,000 00	28,000 00	35,000 00	40,000 00
Streets, ...	3,000 00	3,000 00	6,000 00	50,000 00	5,000 00
Interest,..............	30,000 00	28,000 00	32,000 00	32,000 00	42,000 00
Sinking Fund,.........	10,000 00	10,000 00	10,000 00	10,000 00	10,000 00
City Poor,.............	18,000 00	25,000 00	25,000 00	35,000 00	40,000 00
Schools, ...	34,000 00	31,000 00	31,700 00	39,530 00	42,979 44
Police, ...	40,000 00	40,000 00	40,000 00	45,000 00	80,123 61
County of Albany, ...	5,114 94	6,312 97	5,512 94	7,080 60	8,440 06
Totals, ...	$246,614 94	$246,312 27	$286,212 94	$422,080 60	$455,143 11

City Debt.

The general debt of the city on the 1st day of November, 1865, was $330,250. During the past year the Trustees of the Sinking Fund have paid bonds to the amount of $75,750, and the city has issued its bonds for $190,000, being the sum required to pay for the purchase of Congress Hall block, thus adding $114,250 to the debt as it existed on the 1st of November, 1865. The details of the general debt are shown in the following table:

BONDS, WHEN PAYABLE.	RATE OF INTEREST.			When and where payable.	Total.
	5 per cent.	6 per cent.	7 per cent.		
On demand, ..	....	$3,000	$1,500	Chamberlain's Office, ...	$4,500
1867,..........	....	20,000	....	New York, Jan. 1, July 1,....	20,000
1868,..........	....	20,000	....	New York, Jan. 1, July 1,....	20,000
1869,..........	....	10,000	....	New York, Jan. 1, July 1,....	10,000
1870,..........	$21,000	....	....	New York, June 1, Dec. 1,....	21,000
1871,..........	20,000	....	....	New York, June 1, Dec. 1,....	20,000
1872,..........	20,000	....	....	New York, June 1, Dec. 1,....	20,000
1873,..........	20,000	....	....	New York, June 1, Dec. 1,....	20,000
1874,..........	19,000	....	....	New York, June 1, Dec. 1,....	19,000
1880,*	....	20,000	....	New York, June 1, Dec. 1,....	20,000
1881,*	....	20,000	....	New York, June 1, Dec. 1,....	20,000
1882,*	....	20,000	....	New York, June 1, Dec. 1,....	20,000
1883,*	....	20,000	....	New York, June 1, Dec. 1,....	20,000
1884,*	....	20,000	....	New York, June 1, Dec. 1,....	20,000
1885,†.........	....	10,000	....	Boston, Feb. 1, Aug. 1,....	10,000
1886,†.........	....	20,000	....	Boston, Feb. 1, Aug. 1,....	20,000
1887,†.........	....	20,000	....	Boston, Feb. 1, Aug. 1,....	20,000
1888,†.........	....	20,000	....	Boston, Feb. 1, Aug. 1,....	20,000
1889,†.........	....	20,000	....	Boston, Feb. 1, Aug. 1,....	20,000
1890,†.........	....	20,000	....	Boston, Feb. 1, Aug. 1,....	20,000
1891,†.........	....	20,000	....	Boston, Feb. 1, Aug. 1,....	20,000
1892,†.........	....	20,000	....	Boston, Feb. 1, Aug. 1,....	20,000
1893,†.........	....	20,000	....	Boston, Feb. 1, Aug. 1,....	20,000
1894,†.........	....	20,000	....	Boston, Feb. 1, Aug. 1,....	20,000
Totals,......	$100,000	$343,000	$1,500		$444,500

* War debt, created under an act of Legislature.
† Debt for purchase of Congress Hall property for new State Capitol.

Albany Northern Railroad Debt.

In addition to the foregoing, are the bonds of the city, loaned to the Albany Northern Railroad Company, amounting to the sum of $300,000, bearing interest, at the rate of six per cent. per annum, payable semi-annually, and the principal re-imbursable May 1, 1879.

Water Debt.

The amount of debt contracted for supplying the city with water was $850,000, for which bonds were issued bearing interest at the rate of six per cent. per annum, payable semi-annually, and the principal redeemable as follows:

YEARS.	Amount.	YEARS.	Amount.
1870,	$15,000 00	1876,	$250,000 00
1871,	285,000 00	1881,	250,000 00
1872,	50,000 00		$850,000 00

It will be seen by reference to the report of the Trustees of the Sinking Fund, that they have in cash, on deposit and investments in city bonds, the sum of $115,674.95, applicable to the redemption of the above debt.

Contingent Debt.

In accordance with the agreements made April 23, 1840, and June 26, 1841, between the city, the Albany and West Stockbridge Raillroad Company, and the Western Railroad Corporation, the bonds of the city were issued and delivered to the latter, to the amount of $1,000,000, maturing as follows:

YEARS.	Amount.	YEARS.	Amount.
1870,	$300,000 00	1876,	$250,000 00
1871,	200,000 00		$750,000 00

The Sinking Fund established for the redemption of this debt amounted, November 30, 1866, to the sum of $995,841.34. In this amount is included the sum of $311,000 of the original issue of bonds, viz.: 1866, $246,000; 1870, $38,000; 1871, $9,000; 1876, $18,000. These bonds have since been returned to the city, carefully examined and destroyed, thus reducing the debt to the sum of $689,000.

During the past year, pursuant to an act of the Legislature of this State, passed April 10, 1852, the city has issued its bonds to the amount of $500,000, and loaned the same to the Albany and Susquehanna Railroad Company. These bonds bear interest at the rate of six per cent., payable semi-annually, and the principal is redeemable at the expiration of thirty years from the date of issue.

To secure this loan, a joint mortgage has been executed by the company, in the sum of $2,000,000, on the entire line of road between Albany and Binghamton, including the depot grounds and all the real estate, road and appurtenances of the company, and in addition, the company are required to pay one per cent annually on the amount of bonds loaned to the Trustees of the Sinking Fund, to be by them invested and held as a fund toward the payment and redemption of the said bonds.

Expenditures during the last five years.

OBJECT.	1862.	1863.	1864.	1865.	1866
Markets,,	$887 95	$1,089 00	$1,011 97	$2,064 33	$2,070 79
Ferry,	114 58	96 50	112 00	18,759 76	10,796 47
Assessments for streets and drains,.	11,095 97	47,477 78	53,503 92	51,175 77	38,447 33
Street contingents,	17,088 12	31,001 60	27,755 19	29,816 02	22,903 17
Contingents, ,	21,867 53	30,007 36	23,837 88	30,120 90	51,834 09
City poor,	22,598 86	33,128 57	39,480 35	50,477 52	42,612 05
Almshouse,	40,756 76	23,470 51	24,115 53	30,417 08	47,439 16
City lamps,	22,247 73	27,436 82	36,064 41	41,344 43	44,257 97
Fire Department,	21,012 48	26,027 98	40,098 88	34,016 02	46,622 36

AUBURN.

The indebtedness of this city is $100,000, incurred in 1852 and due in 1872. There is also a floating debt of about $6,000, which has been incurred by exceeding the limitation of the charter, commencing some six years since. The Council have authority to liquidate the present year, and expect to do so, leaving the debt at $100,000.

BINGHAMTON.

This city was incorporated by the Legislature in 1867. Its only indebtedness is $50,000, contracted in aid of the Syracuse and Binghamton Railroad.

BROOKLYN.

Summary of Indebtedness.

Bonds issued by the city of Brooklyn and outstanding on the first day of January, 1867:

City Hall Loan of 1846, due in 1867–74,	$40,000 00
Washington Park Loan of 1848, due in 1869,	121,540 42
City Hall Loan of 1849, due in 1872–76,	50,000 00
do do 1850, due in 1875,	15,000 00
Current expense Loan of 1851, due in 1871,	150,000 00
Water Loan of 1851, due in 1873,	55,000 00
Debts of Williamsburgh, 1855, due in 1875,	150,000 00
Mount Prospect Square Loan of 1856, due in 1887,	90,000 00
Williamsburgh streets Liabilities Loan of 1857, due in 1872,	92,000 00
Local Improvement Loan of 1859, due in 1879,	100,000 00
do do do 1861, due in 1891,	213,000 00
Deficiency Loan of 1861, due in 1867–68,	15,000 00
Water Loan of 1856, due in 1881,	1,700,000 00
do do 1857, due in 1886,	749,000 00
do do 1857, due in 1891,	819,000 00
do do 1857, due in 1896,	1,432,000 00
do do 1859	1,488,000 00
Williamsburgh Local Improvement Loan of 1861, due in 1881,	38,000 00
Third street Improvement Loan of 1861, due in 1881,	166,000 00
Carried forward,	$7,483,540 42

Brought forward,	$7,483,540 42
War Loan 1862, due in 1868,	115,000 00
Atlantic avenue Improvement Loan of 1861, due in 1868-72,	88,000 00
Soldiers' Aid Fund Bonds of 1865, due in 1889-94,	615,000 00
National Guard and Volunteer Firemen's Bonds of 1864, due in 1881,	27,000 00
do do Bonds of 1864,	32,000 00
Public Park Bonds of 1864,	1,647,000 00
do do Bonds of 1866 (second series),	159,000 00
Fourth avenue Improvement Loan of 1861, due in 1868-95,	290,000 00
Bushwick avenue Improvement Loan of 1865, due in 1871-74,	140,000 00
South Seventh street Improvement Loan of 1866,	324,500 00
Gowanus Canal Improvement Loan of 1866,	175,000 00
Williamsburgh City Bonds of 1852,	15,350 00
do Village Bonds of 1852,	2,029 50
	$11,113,419 92

Dates of Maturity of the Brooklyn City Debt.

YEARS.	Amount.	YEARS.	Amount.
1867,	$59,000 00	1885,	$104,000 00
1868,	168,100 00	1886,	853,000 00
1869,	169,069 92	1887,	185,000 00
1870,	46,750 00	1888,	95,000 00
1871,	208,500 00	1889,	95,000 00
1872,	155,000 00	1890,	95,000 00
1873,	107,000 00	1891,	1,104,000 00
1874,	52,000 00	1892,	70,000 00
1875,	249,000 00	1893,	71,000 00
1876,	52,000 00	1894,	70,000 00
1877,	42,000 00	1895,	10,000 00
1878,	42,000 00	1896,	1,432,000 00
1879,	142,000 00	1899,	1,488,000 00
1880,	42,000 00	1915,	430,000 00
1881,	1,973,000 00	1916,	159,000 00
1882,	42,000 00	1924,	1,217,000 00
1883,	42,000 00		
1884,	44,000 00	Total,	$11,113,419 92

BUFFALO.

Previous to 1854, the Common Council of this city was limited by law to the amount to be raised by tax for the contingent expenses of the city government, while at the same time the expenditures were unlimited. It was then necessary to go to the Legislature from time to time for authority to fund the Floating Debt. By the present city charter, the Common Council has unlimited powers in regard to the amount to be raised by tax, and the expenditures are limited only by the necessities of the corporation.

STATEMENT of the amount raised by General Tax, and the annual Expenditures since 1854, *as shown by the annual Reports.*

YEARS.	General Tax.	Expenditures.	YEARS.	General Tax.	Expenditures.
1854,	$322,150 00	$279,585 03	1861,	$224,901 08	$299,608 52
1855,	275,580 00	301,213 32	1862,	270,335 28	302,306 27
1856,	310,000 00	317,478 56	1863,	301,943 00	354,369 35
1857,	297,825 00	345,834 47	1864,	381,247 70	432,015 71
1858,	293,777 25	364,904 48	1865,	582,305 97	551,655 00
1859,	239,419 90	304,793 33	1866,	460,262 03	514,257 50
1860,	255,073 60	302,443 18			

STATEMENT of the amount of the funded debt of the city of Buffalo, and the purposes for which the same was incurred, &c.

Bonds issued July 1, 1852, at 7 per cent., for Buffalo & Brantford Railroad stock, payable in 1872,		$150,000
Bonds issued May 1, 1853, at 6 and 7 per cent., for Franklin street property, payable in 1873,		85,000
Bonds issued August 1, 1853, at 6 per cent., for Elk street market, payable in 1871,		32,000
Bonds issued December 1, 1853, at 6 per cent., for Franklin street property, payable in 1873,		10,000
Bonds issued December 27, 1853, at 7 per cent., for market grounds, corner Court and State streets, payable in 1878,		35,000
Bonds issued December 31, 1853, at 6 per cent., for Central School property, payable in 1879,		31,000
Bonds issued December 31, 1853, at 6 per cent., for market grounds on Batavia street, payable in 1876,		36,000
Bonds issued February 2, 1857, at 7 per cent., for building markets, payable in 1877,		62,000
Bonds issued June 1, 1859, at 6 per cent., to pay judgments against the city in the Ship Canal cases, payable in 1867,		18,000
Bonds issued June 2, 1862, at 7 per cent., to fund floating debt, payable in 1882,		15,000
Bonds issued November 15, 1862, at 7 per cent., for construction of Ship Canal, payable in 1882,		11,000
Bonds issued November 15, 1862, at 7 per cent., to fund floating debt, payable in 1882,		11,000
Bonds issued December 15, 1862, at 7 per cent., to create the fund for the defense of the Federal Union, payable in 1882,		6,000
Bonds issued January 1, 1863, at 7 per cent., to create the fund for the defense of the Federal Union, payable in 1868,	$10,000	
Payable in 1869,	12,000	22,000
Bonds issued May 1, 1863, at 7 per cent., to create the fund for the defense of the Federal Union, payable in 1883,		12,000
Bonds issued August 20, 1863, at 7 per cent., for the purpose of relieving conscripts, payable in 1868,	$1,000	
Payable in 1870,	3,000	
Payable in 1874,	1,000	
Payable in 1875,	1,000	
Payable in 1881,	10,000	
Payable in 1883,	10,000	
		26,000
Bonds issued May 2, 1864, for the relief of families of volunteers, payable in 1874,	$25,000	
Payable in 1880,	25,000	50,000
Total amount of funded debt, January 1, 1867,		$612,000

ELMIRA.

Statement of Permanent Debt of the City of Elmira.

Cemetery Bonds, and interest due July,			1867,		$2,140 00
Academy Bonds,	do	do	1867,	$1,420 00	
do	do	do	1868,	1,350 00	
do	do	do	1869,	1,280 00	
do	do	do	1870,	1,210 00	
do	do	do	1871,	1,140 00	
do	do	do	1872,	1,070 00	
Total amount Academy Bonds and interest,					7,470 00
Bounty Bonds and interest due February,			1868,	$20,040 00	
do	do	do	1869,	18,488 00	
do	do	do	1870,	17,578 00	
do	do	do	1871,	16,068 00	
do	do	do	1872,	16,100 00	
do	do	do	1873,	14,969 00	
do	do	do	1874,	14,552 00	
Total amount Bounty Bonds and interest,					117,795 00
New School-House Bonds, due			1868,	$12,100 00	
do	do		1869,	11,400 00	
do	do		1870,	10,700 00	
Total amount New School-House Bonds and interest,					34,200 00
Total bonded debt and interest,					$161,605 00

Floating Debt.

Street account,		$2,042 60
Hose tower, bell, &c.,		5,700 00
Sewer account,		1,856 17
Board of Education,		4,879 73
The amount which should be in Treasury, credited as above, is,		$14,478 50
The amount actually in the Treasury at settlement was,		2,100 36
Showing the amount drawn from the above special funds to be,		$12,369 14
There is money and uncollected taxes in the hands of the Collector, which can be applied to the purpose of replacing the amount above appropriated, amounting to,		11,000 00
Leaving a balance appropriated from special funds, without funds to replace, of,		$1,369 14
There are outstanding orders and unpaid bills against contingent fund of,		2,000 00
The condition of the pavement fund is as follows:		
Whole cost of pavement,	$28,130 64	
Less notes, &c., given, for pavement, which have been paid, $5,088 27		
Amount due from owners of property on pavement, 17,166 43	22,254 81	
Leaving balance due on pavement as above,	$5,875 93	
Deduct from this amount the balance credited to sewer account, appropriated to this purpose by Common Council,	1,856 17	
Leave balance due on pavement,		4,019 96
Rebuilding of a burnt school-house,		4,252 62
Total floating debt,		$11,641 72

Total Indebtedness.

Bonded debt and interest,	$161,605 00
Floating contingent debt,	11,641 72
Total,	$173,246 72
Due the city,	$4,357 50
Special tax voted and raised to build hose tower, &c.,	5,700 00
Total,	$10,057 50
To be appropriated as follows, viz.:	
New hose,	$1,000 00
Fire alarm bell,	1,200 00
Engine house and hose tower,	7,857 50
Total,	$10,057 50

The payment of that portion of the debt which is bonded, is provided for in the charter, section 2, title 5.

The amount which by the charter the Common Council can raise for all purposes, exclusive of the amount authorized to pay the permanent debt mentioned above, is as follows:

For contingent expenses,	$8,000 00
For street expenses,	10,000 00
For extraordinary and special purposes,	10,000 00
For Board of Education for purchase, &c.,	2,000 00
Total,	$30,000 00

HUDSON.

Statement of the present City Debt.

Bond to State of New York, dated 1st December, 1854, at 7 per cent. interest, payable in annual installments of $1,000, on the 10th day of February, each year,	$4,000 00
Eighty-four bonds of $250 each, dated December 23d, 1854, with interest at 7 per cent., payable semi-annually on the 10th day of February and August, for the purpose of erecting a City Hall,	21,000 00
Forty-five bonds, of $250 each, dated March 22d, 1859, with interest at 7 per cent., payable semi-annually, on the 10th day of February and August, for the purpose of funding the floating debt,	11,250 00
Carried forward,	$36,250 00

Brought forward,	$36,250 00
Mortgage assumed by the city of Hudson on purchase of lot for engine-house,	250 00
Twenty-three city bonds, of $500 each, bounty loan, one payable April 1, 1867, and one payable each succeeding year, interest on which is payable 1st April in each year, at 6 per cent.,	11,500 00
Twenty-five city and county bonds, of $1,000 each, and one bond of $1,500, issued by resolution of Council of November 25, 1864, payable as follows: the $1,500 bond on the first day of April, 1870, and one bond of $1,000 annually thereafter, interest payable annually at 7 per cent. Bonds dated November 1, 1864,	26,500 00
Ten city bonds, of $1,000 each, issued under resolution of Council, passed May 25, 1865, for closing up war expenses; first bonds payable April 1, 1870,	10,000 00
Eight city bonds, of $1,000 each, issued under resolution of Council, passed March 29, 1866, payable as follows: the first bond on the 1st day of April, 1880, and one bond on the first day of April in each year thereafter, until the whole principal is paid. Interest payable semi-annually on the 1st days of October and April in each year. Bonds dated April 1, 1866,	8,000 00
There is also now owing what is known as the "floating debt,"	8,000 00
	$100,500 00

City Disbursements in 1866.

Finance Account,	$17,911 53
Fire,	6,187 91
Street,	5,430 46
Police,	3,124 98
Lamp,	2,140 80
Public Buildings,	1,731 21
Burying-Grounds,	411 95
Ferry,	542 68
Commissioners of Highways,	50 00
Board of Health,	146 25
Poor and Relief,	2,000 00
Superintendents of Common Schools,	4,500 00
R. F. Clark, County Treasurer,	82,338 44
Total,	$126,516 21

LOCKPORT.

This city has no funded or other debt.

NEWBURGH.

Indebtedness of the City of Newburgh, May 1st, 1867.

Water Bonds,	$109,000 00
Contingent Bonds,	14,300 00
Street Improvement Note,	4,500 00
Bounty Fund Debt of township and city of Newburgh, jointly,	161,300 00
	$289,100 00

Water Bonds issued as follows:

50 bonds of $1,000 each, issued 1853, due 1873,	$50,000 00	
25 bonds of $1,000 each, issued 1858, due 1873,	25,000 00	
3 bonds of $1,000 each, issued 1860, due 1864,	3,000 00	
15 bonds of $1,000 each, issued 1865, due from 1868 to 1872,	15,000 00	
16 bonds of $1,000 each, issued 1866, due 1876,	16,000 00	
		$109,000 00

The above Water Bonds were issued under the "Act to provide a supply of water in the village of Newburgh," passed March 30th, 1852, and subsequent acts.

The revenue from the water rents is sufficient at the present time to pay the expense of repairs and maintenance, and the interest on the bonds, and to create a sinking fund of some $2,000 to $4,000 per annum.

Contingent Bonds.

These are of various dates and amounts, all past due, amounting to $14,300.

The village of Newburgh was authorized, by act of the Legislature passed April 3d, 1837, to purchase $150,000 of the capital stock of the Hudson and Delaware Railroad Company, and by resolution of the

Board of Trustees passed April 17th, 1837, the Trustees became subscribers for or purchasers of $150,000 of the stock of said Company, and soon afterward three notes of $5,000 each were paid to said Company in settlement of the first installment of 10 per cent. Bonds given for money borrowed to pay the foregoing notes, constitute the most part of the above amount.

Street Improvement Note.

Note issued February 10th, 1864, to pay the contractor for grading Washington street, for which improvement the assessment has not been collected.

Bounty Fund Debt of Township and City of Newburgh, jointly.

WHEN DUE.	Principal.	Interest.	Total.
1868,	$10,700 00	$11,291 00	$21,991 00
1869,	19,500 00	10,542 00	30,042 00
1870,	23,600 00	9,177 00	32.777 00
1871,	16,800 00	7,525 00	24,325 00
1872,	26,100 00	6,349 00	32,449 00
1873,	22,700 00	4,522 00	27,222 00
1874,	24,000 00	2,933 00	26,933 00
1875,	17,900 00	1,253 00	19,153 00
	$161,300 00	$53,592 00	$214,892 00

NEW YORK.

Debt of the City of New York, December 31st, 1866.

FUNDED DEBT.	HOW PAYABLE.		Total.
For what purpose incurred.	From Sinking Fund.	From taxation.	
For introduc'g and distrib'g the Croton water,	$10,785,800 00	....	$10,785,800 00
For lands for Cent. Park, and improv'g same,	9,648,571 00	....	9,648,571 00
For State Arsenal in Central Park,	275,000 00	....	275,000 00
For buildings blown up during the great fire in 1835,	402,768 00	....	402,768 00
For erection and repairs of public buildings,	190,000 00	$51,000 00	241,000 00
For West Washington Market property,	600,000 00	....	600,000 00
For Fort Gansevoort property,	533,437 50	....	533,437 50
For erection and repairs of docks and slips,	....	500,000 00	500,000 00
For property of N. Y. Public School Society,	....	154,000 00	154,000 00
For liquidation of the floating debt of 1859,	....	2,748,000 00	2,748,000 00
For relief of families of volunteer soldiers,	....	4,266,500 00	4,266,500 00
For bounties to volunteer soldiers,	....	490,000 00	490,000 00
Totals,	$22,435,576 50	$8,209,500 00	$30,635,076 50

TEMPORARY DEBT.

For what purpose incurred.	From collect'n of assessm'ts.	From taxes of the year 1866.	Total.
For opening, widening and improving streets,	$2,042,600 00	....	$2,042,600 00
For payment of general expenses of the Corporation (revenue bonds),	....	$683,800 00	683,800 00
	$2,042,600 00	$683,800 00	$2,726,400 00

RECAPITULATION.

Total Funded Debt as above,		$30,645,076 50
Total Temporary Debt as above,		2,726,400 00
Total,		$33,371,476 50
The Commissioners of the Sinking Fund held securities applicable to the payment of the funded debt on December 31st,	$10,627,587 00	
Also, cash deposited with the Chamberlain, December 31st,	601,644 49	
		$11,229,231 49
Net indebtedness for all purposes on city account, December 31st, 1866,		$22,142,245 01

Debt of the County of New York, December 31st, 1866.

FUNDED DEBT.	HOW PAYABLE.		Total.
For what purpose incurred.	From taxes of the year 1866.	From taxation.	
For paying for the land and building court-house thereon,	....	$1,800,000 00	....
For bounties to volunteer soldiers,	....	8,069,100 00	....
For damage claims by riots of July, 1863,	....	1,620,000 00	....
For bridge at McComb's dam,	....	20,000 00	....
		$11,509,100 00	$11,509,100 00
TEMPORARY DEBT.			
For payment of general expenses of the county (revenue bonds),	$307,200 00	....	307,200 00
Total debt,			$11,816,300 00

RECAPITULATION.

Funded debt, as above, payable from taxation,	$11,509,100 00
Temporary debt, as above, payable from taxes of 1866,	307,200 00
Total,	$11,816,300 00

OSWEGO.

Under the charter granted to this city in 1848, the income of the corporation was limited to $10,000 for contingent fund, $5,000 for highways, and $5,000 for police. No provision was made for future expansion or increased rates of expenditure from the growth of the city, until 1867, when the Legislature authorized the contingent and highway expenses to be doubled, and the police fund to be raised to $7,500. The increased prices of labor and materials since the war had rendered this measure the more necessary. During the last year there was expended on the streets, above $20,000, while but $5,000 could be raised by law. On the fire department, above the whole amount of the contingent fund ($10,000), was required, leaving nothing to provide for the other necessary expenses of the city government. The police expenses during the same period were $7,100, being $2,100 in excess of the amount authorized to be raised for this purpose.

These accumulated debts have recently been funded, and bonds for $60,000, payable through twenty years, have been issued, which, it is supposed, will pay off all the old orders drawn upon the city treasury, the expenses of the Board of Education, the old poor orders, and the orders of the new Board of Commissioners of Public Charity, up to March 12, 1867, leaving the present year's tax levy to pay the present year's expenses.

In addition to this debt, there are outstanding debts as follows:

Iron Bridge Bonds.—These bonds were issued to commissioners for building the iron bridge over the Oswego river, pursuant to act of March 31, 1855, payable at the American Exchange Bank, New York, dated September 19, 1855, with interest from January 1, 1855, payable annually. There are now outstanding of these bonds $10,500, payable in equal annual installments on the first day of January, 1868, 1869, and 1870.

Baldwin Judgment Bonds.—These bonds were issued to pay the judgment obtained against the city by WILLIAM BALDWIN, pursuant to act of January 17, 1866, payable at the City Bank, Oswego, and dated February 21, 1866, interest commencing January 1, 1866, and payable annually thereafter, leaving due $3,000 annually January 1, 1868, 1869, 1870, and 1871, and $4,000 due January 1, 1872. Total, $16,000. Total bonded debt, $86,500. Due in 1868, 1869, and 1870, each, $9,500; in 1871, $6,000; in 1872, $7000; and $3,000 annually thereafter to 1887, inclusive.

LIABILITIES OF THE CITY GOVERNMENT, FEB. 20, 1867.		ASSETS.	
Outstanding Treasury Warrants, issued prior to 1859,........	$203 53	Lands bought at Tax Sale,.... ...	$1,980 41
Outstanding Treasury Warrants issued since 1859,.................	36,551 43	Local Assessments,...............	5,650 41
Outstanding Poor Warrants,..... ..	298 65	Pound in Third Ward,............	275 00
Board of Education,...............	13,318 20	Forward & Smith,....	14 55
Unpaid bills before the Council,...	980 76	City Hall Lot,.........	10,000 00
Balance of salaries,................	2,391 25	Ontario Dock Company,...........	7,355 16
Montcalm Park,....................	2,536 00	Milton Harman,.........	975 84
City Hall Fund,....................	11,984 65	A. S. Crolius, Treasurer,..........	13,682 26
Training School,...................	608 11	Amount due from Collectors,......	13,916 94
Board of Public Charity,...........	22,572 20	Lamp and Watch Assessment,....	1,472 30
Oswego City Library,.......	250 00	Montcalm Park,......	4,771 30
			$60,114 47
	$92,695 78		

POUGHKEEPSIE.

Historical Notes concerning the funded debt created by the Village and City of Poughkeepsie.

VILLAGE LOANS.

Market Loan.—Created May 7, 1831; $6,000 for site. In June, twelve bonds of $1,000 each issued. Additions to market lot, $1,000. This loan was canceled and interest extinguished December 1, 1846. It bore 6½ per cent.

First Water Loan.—Created by village vote, May 21, 1833; $15,000 borrowed for reservoir. Last installment paid December 1, 1861. It bore 6 per cent. interest.

Second Water Loan.—Created by village May 20, 1834; $8,000 paid in December, 1862, by borrowing from other funds, and a Renewed Second Water Loan was created by authority of the Legislature, to be paid December 1, 1869; 6 per cent. (See Class 13.)

Third Water Loan.— Created October 28, 1835; $8,000, to be paid in eight installments of $1,000 each. The last will be due in 1877; 6 per cent.

Free School Loan.— Created under an act of April 18, 1843; $3,000, in installments of $500. Extinguished January 1, 1854. It bore 6 per cent. interest.

CITY LOANS.

Class 1.— $8,415, April 3, 1856, to pay old indebtedness. Extinguished May 1, 1861, in annual installments of $1,683.

Class 2.—$9,000, March 5, 1857, under act of February 21, 1857, for bridges destroyed in freshet of 1855. Extinguished March 1, 1862, by installments of $1,800 annually.

Class 3.— $7,500, September, 1857, for school-houses and engine-houses. Extinguished March 15, 1862, by installments of $1,500.

Class 4.— $2,100, September, 1858, for fencing school-house, purchase of new hose, and for building engine-house. Extinguished May, 1860, by installments of $700.

Class 5.—$2,000, September, 1860, for a new bridge over the Fallkill. Extinguished March 1, 1864, by installments of $500.

Class 6.— $6,000, September 10th, 1860, for a school-house and lot. By installments of $300, and the interest on the first $4,200 is at six, and on the last $1,800 at seven per cent., paid semi-annually. It will be extinguished March 1st, 1880.

Class 7.—$6,300, May 1st, 1861, for a steam fire engine, $3,100; for the deficiency in the cost of the bridge over the Fallkill, $2,100; for new hose $800, and for a new bridge, $300. The interest was on $3,200 at 6, on $2,260, at 6½, and on $840 at 7 per cent., paid semi-annually. On this loan the last installment ($1,260), was paid May 1st, 1866.

Class 8.—$10,000, issued May 1st, 1862, under an act of March 22d, 1862, "for the relief of the families of soldiers from the city of Poughkeepsie, who have enlisted in the service of the United States." An installment of $500, is due each year. This loan will be extinguished March 1st, 1882. Now due, $7,500.

Class 9.—The "Arrearage Loan," was for $23,597.70, issued May 1st, 1862, under an act of March 22d, 1862, to pay the floating debt of the city, so that the necessity of borrowing in anticipation of the taxes might be avoided. Installments, $1,000 each, are due one in each year, except the last, which is for $597.70. Will be paid and the loan extinguished March 1st, 1886.

Class 10.—$6,000, September 1st, 1862, for a new school-house, lot and furniture. By installments of $300. Will be extinguished March 1st, 1882.

Class 11.—$4,000, issued September 1st, 1862, for a new steam fire engine and new hose. By installments of $800. It was extinguished March 1st, 1867.

Class 12.—First county loan, issued April 15th, 1863, by virtue of an act passed March 26th, 1863, and was for $48,000, to pay the indebtedness caused by the payment of bounties to soldiers. By installments of $2,000. Will be extinguished March 1st, 1887.

Class 13.—Renewed second water loan, for $6,000, issued October 1st, 1863, by an act of March 26th, 1863, to return to the currency fund the amount borrowed to take up the second village water loan. By installments of $1,000. Will be extinguished March 1st, 1869.

Class 14.—"The First Almshouse Loan," $9,000, issued April 1st, 1864, for the purchase of the Almshouse lot, buildings, &c., will be extinguished April 1st, 1884.

Class 15.—"The Second Bounty Loan," $246,100, issued March 1st, 1865, by virtue of an act passed February 27th, 1864, to pay the indebtedness incurred by the payment of bounties to soldiers, under the call of 1864.

The Loan is as follows:

A.	$25,000	in bonds of $1,000 each, with interest at 6½ per cent.
B.	156,000	" " " " " " " 7 "
C.	65,100	" " $700 " " " " 6 "
	$246,100	

Interest payable semi-annually by coupons.

The bonds entitled "A" are held by the Poughkeepsie Savings Bank. Of the bonds entitled "B," sixty-five are also held by the same institution, and the other ninety by many different persons. The bonds entitled "C" were issued to take up the certificates in the hands of persons who furnished substitutes. No installments have yet been paid. The Loan will be extinguished March 1st, 1887. The several bonds fall due as follows:

A.	Five,	Nos.	1 to 5	inclusive,	March	1st,	1871,	$5,000
"	Five,	"	6 to 10	"	"	"	1872,	5,000
"	Ten,	"	11 to 20	"	"	"	1873,	10,000
"	Five,	"	21 to 25	"	"	"	1874,	5,000
B.	Five,	"	1 to 5	"	"	"	1874,	5,000
"	Ten,	"	6 to 15	"	"	"	1875,	10,000
"	Ten,	"	16 to 25	"	"	"	1876,	10,000
"	Ten,	"	26 to 35	"	"	"	1877,	10,000
"	Fifteen,	"	36 to 50	"	"	"	1878,	15,000
"	Fifteen,	"	51 to 65	"	"	"	1879,	15,000
"	Seventeen,	"	66 to 82	"	"	"	1880,	17,000
"	Seventeen,	"	83 to 99	"	"	"	1881,	17,000
"	Seventeen,	"	100 to 116	"	"	"	1882,	17,000
"	Twenty,	"	117 to 136	"	"	"	1883,	20,000
"	Twenty,	"	137 to 156	"	"	"	1884,	20,000
C.	Thirty-one,	"	1 to 31	"	"	"	1885,	21,700
"	Thirty-one,	"	32 to 62	"	"	"	1886,	21,700
"	Thirty-one,	"	63 to 93	"	"	"	1887,	21,700
								$246,100

Class 16.—"The School Arrearage Loan," $12,500, issued May 1st, 1865, by virtue of an act passed March 28th, 1865, to pay the floating debt of the Board of Education. Each bond is for $500. Five ($2,500) are due in 1867; ten ($5,000) in 1868; ten ($5,000) in 1869. Interest semi-annually, payable by coupons, 7 per cent.

Class 17.—"City Loan for Hudson River Asylum for the Insane," $48,000, in bonds of $1,000 each, due as follows: 1 to 16, 1888; 17 to 32, in 1889, and 33 to 48, 1890, bearing interest at 7 per cent., semi-annually, on the 1st of March and September. The county gave an additional sum of $32,000 for the purchase of a site for this asylum.

Statement of the Funded Debt of the City of Poughkeepsie, dated March 14th, 1867.

CITY LOANS.

When issued.	WHAT FOR.	Amount yet to be paid.	Rate of interest.	When extinguished.
1835,* ...	Third. Water Loan, ...	$8,000 00	6 per cent.	1877
1860, ...	Sixth. City Loan for First Ward School House, ...	2,100 00	6 do	1874
1860, ...	Sixth. City Loan for First Ward School House, ...	1,800 00	7 do	1880
1862, ...	Eighth. City Loan for Relief of Soldiers' Families, ...	7,500 00	6½ do	1882
1862, ...	Ninth. City Loan for Funding the Floating Debt, ...	18,000 00	6½ do	1886
1862, ...	Ninth. City Loan for Funding the Floating Debt, ...	597 70	7 do	1886
1862, ...	Tenth. City Loan for Second Ward School House, ...	4,500 00	6½ do	1882
1863, ...	Twelfth. City Loan for First B'nty Loan,	40,000 00	6 do	1887
1863, ...	Thirteenth. City Loan for Renewed Second Water Loan, ...	2,000 00	6 do	1869
1864, ...	Fourteenth. City Loan for First Almshouse Loan, ...	8,500 00	6 do	1884
1865, ...	Fifteenth. City Loan for Second Bounty Loan, ...	65,100 00	6 do	1887
1865, ...	Fifteenth. City Loan for Second Bounty Loan, ...	25,000 00	6½ do	1874
1865, ...	Fifteenth. City Loan for Second Bounty Loan, ...	156,000 00	7 do	1884
1865, ...	Sixteenth. City Loan for School Arrearage Loan, ...	10,000 00	7 do	1869
1867, ...	Seventeenth. City Loan for Hudson River Asylum Loan, ...	48,000 00	7 do	1890
Total of Funded Debt, ...		$397,097 70		

Summary of the Village and City Debt of Poughkeepsie, showing the amount payable in each year until the whole shall have been extinguished.

YEARS.	Amount due, including interest.	YEARS.	Amount due, including interest.
1868, ...	$33,157 32	1878, ...	$33,601 82
1869, ...	32,462 32	1879, ...	32,263 82
1870, ...	26,924 32	1880, ...	32,855 82
1871, ...	31,434 82	1881, ...	31,088 32
1872, ...	30,764 82	1882, ...	29,631 32
1873, ...	34,332 32	1883, ...	30,295 32
1874, ...	33,924 82	1884, ...	28,680 32
1875, ...	32,899 82	1885, ...	28,329 32
1876, ...	31,842 82	1886, ...	26,451 61
1877, ...	30,794 82	1887, ...	24,411 00

Amount originally issued, ... $501,512 70
Reduced in 1867 to 397,097 70

* The first loan was a village loan, the remainder are city loans.

ROCHESTER.

Statement of the Debt and Assets of the city of Rochester, March 16, 1867.

BONDED DEBT.

Date of bonds.	Number of bonds.	Amount of bonds.	Aggregate amount.	For what purpose issued.	Rate per cent.	When payable.
July 1, 1850	5	$1,000	$5,000	City Stock,..................	6	July 1, 1868
do 1, 1850	25	1,000	25,000	do	6	do 1, 1870
do 1, 1850	5	1,000	5,000	City Hall, ...	6	do 1, 1870
do 1, 1850	15	1,000	15,000	do	6	do 1, 1872
do 1, 1850	10	1,000	10,000	do	6	do 1, 1873
May 10, 1858	20	1,000	20,000	Floating debt,..........	7	May 10, 1873
do 10, 1858	20	1,000	20,000	do do	7	do 10, 1876
do 10, 1858	17	1,000	17,000	do do	7	do 10, 1878
April 15, 1862	3	1,000	3,000	do do	7	April 15, 1874
do 15, 1862	3	1,000	3,000	do do	7	do 15, 1875
do 15, 1862	3	1,000	3,000	do do	7	do 15. 1876
do 15, 1862	3	1,000	3,000	do do	7	do 15, 1877
do 15, 1862	3	1,000	3,000	do do	7	do 15, 1878
do 15, 1862	51	1,000	51,000	do do	7	do 15, 1882
June 10, 1864	20	1,000	20,000	Relief of Soldiers' families,	6	Sept. 1, 1869
do 10, 1864	20	1,000	20,000	do do do	6	do 1, 1871
do 10, 1864	20	1,000	20,000	do do do	6	do 1, 1877
do 10, 1864	20	1,000	20,000	do do do	6	do 1, 1880
do 10, 1864	20	1,000	20,000	do do do	6	do 1, 1881
Jan'y 1, 1853	100	1,000	100,000	Roch. and G. V. R. R.Stock,	6	Jan. 1, 1873
July 1, 1853	140	1,000	140,000	do do do	6	do 1, 1873
do 1, 1853	1	1,000	2,000	do do do	6	do 1, 1868
do 1, 1853	1	1,000	2,000	do do do	6	do 1, 1869
do 1, 1853	1	1,000	2,000	do do do	6	do 1, 1870
do 1, 1853	1	1,000	2,000	do do do	6	do 1, 1871
do 1, 1853	1	1,000	2,000	do do do	6	do 1, 1872
do 1, 1853	1	1,000	2,000	do do do	6	do 1, 1873
Aug. 28, 1855	20	1,000	20,000	Building Main st. bridge,...	6	do 1, 1876
do 12, 1857	18	1,000	18,000	do Andrews do	7	Aug. 12, 1877
Sept. 1, 1857	32	1,000	32,000	Court and Main st. bridge, ,	6	Sept. 1, 1877
May 15, 1859	3	1,000	3,000	Deep Hollow Improvement,	7	do 1, 1867
do 15, 1859	3	1,000	3,000	do do do	7	do 1, 1869
July 1, 1861	6	1,000	6,000	Steam fire engines,.........	6	July 1, 1881
do 1, 1861	1	800	800	do do	6	do 1, 1881
do 1, 1861	1	250	250	do do	6	do 1, 1881
do 1, 1862	15	1,000	15,000	Building Clarissa st. bridge,	7	do 1, 1882
do 1, 1862	25	1,000	25,000	Widening Main street, ...	6	do 1, 1882
Sept. 16, 1862	12	1,000	12,000	Steam fire engines,....	6	Sept. 16, 1882
do 16, 1862	1	......	950	do do	6	do 16, 1882
do 15, 1864	10	5,000	50,000	Bounties to volunteers,.....	7	Oct. 1, 1867
do 15, 1864	100	500	50,000	do do	7	do 1. 1867
Oct. 6, 1864	125	400	50,000	do do	7	do 1, 1868
do 6, 1864	100	500	50,000	do do	7	do 1, 1868
do 6, 1864	95	600	57,000	do do	7	do 1, 1869
do 6, 1864	43	1,000	43,000	do do	7	do 1, 1869
do 6, 1864	61	500	30,000	do do	7	do 1, 1869
						do 1, 1870
Total.	....	......	$1,001,500			

Amount of Bonds falling due in each year.

YEARS.	Amount.	YEARS.	Amount.	YEARS.	Amount.
1867, ...	$103,000 00	1873, ...	$272,000 00	1880, ...	$20,000 00
1868, ...	107,000 00	1874, ...	3,000 00	1881, ...	27,050 00
1869, ...	125,000 00	1875, ...	4,000 00	1882, ...	103,950 00
1870, ...	62,500 00	1876, ...	43,000 00		
1871, ...	22,000 00	1877, ...	73,000 00	Total,......	$1,001,500 00
1872, ...	17,000 00	1878, ...	20,000 00		

Assets.

City Hall,	$50,000
Center Market,	30,000
Fire Department property—houses, lands, apparatus, &c.,	75,000
Rochester and Genesee Valley Railroad stock,	300,000
Public school property—houses, lands, libraries, &c.,	200,000
Mortgage on property corner Main and Front streets,	7,000
Unpaid taxes, being first lien and drawing 15 per cent per annum,	22,000
Public Parks—"Mechanics'," "Brown's," "Jones'," "Franklin," "Wadsworth," "Center" and "Caledonia,"	150,000
Public Bridges—Andrews st., Main st., Court st., Clarissa st. and Deep Hollow,	150,000
	$984,000

Annual Statement of Expenditures, valuation and tax, since 1846.

YEARS.	General city expenses.	School expenses.	Bonds and interest.	Unpaid taxes.	Bonds issued.	Assessed valuation.	Levied by tax.
1847,	$26,600	$12,945	$4,060	$443	....	....	$43,905
1848,	29,360	12,854	4,060	626	....	....	46,574
1849,	33,300	12,901	4,280	1,348	....	....	51,481
1850,	38,300	23,291	9,440	775	$65,000	$5,072,633	70,063
1851,	35,000	20,321	14,680	1,107	....	9,717,057	70,000
1852,	44,866	23,821	11,065	705	....	10,233,635	79,753
1853,	41,268	29,250	13,983	268	280,000	11,510,707	84,500
1854,	63,333	35,870	14,051	3,797	....	12,045,653	113,454
1855,	69,764	40,497	38,400	2,545	20,000	12,553,031	148,661
1856,	63,903	37,134	34,285	4,180	....	13,071,076	135,323
1857,	72,135	40,634	44,721	15,215	50,000	13,245,877	157,500
1858,	68,876	35,760	38,011	12,980	57,000	11,957,963	142,647
1859,	63,174	36,189	42,454	6,305	13,000	11,150,678	141,817
1860,	69,964	52,573	41,710	9,901	....	11,252,157	164,247
1861,	81,723	43,877	50,130	7,845	7,050	11,353,463	175,732
1862,	83,014	38,740	50,494	7,642	118,950	11,257,642	172,248
1863,	93,346	36,572	58,671	3,772	....	10,717,614	188,559
1864,	113,414	55,916	57,745	4,809	677,800	11,232,159	232,075
1865,	170,250	61,242	229,858	7,285	....	9,629,118	489,350
1866,	137,613	58,000	143,096	5,257	....	11,126,390	348,709

Relief of soldiers families, $31,656 in 1863; $5,000 in 1864; $28,000 in 1865, and $10,000 in 1866.

Bounties for volunteers, $14,000 in 1861; $59,000 in 1863, and $555,000 in 1864.

SCHENECTADY.

Statement of the Debt of the City of Schenectady, May 1st, 1867.

Date.	When due.	For what Incurred.	Amount.
March 24, 1855	March 24, 1865,	To purchase School Buildings,	$6,000 00
April 1, 1857,	April 1, 1868,	To pay City Debt,	2,000 00
do 1, 1857,	do 1, 1869,	do	2,000 00
do 1, 1857,	do 1, 1870,	do	2,000 00
do 1, 1857,	do 1, 1871,	do	2,000 00
do 1, 1857,	do 1, 1872,	do	2,000 00
do 1, 1857,	do 1, 1873,	do	2,000 00
do 1, 1857,	do 1, 1874,	do	2,000 00
July 1, 1865,	July 1, 1875,	To purchase Steam Fire Engine,	3,000 00
May 1, 1865,	May 1, 1868,	To pay Bounty Debt,	45,000 00
Total,			$68,000 00

Principal financial items of Expenditures for the year ending March 1st, 1866.

For Fire Department,	$7,336 31
For Relief of Poor,	5,583 49
For Lighting Streets,	4,519 86
For Repairs to Streets,	5,580 34
For Police Department (under the old system),	1,952 69
For Salaries of Officers,	1,783 24
For Election Expenses,	637 00
The whole amount of debt incurred for bounties and expenses during the war, not including the amount received from the State,	$240,054 65

SYRACUSE.

The present indebtedness of the city is as follows:

Fifty bonds of $1,000 each, payable at the Bank of the Commonwealth, in the city of New York, $5,000 of which will be due on the 1st day of January, 1875, and $5,000 per year thereafter until paid, with semi-annual interest at six per cent., due June 1st and December 1st,	$50,000 00
There are two bonds of $5,000 each, held by Rufus H. King, which were due on the 1st day of December, 1863, and by a stipulation made with said King, they were made payable on the 1st day of December, 1865, at 7 per cent. interest per annum, payable semi-annually, June 1st and December 1st,	10,000 00
There are six bonds of $2,500 each, payable at the Bank of the Commonwealth, in the city of New York, $2,500 of which will be due on the 1st day of January, 1868, and $2,500 per year thereafter until paid, with semi-annual interest at 6 per cent., due July 1st and January 1st,	15,000 00
There are four bonds of $2,000 each, payable at the Bank of the,Commonwealth, in the city of New York, $2,000 of which will be due on the 1st day of January, 1868, and $2,000 per year thereafter until paid, with semi-annual interest at 7 per cent., due July 1st and January 1st,	8,000 00
Total amount of funded debt,	$83,000 00

This debt was created for the ordinary expenses of the city, with the exception of $40,000, which was for funds raised for the support of families of volunteers, and other expenses during the war. The city is allowed to raise in each year a sum not exceeding $60,000, to pay the ordinary expenses of the city, such as the amount due on the funded debt and interest, salaries of officers, water, gas, cleaning streets, printing, fire department, and all incidental expenses; and a further sum of $10,000, to pay the city's share of new bridges, paving, repaving, macadamizing and sewers. It also receives for collecting taxes, for licenses, weighing of hay, &c., the annual sum of about $4,500.

Total city expenses for the year ending February 23, 1867,	$262,745 05
Assets,	16,830 08
Liabilities,	25,550 30

TROY.

Receipts and Expenditures from March 6th, 1866, to March 4th, 1867, (both inclusive).

EXPENDITURES.		RECEIPTS.	
Assessments,	$15,881 38	Balance at last report,	$55,361 56
Streets, Alleys and Sewers,	26,468 62	Assessments,	4,718 95
Highways and Bridges,	40,176 11	Streets, Alleys and Sewers,	48 00
City Poor,	44,115 28	City Poor,	458 94
Lighting Streets,	25,207 85	Lighting Streets,	8 00
Elections,	986 20	Highways and Bridges,	1 50
Police,	73,793 38	Navigation,	8,155 00
Fire Department,	37,187 28	Police,	1 25
Board of Education,	68,247 13	Fire Department,	878 00
Advertising and Printing,	2,467 16	Board of Education,	14,102 19
Justices' Court,	5,117 26	Justices' Court,	2,588 75
Burial Grounds,	780 89	Troy Union R. R. Compromise,	25,300 00
Board of Health,	3,911 59	Burial Grounds,	244 00
Female Seminary,	113 59	Board of Health,	289 50
Interest on Revenue Bonds,	8,814 32	Female Seminary,	1,100 00
Commissioners of Sinking Fund,	48,831 41	Revenue Bonds,	274,654 70
Revenue Bonds,	252,759 00	Water Works,	7,684 03
Water Works,	17,469 47	Interest on City Debt,	22,302 00
Redemption of Lands,	807 32	Percentage on Taxes,	7,017 13
Fulton Market,	411 88	Permits,	263 00
Washington Market,	18 75	Redemption of Lands,	772 64
City Taxes Refunded,	2,190 08	Fulton Market,	2,169 96
County Taxes,	266,245 83	Washington Market,	7,033 56
Fractional Notes,	43 00	City Taxes,	377,448 68
Contingent,	18,852 05	County Taxes,	273,315 09
Interest on City Debt,	89,937 50	Contingent,	1,800 00
Bounties,	1,589 77	Bounties,	948 88
Albany Bridge,	2,330 25	New York State Bonds,	10,000 00
Interest on State Bonds,	2,292 50	Interest on State Bonds,	11,007 50
Navigation,	7,634 60		
Military,	400 00		$1,109,672 81
Balance,	44,591 36		
	$1,109,672 81		

STATEMENT of the several Funded Debts of the city in March, 1867, *the times when they respectively fall due, and the provision for paying the principal and interest.*

SCHENECTADY AND TROY RAILROAD DEBT.

Contracted for the construction of the Schenectady and Troy Railroad. The sum bears 5½ per cent. interest, payable April 1, annually. Total amount $106,000.

To provide for the payment of principal and interest of this debt, the Common Council is required by law to raise yearly, by tax, twenty thousand dollars, to be paid to the Commissioners of the Sinking Fund, to be by them applied to the payment of this debt; and also to raise yearly, from year to year, a sum sufficient to pay the accruing interest.

THE WATER WORKS DEBT.

Contracted for the construction of the Troy Water Works. Interest 5 per cent. Payable semi-annually, on the 1st of May. Amount $51,000.

It is provided by law that $2,500 shall be raised annually by tax, and paid to the Commissioners of the Sinking Fund, to be applied to the payment of the principal of this debt; and that the rent of the Troy Female Seminary, after deducting expenses of repair, &c., shall be paid to the said Board of Commissioners, to be applied in like manner. The net income of the Water Works is also, by law, appropriated exclusively to the payment of the interest and principal of the money borrowed for the construction of the Water Works. There has been no "net income" from the Water Works for several years. The surplus income has been appropriated by the Common Council to the use of the Water Commissioners.

LOAN UNDER ACT OF 28TH FEBRUARY, 1861.

Contracted for the payment of the Floating Contingent Debt of the city. Interest 7 per cent. Payable semi-annually, on the 1st March. Total amount $70,000.

LOAN UNDER ACT OF 24TH MARCH, 1862.

Contracted for the payment of the Floating Contingent Debt of the city. Interest 7 per cent. Payable semi-annually, April 1st. Total amount, $70,000.

The laws authorizing these loans require the Common Council to raise by tax, such sums of money as shall be necessary from year to year to pay the interest accruing yearly upon the bonds to be issued by virtue of the acts; and to raise in like manner a sufficient sum of money to pay the bonds becoming due in any year.

BONDS OF JUNE 1ST, 1864.

Contracted under the acts of February 9th and of April 30th, 1864, for the payment of the Floating Contingent Debt of the city, and of money raised for war purposes. Interest, 6 per cent. Payable semi-annually on the 1st days of June and December. Total amount, $300,000.

BONDS OF NOVEMBER 1ST, 1864.

Contracted under the act of February 9th, 1864, for the payment of money raised for bounties. Interest 7 per cent. Payable semi-annually, on the 1st day of May and November. Total amount, $264,000.

BONDS ISSUED TO THE TROY UNION RAILROAD.

The city issued its bonds for the benefit of the Troy Union Railroad Company, amounting to $680,000. The Railroad Companies having failed to meet their engagements according to agreement, after considerable litigation, it was found expedient to enter into a compromise for the payment of the bonds and the interest; and the principal of the debt was assumed as follows:

By the New York Central Railroad Company,	$170,000
By the Hudson River Railroad Company,	170,000
By the Rensselaer and Saratoga Railroad Company,	125,000
By the Troy and Boston Railroad Company,	100,000
And by the Corporation of the city of Troy,	115,000
	$680,000

On the 1st of January, 1863, there fell due $100,000. Toward the payment of this amount there had been received $44,000, leaving a balance of $56,000, for which the city isssued bonds payable January 1st, 1869. Therefore there are now outstanding, on account of the Troy Union Railroad Company, bonds, with interest payable semi-annually, the sum of $592,000, of which the city has assumed as its share $115,000.

The Railroad companies have, according to the terms of the above compromise, paid their installments with interest as they became due. The principal is paid over to the Commissioners of the Sinking Fund, and the interest applied toward the interest on the Union Railroad debt, the balance being provided for by the city tax.

General Summary.

By the foregoing statement it appears that the Funded Debt of the city was, on the 5th day of March, 1867, as follows:

The Schenectady and Troy Railroad Debt,	$106,000 00
The Water Works Debt,	51,000 00
The debt contracted under the Act 28th February, 1861,	70,000 00
The debt contracted under the Act 24th March, 1862,	70,000 00
Bonds issued to the Union Railroad, assumed by the city,	115,000 00
Bonds of June 1st, 1864,	300,000 00
Bonds of November 1, 1864,	264,000 00
	$976,000 00

The Floating Debt in 1866 was as follows:

Revenue Bonds outstanding, March 5, 1866,		$32,939 00
Fractional Notes outstanding, March 5, 1866,		4,850 15
Making the whole city debt,		$1,013,789 15
Toward the payment of this debt the Commissioners of the Sinking Fund hold bonds to the amount of	$25,500 00	
And the city holds New York State 7 per cent. bonds to the amount of	132,000 00	
		157,500 00
Total indebtedness,		$856,289 15

TABLE showing the sums that will become due in each year upon the several descriptions of bonds constituting the city debt.

YEARS WHEN PAYABLE.	Schenectady and Troy Railroad debt.	Water-works debt.	Loan under act of Feb. 28, 1861.	Loan under act of March 24, 1862.	Bonds of June 1, 1864.	Bonds of November 1, 1864.	Troy Union Railroad bonds.
1867,	$11,500						
1868,	20,000						
1869,	20,000	$10,000				$53,000	
1870,	20,000						
1871,	20,000						
1872,	14,500	6,000					
1873,			$10,000	$10,000			
1874,			10,000	10,000		53,000	
1875,		15,000	10,000	10,000			
1876,			10,000	10,000			
1877,			10,000	10,000			
1878,			10,000	10,000			
1879,			10,000	10,000		104,000	
1880,		20,000			$30,000		
1881,					30,000		
1882,					30,000		
1883,					30,000		
1884,					30,000	54,000	
1885,					30,000		
1886,					30,000		
1887,					30,000		
1888,					30,000		
1889,					30,000		
Date of maturity not stated,							$115,000

Summary of valuation, rate of tax, and receipts and expenditures, annually since 1825, inclusive.

YEAR.	Real estate.	Personal estate.	Total valuation.	Rate of city tax.	Rate of State and county tax.	Total rate.	Receipts and expenditures.*
1825,.....	$1,362,481	$1,780,662	$3,143,143	.24	.23	.47	$16,892 56
1826,.....	1,557,510	1,852,168	3,409,678	.21	.20	.41	22,231 67
1827,.....	1,653,353	1,765,084	3,418,437	.33	.22	.55	28,999 19
1828,.....	1,861,448	1,748,299	3,609,747	.47	.26	.73	33,582 68
1829,.....	1,867,471	1,687,158	3,554,629	.37	.27	.64	31,412 20
1830,.....	1,949,009	1,908,784	3,857,793	.25	.34	.59	31,775 35
1831,.....	2,021,702	2,103,055	4,124,757	.28	.43	.71	30,972 77
1832,.....	2,075,113	2,146,490	4,221,603	.38	.33	.71	51,229 77
1833......	2,279,526	2,169,360	4,448,886	.36	.44	.80	67,751 75
1834,....	2,343,618	2,156,775	4,500,393	.52	.33	.85	80,857 04
1835,.....	2,551,047	2,328,194	4,879,241	.52	.38	.90	83,238 10
1836,.....	3,029,256	2,511,528	5,540,784	.47	.33	.80	82,301 86
1837,....	2,974,334	2,246,244	5,220,578	.70	.41	1.11	107,830 72
1838,.....	3,238,627	2,257,642	5,496,269	.66	.39	1.05	91,946 30
1839,.....	3,317,477	2,214,916	5,532,393	.65	.36	1.01	90,591 68
1840,.....	3,374,205	2,198,762	5,572,967	.65	.35	1.00	128,837 62
1841,.....	3,570,283	3,024,912	6,595,195	.67	.33	1.00	96,079 86
1842,.....	3,647,586	2,900,427	6,548,013	1.30	.42	1.72	124,342 06
1843,.....	3,526,549	2,960,248	6,486,797	1.75	.39	2.14	170,226 52
1844,.....	3,719,779	2,720,836	6,440,615	1.75	.41	2.16	170,820 84
1845,.....	3,837,997	2,938,326	6,776,323	1.55	.35	1.90	165,628 95
1846,.....	3,989,635	2,949,669	6,939,304	1.53	.33	1.86	165,237 88
1847,.....	4,201,942	3,160,352	7,362,294	1.32	.36	1.68	269,834 06
1848,.....	4,542,136	3,156,852	7,698,988	1.10	.50	1.60	204,909 46
1849,.....	4,627,704	3,170,830	7,798,534	1.21	.49	1.70	208,317 75
1850,.....	4,828,405	3,143,981	7,972,386	1.38	.51	1.89	245,573 63
1851,....	8,347,861	4,263,926	12,611,787	.99	.33	1.32	275,803 52
1852,.....	9,933,366	4,119,180	14,052,546	1.16	.42	1.58	362,227 93
1853,.....	10,103,090	4,822,455	14,925,545	.99	.42	1.41	373,821 96
1854,.....	9,210,755	4,769,028	13,979,783	1.09	.45	1.54	472,798 04
1855,.....	9,133,853	5,173,812	14,307,665	1.18	.61	1.79	400,566 34
1856,.....	8,545,720	5,052,588	13,598,308	1.16	.60	1.76	406,943 74
1857,.....	8,207,270	5,089,859	13,297,129	1.18	.60	1.78	521,452 72
1858,.....	7,919,520	4,899,675	12,819,195	1.28	.65	1.93	576,079 16
1859,.....	7,937,575	4,915,715	12,853,290	1.20	.59	1.79	528,739 55
1860,.....	8,065,305	4,936,310	13,001,615	1.14	.88	2.02	600,348 61
1861,.....	8,162,500	4,917,180	13,079,680	1.15	.79	1.94	530,611 03
1862,.....	8,028,989	4,838,089	12,867,078	1.18	1.02	2.20	815,523 98
1863,.....	8,736,302	5,237,333	13,973,635	1.19	1.45	2.64	898,426 42
1864,.....	8,978,124	5,633,144	14,611,268	3.04	1.66	4.70	2,247,372 71
1865,.....	9,171,506	3,195,283	12,366,789	3.40	1.93	5.33	1,719,789 74
1866,.....	....	....	....	......	......	......	1,109,672 81
Total,.....						....	$14,641,600 53

UTICA.

The funded debt of the city is as follows:

Black River and Utica Railroad Bonds.—$250,000, bearing 7 per cent. interest, city bonds sold, and the amount subscribed and paid for stock in this railroad. They mature in 1875.

Utica and Chenango Valley Railroad Bonds.—$500,000, in like manner subscribed to aid a railroad now in course of construction. These bonds bear 7 per cent. interest, and are divided into five classes of $100,000 each, and mature in from fifteen to twenty years.

By an act of April 16, 1867, the Common Council was authorized to borrow $17,200, to erect two new school-houses, and to issue bonds payable

* The sums here given are for the years beginning on the dates in the left hand column, The amount for 1838–9 is for ten months.

in three equal installments. The School Commissioners call for this money in small sums as needed, and the money is collected by the next tax. This is not, therefore, properly a funded debt.

The accounts of the City Treasurer, rendered on the 20th of February, 1867, show the following receipts for the preceding year:

From city tax of 1866,	$101,245 12
Sundry fines under ordinances,	1,168 69
Police service,	2,946 57
School moneys from State,	8,062 29
Balance of Bounty Fund,	7,596 72
Licenses,	1,131 75
City bonds for Building Fund, due November 1, 1867,	6,000 00
Rents of City Hall,	535 36
Fire department (J. Nelback),	323 60
Other sources,	773 04
	$129,783 14

This income was transferred as follows:

To City Fund,	$51,259 12
To Special Fund,	31,577 66
To School Fund,	33,562 29
To Building Fund,	14,381 07

VILLAGE DEBTS.

Letters were addressed to the Presidents of about one hundred and twenty incorporated villages of the State, inquiring for a statement of the amount of local debt owed by their several corporations, with the purposes for which it was contracted, and the time when it should become due. The following list embraces the result of these inquiries, and show that the total amount of public indebtedness of this description, so far as reported, amounts to $114,710.88. It will be observed that nearly the whole of this debt was incurred for permanent local improvements, and that none of it was contracted for war purposes:

Albany—West Troy, $19,000; in five installments, October 1, 1867–71, and $4,000 in '72, with interest. Incurred under chap. 36, Laws of 1863, for purposes therein specified.

Cortland—Cortland Village, $3,500, in four installments, for paving street. A normal school building in prospect, costing the village $80,000.

Greene—Athens, $350, incurred 25 years ago for ferry and contingent expenses.

Herkimer—Frankfort, $700 for fire engine.

Jefferson—Brownville, $250 for Cemetery grounds. Carthage, $200 for highways and contingencies.

Monroe—Brockport, $13,182.54, loans for Normal School, and $1,000 temporary loan.

Oneida—Clinton, $1,525.45 for contingencies and over-drafts.

Oswego—Fulton, $2,510.25 for a fire engine, due 1868-9. Mexico, $3,000, due for railroad subscription; payable in 1867.

Rensselaer — Greenbush, $1,500, for local purposes. Lansingburgh, $5,481.16, fire, road, gas and general fund.

St. Lawrence — Potsdam, $8,000 for Normal School establishment.

Seneca — Waterloo, $3,737.75, fire engine and engine house.

Tompkins — Ithaca, $19,273.73, chiefly from a flood in 1857, bridges, &c.

Washington — Whitehall, $8,500, balance of a water loan of 1854.

Wayne — Palmyra, $20,000 for a public hall; due $1,000 annually, with interest.

Westchester — Sing Sing, $500 for a free academy; due Jan. 1, 1868.

Yates — Penn Yan, $2,500 claimed, balance for a bridge.

No Village Debts

Were reported in Fredonia and Mayville, Chautauqua county; Norwich and Oxford, Chenango county; Plattsburgh and Keeseville, Clinton county; Homer, Cortland county; Deposit, Broome and Delaware counties; Malone, Franklin county; Gloversville, Fulton county; Le Roy, Genesee county; Cape Vincent and Sackett's Harbor, Jefferson county; Lowville, Lewis county; Geneseo and Mount Morris, Livingston county; Cazenovia, Madison county; Fonda, Montgomery county; Lewiston and Niagara Falls, Niagara county; Geddes and Skaneateles, Onondaga county; Phelps, Canandaigua, and Gorham, Ontario county; Middletown, Orange county; Albion and Medina, Orleans county; Piermont, Rockland county; Canton, Gouverneur and Ogdensburgh, St. Lawrence county; Havana, Schuyler county; Seneca Falls, Seneca county; Corning and Hornellsville, Steuben county; Sag Harbor, Suffolk county; Owego, Tioga county; Saugerties, Ulster county; Glens Falls, Warren county; Fort Edward, Washington county; Lyons, Wayne county; New Rochelle and Yonkers, Westchester county.

FINANCIAL CONDITION OF COUNTIES.

At an early period in the preparation of this volume, circulars were addressed to the treasurer of each county in the State, requesting them to report the following items of information concerning the debts owed by their counties on the first day of March, 1867. The blanks embraced the following inquiries, and, concerning each, the sum, time when incurred, rate of interest, and when and how payable:

Bounties to volunteers;

Other war expenses;

Aid to railroads, giving the name of the road aided;

For roads and bridges;

For public buildings;

For other purposes, specifying each.

Answers were promptly received from every county in the State, and are embraced in the following tables:

Summary of County Debt.

COUNTIES.	Total amount of county debt.	Amount bearing six per cent. interest. *	Amount bearing seven per cent. interest.	Incur'd for bounties to volunteers and other war expenses.	Incur'd for county buildings and other purposes.
Albany, ...	$1,744,250 00	$134,000 00	$1,610,250 00	$1,744,250 00	....
Allegany, ...	36,277 00	....	36,277 00	19,277 00	$17,000 00
Broome, ...	267,685 00	....	267,685 00	220,058 00	47,627 00
Cattaraugus, .	None.	....	....	....	....
Cayuga, ...	632,498 46	....	632,498 46	629,165 13	3,333 33
Chautauqua, .	None.	....	....	....	....
Chemung, ...	28,250 00	8,250 00	20,000 00	See towns.	28,250 00
Chenango, ...	178,000 00	....	178,000 00	178,000 00	....
Clinton, ...	166,700 00	....	167,000 00	163,100 00	3,600 00
Columbia, ...	244,283 95	244,283 95	....	244,283 95	....
Cortland, ...	341,970 00	....	341,000 00	339,970 00	2,000 00
Delaware, ...	None.	....	....	....	....
Dutchess, ...	416,000 00	66,000 00	350,000 00	371,000 00	45,000 00
Erie, ...	692,837 59	60,000 00	632,837 59	692,837 59	....
Essex, ...	None.	....	....	See towns.	....
Franklin, ...	24,795 00	5,000 00	19,795 00	19,795 00	5,000 00
Fulton, ...	89,000 00	....	89,000 00	74,000 00	15,000 00
Genesee, ...	339,418 00	....	339,418 00	339,418 00	....
Greene, ...	527,300 00	....	527,300 00	527,300 00	....
Hamilton, ...	25,000 00	....	25,000 00	25,000 00	....
Herkimer, ...	19,000 00	....	19,000 00	19,000 00	....
Jefferson, ...	1,128,300 00	1,000 00	1,127,988 64	1,112,300 00	16,000 00
Kings, ...	3,462,000 00	2,462,000 00	810,000 00	2,987,000 00	475,000 00
Lewis, ...	84,350 00	....	84,350 00	67,800 00	16,550 00
Livingston, ..	154,697 73	....	154,697 73	154,697 73	....
Madison, ...	22,423 05	....	22,423 05	6,342 75	16,080 30
Monroe, ...	1,564,566 67	38,000 00	1,465,066 67	1,503,066 67	61,500 00
Montgomery,	111,200 00	....	111,200 00	111,200 00	....
New York, ...	†11,816,300 00	3,420,000 00	8,089,100 00	8,069,100 00	3,747,200 00
Niagara, ...	372,800 00	....	372,800 00	372,800 00	....
Oneida, ...	None.	....	....	See towns.	....
Onondaga, ...	1,284,199 98	....	1,248,199 98	1,279,200 00	4,999 98
Ontario, ...	498,060 00	....	498,060 00	498,060 00	....
Orange, ...	231,600 00	....	231,600 00	231,600 00	....
Orleans, ...	239,860 00	....	239,860 00	239,860 00	....
Oswego, ...	813,545 44	....	813,545 44	800,500 00	13,045 44
Otsego, ...	None.	....	....	See towns.	....
Putnam, ...	35,000 00	....	35,000 00	35,000 00	....
Queens, ...	1,085,000 00	11,500 00	1,074,500 00	1,085,000 00	....
Rensselaer, ..	792,200 00	....	792,200 00	792,200 00	....
Richmond, ...	867,054 28	....	867,054 28	801,850 00	65,204 28
Rockland, ...	None.	....	....	See towns.	....
St. Lawrence,	748,350 00	....	748,350 00	688,350 00	60,000 00
Saratoga, ...	146,784 00	....	146,784 00	146,784 00	....
Schenectady, .	24,400 00	....	24,400 00	20,000 00	4,400 00
Schoharie, ...	None.	....	....	See towns.	....
Schuyler, ...	81,943 93	....	71,943 93	71,943 93	10,000 00
Seneca, ...	224,209 00	....	224,209 00	216,209 00	8,000 00
Steuben, ...	283,050 00	....	283,050 00	283,050 00	....
Suffolk, ...	875 00	....	875 00	See towns.	875 00
Sullivan, ...	263,750 00	....	263,750 00	257,400 00	6,350 00
Tioga, ...	141,700 00	....	141,700 00	141,700 00	....
Tompkins, ...	None.	....	....	See towns.	....
Ulster, ...	1,584,175 00	....	1,584,175 00	1,584,175 00	....
Warren, ...	3,408 32	....	3,408 32	See towns.	3,408 32
Washington, .	None.	....	....	See towns.	....
Wayne, ...	228,900 00	....	....	228,900 00	....
Westchester, .	1,145,278 00	....	1,145,278 00	‡1,121,278 00	24,000 00
Wyoming, ...	None.	....	....	See towns.	....
Yates, ...	20,524 00	....	20,524 00	17,524 00	3,000 00
	$35,233,769 40	$6,450,033 95	$27,950,525 79	$30,531,345 75	§ $4,702,423 65

* Except $60,000 in Erie county, which bears 6½ per cent. interest.
† Of this, $1,620,00 was on account of damages in the riots of July, 1863.
‡ Of this, $10,078 was for relief of families of volunteers.
§ Of this sum, $82,031.04 was incurred for roads and bridges, viz.: $3,333.33 in Cayuga county; $38,000 in Monroe county; $20,000 in New York; $4,999.98 in Onondaga county; $875 in Suffolk county; $3,350 in Sullivan county; $2,472.73 in Warren county, and $9,000 in Westchester county.

Dates of Maturity of County Debts.

COUNTIES.	Due on demand, and date of maturity not reported.	1867.*	1868.	1869.	1870.
Albany, ...	....	....	$248,400 00	$378,500 00	$148,900 00
Allegany, ...	$17,000 00	....	9,638 50	9,638 50	....
Broome, ...	47,627 00	....	57,482 00	40,000 00	37,616 00
Cayuga, ...	3,333 33	....	151,475 00	159,850 00	135,150 00
Chemung, ...	8,250 00	$1,000 00	1,000 00	1,000 00	1,000 00
Chenango, ...	....	....	14,000 00	14,000 00	14,000 00
Clinton, ...	3,600 00	....	23,150 00	56,500 00	1,300 00
Columbia, ...	....	....	14,283 95	10,000 00	10,000 00
Cortland, ...	....	....	78,700 00	63,100 00	67,200 00
Dutchess, ...	3,000 00	....	20,000 00	20,000 00	20,000 00
Erie, ...	....	38,835 00	96,800 00	76,500 00	24,962 59
Franklin, ...	5,000 00	....	4,995 00	3,700 00	3,700 00
Fulton, ...	....	....	14,321 43	14,321 43	14.321 43
Genesee, ...	....	....	55,566 00	62,662 00	111,600 00
Greene, ...	305,000 00	12,000 00	12,000 00	12,000 00	12,000 00
Hamilton, ...	25,000 00	....	....	....	....
Herkimer, ...	....	....	10,000 00	9,000 00	....
Jefferson, ...	1,000 00	....	88,600 00	84,400 00	84,300 00
Kings, ...	3,462,000 00	....	....	....	....
Lewis, ...	11,200 00	....	71,150 00	....	....
Livingston, ..	....	....	78,491 53	76,206 20	....
Madison, ...	6,342 75	....	8,040 15	8,040 15	....
Monroe, ...	....	61,500 00	120,966 67	112,550 00	96,050 00
Montgomery,	....	....	12,355 55	12,355 55	12,355 55
New York, ...	7,546,800 00	....	....	....	....
Niagara, ...	....	....	128,600 00	86,700 00	62,500 00
Onondaga, ...	....	....	112,566 66	111,166 66	111,766 66
Ontario, ...	....	....	147,910 00	118,750 00	85,300 00
Orange, ...	....	....	59,400 00	60,300 00	46,400 00
Orleans, ...	....	76,880 00	50,000 00	46,000 00	45,980 00
Oswego, ...	....	166,100 00	109,700 00	89 545 44	73,800 00
Putnam, ...	....	....	15,000 00	15,000 00	5,000 00
Queens, ...	....	....	36,500 00	65,000 00	65,000 00
Rensselaer, ..	....	....	110,500 00	136,400 00	76,000 00
Richmond, ...	24,900 00	....	16,434 76	33,584 76	37,434 76
St. Lawrence,	....	....	132,700 00	135,450 00	74,100 00
Saratoga, ...	....	....	87,150 00	5,884 00	2,000 00
Schenectady, .	4,400 00	....	2,000 00	2,000 00	2,000 00
Schuyler, ...	10,000 00	....	23,981 31	23,981 31	23,981 31
Seneca, ...	8,000 00	30,887 00	30,887 00	30,887 00	30,887 00
Steuben, ...	....	....	172,050 00	111,000 00	....
Suffolk, ...	875 00	....	....	....	....
Sullivan, ...	6,350 00	....	53,800 00	53 800 00	53,800 00
Tioga, ...	....	....	43,900 00	40,000 00	57,800 00
Ulster, ...	....	....	74,400 00	88,275 00	....
Warren, ...	156 67	....	442 00	442 00	442 00
Wayne, ...	....	....	107,700 00	82,300 00	21,200 00
Westchester, .	....	67,078 00	84,200 00	99,000 00	53,000 00
Yates, ...	....	....	20,525 00	....	....
Total, ...	$11,499,834 75	$454,280 00	$2,811,762 51	$2,659,790 00	$1,722,847 30

* Most of the county debts due in 1867, were due and paid near the beginning of the year.

Dates of Maturity of County Debts — (Continued).

COUNTIES.	1871.	1872.	1873.	1874.	1875.
Albany,.......	$136,550 00	$174,000 00	$174,000 00	$183,000 00	$174,900 00
Broome,......	27,390 00	23,700 00	16,675 00	11,550 00	5,000 00
Cayuga,.. ...	150,790 13	31,900 00	....	....	....
Chemung,....	1,000 00	1,000 00	1,000 00	1,000 00	1,000 00
Chenango,....	14,000 00	14,000 00	14,000 00	14,000 00	14,000 00
Clinton,......	59,000 00	23,150 00	....	....	....
Columbia, ...	10,000 00	10,000 00	10,000 00	10,000 00	10,000 00
Cortland, ...	64,200 00	59,770 00	....	....	9,000 00
Dutchess,.....	20,000 00	20,000 00	18,000 00	18,000 00	20,000 00
Erie,..........	36,000 00	20,000 00	30,640 00	76,000 00	56,000 00
Franklin,.....	3,700 00	3,700 00	....	....	....
Fulton, ...	14,321 43	10,571 43	10,571 43	10,571 47	....
Genesee,.	109,600 00	....	....	....	....
Greene, ...	12,000 00	12,000 00	12,000 00	149,300 00	....
Jefferson, ...	82,500 00	83,800 00	84,400 00	76,900 00	78,500 00
Lewis, ...	2,000 00	....	....	....	....
Monroe,......	244,600 00	172,500 00	44,800 00	98,900 00	99,200 00
Montgomery,	12,355 55	12,355 55	12,355 55	12,355 55	12,355 55
New York,...	....	....	....	....	100,000 00
Niagara,......	49,000 00	6,000 00	5,000 00	....	....
Onondaga, ...	123,000 00	128,000 00	139,000 00	140,000 00	150,000 00
Ontario, ...	46,600 00	32,300 00	9,000 00	21,150 00	21,600 00
Orange, ...	40,000 00	25,000 00	500 00	....	....
Orleans, ...	21,000 00	....	....	....	....
Oswego,......	36,500 00	35,000 00	34,800 00	38,500 00	34,000 00
Queens, ...	65,000 00	65,000 00	65,000 00	65,000 00	65,000 00
Rensselaer,...	55,500 00	62,000 00	98,500 00	89,500 00	68,300 00
Richmond, ...	....	....	25,000 00	58,700 00	28,800 00
St. Lawrence,	72,000 00	72 000 00	62,000 00	63,000 00	62,000 00
Saratoga,.....	25,550 00	10,600 00	4,600 00	11,000 00	....
Schenectady,.	2,000 00	2,000 00	2,000 00	2,000 00	2,000 00
Seneca,.......	30,887 00	30,887 00	30,887 00	....	....
Sullivan,.	38,000 00	38,000 00	10,000 00	10,000 00	....
Ulster, ...	98,500 00	84,800 00	41,700 00	95,800 00	94,900 00
Warren, ...	442 00	247 27	247 27	247 27	247 28
Wayne, ...	4,400 00	3,900 00	1,300 00	6,100 00	2,000 00
Westchester,.	50,000 00	50,000 00	60,000 00	60,000 00	60,000 00
Total, ...	$1,758,386 11	$1,318,181 25	$1,017,976 25	$1,322,574 29	$1,179,902 83

COUNTIES.	1876.	1877.	1878.	1879.	1880.
Albany,......	$126,000 00	....	....	....	....
Broome,.....	400 00	$245 00	....	....	....
Chemung, ...	1,000 00	1,000 00	$1,000 00	$1,000 00	$1,000 00
Chenango,,..	14,000 00	14,000 00	14,000 00	14,000 00	10,000 00
Columbia,....	10,000 00	10,000 00	10,000 00	10,000 00	10,000 00
Dutchess,....	20,000 00	23,000 00	23,000 00	23,000 00	23,000 00
Erie,........	21,100 00	27,000 00	68,000 00	34,000 00	97,000 00
Jefferson,....	78,800 00	64,100 00	60,800 00	52,100 00	54,900 00
Monroe,.....	99,700 00	194,200 00	69,600 00	100,000 00	60,000 00
Montgomery,	12,355 55	....	....	....	....
New York,...	100,000 00	100,000 00	100,000 00	100,000 00	100,000 00
Niagara,......	35,000 00	....	....	....	....
Onondaga,...	148,700 00	140,000 00	....	....	....
Ontario,.	....	....	....	....	5,800 00
Oswego,.....	28,600 00	25,500 00	24,500 00	40,000 00	15,500 00
Queens, ...	65,000 00	65,000 00	65,000 00	65,000 00	65,000 00
Rensselaer,..	95,500 00	....	....	....	....
Richmond, ..	....	....	....	52,300 00	34,000 00
St. Lawrence,	60,000 00	15,000 00	100 00	....	....
Schenectady,	2,000 00	2,000 00	....	....	....
Ulster,.......	98,300 00	141,900 00	145,400 00	143,800 00	145,900 00
Warren,....	247 28	247 28	....	....	....
Westchester,	....	100,000 00	100,000 00	100,000 00	100,000 00
Total,......	$1,016,702 83	$923,192 28	$681,400 00	$735,200 00	$722,100 00

Dates of Maturity of County Debts — (Continued).

COUNTIES.	1881.	1882.	1883.	1884.	1885.
Chemung, ...	$1,000 00	$1,000 00	$1,000 00	$1,000 00	$1,000 00
Columbia,....	10,000 00	10,000 00	10,000 00	10,000 00	10,000 00
Dutchess, ...	23,000 00	23,000 00	18,000 00	13,000 00	13,000 00
Jefferson, ...	51,900 00	49,000 00	28,600 00	23,700 00	....
New York,...	100,000 00	192,900 00	100,000 00	100,000 00	100,000 00
Ontario, ...	9,650 00	....	....	....	....
Oswego, ...	15,500 00	15,500 00	15,500 00	15,000 00	....
Queens, ...	115,000 00	40,000 00	40,000 00	40,000 00	44,000 00
Richmond, ..	....	....	84,500 00	250,400 00	23,000 00
Ulster, ...	156,300 00	184,200 00	....	....	....
Westchester,.	62,000 00	....	....	....	....
Totals, ...	$544,350 00	$515,600 00	$297,600 00	$453,100 00	$191,000 00

COUNTIES.	1886.	1887.	1888.	1889.	1890.
Chemung, ...	$1,000 00	....	....	....	....
Columbia, ...	10,000 00	$10,000 00	$10,000 00	$10,000 00	$10,000 00
Dutchess, ...	13,000 00	12,000 00	10,000 00	10,000 00	10,000 00
New York,...........	100,000 00	100,000 00	100,000 00	100,000 00	100,000 00
Richmond, ...	....	....	....	218,000 00	....
Totals,..............	$124,000 00	$122,000 00	$120,000 00	$338,000 00	$120,000 00

COUNTIES.	1891.	1895.	1896.	1897.	1898.
Columbia, ...	$10,000 00	....	....	....	....
New York,...........	585,089 00	$500,000 00	$500,000 00	$500,000 00	$500,000 00
	$595,089 00	$500,000 00	$500,000 00	$500,000 00	$500,000 00

FINANCIAL CONDITION OF TOWNS.

To ascertain the present indebtedness of towns, a circular nearly similar to the one for County Treasurers, noticed on a preceding page, was addressed to the several Supervisors. The returns from these inquiries are presented in the following statement. It will be seen that of the 928 towns of the State, returns were received from all but 46, and that in 365 towns there is no public debt. The principal difficulty encountered in collecting these statistics was from the want of the names and address of the present Supervisors. Town elections had been recently held throughout the State, and it required much time and correspondence to obtain the proper address of these officers, and some were not received until a very late period. After waiting a reasonable time letters were addressed a second time, and if no answer was obtained, application was made to Town Clerks, or to a former Supervisor. Most of the towns not heard from are believed to be free from debt.

ALBANY COUNTY.

No debts, in Guilderland, Knox, Rensselaerville, Watervliet and Westerlo — 5.

Albany (city). $2,779,500. For detail, see statement of city debt.

Berne. $975, 7 per cent. (roads and bridges, 1863), due January, 1868.

Bethlehem. $650, 7 per cent. (object not stated), due in 9 months.

Coeymans. $775.75, 7 per cent. (roads and bridges), due.

New Scotland. $200, 7 per cent. (object not stated), due.

ALLEGANY COUNTY.

No debts, in Alfred, Allen, Alma, Amity, Andover, Birdsall, Centreville, Clarksville, Cuba, Genesee, Granger, Grove, Hume, Independence, Rushford, Scio, Ward, Wellsville and Willing — 19.

Almond. $1,600, 7 per cent. (bounties), due in 1867, with 2 years' interest.

Angelica. $3,100, 7 per cent. (bounties, 1864), due in 1868; for cemetery, $100; roads and bridges, $1,250, both 1867.

Belfast. $5,000, 7 per cent. (bounties, 1864), due March 23, 1868.

Bolivar. $300, 7 per cent. (bounties, 1863), balance over due since 1865; the party being dead, it has not been called for.

Burns. $3,000, 7 per cent. (bounties, 1864), balance of war debt, due 1868.

Caneadea. $30.05, 7 per cent. (war debt, 1865, due January, 1868), object not stated, $333, due January 1, 1868.

Friendship. $9,900, 7 per cent (bounties, 1864, '65, '66), $5,100 due 1868; $4,800 in three installments from 1868.

New Hudson. $1,868, 7 per cent. (bounties, &c., 1866), due March 1, 1868.

West Almond. $22,973.54, 7 per cent. (bounties, &c., 1862–'65), due in three payments. In 1864, paid $11,623.50.

Wirt. $7,500, 7 per cent. (bounties, 1864, '65), due in 1867, also $265 for roads and bridges.

BROOME COUNTY.

No debts, in Chenango, Conklin, Lisle, Maine, Sanford, Triangle and Vestal — 7.

Barker. $2,956, 7 per cent. (bounties, 1864), due February 1, 1868. Bridge, $500, 7 per cent., due February 1, 1868.

Binghamton (city). $50,000 (Syracuse and Binghamton Railroad).

Binghamton (town). $22,900, 7 per cent. (bounties, 1864), due $7,800 in '68; $7,700 in '69; $7,400 in '70. Bridge, $7,400, 7 per cent., 1865, due $5,650 in '68; $500 in '69; $1,250 in '71.

Colesville. $2,800, 7 per cent. (bounties, 1864), due February 1, 1868 with one year's interest. Railroad debt, $50,000, 7 per cent., 1862, '63, '64.

Fenton. $3,800, 7 per cent. (bounties, 1863), due February 1, 1868.

Kirkwood. $5,200, 7 per cent. (bounties, 1864), due February 1, 1868.

Nanticoke. $1,843.82, 7 per cent. (bounties, 1864), due in two installments, February, 1868–9.

Union. $4,530, 7 per cent. (bounties, 1864), due in 1868.

Windsor. $2,000, 7 per cent. (bounties, 1864), due January 1, 1868.

CATTARAUGUS COUNTY.

No debts, in Cold Springs, Conewango, Dayton, East Otto, Ellicottville, Farmersville, Franklinville, Freedom, Great Valley, Humphrey, Ischua, Machias, Mansfield, New Albion, Otto, Perrysburgh, Portville, Randolph, Salamanca and South Valley — 20.

No returns, from Lyndon — 1.

Allegany. $900, 7 per cent. (bounties, 1864), due July, 1867.

Ashford. $350, 7 per cent. (bounties, 1864), date of maturity not specified. Also $100 (roads and bridges) due in 1868.

Carrolton. $366.72, 7 per cent. (bounties, 1864), due April 1, 1868.

Hinsdale. $1,728, 7 per cent. (bounties, 1864), due in 1868.

Little Valley. $15,000 (public buildings), due in ten installments.

Leon. $100 (highway money), date of maturity not specified.

Napoli. $3.000, 7 per cent. (county buildings, 1866), due in six installments, from 1867.

Olean. $7,000, 7 per cent. (bounties, 1862–3), due in two annual payments; $1,000, 7 per cent. (Academy bond and bridges), due in 1867 and 1868.

Persia. $450 (bridges), date of maturity not given.

Yorkshire. $200, 7 per cent. (bounties, 1865), due September 1, 1867. Railroad debt $18,000, 1866, due in three installments on completion of railroad.

CAYUGA COUNTY.

No debts, in Aurelius, Brutus, Conquest, Fleming, Ira, Ledyard, Montezuma, Niles, Owasco, Sempronius, Throop and Victory — 12.

Auburn (city). $100,000. For detail, see statement of city debt.

Cato. $4,657.06, 7 per cent. (bounties, 1864), due 1868. Also for an iron bridge over Seneca river, $3,333.33, 7 per cent, 1865, due in three annual installments.

Genoa. $25,000. (Railroad debt in 1853). In litigation, road not built.

Locke. $45,000. (Railroad debt), due in 30 years. Bonds not yet issued.

Mentz. $4,815, 7 per cent. (bounties, 1864), due March 1, 1868; of this sum $315 is interest.

Moravia. $86,000. (Railroad debt). Town pledged for Southern Central railroad, but bonds not issued.

Sennett. $4,752, 7 per cent. (bounties, 1863), due in 1867.

Springport. $3,900, 7 per cent. (bounties, 1864). In litigation, thirteen claims, $300 each.

Sterling. $25,000, 7 per cent. (railroad debt, 1853), due. Also $12,250, interest on bonds for 1861, '62, '63, '64, '65, '66 and '67, which has not been paid.

Summer Hill. $700, 7 per cent. (bounties), 1865, due. Not audited.

Throop. No debt. Has paid $12,850 for bounties, and $2,000 as volunteer fund.

Venice. $25,000. (Railroad debt), due in twenty installments.

CHAUTAUQUA COUNTY.

No debts, in Arkwright, Busti, Carroll, Charlotte, Chautauqua, Cherry Creek, Ellery, Ellicott, Ellington, Kiantone, Mina, Poland, Pomfret, Ripley, Sheridan, Stockton, Villenova and Westfield — 18.

Clymer. $20,000, 7 per cent. (railroad debt, 1866), due in 20 installments. Also, $816.66 (interest on bonds), due March 1, 1867.

Dunkirk. $3,000, 7 per cent. (object not stated), due in 1867, $2,000, and $1,000 in '68. Also, $100,000 (railroad debt). Bonds not yet issued.

Ellery. From excess of men furnished, received $22,000, which bonds were sold to pay tax.

French Creek. $209.62 (object not stated), due to county.

Gerry. $387.30 (roads and bridges); date of maturity not specified.

Hanover. $5,900, 7 per cent. (bounties, 1864), due in 1868, $2,300, and $3,600 in '69.

Harmony. No debt. $124,666; paid during the war.

Portland. $20,000, 7 per cent. (railroad debt), payable in 1886.

Sherman. $30,000, 7 per cent., sum due (railroad debt), due in twenty installments. Also, $500 (roads and bridges); date of maturity not specified.

CHEMUMG COUNTY.

Baldwin. $4,929, 7 per cent. (bounties), due in seven installments, viz.: $873 in '68; $831 in '69; $789 in '70; $747 in '71; $705 in '72; $663 in '73; and $321 in '74.

Big Flats. $26,880, 7 per cent. (bounties), due in seven installments, viz.: $8,768 in '68; $5,864 in '69; $5,028 in '70; $2,328 in '71; $1,194 in '72; $1,131 in '73; and $2,568 in '74.

Catlin. $12,161.75, 7 per cent. (bounties), due in 7 installments, viz.: $4,012.75 in '68; $1,855 in '69; $975 in '70; $1,215 in '71; $1,452 in '72; $1,368 in '73; and $1,284 in '74.

Chemung. $32,305, 7 per cent. (bounties), due in 7 installments, viz.: $7,327 in '68; $6,642 in '69; $5,478 in '70; $4,970 in '71; $1,676 in '72; $1,592 in '73; and $4,620 in '74.

Elmira (city). $173,246.72, total bonded and floating debt. For details, see statement of city finances.

Elmira (town). $3,714, 7 per cent. (bounties), due in seven installments, viz.: $810 in '68; $768 in '69; $726 in '70; $384 in '71; $363 in '72; $342 in '73; and $321 in '74.

Erin. $26,726.50, 7 per cent. (bounties), due in seven installments, viz.: $4,159.50 in '68; $4,270.50 in '69; $4,060.50 in '70; $3,850.50 in '71; $3,790.50 in '72; $3,920 in '73; $2,675 in '74. Also, $9,174.91 for other war expenses, date of maturity not given, and $250 for roads and bridges.

Horseheads. $3,350, 7 per cent. (bounties), due in two installments, viz.: $1,210 in '68; and $2,140 in '69. For other purposes not stated, $1,101.

Southport. $64,516, 7 per cent. (bounties), due in seven installments, viz.: $11,542 in '68; $10,282 in '69; $9,471 in '70; $9,251 in '71; $8,470 in '72; $7,980 in '73; and $7,490 in '74.

Van Etten. $13,768, 7 per cent. (bounties), due in three installments, viz.: $5,854 in '68; $4,704 in '69; and $3,210 in '70.

Veteran. $26,074, 7 per cent. (bounties), due in seven installments, viz.: $8,240 in '68; $6,771 in '69; $4,372 in '70; $3,613 in '71; $1,089 in '72; $1,026 in '73; and $963 in '74.

CHENANGO COUNTY.

No debts, in Macdonough — 1.

Afton. $6,899.63, 7 per cent. (bounties, 1864–5), due in two installments. Also $30,000, 7 per cent. (railroad debt), due in 1882.

Bainbridge. $30,348.54, 7 per cent. (railroad debt, 1863–5), due twenty-five years from date.

Columbus. $1,505, 7 per cent. (bounties, 1864–5), due in two installments.

Coventry. $7,100, 7 per cent. (bounties, 1863–4), due January, 1868, $5,900; and $1,200 in '69.

German. $3,445, 7 per cent. (bounties, 1863–4), due in four installments.

Greene. $63,800, 7 per cent. (bounties, 1864), due in 1868, $5,400; $5,400 in '69; $18,000 in '70; $12,000 in '71; $8,700 in '72; and $14,300 in '73.

Guilford. $14,000, 7 per cent. (bounties, 1864), due in 1868, $6,000, and $8,000 in '69.

Lincklaen. $15,756, 7 per cent. (bounties, 1863–4), due February 1, 1868, $5,752; in '69, $5,716; and in '70, $4,288.

New Berlin. $18,050, 7 per cent. (bounties, 1863–4–5), due February 1, 1868, $8,850; and $9,200 in '69.

North Norwich. $13,797.54, 7 per cent. (bounties, 1864), due February 1, 1868, $5,297.54; $3,700 in '69; and $4,800 in '70.

Norwich. $24,695, 7 per cent. (bounties, 1864), due February 1, 1868, $17,058; $1,452 in '69: and $6,185 in '70. Also $371,000, railroad debt. It is understood that the consent of the inhabitants has been obtained. No papers are filed or bonds issued.

Otselic. $13,600, 7 per cent. (bounties, 1864–5), due in three installments.

Oxford. $32,000, 7 per cent. (bounties, 1864), due in four installments. Also $200,000 (railroad debt). Bonds not issued, but the town is pledged.

Pharsalia. $13,360, 7 per cent. (bounties, 1864), due February 1, 1868, $7,500; and in '69, $5,860.

Pitcher. $10,044, 7 per cent. (bounties, 1864), due in 1868, $6,544; and $3,500 in '69.

Plymouth. $1,500, 7 per cent. (bounties, 1862), due January 1, 1868. Also $100,000 (railroad). Pledged if located in our town, not otherwise.

Preston. $1,768, 7 per cent. (bounties, 1864), due in two installments. Also $20,000 (railroad). Bonded.

Sherburne. $35,075, 7 per cent. (bounties, 1863–4), due in six installments. Also $145,000, 7 per cent. (railroad debt), due in twenty installments; bonds not issued.

Smithville. $4,152, 7 per cent. (bounties, 1864), due in two installments.

Smyrna. $15,000 (railroad). The effort is being made to bond, with probable success.

CLINTON COUNTY.

No debts, in Altona, Black Brook, Clinton and Plattsburgh — 4.

Ausable. $1,251, 7 per cent. (bounties, 1864), due March 1, 1868, $201; and in '70, $1,050.

Beekmantown. $27.75, 7 per cent. (bounties, 1864), due in 1868.

Champlain. $663.29 (roads and bridges), due in 1868.

Chazy. $3,897, 7 per cent. (bounties, 1864–5), due in 1870.

Dannemora. $350, 7 per cent. (Roads and bridges, 1866.)

Ellenburgh. $3,950, 7 per cent. (bounties, 1864), due April 1, 1868.

Mooers. $17,007.40, 7 per cent. (bounties), due in yearly installments.

Peru. $1,307.50, 7 per cent. (bounties, 1865), due February 1, 1868.

Saranac. $1,000 (bridge across the Saranac river), due in four installments.

Schuyler Falls. $1,350, 7 per cent. (bounties, 1863), due January 1, 1868.

COLUMBIA COUNTY.

No debts, in Austerlitz, Canaan, Clermont, Greenpoint, Hillsdale, Kinderhook, Livingston, Taghkanick — 8.

No returns, from Stockport — 1.

Ancram. $4,000, 7 per cent. (bounties, 1863), due in 1868.

Chatham. $55,000 (bonds for Lebanon Springs Railroad), bonds not yet issued. The consent of taxpayers has been obtained.

Claverack. $3,500, 7 per cent. (bounties, 1865), due in 1868.

Copake. $400, 7 per cent. (object not stated), due February, 1868.

Gallatin. $4,400, 7 per cent. (bounties, 1864), due March 1, 1867.

Germantown. $2,875, 7 per cent. (bounties, 1863–5), Due in 1868. Also $4,000, for 7 per cent., a public dock (1866), due in four installments.

Ghent. $11,000, 7 per cent. (bounties 1864, 5), due $7,000, March 1, 1868, $1,000 each in 1869, 1870, 1871 and 1872, March 1st each year.

Hudson (city). $100,500. See details in statement of city debts.

Lebanon. $100,000, (Lebanon Springs Railroad), bonds not issued. The consent of tax payers obtained.

Stuyvesant. $18,200, 7 per cent. (bounties, 1865), payable in 12 years.

Stockport. For roads $500.

CORTLAND COUNTY.

Cincinnatus. $19,924.21, 7 per cent. (bounties), due in six installments, viz.: $4,555.33 in '68; $3,639.54 in '69; $3,938.10 in '70; $3,762.41 in '71; $3,502.87 in '72; and $527.46 in '75.

Cortlandville. $76,504.38, 7 per cent. (bounties), due in six installments, viz.: $17,505.36 in '68; $13,991.06 in '60; $15,141 in '70; $14,463.50 in '71; $13,465.81 in '72; and $2,027.65 in '73.

Cuyler. $18,145.16, 7 per cent. (bounties), due in six installments, viz.: $4,147.09 in '68; $3,314.54 in '69; $3,586.60 in '70; $3,426.46 in '71; $3,190.10 in '72; and $480.37 in '73.

Freetown. $11,517.07, 7 per cent. (bounties), due in six installments, viz.: $2,632.22 in '68; $2,103.81 in '69; $2,276.48 in '70; $2,174.84 in '71; $2,024.82 in '72; and $304.90 in '73.

Harford. $15,369.01, 7 per cent. (bounties), due in six installments, viz.: $3,512.66 in '68; $2,807.51 in '69; $3,037.77 in '70; $2,902.12 in '71; $2,702.09 in '72; and $406.86 in '73. Bonds for railroad, $21,290, 7 per cent, authorized in 1866, not issued; also $16,710, 7 per cent, consent now being obtained.

Homer. $48,298.56, 7 per cent. (bounties and other war expenses), due in six installments, viz.: $11,038.64 in '68; $8,822.65 in '69; $9,546.77 in '70; $9,120.52 in '71; $8,491.38 in '72; and $1,278.60 in '73.

Lapeer. $8,124.46, 7 per cent. (bounties), due in six installments, viz.: $1,856.84 in '68; $1,484.09 in '69; $1,605.89 in '70; $1,534.20 in '71; $1,428.36 in '72; and $215.08 in '73.

Marathon. $22,260.22, 7 per cent. (bounties), due in six installments, viz.: $5,087.59 in '68; $4,066.24 in '69; $4,399.99 in '70; $4,203.52 in '71; $3,913.59 in '72; and $589.29 in '73.

Preble. $20,949.57, 7 per cent. (bounties), due in six installments, viz.: $4,788 in '68; $3,826.81 in '69; $4,140.90 in '70; $3,956.12 in '71; $3,683.14 in '72; and $554.60 in '73.

Scott. $10,331.94, 7 per cent. (bounties), due in six installments, viz.: $2,361.38 in '68; $1,885.65 in '69; $2,042.22 in '70; $1,952.72 in '71; $1,816.45 in '72; and $273.52 in '73.

Solon. $1,542.10, 7 per cent. (bounties), due in six installments, viz.: $352.45 in '68; $281.70 in '69; $304.82 in '70; $291.20 in '71; $271.11 in '72: and $40.82 in '73.

Taylor. $20,715.27, 7 per cent. (bounties), due in six installments, viz.: $4.734.47 in '68; $3,784.03 in '69; $4,094.62 in '70; $3,911.80 in '71; $3,641.96 in '72; and $548.39 in '73.

Truxton. $15,820.46, 7 per cent. (bounties), due in six installments, viz.: $3,615.64 in '68; $2,889.95 in '69; $3,127.12 in '70; $2,987.50 in '71; $2,781.43 in '72; and $418.82 in '73. For roads and bridges $250, due in 1868.

Virgil. $34,234.28, 7 per cent. (bounties), due in six installments, viz.: $7,824.27 in '68; $6,253.53 in '69; $6,766.81 in '70; $6,464.65 in '71; $6,018.73 in '72; and $906.29 in '73.

Willett. $16,143.31, 7 per cent. (bounties), due in six installments, viz.: $3,689.56 in '68; $2,948.89 in '69; $3,190.91 in '70; $3,048.44 in 71; $2,838.16 in '72; and $427.35 in '73.

DELAWARE COUNTY.

No debts, in Bovina, Masonville, Tompkins — 3.

No returns, from Kortright.

Andes. $23,490.20, 7 per cent. (bounties, 1864), due in 1868 $9,530.20; $6,980 in '69; and $6,980 in '70.

Colchester. $2,500, 7 per cent. (bounties, 1864), due Feb. 1, 1868.

Davenport. $13,276.25, 7 per cent. (bounties, 1864), due $12,276.25 in '68; and $1,000 in '69. Also, railroad bonds, $32,100, 7 per cent. (Dated $3,000 Nov. 15, 1863, and $27,000 August 31, 1866). Due by installments during twenty-five years.

Delhi. $10,000, 7 per cent. (bounties, 1864), due February 1, 1868.

Franklin. $164,720 (railroad debt). Pledged, but bonds not issued.

Hamden. $7,000, 7 per cent. (bounties, 1863 and '64), due in three installments.

Harpersfield. $4,942, 7 per cent. (bounties, 1864), due February 11, 1868, $3,750; in '69, $1,250; and in '70, $200. Also, $150,000 (railroad debt), bonds not yet issued.

Hancock. $17,120 (bounties), due August 1, 1867, $15,515; and in '68, $1,605.

Meredith. $18,000, 7 per cent. (bounties, 1864 and '65), due in three installments, February 1, 1868, $8,000; $7,000 in '69; and $3,000 in '70.

Middletown. $100,000 (railroad debt), pledged, but no bonds issued.

Roxbury. $150,000 (railroad debt), pledged, but bond not issued.

Sidney. $50,000, 7 per cent. (railroad debt), payable within twenty years. Also, $150, 7 per cent. (for support of poor), due.

Stamford. $2,100, 7 per cent. (bounties, 1864), due in 1868. Also, $60,000 for (railroad debt), bonds not issued.

Walton. $12,000, 7 per cent. (bounties, 1864), due in two installments.

DUTCHESS COUNTY.

No debts, in Beekman, Hydepark, La Grange, Milan, Pawling, Pleasant Valley, Pine Plains, Red Hook, Stanford, Union Valley, Washington and Poughkeepsie—11.

No returns, from Dover.

Amenia. $12,000, 7 per cent. (bounties, 1865), due in six installments.

Clinton. $9,900, 7 per cent. (bounties, 1864), due in two installments. Also $86 for (roads and bridges), date of maturity not specified.

East Fishkill. $48,500, 7 per cent. (bounties, 1864), due in ten installments.

Fishkill. $84,000, 7 per cent. (bounties, 1864), due in sixteen installments.

Northeast. $16,000, 7 per cent. (bounties, 1864, '65), March 1, 1868, $5,000; 1869, $5,000; and 1870, $6,000.

Poughkeepsie (city). $397,097.70. For detail, see statement of city debt.

Rhinebeck. $6,000, 7 per cent. (bounties), due in two installments.

ERIE COUNTY.

No debts, in Alden, Boston, Brandt, Clarence, Colden, Collins, East Hamburgh, Evans, Grand Island, Hamburgh, Holland, Lancaster, Marilla, Newstead, North Collins, Tonawanda, Wales and West Seneca — 18.

Amherst. $6,601.32, 7 per cent (bounties and war expenses), due 1868.

Aurora. $271, 7 per cent. (roads and bridges, 1862), due October 1, 1867.

Buffalo (city). $612,000. For detail, see statement of city debts.

Chictawauga. $2,818, 7 per cent. (bounties, 1862), due 1868.

Concord. $500 (road), due.

Eden. $500 (bridge, 1866), due.

Elma. $925 (roads and bridges, 1866, '67), due in 1868.

Sardinia. Pledged to pay the cost of right of way through the town for Buffalo and Washington Railroad.

ESSEX COUNTY.

Chesterfield. $13,500, 7 per cent. (bounties, August 1, 1864), due $5,000 in 1868; $6,000 in 1869; and $2,500 in 1870.

Crown Point. $22,000, 7 per cent. (bounties, 1863), due in two installments.

Elizabethtown. $11,295, 7 per cent. (bounties, 1863, '64, '55), $2,700 due in 1868; $2,000 in 1869; $2,025 in 1870; $1,571 in 1871; 2,500 in 1872; and $1,570 in 1873. Roads and bridges $301,04, 7 per cent. (roads and bridges, 1866), due in 1868.

Jay. $6,800, 7 per cent. (bounties, 1864), due in two installments.

Keene. $1,060, 7 per cent. (bounties, 1863), due in two installments.

Lewis. $13,410, 7 per cent. (war expenses, 1863, '64), due in two installments.

Minerva. $3,000 (bounties, 1864), due in two installments.

Moriah. $27,200, 7 per cent. (bounties, 1863, '64), due in two installments.

Newcomb. $1,768, 7 per cent. (bounties, 1864), due $912 in 1868, and $856 in 1869.

North Elba. $3,252.93, 7 per cent. (bounties, 1863, '64, '65), due in seven installments.

North Hudson. $1,210, 7 per cent. (bounties, 1863), due in two installments.

St. Armand. $1,100, 7 per cent. (bounties, 1864), due in three installments.

Schroon. $7,760, 7 per cent. (bounties, 1863, '64), due in two installments.

Ticonderoga. $58,300, 7 per cent. (bounties, 1863, '64, '65) date of maturity not specified.

Westport. $9,027, 7 per cent. (bounties, 1863,'64), due in 1867, '68.

Willsborough. $10,080, 7 per cent. (bounties, 1863, '64), due, $2,680 in 1868; $3,400 in 1869; $4,000 in 1870. Also $200 (bridges, 1866), due in 1868.

Wilmington. $893.56, 6 per cent. (bounties, 1864, '65), due in four installments. $2,100, (State bonds, for war purposes), due.

FRANKLIN COUNTY.

No debts, in Moira and Westville — 2.

No returns, from Brighton and Duane — 2.

Bangor. $9,000, 7 per cent. (bounties, 1864), due in 1868, $4,600; and in '61, $4,400.

Bellmont. $10,300, 7 per cent. (bounties, 1863–4), due in five installments. Also $500 for a bridge.

Bombay. $1,500, 7 per cent. (bridge across St. Regis river, 1863), due in five installments.

Brandon. $6,600, 7 per cent. (bounties, 1864), due in 1868, $3,000; in '69, $3,600.

Burke. $17,500, 7 per cent. (bounties, 1864), due, $3,100 in '68; $2,900 in '69; $3,100 in '70; $2,900 in '71; $1,300 in '72; $2,100 in '73; and $2,100 in '74.

Chateaugay. $16,127.75, 7 per cent. (bounties, 1863–4), due in four installments.

Constable. $6,035, 7 per cent. (bounties, 1864), date of maturity not stated.

Dickinson. $6,900, 7 per cent. (bounties, 1864), due in three installments.

Fort Covington. $12,400, 7 per cent. (bounties, 1864), due in four installments. $175 (roads and bridges), date of maturity not stated.

Franklin. $551, 7 per cent. (bounties), due, date of payment not given.

Harrietstown. $350, 7 per cent. (bounties, 1864), due in 1868.

Malone. $44,300, 7 per cent. (bounties, 1863–4–5), due in 1868, $11,100; and balance in annual payments from 1875 to 1880.

FULTON COUNTY.

No debts, in Caroga and Northampton — 2.

No returns, from Oppenheim — 1.

Bleecker. $1,070. 7 per cent. (bounties. 1863), due 1868. Also $385 (for bridges and roads), due 1868.

Broadalbin. $19,466, 7 per cent. (bounties), due $4,770 in 1867; $4,326 in in 1868; $4,670 in 1869; and $5,700 in 1870.

Ephratah. $16,000, 7 per cent. (bounties, 1864), due in 1868; also $250, 7 per cent.; date of payment not given.

Johnstown. $27,000, 7 per cent. (bounties, 1864), due March 1, 1868, $21,000; $3,000 in 1869; and $3,000 in 1870. Also $275,674 (railroad debt), pledged but bonds not issued.

Mayfield. $3,690, 7 per cent. (bounties, 1864), due 1868.

Perth. $6,100, 7 per cent. (bounties), due 1868.

Stratford. $1,100 (bridges, 1867); date of payment not given.

GENESEE COUNTY.

No debts, in Bergen, Byron, Pavilion and Stafford — 4.

Alabama. $8,900, 7 per cent. (bounties, 1864), due in three installments, viz.: $3,200 in 1868; $3,000 in '69; and $2,700 in '70.

Alexander. $10,000, 7 per cent. (war expenses), due in three installments.

Batavia. $17,029, 7 per cent. (bounties, 1864), due in three installments.

Bethany. $500 (object not stated); date of payment not given.

Darien. $4,800, 7 per cent. (bounties, 1864), due $2,700 in 1868, and $2,100 in 1869.

Elba. $11,300, 7 per cent. (bounties, 1864), due in 1868, $3,800; $3,800 in '69; and $3,700 in '70. Interest from February 15, 1867.

Le Roy. $11,400, 7 per cent. (bounties, 1864), due February 15, 1868. Also $10,000, 7 per cent. (1867), for academic purposes, due in ten installments.

Oakfield. $11,400, 7 per cent. (bounties, 1865), due in 1868, $3,800; in '69, $3,900; and in '70, $3,700.

Pembroke. $9,100, 7 per cent. (war expenses, 1865), due in three installments.

GREENE COUNTY.

No debts, in Ashlands, Athens, Cairo, Catskill, Coxsackie, Durham, Greenville and Prattsville — 8.

No returns, from Jewett — 1.

Halcott. $10,000 (Rondout and Oswego Railroad), bonds not yet issued; credit of the town pledged.

Hunter. $876.40, 7 per cent. (roads and bridges), due in 1868.

Lexington. $612.82, 7 per cent. (roads and bridges), due in sums of $250 annually.

Windham. $200 (bridges), due in 1868.

New Baltimore. $50 (election debt), due in 1868.

HAMILTON COUNTY.

No debts, in Arietta, Benson and Hope — 3.

No returns, from Gilman and Lake Pleasant — 2.

Indian Lake. $3,000, 7 per cent. (bounties, 1864), date of payment not given.

Long Lake. $2,000, 7 per cent. (bounties, 1863), to be paid in October, 1867.

Morehouse. $721, 7 per cent. (bounties, 1864), due. Also, $730, 7 per cent. (object not stated), due.

Wells. $8,000, 7 per cent. (bounties, 1863), due. Also, $3,850, 7 per cent., for a bridge. Date of payment not given.

HERKIMER COUNTY.

No debts, in Litchfield, Schuyler, Stark, Warren and Wilmurt — 5.

Columbia. $6,900, 7 per cent. (bounties, 1863, '64) due in two installments. $10,800 (other war expenses), date of maturity not stated. $50,000 (railroad debt), pledged, but bonds not yet issued.

Danube. $1,333.33, 7 per cent. (Fink's bridge, 1861), due in four installments.

Fairfield. $8,147.80 (bounties, 1863, '64), $2,647.80 in 1868; $1,000 annually after.

Frankfort. $7,000, 7 per cent. (bounties, 1864), due in 1867, $1,000; in '68, $5,000; and in '69, $1,000.

German Flats. $13,800 7 per cent. (bounties), due in five equal installments, 1868–72

Herkimer. $1,300, 7 per cent. (bounties, 1864), due Feb. 1, 1868.

Little Falls. $46,450.76, 7 per cent. (bounties, 1862, '65), due in installments of $4,000 annually until paid. Also $333.33 (Fink's bridge), due.

Manheim. $1,500, 7 per cent. (bounties, 1864), due Feb. 1, 1868. $2,508 (other war expenses), due in 1868. $1,333.33 (bridge over Mohawk), due in four installments.

Newport. $6,400, 7 per cent. (bounties, 1863, '64), due $1,200 in '68; $1,900 in '69; $1,000 in '70; $1,000 in '71; and $1,300 in '72.

Norway. $10,755 (bounties, 1863, '64), due Feb. 1, 1868, $4,455; in '69, $3,580, and in '70, $2,740.

Ohio. $2,216.68, 7 per cent. (bounties, 1864), due Jan. 1868. $500, 7 per cent. (bridges, 1863 and '65), due in 1868.

Russia. $4,000, 7 per cent. (bridge, 1866), due Feb. 1, 1868.

Salisbury. $4,055.30, 7 per cent. (bounties, Feb. 21, 1863), due Feb. 1, 1868.

JEFFERSON COUNTY.

No debts, in Henderson and Hounsfield — 2.

Adams. $2,000, 7 per cent. (bounties), due in two installments.

Alexandria. $5,830.60, 7 per cent. (bounties, 1863, '64), $1,830.60 in 2, and $4,000 in 4 years.

Antwerp. $1,150, 7 per cent. (bounties, 1863), due in 1868.

Brownville. $14,200, 7 per cent. (bounties, 1863), due in seven installments.

Cape Vincent. $13,100, 7 per cent. (bounties, 1864), due $5,300 in '67; $3,300 in '68; $4,500 in '69; also $1,000, 6 per cent. (roads and bridges), date of payment not specified.

Champion. $8,796, 7 per cent. (bounties, 1862, '64), also $8,800 (war expenses), dates of maturity not specified.

Clayton. $10,000, 7 per cent, (bounties, 1864), due in three installments; also $422, 7 per cent. (bridge), due March 1, 1868.

Ellisburgh. $361.45, 7 per cent. (bounties, 1864), due February 15, 1868; also $850, 7 per cent. (roads and bridges), due.

Le Ray. $4,275, 7 per cent. (roads and bridges), date of payment not specified.

Lorraine. $1,000, 7 per cent. (bounties, 1864), due in 1868, $490.63, 7 per cent. (roads and bridges, 1866), due in 1867.

Lyme. $18,946.95, 7 per cent. (bounties, 1863, '64), due in seven installments; $727 (war expenses), due in 1869.

Orleans. $13,070, 7 per cent. (bounties, 1863, '64, '65), due $5,853.34 in '68; $2, 683.33 in '69; $3,133.33 in '70; $600 in '71; and $770 in '72.

Pamelia. $9,157.50, 7 per cent. (bounties), due in 1868, $3,052; '69, $2,035; '70, $2,035; and '71, $2,035.

Philadelphia. $1,770 (roads and bridges), date of maturity not stated.

Rodman. $1,300 (bounties, 1864), due $300 (6 per cent.) in '68, and $1,000 (7 per cent.) in 1869; also $2,262.73 (bridges), date of payment not stated; also $100,000 conditional pledge for a railroad not bonded and construction doubtful.

Rutland. $3,500, 7 per cent. (roads and bridges), due in four installments.

Theresa. $11,442, 7 per cent. (bounties, 1863, '64), due in eleven installments; also $600 (bridge), date of payment not specified.

Watertown. $30,300, 7 per cent. (bounties, 1863, '64), due from 1867 to '74; also $4,436.49 for other purposes ($1,000 at 6 per cent., balance at 7 per cent.) date of maturity not stated.

Wilna. $50,000 (railroad) pledged, bonds not issued; $1,100 (bridge), due in 1868.

Worth. $1,600, 7 per cent. (bounties 1864), due in three installments.

KINGS COUNTY.

No debts, in Flatlands and New Utrecht — 2.

No returns, from Gravesend and New Lots — 2.

Brooklyn. $11,113,415.92. For detail see statement of city debt.

Flatbush. $2,000 (engine house for fire company), due January 1, 1868.

LEWIS COUNTY.

No debts, in Croghan, Greig, Harrisburgh, High Market, Lewis and Leyden — 6.

No returns, from Montague.

Denmark. $50,000 (railroad debt); pledged, but not bonded.

Diana. $300 (roads and bridges), due 1868. Also $500 (object not stated), due 1868.

Lowville. $100,000 (railroad debt); pledged, but bonds not issued.

Martinsburgh. $30,000 (railroad debt); pledged, but bonds not issued.

New Bremen. $6,250, 7 per cent. (bounties, 1864), due February 10, 1868.

Osceola. $81.22 (balance of war debt), due.

Pinckney. $30,000 (railroad debt), bonds not issued. Also $200 (object not stated), due 1867.

Turin. $230 (roads and bridges), date of maturity not stated.

Watson. $169.46 (roads and bridges), due in 1867.

LIVINGSTON COUNTY.

No debts, in Avon, Caledonia, Conesus, Geneseo, Groveland, Mount Morris, Nunda, Ossian, Portage, Sparta, Springwater and York — 13.

No returns, from Livonia and West Sparta — 2.

Leicester. $9,000 (bridge across Genesee river), contested in litigation.

Lima. $254, 7 per cent. (war debt), due January 1, 1868. Also $500 for repairs of town-house, due January 1, 1868.

North Dansville. $100,000 (for railroad); not pledged, nor bonds issued.

MADISON COUNTY.

No debt, in Cazenovia, Eaton, Fenner, Georgetown, Lenox, Madison, Nelson, Smithfield and Stockbridge — 9.

Brookfield. $60,000, 6 per cent. (railroad debt), payable in twenty years. Bonds not issued.

De Ruyter. $102,300 (railroad debt), conditioned to the location of a railroad on a certain line, or, if not, to be void. Bonds not issued.

Hamilton. $100,000 (railroad debt), pledged but no bonds issued yet.

Lebanon. $125,000 (railroad debt), conditioned to the location of Midland railroad in town, with six miles and a station in town. No bonds yet issued. Also $200 to defend a suit for town.

Sullivan. $1,400 (repairing roads and bridges), due. Also $109.79 to be paid to different individuals for taxes illegally assessed and collected in 1865 and 1866.

MONROE COUNTY.

No debts, in Brighton, Chili, Clarkson, Gates, Henrietta, Irondequoit, Parma, Perrinton, Riga and Sweden — 10.

No returns, from Pittsford and Wheatland — 2.

Greece. $24,900, 7 per cent. (bounties, 1864), due in three installments, February 15.

Hamlin. $50 (war expenses), due March 1, 1868.

Mendon. $2,255.21, 7 per cent. (roads and bridges, 1865, '66), due February 15, 1868.

Ogden. $11,823.50, 7 per cent. (bounties, 1864), due February 15, 1868. Also $900 (object not specified, 1867), due in 1868.

Penfield. $160 (roads and bridges), and $300 (poor), due February 15, 1868.

Rochester (city), $1,001,500. For details, see statement of city debt.

Rush. $3,600 (iron bridge over Honeoye creek), due in three installments.

MONTGOMERY COUNTY.

No debts, in Palatine — 1.

Amsterdam. $75,278.80, 7 per cent. (bounties, 1864, '65), due in six installments, 1867–72.

Canajoharie. $25,749, 7 per cent. (bounties, 1864), due in four installments.

Charleston. $8,000, 7 per cent. (bounties, 1864), due in 1868.

Florida. $44,500, 7 per cent. (bounties, 1864), due in three installments. Also $345.59, 7 per cent. (roads and bridges), and $172.50 for other expenses.

Glen. $4,000, 7 per cent. (bounties, 1864), due in 1868, $1,000; in 1870, $3,000. Also $8,500, 7 per cent., for free bridge, due $1,000 in 1867; $2,500 in 1869; and $3,000 in 1871.

Minden. $2,400, 7 per cent. (bounties, 1863), due Feb. 1, 1868.

Mohawk. $3,000 (bridge across the Mohawk river), due.

Root. $10,600, 7 per cent. (bounties, 1864), due Feb. 1, 1868.

St. Johnsville. $5,000, 7 per cent. (bounties, 1865), due Feb. 1, 1868.

NEW YORK COUNTY.

New York (city). $22,142,254.01. For detail, see statement of city debt.

NIAGARA COUNTY.

No debts, in Cambria, Hartland, Lewiston, Lockport, Niagara, Pendleton, Porter, Royalton, Somerset, Wheatfield and Wilson — 11.

Newfane. $2,000 (roads and bridges), due in 1868.

ONEIDA COUNTY.

No debts, in Annsville, Augusta, Ava, Bridgewater, Camden, Florence, Floyd, Kirkland, Lee, Marcy, Marshall, New Hartford, Remsen, Rome, Steuben, Trenton, Vernon, Verona, Western and Westmoreland — 20.

Boonville. $166.33, 7 per cent. (roads and bridges, 1866), due next tax.

Deerfield. $2,200, 7 per cent. (roads and bridges, 1865, '66), due in two installments.

Paris. $3,550 (bounties), due in two installments. Also, $150,000 for railroad, bonded, and payable in twenty-five years.

Sangerfield. $65,000 (railroad debt), due.

Utica (city). $750,000. For detail, see statement of city debt.

Vienna. $45 (damage for a horse drowned).

Whitestown. $3,991.92 (roads and bridges), due January 1, 1868.

ONONDAGA COUNTY.

No debts, in Camillus, Cicero, Eldridge, Geddes, Lafayette, Lysander, Marcellus, Pompey, Spofford, Salina, Tully, and Van Buren — 12.

No returns, from De Witt.

Clay. $650 (roads, bridges, &c.), due.

Fabius. $620, 7 per cent. (bounties), due January 15, 1868.

Manlius. $900, 7 per cent. (bounties, 1864), due February 1, 1870.

Onondaga. $9,500, 7 per cent. (bridge), due in nine installments.

Otisco. $1,400, 7 per cent. (war expenses), due.

Skaneateles. $30,000, 7 per cent. (railroad debt, 1866), due in ten installments.

Syracuse. $83,000. For detail, see statement of city debt.

ONTARIO COUNTY.

No debts, in Bristol, Canadice, Canandaigua, East Bloomfield, Farmington, Gorham, Hopewell, Manchester, Richmond, Seneca, South Bristol, and West Bloomfield — 12.

Naples. $300 (local purposes), due.

Phelps. $1,000 (roads and bridges), due 1868. Also $1,620 (objects not stated), due 1868.

ORANGE COUNTY.

No debts, in Chester and Hamptonburgh — 2.

Blooming Grove. $3,248.49, 7 per cent. (bounties, 1863), due by installments to 1870.

Cornwall. $57,500, 7 per cent. (bounties, 1864, '65), due by installments to 1875.

Crawford. $6,250, 7 per cent. (bounties, 1864), due February 1, 1868.

Deer Park. $114,300, 7 per cent. (bounties, 1864), due by annual installments to 1876. Also $1,221.65, for relief of soldiers' families in 1864, '65; date of maturity not stated.

Goshen. $21,250, 7 per cent. (bounties, 1864), due in 1868, $5,650; in '69, $4,600; in '70, $4,000; in '71, $2,000; and in '72, $5,000.

Greenville. $14,500, 7 per cent. (bounties, 1864), due in 1868, $3,700; in '69, $3,700; in '70, $3,400; and in '71, $3,700.

Minisink. $15,350, 7 per cent. (bounties, 1864, '65), due in five annual installments from February, 1867.

Monroe. $55,243.62, (bounties), due in 1868, $8,100; in '69, $8,318.62; in '70, $8,100; in '71, $8,025; in '72, $8,000; in '73, $7,250; in '74, $2,000; in '75, $1,500; in '76, $1,450; and in '77, $2,500.

Montgomery. $24,420, 7 per cent. (bounties, 1864), due in three installments. Also $120,000, 7 per cent. (railroad), due in thirty years.

Mount Hope. $13,878, 7 per cent. (bounties, 1864), due $6,000 in 1868; $4,578 in '69; and $3,300 in '70.

Newburgh (city and town). $161,300, 7 per cent. (bounties, 1864, '65), due $10,700 in 1868; $19,500 in '69; $23,600 in '70; $16,800 in '71; $26,100 in '72; $22,700 in '73; $24,000 in '74; and $17,900 in '75. Also $6,700, due in 1867, for bridges.

New Windsor. $8,700, 7 per cent. (bounties, 1864), due in five years, 1868–'72. Also $1,050, 7 per cent. (roads and bridges), due in two years.

Warwick. $66,000, 7 per cent. (bounties, 1864, '65), due in six installments.

Wawayanda. $21,800, 7 per cent. (bounties, 1864, '65), due $2,500 in 1868, '69; $3,900 in '70; $3,600 in '71; $4,800 in '72; $1,900 in '73; and $2,600 in '74.

Wallkill. $88,000, 7 per cent. (bounties, 1864), due in ten installments.

ORLEANS COUNTY.

No debts, in Barre, Carlton, Clarendon, Gaines, Kendall, Murray, Shelby and Yates — 8.

Ridgeway. $2,000, 7 per cent. (roads and bridges, 1867), due in 1868.

OSWEGO COUNTY.

No debts, in Albion, Constantia, Hannibal, Hastings, Mexico, New Haven, Orwell, Oswego, Palermo, Redfield, Richland, Sandy Creek, Scriba and West Monroe — 14.

No returns, from Boylston and Williamstown — 2.

Amboy. $4.800, 7 per cent. (bounties, 1864), due in 16 years.

Granby. $2,611, per cent. (bounties, 1864), due April 1, 1868.

Oswego City. $86,500. For detail, see statement of city debt.

Parish. $9,600, 7 per cent. (bounties, 1864), due in three installments.

Schroeppel. $65,000 (Midland railroad subscription), bonds not issued.

Volney. $1,824.30 (town expenses), due in next tax levy.

OTSEGO COUNTY.

No debts, in Burlington, Cherry Valley, Edmeston and Roseboom — 4.

Butternuts. $16,205, 7 per cent. (bounties, 1863, '64, '65), due in three installments.

Decatur. $20,000, 7 per cent. (Albany and Susquehanna railroad aid), 1858.

Exeter. $90,000 (Utica and Susquehanna Valley railroad subscription), bonds not issued.

Hartwick. $50,000 (railroad debt), town not yet bonded.

Laurens. $15,350, 7 per cent. (bounties, 1864, '65), due in two installments.

Maryland. $3,750, 7 per cent. (bounties, 1864), due in 1867, $2,500; in '68, $1,250. Also, $70,000 (Albany and Susquehanna railroad bonds, 1862), due May 1, 1882.

Middlefield. $7,000 (bounties), due. Also $50,000 (railroad debt), due, and $2,000 for bridge, due.

Milford. $60,000, 7 per cent. (Albany and Susquehanna railroad bonds).

Morris. $25,735.45 (bounties), due, $11,523.25 in '68; $10,574.20 in '69; and $3,638 in '70.

New Lisbon. $16,000, 7 per cent. (bounties, 1864), due in two installments.

Oneonta. $7,538, 7 per cent. (bounties, 1864), due Feb. 1, 1868. Also, $70,000, 7 per cent. (Albany and Susquehanna railroad bonds, 1857).

Otego. $70,000, 7 per cent. (railroad bonds, 1863, '64).

Otsego. $100,000 (railroad subscription), bonds not issued.

Pittsfield. $850, 7 per cent. (bounties, 1865), due in 1868.

Plainfield. $25,000, 7 per cent. (Utica, Chenango and Susquehanna railroad subscription), bonds not issued. Debt conditional to location on a certain route.

Richfield. $8,867.50, 7 per cent. (bounties, 1864), due Jan. 1, 1868.

Springfield. $100,000 (railroad subscription), subscribed March, 1867. Conditional.

Unadilla. $6,700, 7 per cent. (bounties, 1864), due in two installments. Also $66,000, 7 per cent. (railroad bonds, 1864, '65), due $4,000 annually.

Westford. $30,000, 7 per cent. (railroad, 1862), due May 1, 1882. Also $200, due in 1868, for roads and bridges.

Worcester. $4,000 (bounties), due in 1868. Also $65,000 (railroad debt), due 1883.

PUTNAM COUNTY.

No debts, Patterson and Southeast — 2.

Carmel. $11,645.80, 7 per cent. (bounties), due in five installments.

Kent. $6,200, 7 per cent. (war expenses, 1863), due in two installments.

Phillipstown. $35,505.91, 7 per cent. (bounties, 1864), due February 1, 1879. Also $13,920, 7 per cent. (for town hall), payable within ten years.

Putnam Valley. $5,000, 7 per cent. (bounties, 1864), due in two installments.

QUEENS COUNTY.

No debts, in Hempstead, Newtown and North Hempstead — 3.

Flushing. $32,000 (town hall debt, 1862), payable by installments of $2,000 yearly. Also $6,000 (roads), due.

Jamaica. $21,000, 7 per cent. (bounties, 1864), due in seven installments. Also, $8,000, 7 per cent. (town hall), due $2,500 annually.

Oyster Bay. $53,651, 7 per cent. (bounties, 1862–65), $21,500 payable from March 1, 1869 to March 1, 1885; $32,150, due from 1868 to 1874.

RENSSELAER COUNTY.

No debts, in Brunswick — 1.

Berlin. $11,696.89, 7 per cent. (bounties, 1864), due in nine installments.

East Greenbush. $10,085, (7 per cent. (bounties, 1863), due by installments to 1884.

Grafton. $7,[illegible]98.25, 7 per cent. (bounties, 1864), payable when county bonds become due.

Greenbush. $33,000, 7 per cent. (bounties, 1864), due in 1868, $10,000; $14,000 in '69; $4,500 in '70; and $4,500 in '71.

Hoosick. $24,911.31, 7 per cent. (bounties, 1863–'64), date of maturity not specified.

Lansingburgh. $15,070.72, 7½ per cent. (bounties, 1863–'64), due by installments to 1876.

Nassau. $500, 6 per cent. (bounties, 1863), due in 1868.

North Greenbush. $16,388.19, 7 per cent. (bounties, 1864), due in 1868, $5,462.81; $5,462.69 in '69; and $5,462.69 in '70.

Petersburgh. $13,985.20, 7 per cent. (bounties, 1863–'64–'65), date of maturity not specified. $20,000 (railroad debt), pledged but no bonds issued. Also $4,000 (object not stated), date of maturity not specified.

Pittstown. $684.84, 7 per cent. (poor expenses), date of maturity not specified.

Poestenkill. $23,180.60 (bounties, 1864, '5), payable at option of loan.

Sandlake. $7,829.22, 7 per cent. (bounties, 1864), due in two installments.

Schaghticoke. $18,809, 7 per cent. (bounties, 1863–64), due in nine installments. Also $1,775.28, 7 per cent. (roads and bridges), and $187 (poor), all due.

Schodack. $36,994, 7 per cent. (bounties, 1863–4), when due not stated.

Stephentown. $8,775.82, per cent. (bounties, 1864), due in 1876. Also $30,000, 7 per cent. (railroad debt), due in thirty installments.

Troy. $976,000. For detail, see statement of city debt.

RICHMOND COUNTY.

No debts in Castleton, Southfield and Westfield — 3.

Middletown. $3,210, 7 per cent. (object not stated), due August, 1867.

Northfield. $9,000, 7 per cent. (macadamized road, 1864,) due in three installments.

ROCKLAND COUNTY.

Clarkstown. $2,583.89, 7 per cent. (bounties), due in five installments; $100 for other purposes, 1866, payable this year.

Haverstraw. $36,700, 7 per cent. (bounties, 1864), due in seven installments.

Orangetown. $62,000, 7 per cent. (bounties, 1863, '64, '65), due in 1868, $1,900; in '69, $5,570; in '70, $19,000; in '71, $2,500; in '72, $800; in '73, $1,000; and in '74, $31,300.

Ramapo. $22,768, 7 per cent. (bounties, 1863, '64), due in three installments.

Stony Point. $16,015.19, 7 per cent. (war expenses, 1862, '63, '64), $2,967.49 due in 1867; $1,530.29 in '68; $1,408.48 in '69; $2,828.81 in '70; $3,221.68 in '71; $1,731.64 in '72; and $2,336.82 in '74. Also $3,000, 7 per cent. (bridge, 1866), due in 1868.

ST. LAWRENCE COUNTY.

No debts, in De Peyster, Fine, Gouverneur, Hermon, Hopkinton, Lawrence, Lisbon, Louisville, Macomb, Massena, Parishville, Pierrepont, Rossie and Russell — 14.

No returns, from Colton and Pitcairn — 2.

Brasher. $8,678, 7 per cent. (bounties, 1864), $1,600 due in '67; $2,678 in '68; and $4,400 in '70.

Canton. $1,500, 7 per cent. (bounties), due March 1, 1868. Also $8,000 for other purposes, due in two installments.

De Kalb. $7,800, 7 per cent. (bounties, 1864), due March 1, 1868, $4,700; in '69, $1,100; and in '70, $2,000.

Edwards. $600, 7 per cent. (bounties), due March 1, 1868.

Fowler. $2,000, 7 per cent. (bounties, 1864), due in 1867. $650 (roads and bridges), due in 1867.

Hammond. $1,456, 7 per cent. (bounties, 1864), due January 1, 1868.

Madrid. $6,600, 7 per cent. (war expenses, 1863), due in 1867.

Morristown. $1,300, 7 per cent. (bounties, 1864), due in 1867.

Norfolk. $1,500, 7 per cent. (bounties, 1863, '64), and $4,000 (roads and bridges), all due in December, 1867.

Oswegatchie. $19,500, 7 per cent. (iron bridge, under act of 1866, chapter 240), due in 1868, '69, '70, $3,000 each; in 1871, '72, '73, $1,500 each; and in 1874, '75, '76, $2.000 each.

Potsdam. $8.700, 7 per cent. (bounties, 1864), due in 1870. Also $35,000, 7 per cent. (foundation of a normal school), due in five installments.

Stockholm. $21,929.85, 7 per cent. (bounties, 1864, '65); $3,931 due in '68; $3.300 in '69; $2,700 in '70; and $11,998.85 in '71.

Waddington. $1,400, 7 per cent. (bridge, 1866), due January 1, 1868.

SARATOGA COUNTY.

No debts, in Clifton Park — 1.

No returns, from Day — 1.

Ballston. $19,758.76, 7 per cent. (bounties, 1864), due in three installments. Also for roads and bridges $150, due.

Charlton. $10,627.70, 7 per cent. (bounties, 1864), due in three installments.

Corinth. $14,559.10, 7 per cent. (bounties, 1864), due in three installments.

Edinburgh. $9,508.41, 7 per cent. (bounties, 1863,) due by the year 1870, $7,708.41, and by 1873, $1,800.

Galway. $16,002.58, 7 per cent. (bounties, 1864), due in three installments.

Greenfield. $15,809.39, 7 per cent. (bounties, 1864), due in three installments.

Hadley. $8,472.02, 7 per cent. (bounties, 1864), due in three installments.

Malta. $15,134.66, 7 per cent. (bounties, 1864), due in three installments. Also $200 for other purposes.

Milton. $36,955.18, 7 per cent. (bounties, 1864), due in three installments. Also, object not stated, $5,250, 7 per cent., due.

Moreau. $21,177.11, 7 per cent. (bounties, 1864), due in annual installments. Also, object not stated, $535, 7 per cent., due April 1, 1868.

Halfmoon. $24,000 (bounties), date of maturity not specified.

Northumberland. $1,696.91, 7 per cent. (bounties 1863), due February 15, 1868.

Providence. $6,972.25, 7 per cent. (bounties), due in three installments.

Saratoga. $250, 7 per cent. (bounties, 1863), due February 15, 1868.

Saratoga Springs. $88,500 (bounties), due in fifteen installments, 1868, 1882.

Stillwater. $22,511.43, 7 per cent. (bounties, 1864), due in three installments.

Waterford. $25.075.56, 7 per cent. (bounties), due in three installments.

Wilton. $6,120, 7 per cent. (bounties, 1864), due, $1,338.34 in 1868; $1,326.25 in '69; and $3,455.51 in '70.

SCHENECTADY COUNTY.

Duanesburgh. $5,833.83, 7 per cent. (bounties, 1862, '63), due in two installments. Also $30,000 (railroad), in litigation, not yet decided.

Glenville. $38,600, 7 per cent. (bounties, 1863, '64, '65), due in '68, '69, '70, each $52,000; in '71, '72, '73, each $3,000; and in '74 to '80, inclusive, each $2,000.

Niskayuna. $6,000, 7 per cent. (bounties, 1864, '65), due February 1st, 1868, $500; in '69, $2,000; in '70, $1,500; and in '71, $2,000.

Princetown. $13,000, 7 per cent. (bounties, 1864), due in 1868, $4,000; in '69 to '74, $1,000 each; in '75, '76, $1,500 each.

Rotterdam. $5,000, 7 per cent. (bounties), due February, 1868.

Schenectady (city). $68,000. For detail, see statement of city debt.

SCHOHARIE COUNTY.

No debts, in Conesville, Fulton and Jefferson — 3.

Blenheim. $62.67, 7 per cent. (object not stated), due.

Broome. $17,871, 7 per cent. (bounties), due in 1868, $4,029; in '69, $4,119; in '70, $3,088; in '71, $2,913; in '72, $2,438, and in '73, $1,284. Total war debt originally $87,647.23.

Carlisle. $8,400, 7 per cent. (bounties, 1864, '65), due in two installments, 1869, '70.

Cobleskill. $60,000, 7 per cent. (railroad, 1858,), due in twenty installments, with interest from 1867.

Esperance. $24,878, 7 per cent. (bounties), due in seven installments to 1874. Also $30,000, 7 per cent. (railroad bonds, 1862), due in twenty installments.

Gilboa. $2,200, 7 per cent. (bounties, 1864), due in 1868. The town has consented to bond itself for the Oswego and Rondout railroad, but has not done so. The proposed amount is $20,000.

Middleburgh. $6,510, 7 per cent. (bounties, 1864), due as follows: $4,200 in 1868; $600 in 1869, and $1,710 in 1870. Railroad debt of $50,000 proposed, but not contracted at date of report. For poor, $350. For roads and bridges, $250, due.

Richmondville. $50,000 (railroad debt), due within eight or ten years.

Schoharie. $2,600, 7 per cent. (bounties, 1864, '65), $2,300 due in 1865, and $300 in 1874. Also $30,000 for railroad, at 7 per cent. (1863), due May 1, 1882, and $29,000 at 7 per cent. for railroad (1863), due in sums of $1,000, annually.

Seward. $3,000, 7 per cent. (bounties, 1864), due 1868. Railroad debt $30,000, due in twenty years; contracted in 1858. Also $500 for roads and bridges, due in 1868.

Sharon. $11,975, 7 per cent., (bounties, 1864). Due in 1868, $4,875; $500 in 1869, and $6,600 in 1872.

Summit. $3,000, 7 per cent. (bounties, 1864), due. The credit of the town has been pledged for $25,000 for railroad purposes, but the bonds have not been issued, and the matter is now in litigation.

Wright. $13,550, seven per cent. (bounties, 1864), due in two installments.

SCHUYLER COUNTY.

Catharine. $4,400, 7 per cent. (bounties, 1864), due in two installments. Also $194, for roads and bridges.

Cayuta. $600, 7 per cent. (bounties, 1864), due April 1, 1868. Also $50, for roads and bridges.

Dix. $22,750 (bounties, 1864, '65), due in 1868, $4,900; in '69, $4,600; in '70, $4,800; in '71, $2,400; in '72, $2,400; in '73, $2,350; and in '74, $1,300.

Hector. $10,998, 7 per cent. (bounties, 1863), due in '67, $6,093; in '68, $4,815.

Montour. $6,000, 7 per cent. (bounties, 1864), due in 1867, '68, each $2,100; in '69, $1,800.

Orange. $10,079.11, 7 per cent. (bounties, 1864), due annually till 1874. Also $300, for roads and bridges, due.

Reading. $6,648, 7 per cent. (bounties, 1863, '64). due in '68, $2,374; in '69, $2,474; in '70, $900; and in '71, $900. Also $2,773, 7 per cent. (roads and bridges), and $1,641.70, 7 per cent. (object not stated), due.

Tyrone. $7,800, 7 per cent. (bounties, 1863, '64), due in six installments.

SENECA COUNTY.

No debts, in Tyre — 1.

Covert. $5,000 (bounties), due in 1868.

Fayette. $22,000, 7 per cent. (bounties, 1864, '65), $18,900 due in four installments, 1868–71; and $3,100 due in three installments, 1869–71.

Junius. $10,300, 7 per cent. (bounties, 1864), due March 1, 1868.

Lodi. $2,200, 7 per cent. (bounties, 1863), date of payment not reported.

Ovid. $10,943, 7 per cent. (bounties, 1864, '65), due in three installments.

Romulus. $4,700, 7 per cent. (bounties, 1863, '64), due in 1868. Also $750 (roads and bridges), due in 1868.

Seneca Falls. $56,600 (bounties), due in 1868, $16,000; in '69, $20,000; in '70, $16,600; and in '71, $4,000.

Varick. $25,440, 7 per cent. (bounties, 1864), due $12,900 in '69; $12,540 in '70.

Waterloo. $17,743.33, 7 per cent. (bounties, 1863, '64, '65), due March 1, 1868. Also $1,000, object not stated, due in 1874.

STEUBEN COUNTY.

No debts, in Addison, Erwin, Hartsville, Hornellsville, and West Union — 5.

No returns, from Bath, Cohocton, Hornby, Savona and Wayne — 4.

Avoca. $13,000, 7 per cent. (bounties, 1866), due in two installments, March 1, 1868, '69.

Bradford. $5,500, 7 per cent. (bounties, 1864), due March 1, 1868.

Cameron. $11,450, 7 per cent. (bounties), due March 1, 1868, '69.

Campbell. $11,000, 7 per cent. (bounties, 1864), due in two installments. Also $500 (roads and bridges, 1867), date of maturity not specified.

Canisteo. $200 (roads and bridges), date of maturity not specified.

Caton. $18,200, 7 per cent. (bounties, 1864), due in two installments.

Corning. $79,733.82, 7 per cent. (bounties, 1864), due March 1, 1867, $37,733.82; in '68, $22,000; and in '69, $20,000.

Dansville. $10,000 (bounties), due in two installments.

Fremont. $100 (repairing roads and bridges), due 1867.

Greenwood. $6,000 (bounties), date of maturity not specified.

Howard. $13,855.82, 7 per cent. (bounties, 1864), due March 1, 1868.

Jasper. $10,000, 7 per cent. (bounties, 1866), due 1868.

Lindley. $168.24, 7 per cent. (bounties, 1864), due March 1, 1868. Also $3,000 (object not stated), due March 1, 1868.

Prattsburgh. $5,000, 7 per cent. (bounties, 1864), due March 1, 1868.

Pultney. $16,000, 7 per cent. (bounties, 1864), due in two installments.

Rathbone. $10,116.78, 7 per cent. (bounties, 1864), due in two installments. Also $1,765 (bridges), due.

Thurston. $8,000, 7 per cent. (bounties, 1865), due in two installments.

Troupsburgh. $32,000, 7 per cent. (bounties, 1864), due March 1, 1868, $16,000; and in '69, $16,000.

Tuscarora. $7,000, 7 per cent. (bounties), due in two installments.

Urbana. $18,000, 7 per cent. (bounties, 1866), due March 1, 1868, $11,500; and in '69, $6,500.

Wayland. $14,300, 7 per cent. (bounties, 1864), due in 1868, $13,000, and $13,000 in '69.

Wheeler. $2,000, 7 per cent. (bounties, 1864), due March 1, 1868.

Woodhull. $6,000, 7 per cent. (bounties, 1864), due in two installments,

SUFFOLK COUNTY.

No debts, in Shelter Island — 1.

Brookhaven. $30,203, 7 per cent. (bounties, 1864), due in 1868, $6,100; in '69, $6,585; in '70, $6,545; in '71, $5,795; in '72, $5,178.

East Hampton. $850, 7 per cent. (poor expenses, 1866, '67), due in 1868.

Huntington. $60,109, 7 per cent. (bounties, 1863, '64), due in seven installments.

Islip. $31,500, 7 per cent. (bounties, 1864), due in eleven installments.

Riverhead. $44,600 (bounties, 1863, '64), $39,000 at 7 per cent., and $5,600 at 5 per cent.

Smithtown. $6,500, 7 per cent. (bounties, 1864), due April 1, 1868.

Southampton. $58,637.94, 5 and 6 per cent. (bounties and other war expenses). Of this $2,500, due 1868; $15,000 in five installments, 1869–73, bonds of 1864; $3,568 in '68; $3,300 in '69; $3,200 in '70; $4,200 in '71, '72, '73 and '74 each; $726.94 uncertain. Supervisor's notes for $10,611 at 5 per cent., given July, 1864, and due in 1867, '68.

Southold. $18,200, 7 per cent. (war debt), installments from 1868 to '72 inclusive. Due in five installments.

SULLIVAN COUNTY.

No debts, in Callicoon, Lumberland, Neversink and Thompson — 4.

No returns, from Rockland and Tusten — 2.

Bethel. $5,764, 7 per cent. (bounties, 1864), due in three installments.

Cochecton. $12,000, 7 per cent. (bounties, 1864), due in 1868, $6,000; in '69, $5,000; and in '70, $1,000.

Fallsburgh. $840, 7 per cent. (bounties, 1864), date of maturity not specified.

Forrestburgh. $7,817, 7 per cent. (war debt, 1864), due in three installments.

Fremont. $500, 7 per cent. (bounties, 1864), due March 1, 1868.

Highland. $9,713, 7 per cent. (bounties, 1864), due in four installments

Liberty. $2,000, 7 per cent. (bounties, 1865)) due March 1, 1868. Also $108,500 (for railroad), pledged, but bonds not issued; doubtful.

Mamakating. $30,377, 7 per cent. (bounties, 1864), due March 1, 1868, $16,182, and $14,195 in '69.

TIOGA COUNTY.

No debts, in Owego, Richford, Spencer and Tioga — 4.

No returns, from Nichols — 1.

Barton. $850, 7 per cent. (bounties), due March 1, 1868; $300 for bridges, due.

Berkshire. $22,000 (Southern Central Railroad), time of maturity of this debt not stated.

Candor. $8,250, 7 per cent. (bounties, 1864), due February 1, 1868.

Newark Valley. $4,000, 7 per cent. (bounties, September 12, 1864), due $600 in 1867; $1,400 in '68; $1,100 in '69; and $900 in '70. The credit of the town has been pledged $45,000 for Southern Central railroad, but no bonds issued.

TOMPKINS COUNTY.

No debts, in Danby, Ithaca, Lansing and Dryden — 4.

No returns, from Enfield — 1.

Caroline. $6,677.60, 7 per cent. (bounties), due in 1868.

Groton. $7,761.72, 7 per cent. (bounties, 1864), due February 1, 1869. Also $50,000 (for railroad) pledged, bonds not yet issued, and $150 for support of the poor, not stated when due.

Newfield. $12,696.25, 7 per cent. (bounties), due in 1868.

Ulysses. $1,500, 7 per cent. (highway and bridges), due in two installments.

ULSTER COUNTY.

No debts, in Esopus, Hardenburgh, Lloyd, Marbletown, Marlborough, Plattekill and Rosendale — 7.

No returns, from Hurley, Saugerties and Wawarsing — 3.

Deming. $340 (roads and bridges), due March 1st, 1868.

Gardiner. $83,400 (railroad debt), pledged, but no bonds issued.

Kingston. $600,000 (railroad debt), pledged. Bonds not issued.

New Paltz. $100,000 (railroad debt), pledged. Bonds not issued.

Olive. $75,000, seven per cent. (railroad debt, 1867). Consent of inhabitants obtained. Bonds not issued.

Rochester. $1,700 (bounties, 1863,) contested, now in litigation.

Shandaken. $47,538 (railroad debt). Pledged, but not paid.

Shawangunk. $106 813.65 railroad debt. Pledged, but not paid.

Woodstock. $750, 7 per cent. (roads and bridges, 1866), due February 15th, 1868.

WARREN COUNTY.

No debts, in Horicon and Queensburgh — 2.

No returns, from Stony Creek.

Bolton. $500, 7 per cent. (bounties, 1862), due in 1868, $75, (other war expenses, 1864), due in 1868.

Caldwell. $6,776.48 (bounties, 1864), due in two installments.

Chester. $370, 7 per cent. (bounties, 1864), due; $250, 7 per cent. (roads and bridges, 1866), due in 1868.

Hague. $500, 7 per cent. (bounties, 1864), due in 1865.

Johnsburgh. $15,045, 7 per cent. (bounties, 1864), due in 1867 $1,500; $5,848 in 1868, and $7,697 in 1869.

Luzerne. $1,761.57, 7 per cent. (bounties 1864), due in 1867, $50; in 1868, $1,141.57, and in 1869, $570.

Thurman. $3,200, 7 per cent. (bounties, 1864), due March 1, 1868. Also $150 (object not stated), due.

Warrensburgh. $9,500, 7 per cent. (bounties, 1864), due in three installments.

WASHINGTON COUNTY.

No debts, in Dresden, Hampton, Hartford, Jackson, Putnam and White Creek — 6.

Argyle. $33,800, 7 per cent, (bounties, 1864), due, $14,000 in '68; $7,100 in '69; and $12,700 in '70.

Cambridge. $26,200, 7 per cent. (bounties) due, $10,000 in '68; $12,000 in '69; and $4,200 in '70.

Easton. $38,050, 7 per cent. (bounties, 1864), due, $27,550 in '68; and $10,500 in '69.

Fort Ann. $42,050, 7 per cent. (bounties, 1864, '65), due, $4,700 in '68; $4,750 in '69; $7,000 in '70; $11,000 in '71; $4,000 in '72; $2,500 in '73; and $3,000 in '74.

Fort Edward. $34,150, 7 per cent. (bounties, 1864, '65), due, $4.700 in '68; $4,750 in '69; $5,000 in '70; $7,000 in '71; $8,000 in '72; and $4,700 in '73.

Granville. $3,000, 7 per cent. (bounties), due in 1868.

Greenwich. $47,485, 7 per cent. (bounties, 1865), due, $13,900 in '68; $13,685 in '69; $10,000 in '70; and $9,900 in '71.

Hebron. $11,700, 7 per cent. (bounties, 1864), due in 1868.

Kingsbury. $35,300, 7 per cent. (bounties), due, $19,400 in '68; $12,200 in '69; and $3,700 in '70.

Salem. $14,700, 7 per cent. (bounties), due in 1868.

Whitehall. $18,000, 7 per cent. (bounties, 1864), due March 1, 1868.

WAYNE COUNTY.

No debts, in Butler, Lyons, Macedon, Marion, Ontario, Palmyra, Rose, Savannah, Sodus, Walworth and Williamson — 11.

Arcade. $9,400 (bounties). Date of maturity not given.

Galen. $41,675 (bounties), $14,594 (war expenses), due in 1868, $7,750 (bridge), due in 1868.

Huron. $9,500, 7 per cent. (bounties, 1864, '65). Due in 1868, $7,100, and in 1869 $2,400.

Wolcott. $250 (roads and bridges, 1866), due February 1, 1868.

WESTCHESTER COUNTY.

No debt, in North Salem, Somers and White Plains — 3.

No returns, from Pelham, Scarsdale, Westchester and West Farms — 4.

Bedford $31,222, 7 per cent. (bounties, 1864), last installment due in 1875.

Cortlandt. $9,700, 7 per cent. (bounties, 1864), $3,200 due in 1868; $2,500 in '69; $2,900 in '70; and $1,100 in '71. Also $3,500, 7 per cent, for a jail, due in 1868.

Eastchester. $83,700, 7 per cent. (bounties, 1863, '64), due from 1868 to 1875.

Greensburgh. $68,000, 7 per cent. (bounties, 1864), payable in installments to 1881.

Harrison. $17,250, 7 per cent. (bounties, 1864, '65), due in installments, last in 1877.

Lewisboro. $17,300, 7 per cent. (bounties), due in 1868 and '69, each $2,400; and in 1870, '71, '72, '73, '74, each $2,500.

Mamaroneck. $5,374, 7 per cent. (bounties, 1864), due in 1869, '70, '71, '73.

Morrisania. $26,700, 7 per cent. (bounties, 1863, '64), due in nine installments. Also $425 for roads, &c.

Mount Pleasant. $22,000, 7 per cent. (bounties, 1863, '64, '65), due $1,000 in 1867; $2,000 in '68; $2,500 in '69; $3,000 in '70; $2,000 in '71; $2,000 in 72; $2,000 in '73; $1,500 in '74; $3,000 in '75; and $3,000 in '76.

Newcastle. $8,335, 7 per cent. (bounties, 1864), due in five installments, ending in 1872.

New Rochelle. $27,500, 7 per cent. (bounties, 1864), due in seven installments.

North Castle. $4,315, 7 per cent. (bounties, 1864, '65), due $515 in '68; $1,000 in '69; $500 in '70; $500 in '71; and $1,800 in '72.

Ossining. $25,500, 7 per cent. (bounties, 1863, '64, '65), due in eight installments. Also $12,000, 7 per cent. (roads and bridges, 1861), due in twelve installments.

Pelham. $11,027.67 (bounties), due $1,962.18 in each of the following years: 1876, '77, '78, '79, '80; and $1,216.59 in 1881. Also $6,700 (object not stated), due January 1, 1868, $2,500; in '69, $2,400; and in '70, $2,000.

Poundridge. $18,500, 7 per cent. (bounties, 1863, '64), due $1,000 annually; also $1,000 for war expenses; date of maturity not specified.

Rye. $67,000, 6 per cent. (bounties, 1863, '64), due, $17,000 in '67, the balance in six installments.

Westchester. $62,000, 7 per cent. (bounties, 1863, '64, '65), due in thirty-one installments.

Yonkers. $290,834, 7 per cent. (bounties, 1863, '64), due in ten installments. Also $60,000 (roads, 1865, '66, 67), due in ten installments.

Yorktown. $2,001.08, 7 per cent. (bounties, 1864), due $100 in '68; 351.08 in '69; $500 in '71; $450 in '72; $400 in 73; and $200 in 74.

WYOMING COUNTY.

No debts, in Arcade, Attica, Covington, Castile, Eagle, Gainesville, Genesee Falls, Middlebury, Orangeville, Perry, Pike, Sheldon and Warsaw — 17.

No returns, from China — 1.

Bennington. $1,000 (roads and bridges), due in 1867.

Java. $3,850, 7 per cent. (bounties, 1864), due in 1868.

Wethersfield. $200 (roads and bridges), due in 1867.

YATES COUNTY.

No debts, in Barrington, Benton, Potter and Torrey — 4.

Italy. $100 (roads and bridges, 1867), due.

Jerusalem. $662.32 (for roads and bridges, except $100 for poor).

Middlesex. $350 (roads and bridges), due in 1867.

Milo. $600 (object not stated, 1867), due.

Starkey. $5,898.38, 7 per cent. (bounties, 1864), due in 1868.

Summary of City and Town Debts.

COUNTIES.	Towns with no debt.	Towns not reported.	Bounties to volunteers.	Other war expenses.	Railroad construction.
Albany,	5	..	....	....	....
Allegany,	19	..	$55,271 59	....	$800,000 00
Broome,	7	..	46,029 82	....	100,000 00
Cattaraugus,	20	1	10,544 72	....	18,000 00
Cayuga,	12	..	18,824 06	....	193,250 00
Chautauqua,	18	..	5,900 00	....	170,000 00
Chemung,	...	..	332,219 25	$9,174 91	....
Chenango,	1	..	279,347 17	1,200 00	911,348 54
Clinton,	3	1	28,790 15	....	....
Columbia,	8	1	55,475 00	10,000 00	155,000 00
Cortland,	...	..	339,970 00	....	38,000 00
Delaware,	3	1	110,428 45	....	606,820 00
Dutchess,	12	1	176,400 00	....	....
Erie,	18	..	68,454 69	56,964 63	150,000 00
Essex,	...	..	177,189 49	15,510 00	....
Franklin,	2	2	130,063 75	....	....
Fulton,	2	1	73,326 00	....	275,674 00
Genesee,	4	..	83,929 00	....	....
Greene,	8	1	....	....	10,000 00
Hamilton,	3	2	13,721 00	....	....
Herkimer,	5	..	108,525 59	13,308 00	50,000 00
Jefferson,	2	..	142,254 48	9,527 00	150,000 00
Kings,	2	2	730,000 00	....	....
Lewis,	6	1	6,250 00	81 22	180,000 00
Livingston,	13	2	....	254 00	100,000 00
Madison,	9	..	....	....	387,300 00
Monroe,	10	2	367,223 50	80,050 00	252,000 00
Montgomery,	1	..	175,527 80	....	....
New York,	...	..	....	....	....
Niagara,	11	..	....	....	....
Oneida,	20	..	3,550 00	....	215,000 00
Onondaga,	12	1	1,520 00	1,400 00	30,000 00
Ontario,	12	..	....	....	....
Orange,	2	..	671,750 11	....	120,000 00
Orleans,	8	..	....	....	....
Oswego,	14	2	17,011 00	....	65,000 00
Otsego,	4	..	111,995 95	....	856,000 00
Putnam,	2	..	52,151 71	6,200 00	....
Queens,	3	..	74,651 00	....	....
Rensselaer,	1	..	228,524 20	....	271,000 00
Richmond,	3	..	....	....	12,210 00
Rockland,	...	..	140,067 08	....	....
St. Lawrence,	14	2	53,963 85	8,100 00	....
Saratoga,	1	1	352,015 30	....	....
Schenectady,	...	..	113,433 83	....	30,000 00
Schoharie,	3	..	93,984 00	....	324,000 00
Schuyler,	...	..	69,185 11	....	....
Seneca,	1	..	154,926 33	....	....
Steuben,	5	4	300,574 66	....	....
Suffolk,	1	4	250,099 94	....	....
Sullivan,	4	3	61,194 00	7,817 00	108,500 00
Tioga,	4	1	13,100 00	....	67,600 00
Tompkins,	3	1	27,134 85	....	50,000 00
Ulster,	7	3	1,700 00	....	1,094,008 15
Warren,	2	1	37,203 05	75 00	....
Washington,	6	..	299,335 00	....	....
Wayne,	11	..	60,575 00	14,494 00	....
Westchester,	3	4	798,208 55	1,000 00	....
Wyoming,	14	1	3,840 00	....	....
Yates,	4	..	5,898 38	....	....
Total,	368	46	$7,533,248 36	$235,155 76	$7,790,710 69

Summary of City and Town Debts.—(Continued).

COUNTIES.	Roads and bridges.	Public buildings.	City debts not included in other columns.	Miscellaneous objects.	Total.
Albany,	$1,750 75	....	$1,229,500 00	$750,850 00	$2,050,250 75
Allegany,	1,515 00	....	....	433 00	57,219 59
Broome,	7,900 00	....	....	....	153,929 82
Cattaraugus,	650 00	$18,000 00	....	1,000 00	48,194 72
Cayuga,	3,333 33	....	100,000 00	....	315,407 39
Chautauqua,	887 30	....	....	4,026 28	180,813 58
Chemung,	250 00	....	55,451 72	1,101 00	398,196 88
Chenango,	....	....	....	....	1,176,895 71
Clinton,	1,013 29	....	....	....	29,803 44
Columbia,	500 00	....	79,000 00	4,400 00	304,375 00
Cortland,	250 00	....	....	....	378,220 00
Delaware,	....	....	....	160 00	717,398 45
Dutchess,	86 00	....	397,097 70	....	573,583 70
Erie,	2,196 00	162,000 00	184,000 00	....	623,615 32
Essex,	1,290 94	....	....	....	193,990 43
Franklin,	2,175 00	....	....	....	132,238 75
Fulton,	1,735 00	10,000 00	....	....	350,734 00
Genesee,	....	....	....	500 00	94,429 00
Greene,	1,689 22	....	....	50 00	11,739 22
Hamilton,	3,850 00	....	....	730 00	18,301 00
Herkimer,	7,499 99	....	....	....	179,386 28
Jefferson,	16,270 36	....	....	4,436 49	322,488 33
Kings,	....	105,000 00	10,278,419 92	2,000 00	11,115,419 92
Lewis,	699 46	....	....	500 00	187,530 68
Livingston,	9,000 00	....	....	500 00	109,754 00
Madison,	1,400 00	....	....	309 79	389,009 79
Monroe,	122,015 21	30,000 00	193,000 00	1,200 00	1,045,488 71
Montgomery,	11,845 59	....	....	172 50	187,545 89
New York,	....	....	22,142,245 01	....	22,142,245 01
Niagara,	2,000 00	....	....	....	2,000 00
Oneida,	6,358 25	....	750,000 00	45 00	974,953 25
Onondaga,	10,150 00	....	83,000 00	....	126,070 00
Ontario,	1,000 00	....	....	1,920 00	2,920 00
Orange,	7,750 00	....	....	1,221 65	800,721 76
Orleans,	2,000 00	....	....	....	2,000 00
Oswego,	12,324 30	....	76,000 00	....	170,335 30
Otsego,	2,200 00	....	....	....	970,195 95
Putnam,	....	13,920 00	....	....	72,271 71
Queens,	....	40,000 00	....	....	114,651 00
Rensselaer,	5,775 28	....	755,000 00	871 84	1,261,171 32
Richmond,	....	....	....	....	12,210 00
Rockland,	3,000 00	....	....	100 00	143,167 08
St. Lawrence,	25,550 00	....	....	43,000 00	130,613 85
Saratoga,	150 00	....	....	835 00	352,015 30
Schenectady,	....	6,000 00	17,000 00	....	166,433 83
Schoharie,	750 00	....	....	422 67	419,146 67
Schuyler,	3,317 00	....	....	1,641 71	74,143 82
Seneca,	750 00	....	....	1,000 00	156,676 33
Steuben,	2,465 00	....	....	3,100 00	306,139 66
Suffolk,	....	....	....	850 00	250,949 94
Sullivan,	....	....	....	....	177,511 00
Tioga,	300 00	....	....	....	81,000 00
Tompkins,	1,500 00	....	....	150 00	78,784 85
Ulster,	1,090 00	....	....	....	1,096,798 15
Warren,	250 00	....	....	150 00	37,678 05
Washington,	....	....	....	....	299,335 00
Wayne,	8,000 00	....	....	....	83,069 00
Westchester,	114,500 00	3,500 00	....	6,700 00	923,908 55
Wyoming,	1,200 00	....	....	....	5,040 00
Yates,	1,012 32	....	....	700 00	7,610 70
Total,	$413,194 59	$388,240 00	$36,339,714 35	$835,076 93	$52,787,721 42

Dates of Maturity of Town and City Debts.

COUNTIES.	Dates of maturity not given.	1867.	1868.	1869.	1870.
Albany,	$5,275 75	$20,200 00	$21,625 00	$10,000 00	$336,000 00
Allegany,	2,331 00	10,450 00	27,102 59	8,668 00	8,668 00
Broome,	100,000 00	....	36,158 82	9,121 00	7,400 00
Cattaraugus,	19,550 00	2,450 00	7,194 72	5,500 00	2,000 00
Cayuga,	227,050 00	6,563 11	13,433 17	3,861 11	2,750 00
Chautauqua,	100,887 30	3,026 28	5,800 00	6,100 00	2,500 00
Chemung,	21,917 63	3,810 00	86,286 25	75,295 50	63,597 50
Chenango,	886,348 54	305 00	95,901 80	76,928 24	59,763 43
Clinton,	350 00	....	8,756 44	1,250 00	6,197 00
Columbia,	274,200 00	4,400 00	18,775 00	2,000 00	2,000 00
Cortland,	38,000 00	....	77,950 00	62,100 00	67,200 00
Delaware,	606,970 00	15,515 00	58,836 79	24,563 33	12,513 33
Dutchess,	86 00	....	24,350 00	36,450 00	23,450 00
Erie,	1,000 00	18,271 00	21,344 32	12,000 00	3,000 00
Essex,	59,089 90	5,650 39	57,137 83	54,003 79	8,579 72
Franklin,	7,261 00	2,060 00	33,941 94	22,691 94	14,891 94
Fulton,	277,024 00	4,770 00	52,571 00	7,670 00	8,700 00
Genesee,	500 00	....	37,943 02	25,842 99	23,142 99
Greene,	1,050 00	....	1,326 40	250 00	112 82
Hamilton,	16,301 00	2,000 00	....	....	....
Herkimer,	75,633 88	1,000 00	38,942 40	15,456 66	10,166 66
Jefferson,	228,499 17	11,065 63	27,696 82	19,903 86	13,938 56
Kings,	....	59,000 00	170,100 00	169,069 92	46,750 00
Lewis,	108,230 00	169 46	7,131 22	....	....
Livingston,	109,000 00	....	754 00	....	....
Madison.	329,009 79	....	3,000 00	3,000 00	3,000 00
Monroe,	....	103,000 00	131,988 71	146,000 00	72,000 00
Montgomery,	78,796 89	3,000 00	60,249 00	17,000 00	17,500 00
New York,	22,142,254 01	....	....	....	....
Niagara,	....	....	2,000 00	....	....
Oneida,	765,045 00	....	7,033 25	2,875 00	....
Onondaga,	10,000 00	....	11,670 00	8,500 00	9,400 00
Ontario,	2,920 00	....	....	....	....
Orange,	186,221 65	9,770 00	87,265 84	87,562 45	102,189 32
Orleans,	....	....	2,000 00	....	....
Oswego,	69,800 00	....	17,135 30	12,700 00	12,700 00
Otsego,	810,000 00	6,500 00	54,655 42	50,107 53	9,039 66
Putnam,	13,920 00	....	7,929 16	7,929 16	2,329 16
Queens,	6,000 00	....	13,093 00	14,357 80	14,357 70
Rensselaer,	287,330 65	11,500 00	45,383 31	110,377 30	32,962 69
Richmond,	....	3,210 00	3,000 00	3,000 00	3,000 00
Rockland,	....	7,367 49	18,336 40	18,514 59	36,924 93
St. Lawrence,	....	26,350 00	31,265 00	18,400 00	18,100 00
Saratoga,	38,908 41	....	82,987 97	76,444 83	76,974 09
Schenectady,	36,000 00	....	64,616 91	13,116 92	9,700 00
Schoharie,	120,000 00	62 67	47,233 00	27,748 00	16,352 00
Schuyler,	19,520 82	8,493 00	20,006 00	11,074 00	5,700 00
Seneca,	2,200 00	....	62,866 00	42,305 99	38,546 00
Steuben,	5,405 82	37,833 82	154,032 02	108,808 00	....
Suffolk,	45,326 94	5,311 00	39,840 63	27,975 63	27,835 63
Sullivan,	119,053 00	....	29,210 01	23,721 00	5,526 99
Tioga,	67,600 00	900 00	10,500 00	1,100 00	900 00
Tompkins,	50,150 00	....	20,123 85	8,511 00	....
Ulster,	1,095,708 15	....	1,090 00	....	....
Warren,	150 00	1,920 00	17,619 48	14,821 91	3,166 66
Washington,	....	....	141,650 00	64,985 00	42,600 00
Wayne,	51,075 00	....	29,594 00	2,400 00	....
Westchester,	797,265 00	18,000 00	17,015 00	19,151 08	17,600 00
Wyoming,	....	1,200 00	3,840 00	....	....
Yates,	1,712 32	....	5,898 38	....	....
Total,	$30,317,928 62	$414,493 85	$2,175,187 17	$1,521,213 53	$1,301,726 78

Dates of Maturity of Town and City Debts — (Continued).

COUNTIES.	1871.	1872.	1873.	1874.	1875.
Albany,	$505,000 00	$71,000 00	$20,000 00	$19,000 00	....
Broome,	1,250 00	....	....	....	....
Cattaraugus,	2,000 00	2,000 00	1,500 00	1,500 00	$1,500 00
Cayuga,	2,750 00	2,750 00	2,750 00	2,750 00	2,750 00
Chautauqua,	2,500 00	2,500 00	2,500 00	2,500 00	2,500 00
Chemung,	43,595 50	35,909 50	32,991 00	34,794 00	....
Chenango,	33,957 10	29,795 85	27,395 75	7,250 00	7,250 00
Clinton,	1,250 00	1,000 00	1,000 00	1,000 00	1,000 00
Columbia,	2,000 00	1,000 00	....	....	....
Cortland,	64,200 00	69,770 00	9,000 00	....	....
Dutchess,	22,450 00	22,450 00	27,450 00	25,450 00	25,450 00
Erie,	32,000 00	160,000 00	95,000 00	26,000 00	1,000 00
Essex,	1,964 71	2,964 70	2,034 70	464 70	....
Franklin,	12,391 93	1,600 00	2,100 00	2,100 00	5,533 93
Genesee,	1,000 00	1,000 00	1,000 00	1,000 00	1,000 00
Herkimer,	7,426 68	6,760 00	4,000 00	4,000 00	4,000 00
Jefferson,	7,538 57	3,798 57	3,028 58	1,000 00	1,000 00
Kings,	218,500 00	155,000 00	107,000 00	152,000 00	249,000 00
Madison,	3,000 00	3,000 00	3,000 00	3,000 00	3,000 00
Monroe,	22,000 00	17,000 00	272,000 00	3,000 00	3,000 00
Montgomery,	3,000 00	....	....	....	....
Onondaga,	8,500 00	6,500 00	6,500 00	4,000 00	9,000 00
Orange,	78,622 50	85,327 50	71,537 50	57,287 50	48,087 50
Oswego,	6,000 00	7,000 00	3,000 00	3,000 00	3,000 00
Putnam,	2,329 16	2,329 16	....	....	....
Queens,	12,357 70	11,857 70	11,857 70	11,857 70	4,264 70
Rensselaer,	27,500 00	23,500 00	23,000 00	76,000 00	38,000 00
Rockland,	13,238 45	7,348 41	6,800 00	33,636 80	....
St. Lawrence,	20,498 85	8,500 00	1,500 00	2,000 00	2,000 00
Saratoga,	8,150 00	6,500 00	4,000 00	3,600 00	8,600 00
Schenectady,	8,000 00	6,000 00	6,000 00	6,000 00	6,500 00
Schoharie,	14,467 00	20,592 00	12,838 00	11,854 00	8,000 00
Schuyler,	3,300 00	2,400 00	2,350 00	1,300 00	....
Seneca,	9,758 34	....	....	1,000 00	....
Suffolk,	28,085 63	27,468 63	18,650 63	18,650 63	2,863 63
Washington,	27,900 00	12,000 00	7,200 00	3,000 00	....
Westchester,	9,600 00	9,750 00	7,900 00	6,700 00	5,000 00
Total,	$1,268,082 12	$826,372 02	$796,883 86	$526,695 33	$443,299 76

COUNTIES.	1876.	1877.	1878.	1879.	1880.
Albany,	$500,000 00	....	....	....	$20,000 00
Cattaraugus,	1,500 00	$1,500 00	....	....	....
Cayuga,	2,750 00	2,750 00	$2,750 00	2,750 00	2,750 00
Chautauqua,	2,500 00	2,500 00	2,500 00	2,500 00	2,500 00
Chenango,	7,250 00	7,250 00	7,250 00	7,250 00	7,250 00
Clinton,	1,000 00	1,000 00	1,000 00	1,000 00	1,000 00
Dutchess,	25,450 00	....	....	....	....
Erie,	36,000 00	62,000 00	35,000 00	31,000 00	25,000 00
Franklin,	5,533 33	5,533 33	5,533 33	5,533 34	5,533 34
Genesee,	1,000 00	1,000 00	....	....	....
Herkimer,	4,000 00	4,000 00	4,000 00	....	....
Jefferson,	1,000 00	1,000 00	....	....	....
Kings,	52,000 00	42,000 00	42,000 00	142,000 00	142,000 00
Madison,	3,000 00	3,000 00	3,000 00	3,000 00	3,000 00
Monroe,	43,000 00	73,000 00	20,000 00	....	21,000 00
Onondaga,	9,000 00	8,000 00	5,000 00	5,000 00	5,000 00
Orange,	22,950 00	11,300 00	8,800 00	8,800 00	....
Oswego,	3,000 00	3,000 00	3,000 00	3,000 00	3,000 00
Putnam,	....	....	....	35,505 00	....
Queens,	4,264 70	4,264 70	3,264 70	1,264 70	1,264 70
Rensselaer,	46,846 54	21,000 00	20,000 00	124,000 00	50,000 00
St. Lawrence,	2,000 00	....	....	....	....
Saratoga,	8,425 00	8,425 00	4,800 00	5,200 00	7,000 00
Schenectady,	3,500 00	2,000 00	2,000 00	2,000 00	2,000 00
Schoharie,	8,000 00	8,000 00	8,000 00	8,000 00	8,000 00
Suffolk,	2,863 63	2,863 63	2,863 63	....	....
Westchester,	6,962 18	1,962 18	1,962 18	1,962 18	1,962 18
Total,	$803,795 38	$277,348 84	$182,723 84	$389,765 26	$308,260 22

Dates of Maturity of Town and City Debts — (Continued).

COUNTIES.	1881.	1882.	1883.	1884.	1885.
Albany,	$270,000 00	$20,000 00	$20,000 00	$20,000 00	$10,000 00
Cayuga,	2,750 00	2,750 00	2,750 00	2,750 00	2,750 00
Chautauqua,	2,500 00	2,500 00	2,500 00	2,500 00	2,500 00
Chenango,	7,250 00	37,250 00	7,250 00	7,250 00	7,250 00
Clinton,	1,000 00	1,000 00	1,000 00	....	....
Erie,	10,000 00	44,000 00	22,000 00	....	....
Kings,	1,973,000 00	42,000 00	142,000 00	44,000 00	104,000 00
Madison,	3,000 00	3,000 00	3,000 00	3,000 00	3,000 00
Monroe,	27,000 00	123,950 00	....	....	....
Onondaga,	5,000 00	5,000 00	5,000 00	5,000 00	....
Oswego,	3,000 00	3,000 00	3,000 00	3,000 00	3,000 00
Queens,	1,264 70	1,264 70	1,264 70	1,264 70	1,264 70
Rensselaer,	30,000 00	30,000 00	30,000 00	94,085 00	30,000 00
Saratoga,	8,000 00	5,000 00	....	....	....
Schoharie,	8,000 00	38,000 00	8,000 00	8,000 00	8,000 00
Westchester,	1,216 57	....	....	....	....
Total,	$2,352,981 27	$358,714 70	$247,764 70	$190,849 70	$171,764 70

COUNTIES.	1886.	1887.	1888.	1889.	1890.
Albany,	$20,000 00	$20,000 00	$20,000 00	$20,000 00	$20,000 00
Cayuga,	2,750 00	2,750 00	1,500 00	1,500 00	1,500 00
Chautauqua,	22,500 00	2,500 00	....	....	....
Chenango,	7,250 00	7,250 00	....	....	....
Kings,	853,000 00	185,000 00	95,000 00	95,000 00	95,000 00
Madison,	3,000 00	3,000 00	....	....	....
Oswego,	3,000 00	3,000 00	....	....	....
Rensselaer,	30,000 00	30,000 00	30,000 00	30,000 00	....
Schoharie,	8,000 00	8,000 00	2,000 00	2,000 00	2,000 00
Total,	$949,500 00	$261,500 00	$148,500 00	$148,500 00	$118,500 00

COUNTIES.	1891.	1892.	1893.	1894.	1895.
Albany,	$20,000 00	$20,000 00	$20,000 00	$20,000 00	....
Cayuga,	1,500 00	1,500 00	1,500 00	1,500 00	$1,500 00
Kings,	1,104,000 00	70,000 00	71,000 00	70,000 00	10,000 00
Schoharie,	2,000 00	2,000 00	1,000 00	1,000 00	1,000 00
Total,	$1,127,500 00	$93,500 00	$93,500 00	$92,500 00	$12,500 00

COUNTIES.	1896.	1897.	1899.	1915.	1916.	1924.
Cayuga,	$1,500 00	$1,500 00	....	....	....	....
Kings,	1,432,000 00	....	$1,488,000 00	$430,000 00	$159,000 00	$1,217,000 00
Schoharie,	1,000 00	....	....	....	....	....
Total,	$1,434,500 00	$1,500 00	$1,488,000 00	$430,000 00	$159,000 00	$1,217,000 00

Consolidated Summary of County, City, Town and Village Debts; their amount, and the objects for which incurred.

COUNTIES.	Total amount of debts.	For bounties to volunteers and other war expenses.	For railroad subscription and aid.	For roads and bridges.	Miscellaneous, county, city, town and village debts.
Albany, ...	$4,545,350 75	$1,744,250 00	. $800,000 00	$20,750 75	$1,980,350 00
Allegany, ...	93,496 59	74,548 59	....	1,515 00	17,433 00
Broome, ...	421,614 82	266,087 82	100,000 00	7,900 00	47,627 00
Cattaraugus, ..	48,194 72	10,544 72	18,000 00	650 00	19,000 00
Cayuga, ...	947,905 85	647,989 19	193,250 00	3,333 33	103,333 33
Chautauqua, ..	180,813 58	5,900 00	170,000 00	887 30	4,026 28
Chemung, ...	544,491 88	341,394 16	....	250 00	202,847 72
Chenango, ...	1,369,895 71	458,547 17	911,348 54	....	....
Clinton, ...	196,503 44	191,890 15	....	1,013 29	3,600 00
Columbia,.....	548,658 95	309,758 95	155,000 00	500 00	83,400 00
Cortland,.....	803,690 00	679,940 00	38,000 00	3,750 00	82,000 00
Delaware, ...	717,398 45	110,428 45	606,820 00	....	150 00
Dutchess, ...	989,583 70	547,400 00	....	86 00	442,097 70
Erie, ...	1,316,452 91	818,256 91	150,000 00	2,196 00	346,000 00
Essex, ...	193,990 43	192,699 49	... .	1,290 94	....
Franklin, ...	157,033 75	149,858 75	....	2,175 00	5,000 00
Fulton, ...	439,735 00	147,326 00	275,674 00	1,735 00	15,000 00
Genesee, ...	433,847 00	423,347 00	... .	....	10,500 00
Greene, ...	538,389 22	526,300 00	10,000 00	1,689 22	400 00
Hamilton, ...	43,301 00	38,721 00	....	3,850 00	730 00
Herkimer, ...	199,033 53	140,833 54	50,000 00	7,499 99	700 00
Jefferson, ...	1,451,238 33	1,264,081 48	150,000 00	16,470 36	20,686 49
Kings, ...	14,577,419 92	3,717,000 00	....	....	10,860,419 92
Lewis, ...	271,880 68	74,131 22	180,000 00	699 46	17,050 00
Livingston, ...	264,451 83	154,951 73	100,000 00	9,000 00	500 00
Madison,......	411,432 84	6,342 75	387,300 00	1,400 00	16,390 09
Monroe,.......	2,624,237 92	1,950,340 17	252,000 00	122,015 21	299,882 54
Montgomery,..	298,745 89	286,727 80	....	11,845 59	172 50
New York, ...	33,958,545 01	8,069,100 00	....	....	25,889,445 01
Niagara, ...	374,800 00	372,800 00	....	2,000 00	....
Oneida, ...	976,478 70	3,550 00	215,000 00	6,358 25	751,570 45
Onondaga, ...	1,410,269 98	1,282,120 00	30,000 00	10,150 00	87,999 98
Ontario,.......	500,980 00	498,060 00	....	1,000 00	1,920 00
Orange, ...	1,032,321 76	903,350 11	120,000 00	7,750 00	1,221 65
Orleans,.......	241,869 00	239,860 00	....	2,000 00	....
Oswego, ...	989,390 99	817,511 00	68,000 00	12,324 30	91,555 69
Otsego, ...	970,195 95	111,995 95	856,000 00	2,200 00	....
Putnam, ...	107,271 71	93,351 71	....	....	13,920 00
Queens, ...	1,199,651 00	1,159,651 00	....	....	40,000 00
Rensselaer, ...	2,060,352 48	1,020,724 20	271,000 00	5,775 28	762,853 00
Richmond,...	879,264 28	801,850 00	12,210 00	....	65,204 28
Rockland,.....	143,157 08	140,057 08	....	3,000 00	100 00
St. Lawrence,.	886,963 85	750,413 85	....	25,550 00	111,000 00
Saratoga	499,784 30	498,799 30	....	150 00	835 00
Schenectady,..	190,833 83	133,433 83	30,000 00	....	27,400 00
Schoharie, ...	419,156 67	93,984 00	324,000 00	750 00	422 67
Schuyler, ...	156,087 75	141,129 04	....	3,317 00	11,641 71
Seneca, ...	384,623 08	371,135 33	....	750 00	12,737 75
Steuben, ...	589,189 66	583,624 66	....	2,465 00	3,100 00
Suffolk, ...	251,824 94	250,099 94	....	....	1,725 00
Sullivan, ...	441,261 00	326,411 00	108,500 00	....	6,350 00
Tioga, ...	222,700 00	151,800 00	67,600 00	300 00	....
Tompkins,....	98,058 58	27,134 85	50,000 00	20,773 73	150 00
Ulster, ...	2,680,973 15	1,585,875 00	1,094,008 15	1,090 00	....
Warren,.......	41,086 37	37,278 05	....	250 00	3,558 32
Washington, ..	307,835 00	299,335 00	....	....	8,500 00
Wayne, ...	331,969 00	303,969 00	....	8,000 00	20,000 00
Westchester,..	2,069,686 55	1,920,486 55	....	114,500 00	34,700 00
Wyoming,.....	5,040 00	3,840 00	....	1,200 00	....
Yates,.........	30,634 70	23,422 38	....	3,512 32	3,700 00
Total, ...	$89,081,035 96	$38,298,749 87	$7,793,710 69	$457,668 32	$42,530,907 08

*General Summary of the years when the aggregate County, City, Village and Town Debts reported in the foregoing tables become due.**

YEARS.	County debts.	City, town and village debts.	Total.
Not reported,	$11,499,834 75	$31,436,437 54	$42,936,272 29
1867,	454,280 00	429,832 05	884,112 05
1868,	2,811,762 51	2,183,762 17	4,995,524 68
1869,	2,659,790 00	1,529,721 07	4,189,511 07
1870,	1,722,847 30	1,311,212 03	3,034,059 33
1871,	1,758,386 11	1,274,082 12	3,032,468 23
1872,	1,318,181 25	831,372 02	2,149,553 27
1873,	1,017,976 25	797,883 86	1,815,860 11
1874,	1,322,574 29	527,695 33	1,850,269 62
1875,	1,168,802 83	447,299 76	1,616,102 59
1876,	1,016,702 83	807,795 38	1,824,498 21
1877,	923,192 28	282,348 84	1,205,541 12
1878,	681,400 00	183,723 84	865,123 84
1879,	735,200 00	390,765 26	1,125,965 26
1880,	722,100 00	309,260 22	1,031,360 22
1881,	544,350 00	2,353,981 27	2,898,331 27
1882,	515,600 00	359,714 70	875,314 70
1883,	297,600 00	248,764 70	546,364 70
1884,	453,100 00	191,849 70	644,949 70
1885,	191,000 00	172,764 70	363,764 70
1886,	124,000 00	950,500 00	1,074,500 00
1887,	122,000 00	261,500 00	383,500 00
1888,	120,000 00	148,500 00	268,500 00
1889,	338,000 00	148,500 00	486,500 00
1890,	120,000 00	118,500 00	238,500 00
1891,	595,089 00	1,127,500 00	1,722,589 00
1892,	....	93,500 00	93,500 00
1893,	....	93,500 00	93,500 00
1894,	....	92,500 00	92,500 00
1895,	500,000 00	12,500 00	512,500 00
1896,	500,000 00	1,434,500 00	1,934,500 00
1897,	500,000 00	1,500 00	501,500 00
1898,	500,000 00	....	500,000 00
1899,	....	1,488,000 00	1,488,000 00
1915,	....	430,000 00	430,000 00
1916,	....	159,000 00	159,000 00
1924,	....	1,217,000 00	1,217,000 00
Total,	$35,233,769 40	$53,847,266 56	$89,081,035 96

* In many cases an uncertainty existed in the returns, which rendered an exact classification by years, impossible. For example, "payable in thirty years," may have been intended "by installments during thirty years," or "at the end of thirty years in one sum." The summary above given is therefore but an approximation. The large amount of "unknown," arises in part from its including most of the New York city debt, which was reported only in the aggregate

ALBANY COUNTY.

TOWNS.	Population.	Aliens.	Colored persons not taxed.	Whole number of persons of color.	Number, deducting aliens and colored persons not taxed.	Population, excluding aliens only.	Population, excluding persons of color not taxed only.	Population, excluding all persons of color.	Voters.
Albany city:									
1st ward,	9,620	1,323	49	77	8,248	8,297	9,671	9,543	1,789
2d ward,	4,924	659	18	19	4,247	4,265	4,906	4,905	1,030
3d ward,	4,573	185	59	60	4,329	4,388	4,514	4,713	1,192
4th ward,	3,826	466	53	54	3,307	3,360	3,773	3,772	894
5th ward,	1,888	357	48	65	1,483	1,531	1,840	1,823	423
6th ward,	3,191	433	1	2	2,757	2,758	3,190	3,189	757
7th ward,	5,688	426	3	5	5,259	5,262	5,685	5,683	1,174
8th ward,	8,701	766	130	157	7,805	7,935	8,571	8,544	1,791
9th ward,	8,932	789	50	57	8,093	8,143	8,882	8,875	1,876
10th ward,	11,270	767	239	247	10,264	10,503	11,031	11,023	2,270
Total Albany city,	62,613	6,171	650	743	55,792	56,442	61,963	61,870	13,196
Berne,	2,851	7	2	2	2,842	2,844	2,849	2,849	757
Bethlehem,	5,928	654	88	98	5,186	5,274	5,840	5,830	1,243
Coeymans,	3,264	216	60	66	2,988	3,048	3,204	3,198	796
Guilderland,	3,207	47	1	9	3,159	3,160	3,206	3,198	815
Knox,	1,809	6	....	....	1,803	1,803	1,809	1,809	470
New Scotland,	3,311	60	18	19	3,233	3,251	3,293	3,292	818
Rensselaerville,	2,745	16	1	2	2,728	2,729	2,744	2,743	759
Watervliet,	27,279	3,236	40	64	24,003	24,043	27,239	27,215	5,177
Westerlo,	2,497	9	6	11	2,482	2,488	2,491	2,486	692
Total,	115,504	10,422	866	1,014	104,216	105,082	114,638	114,490	24,723

ALLEGANY COUNTY.

TOWNS.	Population.	Aliens.	Colored persons not taxed.	Whole number of persons of color.	Number, deducting aliens and colored persons not taxed.	Population, excluding aliens only.	Population, excluding persons of color not taxed only.	Population, excluding all persons of color.	Voters.
Alfred,	1,335	14	6	6	1,315	1,321	1,329	1,329	338
Allen,	870	17	....	....	853	853	870	870	220
Alma,	611	16	....	....	595	595	611	611	141
Almond,	1,655	12	....	....	1,643	1,643	1,655	1,655	455
Amity,	2,073	56	5	7	2,012	2,017	2,068	2,066	478
Andover,	1,812	93	....	....	1,719	1,719	1,812	1,812	424
Angelica,	1,663	51	13	13	1,599	1,612	1,650	1,650	418
Belfast,	1,689	35	3	3	1,651	1,654	1,686	1,686	434
Birdsall,	766	19	....	....	747	747	766	766	169
Bolivar,	1,005	1	....	....	1,004	1,004	1,005	1,005	258
Burns,	1,064	14	....	....	1,050	1,050	1,064	1,064	276
Caneadea,	1,948	43	22	31	1,883	1,905	1,926	1,917	451
Centreville,	1,181	36	....	....	1,145	1,145	1,181	1,181	316
Clarksville,	879	3	....	...	876	876	879	879	219
Cuba,	1,978	32	7	17	1,939	1,946	1,971	1,961	523
Friendship,	1,725	32	6	17	1,687	1,673	1,719	1,708	464
Genesee,	922	2	....	1	920	920	922	921	236
Granger,	1,054	17	4	4	1,033	1,037	1,050	1,050	271
Grove,	1,038	37	....	....	1,001	1,001	1,038	1,038	237
Hume,	2,016	35	....	....	1,981	1,981	2,016	2,016	528
Independence,	1,126	2	2	2	1,122	1,124	1,124	1,124	309
New Hudson,	1,218	24	...	....	1,194	1,194	1,218	1,218	341
Rushford,	1,680	34	14	15	1,632	1,646	1,666	1,665	433
Scio,	1,721	31	49	95	1,641	1,690	1,672	1,626	401
Ward,	833	24	1	1	808	809	832	832	202
Wellsville,	3,070	219	10	10	2,841	2,851	3,060	3,060	656
West Almond,	893	1	....	....	892	892	893	893	231
Willing,	1,093	12	....	....	1,081	1,081	1,093	1,093	277
Wirt,	1,367	4	7	44	1,356	1,363	1,360	1,323	382
Total,	40,285	916	149	266	39,220	39,369	40,136	40,019	10,088

BROOME COUNTY.

TOWNS.	Population.	Aliens.	Colored person not taxed.	Whole number of persons of color.	Number, deducting aliens and colored persons, not taxed.	Population, excluding aliens only.	Population, excluding persons not taxed only.	Population, excluding all persons of color.	Voters.
Barker,	1,339	3	....	....	1,336	1,336	1,339	1,339	341
Binghamton,*	10,092	677	179	289	9,236	9,415	9,913	9,803	2,468
Chenango,	1,671	2	....	1	1,669	1,669	1,671	1,670	461
Colesville,	3,202	55	2	7	3,145	3,147	3,200	3,195	876
Conklin,	1,282	32	1	1	1,249	1,250	1,281	1,281	299
Fenton,†	1,503	6	....	....	1,373	1,377	1,503	1,503	358
Kirkwood,	1,440	63	4	20	1,497	1,497	1,436	1,420	400
Lisle,	2,066	27	....	5	2,039	2,039	2,066	2,061	537
Maine,	2,061	15	....	....	2,046	2,046	2,061	2,061	523
Nanticoke,	972	22	....	....	950	950	972	972	242
Sanford,	3,262	141	27	28	3,094	3,121	3,235	3,234	739
Triangle,	1,875	19	2	5	1,854	1,856	873	1,870	510
Union,	2,532	46	42	46	2,444	2,486	2,490	2,486	644
Vestal,	1,939	11	1	12	1,927	1,928	1,938	1,927	480
Windsor,	2,697	15	....	....	2,682	2,682	2,697	2,697	684
Total,	37,933	1,134	258	414	36,541	36,799	37,675	37,519	9,562

CATTARAUGUS COUNTY.

TOWNS.	Population.	Aliens.	Colored person not taxed.	Whole number of persons of color.	Number, deducting aliens and colored persons, not taxed.	Population, excluding aliens only.	Population, excluding persons not taxed only.	Population, excluding all persons of color.	Voters.
Allegany,	2,151	162	....	....	1,989	1,989	2,151	2,151	459
Ashford,	1,838	95	....	1	1,743	1,743	1,838	1,837	409
Carrolton,	1,037	121	7	7	909	916	1,030	1,030	237
Cold Spring,	711	19	....	....	692	692	711	711	182
Connewango,	1,229	47	1	1	1,181	1,182	1,228	1,228	333
Dayton,	1,247	25	8	8	1,214	1,222	1,239	1,239	307
East Otto,	1,152	23	....	6	1,129	1,129	1,152	1,146	309
Ellicottville,	1,862	40	11	15	1,811	1,822	1,851	1,847	416
Farmersville,	1,197	9	....	....	1,188	1,188	1,197	1,197	286
Franklinville,	1,510	33	1	1	1,476	1,477	1,509	1,509	378
Freedom,	1,398	70	....	....	1,328	1,328	1,398	1,398	364
Great Valley,	1,565	118	8	8	1,439	1,447	1,557	1,557	354
Hinsdale,	1,645	35	2	2	1,608	1,610	1,643	1,643	393
Humphrey,	948	30	....	....	918	918	948	948	218
Ischua,	858	4	....	....	854	854	858	858	234
Leon,	1,310	36	....	....	1,274	1,274	1,310	1,310	347
Little Valley,	1,010	48	....	3	962	962	1,010	1,007	250
Lyndon,	1,011	11	....	....	1,000	1,000	1,011	1,011	256
Machias,	1,190	43	....	....	1,147	1,147	1,190	1,190	290
Mansfield,	1,217	22	....	....	1,195	1,195	1,217	1,217	305
Napoli,	1,231	13	1	1	1,217	1,218	1,230	1,230	330
New Albion,	1,696	88	2	2	1,606	1,608	1,694	1,694	408
Olean,	2,701	238	69	78	2,394	2,463	2,632	2,623	569
Otto,	1,106	100	....	....	1,006	1,006	1,106	1,106	290
Perrysburgh,	1,453	15	5	4	1,433	1,432	1,448	1,449	378
Persia,	1,291	24	4	15	1,263	1,267	2,287	1,276	309
Portville,	1,638	34	5	14	1,599	1,604	1,633	1,624	394
Randolph,	1,846	76	1	1	1,769	1,770	1,845	1,845	464
Salamanca,	1,801	204	4	4	1,593	1,597	1,797	1,797	377
South Valley,	639	19	....	....	620	620	639	639	147
Yorkshire,	1,670	15	4	14	1,651	1,655	1,666	1,656	341
Allegany Ind. Res'n,	814	......	....	....	......	......	......	......	......
Cattaraugus do ‡	233	......	....	....	......	......	......	......	......
Total,	44,205	1,817	133	185	41,208	41,341	43,025	42,973	10,334

* The city of Binghamton, with five wards, has been formed since the census was taken, leaving still a town of this name.

† Changed from Port Crane by the Legislature, in 1867.

‡ A part of this reservation in Erie and Chautauqua counties. The whole number is 1,347.

CAYUGA COUNTY.

TOWNS.	Population.	Aliens.	Colored persons not taxed.	Whole number of persons of color.	Number, deducting aliens and colored persons, not taxed.	Population excluding aliens only.	Population excluding persons of color not taxed only.	Population excluding all person of color.	Voters.
Auburn City:									
1st ward, ...	4,085	507	11	19	3,567	3,578	4,074	4,066	864
2d ward, ...	2,405	297	68	80	2,040	2,108	2,337	2,325	520
3d ward, ...	2,337	325	28	56	1,984	2,012	2,309	2,281	525
4th ward, ...	3,740	447	29	70	3,264	3,293	3,711	3,670	622
Total Auburn City,	12,567	1,576	136	225	10,855	10,991	12,431	12,342	2,531
Aurelius, ...	2,470	152	....	9	2,318	2,318	2,470	2,461	555
Brutus, ...	2,588	90	3	19	2,495	2,498	2,585	2,569	638
Cato, ...	2,192	104	1	1	2,087	2,088	2,191	2,191	560
Conquest, ...	1,809	45	....	....	1,764	1,764	1,809	1,809	465
Fleming, ...	1,248	101	14	14	1,133	1,147	1,234	1,234	294
Genoa, ...	2,362	91	5	9	2,266	2,271	2,357	2,353	638
Ira, ...	2,175	37	2	2	2,136	2,138	2,173	2,173	586
Ledyard, ...	2,065	102	55	66	1,908	1,963	2,010	1,999	486
Locke, ...	1,125	9	....	....	1,116	1,116	1,125	1,125	342
Mentz, ...	2,366	54	26	34	2,286	2,312	2,340	2,332	608
Montezuma, ...	1,314	21	9	17	1,284	1,293	1,305	1,297	336
Moravia, ...	1,881	31	3	6	1,847	1,850	1,878	1,875	518
Niles, ...	1,876	46	6	6	1,824	1,830	1,870	1,870	527
Owasco, ...	1,284	54	3	7	1,227	1,230	1,281	1,277	304
Scipio, ...	2,047	133	19	28	1,895	1,914	2,028	2,019	490
Sempronius, ...	1,203	18	....	....	1,185	1,185	1,203	1,203	322
Sennett, ...	1,722	119	1	3	1,602	1,603	1,721	1,719	462
Springport, ...	2,184	108	30	38	2,046	2,076	2,154	2,146	507
Sterling, ...	2,915	172	1	2	2,742	2,743	2,914	2,913	723
Summer Hill, ...	1,112	....	....	....	1,112	1,112	1,112	1,112	306
Throop, ...	1,291	39	....	4	1,252	1,252	1,291	1,287	332
Venice, ...	1,943	89	5	21	1,849	1,854	1,938	1,922	518
Victory, ...	1,991	19	4	4	1,968	1,972	1,987	1,987	542
Total, ...	55,730	3,210	323	515	52,197	52,520	55,407	55,215	13,590

CHAUTAUQUA COUNTY.

TOWNS.	Population.	Aliens.	Colored persons not taxed.	Whole number of persons of color.	Number, deducting aliens and colored persons, not taxed.	Population excluding aliens only.	Population excluding persons of color not taxed only.	Population excluding all person of color.	Voters.
Arkwright, ...	1,116	37	....	11	1,079	1,079	1,116	1,105	276
Busti, ...	1,976	55	26	28	1,895	1,921	1,950	1,948	484
Carroll, ...	1,454	5	1	1	1,448	1,449	1,453	1,453	371
Charlotte, ...	1,664	42	5	5	1,617	1,622	1,659	1,659	428
Chautauqua, ...	2,698	128	2	4	2,568	2,570	2,696	2,694	729
Cherry Creek, ...	1,304	13	....	....	1,291	1,291	1,304	1,304	350
Clymer, ...	1,322	54	1	1	1,267	1,268	1,321	1,321	331
Dunkirk, ...	7,452	1,349	36	49	6,067	6,103	7,416	7,403	1,482
Ellery, ...	1,609	7	....	....	1,602	1,602	1,609	1,609	411
Ellicott, ...	5,556	447	27	53	5,082	5,109	5,529	5,503	1,337
Ellington, ...	1,722	6	1	1	1,715	1,716	1,721	1,721	441
French Creek, ...	901	20	....	....	881	881	901	900	216
Gerry, ...	1,129	13	....	....	1,116	1,116	1,129	1,129	311
Hanover, ...	4,087	159	17	23	3,911	3,928	4,070	4,064	1,029
Harmony, ...	3,653	146	1	3	3,506	3,507	3,652	3,650	880
Kiantone, ...	574	27	....	....	547	547	574	574	135
Mina, ...	1,188	23	....	....	1,165	1,165	1,188	1,188	292
Poland, ...	1,575	101	3	6	1,471	1,474	1,572	1,569	383
Pomfret, ...	4,065	231	2	7	3,832	3,834	4,063	4,058	1,005
Portland, ...	1,816	57	1	1	1,758	1,759	1,815	1,815	462
Ripley, ...	1,870	82	2	2	1,786	1,788	1,868	1,868	430
Sheridan, ...	1,688	111	....	....	1,577	1,577	1,688	1,688	412
Sherman, ...	1,353	21	1	1	1,331	1,332	1,352	1,352	339
Stockton, ...	1,665	9	....	....	1,656	1,656	1,665	1,665	475
Villenova, ...	1,503	21	4	8	1,478	1,482	1,499	1,495	398
Westfield, ...	3,559	342	26	26	3,191	3,217	3,533	3,533	821
Total, ...	58,528*	3,506	156	230	54,837	54,993	58,343	58,269	14,228

* Including twenty-nine Indians on the Cattaraugus Reservation.

CHEMUNG COUNTY.

TOWNS.	Population.	Aliens.	Colored persons not taxed.	Whole number of persons of color.	Number, deducting aliens and colored persons, not taxed.	Population, excluding aliens only.	Population, excluding persons of color not taxed, only.	Population, excluding all persons of color.	Voters.
Baldwin,	923	11	...	...	912	912	923	923	224
Big Flats,	1,891	33	3	6	1,855	1,858	1,888	1,885	499
Catlin,	1,440	2	2	6	1,436	1,438	1,438	1,434	380
Chemung,	1,950	54	1	1	1,895	1,896	1,949	1,949	457
Elmira (town),	1,169	41	10	14	1,118	1,128	1,159	1,155	261
Elmira (city):									
1st ward,	1,489	135	10	16	1,344	1,354	1,479	1,473	386
2d ward,	3,898	698	24	30	3,176	3,200	3,874	3,868	810
3d ward,	3,219	344	243	414	2,632	2,875	2,976	2,805	631
4th ward,	2,595	291	31	44	2,273	2,304	2,564	2,551	541
5th ward,	1,929	220	15	34	1,694	1,709	1,914	1,895	392
Total Elmira city,	13,130	1,688	323	538	11,119	11,442	12,807	12,592	2,760
Erin,	1,256	1	6	10	1,249	1,255	1,250	1,246	295
Horseheads,	2,838	36	64	68	2,738	2,802	2,774	2,770	720
Southport,	3,412	115	2	6	3,295	3,297	3,410	3,406	844
Van Etten,	1,485	9	...	...	1,476	1,476	1,485	1,485	363
Veteran,	2,429	25	11	11	2,393	2,404	2,418	2,418	647
Total,	31,923	2,015	422	660	29,486	29,908	31,501	31,263	7,450

CHENANGO COUNTY.

TOWNS.	Population.	Aliens.	Colored persons not taxed.	Whole number of persons of color.	Number, deducting aliens and colored persons, not taxed.	Population, excluding aliens only.	Population, excluding persons of color not taxed, only.	Population, excluding all persons of color.	Voters.
Afton,	1,827	2	....	3	1,825	1,825	1,827	1,824	490
Bainbridge,	1,699	16	11	11	1,672	1,683	1,688	1,688	468
Columbus,	1,273	21	....	....	1,252	1,252	1,273	1,273	345
Coventry,	1,522	14	....	....	1,508	1,508	1,522	1,522	425
German,	778	13	1	1	764	765	777	777	190
Greene,	3,314	21	21	27	3,272	3,293	3,293	3,287	900
Guilford,	2,423	15	2	5	2,406	2,408	2,421	2,418	671
Lincklaen,	988	2	....	....	986	986	988	988	270
Macdonough,	1,306	4	1	1	1,301	1,302	1,305	1,305	356
New Berlin,	2,459	11	1	5	2,447	2,448	2,458	2,454	701
North Norwich,	1,078	21	....	....	1,057	1,057	1,078	1,078	274
Norwich,	4,331	130	99	122	4,102	4,201	4,232	4,209	1,132
Otselic,	1,468	5	....	....	1,463	1,463	1,468	1,468	424
Oxford,	2,996	49	10	25	2,937	2,947	2,986	2,971	817
Pharsalia,	1,112	11	....	....	1,101	1,101	1,112	1,112	290
Pitcher,	1,186	......	....	1	1,186	1,186	1,186	1,185	330
Plymouth,	1,487	17	3	3	1,467	1,470	1,484	1,484	382
Preston,	982	21	5	4	956	961	977	978	273
Sherburne,	2,820	104	3	23	2,709	2,712	2,817	2,797	729
Smithville,	1,634	12	....	2	1,622	1,622	1,634	1,632	425
Smyrna,	1,677	21	....	....	1,656	1,656	1,677	1,677	444
Total,	38,360	514	157	233	37,689	37,846	38,203	38,127	10,336

CLINTON COUNTY.

TOWNS.	Population.	Aliens.	Colored persons not taxed.	Whole number of persons of color.	Number, deducting aliens and colored persons, not taxed.	Population, excluding aliens only.	Population, excluding persons of color not taxed, only.	Population, excluding all persons of color.	Voters.
Altona,	1,820	324	4	8	1,492	1,496	1,816	1,812	281
Ausable,	2,694	220	1	7	2,473	2,474	2,693	2,687	542
Beekmantown,	2,708	162	14	24	2,532	2,546	2,694	2,684	578
Black Brook,	3,282	601	....	....	2,681	2,681	3,282	3,282	439
Champlain,	5,774	1,204	11	11	4,559	4,570	5,763	5,763	898
Chazy,	3,381	361	12	15	3,008	3,020	3,369	3,366	655
Clinton,	1,786	242	...	....	1,544	1,544	1,786	1,786	282
Dannemora,	1,371	306	16	17	1,049	1,065	1,355	1,354	130
Ellenburgh,	2,919	388	5	16	2,526	2,531	2,914	2 903	553
Mooers,	4,202	658	....	....	3,544	3,544	4,202	4,202	746
Peru,	3,087	158	4	6	2,925	2,929	3,083	3,081	648
Plattsburgh,	7,195	923	4	7	6,268	6,272	7,191	7,188	1,291
Saranac,	3,623	440	6	6	3,177	3,183	3,617	3,617	588
Schuyler's Falls,	1,871	107	7	7	1,757	1,764	1,864	1,864	421
Total,	45,713	6,094	84	124	39,535	39,619	45,629	45,589	8,052

COLUMBIA COUNTY.

TOWNS.	Population.	Aliens.	Colored persons not taxed.	Whole number of persons of color.	Number, deducting aliens and colored persons, not taxed.	Population, excluding aliens only.	Population, excluding persons of color not taxed only.	Population, excluding all persons of color.	Voters.
Ancram,	1,651	91	....	8	1,560	1,560	1,651	1,643	422
Austerlitz,	1,443	46	30	54	1,367	1,397	1,413	1,389	379
Canaan,	2,000	87	24	25	1,889	1,913	1,976	1,975	493
Chatham,	4,285	246	112	218	3,927	4,039	4,173	4,067	994
Claverack,	3,353	104	39	56	3,210	3,249	3,314	3,297	813
Clermont,	942	44	4	4	894	898	938	938	226
Copake,	1,738	112	....	2	1,626	1,626	1,738	1,736	423
Gallatin,	1,392	7	9	10	1,376	1,385	1,383	1,382	378
Germantown,	1,278	13	13	25	1,252	1,265	1,265	1,253	308
Ghent,	2,661	113	95	129	2,453	2,548	2,566	2,532	669
Greenport,	1,130	44	13	40	1,073	1,086	1,117	1,090	262
Hillsdale,	2,142	53	5	8	2,084	2,089	2,137	2,134	566
Hudson city:									
1st ward,	1,609	148	9	23	1,452	1,461	1,600	1,586	344
2d ward,	2,078	119	104	138	1,855	1,959	1,974	1,940	401
3d ward,	1,828	85	17	18	1,726	1,743	1,811	1,810	443
4th ward,	2,316	119	83	116	2,114	2,197	2,233	2,200	494
Total Hudson city,	7,831	471	213	295	7,147	7,360	7,618	7,536	1,682
Kinderhook,	4,008	253	126	143	3,629	3,755	3,882	3,865	899
Livingston,	1,904	39	7	7	1,858	1,865	1,897	1,897	487
New Lebanon,	2,086	140	5	8	1,941	1,946	2,081	2,078	489
Stockport,	1,355	51	47	55	1,257	1,304	1,308	1,300	310
Stuyvesant,	2,234	76	107	135	2,051	2,158	2,127	2,099	469
Taghkanick,	1,472	19	6	6	1,447	1,453	1,466	1,466	366
Total,	44,905	2,009	855	1,228	42,041	42,896	44,050	43,677	10,635

CORTLAND COUNTY.

TOWNS.	Population.	Aliens.	Colored persons not taxed.	Whole number of persons of color.	Number, deducting aliens and colored persons, not taxed.	Population, excluding aliens only.	Population, excluding persons of color not taxed only.	Population, excluding all persons of color.	Voters.
Cincinnatus,	1,169	4	1	1	1,164	1,165	1,168	1,168	340
Cortlandville,	5,008	107	12	16	4,889	4,901	4,996	4,992	1,360
Cuyler,	1,447	20	....	....	1,427	1,427	1,447	1,447	374
Freetown,	942	18	1	1	923	924	941	941	266
Harford,	888	4	1	1	883	884	887	887	240
Homer,	3,856	141	5	6	3,710	3,715	3,851	3,850	983
Lapeer,	762	......	....	....	762	762	762	762	198
Marathon,	1,485	29	1	1	1,455	1,456	1,484	1,484	385
Preble,	1,267	30	....	....	1,237	1,237	1,267	1,267	338
Scott,	1,149	12	....	9	1,137	1,137	1,149	1,140	331
Solon,	995	7	....	....	988	988	995	995	271
Taylor,	1,167	2	1	2	1,164	1,165	1,166	1,165	310
Truxton,	1,689	112	....	....	1,577	1,577	1,689	1,689	409
Virgil,	2,009	28	....	1	1,981	1,981	2,009	2,008	520
Willet,	982	19	....	....	963	963	982	982	267
Total,	24,815	533	22	38	24,260	24,282	24,793	24,777	6,592

DELAWARE COUNTY.

TOWNS.	Population.	Aliens.	Colored persons not taxed.	Whole number of persons of color.	Number, deducting aliens and colored persons, not taxed.	Population, excluding aliens only.	Population, excluding persons of color not taxed only.	Population, excluding all persons of color.	Voters.
Andes,	2,815	51	2	3	2,762	2,764	2,813	2,812	674
Bovina,	1,146	27	....	....	1,119	1,119	1,146	1,146	306
Colchester,	2,446	23	1	12	2,422	2,423	2,445	2,434	627
Davenport,	2,238	37	1	1	2,200	2,201	2,237	2,237	576
Delhi,	2,785	67	40	64	2,678	2,718	2,745	2,721	706
Franklin,	3,136	27	...	....	3,109	3,109	3,136	3,136	832
Hamden,	1,836	19	1	14	1,816	1,817	1,835	1,822	466
Hancock,	2,933	184	....	1	2,749	2,749	2,933	2,932	660
Harpersfield,	1,446	22	12	12	1,412	1,424	1,434	1,434	362
Kortright,	1,897	32	....	....	1,865	1,865	1,897	1,897	498
Masonville,	1,700	3	....	....	1,697	1,697	1,700	1,700	447
Meredith,	1,507	44	....	....	1,463	1,463	1,507	1,507	379
Middletown,	3,119	74	8	8	3,037	3,045	3,111	3,111	756
Roxbury,	2,335	41	....	9	2,294	2,294	2,335	2,326	610

DELAWARE COUNTY — (Continued).

TOWNS.	Population.	Aliens.	Colored persons not taxed.	Whole number of persons of color.	Number, deducting aliens and colored persons, not taxed.	Population, excluding aliens only.	Population, excluding persons of color not taxed, only.	Population, excluding all persons of color.	Voters.
Sidney,	1,753	12	....	....	1,741	1,741	1,763	1,753	510
Stamford,	1,556	26	....	....	1,530	1,530	1,556	1,556	407
Tompkins,	4,064	74	34	38	3,956	3,990	4,030	4,026	988
Walton,	2,926	7	31	35	2,888	2,919	2,895	2,891	778
Total,	41,638	770	130	197	40,738	40,868	41,508	41,441	10,582
DUTCHESS COUNTY.									
Amenia,	2,512	341	89	96	2,082	2,171	2,423	2,416	524
Beekman,	1,208	34	18	38	1,156	1,174	1,190	1,170	310
Clinton,	1,719	42	1	3	1,676	1,677	1,718	1,716	482
Dover,	2,093	119	32	38	1,942	1,974	2,061	2,055	522
East Fishkill,	2,448	121	85	107	2,242	2,327	2,363	2,341	575
Fishkill,	9,949	1,082	370	431	8,497	8,867	9,579	9,518	2,035
Hyde Park,	2,654	212	50	60	2,392	2,442	2,604	2,594	619
La Grange,	1,817	81	35	46	1,701	1,736	1,782	1,771	487
Milan,	1,545	15	11	35	1,519	1,530	1,534	1,510	411
Northeast,	2,007	132	63	73	1,812	1,875	1,944	1,934	486
Pawling,	1,742	79	7	12	1,656	1,663	1,735	1,730	437
Pine Plains,	1,339	25	17	26	1,297	1,314	1,322	1,313	376
Pleasant Valley,	1,920	18	56	58	1,846	1,402	1,864	1,862	530
Poughkeepsie (town),	3,073	347	70	86	2,656	2,726	3,003	2,987	736
Poughkeepsie (city):									
1st ward,	3,669	458	1	1	3,210	3,211	3,668	3,668	680
2d ward,	3,467	271	61	75	3,135	3,196	3,406	3,392	723
3d ward,	2,188	182	24	25	1,982	2,006	2,164	2,163	490
4th ward,	2,802	217	136	156	2,449	2,585	2,666	2,646	647
5th ward,	2,123	126	101	144	1,896	1,997	2,022	1,979	493
6th ward,	1,824	125	17	22	1,682	1,699	1,807	1,802	384
Total city,	16,073	1,379	340	423	14,354	14,694	15,733	15,650	3,417
Red Hook,	3,128	164	42	49	2,922	2,964	3,036	3,079	721
Rhinebeck,	3,610	228	73	92	3,309	3,382	3,537	3,518	862
Stanford,	2,216	90	51	53	2,075	2,126	2,165	2,163	561
Union Vale,	1,420	28	8	18	1,384	1,392	1,412	1,402	374
Washington,	2,719	269	96	129	2,354	2,450	2,623	2,590	654
Total,	65,192	4,806	1,514	1,873	58,872	60,386	63,678	63,319	15,119
ERIE COUNTY.									
Alden,	2,520	128	3	7	2,389	2,392	2,517	2,513	339
Amherst,	4,575	283	....	3	4,292	4,292	4,575	4,572	858
Aurora,	2,486	171	5	6	2,310	2,315	2,481	2,480	496
Boston,	1,734	91	....	....	1,643	1,643	1,734	1,734	393
Brandt,	1,376	230	....	15	1,146	1,146	1,376	1,361	277
Buffalo city:									
1st ward,	10,009	2,798	4	4	7,207	7,211	10,005	10,005	1,486
2d ward,	6,402	892	23	31	5,487	5,510	6,379	6,371	1,325
3d ward,	7,013	1,236	10	30	5,767	5,777	7,003	6,983	1,192
4th ward,	7,752	1,287	208	213	6,257	6,465	7,544	7,539	1,383
5th ward,	12,741	1,671	79	147	10,991	11,070	12,662	12,594	2,213
6th ward,	10,132	1,116	102	122	8,914	9,016	10,030	10,010	1,770
7th ward,	10,329	1,425	7	19	8,897	8,904	10,322	10,310	1,762
8th ward,	6,202	1,524	50	59	4,628	4,678	6,152	6,143	1,094
9th ward,	5,864	1,054	21	23	4,739	4,810	5,843	5,841	1,257
10th ward,	6,363	734	4	9	5,625	5,629	6,359	6,354	1,253
11th ward,	4,450	1,299	6	9	3,145	3,151	4,444	4,441	526
12th ward,	5,132	890	7	26	4,235	4,242	5,125	5,106	852
13th ward,	2,113	377	....	19	1,736	1,736	2,113	2,094	347
Total Buffalo city,	94,502	16,303	521	711	77,678	78,199	93,981	93,791	16,460

ERIE COUNTY — (Continued).

TOWNS.	Population.	Aliens.	Colored persons not taxed.	Whole number of persons of color.	Number, deducting aliens and colored persons not taxed.	Population, excluding aliens only.	Population, excluding persons of color not taxed only.	Population, excluding all persons of color.	Voters.
Chictawauga, ...	2,657	276	2	3	2,379	2,381	2,655	2,654	477
Clarence, ...	3,610	308	....	1	3,302	3,302	3,610	3,609	776
Colden, ...	1,386	3	2	2	1,381	1,383	1,384	1,384	360
Collins, ...	2,054	101	....	2	1,953	1,953	2,054	2,052	554
Concord, ...	2,811	62	1	2	2,748	2,749	2,810	2,809	727
East Hamburgh, ...	2,128	131	....	....	1,997	1,997	2,128	2,128	497
Eden, ...	2,392	108	....	....	2,284	2,284	2,392	2,392	538
Elma, ...	2,907	333	....	6	2,574	2,574	2,907	2,901	549
Evans, ...	2,626	193	....	4	2,433	2,433	2,626	2,622	600
Grand Island, ...	1,229	215	27	37	987	1,014	1,202	1,192	197
Hamburgh, ...	3,139	331	....	1	2,808	2,808	3,139	3,138	646
Holland, ...	1,523	34	....	1	1,489	1,489	1,523	1,522	354
Lancaster, ...	4,112	252	8	17	3,852	3,860	4,104	4,095	825
Marilla, ...	1,630	30	....	....	1,600	1,600	1,630	1,630	425
Newstead, ...	3,206	203	2	10	3,001	3,003	3,204	3,196	759
North Collins, ...	1,813	40	....	....	1,773	1,773	1,813	1,813	395
Sardinia, ...	1,821	12	....	9	1,809	1,809	1,821	1,812	482
Tonawanda, ...	3,040	345	....	....	2,695	2,695	3,040	3,040	605
Wales, ...	1,441	57	....	....	1,384	1,384	1,441	1,441	343
West Seneca, ...	3,347	598	....	4	2,749	2,749	3,347	3,343	599
Part of Cattaraugus Indian Reservation,	1,085	......	....	....	......	... ..	......	......	......
Total, ...	157,150	20,838	571	841	134,656	135,227	156,579	155,224	29,441
				ESSEX COUNTY.					
Chesterfield, ...	2,787	244	15	15	2,528	2,543	2,772	2,772	523
Crown Point, ...	2,636	174	1	1	2,461	2,462	2,635	2,635	617
Elizabethtown, ...	1,592	131	12	12	1,449	1,461	1,580	1,580	352
Essex, ...	1,501	84	6	7	1,411	1,417	1,495	1,494	328
Jay, ...	2,279	126	....	....	2,153	2,153	2,279	2,279	479
Keene, ...	770	11	....	....	759	759	770	770	180
Lewis, ...	1,774	79	....	....	1,695	1,695	1,774	1,774	412
Minerva, ...	1,082	149	2	2	931	933	1,080	1,080	200
Moriah, ...	4,640	721	....	5	3,919	3,919	4,640	4,635	868
Newcomb, ...	149	6	....	....	143	143	149	149	35
North Elba, ...	339	1	7	17	331	338	332	322	92
North Hudson, ...	575	85	....	....	490	490	575	575	112
St. Armand, ...	299	4	....	....	295	295	299	299	83
Schroon, ...	1,688	157	....	....	1,531	1,531	1,688	1,688	364
Ticonderoga, ...	2,606	181	....	....	2,425	2,425	2,606	2,606	607
Westport, ...	1,687	77	6	7	1,604	1,610	1,681	1,680	375
Willsborough, ...	1,432	92	11	11	1,329	1,340	1,421	1,421	317
Wilmington, ...	808	17	....	....	791	791	808	808	177
Total, ...	28,644	2,339	60	77	26,245	26,305	28,584	28,567	6,121
				FRANKLIN COUNTY.					
Bangor, ...	2,180	94	....	....	2,086	2,086	2,180	2,180	511
Bellmont, ...	1,492	227	1	1	1,264	1,265	1,491	1,491	258
Bombay, ...	1,689	181	....	....	1,508	1,508	1,689	1,689	304
Brandon, ...	821	40	....	....	781	781	821	821	182
Brighton, ...	160	10	....	1	150	150	160	159	37
Burke, ...	1,929	169	....	....	1,760	1,760	1,929	1,929	359
Chateaugay, ...	2,843	308	....	....	2,535	2,535	2,843	2,843	524
Constable, ...	1,520	180	....	....	1,340	1,340	1,520	1,520	308
Dickson, ...	1,783	22	....	....	1,761	1,761	1,783	1,783	387
Duane, ...	270	16	1	1	253	254	269	269	57
Fort Covington, ...	2,383	347	....	....	2,036	2,036	2,383	2,383	450
Franklin, ...	1,070	59	5	12	1,006	1,011	1,065	1,058	218
Harrietstown, ...	305	5	....	...	300	300	305	305	71
Malone, ...	6,330	914	4	5	5,412	5,416	6,326	6,325	1,190

FRANKLIN COUNTY — (Continued).

TOWNS.	Population.	Aliens.	Colored persons not taxed.	Whole number of persons of color.	Number, deducting aliens and colored persons, not taxed.	Population, excluding aliens only.	Population, excluding persons of color not taxed only.	Population, excluding all persons of color.	Voters.
Moira,	1,695	54	...	....	1,641	1,641	1,695	1,695	356
Westville,	1,675	206	....	....	1,469	1,469	1,675	1,675	293
St. Regis Ind. Res'n,	430	......	....	....	......	......	......	......	.....
Total,	28,575	2,832	11	20	25,302	25,313	28,134	28,125	5,505
FULTON COUNTY.									
Bleecker,	993	49	....	....	944	944	993	993	194
Broadalbin,	2,335	19	16	16	2,300	2,316	2,319	2,319	562
Caroga,	631	17	8	19	606	614	623	612	142
Ephratah,	2,189	7	5	6	2,177	2,182	2,184	2,183	535
Johnstown,	9,805	332	80	117	9,393	9,473	9,725	9,688	2,278
Mayfield,	2,280	39	7	12	2,234	2,241	2,273	2,268	571
Northampton,	1,903	9	....	4	1,894	1,894	1,903	1,899	499
Oppenheim,	2,213	12	10	11	2,191	2,201	2,203	2,202	606
Perth,	1,053	62	....	....	991	991	1,053	1,053	245
Stratford,	1,110	17	....	1	1,093	1,093	1,110	1,109	263
Total,	24,512	563	126	186	23,823	23,949	24,386	24,326	5,895
GENESEE COUNTY.									
Alabama,	1,839	103	31	33	1,700	1,731	1,808	1,806	430
Alexander,	1,828	107	3	5	1,718	1,721	1,825	1,823	445
Batavia,	6,004	548	28	42	5,423	5,456	5,976	5,962	1,349
Bergen,	1,908	93	2	6	1,813	1,815	1,906	1,902	504
Bethany,	1,734	103	....	....	1,631	1,631	1,734	1,734	451
Byron,	1,645	278	1	1	1,366	1,357	1,644	1,644	359
Darien,	2,168	121	1	1	2,046	2,047	2,167	2,167	527
Elba,	2,044	121	1	2	1,922	1,923	2,043	2,042	504
Le Roy,	4,304	320	9	16	3,975	3,984	4,295	4,288	1,032
Oakfield,	1,511	110	....	....	1,401	1,401	1,511	1,511	344
Pavilion,	1,611	101	....	....	1,510	1,510	1,611	1,611	419
Pembroke,	2,825	123	....	....	2,702	2,702	2,825	2,825	696
Stafford,	1,798	194	....	....	1,604	1,604	1,798	1,798	405
Tonawanda In. Res,.*	509	......	....	....	......	......	......	......	......
Total,	31,728	2,327	76	106	28,816	28,892	31,143	31,113	7,465
GREENE COUNTY.									
Ashland,	1,080	3	1	1	1,076	1,077	1,079	1,079	267
Athens,	2,978	80	60	103	2,838	2,898	2,918	2,875	736
Cairo,	2,343	13	24	29	2,306	2,330	2,319	2,314	612
Catskill,	6,679	306	176	218	6,197	6,373	6,503	6,461	1,482
Coxsackie,	3,561	127	212	238	3,222	3,434	3,349	3,323	835
Durham,	2,412	12	14	22	2,386	2,400	2,398	2,390	650
Greenville,	2,246	23	38	40	2,185	2,223	2,208	2,206	582
Halcott,	436	....	....	......	436	436	436	436	106
Hunter,	1,641	43	....	6	1,598	1,598	1,641	1,635	381
Jewett,	1,110	2	....	......	1,108	1,108	1,110	1,110	280
Lexington,	1,520	1	...	......	1,519	1,519	1,520	1,520	381
New Baltimore,	2,629	91	40	57	2,498	2,538	2,589	2,572	652
Prattsville,	1,484	10	11	29	1,463	1,474	1,473	1,455	366
Windham,	1,591	10	1	1	1,580	1,581	1,590	1,590	415
Total,	31,710	721	577	744	30,412	30,989	31,133	30,966	7,745

* A cmall portion of those reside in Niagara County.

HAMILTON COUNTY.

TOWNS.	Population.	Aliens.	Colored persons not taxed.	Whole number of persons of color.	Number, deducting aliens and colored persons, not taxed.	Population, excluding aliens only.	Population, excluding persons of color not taxed only.	Population, excluding all persons of color.	Voters.
Arietta,	82	......	....	....	82	82	82	82	27
Benson,	315	......	....	....	315	315	315	315	79
Hope,	621	10	....	....	611	611	621	621	139
Indian Lake,	174	9	....	1	165	165	174	173	34
Lake Pleasant,	280	3	....	....	277	277	280	280	72
Long Lake,	270	2	....	....	268	268	270	270	62
Morehouse,	219	8	....	....	211	211	219	219	59
Wells,	692	6	1	1	685	686	691	691	186
Total,	2,653	38	1	2	2,614	2,615	2,652	2,651	657

HERKIMER COUNTY.

TOWNS.	Population.	Aliens.	Colored persons not taxed.	Whole number of persons of color.	Number, deducting aliens and colored persons, not taxed.	Population, excluding aliens only.	Population, excluding persons of color not taxed only.	Population, excluding all persons of color.	Voters.
Columbia,	1,732	31	2	3	1,699	1,701	1,730	1,729	493
Danube,	1,343	26	1	1	1,316	1,317	1,342	1,342	357
Fairfield,	1,649	122	3	3	1,524	1,527	1,646	1,646	419
Frankfort,	3,087	150	1	3	2,936	2,937	3,086	3,084	758
German Flats,	5,074	295	41	42	4,738	4,779	5,033	5,032	1,347
Herkimer,	2,922	153	14	16	2,755	2,769	2,908	2,906	722
Litchfield,	1,397	75	11	11	1,311	1,322	1,386	1,386	256
Little Falls,	5,588	500	43	66	5,045	5,088	5,545	5,522	1,288
Manheim,	1,831	109	17	18	1,705	1,722	1,814	1,813	437
Newport,	1,983	85	8	20	1,890	1,898	1,975	1,963	471
Norway,	1,080	58	....	....	1,022	1,022	1,080	1,080	241
Ohio,	928	15	....	....	913	913	928	928	229
Russia,	2,030	89	....	1	1,941	1,941	2,030	2,029	527
Salisbury,	2,123	116	1	3	2,006	2,007	2,122	2,120	511
Schuyler,	1,589	62	1	1	1,526	1,527	1,588	1,588	394
Stark,	1,522	31	....	5	1,491	1,491	1,522	1,517	405
Warren,	1,611	36	1	1	1,574	1,575	1,610	1,610	437
Wilmurt,	148	6	....	....	142	142	148	148	32
Winfield,	1,517	68	3	3	1,446	1,449	1,514	1,514	396
Total,	39,154	2,027	147	197	36,980	37,127	39,007	38,957	9,720

JEFFERSON COUNTY.

TOWNS.	Population.	Aliens.	Colored persons not taxed.	Whole number of persons of color.	Number, deducting aliens and colored persons, not taxed.	Population, excluding aliens only.	Population, excluding persons of color not taxed only.	Population, excluding all persons of color.	Voters.
Adams,	3,418	240	13	14	3,165	3,178	3,405	3,404	881
Alexandria,	3,614	221	....	14	3,393	3,393	3,614	3,600	826
Antwerp,	3,132	221	1	2	2,910	2,911	3,131	3,130	747
Brownville,	3,495	165	6	6	3,324	3,330	3,489	3,489	879
Cape Vincent,	3,479	510	2	2	2,967	2,969	3,477	3,477	683
Champion,	2,062	82	....	....	1,980	1,980	2,062	2,062	535
Clayton,	4,446	433	3	3	4,010	4,012	4,443	4,443	694
Ellisburgh,	5,286	124	1	3	5,161	5,162	5,285	5,283	1,373
Henderson,	1,962	119	1	1	1,842	1,843	1,961	1,961	497
Hounsfield,	2,754	140	8	15	2,606	2,614	2,746	2,739	721
Le Ray,	2,986	123	....	1	2,863	2,863	2,986	2,985	778
Lorraine,	1,580	63	....	2	1,517	1,517	1,580	1,578	378
Lyme,	2,377	116	....	....	2,261	2,261	2,377	2,377	590
Orleans,	2,791	169	....	....	2,622	2,622	2,791	2,791	640
Pamelia,	2,492	236	3	10	2,253	2,256	2,489	2,482	589
Philadelphia,	1,715	74	....	1	1,641	1,641	1,715	1,714	426
Rodman,	1,654	52	6	7	1,596	1,602	1,648	1,647	449
Rutland,	1,964	156	....	....	1,808	1,808	1,964	1,964	494
Theresa,	2,515	142	....	....	2,373	2,373	2,515	2,515	592
Watertown,	8,194	1,136	65	75	6,993	7,058	8,129	8,119	1,686
Wilna,	3,921	317	9	12	3,595	3,604	3,912	3,909	918
Worth,	611	26	12	13	573	585	599	598	150
Total,	66,448	4,865	130	181	61,453	61,583	66,318	66,267	15,526

KINGS COUNTY.

TOWNS.	Population.	Aliens.	Colored persons not taxed.	Whole number of persons of color.	Number, deducting aliens and colored persons, not taxed.	Population, excluding aliens only.	Population, excluding persons of color not taxed only.	Population, excluding all persons of color.	Voters.
Brooklyn city:									
1st ward,	6,128	1,537	22	29	4,569	4,591	6,106	6,099	1,267
2d ward,	8,760	1,903	65	75	6,792	6,857	8,695	8,185	1,627
3d ward,	8,890	2,107	91	99	6,692	6,783	8,799	8,791	1,955
4th ward,	11,506	1,639	402	423	9,465	9,867	11,104	11,083	2,556
5th ward,	17,820	2,792	223	249	14,805	15,028	17,597	17,571	3,482
6th ward,	26,407	7,235	60	62	19,112	19,172	26,347	26,345	4,157
7th ward,	15,968	2,408	43	70	13,517	13,560	15,925	15,898	2,999
8th ward,	9,829	1,728	59	72	8,042	8,101	9,770	9,757	1,766
9th ward,	23,443	3,846	593	687	19,004	19,597	22,850	22,756	3,816
10th ward,	28,668	5,504	151	171	23,013	23,164	28,517	28,497	4,970
11th ward,	18,242	2,942	606	689	14,694	15,300	17,636	17,553	3,609
12th ward,	13,085	2,963	....	1	10,122	10,122	13,085	13,084	2,143
13th ward,	17,791	2,499	93	139	15,199	15,292	17,698	17,652	3,788
14th ward,	15,425	2,232	52	61	13,141	13,193	15,373	15,364	2,904
15th ward,	11,449	1,288	367	388	9,794	10,161	11,082	11,061	2,097
16th ward,	24,379	3,564	557	783	20,258	20,815	23,822	23,596	4,300
17th ward,	10,234	1,163	3	11	9,068	9,071	10,231	10,223	2,102
18th ward,	6,319	752	5	13	5,296	5.301	6,048	6,040	1,160
19th ward,	8,055	964	10	31	7,081	7,091	8,045	8,024	1,726
20th ward,	13,980	1,717	125	136	12,138	12,263	13,855	13,844	3,060
Total Brooklyn,	296,378	50,783	3,527	4,189	241,802	245,329	292,585	291,923	55 484
Flatbush,	2,778	502	154	187	2,122	2,276	2,624	2,591	463
Flatlands,	1,904	240	49	129	1,615	1,664	1,855	1,775	367
Gravesend,	1,627	313	26	166	1,288	1,314	1,601	1,461	366
New Lots,	5,009	874	75	81	4,060	4,135	4,934	4,928	908
New Utrecht,	3,394	716	106	109	2,572	2,678	3,288	3,285	579
Total,	311,090	53,428	3,937	4,861	253,459	257,396	306,887	305,963	58,167

LEWIS COUNTY.

TOWNS.	Population.	Aliens.	Colored persons not taxed.	Whole number of persons of color.	Number, deducting aliens and colored persons, not taxed.	Population, excluding aliens only.	Population, excluding persons of color not taxed only.	Population, excluding all persons of color.	Voters.
Croghan,	2,146	189	...	6	1,957	1,957	2,146	2,140	450
Denmark,	2,222	86	17	20	2,119	2,136	2,205	2,202	602
Diana,	1,645	141	....	....	1,504	1,504	1,645	1,645	367
Greig,	1,946	113	....	....	1,833	1,833	1,946	1,946	479
Harrisburgh,	1,238	37	2	7	1,199	1,201	1,236	1,231	330
High Market,	1,130	85	....	....	1,045	1,045	1,130	1,130	217
Lewis,	1,259	78	....	....	1,181	1,181	1,259	1,259	250
Leyden,	1,828	86	....	9	1,742	1,742	1,828	1,819	467
Lowville,	2,574	95	3	8	2,476	2,479	2,571	2,566	656
Martinsburgh,	2,480	104	3	6	2,373	2,376	2,477	2,474	581
Montague,	643	9	....	....	634	634	643	643	142
New Bremen,	1,966	136	....	....	1,830	1,830	1,966	1,966	434
Osceola,	712	15	....	....	697	697	712	712	172
Pinckney,	1,291	53	....	1	1,238	1,238	1,291	1,290	318
Turin,	1,683	31	....	....	1,652	1,652	1,683	1,683	441
Watson,	949	25	....	....	924	924	949	949	264
West Turin,	2,128	114	....	....	2,014	2,014	2,128	2,128	507
Total,	27,840	1,397	25	57	26,418	26,443	27,815	27,783	6,677

LIVINGSTON COUNTY.

TOWNS.	Population.	Aliens.	Colored persons not taxed.	Whole number of persons of color.	Number, deducting aliens and colored persons, not taxed.	Population, excluding aliens only.	Population, excluding persons of color not taxed only.	Population, excluding all persons of color.	Voters.
Avon,	2,930	374	11	11	2,545	2,556	2,919	2,919	628
Caledonia,	1,725	225	....	....	1,500	1,500	1,725	1,725	372
Conesus,	1,346	49	5	5	1,292	1,297	1,341	1,341	320
Geneseo,	3,001	210	21	46	2,770	2,791	2,980	2,955	749
Groveland,	1,430	106	1	1	1,323	1,324	1,429	1,429	303
Leicester,	1,651	95	2	28	1,554	1,556	1,649	1,623	403
Lima,	2,925	176	7	21	2,742	2,749	2,918	2,904	684
Livonia,	2,605	94	1	1	2,510	2,510	2,604	2,604	667

LIVINGSTON COUNTY—(Continued).

TOWNS.	Population.	Aliens.	Colored persons not taxed.	Whole number of persons of color.	Number, deducting aliens and colored persons, not taxed.	Population, excluding aliens only.	Population, excluding persons not taxed only.	Population, excluding all persons of color.	Voters.
Mount Morris, ...	3,770	169	4	6	3,597	3,601	3,766	3,764	964
North Dansville, ...	3,724	162	13	13	3,549	3,562	3,711	3,711	875
Nunda, ...	2,843	128	5	5	2,710	2,715	2,838	2,838	698
Ossian, ...	884	15	4	4	865	869	880	880	237
Portage, ...	1,407	50	....	....	1,357	1,357	1,407	1,407	334
Sparta, ...	1,183	14	....	....	1,169	1,169	1,183	1,183	349
Springwater, ...	2,227	28	....	11	2,199	2,199	2,227	2,216	574
West Sparta, ...	1,383	31	....	....	1,352	1,352	1,383	1,383	339
York, ...	2,521	318	7	16	2,196	2,203	2,514	2,505	559
Total, ...	37,555	2,244	81	168	35,230	35,311	37,474	37,387	9,055

MADISON COUNTY.

TOWNS.	Population.	Aliens.	Colored persons not taxed.	Whole number of persons of color.	Number, deducting aliens and colored persons, not taxed.	Population, excluding aliens only.	Population, excluding persons not taxed only.	Population, excluding all persons of color.	Voters.
Brookfield, ...	3,593	92	1	7	3,500	3,501	3,592	3,586	997
Cazenovia, ...	4,157	127	9	33	4,021	4,030	4,148	4,124	1,094
De Ruyter, ...	1,820	33	....	2	1,787	1,787	1,820	1,818	502
Eaton, ...	3,861	240	11	14	3,610	3,621	3,850	3,847	965
Fenner, ...	1,387	18	7	7	1,362	1,369	1,380	1,380	383
Georgetown, ...	1,479	15	....	....	1,464	1,464	1,479	1,479	396
Hamilton, ...	3,434	84	26	26	3,324	3,350	3,408	3,408	960
Lebanon, ...	1,557	71	13	17	1,473	1,486	1,544	1,540	409
Lenox, ...	8,456	334	32	52	8,090	8,122	8,424	8,404	2,170
Madison, ...	2,414	116	....	...	2,298	2,298	2,414	2,414	611
Nelson, ...	1,717	42	....	....	1,675	1,675	1,717	1,717	462
Smithfield, ...	1,366	25	42	85	1,299	1,341	1,324	1,281	353
Stockbridge, ...	1,925	91	13	13	1,821	1,834	1,912	1,912	559
Sullivan, ...	5,340	286	60	69	4,994	5,054	5,280	5,271	1,299
Oneida Indians, ...	101	.....	....	....	......	.....	......	......	......
Total, ...	42,607	1,574	214	325	40,718	40,932	42,292	42,181	11,160

MONROE COUNTY.

TOWNS.	Population.	Aliens.	Colored persons not taxed.	Whole number of persons of color.	Number, deducting aliens and colored persons, not taxed.	Population, excluding aliens only.	Population, excluding persons not taxed only.	Population, excluding all persons of color.	Voters.
Brighton, ...	3,590	731	36	46	2,823	2,859	3,554	3,544	666
Chili, ...	2,242	229	10	10	2,003	2,013	2,232	2,232	498
Clarkson, ...	1,843	138	1	3	1,704	1,705	1,842	1,840	419
Gates, ...	2,783	223	3	6	2,557	2,560	2,780	2,777	541
Greece, ...	4,400	633	9	14	3,758	3,767	4,391	4,386	877
Henrietta, ...	2,207	182	....	4	2,025	2,025	2,207	2,203	515
Hamlin, ...	2,392	169	....	....	2,223	2,223	2,392	2,392	584
Irondequoit, ...	3,420	261	11	11	3,148	3,159	3,409	3,409	697
Mendon, ...	2,959	247	1	3	2,711	2,712	2,958	2,956	727
Ogden, ...	2,791	194	2	2	2,595	2,597	2,789	2,789	681
Parma, ...	2,936	198	2	4	2,736	2,738	2,934	2,932	705
Penfield, ...	3,059	255	3	3	2,801	2,804	3,056	3,056	728
Perrinton, ...	3,219	286	4	6	2,929	2,933	3,215	3,213	792
Pittsford, ...	2,029	153	1	1	1,875	1,876	2,028	2,028	459
Riga, ...	2,141	233	....	....	1,908	1,908	2,141	2,141	464
Rochester city:									
1st ward, ...	2,220	432	24	29	1,764	1,788	2,196	2,191	487
2d ward, ...	3,468	650	....	1	2,818	2,818	3,468	3,467	661
3d ward, ...	4,820	715	110	149	3,995	4,105	4,710	4,671	984
4th ward, ...	3,236	462	12	16	2,762	2,774	3,224	3,220	656
5th ward, ...	4,616	546	8	8	4,062	4,070	4,608	4,608	876
6th ward, ...	3,613	340	3	7	3,270	3,273	3,610	3,606	817
7th ward, ...	2,605	183	6	21	2,416	2,422	2,599	2,584	556
8th ward, ...	4,480	367	64	93	4,049	4,113	4,416	4,387	807
9th ward, ...	5,084	727	20	20	4,337	4,357	5,064	5,064	845
10th ward, ...	2,732	342	12	16	2,378	2,390	2,720	2,716	539
11th ward, ...	4,300	563	....	3	3,737	3,737	4,300	4,297	762
12th ward, ...	3,245	374	8	33	2,863	2,871	3,237	3,212	655
13th ward, ...	3,228	284	4	5	2,940	2,944	3,224	3,223	591
14th ward, ...	3,293	425	16	28	2,852	2,868	3,277	3,265	634
Total Rochester, ...	50,940	6,410	287	429	44,243	44,530	50,653	50,511	9,870

MONROE COUNTY — (Continued).

TOWNS.	Population.	Aliens.	Colored persons not taxed.	Whole number of persons of color.	Number, deducting aliens and colored persons, not taxed.	Population, excluding aliens only.	Population, excluding persons of color not taxed only.	Population, excluding all persons of color.	Voters.
Rush,	1,708	229	4	4	1,475	1,479	1,704	1,704	385
Sweden,	4,126	311	13	28	3,802	3,815	4,113	4,098	916
Webster,	2,775	112	12	19	2,651	2,663	2,763	2,756	699
Wheatland,	2,675	294	2	2	2,379	2,381	2,673	2,673	554
Total,	104,235	11,488	401	595	92,346	92,747	103,834	103,640	21,777
MONTGOMERY COUNTY.									
Amsterdam,	5,135	345	26	40	4,764	4,790	5,109	5,095	1,215
Canajoharie,	4,248	106	44	72	4,098	4,142	4,204	4,176	903
Charleston,	1,687	6	....	....	1,681	1,681	1,687	1,687	472
Florida,	2,885	111	20	20	2,754	2,774	2,865	2,865	732
Glen,	2,737	56	36	39	2,645	2,681	2,701	2,698	701
Minden,	4,637	126	39	44	4,472	4,511	4,598	4,593	1,174
Mohawk,	2,948	92	81	89	2,775	2,856	2,867	2,859	680
Palatine,	2,561	34	10	12	2,517	2,527	2,551	2,549	645
Root,	2,456	35	4	14	2,417	2,421	2,452	2,442	643
St. Johnsville,	2,153	61	13	13	2,079	2,092	2,140	2,140	529
Total,	31,447	972	273	343	30,202	30,475	31,174	31,104	7,694
NEW YORK COUNTY.									
New York city:									
1st ward,	9,852	1,827	75	78	7,930	8,025	9,877	9,774	1,906
2d ward,	1,194	282	28	34	884	912	1,166	1,160	277
3d ward,	3,367	1,130	39	45	2,198	2,237	3,328	3,322	744
4th ward,	17,352	4,558	30	48	12,764	12,794	17,322	17,304	3,088
5th ward,	18,205	4,906	809	865	12,490	13,299	17,396	17,340	3,295
6th ward,	19,754	3,674	275	289	15,805	16,080	19,479	19,465	4,145
7th ward,	36,962	9,863	45	70	27,054	27,099	36,917	36,892	6,150
8th ward,	30,098	5,334	2,076	2,174	22,688	24,764	28,022	27,924	5,499
9th ward,	38,504	5,494	313	476	32,697	33,010	38,191	38,028	7,999
10th ward,	31,537	8,478	88	96	22,971	22,059	31,449	31,441	5,462
11th ward,	58,953	12,651	118	124	46,184	46,302	58,835	58,829	9,222
12th ward,	28,259	4,361	369	436	23,529	23,898	27,890	27,823	4,720
13th ward,	26,388	4,275	252	302	21,861	22,113	26,136	26,086	4,799
14th ward,	23,382	5,050	628	683	17,704	18,332	22,754	22,699	4,324
15th ward,	25,572	6,672	797	962	18,103	18,900	24,775	24,610	5,313
16th ward,	41,972	8,388	672	721	32,912	33,584	41,300	41,251	6,989
17th ward,	79,563	17,895	213	253	61,455	61,668	79,350	79,310	13,361
18th ward,	47,613	10,197	259	302	37,157	37,416	47,354	47,311	8,576
19th ward,	39,945	7,336	270	295	32,339	32,609	39,675	39,650	7,286
20th ward,	61,884	12,658	1,128	1,224	48,098	49,226	60,756	60,660	10,643
21st ward,	38,669	8,353	206	258	30,110	30,316	38,463	38,411	7,064
22d ward,	47,361	8,456	189	208	38,716	38,905	47,172	47,153	8,113
Total,	726,386	151,838	8,879	9,943	565,649	574,548	717,607	716,443	128,975
NIAGARA COUNTY.									
Cambria,	2,115	174	2	2	1,939	1,941	2,113	2,113	481
Hartland,	3,445	281	1	1	3,163	3,164	3,444	3,444	794
Lewiston,	2,998	472	27	29	2,499	2,526	2,971	2,969	537
Lockport,*	13,937	1,512	164	240	12,261	12,425	13,773	13,697	2,846
Newfane,	3,246	249	8	8	2,989	2,997	3,238	3,238	782
Niagara,	6,186	1,229	114	126	4,843	4,957	6,072	6,060	988

* The town of Lockport. Since the census was taken, a town and a city of five wards have been formed from the territory of this town.

NIAGARA COUNTY — (Continued).

TOWNS.	Population.	Aliens.	Colored persons not taxed.	Whole number of persons of color.	Number, deducting aliens and colored persons not taxed.	Population, excluding aliens only.	Population, excluding persons of color not taxed only.	Population, excluding all persons of color.	Voters.
Pendleton,	1,731	156	....	....	1,575	1,575	1,731	1,731	368
Porter,	2,366	271	3	3	2,092	2,095	2,363	2,363	496
Royalton,	4,691	469	2	4	4,220	4,222	4,689	4,687	1,087
Somerset,	1,787	141	....	....	1,646	1,646	1,787	1,787	443
Wheatfield,	3,517	493	2	2	3,022	3,024	3,515	3,515	669
Wilson,	3,264	263	8	8	2,993	3,001	3,256	3,256	731
Tuscarora Ind. Res.,	372	......	....	....	.....	......	......	......	......
Total,	49,655	5,710	331	423	43,242	43,573	48,952	48,860	10,222

ONEIDA COUNTY.

TOWNS.	Population.	Aliens.	Colored persons not taxed.	Whole number of persons of color.	Number, deducting aliens and colored persons not taxed.	Population, excluding aliens only.	Population, excluding persons of color not taxed only.	Population, excluding all persons of color.	Voters.
Annsville,	2,685	61	....	....	2,624	2,624	2,685	2,685	671
Augusta,	2,061	76	3	3	1,982	1,985	2,058	2,058	551
Ava,	1,121	27	3	3	1,091	1,094	1,118	1,118	272
Boonville,	4,228	245	...	....	3,983	3,983	4,228	4,228	1,071
Bridgewater,	1,252	56	....	....	1,196	1,196	1,252	1,252	346
Camden,	3,533	167	27	28	3,339	3,366	3,506	3,505	903
Deerfield,	2,071	159	3	3	1,909	1,912	2,068	2,068	511
Florence,	2,467	93	2	12	2,372	2,374	2,465	2,455	588
Floyd,	1,227	29	....	....	1,198	1,198	1,227	1,227	332
Kirkland,	4,044	296	32	34	3,716	3,748	4,012	4,010	909
Lee,	2,714	33	8	13	2,673	2,681	2,706	2,701	730
Marcy,	1,517	69	....	....	1,448	1,448	1,517	1,517	403
Marshall,	2,141	99	9	9	2,033	2,042	2,132	2,132	540
New Hartford,	3,654	285	7	8	3,362	3,369	3,647	3,646	843
Paris,	3,595	204	6	8	3,385	8,391	3,589	3,587	889
Remsen,	2,650	170	5	11	2.475	2,480	2,645	2,639	708
Rome,	9,478	678	55	78	8,745	8,800	9,423	9,400	2,197
Sangerfield,	2,357	184	24	47	2,149	2,173	2,333	2,310	566
Steuben,	1,416	33	7	7	1,376	1,383	1,409	1,409	390
Trenton,	3,199	165	3	3	3,031	3,034	3,196	3,196	810
Utica city:									
1st ward,	1,309	195	3	3	1 111	1,114	1,306	1,306	308
2d ward,	2,733	283	1	16	2,449	2,450	2,732	2,717	630
3d ward,	3,190	272	4	4	2,914	2,918	3,186	3,186	709
4th ward,	3,667	230	143	154	3,294	3,437	3,524	3,513	798
5th ward,	3,246	314	3	4	2,929	2,932	3,243	3,242	669
6th ward,	5,527	408	2	2	5,117	5,119	5,525	5,525	1,006
7th ward,	4,014	248	34	53	3,732	3,766	3,980	3,961	800
Total Utica,	23,686	1,950	190	236	21,546	21,736	23,496	23,450	4,920
Vernon,	2,931	126	9	12	2,796	2,805	2,922	2,919	736
Verona,	5,964	313	3	7	5,648	5,651	5,961	5,957	1,453
Vienna,	3,408	59	1	1	3,348	3,349	3,407	3,407	921
Western,	2,352	61	18	50	2,273	2,291	2,334	2,302	585
Westmoreland,	2,978	147	15	16	2,816	2,831	2,963	2,962	736
Whitestown,	3,984	260	25	32	3,699	3,724	3,959	3,952	908
Total,	102,713	6,045	455	621	96,213	96,668	102,258	102,092	24,489

ONONDAGA COUNTY.

TOWNS.	Population.	Aliens.	Colored persons not taxed.	Whole number of persons of color.	Number, deducting aliens and colored persons not taxed.	Population, excluding aliens only.	Population, excluding persons of color not taxed only.	Population, excluding all persons of color.	Voters.
Camillus,	2,552	104	3	3	2,445	2,448	2,549	2,549	598
Cicero,	3,166	67	22	22	3,077	3,099	3,144	3,144	807
Clay,	3,069	75	4	5	2,990	2,994	3,065	3,064	764
De Witt,	3,001	181	8	9	2,812	2,820	2,993	2,992	685
Elbridge,	4,318	211	29	32	4,078	4,107	4,289	4,286	966
Fabius,	2,201	107	5	5	2,089	2,094	2,196	2,196	575
Geddes,	3,246	424	2	3	2,820	2,822	3,244	3,243	605
Lafayette,	2,397	73	4	4	2,320	2,324	2,393	2,393	642
Lysander,	4,813	211	17	17	4,585	4,602	4,796	4,796	1,156

ONONDAGA COUNTY—(Continued).

TOWNS.	Population.	Aliens.	Colored persons not taxed.	Whole number of persons of color.	Number, deducting aliens and colored persons not taxed.	Population, excluding aliens only.	Population, excluding persons of color not taxed only.	Population, excluding all persons of color.	Voters.
Manlius,.	6,276	259	30	32	5,987	6,017	6,246	6,244	1,519
Marcellus,	2,577	195	....	1	2,382	2,382	2,577	2,576	592
Onondaga,	5,312	374	53	75	4,885	4,938	5,259	5,237	1,320
Otisco,	1,696	71	....	5	1,625	1,625	1,696	1,691	438
Pompey,	3,502	154	1	3	3,347	3,348	3,501	3,499	907
Salina,	2,754	206	1	1	2,547	2,548	2,753	2,753	633
Skaneateles,	4,128	426	12	14	3,690	3,702	4,116	4,114	932
Spafford,	1,566	45	2	3	1,519	1,521	1,564	1,563	422
Syracuse city:									
1st ward,	3,870	450	....	....	3,420	3,420	3,870	3,870	773
2d ward,	4,661	515	18	33	4,128	4,146	4,643	4,628	903
3d ward,	2,473	426	....	1	2,047	2,047	2,473	2,472	520
4th ward,	4,880	544	44	58	4,292	4,336	4,836	4,822	926
5th ward,	3,749	486	....	1	3,263	3,263	3,749	3,748	816
6th ward,	3,514.	450	7	8	3,057	3,064	3,507	3,506	828
7th ward,	5,627	586	24	28	5,017	5,041	5,603	5,599	1,207
8th ward,	3,010	204	93	168	2,713	2,806	2,917	2,842	638
Total Syracuse,	31,784	3,661	186	297	27,937	28,123	31,598	31,487	6,611
Tully,	1,583	66	....	1	1,517	1,517	1,583	1.582	443
Van Buren,	3,031	85	3	5	2,943	2,946	3,028	3,026	794
Onondaga Ind. Res.,	360	......	....	....	......	......	......	......	......
Total,	93,332	6,995	382	537	85,595	85,977	92,590	92,435	21,409
ONTARIO COUNTY.									
Bristol,	1,637	48	2	2	1,587	1,589	1,635	1,635	444
Canadice,	889	16	....	....	873	873	889	889	226
Canandaigua,	7,121	492	97	152	6,532	6,629	7,024	6,969	1,613
East Bloomfield,	2,177	184	12	12	1,981	1,993	2,165	2,165	506
Farmington,	1,773	187	2	4	1,584	1,586	1,771	1,769	411
Gorham,	2,341	117	3	3	2,221	2,224	2,338	2,338	605
Hopewell,	1,788	139	2	6	1,647	1,649	1,786	1,782	445
Manchester,	3,238	119	40	52	3,079	3,119	3,198	3,186	833
Naples,	2,028	13	3	3	2,012	2,015	2,025	2,025	561
Phelps,	5,200	269	8	14	4,923	4,931	5,192	5,186	1,267
Richmond,	1,454	90	5	5	1,359	1,364	1,449	1,449	380
Seneca,	8,553	701	173	290	7,679	7,852	8,380	8,263	1,931
South Bristol,	1,162	17	....	....	1,145	1,145	1,162	1,162	283
Victor,	2,371	220	11	11	2,140	2,151	2,360	2,360	582
West Bloomfield,	1,584	103	3	3	1,478	1,481	1,581	1,581	400
Total,	43,316	2,715	361	557	40,240	40,601	42,955	42,759	10,487
ORANGE COUNTY.									
Blooming Grove,	2,404	202	135	153	2,067	2,202	2,269	2,251	507
Chester,	1,982	116	113	150	1,753	1,866	1,869	1,832	422
Cornwall,	4,610	274	70	89	4,266	4,336	4,540	4,521	951
Crawford,	2,014	102	16	19	1,896	1,912	1,998	1,995	482
Deerpark,	7,417	564	78	107	6,775	6,853	7,339	7,310	1,699
Goshen,	3,393	297	206	233	2,890	3,096	3,187	3,160	727
Greenville,	1,147	13	....	....	1,134	1,134	1,147	1,147	291
Hamptonburgh,	1,212	110	73	90	1,029	1,112	1,139	1,122	264
Minisink,	1,200	31	12	25	1,166	1,169	1,188	1,175	295
Monroe,	4,722	356	7	8	4,359	4,366	4,715	4,714	963
Montgomery,	3,627	303	103	122	3,221	3,324	3,524	3,505	842
Mount Hope,	1,977	171	23	26	1,783	1,806	1,954	1,951	414
Newburgh,	17,388	2,504	416	538	14,469	14,884	16,972	16,850	3,324
New Windsor,	2,697	361	61	67	2,275	2,336	2,636	2,630	547
Wallkill,	7,382	450	179	263	6,753	6,932	7,203	7,119	1,666

ORANGE COUNTY — (Continued).

TOWNS.	Population.	Aliens.	Colored person not taxed.	Whole number of persons of color.	Number, deducting aliens and colored persons, not taxed.	Population, excluding aliens only.	Population, excluding persons of color not taxed, only.	Population, excluding all persons of color.	Voters.
Warwick,...........	5,077	114	129	177	4,834	4,963	4,948	4,900	1,158
Wawayanda,.........	1,906	78	34	34	1,794	1,828	1,872	1,872	425
Total,..............	70,155	6,046	1,655	2,101	62,464	64,109	68,500	68,054	14,977
ORLEANS COUNTY.									
Barre,................	6,845	527	22	41	6,296	6,318	6,823	6,804	1,647
Carlton,..............	2,461	131	6	8	2,324	2,330	2,455	2,453	619
Clarendon,...........	1,800	92	3	7	1,705	1,708	1,797	1,793	458
Gaines,...............	2,355	159	2	2	2,194	2,196	2,353	2,353	579
Kendall,..............	1,873	115	....	....	1,758	1,758	1,873	1,873	467
Murray,...............	2,616	142	5	7	2,469	2,474	2,611	2,609	626
Ridgeway,...........	5,328	466	34	42	4,828	4,862	5,294	5,286	1,276
Shelby,...............	3,203	244	3	3	2,956	2,959	3,200	3,200	766
Yates,...............	2,122	123	2	2	1,997	1,999	2,120	2,120	518
Total,...............	28,603	1,999	77	112	26,527	26,604	28,526	28,491	6,956
OSWEGO COUNTY.									
Albion,.............	2,366	88	1	2	2,277	2,278	2,365	2,364	599
Amboy,..............	1,423	36	....	....	1,387	1,387	1,423	1,423	356
Boylston,............	960	21	....	....	939	939	960	960	226
Constantia,..........	3,517	133	10	38	3,374	3,384	3,507	3,479	810
Granby,..............	3,956	222	2	11	3,732	3,734	3,954	3,945	897
Hannibal,............	3,322	90	4	10	3,228	3,232	3,318	3,312	827
Hastings,............	3,005	50	....	....	2,955	2,955	3,005	3,005	758
Mexico,..............	3,828	135	15	27	3,678	3,693	3,813	3,801	1,025
New Haven,.........	1,948	47	....	....	1,901	1,901	1,948	1,948	479
Orwell,..............	1,427	46	....	....	1,381	1,381	1,427	1,427	346
Oswego,.............	2,913	188	6	6	2,719	2,725	2,907	2,907	659
Oswego city:									
1st ward,........	4,475	872	15	18	3,588	3,603	4,460	4,457	538
2d ward,........	3,897	756	5	28	3,136	3,141	3,892	3,869	698
3d ward,........	6,004	731	46	56	5,227	5,273	6,958	5,948	1,014
4th ward,........	4,912	765	2	4	4,145	4,147	4,910	4,908	900
Total Oswego city,.	19,288	3,124	68	106	16,096	16,164	19,220	19,182	3,150
Palermo,............	2,219	25	....	....	2,194	2,194	2,219	2,219	585
Parish,..............	1,814	8	1	1	1,805	1,806	1,813	1,813	471
Redfield,............	1,072	46	....	....	1,026	1,026	1,072	1,072	224
Richfield,...........	4,137	217	3	3	3,917	3,920	4,134	4,134	1,040
Sandy Creek,........	2,423	34	5	5	2,384	2,389	2,418	2,418	653
Schroeppel,.........	3,669	131	24	31	3,514	3,538	3,645	3,638	947
Scriba,..............	3,215	174	12	16	3,029	3,041	3,203	3,199	791
Volney,.............	6,472	389	53	76	6,030	6,083	6,419	6,396	1,501
West Monroe,........	1,278	28	....	....	1,250	1,250	1,278	1,278	328
Williamstown,.......	1,948	369	....	....	1,579	1,579	1,948	1,948	389
Total,..............	76,200	5,601	204	332	70,395	70,599	75,996	75,868	17,061
OTSEGO COUNTY.									
Burlington,..........	1,690	28	2	2	1,660	1,662	1,688	1,688	446
Butternuts,..........	2,245	53	2	2	2,190	2,192	2,243	2,243	603
Cherry Valley,.......	2,384	57	2	2	2,325	2,327	2,382	2,382	593
Decatur,............	853	......	1	1	852	853	852	852	241
Edmeston,..........	1,793	21	....	....	1,772	1,772	1,793	1,793	493
Exeter,..............	1,445	32	7	8	1,406	1,413	1,438	1,437	386

OTSEGO COUNTY — (Continued).

TOWNS.	Population.	Aliens.	Colored persons not taxed.	Whole number of persons of color.	Number, deducting aliens and colored persons, not taxed.	Population excluding aliens only.	Population excluding persons of color not taxed only.	Population excluding all persons of color.	Voters.
Hartwick,	2,248	34	1	1	2,213	2,214	2,247	2,247	620
Laurens,	1,885	7	....	1	1,878	1,878	1,885	1,884	518
Maryland,	2,197	48	5	5	2,144	2,149	2,192	2,192	569
Middlefield,	2,690	94	17	18	2,579	2,596	2,673	2,672	716
Milford,	2,208	24	1	1	2,183	2,184	2,207	2,207	612
Morris,	2,191	26	1	12	2,164	2,165	2,190	2,179	574
New Lisbon,	1,649	31	....	....	1,618	1,618	1,649	1,649	350
Oneonta,	2,363	35	6	6	2,322	2,328	2,357	2,357	660
Otego,	1,883	6	1	3	1,876	1,877	1,882	1,880	538
Otsego,	4,292	148	32	32	4,112	4,144	4,260	4,260	1,135
Pittsfield,	1,444	25	12	17	1,407	1,419	1,432	1,427	381
Plainfield,	1,283	32	....	4	1,251	1,251	1,283	1,279	349
Richfield,	1,665	68	19	18	1,578	1,597	1,646	1,647	430
Roseboom,	1,719	14	5	5	1,700	1,705	1,714	1,714	463
Springfield,	2,291	47	6	6	2,238	2,244	2,285	2,285	613
Unadilla,	2,685	163	6	5	2,516	2 522	2,679	2,680	740
Westford,	1,282	8	..	....	1,274	1,274	1,282	1,282	352
Worcester,	2,231	87	4	4	2,140	2,144	2,227	2,227	572
Total,	48,616	1,088	130	153	47,398	47,528	48,486	48,463	12,954
PUTNAM COUNTY.									
Carmel,	2,240	115	11	20	2,114	2,125	2,229	2,220	575
Kent,	1,473	10	8	9	1,455	1,453	1,465	1,464	370
Patterson,	1,476	74	24	25	1,378	1,402	1,452	1,451	366
Phillipstown,	5,436	745	2	2	4,689	4,691	3,434	5,434	1,119
Putnam Valley,	1,622	18	1	1	1,603	1,604	1,621	1,621	408
Southeast,	2,598	223	40	54	2,335	2,375	2,558	2,544	607
Total,	14,845	1,185	86	111	13,574	13,660	14,759	14,734	3,445
QUEENS COUNTY.									
Flushing,	10,813	1,249	437	615	9,127	9,564	10,876	10,198	2,152
Hempstead,	11,764	354	278	372	11,132	11,410	11,486	11,392	2,719
Jamaica,	6,777	726	282	373	5,769	6,051	6,495	6,404	1,436
Newtown,	13,891	1,850	197	675	11,844	12,041	13,694	13,216	2,689
North Hempstead,	5,335	577	592	292	4,166	4,758	4,743	5,043	1,038
Oyster Bay,	9,417	840	746	860	7,831	8,577	8,671	8,557	1,767
Total,	57,997	5,596	2,532	3,187	49,869	52,401	55,465	54,810	11,801
RENSSELAER COUNTY.									
Berlin,	2,149	94	2	3	2,053	2,055	2,147	2,146	529
Brunswick,	3,175	214	2	6	2,959	2,961	3,173	3,169	788
East Greenbush,	1,663	217	7	9	1,439	1,446	1,656	1,654	377
Grafton,	1,673	13	4	5	1,656	1,660	1,669	1,668	402
Greenbush,	4,779	476	36	50	4,267	4,303	4,743	4,729	985
Hoosick,	4,783	403	53	64	4,327	4,380	4,730	4,719	1,097
Lansingburgh,	6,072	419	71	91	5,582	5,653	6,001	5,981	1,219
Nassau,	2,894	106	4	9	2,784	2,788	2,890	2,885	751
North Greenbush,	2,575	156	4	10	2,415	2,415	2,571	2,565	567
Petersburgh,	1,670	35	....	....	1,635	1,635	1,670	1,670	410
Pittstown,	3,831	290	15	19	3,526	3,541	3,816	3,812	912
Poestenkill,	1,952	48	....	....	1,904	1,904	1,952	1,952	475
Sandlake,	2,606	70	13	14	2,523	2,536	2,593	2,592	631
Schaghticoke,	3,054	202	23	23	2,829	2,852	3,031	3,031	710
Schodack,	4,015	231	11	50	3,773	3,784	4,004	3,965	1,001
Stephentown,	2,026	37	1	8	1,988	1,989	2,025	2,018	426

RENSSELAER COUNTY — (Continued).

TOWNS.	Population.	Aliens.	Colored persons not taxed.	Whole number of persons of color.	Number, deducting aliens and colored persons taxed.	Population, excluding aliens only.	Population, excluding persons of color not taxed only.	Population, excluding all persons of color.	Voters,
Troy city:									
1st ward,........	3,920	424	137	182	3,359	3,496	3,783	3,738	775
2d ward,........	4,606	616	138	165	3,852	3,990	4,468	4,441	992
3d ward,........	1,952	422	23	27	1,507	1,530	1,929	1,925	498
4th ward,........	3,164	305	24	29	2,835	2,859	3,140	3,135	759
5th ward,........	2,869	323	1	1	2,545	2,546	2,868	2,868	582
6th ward,........	3,124	534	2	....	2,588	2,590	3,122	3,124	572
7th ward,........	4,923	520	3	17	4,400	4,403	4,920	4,906	983
8th ward,........	5,399	794	3	11	4,602	4,605	5,396	5,388	949
9th ward,........	4,723	828	....	12	3,895	3,895	4,723	4,711	776
10th ward,........	4,613	513	4	4	4,096	4,100	4,609	4,609	932
Total Troy city,....	39,293	5,279	335	448	33,679	34,014	38,958	38,845	7,818
Total,..............	88,210	8,290	581	809	79,339	79,920	87,639	87,401	19,098

RICHMOND COUNTY.

TOWNS.	Population.	Aliens.	Colored persons not taxed.	Whole number of persons of color.	Number, deducting aliens and colored persons taxed.	Population, excluding aliens only.	Population, excluding persons of color not taxed only.	Population, excluding all persons of color.	Voters,
Castleton,............	7,683	1,088	86	88	6,509	6,595	7,597	7,595	1,709
Middletown...........	6,866	1,169	115	204	5,582	5,697	6,751	6,662	1,199
Northfield,...........	5,201	507	81	87	4,613	4,694	5,120	5,114	1,090
Southfield,...........	4,407	874	28	46	3,505	3,533	4,379	4,361	733
Westfield,............	4,052	318	145	218	3,589	3,734	3,907	3,834	896
Total,............	28,209	3,956	455	643	23,798	24,253	27,754	27,566	5,627

ROCKLAND COUNTY.

TOWNS.	Population.	Aliens.	Colored persons not taxed.	Whole number of persons of color.	Number, deducting aliens and colored persons taxed.	Population, excluding aliens only.	Population, excluding persons of color not taxed only.	Population, excluding all persons of color.	Voters,
Clarkstown,..........	4,023	274	76	93	3,673	3,749	3,947	3,930	903
Haverstraw,..........	4,113	558	65	69	3,490	3,555	4,048	4,044	756
Orangetown,..........	6,136	616	260	309	5,260	5,520	5,876	5,827	1,196
Ramapo,.............	4,330	241	82	95	4,007	4,089	4,248	4,235	1,009
Stony Point,.........	2,186	249	....	....	1,937	1,937	2,186	2,186	455
Total,............	20,788	1,938	483	566	18,367	18,850	20,305	20,222	4,319

ST. LAWRENCE COUNTY.

TOWNS.	Population.	Aliens.	Colored persons not taxed.	Whole number of persons of color.	Number, deducting aliens and colored persons taxed.	Population, excluding aliens only.	Population, excluding persons of color not taxed only.	Population, excluding all persons of color.	Voters,
Brasher,..............	3,348	462	....	....	2,886	2,886	3,348	3,348	541
Canton,..............	5,694	555	....	2	5,409	5,409	5,964	5,962	1,267
Colton,...............	1,481	190	....	....	1,291	1,291	1,481	1,481	290
De Kalb,.............	3,102	209	....	....	2,893	2,893	3,102	3,102	666
De Peyster,..........	1,187	107	....	....	1,080	1,080	1,187	1,187	269
Edwards,.............	1,180	46	....	....	1,134	1,134	1,180	1,180	272
Fine,.................	487	59	....	....	428	428	487	487	99
Fowler,..............	1,748	86	....	....	1,662	1,662	1,748	1,748	424
Gouverneur,.........	2,915	255	1	2	2,659	2,660	2,914	2,913	643
Hammond,...........	1,819	140	....	....	1,679	1,679	1,819	1,819	407
Hermon,.............	1,667	80	....	....	1,587	1,587	1,667	1,667	408
Hopkinton,..........	1,941	75	....	....	1,866	1,866	1,941	1,941	418
Lawrence,...........	2,719	207	....	....	2,512	2,512	2,719	2,719	621
Lisbon,..............	5,078	452	....	2	4,626	4,626	5,078	5,076	1,022
Louisville,...........	2,237	358	15	15	1,864	1,879	2,222	2,222	503
Macomb,............	1,788	195	....	....	1,593	1,593	1,788	1,788	310
Madrid,..............	2,109	197	5	5	1,907	1,912	2,104	2,104	503
Massena,............	2,741	255	6	20	2,480	2,486	2,735	2,721	550
Morristown,..........	1,881	137	....	....	1,744	1,744	1,881	1,881	440
Norfolk,..............	1,876	267	....	....	1,609	1,609	1,876	1,876	377
Oswegatchie,........	11,091	2,201	5	16	8,885	8,890	11,086	11,075	1,871
Parishville,..........	2,319	144	4	4	2,171	2,175	2,315	2,315	520
Pierrepont,..........	2,423	130	....	....	2,293	2,293	2,423	2,423	523

ST. LAWRENCE COUNTY — (Continued).

TOWNS.	Population.	Aliens.	Colored persons not taxed.	Whole number of persons of color.	Number, deducting aliens and colored persons, not taxed.	Population, excluding aliens only.	Population, excluding persons of color not taxed, only.	Population, excluding all persons of color.	Voters.
Pitcairn,	558	10	....	....	548	548	558	558	117
Potsdam,	6,441	560	....	2	5,881	5,881	6,449	6,439	1,419
Rossie,	1,836	237	....	....	1,599	1,599	1,836	1,836	347
Russsll,	2,625	117	....	....	2,508	2,508	2,625	2,625	572
Stockholm,	3,770	209	....	....	3,561	3,561	3,770	3,770	816
Waddington,	2,663	370	....	....	2,293	2,293	2,663	2,663	549
Total,	80,994	8,310	36	68	72,648	72,684	80,958	80,926	16,764
SARATOGA COUNTY.									
Ballston,	2,089	78	10	13	2,001	2,011	2,079	2,076	478
Charlton,	1,589	45	3	9	1,541	1,544	1,586	1,580	434
Clifton Park,	2,712	108	38	49	2,566	2,604	2,674	2,663	698
Corinth,	1,491	48	....	....	1,443	1,443	1,491	1,491	374
Day,	1,185	24	....	....	1,161	1,161	1,185	1,185	279
Edinburgh,	1,357	4	....	2	1,353	1,353	1,357	1,355	358
Galway,	2,202	51	1	1	2,150	2,151	2,201	2,201	551
Greenfield,	2,891	136	12	30	2,743	2,755	2,879	2,861	734
Hadley,	1,067	74	....	....	993	993	1,067	1,067	225
Halfmoon,	3,032	153	6	7	2,873	2,879	3,026	3,025	748
Malta,	1,190	52	6	21	1,132	1,138	1,184	1,169	344
Milton,	4,923	313	53	60	4,557	4,610	4,870	4,863	1,075
Moreau,	2,279	145	18	32	2,116	2,134	2,261	2,247	496
Northumberland,	1,705	69	16	16	1,620	1,636	1,689	1,689	411
Providence,	1,295	19	....	2	1,276	1,276	1,295	1,293	331
Saratoga,	3,730	244	10	16	3,476	3,486	3,720	3,714	900
Saratoga Springs,	7,307	700	245	285	6,362	6,607	7,062	7,022	1,563
Stillwater,	3,087	167	23	32	2,897	2,920	3,064	3,055	708
Waterford,	3,399	369	25	31	3,005	3,030	3,374	3,368	719
Wilton,	1,362	29	11	12	1,322	1,333	1,351	1,350	356
Total,	49,892	2,828	477	618	46,587	47,064	49,415	49,274	11,782
SCHENECTADY COUNTY.									
Duanesburgh,	3,099	48	13	20	3,038	3,051	3,086	3,079	787
Glenville,	3,038	116	3	22	2,919	2,922	3,035	3,016	770
Niskayuna,	845	36	7	7	802	809	838	838	105
Princetown,	931	1	1	1	929	930	930	930	244
Rotterdam,	2,290	97	21	24	2,172	2,193	2,269	2,260	541
Schenectady city:									
1st ward,	1,443	136	9	10	1,298	1,307	1,434	1,433	313
2d ward,	1,562	86	5	7	1,471	1,476	1,557	1,555	373
3d ward,	2,592	236	43	60	2,313	2,356	2,549	2,532	512
4th ward,	2,738	80	43	47	2,615	2,658	2,695	2,681	666
5th ward,	2,350	108	6	16	2,236	2,242	2,344	2,344	559
Total city,	10,685	646	106	140	9,933	10,039	10,579	10,545	2,423
Total,	20,888	944	151	214	19,793	19,944	29,737	20,674	4,870
SCHOHARIE COUNTY.									
Blenheim,	1,199	2	3	7	1,194	1,197	1,196	1,192	297
Broome,	1,969	5	....	....	1,964	1,964	1,969	1,969	520
Carlisle,	1,700	17	1	1	1,682	1,683	1,699	1,699	435
Cobleskill,	2,439	66	18	32	2,355	2,373	2,421	2,407	621
Conesville,	1,359	10	....	....	1,349	1,349	1,359	1,359	344
Esperance,	1,383	36	9	9	1,338	1,347	1,374	1,374	351
Fulton,	2,808	2	7	8	2,799	2,806	2,801	2,800	662

SCHOHARIE COUNTY — (Continued).

TOWNS.	Population.	Aliens.	Colored persons not taxed.	Whole number of persons of color.	Number, deducting aliens and colored persons, not taxed.	Population, excluding aliens only.	Population, excluding persons of color not taxed only.	Population, excluding all persons of color.	Voters.
Gilboa,	2,385	13	1	1	2,371	2,372	2,384	2,384	598
Jefferson,	1,718	5	....	....	1,713	1,713	1,718	1,718	432
Middleburgh,	3,267	18	54	59	3,195	3,249	3,213	3,208	757
Richmondville,	2,272	86	....	....	2,186	2,186	2,272	2,272	513
Schoharie,	3,155	41	200	269	2,914	3,114	2,955	2,886	686
Seward,	1,692	6	....	7	1,686	1,686	1,692	1,685	455
Sharon,	2,601	28	22	52	2,551	2,573	2,579	2,549	552
Summit,	1,818	5	....	1	1,813	1,813	1,818	1,817	449
Wright,	1,588	3	7	12	1,578	1,585	1,581	1,576	411
Total,	33,353	343	322	458	32,688	33,010	33,031	32,895	8,083
SCHUYLER COUNTY.									
Catharine,	1,622	6	11	29	1,605	1,616	1,611	1,593	410
Cayuta,	636	1	....	....	635	635	639	636	173
Dix,	3,432	95	20	30	3,317	3,337	3,412	3,402	901
Hector,	5,048	33	17	30	4,998	5,015	5,031	5,018	1,336
Montour,	1,854	28	2	27	1,824	1,826	1,852	1,827	500
Orange,	2,094	20	10	10	2,064	2,074	2,084	2,084	568
Reading,	1,682	79	13	13	1,590	1,603	1,669	1,669	416
Tyrone,	2,073	30	1	5	2,042	2,043	2,072	2,068	570
Total,	18,441	292	74	144	18,075	18,149	18,367	18,297	4,874
SENECA COUNTY.									
Covert,	2,261	124	2	2	2,135	2,137	2,259	2,259	563
Fayette,	3,509	120	5	5	3,384	3,389	3,504	3,504	870
Junius,	1,442	73	2	2	1,367	1,369	1,440	1,440	351
Lodi,	1,892	25	3	6	1,864	1,867	1,889	1,886	501
Ovid,	2.382	58	15	32	2,309	2,324	2,367	2,350	583
Romulus,	1,973	109	6	6	1,858	1,864	1,967	1,967	462
Seneca Falls,	6,490	435	28	38	6,027	6,055	6,462	6,452	1,487
Tyre,	1,348	38	3	3	1,307	1,310	1,346	1,346	349
Varick,	1,833	36	21	32	1,776	1,797	1,812	1,801	461
Waterloo,	4,523	183	27	69	4,313	4,340	4,496	4,454	1,016
Total,	27,653	1,201	112	195	26,340	26,452	27,541	27,458	6,643
STEUBEN COUNTY.									
Addison,	1,819	50	20	20	1,749	1,769	1,799	1,799	396
Avoca,	1,853	37	1	1	1,815	1,816	1,852	1,852	491
Bath,	6,247	180	61	144	6,006	6,067	6,186	6,103	1,513
Bradford,	1,163	2	13	18	1,148	1,161	1,150	1,145	306
Cameron,	1,439	26	1	1	1,412	1,413	1,438	1,438	349
Campbell,	1,794	69	1	1	1,724	1,725	1,793	1,793	430
Canisteo,	2,132	38	....	....	2,094	2,094	2,132	2,132	496
Caton,	1,543	11	2	8	1,530	1,532	1,541	1,535	417
Cohocton,	2,614	85	....	8	2,529	2,529	2,614	2,606	602
Corning,	6,724	695	67	87	5,962	6,029	6,657	6,637	1,421
Dansville,	1,980	33	1	1	1,946	1,947	1,979	1,979	504
Erwin,	1,982	121	13	13	1,848	1,861	1,969	1,969	441
Fremont,	1,011	13	....	....	998	998	1,011	1,011	265
Greenwood,	1,163	29	....	...	1,134	1,134	1,163	1,163	270
Hartsville,	995	23	3	3	969	972	992	992	224
Hornby,	1,193	8	...	....	1,185	1,185	1,193	1,193	314
Hornellsville,	5,338	324	15	19	4,999	5,014	5,323	5,319	1,250
Howard,	2,373	43	....	1	2,330	2,330	2,373	2,372	590
Jasper,	1,678	14	....	1	1,664	1,664	1,678	1,677	424

STEUBEN COUNTY — (Continued).

TOWNS.	Population.	Aliens.	Colored persons not taxed.	Whole number of persons of color.	Number, deducting aliens and colored persons not taxed.	Population, excluding aliens only.	Population, excluding persons of color not taxed only.	Population, excluding all persons of color.	Voters.
Lindley,	940	36	1	2	903	904	939	938	221
Prattsburgh,	2,606	45	20	40	2,541	2,561	2,586	2,566	675
Pultney,	1,387	10	....	....	1,377	1,377	1,387	1,387	388
Rathbone,	1,464	67	....	1	1,397	1,397	1,464	1,463	312
Thurston,	1,176	2	1	1	1,173	1,174	1,175	1,175	285
Troupsburgh,	2,100	21	....	....	2,079	2,079	2,100	2,100	494
Tuscarora,	1,523	23	1	1	1,499	1,500	1,522	1,522	345
Urbana,	1,711	38	8	9	1,665	1,673	1,703	1,702	449
Wayland,	2,621	76	....	....	2,545	2,545	2,621	2,621	574
Wayne,	814	4	....	....	810	810	814	814	198
West Union,	1,382	90	....	....	1,292	1,292	1,382	1,382	281
Wheeler,	1,297	2	3	10	1,292	1,295	1,294	1,287	342
Woodhull,	2,130	17	....	....	2,113	2,113	2,130	2,130	499
Total,	66,192	2,232	232	390	63,728	63,960	65,960	65,802	15,766

SUFFOLK COUNTY.

TOWNS.	Population.	Aliens.	Colored persons not taxed.	Whole number of persons of color.	Number, deducting aliens and colored persons not taxed.	Population, excluding aliens only.	Population, excluding persons of color not taxed only.	Population, excluding all persons of color.	Voters.
Brookhaven,	10,159	301	418	466	9,440	9,858	9,741	9,693	2,383
East Hampton,	2,311	73	158	195	2,080	2,238	2,153	2,116	562
Huntington,	7,809	412	301	361	7,096	7,397	7,508	7,448	1,797
Islip,	4,243	172	131	137	3,940	4,071	4,112	4,106	926
River Head,	3,226	110	47	56	3,069	3,116	3,179	3,170	803
Shelter Island,	570	27	....	1	543	543	570	569	123
Smithtown,	2,085	61	194	198	1,830	2,024	1,891	1,887	449
Southampton,	6,194	156	272	307	5,766	6,038	5,922	5,887	1,434
Southold,	6,272	221	92	159	5,959	6,051	6,180	6,113	1,484
Total,	42,869	1,533	1,613	1,880	39,723	41,336	41,256	40,989	9,961

SULLIVAN COUNTY.

TOWNS.	Population.	Aliens.	Colored persons not taxed.	Whole number of persons of color.	Number, deducting aliens and colored persons not taxed.	Population, excluding aliens only.	Population, excluding persons of color not taxed only.	Population, excluding all persons of color.	Voters.
Bethel,	2,817	111	2	2	2,704	2,706	2,815	2,815	589
Cochecton,	3,076	276	7	7	2,793	2,800	3,069	3,069	622
Collicoon,	2,782	133	....	....	2,649	2,649	2,782	2,782	576
Fallsburgh,	3,271	64	25	25	3,182	3,207	3,246	3,246	754
Forrestburgh,	862	45	....	....	817	817	862	862	200
Fremont.	1,967	139	....	....	1,828	1,828	1,967	1,967	444
Highland,	925	86	8	8	831	839	917	917	195
Liberty,	2,855	24	5	7	2,826	2,831	2,850	2,848	657
Lumberland,	1,026	34	....	....	992	992	1,026	1,026	241
Mamakating,	4,222	92	25	30	4,105	4,130	4,197	4,192	1,036
Neversink,	2,542	50	....	....	2,492	2,492	2,542	2,542	683
Rockland,	1,709	63	....	...	1,646	1,646	1,709	1,709	394
Thompson,	3,713	86	1	2	3,626	3,627	3,712	3,711	883
Tusten,	974	48	....	7	926	926	974	967	199
Total,	32,741	1,251	73	88	31,417	31,490	32,668	32,653	7,473

TIOGA COUNTY.

TOWNS.	Population.	Aliens.	Colored persons not taxed.	Whole number of persons of color.	Number, deducting aliens and colored persons not taxed.	Population, excluding aliens only.	Population, excluding persons of color not taxed only.	Population, excluding all persons of color.	Voters.
Barton,	4,077	89	33	48	3,955	3,988	4,044	4,029	1,042
Berkshire,	1,073	13	2	14	1,058	1,060	1,071	1,059	289
Candor,	4,103	30	3	14	4,070	4,073	4,100	4,039	1,114
Newark Valley,	2,133	38	1	1	2,094	2,095	2,132	2,132	453
Nichols,	1,778	6	6	22	1,766	1,772	1,772	1,756	498
Owego,	8,865	214	112	147	8,539	8,651	8,753	8,718	2,209
Richford,	1,283	......	....	11	1,283	1,283	1,283	1,272	324
Spencer,	1,757	12	1	1	1,744	1,745	1,756	1,756	494
Tioga,	3,094	45	10	22	3,039	3,049	3,084	3,072	791
Total,	28,163	447	168	280	27,548	27,716	27,995	27,883	7,214

TOMPKINS COUNTY.

TOWNS.	Population.	Aliens.	Colored persons not taxed.	Whole number of persons of color.	Number, deducting aliens and colored persons, not taxed.	Population, excluding aliens only.	Population, excluding persons of color not taxed, only.	Population, excluding all persons of color.	Voters.
Caroline,	2,257	72	6	23	2,179	2,185	2,251	2,234	612
Danby,	2,140	4	4	8	2,132	2,136	2,136	2,132	541
Dryden,	4,795	41	5	10	4,749	4,754	4,790	4,785	1,178
Enfield,	1,693	3	...	4	1,690	1,690	1,693	1,689	480
Groton,	3,401	27	5	5	3,369	3,374	3,396	3,396	914
Ithaca,	7,264	244	126	220	6,894	7,020	7,138	7,144	1,837
Lansing,	2,940	40	8	8	2,892	2,900	2,932	2,932	775
Newfield,	2,700	......	1	1	2,699	2,700	2,699	2,699	738
Ulysses,	3,506	78	16	46	3,412	3,426	3,490	3,460	924
Total,	30,696	509	171	325	30,016	30,187	30,525	30,371	7,999

ULSTER COUNTY.

TOWNS.	Population.	Aliens.	Colored persons not taxed.	Whole number of persons of color.	Number, deducting aliens and colored persons, not taxed.	Population, excluding aliens only.	Population, excluding persons of color not taxed, only.	Population, excluding all persons of color.	Voters.
Denning,	939	29	....	....	910	910	939	939	204
Esopus,	4,746	392	12	15	4,342	4,354	4,734	4,731	1,005
Gardiner,	1,951	73	103	109	1,775	1,878	1,848	1,842	442
Hardenburgh,	533	13	2	2	518	520	531	531	117
Hurley,	2,382	135	63	81	2,184	2,247	2,319	2,301	503
Kingston,	17,296	2,002	377	362	14,917	15,294	16,919	16,934	3,227
Lloyd,	2,567	58	13	20	2,496	2,509	2,554	2,547	587
Marbletown,	3,818	51	188	227	3,579	3,767	3,630	3,591	823
Marlborough,	2,733	188	36	43	2,509	2,545	2,697	2,690	567
New Paltz,	2,033	113	67	83	1,853	1,920	1,966	1,950	458
Olive,	3,259	70	16	24	3,173	3,189	3,243	3,235	767
Plattekill,	2,012	68	47	69	1,897	1,944	1,965	1,943	463
Rochester,	3,585	27	16	17	3,542	3,558	3,569	3,568	897
Rosendale,	2,884	289	20	22	2,575	2,595	2,864	2,862	574
Saugerties,	9,426	515	82	110	8,829	8,911	9,344	9,316	2,084
Shandaken,	2,719	135	4	6	2,580	2,584	2,715	2,713	597
Shawangunk,	2,767	75	51	61	2,641	2,692	2,716	2,706	683
Wawarsing,	8,335	303	135	161	7,897	8,032	8,200	8,174	1,823
Woodstock,	1,624	27	....	....	1,597	1,597	1,624	1,162	403
Total,	75,609	4,563	1,232	1,412	69,814	71,046	74,377	74,197	16,224

WARREN COUNTY.

TOWNS.	Population.	Aliens.	Colored persons not taxed.	Whole number of persons of color.	Number, deducting aliens and colored persons, not taxed.	Population, excluding aliens only.	Population, excluding persons of color not taxed, only.	Population, excluding all persons of color.	Voters.
Bolton,	1,221	3	....	....	1,218	1,218	1,221	1,221	325
Caldwell,	979	16	....	....	963	963	979	979	245
Chester,	2,274	69	....	....	2,205	2,205	2,274	2,274	479
Hague,	684	14	....	....	670	670	684	684	174
Horicon,	1,398	22	....	....	1,376	1,376	1,398	1,398	316
Johnsburgh,	2,286	107	....	1	2,179	2,179	2,286	2,285	507
Luzerne,	1,136	15	....	....	1,121	1,121	1,136	1,136	301
Queensbury,	7,623	678	12	28	6,933	6,945	7,611	7,595	1,529
Stony Creek,	935	10	....	....	925	925	935	935	201
Thurman,	1,007	4	...	....	1,003	1,003	1,007	1,007	267
Warrensburgh,	1,585	12	2	2	1,571	1,573	1,583	1,583	396
Total,	21,128	950	14	31	20,164	20,178	21,114	21,097	4,740

WASHINGTON COUNTY.

TOWNS.	Population.	Aliens.	Colored persons not taxed.	Whole number of persons of color.	Number, deducting aliens and colored persons, not taxed.	Population, excluding aliens only.	Population, excluding persons of color not taxed, only.	Population, excluding all persons of color.	Voters.
Argyle,	3,056	200	4	6	2,852	2,856	3,052	3,050	773
Cambridge,	2,453	153	13	13	2,287	2,300	2,440	2,440	547
Dresden,	765	30	6	12	729	735	759	753	194
Easton,	2,929	219	39	42	2,671	2,710	2,890	2,887	664
Fort Ann,	3,155	91	12	22	3,052	3,064	3,143	3,133	781
Fort Edward,	3,997	303	2	2	3,692	3,694	3,995	3,995	901
Granville,	3,670	405	3	4	3,262	3,265	3,667	3,666	750

WASHINGTON COUNTY—(Continued).

TOWNS.	Population.	Aliens.	Colored persons not taxed.	Whole number of persons of color.	Number, deducting aliens and colored persons, not taxed.	Population, excluding aliens only.	Population, excluding persons of color not taxed, only.	Population, excluding all persons of color.	Voters.
Greenwich, ...	3,959	221	31	62	3,707	3,738	3,928	3,897	1,022
Hampton, ...	985	123	2	2	860	862	983	983	185
Hartford, ...	2,088	158	....	....	1,930	1,930	2,088	2,088	526
Hebron, ...	2,590	192	2	2	2,396	2,398	2,588	2,588	621
Jackson, ...	1,757	160	11	17	1,586	1,597	1,746	1,740	416
Kingsbury, ...	3,751	237	23	25	3,491	3,514	3,728	3,526	805
Putnam, ...	746	17	....	....	729	729	746	746	190
Salem, ...	3,239	272	9	12	2,958	2,967	3,230	3,227	782
White Creek, ...	2,682	125	31	88	2,526	2,557	2,651	2,644	698
Whitehall, ...	4,422	458	28	44	3,936	3,964	4,394	4,378	912
Total, ...	46,244	3,364	216	303	42,664	42,880	46,028	45,941	10,767
WAYNE COUNTY.									
Arcadia, ...	5,253	143	18	18	5,092	5,110	5,235	5,235	1,333
Butler, ...	2,083	26	....	....	2,057	2,057	2,083	2,083	540
Galen, ...	5,314	381	23	35	4,910	4,933	5,291	5,279	1,211
Huron, ...	1,972	38	8	25	1,926	1,934	1,964	1,947	486
Lyons, ...	5,007	271	21	28	4,715	4,736	4,986	4,979	1,122
Macedon, ...	2,472	130	9	16	2,433	2,342	2,463	2,456	521
Marion, ...	2,136	83	....	2	2,053	2,053	2,136	2,134	559
Ontario, ...	2,312	119	9	15	2,184	2,193	2,303	2,297	606
Palmyra, ...	4,225	366	42	55	3,817	3,859	4,183	4,170	964
Rose, ...	2,209	95	....	....	2,114	2,114	2,209	2,209	566
Savannah, ...	1,938	67	11	11	1,860	1,871	1,927	1,927	471
Sodus, ...	4,603	117	36	65	4,450	4,486	4,567	4,538	1,094
Walworth, ...	2,179	75	....	17	2,104	2,104	2,179	2,162	543
Williamson, ...	2,571	187	1	1	2,383	2,384	2,570	2,570	611
Wolcott, ...	3,224	65	1	4	3,158	3,159	3,223	3,220	829
Total, ...	47,498	2,163	179	292	45,256	45,335	47,319	47,206	11,456
WESTCHESTER COUNTY.									
Bedford, ...	3,465	179	79	107	3,207	3,286	3,386	3,358	836
Cortlandt, ...	9,393	975	112	158	8,306	8,418	9,281	9,235	1,813
East Chester, ...	5,615	665	54	58	4,896	4,950	5,561	6,557	1,087
Greenburgh, ...	8,463	1,255	127	153	7,081	7,208	8,336	8,310	1,674
Harrison, ...	1,380	174	120	175	1,086	1,206	1,260	1,205	265
Lewisborough, ...	1,653	67	7	10	1,579	1,586	1,646	1,643	433
Mamaroneck, ...	1,393	193	33	35	1,167	1,200	1,360	1,358	258
Morrisania, ...	11,691	1,652	44	81	9,995	10,039	11,647	11,610	2,147
Mount Pleasant, ...	4,339	405	61	77	3,923	3,984	4,328	4,312	945
New Castle, ...	1,879	120	40	54	1,719	1,759	1,839	1,825	423
New Rochelle, ...	3,968	657	124	185	3,187	3,311	3,844	3,783	742
North Castle, ...	2,198	68	110	115	2,020	2,130	2,088	2,083	490
North Salem, ...	1,522	120	33	33	1,369	1,402	1,489	1,489	364
Ossining, ...	6,223	564	80	124	5,579	5,659	6,143	6,099	1,165
Pelham, ...	1,043	145	14	16	884	898	1,029	1,027	222
Pounndridge, ...	1,299	18	3	3	1,278	1,281	1,296	1,296	344
Rye, ...	4,675	502	129	154	4,044	4,173	4,546	4,521	980
Scarsdale, ...	557	126	16	22	415	431	541	535	109
Somers, ...	1,695	131	39	52	1,525	1,564	1,656	1,643	389
Westchester, ...	3,926	484	57	78	3,385	3,442	3,869	3,848	799
West Farms, ...	7,333	1,182	59	98	6,092	6,151	7,274	7,235	1,742
White Plains, ...	2,122	144	55	67	1,923	1,978	2,067	2,055	475
Yonkers, ...	12,756	2,428	81	118	10,247	10,328	12,675	12,638	2,194
Yorktown, ...	2,559	141	49	58	2,369	2,418	2,510	2,501	583
Total, ...	101,197	12,395	1,526	2,031	87,276	87,802	99,671	99,166	20,479

WYOMING COUNTY.

TOWNS.	Population.	Aliens.	Colored persons, not taxed.	Whole number of persons of color.	Number, deducting aliens and colored persons, not taxed.	Population, excluding aliens only.	Population, excluding persons of color not taxed, only.	Population, excluding all persons of color.	Voters.
Attica,	2,367	118	2	2	2,247	2,249	2,365	2,365	588
Bennington,	2,445	128	....	....	2,317	2,317	2,445	2,445	604
Castile,	2,081	53	....	....	2,028	2,028	2,081	2,081	564
China,	1,903	52	....	....	1,851	1,851	1,903	1,903	488
Covington,	1,233	97	....	....	1,136	1,136	1,233	1,233	291
Eagle,	1,211	20	....	....	1,191	1,191	1,211	1,211	313
Gainesville,	1,635	27	4	5	1,604	1,608	1,631	1,630	431
Genesee Falls,	1,070	106	....	....	964	964	1,070	1,070	246
Java,	2,142	37	....	....	2,105	2,105	2,142	2,142	517
Middlebury,	1,724	58	....	2	1,666	1,666	1,724	1,722	463
Orangeville,	1,322	53	1	1	1,268	1,269	1,321	1,321	340
Perry,	2,366	80	....	5	2,286	2,286	2,366	2,361	612
Pike,	1,805	48	....	1	1,757	1,757	1,805	1,804	492
Sheldon,	2,591	225	....	1	2,366	2,366	2,591	2,590	527
Warsaw,	2,824	74	31	41	2,719	2,750	2,793	2,783	729
Wethersfield,	1,314	41	....	....	1,273	1,273	1,314	1,314	328
Total,	30,033	1,217	38	58	28,778	28,816	29,995	29,975	7,533

YATES COUNTY.

TOWNS.	Population.	Aliens.	Colored persons, not taxed.	Whole number of persons of color.	Number, deducting aliens and colored persons, not taxed.	Population, excluding aliens only.	Population, excluding persons of color not taxed, only.	Population, excluding all persons of color.	Voters.
Barrington,	1,469	12	....	....	1,457	1,457	1,469	1,469	384
Benton,	2,400	84	7	7	2,309	2,316	2,393	2,393	648
Italy,	1,452	24	1	2	1,427	1,428	1,451	1,450	364
Jerusalem,	2,682	75	4	12	2,603	2,607	2,678	2,670	729
Middlesex,	1,287	17	3	3	1,267	1,270	1,284	1,284	334
Milo,	4,195	153	24	56	4,018	4,042	4,171	4,139	1,069
Potter,	2,137	82	16	17	2,039	2,055	2,121	2,120	555
Starkey,	2,394	41	25	29	2,328	2,353	2,369	2,365	651
Torrey,	1,322	25	5	20	1,292	1,297	1,317	1,302	348
Total,	19,338	513	85	146	18,740	18,825	19,253	19,192	5,082

Recapitulation by Counties.

COUNTIES.	Total population.	Aliens.	Colored persons not taxed.	Whole number of persons of color.	Number, deducting aliens and colored persons, not taxed.
Albany,	115,504	10,422	866	1,014	104,216
Allegany,	40,285	916	149	266	39,220
Broome,	37,933	1,134	258	414	36,541
Cattaraugus,	44,205	1,817	133	185	41,208
Cayuga,	55,730	3,210	323	515	52,197
Chautauqua,	58,528	3,506	156	230	54,837
Chemung,	31,923	2,015	422	660	29,486
Chenango,	38,360	514	157	233	37,689
Clinton,	45,713	6,094	84	124	39,535
Columbia,	44,905	2,009	855	1,228	42,041
Cortland,	24,815	533	22	38	24,260
Delaware,	41,638	770	130	197	40,738
Dutchess,	65,192	4,806	1,514	1,873	58,872
Erie,	157,150	20,838	571	841	134,656
Essex,	28,644	2,339	60	77	26,245
Franklin,	28,575	2,832	11	20	25,302
Fulton,	24,512	563	126	186	23,823
Genesee,	31,728	2,327	76	106	28,816
Greene,	31,710	721	577	744	30,412
Hamilton,	2,653	38	1	2	2,614
Herkimer,	39,154	2,027	147	197	36,980
Jefferson,	66,448	4,865	130	181	61,453
Kings,	311,090	53,428	3,937	4,861	253,459
Lewis,	27,840	1,397	25	57	26,418
Livingston,	37,555	2,244	81	168	35,230
Madison,	42,607	1,574	214	325	40,718
Monroe,	104,235	11,488	401	395	92,346
Montgomery,	31,447	972	273	343	30,202
New York,	726,386	151,838	8,899	9,943	565,649
Niagara,	49,655	5,710	331	423	43,242
Oneida,	102,713	6,045	455	621	96,213
Onondaga,	93,332	6,995	382	537	85,595
Ontario,	43,316	2,715	361	557	40,240
Orange,	70,165	6,046	1,655	2,101	62,464
Orleans,	28,603	1,999	77	112	26,527
Oswego,	76,200	5,601	204	332	70,395
Otsego,	48,616	1,088	130	153	47,398
Putnam,	14,845	1,185	86	111	13,574
Queens,	57,997	5,596	2,532	3,187	49,869
Rensselaer,	88,210	8,290	581	809	79,339
Richmond,	28,209	3,956	455	643	23,798
Rockland,	20,788	1,938	483	566	18,367
St. Lawrence,	80,994	8,310	36	68	72,648
Saratoga,	49,892	2,828	477	618	46,587
Schenectady,	20,888	944	151	214	19,793
Schoharie,	33,353	343	322	458	32,688
Schuyler,	18,441	292	74	144	18,075
Seneca,	27,653	1,201	112	195	26,340
Steuben,	66,192	2,232	232	390	63,728
Suffolk,	42,869	1,533	1,613	1,880	39,723
Sullivan,	32,741	1,251	73	88	31,417
Tioga,	28,163	447	168	280	27,548
Tompkins,	30,696	509	171	325	30,016
Ulster,	75,609	4,563	1,232	1,412	69,814
Warren,	21,128	950	14	31	20,164
Washington,	46,244	3,364	216	303	42,664
Wayne,	47,498	2,163	179	292	45,256
Westchester,	101,197	12,395	1,526	2,031	87,276
Wyoming,	30,033	1,217	38	58	28,778
Yates,	19,338	513	85	146	18,740
Total,	*3,832,043	399,456	35,049	44,708	3,393,439

* Including Indians residing on reservations and not taxed, nor allowed the rights of citizens.

Recapitulation by Counties — (Continued).

COUNTIES.	Population, excluding aliens only.	Population, excluding persons not taxed only.	Population, excluding all persons of color.	Voters.
Albany,	105,082	114,638	114,490	24,723
Allegany,	39,369	40,136	40,019	10,088
Broome,	36,799	37,675	37,519	9,562
Cattaraugus,	41,341	43,025	42,973	10,334
Cayuga,	52,520	55,407	55,215	13,590
Chautauqua,	54,993	58,343	58,269	14,228
Chemung,	29,908	31,501	31,263	7,450
Chenango,	37,846	38,203	38,127	10,336
Clinton,	39,619	45,629	45,589	8,052
Columbia,	42,896	44,050	43,677	10,635
Cortland,	24,282	24,793	24,777	6,592
Delaware,	40,868	41,508	41,441	10,582
Dutchess,	60,386	63,678	63,319	15,119
Erie,	135,227	156,579	155,224	29,441
Essex,	26,305	28,584	28,567	6,121
Franklin,	25,313	28,134	28,125	5,505
Fulton,	23,949	24,386	24,326	5,895
Gennesee.	28,892	31,143	31,113	7,465
Greene,	30,989	31,133	30,966	7,745
Hamilton,	2,615	2,652	2,651	657
Herkimer,	37,127	39,007	38,957	9,720
Jefferson,	61,583	66,318	66,267	15,526
Kings,	257,662	307,153	306,229	58,167
Lewis,	26,443	27,815	27,783	6,677
Livingston,	35,311	37,474	37,387	9,055
Madison,	40,932	42,393	42,282	11,160
Monroe,	92,747	103,834	103,640	21,777
Montgomery,	30,475	31,174	31,104	7,694
New York,	574,548	717,607	716,443	128,975
Niagara,	43,573	48,952	48,860	10,222
Oneida,	96,668	102,258	102,092	24,489
Onondaga,	85,977	92,590	92,435	21,409
Ontario,	40,601	42,955	42,759	10,487
Orange,	64,109	68,500	68,054	14,977
Orleans,	26,604	28,526	28,491	6,956
Oswego,	70,599	75,996	75,868	17,061
Otsego,	47,528	48,486	48,463	12,954
Putnam,	13,660	14,759	14,734	3,445
Queens,	52 401	55,465	54,810	11,801
Rensselaer,	79,920	87,629	87,401	19,098
Richmond,	24,258	27,754	27,566	5,627
Rockland,	18,850	20,305	20,222	4,319
St. Lawrence,	72,684	80,958	80,926	16,764
Saratoga,	47,064	49,415	49,274	11,782
Schenectady,	19,944	20,737	20,674	4,870
Schoharie,	33,010	33,031	32,895	8,083
Schuyler,	18,149	18,367	18,297	4,874
Seneca,	26,452	27,541	27,458	6,643
Steuben,	63,960	65,960	65,802	15,766
Suffolk,	41,346	41,256	40,989	9,961
Sullivan,	31,490	32,660	32,653	7,473
Tioga,	27,716	27,995	27,883	7,214
Tompkins,	30,187	30,525	30,371	7,999
Ulster,	71,046	74,377	74,197	16,224
Warren,	20,178	21,114	21,097	4,740
Washington,	42,880	46,028	45,941	10,767
Wayne,	45,335	47,319	47,206	11,456
Westchester,	88,802	99,671	99,166	20,479
Wyoming,	28,816	29,995	29,975	7,533
Yates,	18,825	19,253	19,192	5,082
Total,	3,428,057	3,829,406	3,783,493	823,426

Recapitulation of Cities.

CITIES.*	Population.	Aliens.	Colored persons not taxed.	Whole number of persons of color.	Population, excluding aliens and persons of color, not taxed.
Albany,	62,613	6,171	650	743	55,792
Auburn,	12,567	1,576	136	225	10,855
Brooklyn,	296,112	50,783	3,527	4,189	241,802
Buffalo,	94,502	16,303	521	711	77,678
Elmira,	13,130	1,688	323	538	11,119
Hudson,	7,831	471	213	295	7,147
New York,	726,386	151,838	8,899	9,943	565,649
Oswego,	19,288	3,124	68	106	16,096
Poughkeepsie,	16,073	1,379	340	423	14,354
Rochester,	50,940	6,410	287	429	44,243
Schenectady,	10,685	646	106	140	9,933
Syracuse,	31,784	3,661	186	297	27,937
Troy,	39,293	5,279	335	448	33,679
Utica,	23,686	1,950	190	236	21,546
Total,	1,404,890	251,279	15,781	18,723	1,137,830

CITIES.	Population, excluding aliens only.	Population, excluding colored persons not taxed only.	Population, excluding all persons of color.	Voters.
Albany,	56,442	61,963	61,870	13,196
Auburn,	10,991	12,431	12,342	2,531
Brooklyn,	245,329	292,585	291,923	55,484
Buffalo,	78,199	93,981	93,791	6,460
Elmira,	11,442	12,807	12,592	2,760
Hudson,	7,360	7,618	7,536	1,682
New York,	574,548	717,487	716,443	128,975
Oswego,	16,164	19,220	19,182	3,150
Poughkeepsie,	14,694	15,733	15,650	3,417
Rochester,	44,530	50,653	50,511	9,870
Schenectady,	10,039	10,579	10,545	2,423
Syracuse,	28,123	31,598	31,487	6,611
Troy,	34,014	38,958	38,845	7,818
Utica,	21,736	23,496	23,450	4,920
Total,	1,153,611	1,389,109	1,386,167	249,297

*** The cities of Binghamton, Lockport, and Newburgh, are included in the towns from which they were organized.**

Comparative view of Senatorial Districts under the Constitution of 1846.

Dists.	Under Article III of Constitution.	Act of April 13, 1857 (Census of 1855).	Act of April 25, 1866 (Census of 1865).
1	Queens, Richmond and Suffolk counties,	Queens, Richmond and Suffolk counties,	Queens, Richmond and Suffolk counties.
2	Kings county,	1st, 2d, 3d, 4th, 5th, 7th, 11th, 13th and 19th wards of Brooklyn, Kings county,	1st, 2d, 3d, 4th, 5th, 7th, 11th, 13th, 15th, 19th and 20th wards of Brooklyn, Kings county.
3	1st, 2d, 3d, 4th, 5th and 6th wards of New York city,	6th, 8th, 9th, 10th, 12th, 14th, 15th, 16th, 17th and 18th wards of Brooklyn, Kings county,	6th, 8th, 9th, 10th, 12th, 14th, 16th, 17th and 18th wards, Brooklyn, and towns of Kings county.
4	7th, 10th, 13th and 17th wards of New York city,	1st, 2d, 3d, 4th, 5th, 6th, 7th, 8th and 14th wards of New York city,	1st, 2d, 3d, 4th, 5th, 6th, 7th, 13th and 14th wards of New York city.
5	8th, 9th and 14th wards of New York city,	10th, 11th, 13th and 17th wards of New York city,	8th, 9th, 15th and 16th wards of New York city.
6	11th, 12th, 15th 16th, 18th, 19th, 20th, 21st and 22d wards of New York city,	9th, 15th, 16th and 18th wards of New York city,	10th, 11th and 17th wards of New York city.
7	Putnam, Rockland and Westchester counties,	12th, 19th, 20th, 21st and 22d wards of New York city,	18th, 20th and 21st wards of New York city.
8	Columbia and Dutchess counties,	Putnam Rockland and Westchester counties,	12th, 19th and 22d wards of New York city.
9	Orange and Sullivan counties,	Orange and Sullivan counties,	Westchester, Putnam and Rockland counties.
10	Greene and Ulster counties,	Greene and Ulster counties,	Orange and Sullivan counties.
11	Albany and Schenectady counties,	Columbia and Dutchess counties,	Columbia and Dutchess counties.
12	Rensselaer county,	Rensselaer and Washington counties,	Rensselaer and Washington counties.
13	Saratoga and Washington counties,	Albany county,	Albany county.
14	Clinton, Essex and Warren counties,	Delaware, Schenectady and Schoharie counties,	Greene and Ulster counties.
15	Franklin and St. Lawrence counties,	Fulton, Hamilton, Montgomery and Saratoga counties,	Saratoga, Montgomery, Fulton, Hamilton and Schenectady counties.
16	Fulton, Hamilton, Herkimer and Montgomery Cos.	Clinton, Essex and Warren counties,	Clinton, Essex and Warren counties.
17	Delaware and Schoharie counties,	Franklin and St. Lawrence counties,	Franklin and St. Lawrence counties.
18	Chenango and Otsego counties,	Jefferson and Lewis counties,	Jefferson and Lewis counties.
19	Oneida county,	Oneida county,	Oneida county.
20	Madison and Oswego counties,	Herkimer and Otsego counties,	Herkimer and Otsego counties.
21	Jefferson and Lewis counties,	Oswego county,	Madison and Oswego counties.
22	Onondaga county,	Onondaga county,	Cortland and Onondaga counties.
23	Broome, Cortland and Tioga counties,	Chenango, Cortland and Madison counties,	Chenango, Delaware and Schoharie counties.
24	Cayuga and Wayne counties,	Broome, Tioga and Tompkins counties,	Broome, Tioga and Tompkins counties,
25	Seneca, Tompkins and Yates counties,	Cayuga and Wayne counties,	Cayuga and Wayne counties.
26	Chemung and Steuben counties,	Ontario, Seneca and Yates counties,	Ontario, Seneca and Yates counties.
27	Monroe county,	Chemung, Schuyler and Steuben counties,	Chemung, Schuyler and Steuben counties.
28	Genesee, Niagara and Orleans counties,	Monroe county,	Monroe county.
29	Livingston and Ontario counties,	Genesee, Niagara and Orleans counties,	Genesee, Niagara and Orleans counties.
30	Allegany and Wyoming counties,	Allegany, Livingston and Wyoming counties,	Allegany, Livingston and Wyoming counties.
31	Erie county,	Erie county,	Erie county.
32	Cattaraugus and Chautauqua counties,	Cattaraugus and Chautauqua counties,	Cattaraugus and Chautauqua counties.

Comparative view of the distribution of Representation in Assembly, under the Constitution of 1846.

COUNTIES.	Act of March 8, 1846.	Act of April 12, 1857.	Act of April 16, 1866.	COUNTIES.	Act of March 8, 1846.	Act of April 12, 1857.	Act of April 16, 1866.
Albany,	4	4	4	Oneida,	4	4	4
Allegany,	2	2	1	Onondaga,	4	3	3
Broome,	1	1	1	Ontario,	2	2	2
Cattaraugus,	2	2	2	Orange,	3	2	2
Cayuga,	3	2	2	Orleans,	1	1	1
Chautauqua,	2	2	2	Oswego,	2	3	3
Chemung,	1	1	1	Otsego,	3	2	2
Chenango,	2	2	1	Putnam,	1	1	1
Clinton,	1	1	1	Queens,	1	2	2
Columbia,	2	2	2	Rensselaer,	3	3	3
Cortland,	1	1	1	Richmond,	1	1	1
Delaware,	2	2	2	Rockland,	1	1	1
Dutchess,	3	2	2	St. Lawrence,	3	3	3
Erie,	4	4	5	Saratoga,	2	2	2
Essex,	1	1	1	Schenectady,	1	1	1
Franklin,	1	1	1	Schoharie,	2	1	1
Fulton,*	1	1	1	Schuyler,	1	1	1
Genesee,	2	1	1	Seneca,	1	1	1
Greene,	2	1	1	Steuben,	3	3	2
Hamilton,*	....	....	....	Suffolk,	2	2	1
Herkimer,	2	2	1	Sullivan,	1	1	1
Jefferson,	3	3	2	Tioga,	1	1	1
Kings,	3	7	9	Tompkins,	2	1	1
Lewis,	1	1	1	Ulster,	2	3	3
Livingston,	2	2	1	Warren,	1	1	1
Madison,	2	2	2	Washington,	2	2	2
Monroe,	3	3	3	Wayne,	2	2	2
Montgomery,	2	1	1	Westchester,	2	3	3
New York,	16	17	21	Wyoming,	1	1	1
Niagara,	2	2	2	Yates,	1	1	1

DATES OF THE PASSAGE OF LAWS.

The following table shows, for the last twenty years, the number of laws that were signed by the President of the Senate, the Speaker of the House, and the Governor, during the first seventy days from the beginning of the year, and on each day subsequently until the end of the session, with the exception of those years in which an extra meeting was called. It therefore exhibits the amount of legislation finished at these dates, but does not include the number of bills that received final action in either house without becoming laws.

For many years the custom has prevailed, for the Governor to approve of bills that had passed both houses, at any convenient time after the adjournment of the legislature. The number of laws dated later than the day of adjournment has been since 1846, 1,038. Of these, 2 were approved in 1847; 6 in 1852; 38 in 1855; 50 in 1856; 3 in 1858; 1 in 1859; 5 in 1860; 63 in 1861; 12 in 1862; 279 in 1863; 240 in 1864; 173 in 1865; and 166 in 1867.

The Court of Appeals has decided that "The power of the Governor to approve and sign a bill presented to him within ten days previous to the adjournment of the legislature, does not cease with the adjournment." (*The People* v. *Bowen et al.*, Smith's Reports, vii, 517; June, 1860.)

* Fulton and Hamilton form one district.

Dates of Passage of Laws.

DAYS.	1847.			1848.			1849.			1850.		
	S.	A.	G.	S.	A.	G.	S.	A.	G.	S.	A.	G.
First 70,........	37	37	25	104	137	82	138	164	85	87	76	56
March 12,......	....	....	....	....	....	....	....	12	11	3	1	1
do 13,......	....	1	1	2	5	3	3	9	....	6	6	....
do 14,......	....	....	....	5	2	....	....	9	....	....	15	1
do 15,......	2	2	1	6	9	3	....	4	13	7	13	1
do 16,......	5	1	...	5	3	4	14	....	....	2	8	17
do 17,......	....	7	....	5	6	....	1	3	....	....	....	....
do 18,......	3	2	....	2	1	7	....	....	....	3	....	1
do 19,......	2	1	3	....	....	....	4	1	....	....	8	....
do 20,......	11	5	1	8	3	3	5	6	1	5	....	4
do 21,......	....	....	....	4	4	5	5	5	6	1	1	....
do 22,......	....	4	3	...	2	1	1	11	6.	6	1	....
do 23,......	1	1	1	25	2	4	3	5	....	14	13	8
do 24,......	....	...	2	6	5	3	3	8	5	....	....	....
do 25,......	10	....	....	3	10	12	....	....	....	11	39	8
do 26,......	1	....	4	....	....	....	27	2	13	3	19	3
do 27,......	5	....	....	9	18	10	28	2	14	9	2	1
do 28,.....	....	....	....	4	9	2	5	29	8	....	4	13
do 29,......	....	....	4	6	1	10	1	6	8	3	26	6
do 30,......	....	5	1	9	2	1	1	8	11	3	17	2
do 31,......	4	11	6	2	....	8	1	10	5	....	....	....
April 1,......	....	....	....	16	2	....	....	....	....	1	1	16
do 2,......	1	16	1	....	....	....	3	13	6	1	1	3
do 3,......	2	....	....	1	....	8	24	9	2	17	5	2
do 4,......	....	....	....	18	15	7	24	22	16	18	13	7
do 5,......	5	1	1	15	7	12	14	22	26	34	15	9
do 6,......	8	....	2	....	20	6	1	28	17	34	5	30
do 7,......	1	...	3	4	16	9	18	4	30	....	....	....
do 8,......	1	....	1	18	25	4	....	....	....	25	8	41
do 9,......	....	....	....	....	....	....	...	10	16	13	37	19
do 10,......	9	....	....	28	35	14	60	25	45	71	43	129
do 11,......	....	....	....	73	33	45	55	12	95	....	....	....
do 12,......	....	....	2	3	9	118	....	....	....	....	....	....
do 13,......	8	1	...	....	....	....	....	....	....	...	....	....
do 14,......	4	4	....	....	....	....	....	....	....	....	....	....
do 15,......	2	16	10	....	....	....	....	....	....	....	....	....
do 16,......	....	16	7	....	....	....	....	...	....	....	....	....
do 17,......	6	16	2	....	....	....	....	....	....	....	....	....
do 18,......	....	....	....	....	....	....	....	....	....	....	....	....
do 19,......	1	8	13	....	....	....	....	....	....	....	....	....
do 20,......	21	8	6	....	....	....	....	....	....	....	....	....
do 21,......	3	....	19	....	....	....	....	....	....	....	....	....
do 22,......	15	....	....	....	....	....	....	....	....	....	....	....
do 23,......	6	....	11	....	....	....	....	....	....	....	...	....
do 24,.....	4	2	13	....	....	....	....	....	....	....	....	....
do 25,......	....	....	....	....	....	....	....	....	....	....	....	....
do 26,......	....	....	....	....	....	....	....	....	....	....	....	....
do 27,......	12	2	10	....	....	....	....	....	....	....	....	....
do 28,......	6	15	16	....	....	....	....	....	....	....	....	....
do 29,......	4	9	5	....	....	....	....	....	....	....	....	....
do 30,......	10	16	7	....	....	....	....	....	....	....	....	....
May 1,......	2	14	10	....	....	....	....	....	....	....	....	....
do 2,......	....	....	....	....	....	....	....	....	....	....	....	....
do 3,......	11	....	8	....	....	....	....	....	....	....	....	....
do 4,......	9	8	1	....	....	....	....	....	....	....	....	....
do 5,.....	11	3	15	....	....	....	....	....	....	....	...	....
do 6,......	13	13	1	....	...	....	....	....	....	....	....	....
do 7,......	10	11	34	....	....	....	....	....	....	....	...	....
do 8,.....	1	1	4	....	....	....	....	....	....	....	....	....
do 9,......	....	....	....	....	....	....	....	....	....	....	....	....
do 10,......	6	3	7	....	...	....	....	....	....	....	....	....
do 11,......	10	8	2	....	....	....	....	....	....	....	....	....
do 12,......	7	22	35	....	....	....	....	....	....	....	....	....

Dates of Passage of Laws — (Continued).

DAYS.	1851.			1852.			1853.			1854.		
	S.	A.	G.	S.	A.	G.	S.	A.	G.	S.	A.	G.
First 70,........	88	88	56	120	86	32	80	85	58	99	98	28
March 12,......	4	....	3	....	....	4	4	3	....	....	....	....
do 13,......	3	2	1	8	1	1	....	....	....	1	11	4
do 14,......	5	15	....	....	....	....	1	1	3	6	3	1
do 15,......	5	12	5	1	1	....	3	....	....	10	14	....
do 16,......	....	....	....	6	21	1	1	39	....	5	2	1
do 17,......	4	5	10	7	10	....	8	....	....	2	2	....
do 18,......	....	4	....	7	11	1	....	1	....	8	8	2
do 19,......	2	....	....	....	....	11	....	4	3	....	....	....
do 20,......	....	2	4	....	2	4	....	....	....	1	5	....
do 21,......	10	3	2	....	....	....	37	2	....	9	1	8
do 22,......	....	....	....	2	6	3	....	1	5	7	8	1
do 23,......	....	....	....	10	5	4	....	13	10	8	2	5
do 24,......	....	....	....	6	17	1	6	22	2	1	2	....
do 25,......	....	....	5	2	25	15	....	24	6	10	1	....
do 26,......	....	6	....	1	3	9	2	....	1	....	....	....
do 27,......	10	8	....	2	1	3	....	....	....	3	....	....
do 28,......	4	2	4	....	....	....	....	....	....	11	21	18
do 29,......	9	2	8	1	1	1	2	....	9	16	4	....
do 30,......	....	....	....	41	2	3	20	37	....	3	21	1
do 31,......	2	1	2	16	....	3	25	13	3	2	8	4
April 1,......	4	14	2	11	2	3	1	17	1	6	8	33
do 2,......	3	....	....	1	16	16	1	29	15	....	....	....
do 3,......	1	....	6	....	11	4	....	....	....	21	11	6
do 4,......	10	11	1	....	....	....	1	3	13	3	15	8
do 5,......	11	2	14	....	15	....	....	9	29	5	14	19
do 6,......	....	....	....	1	20	8	....	22	....	17	30	3
do 7,......	8	5	14	23	1	9	11	15	1	1	1	6
do 8,......	8	3	10	25	15	5	44	3	2	2	....	2
do 9,......	6	12	14	47	14	22	49	6	7	....	....	....
do 10,......	22	13	5	2	15	18	....	....	....	3	....	17
do 11,......	1	15	26	....	....	....	19	21	4	16	15	2
do 12,......	1	5	16	....	24	31	18	7	43	1	22	3
do 13,......	....	....	....	1	42	25	....	2	13	23	19	22
do 14,......	11	8	6	8	6	37	....	12	....	34	20	1
do 15,......	2	2	6	15	13	18	14	10	29	49	37	110
do 16,......	....	....	6	44	22	78	....	....	....	....	....	....
do 17,......	....	4	32	....	....	....	....	....	....	24	4	68
do 18,......	....	....	....	....	....	....	....	....	....	....	....	....
do 19,......	....	....	....	....	....	....	....	....	....	....	....	....
do 20,......	....	....	....	....	....	....	....	....	....	....	....	....
do 21,......	....	....	....	....	....	....	....	....	....	....	....	....
do 22,......	....	....	....	....	....	....	....	....	....	....	....	....
do 23,......	....	....	....	....	....	....	....	....	....	....	....	....
do 24,......	....	....	....	....	....	....	....	....	....	....	....	....
do 25,......	....	....	....	....	....	....	....	....	....	....	....	....
do 26,......	....	....	....	....	....	....	....	....	....	....	....	....
do 27,......	....	....	....	....	....	....	....	....	....	....	....	....
do 28,......	....	....	....	....	....	....	....	....	....	....	....	....
do 29,......	....	....	....	....	....	....	....	....	....	....	....	....
do 30,......	....	....	....	....	....	....	....	....	....	....	....	....
May 1,......	....	....	....	....	....	....	....	....	....	....	....	....
do 2,......	....	....	....	....	....	....	....	....	....	....	....	....
do 3,......	....	....	....	....	....	....	....	....	....	....	....	....
do 4,......	....	....	....	....	....	....	....	....	....	....	....	....
do 5,......	....	....	....	....	....	....	....	....	....	....	....	....
do 6,......	....	....	....	....	....	....	....	....	....	....	....	....
do 7,......	....	....	....	....	....	....	....	....	....	....	....	....
do 8,......	....	....	....	....	....	....	....	....	....	....	....	....
do 9,......	....	....	....	....	....	....	....	....	....	....	....	....
do 10,......	....	....	....	....	....	....	....	....	....	....	....	....
do 11,......	....	....	....	....	....	....	....	....	....	....	....	....
do 12,......	....	....	....	....	....	....	....	....	....	....	....	....

Dates of Passage of Laws—(Continued).

DAYS.	1855.			1856.			1857.			1858.		
	S.	A.	G.	S.	A.	G.	S.	A.	G.	S.	A.	G.
First 70,........	176	157	62	69	78	34	185	221	97	63	48	32
March 12,......	....	...	3	1	15	1	8	....	....	...	....	....
do 13,......	....	1	....	....	....	....	4	12	5	3	2	....
do 14,......	....	7	1	....	4	....	27	6	5	....	....	....
do 15,......	....	....	3	....	...	1	....	....	....	3	4	1
do 16,......	....	1	....	....	....	....	18	22	....	1	....	....
do 17,......	5	19	2	6	....	....	....	40	12	3	....	1
do 18,......	....	....	....	2	....	1	....	10	6	5	....	....
do 19,......	6	10	9	....	2	....	29	2	10	1	26	1
do 20,......	1	....	....	....	....	6	8	....	14	2	....	2
do 21,......	1	21	....	....	4	5	49	2	1	....	....	....
do 22,......	3	....	1	3	3	1	....	....	....	....	1	....
do 23,......	26	13	....	....	...	....	4	1	22	7	15	1
do 24,......	4	29	2	....	1	....	....	1	8	1	25	1
do 25,......	....	....	....	6	1	....	3	16	....	5	2	5
do 26,......	12	13	3	1	26	7	9	15	3	21	2	2
do 27,......	7	....	18	9	....	1	16	33	8	11	6	4
do 28,......	5	3	5	3	18	5	....	3	6	....	....	....
do 29,......	...	1	4	7	1	1	....	....	....	2	1	7
do 30,......	23	22	12	....	....	....	35	....	....	20	....	6
do 31,......	13	21	8	10	25	6	4	38	24	1	20	....
April 1,......	....	....	...	3	....	20	...	33	11	20	21	17
do 2,......	1	12	7	1	4	....	18	30	8	12	17	16
do 3,......	21	1	11	16	....	3	2	19	10	1	3	2
do 4,......	17	10	....	4	...	7	22	26	....	....	....	....
do 5,......	10	8	13	29	1	2	....	....	...	14	22	3
do 6,......	1	19	17	....	....	....	18	3	34	1	11	3
do 7,......	56	44	3	5	2	36	4	....	22	7	8	21
do 8,......	....	....	....	....	1	6	2	13	1	9	11	4
do 9,......	26	22	47	30	19	12	45	3	7	2	....	1
do 10,......	11	15	63	....	....	....	9	29	23	37	4	5
do 11,......	41	28	5	....	....	....	56	30	....	....	....	...
do 12,......	41	38	48	...	....	....	....	....	....	15	8	27
do 13,......	30	55	78	....	....	...	93	53	62	48	8	18
do 14,......	40	7	64	....	....	....	18	50	55	11	32	39
do 15,......	....	....	....	....	....	....	14	41	168	19	16	42
do 16,......	....	....	....	....	....	....	69	21	63	12	4	31
do 17,......	....	....	....	....	....	....	33	28	96	14	38	60
do 18,......	....	....	....	....	....	...	2	3	18	....	....	....
do 19,......	....	....	....	...	....	....	....	....	....	5	21	24
do 20,......	....	....	....	....	....	....	....	....	....	....	....	....
do 21,......	....	....	....	....	....	....	....	....	....	....	....	....
do 22,......	....	....	....	....	....	....	....	....	....	....	....	....
do 23,......	....	....	....	....	....	....	....	....	....	....	....	....
do 24,......	....	....	....	....	....	....	....	....	....	....	....	....
do 25,......	....	....	....	....	....	....	....	....	....	....	....	....
do 26,......	....	....	....	....	....	....	....	....	....	....	....	....
do 27,......	....	....	....	....	....	....	....	....	....	....	....	....
do 28,......	....	....	....	....	....	....	....	....	....	....	....	....
do 29,......	....	....	....	....	....	....	....	....	....	....	....	....
do 30,......	....	....	....	....	....	....	....	....	....	....	....	....
May 1,......	....	....	....	....	....	...	....	....	....	....	....	....
do 2,......	...	....	....	....	....	....	....	....	....	....	....	....
do 3,......	....	....	....	....	....	....	....	....	....	....	....	....
do 4,......	....	....	....	....	....	....	....	....	....	....	....	....
do 5,......	...	....	....	....	....	....	....	....	....	....	....	....
do 6,......	....	....	....	....	....	....	....	....	....	....	....	....
do 7,......	....	....	....	....	....	....	....	....	....	....	....	....
do 8,......	....	....	....	....	....	....	....	....	....	....	....	....
do 9,......	....	....	....	....	....	...	....	....	....	....	....	....
do 10,......	....	....	....	....	....	....	....	....	....	....	....	....
do 11,......	....	....	....	....	...	....	....	....	....	....	....	....
do 12,......	....	....	....	....	....	....	....	....	....	....	....	....

Dates of Passage of Laws — (Continued).

DAYS.	1859.			1860.			1861.			1862.		
	S.	A.	G.	S.	A.	G.	S.	A.	G.	S.	A.	G.
First 70,	111	98	40	151	140	63	110	86	37	109	83	28
March 12,	13	2	....	....	3	5	10	10	2	4	12	1
do 13,	....	....	....	23	....	....	5	2	6	5	....	....
de 14,	....	1	2	....	....	1	2	1	....	1	1	1
do 15,	2	1	3	10	....	....	3	....	3	....	9	2
do 16,	8	3	1	....	1	....	....	....	1	....	....	....
do 17,	....	25	....	10	6	17	....	....	....	1	1	1
do 18,	....	....	5	....	....	....	....	1	1	3	....	....
do 19,	....	7	1	....	2	4	12	....	6	2	8	....
do 20,	....	....	....	5	29	2	4	7	1	3	....	2
do 21,	12	3	....	7	2	3	7	34	4	11	1	3
do 22,	....	....	3	4	....	6	2	14	....	2	....	7
do 23,	6	....	....	15	1	4	11	8	....	....	....	....
do 24,	....	....	2	9	2	15	....	....	....	28	21	....
do 25,	35	21	5	....	....	....	1	....	....	3	....	1
do 26,	3	16	7	2	....	....	8	1	22	12	29	11
do 27,	....	....	....	6	5	....	8	14	9	13	8	8
do 28,	8	22	3	14	6	....	7	23	....	22	1	14
do 29,	1	30	....	15	....	3	5	....	1	15	16	14
do 30,	2	13	9	9	....	12	14	2	20	....	....	....
do 31,	19	1	4	19	1	10	....	....	....	9	2	7
April 1,	18	32	9	....	....	....	12	....	....	10	8	7
do 2,	....	18	14	6	30	2	6	....	2	9	....	24
do 3,	....	....	....	2	23	13	....	11	14	8	15	3
do 4,	36	19	9	1	40	5	1	....	1	15	1	8
do 5,	....	16	24	29	33	9	5	....	2	4	....	2
do 6,	25	20	16	3	3	28	9	8	5	....	....	....
do 7,	34	10	12	1	....	10	....	....	....	6	19	2
do 8,	7	11	34	....	....	....	....	11	18	11	23	15
do 9,	1	14	17	40	36	4	....	2	....	6	18	6
do 10,	....	....	....	....	21	45	3	18	6	....	23	4
do 11,	33	31	23	32	41	23	12	37	3	25	25	3
do 12,	30	16	26	26	23	41	15	12	17	9	25	47
do 13,	25	15	32	25	21	35	58	19	43	....	....	....
do 14,	....	27	44	32	16	40	....	....	....	2	21	10
do 15,	12	16	37	....	....	....	11	19	39	33	10	26
do 16,	35	7	46	22	30	22	3	4	9	14	78	69
do 17,	....	....	....	12	15	51	....	....	....	16	1	28
do 18,	38	8	53	....	....	....	....	....	....	2	....	32
do 19,	3	14	31	....	....	....	....	....	....	26	20	36
do 20,	....	....	....	....	....	....	....	....	....	....	....	....
do 21,	....	....	....	....	....	....	....	....	....	16	8	37
do 22,	....	....	....	....	....	....	....	....	....	35	5	27
do 23,	....	....	....	....	....	....	....	....	....	2	....	9
do 24,	....	....	....	....	....	....	....	....	....	....	....	....
do 25,	....	....	....	....	....	....	....	....	....	....	....	....
do 26,	....	....	....	....	....	....	....	....	....	....	....	....
do 27,	....	....	....	....	....	....	....	....	....	....	....	....
do 28,	....	....	....	....	....	....	....	....	....	....	....	....
do 29,	....	....	....	....	....	....	....	....	....	....	....	....
do 30,	....	....	....	....	....	....	....	....	....	....	....	....
May 1,	....	....	....	....	....	....	....	....	....	....	....	....
do 2,	....	....	....	....	....	....	....	....	....	....	....	....
do 3,	....	....	....	....	....	....	....	....	....	....	....	....
do 4,	....	....	....	....	....	....	....	....	....	....	....	....
do 5,	....	....	....	....	....	....	....	....	....	....	....	....
do 6,	....	....	....	....	....	....	....	....	....	....	....	....
do 7,	....	....	....	....	....	....	....	....	....	....	....	....
do 8,	....	....	....	....	....	....	....	....	....	....	....	....
do 9,	....	....	....	....	....	....	....	....	....	....	....	....
do 10,	....	....	....	....	....	....	....	....	....	....	....	....
do 11,	....	....	....	....	....	....	....	....	....	....	....	....
do 12,	....	....	....	....	....	....	....	....	....	....	....	....

Dates of Passage of Laws — (Continued.)

DAYS.	1863.			1864.			1865.			1866.		
	S.	A.	G.	S.	A.	G.	S.	A.	G.	S.	A.	G.
First 70,........	84	68	26	107	90	32	209	275	106	202	251	136
March 12,.......	1	...	1	....	1	2	....	....	....	....	6	2
do 13,.......	10	....	....	....	....	....	6	....	5	19	1	3
do 14,.......	4	....	4	....	....	....	2	....	6	20	16	9
do 15,.......	....	....	....	27	....	2	26	16	5	11	9	17
do 16,.......	1	....	....	7	30	....	11	2	11	4	28	18
do 17,.......	13	...	....	1	....	3	16	2	6	2	1	....
do 18,.......	6	16	....	3	31	....	....	11	10	....	....	....
do 19,.......	1	19	5	5	1	5	....	....	....	....	....	6
do 20,.......	4	12	....	....	....	...	....	5	3	19	41	1
do 21,......	1	1	....	....	....	1	25	39	7	9	2	2
do 22,.......	....	....	....	19	....	5	18	9	16	11	5	31
do 23,......	...	....	7	2	14	4	12	9	2	28	1	...
do 24,.......	3	27	....	12	1	1	26	21	19	7	1	3
do 25,.......	....	...	8	2	1	8	2	4	16	....	....	....
do 26,.......	4	...	8	2	45	10	....	....	....	10	17	19
do 27,.......	18	39	....	....	....	....	....	....	3	48	25	....
do 28,......	7	16	....	1	4	7	36	6	6	18	8	..
do 29,.......	....	....	....	9	18	4	5	19	24	20	37	4
do 30,.......	2	21	....	7	45	4	5	14	2	28	22	56
do 31,.......	7	....	7	2	....	10	20	9	19	2	17	19
April 1,.......	1	13	1	3	14	3	22	27	15	....	...	....
do 2,.......	11	2	....	....	5	12	....	....	....	4	29	6
do 3,.......	17	61	3	....	....	....	....	1	9	41	4	40
do 4,.......	9	....	....	....	10	2	27	22	1	23	9	15
do 5,.......	....	....	...	26	54	7	22	13	....	24	29	33
do 6,.......	1	30	1	15	1	1	21	21	27	37	45	19
do 7,.......	18	25	36	5	....	4	17	11	6	27	3	38
do 8,.......	1	19	6	11	36	6	29	7	17	....	....	....
do 9,.......	24	11	2	10	8	18	....	....	....	13	43	1
do 10,......	1	11	2	....	...	....	17	31	20	24	35	27
do 11,.......	3	14	4	7	....	10	21	58	16	27	32	28
do 12,.......	....	....	....	10	7	5	17	3	3	33	93	21
do 13,.......	29	8	1	16	23	6	20	17	36	29	7	26
do 14,.......	29	5	1	....	19	5	19	2	30	27	2	21
do 15,.......	12	32	12	3	....	18	....	....	1	....	....	...
do 16,.......	49	2	1	13	2	15	....	....	....	18	5	31
do 17,.......	31	6	45	....	....	....	....	....	52	30	10	29
do 18,.......	22	4	6	15	28	11	....	....	1	22	31	24
do 19,.......	....	....	....	34	20	13	....	....	....	21	25	15
do 20,.......	12	14	4	19	25	9	....	....	....	40	15	54
do 21,.......	23	7	5	91	18	24	17	47	29	12	5	15
do 22,.......	16	6	3	54	11	20	7	8	23	....	....	....
do 23,.......	36	6	21	48	24	50	1	....	....	....	....	....
do 24,.......	4	25	6	....	....	....	26	23	15	....	....	....
do 25,.......	....	....	....	....	....	....	11	2	....	....	....	....
do 26,.......	....	....	....	....	....	....	4	5	....	....	....	....
do 27,.......	....	....	....	....	....	....	42	25	17	....	....	....
do 28,.......	....	....	....	....	....	....	18	13	16	....	....	....
do 29,.......	....	....	....	....	....	....	....	....	....	....	....	....
do 30,.......	....	....	....	....	....	....	....	....	....	....	....	....
May 1,.......	....	....	....	....	....	....	....	....	....	....	....	....
do 2,.......	....	....	....	....	....	....	....	....	....	....	....	....
do 3,.......	....	....	....	....	....	....	....	....	....	....	....	....
do 4,.......	....	....	....	....	....	....	....	....	....	....	....	....
do 5,.......	....	....	....	....	....	....	....	....	....	....	....	....
do 6,.......	....	....	....	....	....	....	....	....	....	....	....	....
do 7,.......	....	....	....	....	....	....	....	....	....	....	....	....
do 8,.......	....	....	....	....	....	....	....	....	....	....	....	....
do 9,.......	....	....	....	....	....	....	....	....	....	....	....	....
do 10,.......	....	....	....	....	....	....	....	....	....	....	....	....
do 11,.......	....	....	....	....	....	....	....	....	....	....	....	....
do 12,.......	....	....	....	....	....	....	....	....	....	....	....	....

SESSIONS OF THE NEW YORK STATE LEGISLATURE.

Sessions.	Meetings.	Begun.	Ended.	Days in session.	Number of laws passed.	Number of printed pages of laws.‖
1	*1	September 9, 1777,	October 7, 1777,	29	47	300
	†2	January 15, 1778,	April 4, 1778,	80		
	†3	June 22, 1778,	June 30, 1778,	9		
2	†1	October 13, 1778,	November 6, 1778,	25	34	
	†2	January 27, 1779,	March 17, 1779,	50		
3	*1	August 24, 1779,	October 25, 1779,	63	79	
	§2	January 27, 1780,	March 14, 1780,	48		
	*3	April 22, 1780,	July 2, 1780,	72		
4	†1	September 7, 1780,	October 10, 1780,	34	64	
	§2	January 17, 1781,	March 31, 1781,	74		
	†3	June 15, 1781,	July 1, 1781,	17		
5	†1	October 10, 1781,	November 3, 1781,	25	46	
	†2	February 23, 1782,	April 14, 1782,	51		
6	†1	July 8, 1782,	July 25, 1782,	18	54	
	*2	January 27, 1783,	March 27, 1783,	60		
7	‡	do 21, 1784,	May 12, 1784,	113	66	128
8	‡1	October 18, 1784,	November 29, 1784,	43	90	138
	‡2	January 24, 1785,	April 27, 1785,	94		
9	‡	do 16, 1786,	May 5, 1786,	110	67	138
10	‡	do 13, 1787,	April 21, 1787,	99	103	212
11	†	do 11, 1788,	March 22, 1788,	72	95	222
12	§	December 11, 1788,	do 3, 1789,	83	51	82
13	§1	July 6, 1789,	July 16, 1789,	11	59	4
	‡2	January 12, 1790,	April 6, 1790,	85		46
14	‡	do 5, 1791,	March 24, 1791,	79	54	38
15	‡	do 5, 1792,	April 12, 1792,	99	74	74
16	‡	November 6, 1792,	March 12, 1793,	127	67	64
17	§	January 7, 1794,	do 27, 1794,	80	59	36
18	†1	do 6, 1795,	January 14, 1795,	9	76	55
	‡2	do 20, 1795,	April 9, 1795,	80		
19	‡	do 6, 1796,	do 11, 1796,	97	70	54
20	‡1	November 1, 1796,	November 11, 1796,	11	......	......
	2	January 3, 1797,	April 3, 1797,	91	......	340
21	....	do 2, 1798,	do 6, 1798,	95	112	295
22	1	August 9, 1798,	August 27, 1798,	19	94	291
	2	January 3, 1799,	April 3, 1799,	91		
23	....	do 28, 1800,	do 8, 1800,	71	133	294
24	1	November 4, 1800,	November 7, 1800,	4	82	226
	2	January 27, 1801,	April 4, 1801,	68		
25	....	do 26, 1802,	do 5, 1802,	68	119	204
26	....	do 25, 1803,	do 6, 1803,	72	110	360
27	....	do 31, 1804,	do 11, 1804,	72	117	478
28	1	November 6, 1804,	November 12, 1804,	7	137	614
	2	January 23, 1805,	April 10, 1805,	103		
29	....	do 28, 1806,	do 7, 1806,	70	189	648
30	....	do 27, 1807,	do 7, 1807,	71	184	574
31	....	do 26, 1808,	do 11, 1808,	77	479	622
32	1	November 1, 1808,	November 8, 1808,	8	378	380
	2	January 18, 1809,	March 30, 1809,	72		
33	....	do 30, 1810,	April 6, 1810,	67	391	313
34	...	do 29, 1811,	do 9, 1811,	71	248	470
35	....	do 28, 1812,	June 19, 1812,	114	242	503
36	1	November 3, 1812,	November 11, 1812,	9	204	340
	2	January 13, 1813,	April 13, 1813,	91		
37	....	do 25, 1814,	do 15, 1814,	81	218	284
38	1	September 26, 1814,	October 24, 1814,	29	266	288
	2	January 31, 1815,	April 18, 1815,	78		
39	....	do 30, 1816,	do 17, 1816,	79	237	296
40	1	November 5, 1816,	November 12, 1816,	8	295	352
	2	January 14, 1817,	April 14, 1817,	91		
41	....	do 27, 1818,	do 21, 1818,	85	290	314
42	....	do 5, 1819,	do 3, 1819,	89	248	318
43	....	do 4, 1820,	do 14, 1820,	82	249	256
44	1	November 7, 1820,	November 20, 1820,	14	250	268
	2	January 9, 1821,	April 3, 1821,	85		

* Met at Kingston. † Met at Poughkeepsie. ‡ Met at New York city.

§ Met at Albany. After the first meeting of the 20th session, all meetings of the Legislature have been held at Albany.

‖ From 1777 to 1796 inclusive, the laws were printed in folio form.

Sessions of the New York State Legislature — (Continued).

Sessions.	Meetings.	Begun.	Ended.	Days in session.	Number of laws passed.	Number of printed pages of laws.
45	....	January 1, 1822, ...	April 17, 1822, ...	107	275	322
46	...	do 1, 1823, ...	do 24, 1823, ...	114	259	430
47	1	do 6, 1824, ...	do 12, 1824, ...	78	337	392
48	....	do 4, 1825, ...	do 21, 1825, ...	108	326	480
49	....	do 3, 1826, ...	do 18, 1826, ...	106	321	378
50	1	do 2, 1827, ...	do 7, 1827, ...	96	335	376
	2	June 27, 1827, ...	July 24, 1827, ...	28		
	3	September 11, 1827, ...	December 4, 1827, ...	85		
51	1	January 1, 1828, ...	April 21, 1828, ...	112	343	496
	2	September 9, 1828, ...	December 10, 1828, ...	93		
52	....	January 6, 1829, ...	May 5, 1829, ...	100	377	584
53	....	do 5, 1830, ...	April 20, 1830, ...	106	337	428
54	....	do 4, 1831, ...	do 26, 1831, ...	113	323	434
55	1	do 3, 1832, ...	do 26, 1832, ...	115	335	586
	2	June 21, 1832, ...	July 2, 1832, ...	12		
56	....	January 1, 1833, ...	April 30, 1833, ...	120	323	516
57	. ..	do 7, 1834, ...	May 6, 1834, ...	120	320	594
58	....	do 6, 1835, ...	do 11, 1835, ...	126	311	366
59	....	do 5, 1836, ...	do 26, 1836, ...	143	536	814
60	....	do 3, 1837, ...	do 16, 1837, ...	134	478	562
61	. ..	do 2, 1838, ...	April 18, 1838, ...	107	333	340
62	....	do 1, 1839, ...	May 7, 1839, ...	126	390	372
63	....	do 7, 1840, ...	do 14, 1840, ...	129	387	354
64	....	do 5, 1841, ...	do 26, 1841, ...	142	351	378
65	1	do 4, 1842, ...	April 12, 1842, ...	99	326	422
	2	August 16, 1842, ...	September 7, 1842, ...	23		
66	....	January 3, 1843, ...	April 18, 1843, ...	106	240	350
67	....	do 2, 1844, ...	May 7, 1844, ...	127	347	546
68	....	do 7, 1845, ...	do 14, 1845, ...	128	367	448
69	....	do 6, 1846, ...	do 13, 1846, ...	128	337	486
70	1	do 5, 1847, ...	do 13, 1847, ...	129	499	487
	2	September 8, 1847, ...	December 15, 1847, ...	99		
71	....	January 4, 1848, ...	April 12, 1848, ...	100	381	584
72	....	do 2, 1849, ...	do 11, 1849, ...	100	439	736
73	....	do 1, 1850, ...	do 10, 1850, ...	100	378	822
74	1	do 7, 1851, ...	do 17, 1851, ...	101	547	1,024
	2	June 10, 1851, ...	July 11, 1851, ...	32		
75	....	January 6, 1852, ...	April 16, 1852, ...	102	408	734
76	1	do 4, 1853, ...	do 15, 1853, ...	102	654	1,266
	2	May 24, 1853, ...	July 21, 1853, ...	59	.....	......
77	....	January 3, 1854, ...	April 17, 1854, ...	105	407	1,108
78	....	do 2, 1855, ...	do 14, 1855, ...	103	577	1,122
79	....	do 1, 1856, ...	do 9, 1856, ...	109	205	366
80	....	do 6, 1857, ...	do 18, 1857, ...	103	804	1,712
81	....	do 5, 1858, ...	do 19, 1858, ...	105	376	668
82	....	do 4, 1859, ...	do 19, 1859, ...	106	517	1,212
83	....	do 3, 1860, ...	do 17, 1860, ...	106	530	1,080
84	....	do 1, 1861, ...	do 16, 1861, ...	106	344	834
85	....	do 7, 1862, ...	do 23, 1862, ...	107	492	1,006
86	...	do 6, 1863, ...	do 25, 1863, ...	110	515	912
87	....	do 5, 1864, ...	do 23, 1864, ...	110	586	1,360
88	....	do 3, 1865, ...	do 28, 1865, ...	116	777	1,556
89	....	do 2. 1866, ...	do 20, 1866, ...	109	910	2,150
90	....	do 1, 1867, ...	do 20, 1867, ...	110	......	......

PRINTED BILLS.

The custom of printing legislative bills came generally into use in 1832, although for ten years or more, previously, many of the more important bills were printed before their passage as laws. Until 1844, there was but one series of numbers, each bill being designated as "Senate" or "Assembly" according as it originated. Since 1844, inclusive, each house has had its separate series. The number printed annually is shown in the following table:

Number of Bills printed annually.

YEARS.	Senate bills.	Assembly bills.	Total.	YEARS.	Senate bills.	Assembly bills.	Total.
1832,	......	......	*117	1850,	*231	*407	638
1833,	......	......	*139	1851,	*220	*630	850
1834,	......	......	*352	1852,	257	439	696
1835,	......	......	*281	1853,	295	459	754
1836,	......	......	*218	1854,	366	469	835
1837,	......	......	*143	1855,	334	452	786
1838,	......	......	*314	1856,	*405	*460	865
1839,	......	......	*500	1857,	*405	*626	1,031
1840,	......	......	*444	1858,	321	478	799
1841,	......	......	596	1859,	307	617	924
1842,	......	......	*325	1860,	360	588	948
1843,	......	......	391	1861,	289	550	839
1844,	166	431	597	1862,	284	519	803
1845,	263	450	713	1863,	348	493	841
1846,	184	462	646	1864,	373	693	1,066
1847,	230	597	827	1865,	420	708	1,128
1848,	195	545	740	1866,	406	813	1,219
1849,	213	570	783				

* Without indexes.

STATISTICS OF COUNTIES AND OF SUPERVISORS.

COUNTIES.	When organized.	Number of towns.	Number of cities.	Days on which town meetings are held.	BOARDS OF SUPERVISORS.		
					No. of members in Boards of Supervisors.	Days in session in 1866.	Compensation for services in 1866.
Albany,.......	1683	9	1	2d Tuesday in April,..................	19	28	*$6,000 00
Allegany,.....	1806	29	..	1st Tuesday in March,.....	29	5	2,064 16
Broome,......	1806	14	1	2d Tuesday in February, ...	19	14	964 68
Cattaraugus, .	1808	31	..	4th Tuesday in February,............	31	12	1,419 98
Cayuga,..... ..	1799	23	1	1st Tuesday in March,................	27	16	2,086 67
Chautauqua,..	1808	26	..	3d Tuesday in February,†........ ...	26	10	1,259 44
Chemung,.....	1836	10	1	2d Tuesday in February,‡............	15	10	618 52
Chenango,....	1798	21	..	3d Tuesday in February,.............	21	12	1,497 49
Clinton,..... .	1788	14	..	1st Tuesday in March,................	14	11	1,300 95
Columbia,.....	1786	18	1	1st Tuesday in March,............	20	33	1,922 51
Cortland,.....	1808	15	..	3d Tuesday in February,.............	15	16	1,220 48
Delaware,.....	1797	18	..	2d Tuesday in February,....	18	§	§
Dutchess,....	1683	19	1	2d Tuesday in March, ...	23	25	1,354 56
Erie,..........	1821	25	1	1st Tuesday in March,....	51	40	580 32
Essex,........	1799	18	..	1st Tuesday in March,................	18	6	1,001 26
Franklin,.....	1808	16	..	1st Tuesday in March,................	16	4	637 23
Fulton,........	1838	10	..	1st Tuesday in March,....	10	14	1,565 94
Genesee,......	1802	13	..	1st Tuesday in March,................	13	12	437 60
Greene,.......	1800	14	..	1st Tuesday in April,.................	14	7	2,732 29
Hamilton,.....	1816	8	..	1st Tuesday in February,.............	8	5	677 25
Herkimer,....	1791	19	..	2d Tuesday in February, ...	19	12	1,710 95
Jefferson,.....	1805	22	..	1st Tuesday in February,.............	22	13	1,350 40
Kings,........	1683	5	1	1st Tuesday in April..................	27	40	15,952 45
Lewis,........	1805	17	..	3d Tuesday in February,.......	17	10	1,299 60
Livingston,...	1821	17	..	1st Tuesday in March,................	17	24	949 46
Madison,......	1806	14	..	1st Tuesday in March..................	14	11	952 30
Monroe,......	1821	19	1	1st Tuesday after 1st Monday in March.	33	38	2,871 04
Montgomery,.	1772	10	..	2d Tuesday in February,..............	10	14	934 56
New York,....	1683	..	1	....	12	34	24,000 00
Niagara,......	1808	12	1	2d Tuesday in April,....	17	23	1,725 19
Oneida,.......	1798	26	1	1st Tuesday in March,................	33	19	3,651 34
Onondaga,....	1794	19	1	3d Tuesday in February,..............	27	32	830 11
Ontario,......	1789	15	..	1st Tuesday in March,................	15	24	1,338 16
Orange,.......	1683	16	1	Last Tuesday in March,..............	21	16	2,063 03
Orleans,......	1824	9	..	1st Tuesday in April,.................	9	19	1,703 18
Oswego,......	1816	21	1	1st Tuesday in March,................	25	17	2,938 34
Otsego,.......	1791	24	..	2d Tuesday of each year,‖............	24	13	2,174 56
Putnam,......	1812	6	..	1st Tuesday in April, ...	6	10	502 04
Queens,..	1683	6	..	1st Tuesday in April,.................	6	16	800 02
Rensselaer,..	1791	16	1	1st Tuesday in March,................	26	33	3,783 54
Richmond,...	1683	5	..	2d Tuesday in February, ...	5	38	1,020 61
Rockland,....	1798	5	..	3d Tuesday in March, ...	5	18	457 28
St. Lawrence,.	1802	29	..	2d Tuesday in February,..............	29	14	1,830 76
Saratoga,.....	1791	20	..	1st Tuesday in March,........	20	15	1,639 16
Schenectady, .	1809	5	1	1st Tuesday in April,.................	10	20	1,070 80
Schoharie,....	1795	16	..	3d Tuesday in February, ...	16	§	§
Schuyler,.....	1854	8	..	2d Tuesday in February, ...	8	16	686 01
Seneca,.......	1804	10	..	2d Tuesday in March,.................	10	13	683 44
Steuben,.....	1796	32	..	2d Tuesday in February,..............	32	11	1,513 92
Suffolk,.......	1683	9	..	1st Tuesday in April,.................	9	8	696 48
Sullivan,......	1809	14	..	1st Tuesday in March,................	14	7	812 12
Tioga,........	1791	9	..	2d Tuesday in February,..............	9	9	752 90
Tompkins,...	1817	9	..	1st Tuesday in April,.................	9	11	662 34
Ulster,........	1683	19	..	1st Tuesday in March,................	19	14	128 41
Warren,......	1813	11	..	1st Tuesday in March,................	11	8	688 58
Washington, .	1772	17	..	1st Tuesday in March,................	17	12	1,643 98
Wayne,.......	1823	15	..	1st Tuesday in March,................	15	10	991 36
Westchester, .	1683	24	..	Last Tuesday in March,..............	24	20	2,236 72
Wyoming,....	1841	17	..	Last Tuesday in February,............	17	6	370 90
Yates,........	1823	9	..	Last Tuesday in February,............	9	18	929 28
Total,......	......	927	17	....	....	..	$120,696 65

* Including pay of officers.
† Except in Dunkirk, where they are held on the first Tuesday in March.
‡ Charter elections in Elmira on the first Tuesday in March.
§ No data from these counties.
‖ Probably second Tuesday of March in each year, although reported as above.

APPENDIX.

VOTERS.

Under the first State Constitution the franchise was restricted to property qualifications, and the representation was based upon a census taken once in seven years. The following table presents the number and percentage of electors in the State of New York during the period that this Constitution was in force:

Number of Electors, 1790–1821.

CLASSES.	1790.	1795.	1801.	1807.	1814.	1821.
Electors worth freeholds of $100 ($250) or over,	19,369	36,338	52,058	71,159	87,491	100,490
Electors worth freeholds of $20 to $100 ($50 to $250),	23,425	4,838	5,264	5,800	5,231	8,985
Total electors owning freeholds,	42,794	41,176	57,322	82,959	92,722	69,475
Electors not freeholders, but renting estates valued at 40*s.* ($5),	14,674	22,598	28,522	14,330	59,104	93,035
Other electors,*	138	243	63	88	20	†56,877
Total electors of all classes,	57,606	64,017	85,907	121,377	151,846	259,387

Percentage of Electors to Population, 1790–1821.

CLASSES.	1790.	1795.	1801.	1807.	1814.	1821.
Electors worth freeholds of $100 ($250) or over,	5.692	7.825	8.317	8.372	8.446	7.193
Electors worth freeholds of $20 to $100 ($50 to $250),	6.887	1.042	.841	.682	.505	.643
Total electors owning freeholds,	12.579	8.867	9.158	9.054	8.951	7.836
Electors not freeholders, but renting estates valued at 40*s.* ($5),	4.314	4.866	4.558	1.686	5.705	6.659
Other electors,*	.040	.052	.010	.014	.002	4.289
Total electors of all classes,	16.933	13.785	13.726	10.754	14.658	18.784

The number who actually voted for Governor during and before the above period (not including scattering votes) was:

1789. For George Clinton and Robert Yates, ... 12,353
1792. For George Clinton and John Jay, ... 16,772
1795. For John Jay and Robert Yates, ... 25,373
1798. For John Jay and Robert R. Livingston, ... 29,644

* Freemen of New York on the 14th day of October, 1775, and freemen of Albany on the 20th day of April, 1777.

† Free male inhabitants who were citizens of the State, of the age of twenty-one or upward, who were not possessed of freeholds, and who did not rent tenements of the yearly value of $5, but who had been actually rated and paid taxes to this State, or who had enrolled in the militia, or in a uniform company of this State, and served therein, either as an officer or private, or who had done service in any way which, by law, exempts from taxation or military duty, or who had been rated and actually paid highway taxes by commutation or labor.

1801. For George Clinton and Stephen Van Rensselaer, ... 45,651
1804. For Morgan Lewis and Aaron Burr, ... 52,968
1807. For Daniel D. Tompkins and Morgan Lewis, ... 65,063
1810. For Daniel D. Tompkins and Jones Platt, ... 79,578
1813. For Daniel D. Tompkins and Stephen Van Rensselaer, ... 83,042
1816. For Daniel D. Tompkins and Rufus King, ... 84,059
1817. For De Witt Clinton and Peter B. Porter, ... 44,789
1820. For De Witt Clinton and Daniel D. Tompkins, ... 93,437

These electors possessed the freehold qualification of £100 and upward.

Number and percentage of voters, 1825–1865.

YEARS.	Number of voters.	Percentage of voters to total population.	YEARS.	Number of voters.	Percentage of voters to total population.
1825, ...	296,132	18.31	1855, ...	652,322	19.18
1835, ...	422,034	19.77	1865, ...	823,484	21.51
1845, ...	539,379	20.71			

Number and percentage of aliens, 1825–1865.

YEARS.	Number of aliens.	Percentage of aliens to total population.	YEARS.	Number of aliens.	Percentage of aliens to total population.
1825, ...	40,430	2.44	1855, ...	632,746	18.54
1835, ...	82,319	3.83	1865, ...	399,463	10.43
1845, ...	153,717	7.52			

Number of Persons who exercised the privilege of voting annually, from 1826 *to* 1866, *inclusive.**

YEARS.	Number of votes actually cast.	Number of voters in the State as shown by the census.	Percentage of votes cast to number of voters.	YEARS.	Number of votes actually cast.	Number of voters in the State as shown by the census.	Percentage of votes cast to number of voters.
1826, ...	96,074	308,724	31.12	1847, ...	325,013	561,967	53.52
1827, ...	177,809	321,314	55.34	1848, ...	460,166	573,261	80.27
1828, ...	252,757	333,904	75.69	1849, ...	407,059	584,556	69.63
1829, ...	198,603	346,492	57.02	1850, ...	432,597	595,850	72.51
1830, ...	251,381	359,082	70.01	1851, ...	401,083	607,144	66.06
1831, ...	230,489	371,672	62.01	1852, ...	525,391	618,439	84.95
1832, ...	312,776	384,262	81.39	1853, ...	372,100	629,733	59.25
1833, ...	186,540	396,852	47.00	1854, ...	407,595	641,027	79.59
1834, ...	349,055	409,444	85.25	1855, ...	436,419	652,322	66.90
1835, ...	175,278	422,034	41.53	1856, ...	594,347	669,414	88.78
1836, ...	303,859	433,768	70.05	1857, ...	440,022	686,506	64.09
1837, ...	296,430	445,503	65.54	1858, ...	545,529	703,598	77.53
1838, ...	380,623	457,237	83.24	1859, ...	503,063	720,691	69.80
1839, ...	364,141	468,972	77.65	1860, ...	673,469	737,783	91.27
1840, ...	441,552	480,706	91.86	1861, ...	487,567	754,875	64.59
1841, ...	366,087	492,441	76.37	1862, ...	603,038	771,967	78.12
1842, ...	401,542	504,175	79.65	1863, ...	599,439	789,059	75.97
1843, ...	358,897	515,910	69.56	1864, ...	731,010	806,151	90.68
1844, ...	487,334	527,644	92.36	1865, ...	573,421	823,484	69.62
1845, ...	337,496	539,379	62.38	1866, ...	719,195	....	......
1846, ...	406,720	550,673	73.85				

* These numbers in even years were those who voted for Governor, and in odd years for Senators, until 1845, and for Secretary of State since that period. The vote includes all candidates, and the scattering vote for the office, in each year. The table is taken from the census of 1865, pages 80, 81 and 82, where the vote is given by counties.

SUPPLEMENTARY TABLES OF CANAL DEPARTMENT.

A series of tables, embracing specific statements of cost, income and revenue of the canals was in preparation for this volume, when the Auditor was called upon by a resolution of the Convention dated June 26th, 1867, for information embracing substantially the materials in hand, but in a modified form from the arrangement that had been originally designed.

It was, therefore, found necessary to go on with the printing of the other portions of the Manual, and leave these tables and statements that should properly have been placed in connection with the statistics of the Canal Department, to be inserted in the Appendix.

The information called for in the resolution above noticed, was as follows:

"1. The original cost of the several canals of this State, including that of any enlargement or extension thereof.

"2. The aggregate cost of each canal as aforesaid, including superintendence, repairs and legal interest on the cost of construction up to the close of the last fiscal year.

"3. The aggregate receipts or income from each canal, completed in like manner, with interest thereon, to the close of the last fiscal year.

"4. The annual receipts or income of the State from each canal, with the annual cost of superintendence and repairs respectively of such canals up to the close of the last fiscal year.

"6. Also a table which will show with how much each so called lateral canal should be credited for its contributions to the revenues, which in the yearly official tables are credited to the Erie canal.

"7. The amount of outstanding canal debt and when due, and when the same would be paid, assuming as a basis of calculation for the future revenue of the toll receipts, the revenue from the same source for the last seven years."

The reply of the Auditor is embraced in the following pages:

Statement A, is an aggregate recapitulation in a condensed form of the detailed information called for by the first six propositions of the resolution of inquiry. The specific and detailed information in reference to each canal will be found in tables, Nos. 1 to 13, inclusive, following consecutively.

Statement B, is a balance sheet, showing the net cost or profit to the State of each canal as deduced from the tables submitted.

The Auditor submits the following reply to the 7th inquiry of the resolution, which is in these words:

"The amount of outstanding canal debt and when due, and when the same would be paid, assuming as a basis of calculation for the future revenue of the toll receipts the revenue from the same source for the last seven years."

Amount of Debt July 1, 1867.	When due.	Annual interest.	Interest to maturity.
$160 00	July 1, 1837,	No interest.	
10,000 00	After 1860,	do	
247,900 00	October 1, 1868,	$12,395 00	$15,493 75
57,000 00	January 1, 1871,	2,850 00	9,975 00
2,800,000 00	July 1, 1872,	168,000 00	840,000 00
1,000,000 00	January 1, 1873,	60,000 00	330,000 00
2,750,000 00	July 1, 1873,	165,000 00	990,000 00
2,250,000 00	November 1, 1873,	135,000 00	855,000 00
3,000,000 00	January 1, 1874,	150,000 00	975,000 00
2,250,000 00	October 1, 1874,	135,000 00	978,750 00
500,000 00	October 1, 1875,	30,000 00	247,500 00
900,000 00	December 1, 1877,	54,000 00	562,500 00
$15,765,060 00		$912,245 00	
Total interest of debt,			$5,804,218 75
Total principal of debt,			15,765,060 00
Total principal and interest,			$21,569,278 75

In the above statement there is included the sum of $1,700,000 the remainder of the Floating Debt Loan, so called, contracted for canal purposes, under the act, chapter 271 of the Laws of 1859.

The aggregate of the net receipts from tolls or surplus canal revenues, for the seven years ending on the 30th September, 1866, was $20,636,868.26.

This gives an average per year of $2,948,124.03, so that, assuming that the net surplus canal revenues for the next seven years will be as large as the last seven, this debt, principal and interest, can be paid in seven and three-fourths years.

Assume that the whole annual surplus will be,	$2,948,124 03
Deduct from this the annual interest of the whole outstanding canal debt,	912,245 00
Annual remainder to apply on principal,	$2,035,879 03

Multiply this remainder by 7¾ and we have $15,778,062.47.

But these surpluses will not be available to pay this Canal Debt, until after the extinguishment of the General Fund Debt of 1846, amounting to $5,636,622.22, which, by the present Constitution, has a preference in payment to the whole of the above Canal Debt, except $3,257,900, the remainder of the Canal Debt of 1846. The aggregate of the principal of both debts, is $21,401,682.22, and the aggregate of the yearly interest is $1,234,663.35.

On the 30th September, 1867, the actual and estimated balance in the treasury applicable to the payment of the principal and interest of these debts, after deducting the interest on the Canal Debt, and the contribution of $350,000 to the General Fund Debt Sinking Fund, due the 1st of October, 1867, will be $2,755,595.26. If this actual and estimated revenue shall be realized on the 30th of September next, it will not be subject to any deductions for interest due up to that time; and if this actual and estimated balance were then applied to the redemption of the principal of these debts, according to their priority, the results below would be obtained, by applying the seven years' averages.

1867, Sept. 30. Aggregate principal of both debts,		$21,401,682 22
1867, Sept. 30. Apply means on hand,		2,755,595 26
Balance of principal outstanding,		$18,646,086 96
Amount of the seven years average,	$2,948,124 03	
Yearly interest on the remainder of principal deducted,	1,112,170 35	
Yearly balance applicable to principal,	$1,835,953 68	

These figures show that both debts will be wiped out in about ten years, if these averages are maintained, as they probably will be if the canals are not depleted in the future as they have been in the past. The last installment of the Canal Debt is due December 1, 1877, and that of the General Fund Debt, July 1st, 1878.

What have the canals cost the treasury of the State?

This short and literal exposition of a portion of the tables will answer this question.

There was contributed from the treasury prior to 1846, in aid of the canals:

From taxes levied prior to 1846,	$496,496 05
From vendue duty,	3,592,039 05
From duty on salt,	2,055,458 06
From steamboat tax,	73,509 99
From sales of land,*	320,518 15
From General Fund for deficiencies,	1,386,498 88
Total,	$7,924,520 18
Reimbursed to the treasury from the canal tolls, prior to September 30, 1846,	2,537,602 73
Balance advanced by treasury, without interest,	$5,386,917 45

The credit to the treasury of $320,518.15 for the receipts from the sales of public lands, includes the proceeds of the sales of land donated to the Erie and Champlain Canals, and, therefore, to the extent of the means thus derived, nothing was taken from the treasury, nor any means whereby the treasury proper could have been benefited. When the Convention in 1846 adjusted the balances between the canals and the treasury for advances, a perpetual annuity of $200,000 a year was imposed upon the surplus canal revenues, equal to an annual income at five cent. on $4,000,000 invested; a charge was made upon the canals to pay the General Fund Debt and other collateral liabilities which now aggregate $5,636,622.22, and imposed an annual payment upon the canals of $350,-000 to cover the accruing interest on this debt, which is $27,581.65 a year in excess of the actual interest paid by the treasury, and this statement may be given.

Paid to the treasury since 1846, on the $200,000 for the support of government,	$2,151,113 40
Paid to the treasury since 1846, in excess of the actual interest on the General Fund Debt during that period,	551,633 00
Advanced outside of the interest on General Fund Debt,	$2,702,746 40

* The Erie and Champlain Canals received donations of 110,036 acres of land west of the Seneca river, to aid in their construction.

The adjustment and award made by the Convention in 1846, was supposed to be a finality, and the legislative and fiscal departments of the State are bound to consider the question closed under the present fundamental law. The resolutions of inquiry, which the Auditor has endeavored to answer as fully and elaborately as the means at hand and urgency of the occasion will allow, go far behind that finding and award in 1846, and call for information that in its natural characteristics will give a partial and one sided view of the subject, and hence this volunteer addition. The State has not paid or advanced a dollar since 1846 to the canals or their debt, which they will not repay with interest according to the terms of the contract on which the advances were made. The periods for the final liquidation of the General Fund Debt are rapidly approaching and will soon be consummated; the final payments of the Canal Debt will soon be made without any resort to the State for aid; and the advances made since 1846 will be refunded with interest, and the State will have the canals free of charge or cost, as a commission for advances repaid, and a compensation for indorsements.

The canals are indebted to the treasury $14,396,767.97 for taxes levied and received for canal purposes since 1846, besides the interest, which must be refunded out of the canal revenues after the payment of certain preferred claims.

TABLE NO. 1.

Erie and Champlain Canals.

YEAR.	INCOME.				DISBURSEMENTS.							
					FOR CONSTRUCTION.		FOR MAINTENANCE.					
	(1)	(2)	(3)	(4)	(1)	(2)	(3)	(4)	(5)	(6)	(7)	(8)
	Tolls proper.	Legal interest on tolls proper.	Tolls after deducting tolls on contributions from the lateral canals.	Legal interest on tolls after deduct'g tolls on contributions from the lateral canals.	Cost of construction.	Legal interest on cost of construction.	Contractors for repairs.	Superintendents for repairs.	Collectors, inspectors, &c.	Weighmasters.	Tot. payments, including cost of construction and enlargement.	Legal interest on total payments, including cost of construction, &c.
1817,	....	....	....	....	$200,000 00	$686,000 00	....	....	....	....	$200,000 00	$686,000 00
1818,	....	....	....	....	466,900 00	1,568,784 00	....	....	....	....	466,900 00	1,568,784 00
1819,	....	....	....	....	587,467 09	1,932,766 73	....	....	....	....	587,467 09	1,932,766 72
1820,	....	....	....	....	668,900 00	2,153,858 00	....	....	....	....	668,900 00	2,153,858 00
1821,	$6,930 00	$2,200 00	$2,200 00	$6,930 00	1,120,500 00	3,529,575 00	....	....	....	....	1,120,500 00	3,529,575 00
1822,	137,019 10	44,486 72	44,486 72	137,019 10	1,955,012 23	6,021,437 67	....	....	....	....	1,955,012 23	6,021,437 68
1823,	361,164 12	119,988 08	119,988 08	361,164 12	1,784,102 61	5,370,148 86	....	....	....	....	1,784,102 61	5,370,148 85
1824,	850,602 50	289,320 58	289,320 58	850,602 51	1,275,543 82	3,750,098 83	....	....	....	....	1,275,543 82	3,750,098 83
1825,	1,496,257 11	521,343 94	521,343 94	1,496,257 11	990,537 84	2,842,843 60	....	....	....	....	990,537 84	2,842,843 60
1826,	2,356,724 36	841,687 27	841,687 27	2,356,724 36	403,255 91	1,129,116 55	....	$124,652 51	....	....	527,908 42	1,478,143 57
1827,	2,404,072 40	880,978 90	880,978 90	2,405,072 40	153,551 67	419,196 06	....	284,654 16	$26,636 61	$450 00	465,292 44	1,270,248 36
1828,	2,204,991 78	828,944 28	828,244 43	2,203,130 18	92,310 92	245,547 05	....	215,809 25	27,042 33	4,052 87	339,215 37	902 312 90
1829,	2,071,361 33	799,753 41	787,710 42	2,040,169 99	48,698 21	126,128 36	....	234,504 21	26,111 47	5,116 63	314,430 52	814,375 04
1830,	2,567,428 67	1,018,820 90	988,442 31	2,490,874 62	18,255 81	46,004 64	....	211,044 19	22,327 28	4,377 88	256,005 16	645,133 00
1831,	1,786,961 67	729,372 11	692,762 32	1,697,267 68	11,377 68	27,875 32	....	156,553 66	22,973 86	2,023 50	192,928 70	472,675 31
1832,	2,578,983 04	1,083,606 32	1,049,578 17	2,497,996 04	32,890 81	78,280 13	....	333,786 05	22,987 29	4,430 59	394,094 74	937,945 48
1833,	3,117,342 16	1,349,498 77	1,306,869 97	3,018,869 63	35,264 66	81,461 36	....	330,759 44	25,052 14	4,602 25	395,678 49	914,017 31
1834,	3,010,015 14	1,343,756 76	1,272,706 51	2,850,862 57	15,006 17	33,613 82	....	423,517 10	25,162 42	4,511 25	468,196 94	1,048,761 14
1835,	3,007,123 35	1,431,854 08	1,342,189 91	2,912,652 10	52,109 05	113,076 64	....	403,473 90	25,764 64	4,781 30	486,128 89	1,054,899 69
1836,	3,237,829 88	1,541,823 75	1,445,906 35	3,036,403 34	66,259 82	139,145 62	....	300,391 32	26,030 90	4,211 20	396,893 24	833,475 80
1837,	2,586,436 32	1,274,106 81	1,209,145 61	2,454,565 59	694,103 10	1,409,029 29	....	361,714 70	29,912 18	5,671 71	1,091,401 69	2,215,545 43
1838,	2,747,341 50	1,401,704 75	1,310,609 81	2,568,795 23	1,244,398 49	2,439,021 04	....	365,661 95	24,335 97	6,350 32	1,640,746 73	3,215,863 59
1839,	3,033,928 67	1,578,798 24	1,491,065 31	2,818,113 44	2,330,664 11	4,404,955 17	....	299,599 53	38,814 32	6,067 85	2,675,145 81	5,056,025 58
1840,	2,800,798 55	1,538,900 30	1,438,565 13	2,618,188 54	3,287,636 70	5,983,498 79	....	296,913 67	39,740 88	5,719 28	3,630,010 53	6,606,619 16
1841,	3,313,872 70	1,893,641 54	1,751,143 43	3,064,501 00	2,569,327 23	4,496,322 65	....	273,433 22	38,293 30	5,290 22	2,886,343 97	5,051,101 95
1842,	2,868,248 73	1,707,290 91	1,605,574 69	2,697,365 48	1,622,692 72	2,726,123 77	....	303,654 96	37,148 35	5,152 55	1,968,648 58	3,307,329 61
1843,	3,001,954 25	1,864,567 86	1,707,117 75	2,748,459 58	575,548 97	926,633 84	....	294,941 49	33,055 48	4,506 84	908,052 78	1,461,964 93
1844,	3,481,660 55	2,260,818 54	2,009,568 40	3,094,735 34	482,305 64	742,750 70	....	353,688 77	32,372 45	4,724 21	873,091 07	1,344,560 25
1845,	3,257,643 94	2,216,084 31	1,903,687 66	2,798,420 86	259,086 44	380,857 07	....	408,024 59	32,891 53	4,985 60	704,988 16	1,036.332 59
1846,	3,664,256 62	2,617,326 16	2,323,984 53	3,253,578 34	102,029 69	142,841 57	....	368,626 45	33,558 13	4,795 93	509,010 20	712,614 23

1847,	4,336,176 70	3,260,283 23	2,864,660 65	3,809,998 66	83,876 49	111,555 73	....	377,750 22	34,786 68	5,066 65	501,480 04	666,968 45
1848,	3,637,234 19	2,886,693 73	2,519,796 25	3,174,943 28	665,267 02	838,236 45	....	515,687 65	39,990 72	5,885 71	1,226,831 10	1,545,807 19
1849,	3,645,985 39	3,063,853 27	2,682,016 39	3,191,599 50	1,009,909 28	1,201,792 04	....	401,862 55	39,153 72	6,178 80	1,457,104 35	1,733,954 17
1850,	3,424,605 40	3,057,683 39	2,631,020 89	2,946,743 40	1,375,300 98	1,540,337 10	....	429,014 55	35,912 99	6,081 93	1,846,310 45	2,067,867 70
1851,	3,476,033 16	3,310,507 77	2,924,063 52	3,070,266 70	1,026,242 73	1,077,554 87	....	485,158 75	51,162 53	7,412 50	1,569,976 51	1,648,475 33
1852,	2,858,368 02	2,916,702 06	2,534,456 75	2,483,767 62	972,704 92	953,250 82	....	555,594 75	45,928 01	7,076 93	1,581,304 61	1,549,678 52
1853,	2,665,779 85	2,929,428 41	2,439,742 60	2,220,165 77	605,269 10	550,794 88	....	566,833 08	47,830 36	7,468 11	1,227,400 65	1,116,934 59
1854,	2,315,331 99	2,756,351 18	2,423,397 63	2,035,654 01	646,939 43	543,429 12	....	705,307 31	50,422 49	7,873 16	1,410,542 39	1,184,855 61
1855,	1,877,209 43	2,437,934 33	2,040,493 89	1,571,180 30	2,250,282 72	1,732,717 69	$16,873 23	540,707 79	54,113 05	8,093 29	2,870,070 08	2,209,953 96
1856,	1,750,348 59	2,500,497 98	2,029,359 59	1,420,551 71	3,361,764 30	2,353,235 01	53,498 54	387,217 91	55,715 16	7,796 73	3,865,992 64	2,706,194 85
1857,	1,456,859 04	2,312,474 66	1,983,582 23	1,249,656 80	2,416,258 51	1,522,242 86	65,979 25	408,853 91	55,222 28	7,779 10	2,954,093 05	1,861,078 62
1858,	1,055,018 95	1,883,962 41	1,577,469 15	883,382 72	1,491,786 68	835,400 54	66,981 61	369,173 98	59,149 44	8,096 78	1,995,188 49	1,117,305 55
1859,	810,921 74	1,654,942 32	1,316,708 79	645,187 31	540,127 31	264,662 38	80,797 10	357,261 37	46,836 13	6,295 93	1,031,317 84	505,345 74
1860,	911,868 54	2,171,115 57	1,564,098 46	656,921 35	2,445,910 67	1,027,282 48	113,978 42	128,798 07	64,805 75	9,867 67	2,763,360 58	1,160,611 44
1861,	1,096,052 76	3,131,579 31	2,574,023 32	900,908 16	768,792 57	269,077 40	141,819 94	68,752 43	45,099 75	8,111 30	1,032,575 99	361,401 60
1862,	1,271,111 39	4,539,683 55	3,886,262 05	1,088,153 38	863,565 97	241,798 47	153,101 18	76,103 27	42,687 95	8,430 85	1,143,889 22	320,288 98
1863,	1,000,876 28	4,766,077 54	4,165,884 49	874,835 74	355,871 38	74,732 99	197,588 02	99,997 35	42,365 26	9,164 07	704,986 08	148,047 08
1864,	566,104 64	4,043,604 53	3,589,141 69	502,479 84	738,961 09	103,454 55	244,567 10	257,968 69	43,645 77	9,256 88	1,294,399 53	181,215 93
1865,	232,199 99	3,317,142 72	2,771,039 11	193,972 74	626,733 28	43,871 33	495,389 06	360,771 89	49,120 97	9,705 70	1,541,720 90	107,920 46
1866,	....	3,995,548 42	3,375,073 22	....	626,932 37	....	396,302 54	290,035 46	54,558 25	11,306 35	1,379,134 97	....
	$100,339,037 90	$92,116,741 67	$81,057,168 87	$91,399,088 14	$46,018,234 19	$69,232,418 84	$2,026,875 99	$13,728,256 10	$1,548,718 79	$248,770 42	$63,570,855 49	$90,429,363 47

RESULT I. CREDIT—INCOME.

From tolls proper,	$92,116,741 67		
Interest thereon,	100,339,037 90		
Total income and interest,			$192,455,779 57

DEBIT—EXPENDITURES.

For construction,	$46,018,234 19		
Interest thereon,	69,232,418 84		
		$115,250,653 03	
For maintenance,	$17,552,621 30		
Interest thereon,	21,196,944 63		
		38,749,565 93	
Total expenditures and interest,			154,000,218 96
Profit and interest,			$38,455,560 61

RESULT II. CREDIT—INCOME.

From tolls proper,	$92,116,741 67	
Interest thereon,	100,339,037 90	
Total income and interest,		$192,455,779 57
Less tolls on contributions from the lateral canals,	$11,059,572 80	
Interest thereon,	8,939,949 76	
Total contributions from laterals and interest,		19,999,522 56
Net income and interest,		$172,456,257 01

DEBIT—EXPENDITURES.

For construction,	$46,018,234 19		
Interest thereon,	69,232,418 84		
		$115,250,653 03	
For maintenance,	$17,552,621 30		
Interest thereon,	21,196,944 63		
		38,749,565 93	
Total expenditures and interest,			154,000,218 96
Net profit and interest,			*$18,456,038 05

Add to this balance the proportion of repairs and maintenance of the Erie and Champlain Canals chargeable to the lateral canals, viz.:

Oswego Canal,	$2,826,648 19	
Cayuga and Seneca Canal,	579,994 50	
Chemung Canal,	654,879 47	
Crooked Lake Canal,	201,092 20	
Chenango Canal,	51,856 93	
Black River Canal,	53,855 47	
Genesee Valley Canal,	283,961 20	
		4,652,287 96
Balance of profit and interest,		$23,108,326 01

* In the above result all the tolls contributed by the lateral canals have been restored to the contributing canals, as will appear in the following tables; but the lateral canals have been charged nothing for their proportion of repairs and maintenance of the Erie and Champlain Canals, excepting the memorandum at the bottom of each table showing the proportion chargeable to each.

TABLE

Oswego

YEARS.	INCOME.			
	(1)	(2)	(3)	(4)
	Tolls proper.	Tolls contributed to and heretofore credited Erie and Champlain Canals.	Total of tolls proper and contributions.	Legal interest on tolls proper and contributions.
1826,	....	....	....	....
1827,	....	....	....	....
1828,	$2,057 82	$699 85	$2,757 67	$7,335 40
1829,	9,071 93	367 51	9,439 44	24,448 15
1830,	12,430 01	....	12,430 01	31,323 62
1831,	11,465 20	4,805 90	16,271 10	39,864 20
1832,	16,610 65	3,175 55	19,786 20	47,091 16
1833,	22,965 26	....	22,965 26	53,049 75
1834,	22,174 13	20,246 09	42,420 22	95,021 29
1835,	26,267 09	35,989 77	62,256 86	135,097 39
1836,	29,359 93	41,238 11	70,598 04	148,255 88
1837,	24,556 97	18,900 60	43,457 57	88,218 87
1838,	22,961 40	35,923 85	58,885 25	115,415 09
1839,	32,593 80	39,204 68	71,798 48	135,699 13
1840,	29,166 71	35,968 37	65,135 08	118,545 85
1841,	34,630 03	51,605 15	86,235 18	150,911 57
1842,	35,878 82	35,963 70	71,842 52	120,695 43
1843,	31,914 21	63,305 91	95,220 12	153,304 39
1844,	50,013 24	108,753 36	158,766 60	244,500 56
1845,	53,831 17	111,876 25	165,707 42	243,589 91
1846,	60,101 35	128,315 93	188,417 28	263,784 19
1847,	70,839 01	190,161 54	261,000 55	347,130 73
1848,	71,564 58	184,307 60	255,872 18	322,398 95
1849,	86,139 66	224,665 31	310,804 97	369,857 91
1850,	94,524 17	243,590 91	338,115 08	378,688 89
1851,	104,366 58	232,322 30	336,688 88	353,523 32
1852,	82,951 22	237,310 92	320,262 14	313,856 90
1853,	88,839 97	301,962 61	390,802 58	355,630 35
1854,	81,266 00	151,273 51	232,539 51	195,333 19
1855,	64,954 15	234,123 03	299,077 18	230,289 43
1856,	96,136 22	336,379 98	432,516 20	302,761 34
1857,	105,141 39	204,452 79	309,594 18	195,044 33
1858,	83,939 46	173,361 59	257,301 05	144,088 59
1859,	69,348 37	198,234 69	267,583 06	131,115 70
1860,	109,840 03	455,410 02	565,250 05	237,405 02
1861,	131,458 38	452,795 02	584,253 40	204,488 69
1862,	153,006 82	496,703 51	649,710 33	181,918 89
1863,	143,273 75	450,793 05	594,066 80	124,754 03
1864,	142,561 87	321,655 78	464,217 65	64,990 47
1865,	112,063 86	432,047 82	544,111 68	38,087 82
1866,	143,364 27	461,708 04	605,072 31	....
	$2,563,629 48	$6,719,600 60	$9,283,230 08	$6,707,516 38

RESULT.

CREDIT.

By tolls proper,	$2,563,629 48	
By tolls on tonnage contributed to the Erie Canal,	6,719,600 60	
Total income from 1827 to 1866,		$9,283,230 08
Interest on income from 1827 to 1866,		6,707,516 38
Total credit, with interest,		$15,990,746 46

NO 2.

Canal.

DISBURSEMENTS.						
FOR CONSTRUCTION.		FOR MAINTENANCE.				
(1)	(2)	(3)	(4)	(5)	(6)	(7)
Cost of construction.	Legal interest on cost of construction.	Contractors, for repairs.	Superintendents, for repairs.	Collectors, inspectors, &c.	Total payments, including cost of construction.	Legal interest on total payments, including cost of construction.
$237,015 57	$663,643 60	....	....	....	$237,015 57	$663,643 59
175,221 00	478,353 33	....	....	....	175,221 00	439,353 33
83,774 46	222,840 06	....	$8,418 00	....	92,192 46	245,241 94
43,319 99	112,198 80	....	13,186 40	$942 94	57,449 33	137,693 76
3,310 00	8,341 20	....	12,972 51	1,837 25	18,119 76	45,662 79
....	....	....	8,860 48	1,866 77	10,727 25	26,281 76
....	....	....	12,507 99	1,974 39	14,482 38	34,468 06
....	....	....	11,236 72	2,015 03	13,251 75	30,611 54
....	....	....	12,522 48	2,008 51	14,530 99	32,549 41
....	....	....	12,747 26	2,044 97	14,792 23	32,099 13
....	....	....	51,064 14	2,147 44	53,211 58	111,744 31
165 00	334 95	....	54,625 00	2,616 81	57,406 81	116,535 82
1,156 21	2,265 76	....	53,997 56	2,003 13	57,156 90	112,027 52
....	....	....	24,624 60	3,086 62	27,711 22	52,374 20
....	....	....	36,198 40	2,988 44	39,186 84	71,320 04
....	....	....	26,241 95	2,992 96	29,234 91	51,161 09
....	....	....	30,189 57	3,138 64	33,328 21	55,991 39
....	....	....	22,741 60	2,766 86	25,508 46	41,068 62
....	....	....	27,410 68	2,774 31	30,184 99	46,484 88
....	....	....	46,531 82	3,123 21	49,655 03	72,992 89
....	....	....	54,273 11	3,263 75	57,536 86	80,551 60
....	....	....	39,439 41	3,228 30	42,667 71	56,748 05
....	....	....	74,093 10	3,690 67	77,783 77	98,007 55
4,939 70	5,878 60	....	33,470 43	3,855 83	42,265 96	50,296 49
82,507 60	92,408 96	....	29,631 44	3,598 45	115,737 49	129,625 98
60,546 29	63,573 30	....	30,913 20	4,775 91	96,235 40	101,047 17
75,652 45	74,138 96	....	40,972 84	4,468 08	121,093 37	118,671 50
166,726 53	151,721 57	....	39,322 17	4,748 09	210,796 79	191,825 08
308,087 93	258,793 92	....	67,247 64	5,734 16	381,069 73	320,098 57
327,307 14	252,026 39	....	64,635 15	5,708 23	397,650 52	306,190 90
257,828 62	180,480 30	....	59,529 15	6,010 86	323,368 63	226,358 04
214,921 60	135,400 86	....	83,267 97	6,231 47	304,421 04	191,785 25
181,564 60	101,676 40	....	97,565 51	6,668 65	285,798 76	160,047 30
161,053 67	78,916 46	$5,741 08	44,427 25	5,114 67	216,336 67	106,004 96
421,088 67	176,857 38	14,456 55	5,264 93	7,585 87	448,396 02	188,326 32
140,281 93	49,098 70	23,192 76	3,776 53	5,666 25	172,917 47	60,521 11
130,960 61	36,669 08	19,186 96	10,535 49	5,229 85	165,912 91	46,455 61
65,293 12	13,711 53	27,875 71	1,899 18	5,080 09	100,148 10	21,031 10
36,703 92	5,138 56	23,685 80	5,761 16	5,945 10	72,095 98	10,093 43
136,265 89	9,569 28	33,526 93	209,759 45	6,695 61	386,247 88	27,037 35
175,256 74	....	42,259 24	9,956 19	7,199 76	234,671 93	....
$3,490,949 24	$3,174,037 95	$189,925 03	$1,471,818 46	$150,827 93	$5,303,520 66	$4,910,029 43

DEBIT.

To cost of construction, ...	$3,490,949 24		
Interest thereon, ...	3,174,037 95		
		$6,664,987 19	
To cost of maintenance, ...	$1,812,571 42		
Interest thereon, ...	1,735,991 48		
		3,548,562 90	
			$10,213,550 09
			$5,777,196 37
To proportion of cost of repairs and maintenance of Erie and Champlain Canals from 1828 to 1866, ...			2,826,648 19
Net profit, ...			$2,950,548 18

These statements are appended, by request, to Table No. 2, showing the operations of the Oswego Canal.

STATEMENT of property which has passed at Oswego through the Welland Canal, to and from tide water, and also the increase of tolls which would have been produced had all such property passed through the whole line of the Erie Canal for the year named below.

YEAR.	PROPERTY WHICH PASSED THROUGH THE WELLAND CANAL TO WESTERN STATES FROM TIDE WATER.		PROPERTY WHICH PASSED THROUGH THE WELLAND CANAL FROM WESTERN STATES TO TIDE WATER.		INCREASE OF TOLLS PRODUCED IF ALL SUCH PROPERTY HAD PASSED THROUGH THE WHOLE LINE OF THE ERIE CANAL.		
	Tons.	Tolls.	Tons.	Tolls.	From tide water.	To tide water.	Total.
1852,...	75,026	$75,296	186,719	$208,136	$55,841	$154,359	$210,200
1853,...	98,066	95,323	238,790	328,822	70,694	243,903	314,597
1854,...	59,998	56,064	145,985	141,631	41,578	105,027	146,605
1855,...	69,817	66,388	225,080	235,670	49,235	174,825	224,060
1856,...	67,177	79,464	282,533	301,180	58,932	223,363	282,295
1857,...	68,776	112,242	154,338	157,424	81,430	114,210	195,640
1858,...	45,397	37,043	194,468	158,685	26,875	115,125	142,000
1859,...	60,212	24,566	190,593	155,523	17,822	112,831	130,653
1860,...	57,089	46,584	453,103	369,732	33,796	268,236	302,032
1861,...	30,031	24,505	358,536	365,706	17,778	265,316	283,094
1862,...	48,966	39,956	341,188	382,812	28,987	277,727	306,714
1863,...	67,291	54,909	261,692	293,618	39,836	213,017	252,853
1864,...	67,341	41,212	114,081	127,998	29,899	92,861	122,760
1865,...	45,255	27,696	130,473	146,390	20,093	106,204	126,297
1866,...	70,945	43,418	142,222	159,573	31,499	115,788	147,287
	931,387	$824,666	3,419,801	$3,532,900	$604,295	$2,582,792	$3,187,087

In making this statement, it was assumed that all the property which passed through the Welland Canal from Western States to Oswego, came to tide water; and that all the property going from Oswego through the Welland Canal to Western States (except the salt manufactured at the salt works) went from tide water.

There are no returns in the department previous to 1852, from which the property going to, and coming from other States, through the Welland Canal, can be arrived at.

STATEMENT of the salt which passed at Oswego through the Welland Canal, the tolls on the same from Syracuse to Oswego, and also the increase of tolls that would have been produced had such salt passed through the Erie Canal, from Syracuse to Buffalo, for the years named below.

YEARS.	Tons of salt which passed through the Welland Canal to Western States.	Tolls on same on Oswego Canal, from Syracuse to Oswego.	Tolls on same on Erie Canal, from Syracuse to Buffalo.	Increase of tolls produced, if all such salt had passed through Erie Canal to Buffalo.
1852,	43,420	$3,299	$12,852	$9,553
1853,	48,090	3,654	14,234	10,580
1854,	71,575	5,439	21,186	15,747
1855,	62,947	4,783	18,632	13,849
1856,	82,316	6,256	24,365	18,109
1857,	57,409	4,363	16,993	12,630
1858,	77,541	5,893	22,952	17,059
1859,	60,657	4,609	17,954	13,345
1860,	55,651	4,269	16,472	12,203
1861,	60,702	2,306	8,983	6,677
1862,	82,488	6,269	24,416	18,147
1863,	69,812	5,305	20,664	15,359
1864,	50,885	5,800	22,592	16,792
1865,	40,084	4,637	18,663	14,026
1866,	44,315	5,051	19,675	14,624
	907,892	$71,933	$280,633	$208,700

STATEMENT showing the total tons of merchandise going to, and the total tons of all property coming from other States by way of Buffalo and Oswego, for the years named below.

YEAR.	BY WAY OF BUFFALO.		BY WAY OF OSWEGO.		Total merchandise going to other States by way of Buffalo and Oswego.	Total property coming from other States by way of Buffalo and Oswego.	Total merchandise going to and property coming from other States.
	Merchandise going to other States.	Property coming from other States.	Merchandise going to other States.	Property coming from other States.			
1852,...	143,787	770,874	76,013	381,104	219,800	1,151,978	1,371,778
1853,..	163,192	718,493	98,560	495,197	261,752	1,213,690	1,475,442
1854,...	167,550	758,755	64,329	334,511	231,879	1,093,266	1,325,145
1855,...	145,530	752,334	74,936	382,755	220,466	1,135,089	1,355,555
1856,...	114,696	698,774	68,817	513,776	183,513	1,212,550	1,396,063
1857,...	74,733	640,916	43,393	378,196	118,126	1,019,112	1,137,238
1858,...	47,350	790,252	29,540	481,322	76,890	1,271,574	1,348,464
1859,...	72,767	632,017	26,109	403,700	98,876	1,035,717	1,134,593
1860,...	72,030	1,195,466	47,652	700,860	119,682	1,896,326	2,016,008
1861,...	35,278	1,597,893	17,184	559,790	52,462	2,157,683	2,210,145
1862,...	52,945	2,001,669	18,094	592,739	71,039	2,594,408	2,665,447
1863,...	64,124	1,727,082	29,971	448,422	94,095	2,175,504	2,269,599
1864,...	57,338	1,469,808	27,485	435,284	84,823	1,905,092	1,989,915
1865,...	59,175	1,365,776	13,366	536,071	72,541	1,901,847	1,974,388
1866,...	68,375	1,619,272	20,894	509,332	89,269	2,128,604	2,217,873
	1,338,870	16,739,381	656,343	7,153,059	1,995,213	23,892,440	25,887,653

TABLE

Cayuga and

YEARS.	INCOME.			
	(1)	(2)	(3)	(4)
	Tolls proper.	Tolls contributed to and heretofore credited Erie and Champlain Canals.	Total of tolls proper and contributions.	Legal interest on tolls proper and contributions.
1826,	$2,280 75	....	$2,820 75	$7,898 10
1827,	155 19	....	155 19	423 67
1828,	....	....	....	....
1829,	8,370 24	$11,675 48	20,045 72	51,918 41
1830,	13,087 51	30,378 59	43,466 10	109,534 57
1831,	8,859 48	31,803 89	40,663 37	99,625 26
1832,	12,375 77	30,852 60	43,228 37	102,883 52
1833,	15,591 50	42,628 80	58,220 30	134,488 89
1834,	18,053 14	41,451 57	59,504 71	133,290 55
1835,	20,192 61	28,682 84	48,875 45	106,059 73
1836,	19,914 53	29,405 01	49,319 54	103,571 03
1837,	16,648 77	13,146 98	29,795 75	60,485 37
1838,	17,488 82	18,846 17	36,334 99	71,216 60
1839,	19,354 67	18,196 69	37,551 36	70,979 63
1840,	17,787 29	28,949 56	46,736 85	85,061 07
1841,	22,445 46	29,786 96	52,232 42	91,406 74
1842,	17,992 67	19,830 67	37,823 34	63,543 21
1843,	17,938 40	22,548 22	40,486 62	65,183 46
1844,	23,054 19	55,825 82	78,880 01	121,475 20
1845,	28,881 48	40,493 70	69,375 18	101,981 51
1846,	29,395 23	43,263 53	72,658 76	101,722 26
1847,	26,908 78	56,712 97	83,621 75	111,216 93
1848,	28,470 86	52,023 56	80,494 42	101,422 97
1849,	27,735 44	41,013 82	68,749 26	81,811 62
1850,	27,589 59	40,368 51	67,958 10	76,113 07
1851,	26,258 40	29,849 34	56,107 74	58,913 13
1852,	22,524 38	30,546 66	53,071 04	52,009 62
1853,	25,169 84	40,102 05	65,271 89	59,397 42
1854,	24,808 90	37,901 60	62,710 50	52,676 82
1855,	21,915 81	37,596 86	59,512 67	45,824 76
1856,	20,919 78	30,557 15	51,476 93	36,033 85
1857,	19,457 35	31,438 87	50,896 22	32,064 62
1858,	14,400 67	34,121 36	48,522 03	27,172 34
1859,	17,449 54	33,401 14	50,850 68	24,916 83
1860,	20,089 09	39,625 25	59,714 34	25,080 02
1861,	18,778 32	31,601 92	50,380 24	17,633 08
1862,	21,395 82	39,588 13	60,983 95	17,075 51
1863,	25,243 93	39,205 12	64,449 05	13,534 30
1864,	28,040 29	56,644 16	84,684 45	11,855 82
1865,	23,802 22	71,062 62	94,864 84	6,640 54
1866,	34,151 25	67,654 19	101,805 44	....
	$805,517 96	$1,378,782 36	$2,184,300 32	$2,534,142 03

RESULT.

CREDIT.

By tolls proper,	$805,517 96	
By tolls on tonnage contributed to the Erie Canal,	1,378,782 36	
Total income, &c.,		$2,184,300 32
Interest on tolls proper and contributions,		2,534,142 03
Total credits with interest,		$4,718,442 35

Seneca Canal.

DISBURSEMENTS.						
FOR CONSTRUCTION.		FOR MAINTENANCE.				
(1)	(2)	(3)	(4)	(5)	(6)	(7)
Cost of construction.	Legal interest on cost of construction.	Contractors, for repairs.	Superintendents, for repairs.	Collectors, inspectors, &c.	Total payments, including cost of construction.	Legal interest on total payments, including cost of construction.
$42,190 30	$118,132 00			$255 83	$42,446 13	$118,849 64
65,068 75	177,638 37				65,068 75	177,638 37
90,918 54	241,844 54				90,918 54	241,844 54
20,783 50	53,830 56		$8,038 94		28,822 44	74,650 11
6,885 55	17,352 72		5,833 96	826 50	13,546 01	34,135 94
			3,301 39	822 00	4,123 39	10,102 30
100 00	238 00		4,132 85	799 17	5,032 02	11,976 20
			9,338 71	807 91	10,146 62	23,438 69
90 00	201 60		8,926 17	948 73	9,964 90	22,321 37
			10,275 83	1,412 96	11,688 79	25,364 67
			26,301 78	1,422 95	27,724 73	58,221 93
			30,471 56	1,459 73	31,931 29	64,820 51
			19,898 53	1,166 16	21,064 69	41,286 79
			23,594 36	1,712 01	25,306 37	47,829 03
			22,656 16	1,541 09	24,197 25	44,038 99
2,055 41	3,596 25		16,330 33	1,509 56	19,895 30	34,816 77
10,819 24	18,175 92		14,708 75	1,524 10	27,052 09	45,447 51
			10,953 48	1,454 16	12,407 64	19,976 30
4 52	7 70		14,127 13	1,337 65	15,469 30	23,822 72
			13,853 68	1,496 66	15,350 34	22,564 99
			12,947 02	1,567 50	14,514 52	20,320 32
756 40	1,005 48		14,099 37	1,526 51	16,382 28	21,788 43
			13,048 47	1,390 87	14,439 34	18,193 56
51,932 60	61,800 27		11,923 64	1,280 00	65,136 24	77,512 12
70,219 79	78,646 40		10,780 52	1,175 55	82,175 86	92,036 96
7,038 48	7,389 90		20,894 51	1,547 81	29,480 80	30,954 84
2,096 00	2,054 08		27,387 80	1,452 58	31,936 38	31,297 65
14,223 35	12,942 93		14,502 06	1,530 29	30,255 70	27,532 68
64,246 84	53,967 48		16,834 52	1,903 49	82,984 85	69,707 27
117,821 09	90,722 17		10,557 72	2,170 76	130,549 57	100,523 16
168,797 78	118,158 60		10,082 85	2,558 28	181,438 91	127,007 23
136,589 28	86,051 07		12,688 50	3,034 62	152,312 40	95,956 81
124,207 79	69,556 48		30,872 03	3,111 29	158,191 11	88,587 02
36,840 22	18,051 60	$1,113 25	5,278 55	2,397 46	45,629 48	22,358 44
135,590 78	56,948 22	3,360 43	131 24	2,644 40	141,726 85	59,525 27
84,308 31	29,507 80	2,473 08	17,010 38	2,307 26	106,099 03	37,134 66
93,564 74	26,198 20	4,258 70	14,799 98	1,734 80	114,358 22	32,020 30
44,293 70	9,301 74	8,457 48	3,159 49	1,373 21	57,283 88	12,029 61
39,029,63	5,464 20	10,527 92	4,069 54	1,384 39	55,011 48	7,701 60
64,334 92	4,503 45	19,591 65	373 03	1,581 04	85,880 64	6,011 64
25,735 08		14,029 44	2,097 49	1,786 67	43,648 68	
$1,520,542 59	$1,363,287 73	$63,811 95	$496,282 32	$59,955 95	$2,140,592 81	$2,121,346 94

DEBIT.

To cost of construction, ...	$1,520,542 59		
To interest thereon, ...	1,363,287 73		
		$2,883,830 32	
To cost of maintenance, ...	$620,050 22		
To interest thereon, ...	758,059 21		
		1,378,109 43	
			$4,261,939 75
Balance, profit, ...			$456,502 60
To proportion of cost of repairs and maintenance of Erie and Champlain Canals, from 1826 to 1866, ...			$579,994 50
Net cost, ...			$123,491 90

TABLE

Chemung

YEARS.	INCOME.			
	(1)	(2)	(3)	(4)
	Tolls proper.	Tolls contributed to and heretofore credited Erie and Champlain Canal.	Total of tolls proper and contributions.	Legal interest on tolls proper and contributions.
1830,	....	....	....	....
1831,	....	....	....	....
1832,	....	....	....	....
1833,	....	....	....	....
1834,	$2,398 39	$8,685 95	$11,084 34	$24,828 92
1835,	4,153 07	15,364 71	19,517 78	42,353 58
1836,	5,078 37	12,375 63	17,454 00	36,653 40
1837,	4,342 99	12,093 67	16,436 66	33,366 42
1838,	4,478 01	15,005 00	19,483 01	38,186 70
1839,	4,767 62	16,539 63	21,307 25	40,270 70
1840,	5,011 50	14,262 50	19,274 00	35,078 68
1841,	7,158 18	33,133 94	40,292 12	70,511 21
1842,	7,206 28	25,104 97	32,311 25	54,282 90
1843,	9,188 51	44,527 71	53,716 22	86,483 11
1844,	12,950 92	39,183 69	52,134 61	80,287 30
1845,	20,281 70	93,409 37	113,691 07	167,125 87
1846,	15,862 99	56,385 69	72,248 68	101,148 15
1847,	13,677 28	69,674 96	83,352 24	110,858 48
1848,	16,821 58	59,211 68	76,033 26	95,801 91
1849,	16,048 96	50,120 58	66,169 54	78,741 75
1850,	16,276 54	73,711 10	89,987 64	100,786 16
1851,	15,986 04	66,303 79	82,289 83	86,404 32
1852,	15,683 31	61,146 39	76,829 70	75,293 11
1853,	20,810 23	81,822 80	102,633 03	93,396 06
1854,	19,635 35	91,251 47	110,886 82	93,144 93
1855,	19,771 91	80,403 36	100,175 27	77,134 96
1856,	17,111 13	62,975 51	80,086 64	56,060 65
1857,	17,101 71	55,555 87	72,657 58	45,774 28
1858,	13,347 95	51,716 31	65,064 26	36,436 99
1859,	16,868 66	55,445 57	72,314 23	35,433 97
1860,	18,579 46	52,036 90	70,616 36	29,658 87
1861,	15,319 04	39,630 03	54,949 07	19,232 17
1862,	19,901 96	56,123 21	76,025 17	21,287 05
1863,	21,628 77	56,963 24	78,592 01	16,504 32
1864,	23,406 86	43,316 93	66,723 79	9,341 33
1865,	16,745 91	21,395 50	38,141 41	2,669 90
1866,	18,173 04	41,923 68	60,096 72	....
	$455,774 22	$1,556,801 34	$2,012,575 56	$1,894,538 15

RESULT.

DEBIT.

To cost of construction,	$1,273,261 86		
To interest thereon,	1,635,704 70		
		$2,908,966 56	
To cost of maintenance,	$1,139,770 30		
To interest thereon,	970,699 26		
		2,110,469 56	
Total disbursements and interest,			$5,019,436 12

NO. 4.

Canal.

DISBURSEMENTS.						
FOR CONSTRUCTION.		FOR MAINTENANCE.				
(1)	(2)	(3)	(4)	(5)	(6)	(7)
Cost of construction.	Legal interest on cost of construction.	Contractors, for repairs.	Superintendents, for repairs.	Collectors, inspectors, &c.	Total payments, including cost of construction.	Legal interest on total payments, including cost of construction.
$69,190 00	$174,358 80	....	....	....	$69,190 00	$174,358 80
148,291 57	363,315 40	....	....	....	148,291 57	363,314 34
75,410 47	179,475 80	....	....	....	75,410 47	179,476 92
47,793 38	110,401 83	....	$26,448 53	....	74,241 91	171,498 81
2,258 91	5,060 16	....	23,703 48	696 48	26,658 87	59,715 87
9 08	19 53	....	11,175 89	1,036 75	12,221 72	26,521 13
....	....	....	9,623 16	1,037 88	10,661 04	22,388 18
3,558 79	7,224 77	....	15,193 82	1,091 13	19,843 74	40,282 50
1,859 91	3,645 60	....	12,106 16	992 97	14,959 04	29,279 72
....	....	....	14,315 71	1,187 94	15,503 65	29,301 90
68 50	125 58	....	11,969 24	1,268 33	13,306 07	24,217 05
100,056 81	175,099 75	....	23,175 22	1,201 54	124,433 57	217,758 75
185,987 49	312,458 16	....	33,451 59	1,076 23	220,515 31	370,465 72
25,417 46	40,921 37	....	14,486 27	1,159 40	41,063 13	66,111 64
3,467 07	5,339 18	....	12,172 23	1,085 80	16,725 10	25,756 65
9 90	14 70	....	17,280 27	1,239 50	18,529 67	27,238 61
1,646 00	2,304 40	....	14,689 55	1,455 00	17,790 55	24,906 77
4,360 86	5,800 13	....	15,485 39	1,561 15	21,407 40	28,471 84
328 66	414 54	....	27,080 33	2,030 00	29,438 99	37,091 33
19,876 96	23,653 63	....	23,897 06	2,136 00	45,910 02	54,632 92
53,768 39	60,220 16	....	28,885 79	1,896 21	84,550 39	94,696 44
11,044 92	11,597 25	....	42,330 76	2,566 35	55,942 03	58,739 13
2,144 06	2,101 12	....	32,952 17	2,198 36	37,294 59	36,548 70
12,665 24	11,525 15	....	23,883 28	2,214 84	38,763 36	35,274 66
3,047 11	2,559 48	....	33,099 05	2,187 62	38,333 78	32,200 38
6,971 63	5,368 44	....	23,094 86	2,252 97	32,319 46	24,886 14
3,223 28	2,256 10	$11,964 48	4,652 49	2,403 11	22,243 36	15,570 35
29,988 16	18,892 44	9,543 45	66,101 23	2,435 05	108,067 89	67,982 77
28,345 22	15,873 20	....	161,702 33	2,604 82	192,652 37	107,885 33
39,026 44	19,122 74	4,660 46	18,786 02	2,195 01	64,667 93	31,687 29
69,787 13	29,310 54	12,031 48	316 67	3,264 81	85,400 09	35,868 04
20,828 36	7,289 80	18,788 48	6,510 67	2,628 39	48,755 90	17,064 57
81,911 75	22,935 36	17,649 07	7,628 96	2,294 62	109,484 40	30,655 63
34,356 39	7,214 76	19,287 83	53,324 59	2,256 50	109,225 31	22,937 32
48,290 86	6,760 74	23,601 19	12,859 91	2,392 74	87,144 70	12,200 25
43,486 76	3,044 09	71,490 25	16,713 24	2,845 55	134,535 80	9,417 51
94,784 34	....	31,357 24	18,218 19	3,189 21	147,548 98	....
$1,273,261 86	$1,635,704 70	$220,373 93	$857,314 11	$62,082 26	$2,413,032 16	$2,606,403 96

CREDIT.

By tolls proper,...	$455,774 22		
By tolls on tonnage contributed to the Erie Canal,..	1,556,801 34		
Total income, &c.,...		$2,012,575 56	
Interest on tolls proper and contributions,...		1,894,538 15	
Total credits, with interest,...			$3,907,113 71
To balance,...			$1,112,322 41
To proportion of cost of repairs and maintenance of Erie and Champlain Canals from 1830 to 1866,...			654,879 47
Net cost,...			$1,767,201 88

TABLE

Crooked Lake

YEARS.	INCOME.			
	(1)	(2)	(3)	(4)
	Tolls proper.	Tolls contributed to and heretofore credited Erie and Champlain Canals.	Total of tolls proper and contributions.	Legal interest on tolls proper and contributions.
1831,	....	....	....	....
1832,	....	....	....	....
1833,	....	....	....	....
1834,	$1,007 60	$666 64	$1,674 24	$3,750 29
1835,	1,803 76	9,626 85	11,430 61	24,804 42
1836,	1,953 90	12,898 65	14,852 55	31,190 35
1837,	1,547 61	13,091 51	14,639 12	29,717 41
1838,	1,566 06	15,047 31	16,613 37	32,562 20
1839,	1,893 90	13,339 42	15,233 32	28,790 97
1840,	1,613 16	18,561 84	20,175 00	36,718 50
1841,	2,023 46	17,139 58	19,163 04	33,535 32
1842,	1,216 73	11,534 20	12,750 93	21,421 56
1843,	1,341 60	11,181 79	12,523 39	20,162 65
1844,	1,367 21	19,224 97	20,592 18	31,689 95
1845,	1,662 84	27,493 31	29,156 15	42,859 54
1846,	1,846 37	26,986 96	28,833 33	40,366 66
1847,	1,774 55	24,490 26	26,264 81	34,932 19
1848,	1,858 04	22,872 64	24,730 68	31,160 65
1849,	1,819 17	26,340 84	28,160 01	33,510 41
1850,	1,796 17	25,983 27	27,779 44	31,112 97
1851,	1,714 34	19,305 85	21,020 19	22,071 19
1852,	1,246 02	23,314 02	24,560 04	24,068 83
1853,	1,656 75	22,145 64	23,802 39	21,660 17
1854,	1,303 69	11,926 46	13,230 15	11,113 32
1855,	837 48	16,182 35	17,019 83	13,105 26
1856,	1,154 48	16,041 69	17,196 17	12,037 31
1857,	879 26	7,186 64	8,065 90	5,081 51
1858,	520 82	8,527 11	9,047 93	5,066 84
1859,	715 06	6,338 97	7,054 03	3,456 47
1860,	683 34	8,640 96	9,324 30	3,916 20
1861,	699 94	6,982 94	7,682 88	2,689 40
1862,	712 70	11,227 85	11,940 55	3,343 35
1863,	746 40	5,572 54	6,318 94	1,326 97
1864,	585 88	3,613 62	4,199 50	587 93
1865,	290 65	5,740 44	6,031 09	422 17
1866,	534 96	8,815 52	9,350 48	....
	$42,373 90	$478,042 64	$520,416 54	$638,232 96

RESULT.

DEBIT.

To cost of construction,	$333,287 27		
To interest thereon,	535,896 06		
		$869,183 33	
To cost of maintenance,	$258,282 78		
To interest thereon,	236,180 06		
		$494,462 84	
Total disbursements and interest,			**$1,363,646 17**

NO. 5.

Canal.

DISBURSEMENTS.						
FOR CONSTRUCTION.		FOR MAINTENANCE.				
(1)	(2)	(3)	(4)	(5)	(6)	(7)
Cost of construction.	Legal interest on cost of construction.	Contractors, for repairs.	Superintendents, for repairs.	Collectors, inspectors, &c.	Total payments, including cost of construction.	Legal interest on total payments, including cost of construction.
$11,350 00	$27,807 50	....	....	....	$11,350 00	$27,807 50
62,906 46	149,716 28	....	....	....	62,906 46	149,717 37
52,461 30	121,184 91	....	....	....	52,461 30	124,485 60
13,293 82	29,778 56	....	$2,437 67	....	15,731 49	35,238 54
1 70	4 34	....	3,694 66	$350 75	4,047 11	8,782 23
255 90	537 60	....	5,063 82	425 25	5,744 97	12,064 44
402 31	816 06	....	5,743 71	725 13	6,871 15	13,948 44
....	....	....	5,060 07	543 54	5,603 61	10,983 07
....	....	....	2,778 31	885 11	3,663 42	6,833 87
....	....	....	4,559 23	873 65	5,432 88	9,887 84
2 00	3 50	....	9,463 07	987 85	10,452 92	18,292 61
....	....	....	8,016 66	918 13	8,934 79	15,010 45
....	....	....	3,674 16	880 78	4,554 94	7,333 45
....	....	....	3,905 84	842 06	4,747 90	7,321 77
9 00	13 23	....	4,844 67	857 28	5,710 95	8,495 10
26,358 42	36,901 20	....	5,384 00	875 73	32,618 15	45,665 41
46,630 76	62,019 23	....	6,065 89	875 00	53,571 65	71,250 29
57,493 78	72,442 44	....	8,558 88	881 87	66,934 53	84,337 51
2,163 61	2,573 97	....	10,208 40	863 42	13,235 43	15,750 16
10,131 25	11,346 72	....	4,983 72	777 04	15,892 01	17,799 05
6,429 28	6,750 45	....	6,118 94	954 80	13,503 02	14,178 17
1,750 92	1,715 98	....	7,975 12	925 42	10,651 46	10,338 43
....	....	....	5,350 00	958 50	6,308 50	5,740 74
1,719 65	1,444 80	....	5,122 08	922 04	7,763 77	6,521 57
2,565 20	1,975 05	....	5,320 39	888 45	8,774 04	6,756 01
780 00	546 00	$3,204 08	694 16	888 02	5,566 26	3,896 38
7,340 70	4,624 83	4,447 37	199 98	703 86	12,691 91	7,995 90
584 20	327 04	9,803 46	....	542 25	10,929 91	6,120 75
147 78	72 52	4,849 53	....	440 09	5,437 40	2,664 49
467 24	196 14	5,033 63	125 00	670 34	6,296 21	2,644 41
573 10	200 55	6,017 13	....	493 98	7,084 21	2,479 47
284 90	79 80	4,692 38	2,468 94	635 69	8,081 91	2,262 93
2,306 66	484 47	5,141 76	....	555 56	8,003 98	1,680 84
13,446 85	1,882 58	19,995 78	....	579 27	34,021 90	4,763 07
6,432 68	450 31	36,200 58	....	627 53	43,260 79	3,028 26
4,997 80	....	6,770 69	273 00	687 63	12,729 12	....
$333,287 27	$535,896 06	$106,156 39	$128,090 37	$24,036 02	$591,570 05	$772,076 12

CREDIT.

By tolls proper,....................	$42,373 90		
By tolls on tonnage contributed to the Erie Canal,......	478,042 64		
Total income from 1834 to 1866,..		$520,416 54	
Interest thereon,..		638,232 96	
			$1,158,649 50
			$204,996 67
To proportion of cost of repairs and maintenance of Erie and Champlain from 1834 to 1866,..			201,092 20
Net cost,..			$406,088 87

TABLE

Chenango

YEARS.	INCOME.			
	(1)	(2)	(3)	(4)
	Tolls proper.	Tolls contributed to and hertofore credited Erie and Champlain Canals.	Total of tolls proper and contributions.	Legal interest on tolls proper and contributions.
1833,	....	....	....	....
1834,	....	....	....	....
1835,	....	....	....	....
1836,	....	....	....	....
1837,	$4,081 62	$7,728 44	$11,810 06	$23,974 42
1838,	16,751 12	6,272 61	23,023 73	45,126 51
1839,	18,050 33	452 51	18,502 84	34,970 37
1840,	14,023 32	2,592 90	16,616 22	30,241 52
1841,	16,893 02	6,249 83	23,142 85	17,357 14
1842,	15,330 57	1,593 72	16,924 29	28,332 81
1843,	14,668 94	5,578 31	20,247 25	33,598 07
1844,	20,983 05	9,167 32	30,150 37	46,431 57
1845,	23,920 66	13,176 49	37,097 15	54,532 81
1846,	25,578 76	8,209 78	33,788 54	47,303 96
1847,	25,620 01	13,890 42	39,510 43	52,548 87
1848,	28,091 66	10,035 01	38,126 67	48,639 60
1849,	28,028 98	....	28,028 98	30,354 48
1850,	20,343 65	4,283 50	24,627 15	27,582 41
1851,	19,732 35	2,289 96	22,022 31	23,123 43
1852,	16,891 62	2,092 11	18,983 73	18,604 06
1853,	18,107 89	4,331 29	22,439 18	20,419 65
1854,	19,496 15	1,997 39	21,493 54	18,054 57
1855,	20,302 08	1,529 16	21,831 24	16,810 05
1856,	18,634 62	3,174 27	21,808 89	15,266 12
1857,	22,969 47	....	22,969 47	14,470 77
1858,	15,305 64	1,609 38	16,915 02	9,472 41
1859,	17,801 72	2,085 91	19,887 63	9,744 94
1860,	22,214 37	3,087 07	25,301 44	10,626 60
1861,	23,397 24	3,074 52	26,471 76	9,265 12
1862,	22,155 94	2,578 54	24,734 48	6,925 65
1863,	24,354 87	4,169 94	28,524 81	5,990 21
1864,	30,034 43	....	30,034 43	4,204 82
1865,	21,710 98	....	21,710 98	1,519 76
1866,	28,534 53	2,026 02	30,560 55	....
	$614,009 59	$123,276 40	$737,285 99	$708,492 70

RESULT.

DEBIT.

To cost of construction,	$2,782,124 19		
Interest thereon,	5,119,376 29		
		$7,901,500 48	
To cost of maintenance,	$970,169 49		
Interest thereon,	745,683 48		
		1,715,852 97	
Total disbursements and interest,			**$9,617,353 45**

NO. 6.

Canal.

DISBURSEMENTS.						
FOR CONSTRUCTION.		FOR MAINTENANCE.				
(1)	(2)	(3)	(4)	(5)	(6)	(7)
Cost of construction.	Legal interest on cost of construction.	Contractors, for repairs.	Superintendents, for repairs.	Collectors, inspectors, &c.	Total payments, including cost of construction.	Legal interest on total payments, including cost of construction.
$9,222 65	$21,305 13	....	....	....	$9,222 65	$21,304 32
211,013 44	472,669 12	....	....	....	211,013 44	472,680 11
651,782 45	1,414,366 94	....	....	....	651,782 45	1,414,367 92
911,035 10	1,913,173 50	....	....	....	911,035 10	1,913,173 71
480,807 02	976,038 21	....	$18,663 62	....	499,470 64	1,013,825 40
65,759 17	128,887 64	....	20,270 95	$1,074 85	87,104 97	170,725 74
47,458 98	89,697 51	....	16,990 64	1,576 00	66,025 62	124,788 42
12,232 90	22,264 06	....	14,775 24	1,559 66	28,567 80	51,993 40
5,349 47	9,360 75	....	16,638 05	1,931 42	23,918 94	41,858 15
5,075 33	8,526 00	....	18,467 28	1,821 00	25,363 61	42,610 86
668 05	1,075 48	....	15,917 35	1,395 40	17,980 80	28,949 09
3,942 72	6,072 22	....	15,700 51	1,233 02	20,876 25	32,149 43
153 95	226 38	....	18,283 33	1,198 91	19,636 19	28,865 20
152 47	212 80	....	17,827 13	1,332 00	19,311 60	27,036 24
2,704 28	3,596 32	....	18,404 54	1,226 00	22,334 82	29,605 31
119 06	149 94	....	20,471 02	1,418 49	22,008 57	27,730 80
817 88	973 42	....	27,772 21	1,442 12	30,032 21	35,738 33
5,051 91	5,658 24	....	25,071 12	1,237 68	31,360 71	35,124 00
1,064 75	1,118 25	....	31,110 32	1,426 08	33,601 15	35,281 20
6,112 00	5,989 76	....	34,706 26	1,339 94	42,158 20	41,315 04
....	....	....	37,752 37	1,400 79	39,153 16	35,629 38
....	....	....	49,476 20	1,403 37	50,879 57	42,738 84
3,095 35	2,383 15	....	44,250 04	1,557 00	48,902 39	37,654 84
1,589 35	1,112 30	$11,234 30	10,301 24	1,723 86	24,848 75	17,394 13
160 00	100 80	25,806 50	2,276 18	1,923 39	30,166 07	19,004 62
616 21	344 96	20,700 00	23,785 09	1,981 10	47,082 40	26,366 14
1,933 72	947 66	22,611 54	3,450 19	1,383 66	29,379 11	14,395 76
11,757 84	4,938 36	25,175 90	1,893 95	1,761 57	40,589 26	17,047 49
39,097 72	13,684 30	21,431 65	1,210 98	1,744 35	63,484 70	22,219 65
12,577 91	3,521 84	27,828 68	1,215 98	1,860 74	43,478 31	12,173 92
9,357 43	1,964 97	30,266 31	1,620 78	1,904 36	43,148 88	9,061 26
38,410 12	5,377 40	37,647 49	3,210 97	2,107 10	81,375 68	11,392 60
51,983 95	3,638 88	96,443 14	4,039 74	2,654 17	155,121 00	10,858 47
191,021 01	....	75,635 87	12,333 31	2,888 49	281,878 68	....
$2,782,124 19	$5,119,376 29	$394,776 38	$527,886 59	$47,506 52	$3,752,293 68	$5,865,059 77

CREDIT.

By tolls proper,..........	$614,009 59		
By tolls on tonnage contributed to Erie Canal,..........	123,276 40		
		$737,285 99	
Interest thereon,..........		708,492 70	
Total income and interest,..........			1,445,778 69
			$8,171,574 76
To proportion of cost of repairs and maintenance of Erie Canal from 1833 to 1866, .			51,856 93
Net cost, ...			$8,223,431 69

TABLE

Black River

YEARS.	INCOME. (1) Tolls proper.	(2) Tolls contributed and heretofore credited Erie and Champlain Canals.	(3) Total of tolls proper and contributions.	(4) Legal interest on tolls proper and contributions.
1837,	....	....	....	....
1838,	....	....	....	....
1839,	....	....	....	....
1840,	....	....	....	....
1841,	....	....	....	....
1842,	....	....	....	....
1843,	....	....	....	....
1844,	....	....	....	....
1845,	....	....	....	....
1846,	....	....	....	....
1847,	....	....	....	....
1848,	....	....	....	....
1849,	....	....	....	....
1850,	$1,115 73	$1,514 16	$2,629 89	$2,945 47
1851,	3,834 73	2,139 60	5,974 33	6,273 04
1852,	4,166 05	3,626 67	7,792 72	7,636 86
1853,	5,546 32	4,700 45	10,246 77	9,324 56
1854,	5,843 42	7,499 53	13,342 95	11,208 07
1855,	6,808 05	7,640 32	14,448 37	11,125 24
1856,	5,594 10	5,101 64	10,695 74	7,487 01
1857,	6,575 22	6,014 46	12,589 68	7,931 49
1858,	4,998 48	5,572 01	10,570 49	5,919 47
1859,	5,963 02	7,671 08	13,634 10	6,680 70
1860,	6,330 71	8,780 05	15,110 76	6,346 51
1861,	6,112 73	8,139 17	14,251 90	4,988 16
1862,	8,647 82	9,729 22	18,377 04	5,155 57
1863,	10,172 66	12,248 49	22,421 15	4,708 44
1864,	10,078 30	12,466 74	22,545 04	3,156 30
1865,	10,985 87	9,533 74	20,519 61	1,436 37
1866,	11,802 81	15,649 67	27,452 48	....
	$114,576 02	$128,027 00	$242,603 02	$102,323 26

RESULT.

DEBIT.

To cost of construction, ...	$3,224,779 55		
To interest thereon, ...	4,454,243 92	$7,679,023 47	
To cost of maintenance, ...	$445,011 36		
To interest thereon, ...	270,291 78	715,303 14	
Total disbursement and interest, ...			$8,394,326 61

NO. 7.

Canal.

DISBURSEMENTS.						
FOR CONSTRUCTION.		FOR MAINTENANCE.				
(1)	(2)	(3)	(4)	(5)	(6)	(7)
Cost of construction.	Legal interest on cost of construction.	Contractors, for repairs.	Superintendents, for repairs.	Collectors, inspectors, &c.	Total payments, including cost of construction.	Legal interest on total payments, including cost of construction.
$5,255 55	$10,669 68	....	....	....	$5,255 55	$10,668 77
97,735 21	191,560 60	....	....	....	97,735 21	191,561 01
513,154 39	969,861 06	....	....	....	513,154 39	969,861 80
537,794 74	978,786 90	....	....	....	537,794 74	978,789 03
335,973 06	587,952 75	....	....	....	335,973 06	587,952 85
234,824 34	394,504 32	....	....	....	234,824 34	442,504 89
24,928 61	40,135 69	....	....	....	24,928 61	40,135 06
14,528 33	22,373 12	....	....	....	14,528 33	22,373 63
39,147 14	57,546 09	....	....	....	39,147 14	57,546 30
12,852 14	17,992 80	....	....	....	12,852 14	17,993 00
12,326 24	16,393 58	....	....	....	12,326 24	16,393 90
108,522 95	136,738 98	....	....	....	108,522 95	136,738 93
233,373 97	277,715 06	....	....	....	233,373 97	277,715 02
151,492 03	169,671 04	....	$10,014 52	....	161,506 55	180,887 34
95,590 17	100,369 50	....	25,753 83	$317 43	121,661 43	127,744 50
118,356 30	115,988 88	....	29,404 55	529 95	148,290 80	145,324 98
31,957 28	29,080 87	....	24,443 88	525 97	56,927 13	51,803 69
33,026 36	27,741 84	....	30,500 35	554 15	64,080 86	53,827 92
105,539 77	81,265 80	....	35,671 38	752 97	141,964 12	109,312 37
93,437 29	65,405 90	$6,165 28	10,855 81	764 34	111,222 72	77,855 90
61,664 72	38,848 95	12,601 25	1,613 45	783 67	76,663 09	48,297 75
41,297 38	23,126 32	15,406 88	3,062 48	824 40	60,591 14	33,931 04
16,023 62	7,851 76	23,539 65	1,843 98	627 86	42,035 11	20,597 20
101,030 62	42,433 02	21,834 91	366 66	862 67	124,094 86	52,119 84
103,593 31	36,257 55	17,261 63	6,173 28	667 13	127,695 35	41,693 37
33,870 86	9,483 88	18,802,06	2,183 53	640 85	55,497 30	15,539 24
10,053 54	2,111 34	15,582 89	3,491 19	574 76	29,702 38	6,237 50
1,860 84	260 54	15,802 17	6,142 25	503 16	24,308 42	3,483 18
30,229 68	2,116 10	40,227 08	9,582 68	613 25	80,652 69	5,645 69
25,339 11	....	32,697 74	13,745 68	697 76	72,480 29	....
$3,224,779 55	$4,454,243 92	$219,921 54	$214,849 50	$10,240 32	$3,669,790 91	$4,724,535 70

CREDIT.

By tolls proper,..	$114,576 02		
By tolls on tonnage contributed to Erie Canal,........	128,027 00		
Total income, ...		$242,603 02	
Interest thereon, ...		102,323 26	
Total income and interest,...			$344,926 28
Balance,..			$8,049,400 33
To proportion of cost of repairs and maintenance of Erie Canal, from 1837 to 1866,.....			53,855 47
Net cost, ...			$8,103,255 80

TABLE

Genesee Valley

YEARS.	INCOME.			
	(1)	(2)	(3)	(4)
	Tolls proper.	Tolls contributed to and heretofore credited Erie and Champlain Canals.	Total of tolls proper and contributions.	Legal interest on tolls proper and contributions.
1837,	....	....	....	....
1838,	....	....	....	....
1839,	....	....	....	....
1840,	....	....	....	....
1841,	$12,275 44	$4,582 65	$16,858 09	$29,501 66
1842,	12,075 97	7,688 96	19,764 93	33,205 04
1843,	13,734 52	10,308 17	24,042 69	38,708 73
1844,	18,586 52	19,094 98	37,681 50	58,029 51
1845,	20,484 17	25,937 53	46,421 70	68,239 90
1846,	24,182 60	30,179 74	54,362 34	76,107 28
1847,	25,055 20	40,692 43	65,747 63	87,444 35
1848,	26,012 50	38,446 99	64,459 49	81,218 95
1849,	25,234 04	39,696 33	64,930 37	77,267 14
1850,	28,821 98	37,211 05	66,033 03	73,956 99
1851,	25,451 36	34,233 41	59,684 77	62,669 01
1852,	25,064 39	24,208 54	49,272 93	47,287 47
1853,	30,183 73	34,620 97	64,804 70	57,972 28
1854,	30,662 08	31,103 59	61,765 67	51,883 08
1855,	28,390 12	19,965 36	48,355 48	37,233 72
1856,	23,365 84	16,908 15	40,273 99	28,191 79
1857,	25,966 70	24,243 80	50,210 50	31,632 62
1858,	25,651 07	31,585 50	57,236 57	32,052 48
1859,	28,163 93	35,056 17	63,220 10	30,977 85
1860,	30,801 74	39,436 86	70,238 60	29,500 21
1861,	29,189 60	15,332 39	44,521 99	15,582 70
1862,	28,697 27	37,471 04	66,168 31	18,527 02
1863,	32,747 98	31,240 67	63,988 65	13,437 62
1864,	27,562 66	16,765 61	44,328 27	6,205 95
1865,	15,785 16	6,333 49	22,118 65	1,548 30
1866,	17,724 01	22,698 08	40,422 09	....
	$631,870 58	$675,042 46	$1,306,913 04	$1,088,381 65

RESULT.

DEBIT.

To cost of construction,	$5,827,813 72		
Interest thereon,	7,969,085 39		
		$13,796,899 11	
To cost of maintenance,	$1,405,342 66		
Interest thereon,	1,211,081 19		
		2,616,423 85	
Total disbursements and interest,			**$16,413,322 96**

NO. 8.

Canal.

DISBURSEMENTS.						
FOR CONSTRUCTION.		FOR MAINTENANCE.				
(1)	(2)	(3)	(4)	(5)	(6)	(7)
Cost of construction.	Legal interest on cost of construction.	Contractors, for repairs.	Superintendents, for repairs.	Collectors, inspectors, &c.	Total payments, including cost of construction.	Legal interest on total payments, including cost of construction.
$22,371 86	$45,415 16	....	....	....	$22,371 86	$45,424 87
229,161 20	449,155 56	....	....	....	229,161 20	449,155 95
764,182 61	1,444,305 87	....	....	....	764,182 61	1,444,305 13
1,151,653 97	2,096,010 28	....	$2,176 00	....	1,153,829 97	2,099,970 54
612,760 50	1,072,331 75	....	12,750 91	$924 73	626,436 14	1,096,263 24
520,409 56	420,687 12	....	18,062 75	1,308 56	539,780 87	906,831 86
170,667 75	274,775 48	....	13,669 85	1,591 78	185,929 38	299,346 30
202,106 67	311,244 78	....	15,719 96	1,540 55	219,367 18	337,825 45
35,311 25	51,907 17	....	15,776 49	1,381 00	52,468 74	77,129 04
39,328 58	55,060 60	....	17,614 20	1,464 00	58,406 78	81,769 49
10,441 67	13,887 86	....	15,782 32	1,506 01	27,730 00	36,880 90
33,035 89	41,625 36	....	26,987 41	1,545 55	61,568 85	77,576 75
184,768 71	219,875 11	....	17,244 51	1,546 75	203,559 97	242,236 36
375,164 73	420,184 80	....	17,350 00	1,387 15	393,901 88	442,170 10
229,380 52	240,850 05	....	34,478 74	2,221 85	266,081 11	279,385 16
208,930 94	204,752 38	....	73,290 05	3,092 61	285,313 60	279,607 32
182,546 38	166,116 86	....	59,291 41	2,801 88	244,639 67	222,622 09
98,939 79	83,109 60	....	44,759 69	3,123 34	146,822 82	123,331 16
123,680 58	95,234 37	....	51,417 00	2,877 76	177,975 34	137,041 01
123,820 60	86,674 70	$9,845 43	22,192 85	3,367 25	159,226 13	111,458 29
69,879 20	44,024 40	19,666 87	41,032 14	3,891 52	134,469 73	84,715 92
74,256 35	41,583 36	33,468 81	49,136 90	4,634 71	161,496 77	90,438 19
59,856 73	29,329 93	16,380 98	33,372 43	3,691 25	113,301 39	55,517 68
78,949 86	33,159 00	29,197 68	12,261 70	4,488 08	124,897 32	52,456 87
15,164 32	5,307 40	27,169 05	1,707 64	2,982 93	47,023 94	16,458 37
46,413 77	12,995 92	48,279 94	16,261 06	2,609 70	113,564 47	31,798 05
16,989 48	3,567 90	47,418 02	3,413 06	2,664 77	70,485 33	14,801 91
17,702 09	2,478 28	120,567 73	18,499 68	2,762 76	159,532 26	22,334 51
49,062 48	3,434 34	154,798 82	97,346 75	3,278 73	304,486 78	21,314 07
80,875 68	....	85,869 57	14,822 51	3,576 53	185,144 29	....
$5,827,813 72	$7,969,085 39	$592,662 90	$746,418 01	$66,261 75	$7,233,156 38	$9,180,166 58

CREDIT.

By tolls proper,	$631,870 58		
By tolls on tonnage contributed to the Erie Canal,	675,042 46		
		$1,306,913 04	
By interest on tolls proper and contributions,		1,088,381 65	
Total income and interest,			$2,395,294 69
Balance, loss,			$14,018,028 27
To proportion of cost of repairs and maintenance of the Erie and Champlain Canal, from 1837 to 1866,			283,961 20
Net cost,			$14,301,989 47

TABLE

Oneida Lake

YEARS.	INCOME.			
	(1)	(2)	(3)	(4)
	Tolls proper.	Tolls contributed to and heretofore credited Erie and Champlain Canals.	Total of tolls proper and contributions.	Legal interest on tolls proper and contributions.
1841,	$294 58	....	$294 58	$515 51
1842,	471 85	....	471 85	696 70
1843,	475 04	....	475 04	765 45
1844,	683 67	....	683 67	1,052 84
1845,	678 66	....	678 66	997 63
1846,	604 41	....	604 41	846 17
1847,	487 49	....	487 49	648 36
1848,	671 89	....	671 89	846 58
1849,	794 67	....	794 67	945 65
1850,	2,513 19	....	2,513 19	2,815 09
1851,	6,178 57	....	6,178 57	6,487 49
1852,	7,795 05	....	7,795 05	7,639 14
1853,	10,282 18	....	10,282 18	9,356 78
1854,	9,802 11	....	9,802 11	8,233 83
1855,	7,340 81	....	7,340 81	5,652 42
1856,	8,639 04	....	8,639 04	6,047 32
1857,	4,849 34	....	4,849 34	3,055 08
1858,	1,235 32	....	1,235 32	691 77
1859,	701 41	....	701 41	343 69
1860,	290 33	....	290 33	121 93
1861,	218 86	....	218 86	76 60
1862,	121 83	....	121 83	34 11
1863,	45 21	....	45 21	9 49
1864,	5 00	....	5 00	70
1865,	....	....	....	....
1866,	....	....	....	....
	$65,180 51	....	$65,180 51	$57,880 33

RESULT.

DEBIT.

To cost of construction,	$64,837 68		
To interest thereon,	89,452 58	$154,290 26	
To cost of maintenance,	$123,234 92		
To interest thereon,	117,989 42	241,224 34	
Total disbursements,			$395,514 60

NO. 9.

Canal.

DISBURSEMENTS.						
FOR CONSTRUCTION.		FOR MAINTENANCE.				
(1)	(2)	(3)	(4)	(5)	(6)	(7)
Cost of construction.	Legal interest on cost of construction.	Contractors, for repairs.	Superintendents, for repairs.	Collectors, inspectors, &c.	Total payments, including cost of construction.	Legal interest on total payments, including cost of construction.
$50,000 00	$87,500 00	....	$2,332 81	$115 50	$52,448 31	$91,784 52
....	....	....	5,554 15	275 11	5,829 26	9,793 15
....	....	....	2,234 25	254 35	2,488 60	4,006 64
....	....	....	1,619 86	350 00	1,969 86	3,033 58
....	....	....	1,406 45	250 00	1,656 45	2,434 98
....	....	....	18,149 50	250 10	18,399 60	25,759 44
....	....	....	6,130 02	233 25	6,363 27	8,843 14
....	....	....	1,866 05	250 01	2,116 06	2,666 23
....	....	....	1,992 58	249 98	2,242 56	2,668 64
15 88	17 92	....	4,719 29	528 88	5,264 05	5,895 73
....	....	....	3,590 16	725 46	4,315 62	4,531 40
....	....	....	5,403 08	649 07	6,052 15	5,931 10
....	....	....	5,761 92	822 13	6,584 05	5,991 48
....	....	....	11,802 83	986 32	12,789 15	10,742 88
....	....	....	6,235 63	1,057 01	7,292 64	5,615 33
....	....	$2,481 71	107 91	1,018 69	3,608 31	2,525 81
20 86	13 23	3,919 00	....	863 39	4,803 25	3,026 04
....	....	4,103 94	....	762 62	4,866 56	2,725 27
1,150 00	563 50	3,975 00	....	600 87	5,725 87	2,805 67
210 75	88 62	4,058 67	....	937 88	5,207 30	2,187 06
1,064 15	372 40	2,841 61	400 00	755 51	5,061 27	1,771 44
....	....	2,375 01	100 00	329 15	2,804 16	785 16
772 44	162 12	2,375 01	....	....	3,147 45	660 96
2,534 64	354 90	2,543 23	....	....	5,077 87	710 90
5,426 71	379 89	2,365 50	....	....	7,792 21	545 45
3,642 25	....	524 47	....	....	4,166 72	....
$64,837 68	$89,452 58	$31,563 15	$79,406 49	12,265 28	$188,072 60	$207,442 00

CREDIT.

By tolls proper,	$65,180 51	
By interest thereon,	57,880 33	
Total income and interest,		123,060 84
Net cost,		$272,453 76

TABLE

Baldwinsville

YEARS.	INCOME.			
	(1)	(2)	(3)	(4)
	Tolls proper.	Tolls contributed to and heretofore credited Erie and Champlain Canals.	Total tolls proper and contributions.	Legal interest on tolls proper and contributions.
1852,	....	....	....	....
1853,	$472 06	....	$472 06	$429 57
1854,	429 86	....	429 86	361 08
1855,	76 01	....	76 01	58 52
1856,	73 02	....	73 02	51 11
1857,	32 81	....	32 81	20 67
1858,	14 13	....	14 13	7 91
1859,	26 03	....	26 03	12 75
1860,	23 17	....	23 17	9 73
1861,	22 57	....	22 57	7 89
1862,	31 83	....	31 83	8 91
1863,	39 17	....	39 17	8 22
1864,	20 82	....	20 82	2 91
1865,	....	....	....	....
1866,	....	....	....	....
	$1,261 48	....	$1,261 48	$979 27

RESULT.

DEBIT.

To cost of construction,	$23,556 14		
To interest thereon,	16,077 32		
		$39,633 46	
To cost of maintenance,	$25,035 26		
To interest thereon,	7,674 62		
		32,709 88	
Total disbursements and interest,			$72,343 34

NO. 10.

Canal.

DISBURSEMENTS.						
FOR CONSTRUCTION.		FOR MAINTENANCE.				
(1)	(2)	(3)	(4)	(5)	(6)	(7)
Cost of construction.	Legal interest on cost of construction.	Contractors, for repairs.	Superintendents, for repairs.	Collectors, inspectors, &c.	Total payments, including cost of construction.	Legal interest on total payments, including cost of construction.
$2,125 00	$2,082 50				$2,125 00	$2,082 50
				$159 46	159 46	145 10
12,885 00	10,823 40		$2,372 29	432 79	15,690 08	13,179 66
200 00	154 00		2,372 66	375 00	2,947 66	2,269 69
			422 46	377 58	800 04	560 02
885 13	557 55		455 43	178 59	1,519 15	957 06
2,615 00	1,464 40		2,381 61		4,996 62	2,798 10
			413 30		413 30	202 51
			1,069 60		1,069 60	374 36
			174 67		174 67	48 90
4,529 14	951 09		72 33		4,601 47	966 30
316 87	44 38		631 80		948 67	132 81
			499 00		499 00	34 93
			12,646 68		12,646 68	
$23,556 14	$16,077 32		$23,511 84	$1,523 42	$48,591 40	$23,751 94

CREDIT.

By tolls proper,	$1,261 48	
By interest thereon,	979 27	
		2,240 75
Net cost,		$70,102 59

TABLE

Oneida River

YEARS.	INCOME.			
	(1)	(2)	(3)	(4)
	Tolls proper.	Tolls contributed to and heretofore credited Erie and Champlain Canal.	Total of tolls proper and contributions.	Legal interest on tolls proper and contributions.
1839,	....	....	....	....
1840,	....	....	....	....
1841,	....	....	....	....
1842,	....	....	....	....
1843,	....	....	....	....
1844,	....	....	....	....
1845,	....	....	....	....
1846,	....	....	....	....
1847,	$118 22	....	$118 22	$157 23
1848,	200 50	....	200 50	252 63
1849,	230 71	....	230 71	274 54
1850,	5,555 63	....	5,555 63	6,222 30
1851,	18,409 56	....	18,409 56	19,330 03
1852,	24,540 54	....	24,540 54	24,049 72
1853,	31,275 36	....	31,275 36	28,460 57
1854,	31,992 92	....	31,992 92	24,874 05
1855,	24,004 94	....	24,004 94	18,483 80
1856,	29,035 78	....	29,035 78	20,324 74
1857,	15,758 42	....	15,758 42	9,927 80
1858,	3,725 19	....	3,725 19	2,086 10
1859,	2,044 64	....	2,044 64	1,001 87
1860,	1,015 98	....	1,015 98	426 71
1861,	919 63	....	919 63	321 87
1862,	2,311 06	....	2,311 06	647 09
1863,	4,399 07	....	4,399 07	923 80
1864,	3,572 36	....	3,572 36	500 13
1865,	2,489 87	....	2,489 87	174 29
1866,	2,688 53	....	2,688 53	....
	$204,288 91	....	$204,288 91	$158,439 27

RESULT.

CREDIT.

By tolls proper,	$204,288 91	
By interest thereon, 1847 to 1866,	158,439 27	
Total income and interest,		$362,728 18

NO. 11.

Improvement.

DISBURSEMENTS.						
FOR CONSTRUCTION.		FOR MAINTENANCE.				
(1)	(2)	(3)	(4)	(5)	(6)	(7)
Cost of construction.	Legal interest on cost of construction.	Contractors, for repairs.	Superintendents, for repairs.	Collectors, inspectors, &c.	Total payments, including cost of construction.	Legal interest on total payments, including cost of construction.
....	....	....	....	....	....	....
$16,128 94	$29,354 67	....	....	....	$16,128 94	$29,354 67
21,690 05	37,957 58	....	....	....	21,690 05	37,957 58
19,308 13	32,437 65	....	....	....	19,308 13	32,437 65
....	....	....	....	....	....	....
6,094 98	9,386 26	....	....	....	6,094 98	9,386 26
....	....	....	....	....	....	....
....	....	....	....	....	....	....
1,179 87	1,569 22	....	....	....	1,179 87	1,569 22
....	....	....	....	....	....	....
6,080 00	7,235 20	....	....	....	6,080 00	7,235 20
8,727 37	9,774 24	....	$394 67	....	9,122 04	10,216 68
6,913 07	7,258 65	....	2,249 61	....	9,162 68	9,620 81
....	....	....	1,765 37	....	1,765 37	1,730 06
....	....	....	1,707 40	....	1,707 40	1,553 73
....	....	....	2,876 47	....	2,876 47	2,416 23
1,443 75	1,111 88	....	4,518 79	....	5,962 54	4,591 15
....	....	....	2,481 73	....	2,481 73	1,737 21
4,228 42	2,663 64	....	3,590 51	....	7,818 93	4,925 92
....	....	....	2,797 27	....	2,797 27	1,566 47
....	....	....	1,078 83	....	1,078 83	528 62
182 67	76 72	....	....	....	182 67	76 72
15,054 30	5,269 40	....	....	....	15,054 30	5,269 40
928 00	259 84	....	447 76	....	1,375 76	385 21
....	....	....	....	....	....	....
10,141 92	1,419 86	....	....	....	10,141 92	1,419 86
4,623 32	323 61	....	1,097 09	....	5,720 41	400 42
24,269 23	....	....	....	....	24,269 23	....
$146,994 02	$146,098 42	....	$25,005 50	....	$171,999 52	$164,379 07

DEBIT.

To cost of construction, ...	$146,994 02		
To interest thereon, ...	146,098 42		
		$293,092 44	
To cost of maintenance, ...	$25,005 50		
To interest thereon, ...	18,280 65		
		43,286 15	
Total disbursements and interest, ...			336,378 59
Net profit, ...			$26,349 59

NOTE.—The ordinary repairs of this improvement, for some years past, have been included in the contract for repairs of section 2, Oswego Canal.

TABLE

Seneca River

YEARS.	INCOME.			
	(1)	(2)	(3)	(4)
	Tolls proper.	Tolls contributed to and heretofore credited Erie and Champlain Canals.	Total of tolls proper and contributions.	Legal interest on tolls proper and contributions.
1848,	$423 60	....	$422 60	$532 47
1849,	379 65	....	379 65	451 78
1850,	230 45	....	230 45	258 10
1851,	314 22	....	314 22	329 93
1852,	161 45	....	161 45	158 22
1853,	145 62	....	145 62	132 51
1854,	212 15	....	212 15	178 20
1855,	242 56	....	242 56	186 77
1856,	250 51	....	250 51	175 35
1857,	210 23	....	210 23	128 44
1858,	99 69	....	99 69	55 82
1859,	163 82	....	163 82	80 27
1860,	144 05	....	144 05	60 50
1861,	190 38	....	190 38	66 63
1862,	374 55	....	374 55	104 87
1863,	480 57	....	480 57	100 91
1864,	468 17	....	468 17	65 54
1865,	344 36	....	344 36	24 10
1866,	416 66	....	416 66	....
	$5,251 69	....	$5,251 69	$3,090 41

RESULT.

CREDIT.

By tolls proper,	$5,251 69	
By interest thereon,	3,091 41	
Total income and interest,		$8,343 10

NO. 12.

Towing Path.

DISBURSEMENTS.						
FOR CONSTRUCTION.		FOR MAINTENANCE.				
(1)	(2)	(3)	(4)	(5)	(6)	(7)
Cost of construction.	Legal interest on cost of construction.	Contractors, for repairs.	Superintendents, for repairs.	Collectors, inspectors, &c.	Total payments, including cost of construction.	Legal interest on total payments, including cost of construction.
$456 50	$479 85	....	$19 54	....	$476 04	$499 84
1,031 83	72 23	....	....	....	1,031 83	72 23
$1,488 33	$552 08	....	$19 54	....	$1,507 87	$572 07

DEBIT.

To cost of improvement,	$1,488 33		
To interest thereon,	552 08		
		$2,040 41	
To cost of maintenance,	$19 54		
To interest thereon,	19 99		
		39 53	
			$2,079 94
Net profit,			$6,263 16

NOTE.—No account has been kept of the original cost of this improvement, and the repairs thereof have been of late years included in the contract for repairs of section No. Oswego canal.

TABLE

Cayuga

YEARS.	INCOME.			
	(1)	(2)	(3)	(4)
	Tolls proper.	Tolls contributed to and heretofore credited Erie and Champlain Canals.	Total of tolls proper and contributions.	Legal interest on tolls proper and contributions.
1849,	$121 50	....	$121 50	$144 58
1850,	205 96	....	205 96	230 67
1851,	190 41	....	190 41	199 93
1852,	230 14	....	230 14	225 53
1853,	271 78	....	271 78	247 31
1854,	311 16	....	311 16	261 37
1855,	327 86	....	327 86	252 45
1856,	328 13	....	328 13	229 69
1857,	387 82	....	387 82	244 32
1858,	190 18	....	190 18	106 50
1859,	173 95	....	173 95	85 23
1860,	173 44	....	173 44	72 84
1861,	147 97	....	147 97	51 78
1862,	241 94	....	241 94	67 74
1863,	386 40	....	386 40	81 14
1864,	351 85	....	351 85	49 25
1865,	270 03	....	270 03	18 90
1866,	286 44	....	286 44	....
	$4,596 96	....	$4,596 96	$2,569 23

RESULT.

CREDIT.

By tolls proper,	$4,596 96	
By interest thereon,	2,569 23	
Total income and interest,		$7,166 19

NO. 13.

Inlet.

DISBURSEMENTS.						
FOR IMPROVEMENT.		FOR MAINTENANCE.				
(1)	(2)	(3)	(4)	(5)	(6)	(7)
Cost of improvement.	Legal interest on cost of improvement.	Contractors, for repairs.	Superintendents, for repairs.	Collectors, inspectors, &c.	Total payments, including cost of construction.	Legal interest on total payments, including cost of construction.
...	...	...	...	...	...	...
...	...	...	...	...	...	...
...	...	...	...	...	...	...
...	...	...	...	...	...	...
...	...	...	...	...	...	...
$17 63	$14 81	...	...	...	$17 63	$14 81
...	...	...	...	...	...	...
...	...	...	...	...	...	...
...	...	...	...	...	...	...
...	...	...	...	...	...	...
...	...	...	...	...	...	...
...	...	...	...	...	...	...
...	...	...	...	...	...	...
...	...	...	...	...	...	...
1,800 00	378 00	...	...	...	1,800 00	378 00
220 00	30 80	...	...	...	220 00	30 80
...	...	...	...	...	...	...
930 53	...	...	...	...	930 53	...
$2,968 16	$423 61	...	...	...	$2,968 16	$423 61

DEBIT.

To cost of improvements, ...	$2,968 16	
To interest thereon.	423 61	
		$3,391 77
		$3,774 42

NOTE.—The original cost of this improvement, and a portion of the repairs, have been paid by the General Fund. Of late years the ordinary repairs thereof have been included in the contract for repairs of the Cayuga and Seneca Canal.

STATEMENT A.

This is an aggregate recapitulation, in a condensed form, of the detailed information called for by the six first inquiries of the resolution. The specific and detailed information in reference to each canal will be found in tables Nos. 1 *to* 13, *inclusive, following consecutively.*

CANALS.	Cost of construction, enlargement, extension, and improvement.	Interest on cost of construction, &c.	Cost of repairs, maintenance, and collection.	Interest on cost of maintenance, &c.
Erie and Champlain,	$46,018,234 19	$69,232,418 84	$17,552,621 30	$21,196,944 63
Oswego,	3,490,949 24	3,174,037 95	1,812,571 42	1,735,991 48
Cayuga and Seneca,	1,520,542 59	1,363,287 73	620,050 22	758,059 21
Chemung,	1,273,261 86	1,635,704 70	1,139,770 30	970,699 26
Crooked Lake,	333,287 27	535,896 06	258,282 78	236,180 06
Chenango,	2,782,124 19	5,119,376 29	970,169 49	745,683 48
Black River,	3,224,779 55	4,454,243 92	445,011 36	270,291 78
Genesee Valley,	5,827,813 72	7,969,085 39	1,405,342 66	1,211,081 19
Oneida Lake,	64,837 68	89,452 58	123,234 92	117,989 42
Baldwinsville,	23,556 14	16,077 32	25,035 26	7,674 62
Oneida River improvement,	146,994 02	146,098 42	25,005 50	18,280 65
Seneca River towing path,	1,488 33	552 08	19 54	19 99
Cayuga Inlet,	2,968 16	423 61	....	....
	$64,710,836 94	$93,736,654 89	$24,377,114 75	$27,268,895 77

CANALS.	Aggregate cost of each canal, including cost of maintenance and legal interest on cost of construction.	Aggregate cost of each canal, including cost of maintenance and legal interest on cost of construction and maintenance.	Aggregate receipts or income from each canal, with interest thereon.	Revenues contributed to the Erie and Champlain Canals, by the lateral canals.
Erie and Champlain,	$132,803,274 33	$154,000,218 96	$192,455,779 57	....
Oswego,	8,477,558 61	10,213,550 09	4,415,957 01	$6,719,600 60
Cayuga and Seneca,	3,503,880 54	4,261,939 75	1,740,049 42	378,782 36
Chemung,	4,048,736 86	5,019,436 12	884,816 98	1,556,801 34
Crooked Lake,	1,127,466 11	1,363,646 17	94,340 87	478,042 64
Chenango,	8,871,669 97	9,617,353 45	1,204,040 85	123,276 40
Black River,	8,124,034 83	8,394,326 61	162,900 89	128,027 00
Genesee Valley,	15,202,241 77	16,413,322 96	1,158,085 43	675,042 46
Oneida Lake,	277,525 18	395,514 60	123,060 84	....
Baldwinsville,	64,668 72	72,343 34	2,240 75	....
Oneida River improvement,	318,097 94	336,378 59	362,728 18	....
Seneca River towing path,	2,059 95	2,079 94	8,348 10	....
Cayuga Inlet,	3,391 77	3,391 77	7,166 19	....
	$182,824,606 58	$210,093,502 35	$202,619,510 08	$11,059,572 80

STATEMENT B.

BALANCE SHEET showing the net cost or profit to the State of each Canal, as deduced from the foregoing tables.

CANALS.	COST.	PROFIT.	COST.	PROFIT.
	Crediting each lateral canal with its tolls proper, and charging it with its cost of construction, maintenance and repairs, charging and crediting interest at seven per cent.		Crediting each lateral canal with its tolls proper and tolls on its contribution to the Erie and Champlain Canals, and charging it with its own cost of construction, maintenance and repairs; also with its proper proportion of the cost of maintenance of the the Erie and Champlain Canals, charging and crediting interest at seven per cent.	
Erie and Champlain, ...	....	$38,455,560 61	....	$23,108,326 01
Oswego,................	$5,797,593 08	....	....	2,950,548 18
Cayuga and Seneca, ...	2,521,890 33	....	$123,491 90	....
Chemung,...............	4,134,619 14	....	1,767,201 88	....
Crooked Lake,..........	1,269,305 30	....	406,088 87	....
Chenango,..............	8,413,312 60	....	8,223,431 69	....
Black River,...........	8,231,425 72	....	8,103,255 80	....
Genesee Valley,........	15,255,237 53	....	14,301,989 47	....
Oneida Lake,...........	272,453 76	....	272,453 76	....
Baldwinsville,.........	70,102 59	....	70,102 59	....
Oneida river improvem't,	....	26,349 59	....	26,349 59
Seneca river towing path,	....	6,263 16	....	6,265 16
Cayuga inlet,..........	....	3,774 42	....	3,774 42
	$45,965,940 05	$38,491,947 78	$33,268,015 96	$26,095,263 36
Present cost to the State of the entire canal system,..........................		*7,473,992 27		†7,172,752 60
		$45,965,940 05		$33,268,015 96

* To September 30, 1866.
† Crediting the lateral canals with tolls received to December 31, 1866.

NOTE.—The apparent discrepancy of $301,239.67 in the above balance sheet is accounted for from the fact that the result in one case is obtained from the accounts for *fiscal years*, the entire period closing with September 30, 1866, while the result obtained in the other covers the entire period (with the exception of the account of the Erie and Champlain Canals), ending with *December* 31, 1866 — the discrepancy being the amount of revenue or tolls received from the lateral canals from October 1 to December 31, 1866, and the difference in interest.

In ascertaining the amount of tolls contributed by the lateral canals to the Erie, it was necessary (in order to report during the sitting of the Convention) to obtain the result from each year of navigation, instead of for each fiscal year; and this plan favors the lateral canals to the extent of three months' receipts of tolls, without the charge of maintenance and repairs for the corresponding period. If there had been time to ascertain the contributions by fiscal years, the apparent aggregate cost to the State of *all the canals* would have been alike in both results; there would simply have been a difference in the distribution of the cost.

INDEX.

www.ingramcontent.com/pod-product-compliance
Lightning Source LLC
LaVergne TN
LVHW020923110826
845150LV00004B/755

9781425554842